The Tabloid Culture Reader

The Tabloid Culture Reader

Edited by Anita Biressi and Heather Nunn

Open University Press

Open University Press
McGraw-Hill Education
McGraw-Hill House
Shoppenhangers Road
Maidenhead
Berkshire
England
SL6 2QL

email: enquiries@openup.co.uk
world wide web: www.openup.co.uk

and Two Penn Plaza, New York, NY 10121-2289, USA

First published 2008

A catalogue record of this book is available from the British Library

ISBN-10: 0 335 21931 4 (pb)   0 335 21932 2 (hb)
ISBN-13: 978 0 335 21931 5 (pb)   978 0 335 21932 2 (hb)

Library of Congress Cataloging-in-Publication Data
CIP data has been applied for

Typeset by RefineCatch Limited, Bungay, Suffolk
Printed in the UK by Bell and Bain Ltd, Glasgow

The **McGraw·Hill** Companies

Contents

Contributors

Mark Andrejevic is an Assistant Professor in the Department of Communication Studies at the University of Iowa. In addition to his book *Reality TV: The Work of Being Watched,* he is the author of numerous book chapters and articles on popular culture and surveillance and a forthcoming book on new media.

Feona Attwood teaches media and communication studies at Sheffield Hallam University. She has published widely on sex and the media. Her research interests include new pornographies, cybersex, women and sexualization and the study of sexual media in education. She is currently working on online pornography and women's use of online sex sites.

Karin Becker is Professor of Visual Studies and Pedagogy at the University College of Arts, Crafts and Design (Konstfackskolan), Stockholm. Her work is in the area of visual culture studies, with a primary emphasis on the meanings and uses of photographs in various social and cultural contexts, including studies of museum archives and of the press, as well as uses of photography within anthropology, within art and as a vernacular form.

S. Elizabeth Bird is Professor and Chair, Department of Anthropology, University of South Florida. She is the author of *For Enquiring Minds: A Cultural Study of Supermarket Tabloids* (University of Tennessee Press, 1992). Her most recent book, *The Audience in Everyday Life: Living in a Media World* (Routledge, 2003), won the International Communication Association's Outstanding Book Award for 2004. She has published more than 50 academic articles and chapters on media and popular culture.

Anita Biressi is Head of Film, Media and Cultural Studies in the School of Arts, Roehampton University, UK. She is the author of *Crime, Fear and the Law in True Crime Stories* (2001), coauthor of *Reality TV: Realism and Revelation* (2005) and coeditor of *Mediactive: Media War* (2003). Recent publications include articles in *Screen, Feminist Media Studies* and *The Journal For Cultural Research.*

Frances Bonner is a Reader in Television and Popular Culture at the University of Queensland. As well as celebrity she researches non-fiction television and magazines.

She is the author of *Ordinary Television* (Sage, 2003) and currently bringing her research interests together in work on television presenters.

Kate Brooks is a part-time lecturer and researcher at the University of the West of England, Bristol. Previous publications include *Making Sense of Men's Magazines* (with Peter Jackson and Nick Stevenson) and *Knowing Audiences* (with Martin Barker), as well as a number of journal articles and book chapters on a diverse range of topics including urban spaces and fear of crime, retro fashion and alternative consumption practices, and volunteering and social exclusion. She is currently writing up her research on students' investments in teaching and learning practices.

Martin Conboy is a Reader in journalism studies at the University of Sheffield. He is the author of *The Press and Popular Culture* (2002), *Journalism: A Critical History* (2004) *Tabloid Britain: Constructing a Community Through Language* (2006) and *The Language of the News* (2007) as well as being the coeditor of a series of books on Journalism Studies.

Mark Deuze works at Leiden University, The Netherlands, and Indiana University's Department of Telecommunications in Bloomington, the United States. Publications include *Media Work* (Polity Press, 2007), and numerous articles in journals such as *New Media and Society, Journalism Studies,* and the *International Journal of Cultural Studies.*

John Fiske is the author of numerous books and articles on cultural studies and popular culture including *Television Culture* (1987), *Understanding Popular Culture* (1989) and *Reading Popular Culture* (1989).

Bob Franklin is Professor of Journalism Studies in the Cardiff School of Journalism, Media and Cultural Studies. He is Editor of *Journalism Studies* and *Journalism Practice.* Recent books include *Local Journalism and Local Media: Making the Local News* (2006), *Television Policy: The MacTaggart Lectures* and *Packaging Politics: Political Communication in Britain's Media Democracy* (2004).

Des Freedman is a Senior Lecturer in the Department of Media and Communications at Goldsmiths, University of London. He is the author of *The Politics of Media Policy* (forthcoming), *The Television Policies of the Labour Party, 1951–2001* (2003) and coeditor of *War and the Media: Reporting Conflict 24/7* (2003).

Kevin Glynn is Senior Lecturer in the School of Culture, Literature and Society at the University of Canterbury in Aotearoa/New Zealand. He is author of *Tabloid Culture: Trash Taste, Popular Power and the Transformation of American Television.*

Bridget Griffen-Foley is an Australian Research Council (ARC) Queen Elizabeth II Fellow in the Departments of Modern History and Politics at Macquarie University in Sydney. Her publications include *The House of Packer, Sir Frank Packer* and *Party Games: Australian Politicians and the Media from War to Dismissal*. She is now writing a history of Australian commercial radio.

Laura Grindstaff is an Associate Professor of Sociology at the University of California, Davis. Her teaching and research focus on issues of race, gender, class, and sexuality in contemporary American popular culture. She is the author of *The Money Shot: Trash, Class, and the Making of TV Talk Shows* (University of Chicago Press) and is currently researching a new book on cheerleading in American culture.

Jostein Gripsrud is Professor of Media Studies, University of Bergen, Norway. He is the author of numerous articles and books including *The Dynasty Years: Hollywood Television and Critical Media Studies* (1995), *Understanding Media Culture* (2002) and editor of *Television and Common Knowledge* (1999).

Patricia Holland is a Senior Lecturer at the Bournemouth Media School, Bournemouth University. She is the author of numerous books and articles including *Picturing Childhood: The Myth of the Child in Popular Imagery* (2004) and *The Angry Buzz, This Week and Current Affairs Television* (2006).

Su Holmes is Reader in Television at the University of East Anglia. She is the author of *British TV and Film Culture in the 1950s* (Intellect, 2005) and coeditor of *Understanding Reality TV* (Routledge, 2004), *Framing Celebrity* (Routledge, 2006) and *Stardom and Celebrity: A Reader* (Sage, 2007).

Leon Hunt is Senior Lecturer in Film and TV Studies at Brunel University. He is the author of *British Low Culture: From Safari Suits to Sexploitation* and *Kung Fu Cult Masters: From Bruce Lee to Crouching Tiger*. He is currently writing a book on *The League of Gentlemen* for the BFI's TV Classics series.

Anna Maria Jönsson is currently working as a Senior Lecturer and researcher in media studies at Södertörn University College in Sweden. Her main areas of research are media, journalism and the public sphere, and media and science. She has recently published a book on television journalism and commercialization.

Jason Kosovski gained his PhD at the Institute of Communications Research at the University of Illinois. His dissertation, *Wild Boyz and Jackasses: Masculinity and Reality Television*, is an assessment of disturbing images of masculinity on reality television. His research is situated within critical cultural studies in communication especially in the areas of feminist media studies, film theory, and the growing literature on masculinity.

Victoria Mapplebeck is Senior Lecturer in Documentary Practice at Royal Holloway, London University. She writes for the *Guardian* and has contributed to *Reality TV: How Real is Real?* Her TV documentaries include *Meet the Kilshaws* and British TV's first convergence project, *Smart Hearts*, nominated for a 2001 New Media Indie Award.

P. D. Marshall is currently Professor of New Media and Cyberculture at the University of Wollongong. He is the author of many articles on media, new media, popular culture and public personalities and five books including *Celebrity and Power* (Minnesota, 1997), *The Celebrity Culture Reader* (Routledge, 2006) and *New Media Cultures* (Edward Arnold/Oxford, 2004).

Heather Nunn is Reader in Media and Cultural Studies in the School of Arts, Roehampton University, UK. She is the author of *Thatcher, Politics and Fantasy: The Political Culture of Gender and Nation* (2002), coauthor of *Reality TV: Realism and Revelation* (2005) and coeditor of *Mediactive: Media War* (2003). She is currently working on television and the cult of humiliation.

Henrik Örnebring is Axess Research Fellow in Comparative European Journalism at the Reuters Institute for the Study of Journalism, University of Oxford. His main research interests are journalism history, journalism in Europe and journalism and new technology.

Mark Pursehouse is Faculty Manager in Media and Performing Arts at Stafford College, United Kingdom. He is the author of ' "Life's more fun with your Number One Sun": interviews with some *Sun* readers' (1987) and *Looking at the Sun: Into the Nineties with a Tabloid and its Readers* (1991).

Graeme Turner is ARC Federation Fellow and Director of the Centre for Critical and Cultural Studies at the University of Queensland, Brisbane, Australia. His most recent books include *Understanding Celebrity* (2004), *Ending the Affair: The Decline of Television Current Affairs in Australia* (2005) and the fourth revised edition of *Film as Social Practice* (2006).

Pamela Wilson is Associate Professor of Communication at Reinhardt College in Georgia (US). She is the coeditor of *Global Indigenous Media: Cultures, Practices and Politics* (forthcoming from Duke University Press), and has authored pieces in numerous anthologies and journals on topics including early television documentaries, cooking shows, country music, and online communities.

Acknowledgements

We would like to extend our thanks to the following people and institutions. Thanks to the School of Arts at Roehampton University for funding research assistance and Billie Dokur for undertaking that role. The Arts and Humanities Research Council allowed time for Heather Nunn to work on cultural studies approaches to journalism; research that helped inform the planning of this reader. We would like to acknowledge Chris Cudmore, Senior Commissioning Editor at McGraw-Hill, for his encouragement and support. Thanks, too, go to our students on the popular journalism and tabloid culture courses at Middlesex University and then at Roehampton whose critical enthusiasm and always-current knowledge of tabloid media inspired this reader. The research for this course and its pilot materials was partly funded by the ADC-LTSN. And finally, our thanks go to Kathryn, Miri and Berni because girls just want to have fun.

Publisher's acknowledgements

The authors and publisher wish to thank the following for permission to use copyright material:

Franklin, B. 'Newszak: Entertainment versus news and information' from *Newszak and News Media* (Arnold, 1997). Reproduced by permission of Edward Arnold (Publishers) Ltd.

Jönsson, A. M. and Örnebring, H. 'Tabloid journalism and the public sphere: a historical perspective on tabloid journalism' in *Journalism Studies*, 5(2) (Taylor & Francis, 2004). Reprinted by permission of the publisher (Taylor & Francis Ltd, http://www.tandf.co.uk/journals).

Gripsrud, J. 'Tabloidization, popular journalism and democracy' in Spark and Tulloch (eds) *Tabloid Tales* (Rowman & Littlefield, 2000).

Conboy, M. 'The popular press' in *The Press and Popular Culture* (Sage, 2002). Reprinted by permission of Sage Publications Ltd.

Turner, G. 'Ethics, entertainment and the tabloid: the case of talkback radio in Australia' in *Continuum: Journal of Media and Cultural Studies*, 15(3) (Taylor & Francis, 2001). Reprinted by permission of the publisher (Taylor & Francis Ltd, http://www.tandf.co.uk/journals).

Freedman, D. 'The *Mirror* and the war on Iraq: profits, politics and product differentiation' in *Mediactive: Media War*, issue 3.

Becker, K. 'Photojournalism and the tabloid press' in Dahlgren and Sparks (eds) *Journalism and Popular Culture* (Sage, 1992). Reprinted by permission of Sage Publications Ltd.

Attwood, F. 'A very British carnival: women, sex and transgression in *Fiesta* magazine' in *European Journal of Cultural Studies*, 5(1) (Sage, 2002). Reprinted by permission of Sage Publications Ltd.

Conboy, M. 'Integrating approaches to contemporary popular culture' in *The Press and Popular Culture* (Sage, 2002). Reprinted by permission of Sage Publications Ltd.

Fiske, J. 'Excess and the Obvious' in *Understanding Popular Culture* (Routledge, 1989). Reproduced by permission of Taylor & Francis Books UK.

Hunt, L. 'From carnival to crumpet: low comedy in the 1970s' in *British Low Culture: From Safari Suits to Sexploitation* (Routledge, 1998). Reproduced by permission of Taylor & Francis Books UK.

Turner, G., Bonner, F. and Marshall, P. D. (eds) 'The meaning of celebrity' in *Fame Games: The Production of Celebrity in Australia* (Cambridge University Press, 2000).

Biressi, A. and Nunn, H. 'The especially remarkable: celebrity and social mobility in reality TV' in *Mediactive: Celebrity*, issue 2.

Holmes, S. ' "Off-guard, unkempt, unready?" Deconstructing contemporary celebrity in *Heat* magazine' in *Continuum: Journal of Media and Cultural Studies*, 19(1) (Taylor & Francis, 2005). Reprinted by permission of the publisher (Taylor & Francis Ltd, http://www.tandf.co.uk/journals).

Glynn, K. 'The tabloidisation of OJ Simpson' in *Tabloid Culture: Trash Taste, Popular Power and the Transformation of American Television* (Duke University Press, 2000).

Brooks, K. *Loaded with Meaning: Researching Men's Lifestyle Magazines* (2007).

Holland, P. 'The politics of the smile: "soft news" and the sexualisation of the popular press' in Allan *et al.* (eds) *News, Gender and Power* (Routledge, 1998). Reproduced by permission of Taylor & Francis Books UK.

Kosovski, J. Performing masculinity: reflexive-sadomasochism in MTV's *Jackass* (2007).

Deuze, M. 'Popular journalism and professional ideology: tabloid reporters and editors speak out' in *Media, Culture and Society* (Sage, 2005). Reprinted by permission of Sage Publications Ltd.

S. Elizabeth Bird's 'Writing the tabloid' originally appeared in S. Elizabeth Bird's *For Enquiring Minds: A Cultural Study of Supermarket Tabloids*. Copyright 1992, The University of Tennessee Press. Used with permission.

Grindstaff, L. 'Producing trash: class, and the money shot: a behind the scenes account of daytime TV talkshows' in Lull and Hinerman (eds) *Media Scandals: Morality and Desire in the Popular Culture Marketplace* (Polity Press, 1997).

Mapplebeck, V. 'Money shot' in *Reality TV: How Real is Real?* (Institute of Ideas, 2002).

'Looking at the *Sun*' by Mark Pursehouse originally appeared in *Cultural Studies from Birmingham* (1991). Used with permission.

Griffen-Foley, B. 'From tit-bits to big brother: a century of audience participation in the media' in *Media, Culture and Society*, 26(4) (Sage, 2004). Reprinted by permission of Sage Publications Ltd.

Andrejevic, M. 'Reality TV and Voyeurism' in *Reality TV* (Rowman & Littlefield, 2004).

Wilson, P. 'Jamming *Big Brother*: Webcasting, audience intervention and narrative activism' in Murray, S. and Ouellette, L. (eds) *Reality TV: Remaking Television Culture* (New York University Press, 2004).

Every effort has been made to trace the copyright holders but if any have been inadvertently overlooked the publisher will be pleased to make the necessary arrangement at the first opportunity.

Foreword by Martin Conboy

Tabloid culture can no longer be conveniently quarantined in an annexe some distance away from the concerns of mainstream or even elite cultural activity. In some way, it touches the lives of all of us even if our engagement is limited to bemoaning that very influence. It has long been acknowledged that the vicarious coverage of tabloid media in our elite press and by our public service broadcasters is a discreetly acceptable way for these institutions to keep their own idealized audiences abreast of what is commonly known to be going on 'out there'. To this extent, we are all populists now; even if our populism is driven by criticizing the popular influences at play in our media-saturated society. This book demonstrates the extent to which tabloid values have come to permeate our general media culture and in so doing have generated a cultural continuum that critics of culture might have to consider a variant of 'common culture', with all the implications of the word 'common' from vernacular, to the everyday, to the vulgar.

The editors of this volume are to be congratulated for bringing together under one cover a carefully ordered and articulated guide to the range of debate that the phenomenon of tabloid culture has generated in recent years. This range demonstrates the extent to which tabloid culture has impregnated our media, our lives and our media debates.

The paradox of tabloid culture is that it demands attention and critical debate often precisely because of the many discomforting issues about contemporary media products and audiences that it raises. Elite commentators have always sought to place taboos around the assessment of the value of a whole range of popular culture whether that culture has been a folk culture or a mass culture. Critical discussion of tabloid culture keeps popular culture in its contemporary formats very much on our political agendas, asking perennial questions of worth and access of the latest cultural phenomena. Tabloid culture is located within the longer term patterns of popular culture and this means that we need to continue to explore and challenge its various products and audiences in order to give them adequate political and aesthetic consideration whether we approve of them or not. Indeed such explorations may well include a reassessment of the validity of our own presuppositions on vital issues that surround media consumption such as class, gender, ethnicity and taste. Tabloid culture has much to tell us about how our society expresses value, interest and relevance.

The editors provide an examination of the vitality and dynamism of tabloid culture that goes far beyond a mere celebration, for they are astutely aware of the political and cultural dangers in such populist media expression. There is a good summary of the definitions and debates regarding tabloid culture in its various manifestations. This fits well with the broad pedagogic intent of the book, which will serve to engage a range of readers with discussions on the place of these media in our daily lives and that will as a consequence enable us all to better assess the claims made by producers, critics and *aficionados* of the cornucopia of our contemporary tabloid culture.

Introduction

Why 'tabloid culture'?

We have chosen 'tabloid culture' as the umbrella phrase beneath which we can draw together a range of debates, theories and analyses of contemporary popular news and entertainment-based media. The tabloidization of the media has been an ongoing pre-occupation not only of media scholars but also of the media industries themselves. Where public debate takes place about the media, its role and function, concerns about tabloid content are never far away. 'Tabloidization' itself is a tabloid term, a media industry expression rather than a scholarly concept, denoting a dumbing down of media content and a weakening of the *ideal* functions of mass media in liberal democracies (Gripsrud, 2000: 285). Although it was originally deployed to describe a decline in journalistic standards it is now increasingly applied to all forms of popular mainstream media content including talkshows and radio phone-ins, reality television, gross-out comedy, celebrity magazines and even documentary.

To some extent it is far easier to condemn tabloid culture than it is to understand its complex popular appeal. Yet tabloid culture thrives because its rhetoric, attitude and posture (with two fingers stabbing the air in a vulgar salute to high culture and its advocates) consistently speak to the majority of ordinary people and hold our attention. Much of the censure aimed at tabloid journalism and popular entertainment frequently parallels or intersects with earlier criticisms levelled at other 'low' or popular cultural forms such as comic books and true crime magazines, 'video nasties' and pulp fiction, all of which have been the subject of academic study. We suggest, therefore, that in the current moment scholarly debates about the production, values and ethics and con-sumption of tabloidized media can most fruitfully take place in an interdisciplinary arena; an arena in which we can bring together past and present critical thinking in journalism, media and cultural studies around the articulation of the popular in the contemporary media landscape. It is in this context that the term 'tabloid' in conjunction with 'culture' provides a useful shorthand phrase to denote the newer formations of media culture that draw together, in a sustained way, so many of the features that were commonly attributed to older tabloid formats while still retaining their own unique character.

'Tabloid culture' then rather than denoting a particular market, medium, format or content (although it necessarily includes all of these) refers to a changing media landscape or 'mediasphere' and signals the contemporary emphasis of this collection, focusing on tabloid media as both *currently* culturally significant and as part of the content and flow of everyday life. As Gripsrud (2000: 288) observes of tabloid journalism, 'a relative expansion of certain forms of popular journalism affects cultural, political, and public life in general'. It is important, therefore, to consider tabloid forms in the context of this broader cultural field. Consequently, many of the pieces here will refer to diverse questions regarding the tabloid media's impact on the political and social spheres, addressing, for example, tabloid culture with regards to civic responsibility, cultural politics and representation, political affiliation and ideology, the articulation of the private and public spheres and so forth.

Having established that the focus of this Reader is, in the main, on contemporary tabloid culture it is clear that this culture, its forms and discourses, have not emerged from a historical vacuum. Each of these formats and genres will have histories and antecedents and they exhibit continuities as well as differences from those that went before them. This Reader does not include historical readings on the emergence of the tabloid or the broader cultural transformations that accompanied it but this history is important and will be referred to by the editors when appropriate. Several of the pieces included here (e.g. Becker, 1992; Jönsson and Örnebring, 2004; Griffin-Foley, 2004) draw on tabloid histories and these, together with editorial commentary, point towards further reading in this direction. History is important here. For example, many of the features of popular, allegedly 'dumbed down', media today (its accessibility, its use of vernacular, its vulgarity and emphasis on spectacle and excess, its blatant disregard for formal politics and so on) owe something to the influence of the tabloid newspaper and prior to that to earlier modern print and oral folk cultures. But it should also be stressed that the tabloid media today, especially in broadcast form, naturally have their own distinctive characteristics which owe less to the tabloid press (which in any case varies hugely from country to country, where it appears at all) and more to developing technologies, commercial pressures, globalizing imperatives, changes in social attitudes and so on. Indeed, we could argue that the tabloid press in Britain and the United States, for example, continues to appeal to its readers *despite* its fairly traditional presentation precisely because of its close affiliation to the television and online media, which generate much of the everyday news coverage found in popular journalism. The case might even be made that the national tabloid newspaper is in some senses an entertaining and diverting anachronism in the era of 'information-age journalism' (see Campbell 2004: 1–26).

Many of the pieces selected for this Reader explicitly deploy terms such as 'tabloid' or 'tabloidization' but some do not. As already noted 'tabloid culture' refers to formations of media culture that include traditional formats such as the tabloid press but also comprise more unstable and evolving hybrid genres that draw on discourses and practices which were once confined to tabloid journalism and related practices but are now diffused into media culture. Where these pieces do not refer to tabloids or tabloidization overtly they do, nonetheless, explore the populist cultural politics, controversial content or rhetoric that so often inform tabloid culture. Any selection for a Reader such as this is open to challenge or revision and many of the extracts could have been presented in alternative thematic categories. These selections have been chosen not to close down or contain the definitions, readings and debates about tabloid culture but rather to open them up to timely academic scrutiny. Using the index the interested reader will be able to navigate across sections and they will find that many of the pieces selected here can function in a lively dialogue with ideas raised in quite different locations. The Reader will have succeeded most in its intentions if it provokes an inquisitive and questioning attitude towards tabloid culture: towards its nomenclature, towards its status as an academic area of inquiry, towards its origins, genres, values and ethics, industrial contexts, pleasures, modes of production and of consumption.

Almost by definition a Reader whose title encompasses the terms 'tabloid' and culture' and in fact unites them to describe a particularly all-encompassing phenomenon will gather together essays and extracts that cross disciplinary fields. Having said this, we have selected these readings with care and organized them in such a way as to arrive at informative and sometimes provocative groupings around particular themes which should be of relevance whatever the reader's scholarly inclinations. The Reader falls into three parts, which are themselves divided into sections. Each section is preceded by an editors' introduction, which sets out to delineate the important debates and areas of investigation that form the backdrop to our choices. Here we also introduce each piece and make suggestions for further reading.

Part 1 may be viewed as offering a cartography of many of the key debates, concepts and theories that may be drawn on to think through the significance of tabloid culture today. Section 1 considers the origins of tabloids, definitions of tabloidization and the 'problem of tabloidization' today. In doing so it addresses the ideal functions of mass media in liberal democracies, the erosion of distinctions between the public and private spheres and the politics of the popular press. Section 2 examines questions of tabloid values and ethics in relation to talk radio, political journalism and photojournalism. It addresses the tensions between the commercial imperatives of popular media and the regime of ethics to which media professionals are expected to adhere. In different ways, each of the three pieces included here asks us to consider what exactly tabloid journalism is and how it can be evaluated without prejudice but also without the suspension of our critical faculties. Section 3 addresses theories of carnival, spectacle and excess and explores how they might illuminate not only the histories and symbolic meanings of tabloid culture but also the range of pleasures associated with forms that mock or undermine official culture.

Part 2 attends to particular aspects of tabloid culture: celebrity, gender and sexuality. A growing area of interest in media and cultural studies is the prominence of the celebrity as an idealized figure of aspiration (or at least fascination), as a vehicle for consumerism and even as the subject of public mockery and condemnation. Section 4, therefore, considers the meaning, role and function of the celebrity, the rise of the celebrity magazine and the emergence of the ordinary person as celebrity within the context of new developments such as reality TV. Looking at figures as various as O. J. Simpson, Jade Goody and Anna Nicole Smith it considers the loaded cultural politics of media coverage of celebrity issues. Figures such as Smith grab media attention in part because of their highly sexualized image, which lends itself perfectly to tabloid media coverage. Indeed the 'sexualization' of contemporary media is sometimes regarded as the hallmark of tabloid culture. It is viewed as emblematic of the dumbing down of contemporary media which has been brought about by the ongoing deregulation and commercialization of the media together with the more general decline in social mores. With these concerns in mind, Section 5 therefore considers tabloid media in the context of debates around femininity, masculinity and sexuality and the sexual politics of tabloid culture more broadly.

Part 3 encompasses the final two sections, which attend to the production and consumption of tabloid entertainment. Many assumptions are made about how tabloid entertainment is produced, who produces it and what the intentions and values of media professionals might be. Equally, it is easy for students of tabloid culture to jump to conclusions about the ways in which tabloid entertainment is consumed. Section 6 therefore explores professional values in the tabloid market place and Section 7 examines audiences in the market place, considering audiences as readers, consumers and fans and the ways in which tabloid genres might offer news arenas for an alternative public sphere.

PART 1

Debates, concepts, theories

SECTION 1

Origins, definitions and debates: talking about the tabloids

Defining tabloid media is a difficult task as the term 'tabloid' refers not only to changing formats in shifting historical and industrial contexts but also to the attitudes and values that are commonly attached to these formats. The term 'tabloid' is quite often used in a pejorative sense and there are many examples of academic debates that address a perceived 'crisis', 'threat' or even 'panic' in response to the 'tabloidization' of contemporary media culture. Colin Sparks (2000) provides a helpful model for unpacking the various ways in which the term tabloid is used and the values attached to them. Firstly, and originally, the term refers to newspaper and then broadcast journalistic output that prioritizes entertainment, human interest and commercial profitability and which is usually presented as oppositional to 'serious' and socially responsible journalism. Secondly, the term can refer to changing priorities within a given medium such as television leading, for example, to a diminution of serious programming or its marginalization in the schedules and the adoption across the board of entertainment-led values. Finally, it can refer to tabloid content itself. Sparks gives the well-known examples of the *Jerry Springer Show* and the work of American 'shockjock' radio presenter Rush Limbaugh whose shows are open to criticism for their voyeuristic and shameless exploitation of ordinary people in the case of Springer and for controversial populist, highly conservative rhetoric in the case of Limbaugh (Sparks, 2000: 10–11).

There has been longstanding academic interest in the development of the popular and later the tabloid press. From its inception, cultural studies has demonstrated an abiding interest in journalism both for its capacity to articulate common concerns and interests and as a resource when trying to analyse the 'structure of feeling' or the culture of a particular historical period (Williams, 1961: 41). In Barbie Zelizer's words, cultural studies had a 'default regard' for journalism as a 'key strain of resonance for thinking about how culture worked' (Zelizer, 2004: 180–5). For example, Raymond Williams (1961: 171), a founder of what became known as British cultural studies, suggested that the development of the popular press in particular was of major importance in understanding the general expansion of mass culture from the late seventeenth century until the present day. The newspaper was, after all, the most widely distributed of single-issue printed products, it was increasingly affordable, relatively easy to read and set the agenda for public debate on a daily basis. It became, in effect, part and parcel of the common culture of everyday life.

One of the key concerns of scholarship has been the origins of the popular press, the rise of radical politics via popular journalism and then the subsequent transformation of the popular press into distinctively tabloid formats in terms of style and content. Williams observed that although newspapers were originally the creation of the middle class (whose sound commercial footing gave them the resilience to become somewhat independent of government and subsequently to help form public opinion on the events of the day) other kinds of press reflecting the different social bases of the working classes also emerged. Notably, during the late 1770s–1830s these initiatives included attempts (under severe repression) to launch politically radical newspapers and also the establishment of the Sunday newspaper. In the early nineteenth century the former constituted a political voice that was independent of trade advertising and of official political groupings (Curran and Seaton, 2003: 7). The latter was also somewhat radical in tone but its main appeal was its inclusion of stories of fraud, thievery, seduction, murder and executions, sports, human oddities and other diverting content previously found in popular print culture such as ballad sheets, chapbooks and almanacs (Williams, 1961: 175–6, 189; see also Biressi, 2001).

The popular Sunday paper became an established British institution, a 'scandal sheet' seemingly enjoyed (but perhaps for differing reasons) across the social classes (see Orwell, 1946) and a pioneer of tabloid journalistic style. Competition between papers addressing a working-class readership, such as the commercial battles that took place in the 1930s, led to further developments in accessible style and content (Conboy, 2006: 7). The tabloid tone of the Sundays influenced their weekday competitors with the *Daily Mail* perhaps becoming best known of the middle market papers for its adoption of popular address and content. Of the more 'downmarket' papers, the *Daily Mirror*, which was relaunched in the 1930s, was arguably emblematic of the British style of tabloid journalism of the period (Conboy, 2006). The distinguishing features of the tabloid newspaper included not only its content and tone (e.g. sensation, human interest, sentimentality, prurience) but also a growing alliance with the entertainment industries, which, in the United States for example, began as early as the 1890s and was fully realized with the advent of movies and the establishment of Hollywood star system into the 1940s (Ponce de Leon, 2002). The British press, along with many other areas of cultural life, was increasingly marked by the influence of American popular culture such as picture magazines, movies, comics and pulp fiction (see Hoggart, 1957; Nuttall and Carmichael, 1977; Street, 1998). Indeed, since at least the nineteenth century, British journalism had taken on board US tabloid initiatives such as populist campaigning journalism and exposés and the growing coverage of celebrity issues, human interest and scandal (see Ponce de Leon, 2002). In the early part of the twentieth century American journalists also pioneered moves into photojournalism and the heavy deployment of illustration in news reporting (Conboy, 2006: 6) and it could be argued that this emphasis on the visual over the written word in reportage has become symptomatic of the tabloidization of news media in general. Indeed, one of the ways in which the growing tabloidization of the press can be quantified is by tracking whether there are more visuals and less text over a given period of time (McLachlan and Golding, 2000: 75–90).

In the United Kingdom the tightening bond between the entertainment industries, consumerism and the tabloid press became increasingly apparent during the 1970s with the rise to prominence of the *Sun* newspaper, to take one clear example. The *Sun*, acquired in 1969 by a market-wise media conglomerate headed by Rupert Murdoch, made its mark in terms of its reciprocal relationship with the commercial television industry, which is maintained to this day. It also devoted substantial amounts of space to advertising, competitions, TV promotions and tie-ins, sports and lifestyle copy (see Rooney, 1998 and 2000). From the *Sun*'s successful harnessing in the 1970s and 1980s of 'permissive populism' (Hunt, 1998) and political 'authoritarian populism' (Hall and Jacques, 1983: 22) emerged three key components of the tabloid profile – sexual vulgarity, the use of popular vernacular and a radical iconoclastic conservatism that captured the attention of its non-elite audience. In terms of its address to readers it employed a chirpy vernacular and knowing smuttiness and sexualization of content that rendered it a highly distinctive brand in a competitive market. It was also vulnerable to accusations of brandishing overtly jingoistic, xenophobic and sometimes even racist attitudes (see Harris, 1983; Searle, 1989; Campbell, 1995; Law, 2002; Curran, Gaber and Petley, 2005). As such the paper (along with similar competitor titles) has been regarded as a 'scandalous object' (McGuigan, 1992: 175) inviting criticism with regard to questions of representation and cultural politics. As Curran and Seaton (2003: 90) argue, although the paper could all too easily be dismissed as simple minded, it in fact 'evolved a complex editorial formula . . . which was both hedonistic and moralistic, iconoclastic and authoritarian, generally Conservative in its opinions and radical in its rhetoric' and for many the *Sun* remains emblematic of the popular, often politically influential, British mass market tabloid daily.

The *Sun*, which had started life as a trades union supported paper called the *Daily Herald*, also offers a good case study of the ways in which formerly politically radical papers can become transformed into vehicles of conservative values in tandem with tabloid style and content. Many media scholars since Raymond Williams have been concerned with identifying the point at which it could be said that the popular press became the tabloid press or, to frame it another way, the stage at which the popular press became 'depoliticized' and relinquished its commitment to collective working-class politics and leftist values (see Curran and Seaton, 2003: 91–3). Media and communication studies has addressed these questions in the context of broader research into the political economy of the press, taking into account factors such as newspaper ownership, regulation and control, political influence and the public sphere, ideology and agenda setting and the changing commercial landscape of the newspaper market place (see for example Curran and Gurevitch, 1991; Blumler and Gurevitch, 1995; Philo, 1995; Boyd-Barrett and Rantanen, 1998; McChesney, 1999).

The phrase 'public sphere' was first used by Jürgen Habermas (1989) to describe the arena of debate in which 'public opinion' was formed; an arena provided by the rise of the newspaper and its development as a vehicle for public political dialogue. Habermas suggested that the particular circumstances of the emergence of the press together with the circulation of political debate amongst literate society created the conditions for a more democratic and distinctively modern social realm. Many media critics, and indeed journalists themselves, have noted the increasing tabloidization of the news media with dismay, pointing out what has been lost in terms of the media's ability to operate effectively as a public sphere in which rational and informed reflection about the political, economic and social issues of the day might take place. The argument has been made that an increasingly commercialized media, allied with consumerism as noted above, has transformed the public sphere of open citizenship into a privatized sphere in which citizens are primarily defined as consumers (see Garnham, 1986; Rooney, 2000; Street, 2001: 41–2; Campbell, 2004: 55–8; Lewis et al., 2005).

The trajectory of these press analyses has generally been one in which the popular press has been deemed to break away from its radical democratic roots towards a more overt commercialism, which panders to the lowest common denominator in order to sell copy and support a free-market ethos. As such it may be regarded as a process that inexorably erodes serious journalism across all spheres, genres and platforms such as radio and TV broadcast news, documentary, political reportage and online journalism. Debate about tabloidization therefore necessarily addresses the tensions between entertainment and information within an increasingly multimedia and globalized consumerist environment (e.g. Franklin, 1997; Bromley, 1998; Stephenson, 1998; Campbell, 2004). Whether one takes a critical or more positive position in relation to tabloidization one clear concern emerges: that the consumerization of news content and competitive pressures of the media industries allow less time and space for the conduct of serious political reportage and investigative journalism (Barnett and Gaber, 2001: 7).

From a different perspective the colonization of the public sphere and mainstream media by tabloid values and aesthetics has arguably led to the democratization of media by virtue of its frequent inclusion of non elite people, issues and values. It could be said that the relationship between the 'popular' and the 'public sphere' has taken a new turn with the advent of first-person media and reality television leading critics to test and sometimes explicitly challenge outright condemnations of tabloid culture (e.g. Gamson, 1998; Dovey, 2000; Holmes and Jermyn, 2004; Biressi and Nunn, 2005); sometimes proposing new ways of conceptualizing 'the public' within the postmodern public sphere (Hartley, 1992; Couldry, 2000; Moores, 2005). Many of these arguments emerge from the conviction that even the most denigrated forms of popular culture needed to be engaged with at a serious academic level; not merely as vehicles of commercialism and ideological persuasion but also as potential sites of cultural struggle, transgressive pleasures and media visibility for ordinary people and common culture. Whatever one's view of current media culture it is widely acknowledged that tabloid values (e.g. production values, professional values and especially news values) and tabloid content (sensation, the use of vernacular, sexualization, human interest, celebrity culture and so on) have permeated and/or transformed media culture more broadly – producing what we refer to here in shorthand as 'tabloid culture'. Media theory and academic research have expanded to address the political, economic and social implications of the transformations that constitute tabloid culture. While tabloid culture owes its nomenclature and its cultural roots to tabloid journalism it also draws on and intersects with a range of other popular media including TV talkshows, popular factual programming and the aforementioned reality television.

Since the 1990s it has been possible to find studies of journalism, therefore, that have chosen to situate their research either in the context of tabloid culture or in relation to notions and concepts of the popular. In 1992 Colin Sparks and Peter Dahlgren's collection *Journalism and Popular Culture* contended that popular culture had become one of the main sites of investigation not only for cultural studies but also for contemporary mass communication research (Dahlgren and Sparks, 1992: 1; see also Sparks and Tulloch, 2000). Sparks and Dahlgren's aim was to suspend the conventional academic and theoretical boundaries and established lines of inquiry that operated in journalism studies in order to look at journalism from a fresh perspective. This agenda enabled both television and print journalism to be scrutinized as a form of popular culture *per se* as well as considering its relation to issues as diverse as celebrity, melodrama, popular knowledge and folklore. Ten years later the title of Martin Conboy's book *The Press and Popular Culture* (2002) is indicative of the enduring importance of this juxtaposition of journalism studies and popular culture. In this book Conboy begins by reflecting on Sparks and Dahlgren's argument that journalism and popular culture are indissolubly linked. He suggests that the fact that mainstream journalism is a mass media product does not preclude it from being understood as a legitimate form of popular culture. Conboy (2002: 1) notes, 'Successful popular newspapers, like their popular print predecessors, have always managed to articulate a real relationship between the reader and the commercial enterprise and at their most effective involved the reader symbolically in that venture.'

The pieces we have selected for this section all address tabloid journalism and touch on many of the issues we have signalled here. We begin with Bob Franklin's classic exposition of the pressures on news providers to entertain within the context of a highly competitive environment. This account of the emergence of 'newszak' charts the media terrain in which the defining opposition is between news and entertainment and investigates why and how soft news, entertainment and human interest are making inroads across all news genres and formats and on every media platform. This is followed by Anna Maria Jönsson and Henrik Örnebring's reassessment of tabloid journalism as necessarily 'bad' journalism. By tracking the historical development of tabloid journalism and some of the roles it has played in undertaking a populist critique of authority the authors make the case for regarding the tabloid press as an 'alternative public sphere' that may, on occasions, serve the public as well as, if not better than, its more respectable rivals. The piece by Jostein Gripsrud also scrutinizes the value judgements formed about tabloidization and popular journalism; adopting an open-minded but carefully critical evaluation of the functions of popular culture in the context of the ideal of a democratic media sphere. He does this by testing positive (John Fiske) and highly critical (Pierre Bourdieu) views of popular journalism and finding them both wanting in terms of their ability to help us arrive at a sophisticated and pragmatic understanding of what popular journalism can and cannot offer ordinary people. The section concludes with an extract from Martin Conboy's book *The Press and Popular Culture*, which usefully presents an analysis of the current cultural scene by exploring the postmodern dynamics of late capitalism and the ways in which this has fostered the breakdown of established cultural hierarchies and oppositions such as those between elite and popular culture, politics and spectacle. By this route he is able to situate our understanding of the popular press in the context of complex processes of globalization, commercialization and a media sphere in which rhetorical flare and visual images predominate.

Further reading

Calhoun, C. (ed.) (1992) *Habermas and the Public Sphere*, Cambridge, MA: MIT.

Conboy, M. (2006) *Tabloid Britain: Constructing a Community Through Language*, London: Routledge.

Curran, J. and Seaton, J. (1991) *Power Without Responsibility*, London: Routledge, 4th edition.

Engel, M. (1996) *Tickle the Public: One Hundred Years of the Popular Press*, London: Victor Gollancz.

Habermas, J. (1989) *The Structural Transformation of the Public Sphere*, Cambridge: Polity.

McGuigan, J. (1992) *Cultural Populism*, London: Routledge.

McNair, B. (2000) *Journalism and Democracy: An Evaluation of the Political Public Sphere*, London: Routledge.

Sparks, C. and Dahlgren, P (1991) *Communication and Citizenship: Journalism and the Public Sphere*, London: Routledge.

Sparks, C. and Tulloch, J. (eds) (2000) *Tabloid Tales: Global Debates Over Media Standards*, New York: Rowman & Littlefield.

Stephenson, H. (1998) 'Tickle the public: Consumerism rules', in H. Stephenson and M. Bromley (eds) *Sex, Lies and Democracy: The Press and the Public*, Harlow: Longman.

Turner, G. (1999) 'Tabloidization, journalism and the possibility of critique', *International Journal of Cultural Studies*, 2(1): 59–76.

1.1

Newszak: entertainment versus news and information
by Bob Franklin

Criticism of [. . .] recent trends in journalism and news media [. . .] has focused on a more general tendency in contemporary journalism, evident in both print and broadcast media, to retreat from investigative journalism and the reporting of hard news to the preferred territory of 'softer' or 'lighter' stories. Journalism's editorial priorities have changed. Entertainment has superseded the provision of information; human interest has supplanted the public interest; measured judgement has succumbed to sensationalism; the trivial has triumphed over the weighty; the intimate relationships of celebrities from soap operas, the world of sport or the royal family are judged more 'newsworthy' than the reporting of significant issues and events of international consequence. Traditional news values have been undermined by new values; 'infotainment' is rampant.

Since the late 1980s the pressures on news media to win viewers and readers in an increasingly competitive market have generated revised editorial ambitions. News media have increasingly become part of the entertainment industry instead of providing a forum for informed debate of key issues of public concern. Journalists are more concerned to report stories which interest the public than stories which are in the public interest. The phrase which is frequently used to articulate this changing journalistic mood is 'tabloid journalism'. John Pilger regrets this usage since the phrase originally implied a campaigning and crusading tradition of popular journalism which has only recently been perverted into 'cheap, tacky, arcade entertainment' (*Press Gazette*, 7 February 1997); McNair risks falling foul of the tendency he describes, when he offers his preferred designation 'bonk journalism' (McNair, 1994, p. 145). But Malcolm Muggeridge's neologism 'Newszak' captures the phenomenon most closely.

Newszak understands news as a product designed and 'processed' for a particular market and delivered in increasingly homogenous 'snippets' which make only modest demands on the audience. Newszak is news converted into entertainment. [. . .] In television news bulletins, a commitment to newszak is evident in programme formats in which 'one presenter talks to another' that reduce 'crucial events into a cosy chat show' (Sampson, 1996, pp. 46–7). A senior executive at ITN is unequivocal and unapologetic about the nature of the news business at ITN. He suggests that for the contemporary journalist the processing of newszak involves only a minimal exercise of news judgement and little responsibility for constructing the news agenda. The task of journalism has become merely to deliver and serve up whatever the customer wants; rather like a deep-pan pizza.

> ITN news is on contract. We are an independent supplier to ITV. All programmes on ITV are made by suppliers on a contract to the Network Centre which specifies the nature of the programmes it wants. So all I am to denigrate myself, is the guy who gives the customer what they want. I am not taking a higher, purer judgement – this is what the British people deserve or should have. I am saying this is what the customer is paying me £50 million pounds a year to make and I'm pretty unapologetic about that.
>
> (Interview with author. All other unattributed quotations in the text arise from a series of interviews conducted between 1994 and 1996.)

The emergence of newszak has not been without its critics; not least journalists and broadcasters themselves. *Independent* editor, Andrew Marr, criticised the *Guardian* for constantly serving up 'more bite-size McNugget journalism, which is small, tasty, brightly coloured and easy to ingest' (cited in Morgan, 1996, p. 14), while distinguished ex-*Sunday Times* editor, Harold Evans, in a speech to the Guild of Editors warned of the 'drift from substantive news to celebrity hunting, from news to entertainment' and advised editors to guard against 'news mutating into trivia, vigilance into intrusion, public interest into prurient interest'. Evans argues that 'tabloid values appealing to the lowest common denominator have come to prevail' (*Press Gazette*, 1 November 1996, p. 10). This new journalistic environment is not restricted to Britain but approximates closely the phenomenon which McManus has described in America as 'market driven journalism' (McManus, 1992 and 1994). James Fallow believes the changes pose a threat to American democracy, since 'the most influential parts of the media have lost sight of . . . their central values . . . the essence of real journalism which is the search for information of use to the public' (Fallows, 1996, pp. 6–7 and Cronkite, 1997, p. 2). Without an informed citizenry, democracy is impoverished and at risk.

But, in two senses at least, the suggestion of a proliferation of newszak, with all its alleged consequences for public information and democracy, prompts a sense of *déjà vu*. First, critics of contemporary journalism have invariably tended to romanticise and applaud the journalism of an earlier period. As Simon Jenkins observed wryly, 'there is always a golden age of journalism, and it was always when the person discussing the subject came into newspapers' (Engel, 1996a, p. 2). Other observers express weary incredulity and impatience with the succession of visionaries – from T.P. O'Connor, the editor of the *Star* in 1889, to journalist Tom Wolfe in 1973 – who have predicted the emergence of a 'new journalism', only to find their expectations frustrated; 'there is nothing quite so old,' the editor of *British Journalism Review* claims, 'than the periodic bouts of "New Journalism" ' (Goodman, 1994, p. 3). The accusation here is that critics have too frequently been guilty of crying wolf.

Second, newspapers, and more recently broadcast media, have always been driven by the potentially conflictual imperatives of providing information that is essential to citizens in a democracy while at the same time entertaining the public: what one historian of the press has described as the 'two major themes' in 'the development of journalism' (Williams, 1957, p. 5). The history of the press is a history of this shifting balance between informing 'public opinion while drumming up the largest number of paying customers' (ibid. p. 10). From their inception, newspapers have tried to entertain and editorial success has always entailed getting the right mix of information, news, truth, story-telling and good old-fashioned gossip. Given this newspaper history, it seems reasonable to question whether the recent changes in journalism constitute a substantive trend or simply a continuation of previous developments. [. . .] Three unprecedented and significant features of the current changes in journalism and news media seem to suggest otherwise. First, the shifting balance in favour of entertainment in news-media content has rarely, if ever, been so apparent. Second, this shift has been accompanied by a related decline in media attention to news and especially certain kinds of news; foreign and investigative news journalism have virtually disappeared from some news media. Again, the extent of the change is without precedent. Third, this decline in news coverage and the ascendancy of entertainment is evident across all news media, albeit to differing degrees: the broadsheet as well as tabloid newspapers, Radio 4 as much as Talk Radio, television services at BBC (British Broadcasting Corporation), ITN and in the satellite channels. Most significantly, these changes reflect an unprecedented congruence of longer-term changes in the financial, organisational and regulatory structures of news media combined with a deregulatory impulse provided by government media policy which will prove resilient to reversal. Newszak seems set fair to flourish.

Newszak: newspapers, television and radio

The growth of the 'broadloid'

In British newspapers, the emphasis on newszak and entertainment has long been a defining feature of the tabloid press, but recently concern has been expressed about the increasingly tabloid format and content of broadsheet newspapers (Sampson, 1996, p. 44 and Engel, 1996a, pp. 2–3). Every aspect of the modern broadsheet newspaper has changed since the 1980s. The *Guardian* offers a useful illustrative exemplar of many of these changes. So far as newspaper format is concerned, Engel identifies the emergence of the *Independent* with its 'youthful good looks and verve' as the catalyst for the major redesign of the *Guardian* in 1988 and subsequently of the *Daily Telegraph* (Engel, 1996a, p. 3). The front pages of broadsheets now incorporate many of the characteristic formats of the tabloid genre; *The Times*'s commitment to devote its front page to small ads until May 1966 has become an anachronism with remarkable rapidity (Sampson, 1996, p. 44). Since the 1980s, the broadsheets' derision of the tabloid format has increasingly become mimicry. Tabloid-style banner headlines, alliterative and 'punny' headlines, large print, less text, shorter words, bigger pictures, colour pictures and more of them, have become standard components of the broadsheet front page. But it is the changing content of 'quality' newspapers which is most significant.

Four aspects of change are noteworthy. First, broadsheet newspapers contain less news, especially foreign news, parliamentary news and investigative stories (Sampson, 1996; Engel, 1996b). The decline in all three reflects the increasingly competitive market for readers and advertisers combined with the waning financial resources of newspapers and declining journalistic staffs. Foreign correspondents and foreign news are costly items to sustain with shrinking news budgets: the *Independent*'s once renowned foreign reportage has become lean and narrow, reflecting financial restrictions. Lord Cudlipp, former editor-in-chief of the *Mirror*, regrets the extent to which so much foreign news, especially in the *Mirror*, has become bellicose, opinionated and 'relegated to a three inch yapping editorial insulting foreigners' (*Press Gazette*, 7 February 1997). Antony Sampson attributes the decline in foreign reporting to the increased competition for advertising revenues and the consequently enhanced prominence of advertisers in editorial decision-making. Advertisers determine the allocation of space and prefer subjects such as travel and consumer issues above foreign news which has little product tie-in. Consequently 'the world is disappearing out of sight' (Sampson, 1996, p. 45). Worse, foreign news is increasingly reported only when it can be presented as a human-interest story. Pictures of starving and dying children during a famine, limbless victims of land mines left behind after a recent war and seemingly endless trails of 'helpless refugees' fleeing from a current conflict litter the pages of newspapers. The purpose of such pictures seems less to inform than to elicit sympathy – a collective 'Oh, how dreadful' – from the readership.

Parliamentary news and reports of debates from the House have virtually disappeared from the broadsheet papers. Gallery journalism is dead, although few obituaries have mourned the passing of this once significant and vigorous tradition (Franklin, 1996, p. 13). The substantial reports of parliamentary debates, considered essential to the contents of serious newspapers until the early 1990s (the *Financial Times* spiked its parliamentary page as recently as 1993) have been replaced by the less weighty, more entertaining, accounts offered by the cheerful and chirpy sketch writers like Simon Hoggart and Matthew Parris. When parliamentary debates are reported in the press, moreover, they are increasingly trivialised, sensationalist and focused on personal scandals involving individual MPs rather than exploring and constructing a distinctive parliamentary agenda. One senior political journalist explained the collapse of parliamentary coverage as part of a broader 'gravitational force of decline in journalism which has taken place in our lifetime'.

Broadsheet newspapers also undertake considerably less investigative journalism. This is not to deny the welcome and excellent exceptions to this general pattern of neglect, such as John Pilger's report on the Liverpool dockers' strike which broke an otherwise extraordinary media silence or the work of journalists Ed Vulliamy and David Leigh in exposing the furtive lobbying activities of Neil Hamilton and Ian Greer (*Guardian*, 16 January 1997, p. 4). But investigative journalism is costly in terms of financial and journalistic resources and unlikely to flourish when both are scarce. It requires a news organisation to commit its most skilled, able and experienced journalists for perhaps many months or years without any guaranteed outcome in terms of a publishable story. Newszak is less demanding.

The journalistic ground vacated by foreign and investigative reporting has been eagerly colonised by a growing army of columnists. This is the second major change:

views have increasingly replaced *news*. Columnists are not specialist reporters with expertise in a particular area of journalism, but generalists, would-be renaissance figures, and members of the popular literati who routinely appear as guests on late-night chat shows and arts programmes. They seem to possess an endless supply of opinions on every topic and yet the concerns addressed in their columns can be cripplingly banal; columnists may be reduced to telling us 'what happened to them on the way to Sainsburys, what their children did at school, how they enjoyed their holidays' (Sampson, 1996, p. 45). Such routine, if not rather dull and perhaps even private, concerns have become grist to the columnist's mill. But on other occasions, the subject-matter is bizarre. Linda Grant in her *Guardian* column, for example, speculated whether the willingness of novelist Jeanette Winterson (in her early days just after Oxford) to offer sexual services to closet, middle-aged lesbians, in return for Le Creuset ovenware, had a more general relevance for family life and for women's sexual relations with their male partners ('Sex For Money Isn't A Flash In The Pan' *Guardian*, 6 January 1997, p. 13). The following day, perhaps predictably, the *Guardian* made Le Creuset the subject of its regular *Pass Notes* feature (no. 948). As if to underscore its newly acquired tabloid credentials, *The Times* 'scooped' the same story two days earlier under the heading, 'Lesbian Novelist Tells Of Sex For Le Creuset' (*The Times*, 4 January 1997, p. 3). How regrettable that the roar of the 'Thunderer' should have become such a trivial and diminutive squeak. Columns typically begin by posing a question to draw the reader in. Charlotte Raven, for example, asked 'Has Vivienne Westwood gone mad? If recent reports are to be believed, the "no knickers" Queen of punk has joined the moral regeneration brigade' (*Guardian*, 14 January 1997, p. 11). The previous day Angela Neustatter's column devoted to cosmetic surgery inquired 'Could you fancy a man who has had his penis surgically enlarged?' (*Guardian*, 13 January 1997, p. 9). At best such journalism is engaging rather than informing; it is newszak but not news.

Third, broadsheet newspapers are allocating a high news priority to stories which until relatively recently would have been dismissed and disdained as merely tabloid stories. Coverage of the royal family offers an obvious example. On the day after Diana's interview for the BBC's *Panorama* special, broadsheet coverage was extensive (21 November 1995). The *Guardian* allocated five full pages (9120 cm^2) to the interview; the *Daily Telegraph* (7008 cm^2) also provided extensive reports. The *Guardian*'s coverage was tabloid in style with remarkable points of contact with reports in the *Sun*. Both papers assembled a panel of 'experts' to offer Diana 'advice'. The motley crew in the *Sun* included Gary Bushell (the paper's television critic) and Max Clifford ('Stars' PR Guru'), while the *Guardian* managed to recruit a slightly more cerebral collection including Lord St John of Fawsley; but in essence, reports in both papers articulated a tabloid agenda expressed in tabloid format. The broadsheets' discovery of sensational and populist news has not been confined to the royal family. The four broadsheet dailies offered an aggregate 1752 column inches to Hugh Grant's meeting with prostitute Divine Brown (Engel, 1996, p. 2).

Fourth and finally, broadsheet newspapers are recently more likely to include many editorial features which previously were the exclusive preserve of the tabloids. The *Guardian*, for example, publishes a 'problem page', although it is loath to admit it, preferring the title *Private Lives*; but the format is unmistakable. The paper publishes a letter outlining a personal problem and invites readers to respond to the letter including details of their personal experience. 'What can you do when other people's children misbehave in your home?' *Private Lives* asked readers (16 January 1997, p. 25). The following week, the newspaper invited readers' responses to a different dilemma: 'Your sister is in love. The problem? He's your cousin and the family have fallen out over it. What can you do?' (*Guardian*, 23 January 1997, p. 25). At weekends, the *Guardian* offers more tabloid distractions including a *What's On* guide and a 'lonely hearts' contacts section entitled *Soul Mates*.

Given these changes, it is little wonder that some observers are concerned that the line separating broadsheet and tabloid newspapers has 'virtually disappeared' (Sampson, 1996, p. 44) or at the very least has become a 'disappearing frontier' (Engel, 1996, p. 2). *Guardian* editor Alan Rusbridger has in part conceded the case; his neologism 'broadloid' signals the extent to which broadsheet newspapers are adopting tabloid stories and styles. Andrew Marr's allegation that *The Times* can be likened to a 'transvestite, full of dinky, *Daily Mail*, values' similarly acknowledges the convergence between broadsheet and tabloid newspapers (cited in *Press Gazette*, 18 October 1996, p. 14).

Television under siege?

Television news is middle aged. ITN was born on 4 May 1955 (Sendall, 1982, p. 87); the BBC is a little older. Both are displaying unmistakable signs of a mid-life crisis. Broadcast news services expanded rapidly after the 1967 watershed when *News at Ten* went on air. *News at Ten* marked the transition of news broadcasting from the short 10-minute news bulletin into the full-blown half-hour programme and triggered an escalation in television news provision. The BBC moved to a longer *Nine O'Clock News* in 1971, launched *Newsnight* in 1980 and added the *Six O'Clock News* in 1984. ITN increased its output to include lunchtime (12.30) and early evening (5.45) slots and won the contract to provide news for the new Channel 4. The dictates of Birtism in 1987 prompted further expansion: lunchtime news, on-the-hour daytime bulletins with regional news opt-outs, news on breakfast television, and the prospect of a 24-hour news channel. Currently there are 6 hours 25 minutes of news or news analysis daily on BBC television, more than 4 hours on channels 3 and 4 (excluding GMTV), plus Sky News and CNN (Cable and Network News) (Dugdale, 1995a, p. 12).

But television news has witnessed other changes. The investigative television journalism of the 1980s evident in programmes such as *World in Action* and *Panorama* has given way to the story-led, tabloid formats of populist programmes such as *3D* and *The Big Story*. Increased competition, the 'striving for ratings', financial shortages and job cuts offer some explanation, but the government's decision in the Broadcasting Act (1990) to convert ITN from a cost to a profit centre is a major culprit. For the first time in British broadcasting, news had to make a profit. 'We are under siege,' Jon Snow claimed. 'Ratings will be the determinants because the money comes from advertisers.' In America, advertisers know that significant stories like Bosnia make 15 per cent of the audience switch off while 'the stories which got high ratings were ambulance chasing, fires and sadness' even though this coverage generated 'dreadful bulletins. . . . Within a couple of years there could be no serious analytical news programmes on American TV and that is the way we are heading' (cited in *Press Gazette*, 20 September 1996, p. 5 and Snow, 1997, p. 3). David Glencross, chief executive at the ITC (Independent Television Commission) until 1996, expressed similar concerns and regrets that 'factual programming is on a downward path towards the triumph of infotainment over both information and entertainment'. He believes that 'pelvic news' based on the scheduling philosophy of 'if it bleeds it leads' will become increasingly commonplace (Glencross, 1994, pp. 7–8). But despite these shifts in news values, ITV announced further plans in January 1997 to revamp its current-affairs programmes to attract a younger audience and 'avoid being taken on the right flank by Channel 5'. The new channel, which 'will have to be seen to be getting ratings', broadcasts current affairs which are 'non-elitist and bottom up' (Methven, 1997, p. 4). ITV is determined to match these programming ambitions.

The picture, of course, is not wholly bleak. Television, like newspapers, retains a commitment to high-quality news and current affairs which is evident in series such as *Dispatches* and *Cutting Edge*, but such programmes increasingly constitute exceptions in a culture which seems more than ever willing to jettison its public-service commitments. Paul Jackson, director of programming at Carlton, is explicit. 'If *World in Action* were to uncover three more serious miscarriages of justice,' he declared, 'while delivering an audience of . . . five millions, I would cut it. It isn't part of the ITV system to get people out of prison' (quoted in Williams, 1994, p. 16).

At the BBC, audience ratings have similarly assumed a crucial importance if the corporation is to defend the legitimacy of the licence fee, to politicians and the public, in a multi-channel broadcasting environment. Some programme makers concede the significance of audiences in shaping programme contents. Steve Hewlett, editor of *Panorama*, believes the programme must become 'popular and accessible'. 'We live in "zapland" where the remote control is too easy to reach,' he concedes, 'so it is absolutely incumbent upon us to make *Panorama* into something people want to watch' (quoted in *Press Gazette*, 27 September 1996, p. 17). Greg Dyke in his 1994 MacTaggart Lecture offers a more pessimistic thesis concerning the future vitality of news and current affairs. He suggests that the independence of television journalism has been undermined by a growing 'culture of dependency' in which broadcasters are increasingly obliged to 'seek favours' from government and are reliant on politicians for their financial success or even their very existence. In such circumstances it seems less likely than previously that broadcasters might be unduly critical of government (Dyke, 1994, p. 27). In early 1997, the BBC also announced its intention to revamp all of its news provision. The language of moving 'downmarket' is anathema to the BBC, whereas the 'search for new audiences' seems to trip more readily from the tongue. Consequently, Tony Hall, chief executive of BBC News, announced 'one of the central aims will be to encourage not only a younger audience but also one drawn from further down the socio-economic scale.' If the findings of current audience research are accurate, BBC news will have 'less on political ding dongs at Westminster and more on technology and consumer issues' after the review (Culf, 1997, p. 30).

Few research studies of changing news values exist, but early findings are suggestive. A pilot comparison of ITN news at 5.40 p.m., BBC1 news at 6 p.m., SkyNews at 5 p.m. and Radio 4 news at 6 p.m., conducted on behalf of the Voice of the Viewer and Listener, revealed that BBC programmes devoted approximately twice as much airtime to foreign news as ITN, but only half as much attention to items reporting sport, and entertainment. The study concluded that ITN and SkyNews 'operate to a tabloid agenda while BBC TV and radio operate to a more serious one' (Gaber and Barnett, 1993, p. 8). A second study made a longitudinal comparative analysis of the news content of *News at Ten* programmes broadcast before the Broadcasting Act (1990), with an equivalent sample broadcast in 1995. Findings revealed a 65 per cent decline in international news coverage while the focus on sports and 'show business and entertainment' news doubled (Pilling, 1995, p. 13). Across the same period, suggestions that *News at Ten* is moving downmarket to win larger audiences have grown more common-place. A senior broadcasting trade union official identified neatly the various programme elements in *News at Ten* which constitute almost defining characteristics of newszak:

> The number of items, the duration of each item, the range of subject areas that are reported in terms of domestic, foreign, economic and social news are defining characteristics. But there is a more subjective element which is the packaged and conclusive approach of *News at Ten*. Every item has to be snappy, with a beginning, a middle and a very good end and then move on quickly to the next item to keep people's attention.

The recently launched Channel 5 seems set to continue the recent trends of more established broadcasters. Channel 5 controller of news, Tim Gardam, announced that his mission was to prevent news from being 'painful' by offering 'less politics and more consumer, sports and entertainment, news'. Gardam's medium-term ambition, he claims, is 'beating *News At Ten*. That's what I want to be measured against' (*Press Gazette*, 17 February 1997, p. 1).

But newszak is evident in recent changes to programme formats as well as in news content. The increasing gimmickry and circus of news presentation too frequently subverts rather than clarifies the presentation of news stories. 'The technology enables us to package, graphicise and meld five minutes of old TV information into 60 seconds of new TV time,' Jon Snow of *Channel 4 News* claims, 'but the content reduction is so acute that normal debate is in danger of being degraded to the absurd' (Snow, 1997, p. 3). But television has become obsessed with pictures above the story: if there are no pictures, there is no news. The emphasis on presentation is now overwhelming. In 1993, the BBC spent £650,000 to create a virtual-reality news studio which seemed to offer a more appropriate setting for a light-entertainment spectacular rather than a news programme; a year previously, ITN had spent considerable sums on a major 'revamp' of *News at Ten*. News programmes now open with a preview of the major headlines accompanied by apocalyptic theme tunes, eye-catching, hi-tech graphics and virtual-reality backdrops. Constant previewing of 'stories still to come' and reviewing of the headline stories already discussed, suggest broadcaster assumptions about viewers' attention span which are insulting.

Newszak has also encouraged the cultivation of star journalists like Michael Brunson and celebrity presenters such as Trevor McDonald and Jeremy Paxman. But while ITN has replaced two presenters with a single newscaster, the BBC prefers the American 'buddy' style where two news anchors offer a double act. When the presenters are a man and a woman, the 'sexual chemistry' between them is believed to be important for the programme's success. Cheerful and chirpy chatting between presenters and the predictable valedictory banter with the weather presenter have become as routine to the contemporary broadcast as the tail-end item about the skateboarding duck. In Channel 5's 'brightly coloured newsroom' reporters 'chat with presenters who move around to discuss stories and issues' (*Press Gazette*, 17 February 1997, p. 1).

Another contemporary obsession is the 'live two-way', where the presenter in the studio gets the latest news from a correspondent live at the scene of the story; they are typically presented side by side on separate screens clearly and patronisingly labelled to avoid viewer confusion. The suggestion implicit in the 'two-way' is clear: this news programme is so up-to-date that the news is happening and unfolding even as the programme is being transmitted. But too frequently the journalist outside the studio has little or no information to add to what the studio presenter has already made clear. If the viewer is confused, it must surely be about the purpose of programme formats which deliver so little news. But the two-way proliferates and journalists spend an increasing amount of airtime talking to each other when their job is surely to elicit information from others. Why not invite an expert, or someone directly involved in the event which the story is relating, to offer genuine insight into what has occurred or to speculate about future developments?

Radio: the retreat from public-service broadcasting

Radio news has changed throughout the 1990s; and for the worse! Radio, like newspapers and television, seems to have shifted its focus towards entertainment rather than the provision of information, although to date this tendency is more apparent in the commercial than the public sector of broadcasting. That the BBC is not immune to such trends is evident when the *Today* programme on 14 November 1996 devoted 18 minutes' airtime to an interview with Sarah Ferguson. Radio has a distinguished history as a news broadcaster; but its recent history is that of a medium in retreat from its Reithian public-service origins to a medium in which market forces are increasingly influential in determining the range and quality of services in both the public and private sectors.

In the commercial sector of radio newszak is rampant, in part reflecting government policy changes. The Broadcasting Acts of 1990 and 1996 have triggered a proliferation of Independent Local Radio (ILR) stations, created the first three Independent National Radio (INR) stations, relaxed restrictions on ownership and cross-media ownership and created a new regulatory body for local radio intended to operate with a 'lighter touch'. The expansion of ILR stations is undeniable: from 120 in 1992 to 218 in 1996. But what is less clear is whether the government's intention, that market forces should generate greater choice and diversity in radio provision, has been achieved. In reality, the policy outcome may have been precisely the opposite. The market penalises those who stray too far from the mainstream; ILR stations offer a dull, homogeneous and predictable output. Most stations describe their output as 'classic gold' or 'easy listening' which is interrupted only on the hour by two minutes' news feed from Independent Radio News (IRN). On some stations this is complemented by locally generated news, although journalistic staffs are very modest and budgets extremely tight. Commercial local radio has little local identity and reports only a scattering of local news. Whether in Blackpool, Bristol or Basingstoke, ILR offers an unrelentingly tedious and uniform output.

National commercial radio fares little better. Any ambitions that Talk Radio might be a serious competitor to Radio 4 as a news provider have long since been dashed. Arriving on air on 14 February 1995 with a mere £8 million in launch capital, the station has always offered cheap radio. Underfunded, understaffed and committed to an unimaginative schedule comprised almost wholly of phone-in programmes, the station initially failed to reach its audience targets. 'Shock jocks' such as Caesar the Geezer routinely abused their callers, denouncing them as 'sad bastards' (Culf, 2 May 1995, p. 6) but, despite this unpromising start, the station had succeeded in attracting an audience in excess of 2 million listeners within one year of going on air and, by early 1997, enjoyed half the weekly audience reach of the award-winning Radio 5 Live (*Press Gazette*, 17 January 1997, p. 7).

Newszak is less evident in BBC radio programming than at any other point on the news media landscape. But many observers are pessimistic about the prospects for BBC radio and believe that recent trends presage a serious decline. Public-service radio, like its commercial counterpart, has been the subject of close government scrutiny especially in the period immediately prior to the renewal of the BBC's charter. The white paper, *The Future of the BBC: Serving the Nation and Competing Worldwide*, expressed the government's commitment to retaining BBC local radio, but the number of stations has been reduced from 48 to 38 in 1996 because of budgetary cuts which, across the BBC, have fallen inequitably on radio rather than television and on local radio in particular. In truth the battle for public-service radio is lost. BBC radio had 51 per cent of total radio audience share in the first quarter of 1996 but its own estimates predict this figure declining to approximately 30 per cent in the new millennium with the popular-music output of radios 1 and 2 accounting for more than half of that audience share. The remainder of the radio spectrum will be dominated by the commercial stations with their monotonous diet of pop music, formulaic chit-chat and phone-ins with a smattering of news on the hour provided by the same central, rather than local, news agency. The future for British radio is a bleak prospect; audiences will largely be served a rather unwholesome diet of muzak seasoned with newszak.

[. . .]

1.2

Tabloid journalism and the public sphere: a historical perspective on tabloid journalism
by Henrik Örnebring and
Anna Maria Jönsson

Introduction: the problem with tabloid journalism

The problems of tabloid journalism are, of course, all too well known: it allegedly panders to the lowest common denominator of public taste, it simplifies, it personalises, it thrives on sensation and scandal—in short, tabloid journalism lowers the standards of public discourse. Or, even worse, tabloid journalism may even actually be a threat to democracy, breeding cynicism and a lack of interest in politics, while ignoring the real political issues in favour of superficial political scandal.

This view of tabloid journalism is fairly common in contemporary debates on media standards—and it is not merely tabloid journalism that is so criticised. The word *tabloidisation* is sometimes used to describe the perceived tendency for all journalism, even all media, to become more like tabloid journalism (see e.g. Franklin, 1997)—so tabloid journalism seems no longer confined to the medium of its origin, the tabloid press. Indeed, today the case could be made that television is the prime medium for tabloid journalism (Dahlgren, 1992, p. 16; Langer, 1998, p. 1). Tabloid journalism and tabloidisation also become obvious targets when journalists themselves engage in self-reflection and media criticism (see e.g. Rivers, 1996). Rhoufari (2000) interviewed journalists about the role of journalism in Britain and the place of tabloid journalism in particular, and found that a kind of double standard was in place when journalists discussed the role and practices of tabloid journalism:

> . . . all the respondents, from the crime reporter to the deputy editor, developed arguments that led them, more or less explicitly, to distance themselves from the tabloid press and its methods of investigation while endorsing many of its characteristics in discussing their day-to-day activity.
>
> (Rhoufari, 2000, p. 170)

This is potentially a source of problems for social scientists investigating tabloid journalism. The researcher might easily take on the perspective common in the profession and in the media industry and adopt a perspective where tabloid journalism becomes everything which serious, responsible, good-quality journalism is not:

sensationalist, over-simplified, populist etc.: tabloid journalism means, simply, bad journalism. Tabloid journalism becomes a kind of journalistic *other*, used as a warning example and symbol for all that is wrong with modern journalism (for a similar line of reasoning, see Langer, 1998, pp. 8–9). Using this definition, the question whether there can be any quality tabloid journalism becomes impossible to ask, since tabloid journalism by definition is bad, and consequently good tabloid journalism cannot exist. If it was good, then it could not be tabloid journalism!

Recent scholarship on tabloid journalism (Sparks and Tulloch, 2000 provides a very comprehensive selection, for example) has engaged with this normative simplicity, and developed the concept of tabloidisation as well as highlighted how, even though a continually changing news market is also changing journalism, the values by which journalism is judged do not seem to change that much. Lay (and sometimes academic) criticism of journalism continues to be based around simple binary oppositions, where emotional is bad and rational-intellectual is good, sensation is contrasted with contextualisation and tabloid journalism is charged with meeting complexity with dumbing down. But emotionalism, sensation and simplification are not *necessarily* opposed to serving the public good.

The argument of this article is that the journalistic *other* of tabloid journalism has appeared throughout the history of journalism, and that elements and aspects of journalism, defined as "bad" in its own time in many cases did a better job (or at least as good a job) in serving the public good than "respectable" journalism. Tabloid journalism has done so by positioning itself, in different ways, as an alternative to the issues, forms and audiences of the journalistic mainstream—as an *alternative public sphere*, if you will. Looking at the journalism considered "tabloid" in our own time, maybe this is what is happening again. By tracking the development of tabloid journalism through history, we hope to contribute to the reassessment and revision of the normative standards commonly used to assess journalism that is currently taking place within the field of journalism studies. We will do this by first examining what an alternative public sphere can be taken to mean, and how it can be conceptualised, and then relate this to the historical development of tabloid journalism.

Journalism in the public sphere

Following Jürgen Habermas, a number of media scholars have used the concept of the *public sphere* both to describe and evaluate the role of the mass media—particularly news—in public life. Since the publication of Habermas's *The Structural Transformation of the Public Sphere* in 1962 (the first English translation appeared in 1989), his public sphere model has been developed and updated (not least by Habermas himself) to take into account a number of different aspects—one of the more important ones being the changing nature of the media landscape (the book was written when television was only just beginning to gain popularity as a mass medium). Scholars such as John B. Thompson (1995) and Peter Dahlgren (1995), for example, have argued for the increasing centrality of the media as a public arena where the public can access societal dialogues. As such, the media play an important part by providing this access, and it is relevant to talk about a *mediated public sphere* (Dahlgren, 1995, p. 9).

Thompson points out that we have gone rather far from the forms of societal organisation where dialogue and face-to-face communication are viable instruments for day-to-day democracy. Today, we are not able to participate in political life in the same way as described by Habermas, but on the other hand, public life is marked by a much higher degree of visibility—a *mediated publicness* has been created (analogous to Dahlgren's mediated public sphere). Whereas the central struggle in the bourgeois public sphere was the struggle of one particular class to find a new place in society (by criticising traditional authorities and power elites), the central struggle in the mediated public sphere is the struggle for visibility, i.e. the struggle to be heard and seen in the first place (Thompson, 1995, pp. 247ff). This struggle for visibility seems to indicate that there might not be just one mediated public sphere, but instead the media landscape could be described as consisting of a mainstream and a number of alternative spheres—spheres from which marginalised groups strive to gain access to, and representation in, the mainstream.

Alternatives and counterpublics

Even a cursory examination of modern media shows that it is simply not realistic to talk about "the mediated public sphere" as if it constituted a single monolithic entity. Outlets for news, journalism, commentary and debate are numerous and increasingly global in nature. But for the sake of our argument, we assume that one can talk about some kind of *mainstream mediated public sphere*, consisting perhaps of the television and radio news and commentary shows and the daily newspapers that have the largest audience and/or are generally considered most important (in the most general sense of the word) by members of the audience as well as members of the political, economic and cultural elites. We further assume that this mainstream mediated public sphere is dominated by elite sources of different kinds (politicians, corporate representatives, representatives of non-governmental organisations etc.).

This type of structural elitism in the mainstream mediated public sphere in turn creates a need for one or several *alternative* public spheres, where different people debate different issues in different ways. This is a perspective advanced by one of Habermas's key critics, Nancy Fraser (1989, 1992). As Fraser points out, Habermas ". . . stresses the singularity of the bourgeois conception of the public sphere, its claims to be *the* public arena, in the singular" (Fraser, 1992, p. 122). The basic unity and all-encompassing nature of the bourgeois public sphere is an integral part of its attractiveness as an ideal—everyone takes part in public life, playing by the rules of rational debate and equality. Fraser, and others, instead suggest that creating possibilities for alternative public spheres to exist and thrive is a better way to promote democratic participation and open public debate. She writes:

> I contend that in stratified societies, arrangements that accommodate contestation among a plurality of competing publics better promote the ideal of participatory parity than does a single, comprehensive, overarching public.
>
> (Fraser, 1992, p. 122)

and further:

This historiography [the revisionist historiography of the public sphere, our note] records that members of subordinated social groups—women, workers, peoples of colour, and gays and lesbians—have repeatedly found it advantageous to constitute alternative publics. I propose to call these subaltern counterpublics in order to signal that they are parallel discursive arenas where members of subordinated social groups invent and circulate counterdiscourses to formulate oppositional interpretations of their identities interests and needs.

(Fraser, 1992, p. 123)

Fraser uses the late 20th-century feminist movement as an example of such a subaltern counter public, using alternative outlets like journals, publishing companies, bookstores, film and video distribution networks, meeting places, festivals etc. to invent, formulate and spread new concepts and terms (e.g. "sexism" and "sexual harassment") for describing and critiquing social phenomena.

It must be pointed out that Habermas and Fraser to an extent, pursue different theoretical and empirical agendas: Habermas is interested in the public sphere as a locus for *political power*, whereas Fraser is discussing the role of the public sphere as an arbiter of *cultural recognition*. Political power and cultural recognition are related, to be sure (it is difficult to achieve power without recognition). But the emancipatory potential of the public sphere will certainly be judged differently depending on whether the main standard is equality of power or equality of recognition. Needless to say, this discussion is very philosophically complex and intensely debated, and cannot be resolved here. We do wish to point out, however, that criticism of tabloid journalism and tabloid form is more often made using traditional criteria of political power (voting, participation in formal political activities etc.), rather than criteria of cultural recognition (representation, participation in other types of political activities etc.)— see the summary of criticisms of tabloidisation provided by McNair (2003, pp. 46–52), for example. This is something we will return to in our conclusions.

Dimensions of the alternative

Fraser primarily discusses the public sphere in general and not specifically the mediated public sphere. Using Fraser's argument as a basis for conceptualising alternative mediated public spheres, we can say that they can be "alternative" in four different, but related ways. First, alternative might be taken to mean that the discourse itself takes place *somewhere else* other than in the mainstream mediated public sphere—in alternative media outlets, in specialised journals or fanzines, on the Internet, etc. Second, the alternative public sphere may be alternative in the sense that *other participants* than those normally dominating media discourse have access to and a place in the debates and discussions taking place. Third, an alternative public sphere might be alternative in the sense that *other issues* than those commonly debated in the mainstream are discussed—or that issues not even debated at all in the mainstream are discussed in the alternative sphere (much like the privileged position of the church could be debated and defined as a potential obstacle to emancipation in the bourgeois public sphere, for example). Fourth, the "alternativeness" may derive from the usage of *other ways or forms* of debating and discussing common issues than those commonly used in the mainstream, for example forms which encourage citizen participation and non-parliamentary direct action.

As noted at the outset, all these aspects are related: the whole concept of an alternative public discussion being carried out somewhere else than in the mainstream (the first aspect), implies that it will include other participants, be open to other issues and/or use other forms—there is no need to conform to the explicit or implicit rules of the mainstream mediated public sphere. For Fraser, the aspect of creating an entirely new public sphere, based on different networks and media outlets, is clearly the most important one—from this all other aspects follow (Fraser, 1992, pp. 123–4). She points to the dual nature of subaltern counter publics: "On the one hand, they function as spaces of withdrawal and regrouping; on the other hand, they also function as bases and training grounds for agitational activities directed towards wider publics" (Fraser, 1992, p. 124). To have "a space of one's own" is central to the idea of subaltern counter publics and alternative public spheres.

However, this raises the problematic question of integration. According to Fraser, these subaltern counter publics are alienated from the mainstream, or dominant, public sphere both by choice and by necessity. But it would seem that at least part of the goal for subaltern counter publics is acceptance into the mainstream—not acceptance on the terms of the dominant ideology, but rather a dissemination of the subaltern counter public's own definitions and discourses into the mainstream. Indeed, this seems to be one consequence of defining subaltern counter publics as "bases and training grounds for agitational activities directed towards wider publics" (Fraser, 1992, p. 124). Thus, while Fraser's ideal remains a "multiple publics" model, it continues to be important to exert influence over the mainstream, redefining and recontextualising public issues for wider publics.

The discourses created in tabloid journalism are clearly not taking place "somewhere else", in an alternative arena—tabloid journalism must in most ways be said to be solidly within the mediated mainstream. But using a wider definition of the concept of "alternative", tabloid journalism, at least in theory, could provide the three other aspects of an alternative public sphere: it is quite possible that the tabloids would cover different issues using different forms, giving voice to different participants. In the context of the mediated public sphere, we use "alternative" to indicate criticism and questioning of the political, economic and cultural elites and the societal status quo—the possession of some kind of emancipatory potential. Tabloid journalism can help affect social change in addressing issues not previously open to debate, including new publics and using new forms—thus introducing new areas of discourse into the mainstream mediated public sphere. So, there is no theoretical reason why tabloid journalism should not be able to do exactly the same kinds of things Habermas has shown that the early press did during the emergence of the bourgeois public sphere. In the second part of this article, we demonstrate that tabloid journalism has done this many times throughout its history—and that it might well do so again.

Tabloid journalism as alternative public sphere

The word "tabloid" was introduced into the world of media by Alfred Harmsworth (Lord Northcliffe). He stole a term trademarked by a pill manufacturer (*tabloid* was a combination of the words *tablet* and *alkaloid*). Harmsworth wanted his new paper, the *Daily Mail* (established in 1896), to be like a small, concentrated, effective pill, containing all news needs within one handy package, half the size of a conventional broadsheet newspaper. The smaller size made the tabloids easier to handle and read on the bus, tram and other forms of public transport—an adaptation for a new reading public. It must be added that the tabloid format was only one of many strategies Lord Northcliffe used to reach a mass audience: contents, layout, price, distribution and marketing were all factors contributing to the mass-market appeal of the *Daily Mail*. The *Daily Mail* was "the daily time saver", according to Northcliffe, the news format for the quick-paced twentieth century (Seymour-Ure, 2000, p. 10; Tulloch, 2000, pp. 131–2).

The tabloid press thus was synonymous not only with a specific paper format, but also with a certain way of selecting and presenting news. From the very beginning, the tabloid press was criticised for sensationalism and emotionalism, for over-simplification of complex issues, for catering to the lowest common denominator and sometimes for outright lies. But tabloid journalism also managed to attract new publics, by speaking to them about issues previously ignored, in new, clearly understandable ways. Much of the criticism against tabloid journalism came from established power-holders within the media industry, as well as representatives of a pre-industrial, pre-mass society cultural and political elites. Tabloid journalism was damned, in part, for not conforming to the more refined tastes of these elite groups.

[. . .]

Alternative publics: tabloid journalism, new journalism and the yellow press

The first instance of more popular journalism aimed specifically at a non-elite public came with the so-called penny press in America around 1830. The word "tabloid" was of course not yet in use (see the previous section), but the penny press was clearly a forerunner—not least because the penny press also functioned as a kind of journalistic other, being criticised for sensationalism, emotionalism and the other identified characteristics outlined above.

With the introduction of these papers both the reason for publishing newspapers and the content of the newspapers changed. The penny press was more of an economic venture and less a political project than had been the case with most of the papers before that time: ". . . with the penny press a newspaper sold a product to a general readership and sold the readership to advertisers" (Schudson, 1978, p. 25). An important element in this new kind of journalism was an interest for the everyday life of people and it was in the penny press that so-called *human-interest* news was born. This kind of journalism was, and still is, considered less important and noteworthy than so-called hard news. Michael Schudson draws the important conclusion that these changes in journalism and the development of ideals was intimately connected to political as well as economic changes—at the same time the democratic market society was born (Schudson, 1978, pp. 27ff). [. . .]

The year 1833 is considered a watershed year in the history of the American press. On 3 September of that year, New Yorkers saw the arrival of a new daily newspaper: the *New York Sun*. Its founder, Benjamin Day, made a paper for "the common man" in a time where newspapers usually aimed for a more affluent and educated audience. Before the *New York Sun*, the largest dailies were mostly distributed by subscription. Copies bought at newspaper vendors cost six cents. The *Sun* was sold in the streets for one penny, and its customers were the rising American working classes.

The major invention of Day was the redefinition of the concept of news. In earlier papers, news meant reports and comments on political happenings, and even more importantly, commercial information such as shipping news—the audience was the property class, not the working class (DeFleur and Ball-Rokeach, 1989, p. 53). The so-called human-interest story might well have originated in its modern form on the pages of the *Sun*. Scandalous tales of sin, the immoral antics of the upper class, and humorous tales of mishaps of all kinds were a staple of the *Sun*. But so was extended coverage of crime and police news, mostly written by the British veteran police reporter George Wisner (Emery and Emery, 1978, p. 120). In short, it was aimed directly at a newly literate public that did not have much in common with the newspaper public of a mere 10 years earlier.

Inevitably, Day's foray into the newspaper business was met with criticism from other contemporary publicists, who accused the *Sun* of lowering the standards of journalism through its vulgarity, cheapness and sensationalism (DeFleur and Ball-Rokeach, 1989, p. 52; Emery and Emery, 1978, p. 121). The critics became especially vehement after it became apparent that the *New York Sun* was a commercial success. Some of this criticism might seem inappropriate in relation to the modern concept of news, for, as Schudson writes:

> The six-penny papers responded to the penny newcomers with charges of sensationalism. This accusation was substantiated less by the way the penny papers treated the news (there were no sensational photographs, of course, no cartoons or drawings, no large headlines) than by the fact that the penny papers would print "news"—as we understand it—at all.
>
> (Schudson, 1978, p. 23)

Imitators launched new papers almost immediately. The most well known of these competitors are probably James Gordon Bennett, who founded the *New York Herald* in 1835, and Horace Greeley, who founded the *New York Tribune* in 1841. During the years following, the journalism of the penny press changed. Bennett developed crime reporting and a generally more aggressive journalism, used "extras" (special editions) to boost interest in the paper, he included a letters column, where readers could comment on the paper, he developed a financial section and he offered sports news. As with Day, Bennett was roundly criticised by other publicists. A movement to boycott the *Herald* was started, and Bennett was even accused of blasphemy because of his at times flippant treatment of religious news (Emery and Emery, 1978, p. 125). No doubt the *Herald* used sensationalism and emotionalism to bring in the readers, but clearly much of the criticism at the time was motivated by the astounding commercial success of the paper. It was the traditional New York papers, Colonel James Watson Webb's *Courier and Enquirer* and Park Benjamin's *New York*

Signal, that led the war against Bennett's *Herald*, clearly afraid to lose their own position as commercially leading dailies.

When Horace Greeley started his *New York Tribune* in 1841, he used many of Day's and Bennett's ideas, but added something genuinely his own: a tireless crusading journalism and campaigning for a wide range of causes (Smith, 1979, p. 139). Greeley apparently tried to avoid the worst sensationalism of the earlier penny papers, but his sights were still set on "the common man" as audience and public. Greeley, as well as his predecessors, was criticised, mostly for his radicalism and habitual crusading—if it wasn't the evils of alcohol that raised his ire, it was the practice of tobacco consumption. But Greeley's mass paper undoubtedly played an important role in opinion leadership and formation (Tebbel, 1963, pp. 105, 112).

When what is considered to be the next great change in the history of American newspaper came about in the 1880s and 1890s, it is worth noting that the elite's reception of new inventions in journalism changed little. In 1883, Joseph Pulitzer purchased the *New York World* and proceeded to turn it into one of the success stories of the decade. Part of the recipe was the same as Day's five decades earlier: sensation, crime and varied news coverage. Other important parts of Pulitzer's formula were aggressive self-promotion, and, more importantly, a penchant for crusades that rivalled Greeley's. Pulitzer took up several popular causes and campaigned for them in his newspaper, thus both covering and forming public opinion. An immigrant himself, Pulitzer often railed against the inhuman conditions in which many of New York's immigrant labourers lived—particularly against the garment district's sweatshops which employed immigrant women. When, in July 1883, a heat wave caused the deaths of over 700 in the slums (over half of them children under the age of 5), Pulitzer used sensational headlines and shocking narrative in an attempt to force the authorities to recognise the housing problems of the city (Emery and Emery, 1978, p. 224)—a clear illustration of the simple truth that sensational and emotional coverage might have a place and a function within the public sphere, helping to bring about social change and addressing issues not previously addressed in the mediated public sphere.

As could have been expected, Pulitzer came under fire for reviving the coarse and lurid sensationalism of the penny press in the 1830s. He had many imitators and, as before, commentators considered the proliferation of sensationalism and human interest stories a threat to serious journalism (Emery and Emery, 1978, pp. 224–5; Tebbel, 1963, pp. 201–2). The critics became even more vocal when the so-called "yellow journalism war" started in 1895, when William Randolph Hearst bought the *New York Journal* and challenged Pulitzer's new *Sunday World*.

Hearst's sensationalism was considered even more brazen than Pulitzer's and when it came to crusades and campaigning, Hearst consistently strived to go one better than his competitor. The *Journal* soon adopted the tag line "While Others Talk the *Journal* Acts"—among other things, the paper obtained a court injunction that stopped the granting of a city franchise to a gas company. After this success, the *Journal* started similar actions against alleged abuses in government and by large corporations (Emery and Emery, 1978, p. 249; Tebbel, 1963, p. 201). This "journalism that acts" was lauded as well as criticised.

Two points can be made from this short and admittedly selective history of the American penny press. First, that it demonstrates the continuous existence of a journalistic other, that the established institutions of journalism use to define themselves—according to its critics, the penny press, and later the yellow journalism of the 1880s and 1890s, epitomised everything that good journalism should not be. Second, that this journalism obviously played an important role in the public sphere. While it often was sensationalist and emotional rather than measured and rational-intellectual, it can well be described as an alternative public sphere, where a grassroots-based populist critique against established corporate and governmental elites could come to the fore. While the discourse in this populist public sphere might have been limited, the mere fact that it existed where no alternative mediated public sphere of such a size and influence had existed before, demonstrates the potential power of tabloid journalism in widening the public sphere. Being unabashedly emotional does not seem to have stopped the penny press from having a bettering influence on issues of great importance to the poor and disenfranchised in the society of its time.

Alternative issues: a sensationalist crusade

We now move from the United States to the UK. The journalist W. T. (William Thomas) Stead joined the evening penny paper *Pall Mall Gazette* in 1880 as a sub-editor. The *Pall Mall Gazette* was at the forefront of the so-called "new journalism" in the London press. This "new journalism" sought new audiences and was character-ised by a lighter approach and dramatisation of news (especially crime)—in other words, it was the tabloid journalism of its day.

W. T. Stead was soon to move from his position as a sub-editor at the *Pall Mall Gazette* to become one of the most influential and prolific members of the editorial staff. In 1885, he was approached by Benjamin Scott and Josephine Butler, who had for some time and without much success campaigned against juvenile prostitution and for a Bill raising the age of consent (the age of consent at the time was 13). Stead was enlisted to the cause and became a vitriolic critic of juvenile prostitution. He embarked upon a scheme to attract and focus public attention on the issue: he decided to pose as a "vicious man" and try to buy a young girl from her parents, and then try to sell the girl to a house of ill repute. Using a female intermediary, Stead managed to buy a girl and then to sell her, before revealing his ruse and handing the girl into the care of the Salvation Army (Whyte, 1925, pp. 160ff). In July 1885, the first article (of five) on this early form of investigative reporting was published in the *Pall Mall Gazette*. It was entitled *The Maiden Tribute of Modern Babylon: the report of our secret commission*, and had subheadings such as 'The Violation of Virgins', 'The Confessions of a Brothel-Keeper' and 'How Girls are Ruined'. The article took up five and a half of the Gazette's 16 pages. The next day, another five-page article appeared with headings such as 'Unwilling Recruits', 'How Annie was Poisoned', 'You Want a Maid, do you?' and 'I Order Five Virgins'. Headlines like 'The Ruin of the Very Young', 'Entrapping Irish Girls' and 'Ruining Country Girls' continued to appear over the next week (Cranfield, 1978, pp. 212–13; also see Herd, 1952, p. 229 and Whyte, 1925, pp. 163–6). We can see how Stead piqued the readers' interest by using drastic, sensational and even lurid headlines, a typically tabloid strategy.

The reactions caused by the reports of the *Gazette* were many and diverse. Some newsagents refused to sell the *Gazette*, and Stead himself was prosecuted and sentenced to three months in jail, because he had not obtained the consent of the girl's father before "buying" her, and he had also stated in public that he "abducted" her (see Whyte, 1925, pp. 182–6 and Herd, 1952, p. 230). Many readers and advertisers cancelled their orders—but new customers came in their stead. The other London newspapers commented on the *Gazette*'s articles: the *Weekly Times* considered them "a public outrage", whereas *Reynold's News* said that "The *Pall Mall Gazette* has done one of the most courageous and noblest works of our time". But the most common reaction seems to have been, as Whyte puts it, ". . . people . . . were so shocked and scandalized by Stead's methods that they could not take adequately to heart the horrors which he had revealed . . ." (1925, p. 167). For some, the controversial and unorthodox methods Stead used raised far more ire than the widespread practice of juvenile prostitution.

Stead's motives were questioned: was he simply a sensationalist trying to sell papers, or a genuine crusader (Cranfield, 1978, pp. 213–14; Whyte, 1925, pp. 171–2)? It is, of course, quite possible that he was both—the binary opposition between writing-for-profit and writing-for-a-cause is exactly the result of the overly simplistic view of tabloid journalism we have described at the outset of this article. Indeed, Stead's biographer Frederic Whyte describes him as follows:

> As all who knew him can attest, Stead was sincerity itself in his love for, and devotion to, the less fortunate of his fellow-men—he never spared either his time or his purse in his efforts to help them—but his whole-hearted benevolence went hand in hand always with a boyish delight over his own prowess and a showman's eagerness to turn it into practical account.
>
> (Whyte, 1925, p. 105)

Stead's campaigning influenced public opinion and caused much heated public discourse. The culmination of the affair was a mass demonstration in Hyde Park, and the passing of the Criminal Law Amendment Bill, which raised the age of consent to 16 years. Numerous influential public figures came out on Stead's side, and it was clear that the articles and the ensuing debate created a public pressure on the legislators (Cranfield, 1978, p. 214; Whyte, 1925, pp. 166–73, 180–2). The stir that Stead's articles caused cannot be underestimated—he introduced an issue not previously widely debated, using controversial forms of presentation, and clearly also helped bring on a concrete political effect (new legislation) that could be defined as fairly progressive. The *Gazette* helped the formation of public opinion and public discourse on a hotly debated issue—probably not in spite of but rather thanks to its sensationalist bent, using sensationalism and emotional reporting to gain attention and ferment opinion.

[. . .]

The previous examples show that much of the criticism levelled at the journalistic other through history has been based on a set of values that to a large extent coincides with the values of cultural and political elite groups—groups that, in some cases, did not take too kindly to the competition for resources and attention that tabloid journalism offered. This is, of course, not to say that all criticism of tabloid journalism is based on class-based self-interest. Tabloid journalism can be legitimately criticised in many ways. To state the obvious: the fact that sensationalism, emotional appeals and new forms of presentation are not always incompatible with factuality and fairness, does not mean that an incompatibility *never* exists—of course a focus on the emotional and sensational aspects of a news event or story can mean that facts or fairness suffer. And the fact that emotional appeals may serve the public good as well as rational-intellectual reporting and debate, does not mean emotional crusades always serve the public good—but it is possible for it to do so. Again, this is an obvious point, but we still feel it needs to be reiterated: we take a revisionist stance, but of course we do not want to rule out the possibility of criticising tabloid journalism on *any* grounds.

What we are calling for is a greater openness when making normative judgments about tabloid journalism and its effects. What we have referred to as tabloid journalism runs like a spectre through the history of journalism—where there are ideals and ideas about good journalism, there is also a discourse about bad journalism. Bad journalism helps define the good. And the criticism levelled against bad journalism seems to follow similar lines from the 19th century onwards: it is populist, sensationalist, emotionalist, simplifying, uncouth and irresponsible—everything good journalism, is not. Whether we call it tabloid journalism, New Journalism or the penny press, the discourse surrounding journalism more oriented towards the popular and the mass audience seems almost timeless. Popular journalism is immoral, unethical and possibly dangerous precisely because it aims for a different audience than its predecessors or contemporary competitors.

In this study of the development of journalism in history, we have pointed to several examples where the tabloid press actually became an important and influential part of the mainstream mediated public sphere and public discourse, serving the public good. The populist nature of tabloid journalism may have many faults, but it can also be seen as an alternative arena for public discourse, wherein criticism of both the privileged political elites and traditional types of public discourse plays a central role. Tabloid journalism has the ability to broaden the public, giving news access to groups that previously have not been targeted by the prestige press (as was the case when the penny press and the yellow journalism aimed for the mass audience), to effect societal change by redefining previously undebatable issues as in need of debate (as was the case of W. T. Stead's campaigning in the *Pall Mall Gazette*), and give rise to new forms of journalistic discourse that may be more accessible to the audience and less deferent towards traditional authority (as was the case of the interview—a form of journalism that was seen as controversial at least in part because its central element was questioning people in authority). And the often-criticised appeal to emotions prevalent in tabloid journalism can actually stimulate political participation, by speaking to the senses and feelings as well as the rational mind.

[. . .]

1.3

Tabloidization, popular journalism, and democracy
by Jostein Gripsrud

"Tabloidization" is a tabloid term, more of a journalistic buzzword than a scholarly concept. It connotes decay, a lowering of journalistic standards that ultimately undermines the ideal functions of mass media in liberal democracies. In this chapter, I argue that we need a more nuanced understanding of the processes and journalistic forms in question and their relations to the ideals of democratic media. Very briefly put, my view is that some forms of popular and tabloid journalism may be good for some purposes and not for others, while some other forms are probably good for nothing much.

I will first present examples of both very enthusiastic and very critical evaluations of tabloid and other forms of popular journalism, thus presenting my own pragmatic view as a possible third alternative. After looking at the conceptual confusion marking much scholarly discourse on these phenomena, I demonstrate that dichotomies such as "popular" versus "quality" journalism cannot really grasp the complexities of actual journalistic practice, even if they are still partially valid. I argue that many typical forms of popular journalism, perhaps most of them, not least serve as ritual forms of communication, and hence have a purpose that is different from that of journalism, which is more directly relevant for political discourse and action. From the perspective of citizenship and democracy, however, I still argue that both main types of purposes and journalistic forms are important.

Populist enthusiasm

The most prominent representative of a very positive attitude toward tabloid journalism (and other forms of "vulgar" media culture) has no doubt been John Fiske.[1] As an example, I will look at his reading of the (to many or most: quite hilarious) U.S. "supermarket tabloid" *Weekly World News*.

Fiske once argued that the popularity of supermarket tabloids such as the *Weekly World News* is "evidence of the extent of dissatisfaction in a society, particularly among those who feel powerless to change their situation," since such publications demonstrate "the failures of that from which they [the disadvantaged] are excluded" (Fiske 1989, 117). Referring to the front page of an issue of the *Weekly World News*,

Fiske says, "Every headline on the page is a sensational example of the inability of 'the normal' (and therefore of the ideology that produced it) to explain or cope with specific instances of everyday life. . . . It investigates the boundaries of common sense in order to expose its limits" (116). So the headlines "Laser Beam Sets Brain Surgery Patient Ablaze" and "ALIEN MUMMY FOUND: He Looks Like an E.T. Who Never Made It Home" provide antiestablishment pleasures for readers since they represent "the failures or inadequacies of science," or "the pleasures of seeing the dominant, controlling explanations of the world at the point of breakdown, pleasures that are particularly pertinent to those who feel barred from participating in controlling discourses of any sort, scientific or not" (116). And "the story about a top model marrying a leper or a 77-year-old woman eloping with a 90-year-old 'boyfriend' are pleasurable because they enable those whose sexual relationships 'fail' to accord with the romantic ideology of the 'normal' couple to question the norms rather than their own experience" (116).

Many will agree that there are good reasons to take these interpretations with a grain of salt, or perhaps rather quite a few lumps of it. A look at the headlines Fiske does *not* comment on is enough to demonstrate the contrived and inadequate nature of his interpretation. "Hitchhiking Ghost Causes Car Wrecks" may of course also illustrate the inadequacies of science and commonsense ideology in the face of certain "everyday events." But it is harder to make "PARENTS CATCH CHILD ABUSER–ON VIDEOTAPE" fit in with a general resistance to dominant ideologies and controlling discourses. That the story about the alien mummy on the front page is introduced with "finally, the proof we've been waiting for, say scientists" actually smacks more of celebration of scientific progress than pleasures in the breakdown of science as a controlling discourse, and this is probably why Fiske does not mention it. Finally, neither "Was This Man Fired–For Being Too Fat?" nor "QUIZ REVEALS HOW SEXY YOU REALLY ARE" indicate a questioning of the boundaries of the ideological common sense.

A more important problem with this overly sympathetic attitude to publications such as the *Weekly World News* is that it fails to address the problem of how the audiences Fiske and others try to be supportive of are supposed to get information and analysis that is more useful to them if they wish to collectively influence or change their social situation. If political and economic trends and decisions affect them, and international conditions and struggles may be pertinent to their understanding of themselves and their possibilities, how does the *Weekly World News* and other, less entertaining tabloid products serve them? It seems probable that meaningfully active citizenship requires other forms of journalistic information than the pseudo "news" exemplified here.

Utopian critique

The term "tabloidization" is tied to, if not a full-blown moral panic, then at least serious ethical and political worries. Such a discourse has a long history both in public debates and in media theory. Complaints about the deplorable features of much journalism have been voiced ever since the birth of the modern press. (Cf. for instance Keane 1991:44ff.) The fact that such criticism has been around for a long time certainly does not in itself invalidate it. But it should remind us that simplistic narratives about a historical fall from a once ideal, golden age of journalism are unreliable. Furthermore, it indicates that hopes for an entirely serious, enlightening, and ethically impeccable journalism are futile. Jürgen Habermas' classic study of the bourgeois public sphere could be used as an example of such problematic utopianism, but I will instead, for a change, and also because Habermas has since changed his views considerably, point to more recently published work by Pierre Bourdieu.

Bourdieu's sociology of taste has in some Anglo-American circles been perceived as a kind of populist critique of cultural hierarchies and used to demonstrate how the appreciation of high culture is an elitist sin, while the appreciation of any kind of popular culture is an act of solidarity with the people. But Bourdieu himself has actually never been a champion of "equal rights" for popular culture forms. If he does anything in this area aside from the mere social-scientific construction of how culture and society is hierarchically ordered, it is to point out how cultural capital and pure taste are tied to social power and that this is one reason why they are worth having. Cultural capital is not least useful knowledge, and pure taste is not least analytical competence.

This must be kept in mind if we wish to understand the position from which Bourdieu, over the last few years, has been much more engaged in directly political issues than ever before–writing about poverty, unemployment, immigration. It is in connection with this turn that he has also done work on journalism. The little book or pamphlet he published in early 1996, *Sur la télévision*, is a vehement attack on the commercialization and "dumbing down" of, primarily, television journalism.

Bourdieu contends that the field of journalism, like other fields within the realm of culture, is increasingly being deprived of its relative autonomy through the invasion of economic forces that in principle are alien to it. His perspective is in other words strikingly similar to that of Habermas in this respect. But Bourdieu pays closer attention to the actual workings of journalistic practice, pointing out how the increased importance of market research in the printed press and people-meter technology in television significantly increase the pressures on classic enlightenment ideals in journalism. Moreover, he adds, a further consequence to these developments is the effect on other cultural fields, which depend on journalism to reach a wider public. When increased commercial pressures lead to increased reliance on journalistic forms typical of what is known as popular journalism, then this affects also public debate in general, the communication of knowledge produced in various kinds of research, the representation of art in mainstream media, and so on. Sensationalism, personalization, and, not least, the reliance on short, superficial treatment of just about any topic, prevents in-depth, critical coverage of serious issues. The intellectuals who thrive under such circumstances are what Bourdieu calls, using an English phrase, "fast thinkers," an intended reference to fast food. They write one book per year and are ready to comment on anything according to the rules of sound-bite television. They "think faster than their own shadow," Bourdieu says, hinting at the comicbook character Lucky Luc's ability with a gun. This has repercussions within these related fields in that, for instance, academia becomes increasingly orientated toward "stars." Scholars who for largely irrelevant reasons enjoy success in the media can "convert" this "capital of fame" into academic capital plus real money for research, increased salaries, and the like.

Bourdieu's perspective does in other words demonstrate how journalism is central not only to the production and communication of news, but also to the developments in the cultural field at large, that is, the political and cultural public sphere. A relative expansion of certain forms of popular journalism affects cultural, political, and public life in general, not just a set of journalistic formats. I think this is a very important point, often overlooked. Bourdieu's perspective is useful when one tries to get an overall grip of what happens to journalism in today's increasingly competitive media markets, where there also seem to be stronger demands for profits among media owners. Many journalists have experienced how editorial freedom and professional ethos have been set aside by market analyses (i.e., how increased commercialization effectively works as a kind of censorship).

But I also find Bourdieu's attitude toward journalism somewhat problematic. One may sometimes get the impression that he finds almost any coverage of accidents, natural disasters, plane crashes, bank robberies, murders, and calves with two heads what the French call *faits divers*, that is, the favored fare of any popular journalism, illegitimate. It appears as if all newspapers should more or less look and read like *Le Monde*, a paper that tends to pile up in French intellectuals' homes since they never have time to read it as thoroughly as they feel they should and where you find photographs only in the ads. Television should, one may sometimes get the impression Bourdieu suggests, somehow adopt a style analogous to *Le Monde*, exclusively presenting programs where solid analyses are presented at length by rarely interrupted "slow thinkers." This is probably not what he actually has in mind, but the way he phrases his critique of current practices may leave an impression much like such a caricature. His pamphlet may be read as a call for a journalistic Utopia, a nowhere land–and a never-land as well. It is, for instance, quite a while since Villemessant, the founder of *Le Figaro*, said, that to his readers, "an attic fire in the Latin Quarter is more important than a revolution in Madrid" (quoted from Benjamin 1969, 88).

Bourdieu's critique of major trends in today's journalism is, then, in many ways timely and important. But the impression one gets of his alternative to the current situation is not convincing since anything that may belong to the *faits divers* category, anything that is not thoroughly serious, seems to have no place in the journalism he advocates. While I think it is paramount that quality journalism is maintained and further improved, and that it should reach as many as possible, I think a totally intellectual or "literary" journalism is practically unthinkable and politically not desirable: too many citizens would be excluded and so would most probably a number of perspectives based in their life-worlds. For various brands, forms, and concerns of popular journalism do after all have important ties to the everyday lives, values, and interests of "ordinary people." But popular journalism is indeed a mixed bag, and this is why the terms commonly used to describe and understand it are so often confusing.

Conceptual confusion

"Tabloid," derived from the word "tablet," originally designated, as we all know, a particular newspaper format (i.e., half a broadsheet). But the world's first tabloid newspaper, the British *Daily Mirror*, from 1903 on combined this format with an emphasis on certain kinds of brief stories, large pictures, and sensationalist headings.

The connotative link between a certain format and a certain journalistic profile has since then been established. *Le Monde* and all the other tabloid "quality" papers have not been able to alter this. The term "tabloid television" reveals how the original denotative meaning of tabloid as a particular paper format has been almost totally replaced by the form-and-content connotations–it does not refer to TV screens half the normal size.

The meanings of "tabloid journalism" are now in common usage hard to distinguish from those of "popular journalism." This conceptual confusion is well examplified in the title of one of the most interesting books on television journalism in recent years, John Langer's *Tabloid Television* (1998), subtitled *Popular Journalism and the "Other News."* The relations among the three terms in this title (tabloid, popular, "other") are not evident and can hardly be said to get a thorough discussion anywhere in the book. One gets the impression that all three are practically synonymous, and so the title appears pleonastic. But on page ten Langer talks about "reality programming" and "tabloid tv" as "new actuality genres"–which he actually only quite briefly deals with toward the end of the book's final chapter. This may make the book's title less pleonastic, but more odd.

Tabloid Television is actually about the author's own category, "the other news," which consists of all kinds of news that are not directly related to politics, central social issues, and the economy. Earthquakes, traffic accidents, and fires are thus other news, along with human interest stories of various kinds. Crime news are also other news, even if Langer for practical reasons has excluded them from the sample of news material he analyzes. The category in other words contains both "hard" and "soft" news, both socially central information (e.g., a local school was vandalized last night) and material that is less important from an informational point of view (e.g., a lost puppy was found this morning). The term "the other news" is in other words a residual category, only negatively defined. Hence the bewildering diversity of its contents.

Popular, tabloid, trash

The terminological confusion of which the title of Langer's book is an example is clearly problematic. There is an obvious need for distinctions within the field of popular journalism. Many nontabloid forms and contents are popular in the simple sense that they enjoy widespread popularity, both in print and broadcast media. The conflation of *tabloid* and *popular* may thus obscure the existence and potential of a popular journalism, which is different from the forms most typically associated with the first of those terms. Newspaper pages or TV programs devoted to local news of various politically relevant kinds ("Should a new bridge be built?" "Nurses on strike," and so on) could be one example and so could much coverage of health and everyday psychology, wildlife, sports, and the like. Even interviews with celebrities may well serve as examples of nontabloid but still popular journalism, for instance when they focus on the interviewee's professional activities or life experiences with some sort of general relevance.

Tabloidization should thus not simply be seen as a process that shifts the balance between quality and popular journalism, to use the traditional British dichotomy again. Such a view would in practice be in line with the populist defense of tabloid forms put forward by those who produce and profit from them, portraying tabloidization as a sort of liberation from highbrow repression. The process, to the extent that it in fact is going on, might also be a change within the field of popular journalism itself, a move from some popular forms to others. Much of what has traditionally been broadly popular media fare, at least in Europe, has been, and is, too mellow, serious, educational, or whatever to be rubricated as "tabloid," while simultaneously clearly not possible to be categorized as belonging to elite or highbrow culture. The much-referred-to current affairs program once aired by the BBC, *Nationwide*, was not "popular" as opposed to "quality"–it was quality popular journalism, and the same goes for most of the journalism presented by European television channels with public-service obligations. In Scandinavian television, there is a tradition for blending entertainment with more or less socially relevant informational material in family-orientated variety shows–a tradition of broadcast "infotainment" much older than that term. Large regional newspapers read by above 70 percent of all households in their areas in European countries every day carry lots of stories with accessible, engaging social information and diverse political perspectives. Norwegian and Swedish national, popular tabloids (and some also in other countries, of course) contain serious coverage of a number of more and less important issues. The term "middle-brow" might be tempting to use, were it not for its middle-class or petit-bourgeois connotations–nontabloid popular journalism has had much more mixed audiences or readerships.

If there are popular journalistic forms that are not tabloid, the next question might be if there are tabloid forms that are not "trash." The meaning of "tabloid TV" is in common usage often hard to distinguish from that of "trash TV" but such a distinction should probably be made. Trash TV includes, as far as I know, professional wrestling shows, Jerry Springer-type talk shows, certain voyeuristic kinds of "reality TV," and probably phenomena such as "housewife striptease" and other pornographic genres. What all of these have in common is a degree of shock aesthetics, or a particularly pronounced sensationalism. Trash TV is generally not out to please in the sense of something comforting and soothing, as are so many other forms of popular culture. What it wants more is to shake the audience, provide kicks, laughs, and whatever else may increase adrenaline levels. This is clearly related to vital traditions in popular-culture history, from various bloody spectacles to freak shows. But this does not in itself provide a ground for an ethical defense of, say, Jerry Springer's merciless exploitation of the participants in his show. The fact that public decapitations used to be popular spectacles is not a good reason to reintroduce them.

"Tabloid TV" is used in much broader ways than "trash TV," and so the two are not quite identical. There are forms of tabloid news magazines, for instance, which may be rubricated as tabloid but that are closer to mainstream television than shows like Springer's. The emphasis on the personal and personalization as a rhetorical device might suggest that *The Oprah Winfrey Show* belongs to the tabloid category, but it would not at all be fair to label it trash. When Oprah moved her show to Los Angeles after the L.A. riots and let those rebelling in the streets speak for themselves, and in a form of dialogue with opponents, she made innovative use of television in the service of democracy. She once devoted two programs to serious discussions of her own program and related shows, involving both "experts" and members of her core audiences. Consequently, one could imagine the field of popular journalism as containing the subcategory "tabloid," which again contains the subcategory "trash." Tabloid may sometimes be useful and relevant popular journalism; trash may at best be brutal entertainment. Trash is on the whole probably best defined by its disregard of ethics–both ethics in general (exploitation of sources, participants, and so on) and the professional ethos of journalism.

Parameters for categorization

David L. Paletz, in his *The Media in American Politics* (1998), suggests four descriptive categories of news "purveyors"–elite, prestige, popular, and tabloid. Indirectly, this quite simple and commonsensical stratification indicates that one could imagine a sort of *continuum* of journalistic forms and contents, and that distinctions between news media can be made mostly on the basis of which forms and contents *dominate* in them. Paletz describes "elite" purveyors as follows: "The elite press tends to emphasize government and politics, employs or uses foreign correspondents and reports their stories, strives to delve into issues and trends, and indulges in investigative journalism. Its news stories include background and explanations, often containing more than one perspective and source. It treats the news with relative sobriety, downplays flamboyant material, and eschews hyperbolic (but not evocative) language" (Paletz 1998, 65).

According to Paletz, the elite press in the United States is represented by the *New York Times*, the *Washington Post*, the *Los Angeles Times*, the *Wall Street Journal*, a few programs on National Public Radio, and public television's *The NewsHour with Jim Lehrer*. The "prestige" category includes the news magazines *Newsweek, Time*, and *U.S. News & World Report*, and the TV networks' evening news programs. Paletz is not so clear about the defining distinction between elite and prestige purveyors, mostly it seems to be about audience reach and the length of items, plus, possibly, the use of pictures.

The next category, "popular," is more clearly different from the elite standard: these purveyors emphasize "drama, action, entertainment, simplicity, brevity, immediacy, and personalization"[2] (Paletz 1998, 66). *USA Today* is mentioned as the most 'visible' example among newspapers. With 'its simple layout, striking graphics, abundant color, brief stories, and excessive attention to celebrities, it is designed to be simple to read. But it usually gives more space to its colorful weather map than to foreign news' (66). Local TV news in the United States also falls into this category, relying on 'the quartet or crash, casualty, crime, and corpse stories from the police and fire departments, and emphasizes human-interest pieces that evoke audience sympathy, pity, or admiration. Lots of time is given to weather and sports' (67).

Paletz's fourth and final category is "tabloid," and here he places TV shows such as *American Journal, A Current Affair, Hard Copy*, and *Inside Edition* along with supermarket tabloids such as the *National Enquirer* and the *Star*. They all "emphasize sexy crime, celebrities, and scandal; use hyperbolic language; and re-stage events as they may or may not have occurred. They are willing to skirt journalistic ethics by using long-lens cameras, engaging in high-speed chases, paying for interviews and exclusive rights to information. . . . Their stories are often fanciful, if not invented" (68).

Looking at Paletz's (debatable) descriptive categories, it seems reasonable to say that at least four parameters are used when distinctions are made:

1 *Subject matter or content*: The inclusion or exclusion of certain types of stories (crime, accidents, human interest stories, stories about celebrities, and so on versus international news and stories about politics, social movements, the economy, and the like).

2 *Proportions and priorities of various kinds of content*: The amount of space and the priority awarded to the above kinds of contents.

3 *Forms of presentation*: The length of stories, the use of visual elements such as photographs, graphics and colors, layout.

4 *Journalistic techniques and ethics*: The use of single or multiple sources, investigative techniques, "checkbook journalism," respect for privacy, and so on.

If parameters such as these are used to analyze and categorize mainstream newspapers, TV channels, or individual items within them, results will probably in most cases be mixed. This is not least due to the fact that most such media serve highly diverse audiences and hence have to cater to very different tastes and interests. But it also has to do with the fact that events such as plane crashes, the death of a popular princess, or the arrest of a politician smuggling illegal pornography and cocaine cannot possibly be ignored by any news medium worthy of the name. A categorization of specific newspapers or broadcasting channels according to how well they serve as resources for active and informed citizenship is still possible. In my view, parameter numbers 2 and 4 will then be more important than numbers 1 and 3. The interesting question is not whether crime, accidents, and human interest stories are included, but whether and to what extent they dominate in terms of space and priority over, say, international news and stories about politics and the economy, and whether both kinds of stories are produced in accordance with professional and ethical standards. The use of graphics, pictures, colors, an inviting layout, and so on does of course not in itself mean that the medium in question is "tabloid," and the length of a newspaper story or radio/TV program does not in itself guarantee "quality."

Such a multidimensional evaluation is more complicated than litmus tests based on a single binary opposition. It is further complicated by the need to be specific in terms of medium and cultural contexts. For instance, traditions in television as well as newspaper journalism vary from country to country. While attending the Euricom Colloquium on tabloidization in London in September 1998, I came across the headline "Man Denies £1.6m for Mistress Was Gift" in the "quality" newspaper *The Guardian* (Sept. 10, 7). The story was about a "wealthy businessman" who denied in court that he had given his mistress £1.6 million "because he was afraid of losing the only woman who would satisfy his sexual demands." These demands were described as "unusual." There were large photos of the man and his mistress, and both were named. It was indeed hard to see any social, political, or cultural relevance of the story. In other countries, this would be a clear-cut example of tabloid journalism, and, at least in Norway, names and photos would not have been used even in the tabloids. It is hard for a foreigner to tell whether this story is an example of the tabloidization of the British quality press or an example of traditional British quality reporting from the courts.

Still, as the international Euricom Colloquium documented, there seems to be more popular, tabloid, and trash journalism than ever in most countries, even if the overall picture of the situation is highly complex. The question is, then, to what extent, and in what sense, this is a good or a bad thing.

Journalism as ritual communication

The core purpose of journalism is and should be about producing and distributing serious information and debate on central social, political, and cultural matters. Journalists regulate much of what the public gets to know about the world they inhabit, and this activity is vital to a functioning democracy. I would, possibly to some readers' surprise, like to quote John Fiske here, who long ago in his favorable comments to Newcomb's 1953 model of communication said:

> This model assumes, though does not explicitly state, that people need information. In a democracy information is usually regarded as a right but it is not always realized that information is not only a right but a necessity. Without it we cannot feel part of a society. We must have adequate information about our social environment in order both to know how to react to it and to identify in our reaction factors that we can share with the fellow members of our peer group, subculture or culture.
>
> (Fiske 1982, 34)

This paragraph in Fiske's *Introduction to Communication Studies* acknowledges the importance of information and hence also the importance of the linear dimension in models of media communication, here specifically in the context of a working democracy. This is in line with how proper journalism has traditionally been understood. No wonder, then, that approaches that take tabloid or popular journalism seriously and construct various kinds of defense for these forms tend to apply what is known as a *ritual* perspective on media communication to the role(s) of journalism.

The ritual perspective regards media communication primarily as modern society's communication with itself about itself, in ways that reproduce and instill in all its members a sense of community and identity, of shared conditions, values, understandings, and so on. The media are storytellers, reiterating stories that, like ancient myths, serve as ways of thinking about existential and social matters individuals and groups have to deal with in their everyday lives. Such a function overrides distinctions between genres, such as those between factual and fictional genres, between news and other ostensibly informational genres on the one hand and those explicitly dedicated to entertainment on the other.

Studies of "tabloid" or popular journalism reveal their reliance on a ritual perspective of communication in that they focus on the *repetitiousness* or *redundancy* of stories or reports within this field of journalism. Typical studies of typical popular-journalism stories do not focus on either their misconstructing the actual events they report on or on their immediate political or social impact. They take for granted that the mass of individual stories are reducible to a few basic *story types*. Nowhere is structuralist reductionism in textual analysis more alive and kicking than in the studies of popular journalism, and it does not really seem inadequate.

For example, an article which reports an American study of crime news opens like this: "From day to day, many news stories on crime differ only in details about time, place and the identities of victim and defendant. How do daily readers come to take interest in today's report of murder or robbery, given that the story they read yesterday was substantially similar?" (Katz 1987, 47). This study relied on social scientific content analysis of close to two thousand crime news stories from major New York and Los Angeles papers. The final classification arrived at grouped all stories in four categories. The four story types were about (1) *personal competence and sensibility* (vicious, ingenious, and audacious crimes), (2) *collective integrity* (stories about threats to or attacks on symbols of identity), (3) *moralized political crime* (typically terrorism), and (4) *white-collar crime* (obviously related to stories of collective integrity). These thematic categories were of course constructed with a view to the supposed *functions* of crime news for newspaper readers. Katz's thesis is that "crime is made 'news' by a modern public searching for resources to work out sensibilities routinely made problematic in everyday modern life" (48).

> Although people often fear crime and criticize the news as too negative and disturbing, they apparently find it even more unsettling not to read. To understand what makes crime "news," one must explain the voluntary affliction of disturbing emotional experience on the self, on a mass level, day after day, throughout modern society. The reading of crime news appears to serve a purpose similar to the morning shower, routine physical exercise, and shaving . . .: the ritual, non-rational value of experience that is, to a degree, shocking, uncomfortable, and self-destructive, and that is voluntarily taken up by adults in acknowledgement of their personal burden for sustaining faith in an ordered social world.
>
> (Katz 1987, 72)

So clearly, information is not the point and neither is rational reflection on or discussion of crime as such. Crime news is about the daily reconstruction of moral sensibilities on a personal and even private plane.

John Langer's (1998) study of what he calls "the other news" excludes, as mentioned, crime news. His analysis of a large material–341 news items–is solidly based in classical structuralist textual theory (Propp, Lévi-Strauss, Barthes, Todorov) and Marxist theories of ideology put forward in the 1960s and 1970s (Louis Althusser, Stuart Hall). His categorization of the news items is thus, to me at least, more convincing than that of Katz, but it is still quite similar in its results. All of his 341 items can be placed within four categories: (1) *The especially remarkable*–stories about elites and celebrities, or about "triumphs" or achievements of ordinary people. (2) *Victims*–stories about individuals "caught up in untoward and often uncontrollable circumstances which bring radical dislocation to the procedures and routines of everyday life" (Langer 1998, 35). Reports on victims of crime were included here. (3) *Community at risk*–reports on "disrupture and disorder" at a collective rather than an individual level. (4) *Ritual, tradition, and the past*–focus on "community-based obser-vances or commemorations, and more generally, on notions of social memory mani-fested in the remembrance of past deeds and historical moments" (35).

The first three of these seem related to Katz's categories of crime news, especially the middle two. And Langer's analysis also ends in reflections on the relations between the form of journalism he has studied and notions of myth and ritual. "In the multipli-cation of 'other news' stories across bulletins every day, day after day, a structure of sorts, which might be called mythic, does begin to emerge" (Langer 1998, 143). This mythic "structure of sorts" serves to mediate the contradiction in modern life between permanence and change, also formulated as a contradiction between "causal-ity and its disintegration" (142). The "other news" assists people in answering the following question: "How is it possible to conduct a life which is both permanent and changing, that has causal linkages and displays total randomness, that produces continuity yet is simultaneously discontinuous, that progresses with stability and is characterized by resounding instability?" (144).

According to both of these studies, then, typical popular and also tabloid forms provide the audience with existential and moral help, and support in the daily strug-gles to cope with an everyday life marked by the uncertainties characteristic of mod-ernity. Some might say that such forms function primarily as ritual, therapy, and possibly occasions for reflection for audiences or readers as *human beings* rather than as socially and politically relevant information for the audience as *citizens*. But the notion of citizenship must clearly include more than the narrowly political, just as there is more to a democratic society than the immediately political institutions and processes. Democracy as a social form includes cultural life; various forms of reflec-tion on existential matters or "the human condition"; the formation, maintenance, deconstruction, and reformation of identities; and so on. Art and academic phil-osophy are not the only discourses related to these matters; journalism is obviously also important. It is not just, as has long been argued by media scholars, that the reading of newspapers and the watching of television news are rituals in people's everyday life. Through these rituals journalism provides both information related to the more directly political dimensions of democracy and material for ritual or cere-monial "processing" of sociopsychological and existential concerns. Much or most popular journalism can probably be said to concentrate on the latter.

[. . .]

Notes

1   Fiske has since adjusted his position, cf. his *Media Matters* (1996).
2   Paletz here quotes a book review by George Gladney in the *Journal of Communi-cation* 42, no. 3, Summer (1992): 195.

1.4

The popular press: surviving postmodernity
by Martin Conboy

A popular postmodern press

One of the most noticeable features of the current cultural scene is the erosion of the distinctions between popular and high culture and postmodernity's recognition of the ability of the popular to invade all spaces. This does not mean that the popular and the elite have totally colonized each other's spaces, for the debates which rage about dumbing down are indicative that the elite is not prepared to go quietly if at all. Rather than being involved in colonization they are in fact involved in something more akin to switch-flicking, a two-way interchange.

Since this market version of popularity has come to predominate, the popular becomes a key agenda item for postmodernity and therefore changes and continuities in the popular press during an era termed postmodernity may well illuminate broader cultural debates, even if they do take place in that 'introspective world of the press' (Bromley, 1998).

We might consider that the popular press becomes postmodern when its attempts to fulfil the traditional bourgeois functions of the press as a provider of news and political information to a citizenship becomes interchangeable with its function as entertainment. This is a moment of convergence triggered by ever-intensifying communication flows between formats and genres driven by the logic of late capitalism.

For Hal Foster there are two takes on postmodernism: '. . . a postmodernism which seeks to deconstruct modernism and resist the status quo and a postmodernism which repudiates the former to celebrate the latter: a postmodernism of resistance and a postmodernism of reaction' (1985: xi–xii). Whichever definition is used, it is clear that postmodernity is based upon the cultural consequences of a newly assertive wave of popular culture which refuses to play second best aesthetically, economically or politically.

Postmodernity is further understood as a series of crises in representation and rationality, both key terms for the press. McHale has identified postmodernity in its privileging of the ontological over the epistemological (1989: xii); in other words, it isn't the way you relate a unified reality, but the version of competing realities which you choose to narrate.

Foucault claims in *The Order of Things* that transcendental claims to knowledge and the authority of these claims only made sense within the discourse of the liberal humanism of the eighteenth and nineteenth centuries which has been supplanted by discourses of a post-humanist era of knowledge. The discourse of the enlightenment public sphere and of the role of the journalist belong in this epoch as too does the notion of a progressive popular opinion and its ability to be located outside the discourses of capitalism or at least as a credible enemy within.

The contemporary popular press has reasserted much of the sensationalism and distraction which erode the discursive objectivity of the press, in particular its ability to articulate a set of informed discussions on the nature of contemporary society. Norris underlines this relationship between modernity and the 'truth-telling' interests so close to the core of journalism when he writes:

> For it is among the most basic suppositions in Kant and for thinkers (like Habermas) still committed to the 'unfinished project of modernity' that there exists a close relation between truth-telling interests – including the claims of enlightened Ideologiekritik – and those ethical values that likewise depend upon a free and open access to the 'public sphere' of rational, informed discussion.
>
> (1992: 111)

In terms of newspapers, postmodernity's collapse of cultural hierarchies is not only illustrated through debates on 'tabloidization' in the quality press but in concerns over the popular press's erosion of the boundary between politics and entertainment since the boundary between them has always acted as a fulcrum to journalism's own hierarchies and self-definitions. It is no wonder then that such an erosion causes interest and comment as it threatens to demolish a canonical belief in the centrality of political journalism to the genre.

Hartley observes that in postmodernity:

> . . . the image of journalism and of its popular readership has changed; it is neither an image of the 'powers that be' nor of their organized or disorganized radical opponents. Currently – and often to the horror of those brought up in the modernist tradition of 'mainstream adversarial journalism' – the image of both readerships and the meanings circulating via popular journalism suggests a different kind of breakfast reading altogether. Here, and now, the emphasis is not on public life but private meaning, and the readership has morphed from:
>
> > male to female
> > old to young
> > militant to meditative
> > public to private
> > governmental to consumerist
> > law-making to identity-forming.
>
> (1996: 15–16)

Perhaps it may be more accurate to represent these binary distinctions in terms of infective flows, reversible and unstable, hopping backwards and forwards when it suits them. Certainly he is right to point out that political resistance has never been unfailingly organized within the popular press.

Journalism's crisis of representation comes when postmodernity's scepticism about the referent begins to infect journalism's claims to representational truth. In terms of the popular press, rhetoric, up to now simply a vector of the popular, becomes indistinguishable from the claim of the popular press to actually represent the people. It is a popular paper if it presents a persuasive popular rhetoric. As the market comes to dominate more and more, the reduction of the people to market segments accelerates and accentuates this process and the popular is won or lost in terms of style of address.

The popular and the people

At one point the popular and the people were close to synonymous terms. Popular art and culture expressed the worldviews of specific groups of ordinary people. The crisis in representation has loosened the hold of the popular on the people. In the popular press we may now only really use the term 'popular' as denoting the ability of a paper to sell to a large readership. The popular press increasingly is only authenticated by its ability to articulate the 'popular' through its rhetoric. Once the rhetoric emerged from the people; now it is simulacrum standing in for their loss.

Lyotard's 'incredulity towards meta-narratives' (1984: xxiv) claims the discourses of nation, religion and political dogma have lost their ability to persuade, but in terms of the press there is evidence that the contemporary has seen the collapse of the meta-narrative of the 'public sphere' as defined from the emergence of democratic societies in Western Europe. The grand tradition of a press which involved people in a communicative democracy and guided them toward a better future is at least compromised by the developments of newspapers which gear themselves increasingly towards a celebration of consumerist values and the political status quo, not to say anything of the disappearance of an oppositional popular press tradition. The question that we might then ask, paradoxically, is whether the 'popular' in popular culture is also the victim of the collapse of meta-narratives?

Baudrillard's simulacrum – an identical copy without an original – can be applied perhaps to the generation of a popular readership with all the signifiers of community – vernacular, shared tastes, shared habits of media consumption – but without a concrete political community. Newspaper readerships simulate such a community and particularly within the popular press that community is marketed through rhetoric.

If politics and entertainment are blurring and invading each other's spaces, this does not mean that politics has necessarily become entertainment or vice versa. Similarly, if discourse theory helps us to understand the workings and patternings of power in language, this does not lead us inexorably to the conclusion that there is no reality outside the structuring of that language. While we must beware of treating the symptoms of the crisis as a definitive description of reality, there are serious questions for the popular press to answer in terms of the rhetoric which stands in for the people themselves. Is the popular press able to articulate something of the real world of the ordinary people and their political interests unmediated by a simulated rhetoric or does rhetoric go all the way down?

The pressures which have provoked such a generalized crisis in systems of representation and such a proliferation of the reach of popular culture which threaten to turn all discourses of the popular-political into yet another set of empty, depthless signifiers are generally considered to include globalization, commercialization, the intensification of cultural flows and the triumph of the image over narrative (Featherstone, 1993).

Globalization

Globalization, although as a process as old as the capitalist system which prompts its logic, has reached a point of radical intensity due to the increasing availability and improved reliability of transport, particularly long-haul air traffic, the corresponding increase in exchange of people and commodities around the globe, increasing information flows via computer and telecommunications technology; these lead to two parallel and paradoxical trends. The first is a tendency to homogenization as brands such as McDonald's, Nike, Benetton, and CNN become global, sweeping national economies and national borders to one side. The second, driven by these flows of increased density of cultural and economic exchange, because they bring diversity and difference more into the everyday experience of people, have a back-lash effect of causing retreats to ethnie and nationalism among groups who do not perceive the benefits of such increased diversity.

The intensification of the importance of place, of location, in the contemporary popular press in Britain illustrates the point made by Featherstone when defining the relationship between postmodernism and globalization:

> Postmodernism is both a symptom and a powerful cultural image of the swing away from the conceptualization of global culture less in terms of alleged homogenising processes (e.g. theories which present cultural imperialism, Americanization and mass consumer culture as a proto-universal culture riding on the back of Western economic and political domination) and more in terms of the diversity, variety and richness of popular and local discourse, codes and practices . . .
> (1993: 2)

It may be possible to consider the popular press, especially in Britain and Germany where content is robustly national and even xenophobic, as providing evidence that particular cultural groupings in specific places may react against the 'ontological insecurity' of the instabilities inherent in postmodernity (Giddens, 1987). The Hollywood agenda of the American supermarket tabloids, especially those for export such as the *National Enquirer*, act in a supplementary way to more local popular cultures. They have certainly not supplanted them. Consumption and populism have become reconfigured in terms of a series of tropes of nationhood. Such a 'syntax of solidarity' has been postulated as a crucial element in the construction of a national identity in an era of the uncertainties of postmodern and global trends (Billig, 1995: 165–7).

[. . .]

Commercialization

The willing embrace of commerce in public or creative life is seen as a *sine qua non* of postmodernism. Frederic Jameson has defined it in these terms: 'Postmodernism is the consumption of sheer commodification as a process' (1991: x). Yet popular culture had been commercialized since the late Middle Ages with its professional storytellers, singers, almanac and chap-book sellers. Such an orientation of newspapers, in particular the popular end of the market, to the demands of the political economy is nothing new. Curran (1977) has demonstrated how the press has reflected the capitalist organizational rationale of its political economy throughout the modern era. What is distinctive now is the way in which the balance has shifted in favour of the commercial as absolutely dominant as opposed to simply holding an equilibrium with the informational and political imperatives of previous manifestations of popular press.

From as early as the 1840s, in Britain as well as the United States, newspaper popularity was becoming defined in terms of its market appeal. This became an intensifying momentum as the century progressed. The culmination of this has been an intensified commodification of the newspaper and its satellite supplements, its increasing harmonization of a whole package of offers, accessories and defining identities. This illustrates another characteristic of postmodernity in the celebration of the market as a cultural and economic strategy. Newspapers have always been predisposed in terms of their organization and epistemology to be profoundly marked by economic imperatives even in their primary goal of providing information about events in the real world.

This intensified comercialization means that the popular, instead of being articulated primarily as a political category, becomes a consumer category. As McGuigan has written: 'the popular national daily empowers its audiences, not directly as actors in the public sphere but as consumers' (1992: 178). Popular culture has been commodified since the mid-nineteenth century commercializing of the people and their cultures – a process which took place principally through the medium of the popular press.

We will foreground examples from the British popular press here because it presents a broader range of parallels with the traditions of popular print culture. These newspapers all attract a mass readership and are targeted at a readership which is inscribed in their rhetoric. Even more importantly, they retain at least a nominal choice between popular perspectives which even manage a diversity of opinion. This leaves the possibility that there remains a notion of political involvement via the popular press. These papers are to all intents and purposes resistant to the narratives of Hollywood as globalized news and prefer instead a parochial blend of regional and national popular fare. They retain more diversity and miscellany possibly because they are still part of an extremely competitive market. It is predominantly a daily market of preference where the discourse of antagonistic rivalry drives many of the really demotic and sensationalist aspects of their coverage. They are fighting over the people they want to claim as their own readers.

This celebration of consumption is inscribed in the pages of the popular press and explains much of its success in continuing to exercise market dominance. It is in keeping with the spirit of the age. Yet it depends in this on more historical antecedents. Its success has not sprung from a vacuum. The dominance of a consumerist popular press is based on its ability to continue to carry traditions of popular appeal and legitimate its claims to popularity within a commercial framework. The reader is addressed as an interested consumer and within the context of a particular newspaper. Contrasting the insider share-dealing scandal at the *Mirror* where its editor, Piers Morgan, had been censured by the Press Complaints' Commission for taking advantage of privileged information available to the financial experts on the paper to make a stockmarket killing the *Sun* on 25 February 2000 in its 'Sun Says' column indicates the confluence of appealing to the people and its own financial probity: 'Meanwhile, as we say on our front page today, The Sun will continue to be THE PEOPLE'S PAPER.' This enables the *Sun* to present itself as aligned with the interests of those outside the circle of financial experts and thereby draw a virtuous popular glow around its own integrity and support for the common reader. This casts the paper as a whole in a good light.

This is all the more damning as the consumer-reader is very much to the fore in the specialized letters column in the *Sun*'s rival, the *Mirror*, 'Justice with Jacobs', which covers legal matters with a consumer twist as part of a popular consumer-rights agenda. It has an educational slant of a particular populist and raucous style. Jacobs himself, the consumer champion, is featured with gown and wig pointing his finger from the top of the page – the representation in the pages of the press of a particular sort of popular consumer justice. The comic element of this consumer appeal is enhanced by the rhetoric and concentration on bizarre angles on otherwise dull episodes.

Butcher says he was told a porkie
METRIC MESS SPARKED BY SCALES (The *Mirror*, 30 March 2000)

This is matched by the equally vernacular style of 'Sorted', a column set out as investigative journalism into frauds and consumer rip-offs:

THE SCUMBAG WHO PREYED ON A DISABLED WOMAN
Meet Del . . . cowboy builder from hell (The *Mirror*, 18 February 2000)

Quentin Wilson in the *Mirror*, presented as 'the columnist the car industry fears', draws readers and consumer interests into his campaign for cheaper car prices in an on-line buying feature:

Death of the car salesman
YOUR DRIVE FOR FAIRER PRICES IS KILLING THEM (The *Mirror*, 31 March 2000)

The rhetoric employed in these columns is one of resolution within consumer capitalist culture, which speaks of a process of winning battles against the system. In doing so, it distracts from more systemic economic inequalities. The columns point to a more optimistic world of popular consumer power, where people are able to take charge of their own efforts, or a part of them, through the intermediary of their newspaper.

[. . .]

The poverty of image in the public sphere

Another feature which reinforces the sceptical dominance of postmodernity is the elevation of the power of image over rational argument. This springs as much from the blending of advertising and brand into the news media of the public sphere as from any other technological determinants, such as the proliferation of commodified images through the increased availability of television and other visual media of communication. Habermas (1992) has likened the collapse of rationality in this contemporary promotion of the image to a 'refeudalisation of society' (1992: 231). In his view, this society can only grasp the display of the signifiers of importance rather than have access to democratic involvement. In the popular press it has disturbing implications for the political education of popular readerships if they are merely having these signs presented to them without questioning or debate. Jameson suggests that: 'Depth is replaced by surface or multiple surfaces' (1991: 12). The ephemerality of the popular press makes it an interesting contributor to postmodernity in its constant shuffling of the surface elements of its formulaic approach to content. Which celebrity, which scandal, which populist cause? – all seem to be interchangeable. The constant element is the rhetoric and the ventriloquism of the people themselves.

Unlike previous manifestations of popular political involvement through the press that depended on rational debate, the aesthetic of the contemporary popular press is to instruct the reader into being a more adept reader of contemporary patterns of consumption and identity. Political debate is framed by these. The readers of these papers are not presented with a medium that informs them as active participants in the public sphere but interpellates them as consumer identities with a range of intertextual complexity. It is a virtualization and dispersal of the material people.

The imaginary is mediated through the consumption of popular identities including the identity of the reader of a particular newspaper and its opinions. This links to the rhetorical strength of the popular in the popular press, indicating that for our purposes rhetoric is an imagining device, an image of the idealized reader.

In a feature on the popular press in the *Independent* on 14 July 1998, the *Sun's* assistant editor Chris Roycroft-Davis claims: 'A reader who wants to be seriously informed would take the quality press . . . They are not looking for profound analysis of France. It is easier for them to associate the French with an image like "garlic eaters".' In the same article, David Banks, Mirror Group corporate affairs director, reinforces the changing ambition of the tabloid press: 'We are not trying to educate. On the contrary, we go in the direction people want . . . lazy journalism . . . common to journal and readers.'

The association of stereotypes and collective images, once transferred to the public discourse of the popular press, can disrupt the press's traditional claim to provide enlightenment. Rather it feeds, through its shifting of surface realities, a propensity for closure around the lowest common denominator. It provides continuities within an idealized and commodified readership. The image phase of post-modernity may be construed in the popular press as an aesthetics of the popular, without a particular aim or purpose outside the commercial articulation of a credible version of the popular voice and enmeshed within the flows of everyday life and its rich cross-currents of intermedia influences.

[. . .]

SECTION 2

The values and ethics of tabloid media

In his discussion of the reality show *Celebrity Boxing*, a series in which has-been and small-time 'celebrities' fight it out on television Jeffrey Sconce (2004: 258) observes, '. . . critics often judge TV according to obsolete standards of taste, decency and value, while the medium itself – in its crassness, vulgarity, and cutthroat competitiveness – has usually left old aesthetic criteria choking in the dust . . .' Sconce's own analysis of the show draws on a quite different lexicon of 'quality' in order to explain why the show is successful on its own terms. He notes, for example, its careful and knowing selection of combatants whose media histories and personas would provide endless in-jokes for clued-up audiences, its sheer energy and its 'dense semiotic complexity', which generates multiple viewing pleasures. Sconce seems to have little sympathy for the hapless participants in the show but neither will he ally himself with the critics who regard *Celebrity Boxing* as an all-time low in broadcasting and a perfect example of declining standards in an increasingly tabloidized media.

In between these two opposing views is a whole range of critical positions that may be taken towards some of the perceived characteristics of tabloid media as they appear in formats as various as reality television, gross-out and stunt shows, tabloid journalism, celebrity-based media, 'shock documentaries', talkback radio, true crime and so on. One common accusation is that tabloid culture is often vulgar and in poor taste. This is often attributed not only to the topics addressed and behaviours revealed (sex and sexuality, plastic surgery, aggression, profanity, mawkish sentimentality, retrogressive conservatism and personal trauma) but to the types of people who are increasingly given access to media space. As we have noted elsewhere, the visibility of ordinary people in 'unscripted' situations is the watermark of reality TV, to take but one example, and arguably a partial explanation for its success with audiences (Biressi and Nunn, 2005). Reality TV has provided a platform for people from diverse sexual, social and classed backgrounds to gain airtime (see for example Shattuc, 1997; Gamson, 1998; Pullen, 2004; Stephens, 2004). For the few, it offers an opportunity for social mobility as they move on to become celebrities in their own right. For critics of tabloid TV, these new-style celebrities may talk a lot but they have very little of substance to say; their voluble, often unschooled personas seem emblematic of the vulgarity and shallow values of the newer formats (Biressi and Nunn, 2005: 2). For its defenders, this inclusion represents the democratization of the media, a move away from elitist values and towards the inclusion of 'real people and real language' (Biressi and Nunn, 2005: 26).

With the growing inclusion of diverse ordinary people in tabloid media new kinds of ethical considerations arise, for example, about how much control they have over their own representation and whether they are vulnerable to exploitation. Naturally, ordinary people (who are untrained in managing the media) appear across the spectrum of non fiction media: as subjects of news reports (not a new occurrence), in talk shows and talk radio, caught on CCTV, performing in talent shows and docusoaps, featuring in reality programming including makeovers and 'lifeswap' shows and so forth. But many of these representations present participants in a poor light, generating gripping television through TV formats that expose participants as socially inadequate or irresponsible or small-minded or unintelligent. Gareth Palmer (2003: 145 and 156) refers to these as 'spectacles of shame' and we would suggest that these often work through linking the subject's character to their conduct and their conduct to notions of social class and personal failure. The British BBC 3 series *Honey, We're Killing the Kids* is a good example (Biressi and Nunn, 2007). The programme seeks to makeover the unhealthy lives of families and makes clear visual and linguistic associations between these lifestyles and an explicitly lower-class lifeworld. The BBC Web site sums up each family featured in the series quite nicely. Here, we reproduce the synopsis of the McDowell family:

> Single mum Paula McDowell and her four children, Ashlay (aged five), Elena (eight), Connor (ten) and Stacy (13), live in north Wales.
>
> Paula's house acts as a drop-in centre for the whole estate but, while it may offer her some emotional support as a single parent, it means the household lacks any sense of routine and structure.
>
> The kids rule the roost and live for sweets and fights. They're additive addicts and their sugar highs, fatty fry-ups and salted ready meals are having a terrible effect on their behaviour and long-term health.
>
> Five-year-old Ashlay has already lost nine teeth, Connor has behavioural problems and Stacy has a 10-a-day cigarette habit. Expert Kris Murrin says the McDowells are one of the most difficult families she has had to work with.
>
> (http://www.bbc.co.uk/health/tv_and_radio/honey/
> series3honey_families.shtml accessed 8/4/07)

The technical innovation in this series is the part of the show where Kris Murrin (from the government's Institute of Child Health) draws upon digitally manipulated photo-imagery to reveal to the parents what their children will look like when they reach 40 years of age should they continue with their present way of life. We watch with the parents as their children transmute into pallid, slack-jawed obese or undernourished adults who appear older than their projected years. Inevitably, the parents shake, look grief stricken and even cry, invoking what John Langer has called a 'reflex of tears', which he suggests is emblematic of tabloid television. They are sternly informed that if they carry on in this manner their children will be 'at risk' of colon cancer or eating disorders, of morbid obesity and heart disease, of impaired intelligence and so on. At the end of the programme, having followed the new healthy regime, the parents are rewarded with new digital projections, which forecast the children growing into healthy, *attractive* adults. These forecasts are inevitably shot through with class imagery and the symbolism of social difference. In the second set of projections subtle differences in clothes and hairstyles (the substitution of an open necked shirt for a t-shirt or a neat modern haircut instead of a shaven head) suggest that improving one's behaviour and changing one's lifestyle will also spur social or class mobility.

The suggestion overall is that behavioural laxity or incontinence, lack of structure and or discipline – in other words – the 'indisciplinarity' of the 'difficult' family – is the terrain to be struggled over, rather than food and healthiness *per se*. It is difficult to see how the family featured here can be regarded as genuinely participating in its own media representation; it is presented as a chaotic and 'difficult' (albeit loving) family with little scope for it to counterbalance this interpretation. As Kevin Glynn (2000: 227) observes, 'at its worst, tabloidism (like official journalistic forms) surely features the hegemonic and normalizing voices of racism, sexism and homophobia' to which we would add class contempt and a dubious voyeurism. But Glynn goes on: 'At its best, however, it multiplies and amplifies the heterogeneous voices and viewpoints in circulation in contemporary culture.' A key consideration of any discussion of tabloid ethics might then be to ask, on a case-by-case basis, and then perhaps in the round, to what extent and to what effect these voices and viewpoints are really being aired.

What is clear, as Sconce indicates in his reference to 'cutthroat commercialism', is that debates about tabloid ethics and values would also benefit by being aired in the context of the shifting terrain of the media marketplace (see Murray and Ouellette, 2004: 7–9). For example, Chad Raphael (2004) argues in his reflection on the industrial context of reality television that TV programmers have far more on their agenda than pleasing audiences and reflecting the current *Zeitgeist* in terms of programme content. Ultimately TV is a business that looks to the cost of its output, its generation of revenue through advertising, product placement and merchandising, and programmes are made in order to deliver audiences to advertisers in order to maximize profits (Madger, 2004).

An understanding of these issues of cost and rivalry between channels, newspapers, magazines, online sites and so on needs to be counterbalanced by an awareness of formal regulations, industry guidelines or informal professional values and standards by which media workers are governed or choose to follow. We also need to ask why we should worry about whether the tabloid media behave responsibly and what the primary responsibilities and standards at stake might be in any particular case study of tabloid ethics. Karen Sanders (2003: 9) contends that ethics matters because journalism itself matters: 'Journalism matters. Journalists sketch in the contours of our moral landscape. They contribute to the business of telling us who we are, interpreting the world for us, making it legible.' The implication here is that journalism is powerful and influential in helping to determine our view of the world and, crucially, in delineating the moral parameters by which this view is bounded. It is for this reason, perhaps above all others (and there are many others), that the ethics and values of tabloid media are important. Both journalism and other tabloid media (most of which are 'factual', 'unscripted' or allied in some other way to notions of realism and truthfulness) might be held accountable on these grounds and many have been found to fall short of both explicit and unspoken standards of conduct towards their subjects or their audiences. Accusations levelled against tabloid media have included failing a duty of care to a reality show participant, using fake talk-show guests, using unlabelled footage to 'reconstruct' an event, manipulating photographs, using deception to obtain a story, infringing personal privacy, irresponsible overly sensational coverage and cheque-book journalism.

In Section 6 we note the disjunction between the various public and professional expectations of what responsible journalism should be and the pragmatic considerations and working practices of tabloid journalists themselves, whose work, in some cases, may simply not chime with conventional assumptions of what journalism should do. One way to interpret this disjunction would be to accept that different kinds of journalism necessarily follow different protocol, adopts alternative news values and thereby could not reasonably be required (or are simply unable) to take on universal codes of behaviour and ethics. The problem here would be that this would lead to the wholesale dismissal of mechanisms put in place, for example, to protect the public and those featured in the news. A counter argument could be made that these codes should always be adhered to or at least provide a guiding light when it comes to the decision-making processes in whatever field of journalism one works. But as we have noted, some of these guidelines simply make less sense in relation to certain tabloid genres or markets.

Of course, in actuality both of these models fail to reflect the complexity of real-life working practices and their commercial, social and political contexts. As Chris Frost (2000: 61–4) explains, professional morality has to be understood in terms of the loyalties and obligations attached to the role: civic responsibilities, obligations to readers and viewers, to editors and producers, to sponsors and advertisers, proprietors, legal requirements, regularity bodies and professional codes of practice. From this perspective, it makes sense to contextualize fully any discussion of perceived ethical breaches and to try to unpack them in terms of the specificity of each case. The three pieces that we have chosen to include in this section all address questions of ethics and tabloid values without losing sight of the larger technological and/or commercial dynamics of the tabloid industries past and present. In different ways all three pieces remind us of the challenge of asking hard ethical questions effectively about tabloid forms.

Graeme Turner's piece addresses a scandal involving talkback radio hosts in Australia and nicely unravels the complexity of the case; providing a good example of the problems in applying generic ethical standards to tabloid media. In this example, the radio hosts were accused of taking secret payments to endorse the political and commercial interests of companies and even in one case approaching an institution with the offer to change the show's editorial line to favour their interests in return for a cash payment. This caused concern in many quarters, not least because of the programme's capacity to help form public opinion on political matters. The ensuing investigation by the Australian Broadcasting Authority took the form of a contest between civic values and commercial imperatives in which it was remarkably difficult to pinpoint exactly which ethical standard had been breached. There were also real divisions between media professionals about the acceptability of these practices and the defence was made by one host that he was, in fact, an entertainer rather than a journalist proper and was not bound by the established ethical regime. These tensions and contradictions lead Turner to question the relevance of ethical regimes for the entertainment-led tabloid media.

Des Freedman's analysis of the British tabloid newspaper, the *Daily Mirror*, also takes account of the commercial imperatives (in terms of sales figures and market rivalry) that underpin the decision-making processes of tabloid media and their adoption of a particular political editorial line. In this example, he describes a newspaper's attempt to rebrand itself as a serious popular newspaper, to move away from the more conventional tabloid values of gossip and depoliticized journalism and to reposition itself as radical and anti-government. It was certainly the case that in terms of the paper's historical values and political affiliations this move made sense; the paper had a legacy of progressive political views and a mostly loyal readership base. The point is also made that the time was right for press-led political debate as the country was on the brink of going to war against Iraq and many citizens had expressed reservations about this move. The lessons drawn from this case are complex. Firstly, that in an increasingly competitive market, the political values articulated by the press are likely to be 'tactical', bound not only by editorial tradition or current conviction but by marketing assumptions and the need to reach out to readers. But more positively, Freedman's analysis also suggests that in the right climate and with firm resolution tabloid papers are capable of addressing readers as informed and active citizens and of articulating the kinds of public political discourse that, it is assumed, is usually confined to the 'serious' news media.

In the third piece reprinted here Karin Becker addresses the enduring link between photography and the tabloid press and the values attached to different kinds of photo-reportage. She does this by tracking historical developments in photojournalism such as the appearance of new technologies and by highlighting key moments in the press usage of photographic images. In terms of ethics and values, her discussion points to how the sensational content of early tabloid photojournalism attracted criticism for its low ethical standards and for its contamination of press standards more broadly. Becker also observes that the status of photojournalism (and the photojournalist) has risen, noting the artistic values and authority that have been attached to the practice of photographic news in the more upmarket papers even though photography is relatively marginal to serious news reportage. In contrast, she notes that this elevation excludes the work of the tabloid press where a different set of values and indeed aesthetics prevails and where the image often takes priority over the written word.

Further reading

Belsey, A. and Chadwick, R. (eds) (1992) *Ethical Issues in Journalism*, London: Routledge.

Berry, D. (ed.) (2000) *Ethics and Media Culture: Practices and Representations*, Oxford: Focal Press.

Frost, C. (2000) *Media Ethics and Self-Regulation*, Harlow: Longman.

Gross, L., Katz, J. and Ruby, J. (eds) (2003) *Image Ethics in the Media Digital Age*, Minneapolis: University of Minnesota Press.

Lunt, P. and Stenner, P. (2005) '*The Jerry Springer Show* as an emotional public sphere', *Media, Culture and Society*, 27(1): 59–81.

Palmer, G. (2003) *Discipline and Liberty: Television and Governance*, Manchester: Manchester University Press.

Sanders, K. (2003) *Ethics and Journalism*, London: Sage.

Sconce, J. (2004) 'See you in hell, Johnny Bravo!', in S. Murray and L. Ouellete (eds) *Reality TV: Remaking Television Culture*, New York: New York University Press, 251–267.

1.5

Ethics, entertainment, and the tabloid: the case of talkback radio in Australia
by Graeme Turner

In Australia in 1999, a group of conservative and commercially dominant talkback radio hosts—pretty much the epitome of 'the tabloid' in its local incarnation—were involved in a scandal which exposed widespread exploitation of their market power through secret paid endorsements for products, companies and political positions. The consequent official inquiry found it difficult to locate just what was the ethical principle being transgressed, partly because these were not (ethically bound) journalists but (ethically free) 'entertainers' and partly because of the general evacuation of such principles from the codes of practice required of the industry. The privileging of commercial responsibilities and the gradual displacement of community responsibilities which have occurred over the last decade had, in effect, reduced the possibility that an ethical or democratic critique of mass media practice could now be effectively elaborated and understood.

What we now know as the 'Cash for Comment' scandal presents us with a case where, in my view, the media's successful and unregulated pursuit of a mass audience took it beyond the reach of ethical appeal against its specific practices. Tellingly, in its defence, the media organization concerned barely even pretended to acknowledge its responsibility to any broader community interests than those of the mass audience. The contest between commercial and community/democratic imperatives is at its most naked here, and ultimately at issue is the very relevance of an ethical regime within an entertainment-based, rather than an information-based, 'tabloid' media.

The following argument examines the role played by ethics, and by alternative or complementary considerations, within the regulation of an entertainment industry employing the kind of journalism we see in the media today. My starting point is the Cash for Comment scandal and the subsequent Australian Broadcasting Authority inquiry. To recap, this centred on radio talkback hosts John Laws and Alan Jones, as a result of an ABC-TV *MediaWatch* story which revealed that hidden commissions had been paid to the broadcasters in order to secure their on-air editorial support for the political and commercial interests of the companies concerned.[1] Rumours about the existence of such contracts and the payment of large amounts of money had been around for years without generating much media coverage, but the breaking of this particular story provoked broad and intense media scrutiny. The reason, perhaps, is that in this instance Laws' agent had approached the Australian Bankers Association himself, offering to change the editorial line the broadcaster was currently taking on their members' activities in exchange for a substantial payment. More conventional versions of 'payola' (that is, positive treatment for sponsors in return for cash or other rewards) seem to have been tacitly accepted and tolerated by the organizations concerned. However, this approach looked sufficiently like blackmail and constituted a sufficiently clear abuse of market power to raise the level of media interest.

From one point of view, the Cash for Comment scandal could be understood as a story about the decline in the relevance of ethical standards for media practice in Australia. It is possible to regard this decline as a consequence of increased and unregulated competition between broadcasting organizations since the deregulation of the radio industry formalized in the Broadcasting Services Act (1992). The Broadcasting Services Act (1992) understood the media more as a business than a cultural industry and the media have behaved increasingly unequivocally like a business ever since. Issues of media ethics dropped off the regulatory agenda as a result of the so-called co-regulation arrangements that allowed the industry, effectively, to police its own ethical standards. The expectation of civic responsibility which underpins a commitment to media ethics also, necessarily, dropped off the agenda as regulatory environments were increasingly designed to ensure the profitable operation of commercial media companies rather than to serve the interests of citizens (or, even, consumers). So, from July through to November 1999, it was something of a novelty to find media ethics a daily presence on the front page of every newspaper, and debated with implausible sobriety by the hosts of commercial television current affairs programmes.

As a result of this revived attention, a number of ethical issues emerged which were regarded, fairly generally, as worth closer examination and possibly independent regulation. First, it was noted that the line between advertising and editorial content had been deliberately blurred, misleading listeners in order to advantage those paying for the broadcaster's services. This was among the few things expressly forbidden by the codes of practice for the commercial radio industry. Second, while the status of talkback as information rather than entertainment programming is hotly contested (let alone whether it counts as news and current affairs, which is how the ABA presently sees it), it was argued that the standards used to guarantee accuracy, objectivity and independence in news and current affairs should also apply to talkback—whether or not the host is a journalist. Third, the political objectives addressed by the Cash for Comment arrangements were seen to constitute a deliberate abuse of media power, employing secret commissions to influence public debate in order to covertly advantage specific sets of political and commercial interests. Jones' and Laws' sponsors all had specific political objectives in mind; none were simply concerned with maintaining a market image or a commercial competitive advantage.[2] As a result, while some of the media outrage over the affair might be dismissed as opportunistic or hypocritical, there was also serious and widespread democratic and ethical concern about the talkback hosts' manipulation of public debate over important issues of public policy. Fourth, and perhaps most worrying of all, the controversy revealed the inadequacy of the existing codes of practice and the system of co-regulation. Industry suggestions that media-specific codes of practice should be replaced by a commercial code of practice did not convince many observers. Robert Manne, on the ABC's *Lateline* programme (20/7/1999), even suggested that this might be the opportunity for the community to properly investigate business ethics as well, if this was how large and influential business organizations thought they should treat their publics.

One of the most significant factors in this story is that it was actually quite difficult to establish—given the nature of the current codes and standards, and given changes in the kinds of practice tolerated over recent years—exactly what ethical standards had been breached. The issues did not emerge easily. Not only was it difficult to specify a formal breach, but there was also disagreement about what currently constituted legitimate media practice. What some industry observers saw as fundamentally unacceptable, others regarded as totally unexceptionable.

Within the regulatory authority, at first, there seemed to be genuine puzzlement as to whether there had been a breach of the codes or standards and, if so, precisely what it was. This was the first inquiry of its kind since the ABA was established. Hence, while the New South Wales Director of Public Prosecutions was trying to determine whether or not a crime had been committed, Professor David Flint was saying on the ABC's *Lateline* programme (20/7/1999) he didn't know if the BSA did actually prohibit such activities but that he was trying to find out.

On the same edition of *Lateline*, celebrity manager Max Markson and (Sydney radio station) 2GB broadcaster Mike Gibson argued about whether Laws' contracts were in fact normal (and thus acceptable) commercial practice. Max Markson maintained this kind of thing happened all the time, and why not, but Mike Gibson likened the activities of Laws/Jones to prostitution and repudiated them as acceptable practice for a reputable broadcaster: 'I sell my voice but I don't sell my backside' he said. In the *vox pops* around the industry which accompanied most of the early print media stories, broadcasters divided over the issue; some (Wendy Harmer, for instance) deplored the activity, while others (such as Mike Carlton) simply saw it as part of the business of commercial radio.

Given such a split within the industry, it was not entirely disingenuous for Laws to maintain his innocence. Jones simply denied everything, despite the evidence placed in front of him, or else maintained he neither remembered what he had said on air nor the detail of his contracts. It is difficult to determine any kind of principled stand behind what he had to say. But Laws adopted a more substantial defence. He noted that the broadcasting code of ethics was in fact a code for journalists. Since he was not a journalist but an entertainer, he was not bound by the code ('there is no hook for ethics', he famously remarked[3]). As an entertainer using the media, he was not subject to any ethical appeal. This view was not just a convenient fiction invented to protect him at the inquiry. According to evidence given to the inquiry, when 2UE station manager John Conde had issued a warning to his on-air staff about entering into such agreements in breach of the code of practice, Laws told Conde he believed the warning did not apply to him.

Finally, the decline of ethics as a regulatory discourse over the 1990s came home to roost in arguments made by, among others, former journalist and editor Max Suich at the inquiry. Drawing attention to the fact that stories similar to the *MediaWatch* report had been circulated previously, and that the industry was generally aware of the kinds of arrangements now under attack, Suich pointed out that the ABA had not expressed any official interest at all on these previous occasions. As a result, he argued, broadcasters were entitled to believe that they were operating within the ABA's understanding of the code.[4]

While some of the origins of this particular drama do lie in specific policy decisions made by the then Labor government through the late 1980s and into the 1990s, concern about the declining relevance of ethical standards on commercial media practice is not confined to Australia. Indeed, what could be seen as something of a moral panic around tabloidization has been provoked by what is usually regarded as a trend which affects the Western media as a whole, to a greater or lesser extent. In a recent article which focuses on arguments about tabloidization and journalism ethics, Christopher Pieper argues that the current rules for professional behaviour in the United States are also 'obsolete'. The specific performance of the news media in the United States is now, he argues, totally incompatible with the kinds of truth claims customarily made for the press, as well as with the principles of objectivity routinely invoked by members of the news media when defending themselves or attacking their competitors.[5]

Nevertheless, Pieper contests the narrative of decline and contagion usually attached to accounts of tabloidization. First, he argues that it is difficult to find evidence to support the proposition of clear differences between the content and practices employed by mainstream or quality media and the tabloids. While both sectors of the industry claim the status of 'news' for what they do (as distinct from gossip or entertainment), almost all the available promotional tactics are used by almost all the outlets. The only area 'immune' from the so-called contagion of the tabloid in terms of their content and newsgathering practices, according to Pieper, lies outside the commercial domain in the United States: National Public Radio and the News Hour with Jim Lehrer. Pieper concludes that the so-called disease of tabloidization is simply the consequence of unregulated market competition. The problem with the practice of contemporary journalism, he says, is the 'confounding factor' of the profit motive:

> [T]he mainstream media have not been 'infected' in any real sense by the rampaging virus called sensationalism, placing the media in the role of the passive victim and tabloids as the aggressor, but they instead gradually poached techniques from the tabloid side, as needed, to supply what they discerned to be public tastes.

He continues:

> If we understand the tabloid virus to be one that 'invades' by becoming popular and drawing audiences away from mainstream outlets, then the meaning changes. In the post-network era, greater media diversity has shattered the virtual audience monopoly once enjoyed by major news media. The perception that audiences would flock to watch *Inside Edition* over the *CBS Evening News* likely contributed to the networks' ventures into sensationalism, a return from which we have not seen or expect to see. Blaming the tabloids for this change, however is unfair and illogical. The mainstream media was not compelled by any other factor than the

fear of losing their unrealistic and unsustainable market share that they enjoyed for nearly four decades. The true culprit, if we are insistent on finding one, is the hyper-competitive fervour brought on by the need to maintain high levels of profit despite environmental changes to the media landscape. Using the epidemiological metaphor, the source of the system's decay cannot be traced to a virus, as is claimed in popular discourse, but is most likely the result of a congenital defect common to commercial media systems, that of profit maximisation.[6]

Pieper suggests that what is most often discussed as an issue of standards, and represented through metaphors of disease and decline, is actually a structural issue. The commercial media, shorn of any checks and balances to exert a public policy influence over their activities, behave increasingly like a business. As the mainstream media in the US are finding out, this may actually endanger their survival because it constitutes a partial misrecognition of what the media are: that is, they constitute a cultural as well as a commercial industry and many of the normal commercial rules about product development and investment do not apply. As the title of Julianne Schultz's 1994 book says, it is not 'just another business'.[7] Nevertheless, in the United States, where competition has increased and the regulatory hand has never been strong, the media sphere has become a thoroughly commercial domain.

There are other angles we could take onto this debate which accredit the commercial media with more diverse and positive outcomes. John Hartley's *Uses of Television* argues that the media in contemporary culture serve more than the profit motive—perhaps far more than they might realize. For a start, the media provide us with the means to construct a modern citizenship. Not only that, but it may well be an increasingly progressive form of citizenship. According to Hartley's argument, the Western mass media are tightly implicated in what has been a relatively recent move away from addressing what was conventionally thought of as a 'mass', modern but undifferentiated, citizen. Now, the mass media seek a highly differentiated, what Hartley calls a 'DIY', postmodern citizen. They do this through the specialized address we might associate with cult television, fanzines, or slash comics but which is also implicated in the market success of mainstream television programmes such as *The Panel* and talkback radio hosts such as John Laws. Hartley argues in relation to television, in particular, that while it may well aim at something different as its commercial objective, its by-product is in fact a citizenship of the future:

decentralized, post-adversarial, international, based on self-determination not state coercion, right down to the details of identity and selfhood. Its model is the 'remote control' exercised by television audiences, and its manifestations include fan cultures, youth cultures, taste constituencies, consumer-sovereignty movements and those privatizations of previously 'public' cultures that succeed in democratization without politicization: extending to everyone membership of the republic of letters that was once reserved for literate/clerical elites.[8]

This has occurred in the context of an increasingly commercialized, deregulated, and ethically relaxed media. The great irony for Hartley is that what was once thought of as an homogenizing 'mass media' is now actively producing multiple, fragmented, highly differentiated identities—all claiming 'difference' as a right[9] (p. 164). Far from accidental, it would seem, this is a result of the new focus of the media. A centralized and highly selective location for information and entertainment has become a proliferating source for the distribution of information, entertainment and identities as news and journalism move from operating as a 'discourse of power' to operating as a 'discourse of identity'. We can see the result in our programming, argues Hartley; where the 'object of news was once the decision-maker' but is now 'the celebrity' (p. 159)—which is why some decision makers try to become celebrities.

Hartley's position is elaborated within a characteristically optimistic and anti-statist account of the cultural function of the media—an account encapsulated in the neologism he employs throughout *Uses of Television* to label certain aspects of the relationship between the media and the citizen. By using the term 'democratainment', Hartley locates the media as a site of both pleasure and pedagogy, privileging the primacy of entertainment while still reminding us that it is nevertheless through the media that citizens participate in public debate.[10] One doesn't have to accept the full range of implications of this neologism, and I should admit here that I do not, to respond to the notion that a primary cultural function for the media is the construction of personal and public identities. Nor is it difficult to accept that among the effects of the highly commercialized and expanded mediascape of today is the proliferation of new, hitherto marginalized, personal identities, and disrespectful, hitherto silenced, public voices. Their presence is probably reflected, in fact, in the prevalence of the rhetoric of declining standards which is so often used to support the critique of tabloidization.

There is no doubt, I would agree, that the media's size and structure have changed in recent decades. Some of the changes are beneficial, and probably do involve what Hartley refers to as 'transmodern teaching', the 'gathering of audiences' and the creation of 'cultural literacies' which are just as important as those tradition-ally associated with what he refers to as the literate/clerical elite. There is enough evidence to suggest that, as observers or students of the media, we must continue to revise some of the more traditional assumptions about how the media operate, in what configuration of interests they can work, and what kinds of democratic potential they carry.

If there is substance to Hartley's view, then, how seriously should we take the ethical failing that occur along the way to this DIY citizenship? If we are witnessing the democratization of the media sphere, should it matter that certain ethical con-straints will give way in the face of unregulated commercial competition? Does it really matter that the commercialization of the public sphere, and its realignment with the provision of entertainment, effectively sidesteps the traditional claims of journal-ism ethics—claims still implicitly based on the provision of information to the citi-zenry? What, precisely, is the problem if the media disinvest in the culture of public service in order to maximize the benefits of a culture of business?

First of all, it is important to accept that there need not be a categoric answer to this. Certainly, in the specific case we are looking at here, I think it does matter. In this instance, there is clear evidence that the manipulation of public opinion on important matters carries effects that are the reverse of democratic. The connection between the media format and the formation of public opinion has been articulated to private and secret interests. As a result, rather than public opinion being what David Chaney calls 'the creative fiction of a new political order [i.e. democracy]'—and therefore a good thing—the formation of public opinion becomes the 'rhetorical fiction of institutional-ized elites'—definitely a bad thing. The very media structures which ought to *enable* democratic participation work against such an end when 'public opinion' 'is conjured into being by interested groups' through the media 'to rationalise and legitimate the play of institutionalised politics'.[11]

That said, when we move beyond the specific case, there is a comprehensiveness about the claims of an ethical critique that seems insufficiently contingent for our current needs. We need to ask to what extent ethical issues are still relevant for media analysis as well as for media practice. Of course, a code of ethical practice has been a favoured means of protecting the interests of individual members of the national public, as well as those of the nation, in more than the media industries. It had a particular point, though, in its relation to the media industries. The media partici-pated in the cultural formation of the modern citizen and thus carried out a civic responsibility that could be framed in fundamentally democratic terms.

However, the citizen looks a little different to us now. Ideally, today, cultural identity is offered up as the object of choice, DIY, through active identification rather than some form of designation or attribution. The consensual momentum invested in the idea of the nation has lost some of its power. At the same time, the idea of the modern nation is losing some of its democratic furniture as more and more of its operations are privatized, deregulated, and turned over to the market. This has not been such a difficult transaction. The categories of the citizen and the consumer are easily, even unproblematically, merged through the liberal-democratic rhetorics of choice and cultural identity preferred by most Western democracies today.

This makes many of us uncomfortable. It is difficult to reconcile a view of the media that, on the one hand, sees their expansion and plurality as a positively dem-ocratizing force with, on the other hand, a political economy of the media which charts the increasingly concentrated pattern of media influence and ownership around the world. These two principles work against each other. One welcomes the proliferation of voices, access and diversity while the other is intent on controlling and reducing participation to those elements which are profitable for a very small number of beneficiaries.

This conflict requires some managing through a regulatory structure which will privilege 'where necessary' (and this is a minefield I will leave alone in this argument) the interests of the national citizen over those of the commercial consumer. Here, an ethical regulatory regime is still required. The recent Productivity Commission report on Broadcasting pointed out the need for guarantees of ethical media practice within a number of areas: these included the respect for privacy, issues of access, right of reply and redress, and accuracy of reporting.[12] Crucially, they suggested such guarantees should be obligatory conditions of media licences, not just codes of pro-fessional practice. Significantly, also, the Productivity Commission returned to some implicit invocation of the ethical/democratic responsibilities of the media by suggest-ing that, in addition, an outline of what they called 'general condition' should be incorporated into the broadcaster's licence.[13] In the past we have had such general codes—variously articulated as an independently scrutinized regime of 'standards' (which was a taste-based means of policing a particular version of 'quality' as operated by the old Australian Broadcasting Control Board) or the current 'code of ethics' (which effectively established the professional codes of journalism as the only ethical regime required). What the Productivity Commission report implied is more fundamental in that it proposes a charter of fundamental social responsibilities to the citizen and the nation, guaranteed in return for the commerical privilege of ownership of public space. It is only a mild implication, but it represents a significant revival of a less market-oriented construction of the relationship between the media and the nation-state.

Ethics here operates as a means of framing certain aspects of the contract between the media licensee and the licensing state. But it assumes a model of media practice that is still based on journalism or on the provision of information. What kind of regime—if any—do we institute for a media industry concerned primarily with providing entertainment? As someone working within cultural studies, that is now quite a pressing question. An ethical regulatory structure is neither enough nor, on its own, appropriate for managing our relation to these kinds of media.

The media are supplying quite varied needs now, and much media criticism routinely devalues those needs they do not share. We should not forget that ethics is tied not only to issues of citizenship, but also to issues of class. It is not too long ago that the role of the metropolitan intellectual (or Hartley's literate/clerical elite) was explicitly to shape both opinion and taste: to 'civilize' an emerging class by educating them in the values of an elite. Cultural studies has been among the forefront of movements exposing the interests embedded in that role for the intellectual. Previous comfortable agreements about what is an appropriate ethical position or what are acceptable tastes have fallen apart. As a result of the turning of critical attention onto cultural forms based on the experience of women, people of colour, gays and lesbians, what were once considered disinterested ethical positions look a lot more like interested political positions. What was once, according to Andrew Ross, 'exclusively [and unproblematically] thought of as the education of taste', now has to draw upon 'many different schools of ethical action, informed not by "universal" (i.e. Western) humanist values, but by the specific agendas of the new social movements against racism, sexism, homophobia, pollution, and militarism'.[14] Just as in the case of the critiques of tabloidization, these movements have 'run up against the same reactionary consensus of left and right, each unswervingly loyal to their respective narratives of decline'[15] and each of them grounded in an explicit ethics.

We need to accept that even the discourse of ethics is not innocent. This is not to claim that we don't need it, but to argue that we need more than that. As has been found in the Cash for Comment instance, a code of ethics has not been enough to protect us from the effects of the market. However, an obvious alternative, or complementary angle of inspection, involves a regime of content regulation based upon a particular consensus around assumptions of 'quality'—much like that exercised by the old Broadcasting Control Board. This kind of regime still operates in the UK. In June 2000, a storm blew up over the fact that the UK television content regulator (the ITC) intervened on two occasions. It first warned Channel 5 that the populist character of its programming was an object of concern (a naked game show was the provocation here). Then it tested the limits of its powers by instructing ITN to move its News at Eleven back to the previously traditional slot of News at Ten in order to provide access to the news for a larger proportion of the population.[16] I am not recommending this kind of regime at this point, but it is a possibility which deserves revisiting for public debate. Furthermore, it is worth pointing out that such a regime effectively operates in relation to the ABC through the influence of the government of the day (particularly frequent under Minister Richard Alston), while the commercial networks are free of such kinds of scrutiny.

At this point, I am arguing for a much less institutionalized form of cultural criticism of media output that interposes itself against the forces of the market. There has to be a more active and watchful context of consumption—something the Cash for Comment inquiry has helped to create, even if only temporarily. This story was broken by the ABC's *MediaWatch*, taken up by the Fairfax press, debated on *Lateline* and *A Current Affair*, and prosecuted as a public policy issue by the Communications Law Centre. That, it seems to me, is how it *should* happen—only more often. And it should involve people from within media and cultural studies more often. Talkback radio has been virtually ignored by the academy even though it constitutes one of the major influences on the media's shaping of public opinion. There are important modes of critique which do not carry the universalizing assumptions built into the concept of ethics, which will be explicitly motivated and contingent, and which will be mounted on a case-by-case basis.[17] Such modes of critique are among the potential contributions to be made by media and cultural studies to this context of consumption.

The distribution of capital is left largely to the market but few of us are happy with the results. The distribution of cultural capital seems to me far too important to leave to the market, but its regulation is a thorny problem because even the most principled intervention will serve specific interests. On the other hand, of course, we know that the market is not in fact left to its own devices. The Cash for Comment scandal is a perfect example where the possibility of effective political participation was restricted by those who had access to influencing media content. That access was provided by their market power. The power of access can be understood as a significant form of cultural capital in itself. As Chaney says, it is 'not only markedly unevenly distributed, but has also proved to be easily appropriated by dominant organisations. The meaning of the public sphere in different social formations', he goes on to say, 'must be continually inspected, unless its failures are to persistently rob the concept of citizenship of effective meaning.'[18]

I have suggested elsewhere that this has proved difficult for cultural studies over recent years, in that reactionary or populist media forms—indeed, entertainment genres overall—no longer provoke enough attention from a cultural studies which thinks of itself as having left ideology critique behind.[19] With the revival of a context which might encourage informed and case-based critical scrutiny—a context in which there is now a lexicon of ethics as well as commerce, some revival of discussion of what might be the specific point of a culturally regulatory regime over the commercial media, and wider understanding of the fact that media content may no longer have much to do with the provision of information—one would hope to see an expansion in the critical field. Now, more than ever, certainly in relation to Australian talkback radio, there are opportunities to 'contest, reconstruct and redefine existing terms and relations of power'[20] in the media through direct critical engagement. That means more specific studies—not necessarily exemplary, nor theoretically clarifying or programmatic, just inspections of media content in its own right, because it matters.

Correspondence: Graeme Turner, Centre for Critical and Cultural Studies, University of Queensland, St Lucia, Qld 4072, Australia.

Notes

1 I present an account of this in 'Talkback, advertising and journalism', *International Journal of Cultural Studies* 3 (2), 2000, pp. 247–255; a book-length account of the subsequent inquiry is Rob Johnson's *Cash for Comment: the Seduction of Journo Culture* (Sydney: Pluto, 2000).
2 Caroline Overington goes through the political connections in her piece in *The Age*, 'Talk Back Radio', *News Extra, The Age*, 23 October 1999, p. 6.
3 This was reported throughout the media, on 30 October 1999.
4 This was reported and discussed at length, for instance, in *The Australian*, 27 October, p. 3.
5 Christopher Pieper, 'Use your illusion: televised discourse on journalism ethics in the United States' 1992–98, *Social Semiotics* 10 (1), 2000, pp. 61–79.
6 Ibid., p. 74.
7 Julianne Schultz, *Not Just Another Business: Journalists, Citizens and the Media* (Sydney: Pluto, 1994).
8 John Hartley, *Uses of Television* (London: Routledge, 1999), p. 161.
9 Ibid., p. 164.
10 As Liz Jacka pointed out when this paper was presented to the 2000 ANZCA conference, the use of 'democracy' in this formulation is not at all precise. Rather than an increasing 'democratization' of media content, she suggested, what Hartley describes is the increasingly *demotic* content of mainstream media in the Western world. To inscribe this with a democratic politics requires another level of argument and demonstration. I am grateful to her for this observation.
11 *The Cultural Turn: Scene-setting Essays on Contemporary Cultural History* (London: Routledge, 1994), p. 108.
12 Productivity Commission 2000, *Broadcasting*, Report no. 11, Ausinfo, Canberra, p. 455.
13 Ibid., pp. 455–462.
14 Andrew Ross, *No Respect: Intellectuals and Popular Culture* (New York: Routledge, 1989), p. 211.
15 Ibid.
16 At the time of writing, this ruling was to be tested in the courts. For a sample of the debate in the press, see Damian Tambini, 'One watchdog that needs teeth', and (no byline) 'Bring back News at Ten, or else (er, or else what?), *Guardian*, 26 June 2000, p. 5. An academic account can be found in Howard Tumber, '10pm and all that: the battle over UK TV news', in Michael Bromley (ed.) *No News is Bad News: Radio, Television and the Public* (London: Longman, 2001).
17 An elaboration of what this might mean in practice is contained in Graeme

Turner, 'Tabloidisation, journalism and the possibility of critique', *International Journal of Cultural Studies* 2 (1), 1999.

18 Op. cit., p. 112.

19 See 'Tabloidisation, journalism and the possibility of critique', op. cit. See also Graeme Turner, 'Reshaping Australian institutions: popular culture, the market and the public sphere', in Tony Bennett and David Carter (eds), *Culture in Australia: Policies, Public and Programs* (Melbourne: Cambridge University Press, 2001).

20 Ross, op. cit., p. 213.

1.6

The *Daily Mirror* and the war on Iraq
by Des Freedman

Introduction

'You are NOT powerless, You DO have a voice' argued the British tabloid newspaper the *Daily Mirror* (*DM*) on its front page, just above the headline of NO WAR. On that day, 21 January 2003, the newspaper launched its petition to Prime Minister Tony Blair opposing the proposed war on Iraq, a petition that was eventually signed by over 220,000 people. The *Mirror* campaigned tirelessly to rebut the arguments of the British and US administrations that sought to justify a war, and employed the talents of leading political journalists like John Pilger and Jonathan Freedland to make the anti-war case. Celebrity gossip and scandal, once the staple of the *Mirror*'s news agenda, were kicked off the front page to be replaced by hard-hitting critiques of the pro-war lobby. Having backed the Stop the War Coalition's two million-strong demonstration in London on 15 February 2003, the newspaper provided for its readers on the following Monday 'a historic 12-page picture souvenir of our greatest-ever protest march'. Memories of Royal Jubilees, Cup Finals and *Big Brother* seemed a long way off.

Once the war started, the *Mirror* adopted a more cautious political position. It maintained opposition to the war itself but focused more on celebrating the courage and dedication of British soldiers. As the conflict continued, its coverage and editorial position became less distinctive, reducing its identification with the anti-war movement, curtailing its criticism of Tony Blair and returning gossip and showbiz news to more prominent positions in the paper. On 11 April, it was revealed that the *Mirror*'s circulation had dropped below the key psychological barrier of two million copies a day, while its main rival, the pro-war *Sun*, had actually added readers during the war. The following morning saw the paper's first non-war related front page since the beginning of March and the emergence of a more 'balanced' news agenda, juggling celebrity stories, domestic news and the aftermath of the Iraq war.

This chapter examines the *Mirror*'s behaviour in the build-up to and in the course of the war on Iraq. By adopting a highly politicised anti-government stance and by encouraging its readers to be active opponents of the war, the *Mirror* confounded the typical model of the tabloid newspaper as a repository of gossip, and the tabloid reader as a depoliticised, conservative, passive figure. The chapter highlights the constraints facing such a project in the light of the paper's ultimate ambition to make profits for its corporate owners at Trinity Mirror plc and, finally, reflects on the possibilities for and limitations of oppositional media practices in the context of a competitive 'free press' system.

Rebranding the *Mirror*

The *Mirror*'s public and very determined opposition to the war was unprecedented. While the paper supported British involvement in two of the most recent conflicts, the 1991 Gulf War and the 1999 campaign in Kosovo, it also has a long-established anti-war tradition, having opposed both the Suez invasion in 1956 and the Falklands War in 1982. But in opposing the war in Iraq, the *Mirror* was confronting the military plans of a *Labour* government for the first time and was in danger of alienating the Labour supporters who formed the core of its readership. According to David Seymour, the Mirror Group's political editor and leader writer, 'you have to remember who *Mirror* readers are. The *Mirror* was traditionally right-wing Labour because the readers were right-wing Labour and it walked a fine line in all of that.' Some of the paper's coverage of Iraq was, according to Seymour, 'in hindsight, very close to the line, if not over it'.[1]

At another level, the *Mirror*'s anti-war stance could be seen as the logical conclusion of a rebranding exercise that had started following the events of 9/11 and the perceived desire amongst the reading public for a more analytical approach to news in order to understand both the roots and dangers of terrorism. Piers Morgan, the *Mirror*'s editor, shifted the paper away from an unremitting emphasis on celebrity scandal and human interest stories towards a focus on international coverage that included a particularly critical stance towards the US and UK bombing of Afghanistan in late 2001. This approach was consolidated with the £19.5 million formal relaunch of the *Mirror* in April 2002 when the paper's traditional 'red top' masthead was exchanged for a more sombre black one and 'heavyweight' journalists like John Pilger (the leading investigative reporter and long-time *Mirror* writer), *Vanity Fair*'s Christopher Hitchens and the *Guardian*'s Jonathan Freedland were all given regular columns. According to Morgan, the changes were all about the *Mirror* becoming a 'serious paper with serious news, serious sport, serious gossip and serious entertainment' (*DM*, 16 April 2002). While sport, gossip and entertainment were common features of all tabloid papers, Morgan gambled that one way to distinguish the *Mirror* from its rivals would be to adopt a broadly left-wing, 'Old Labour' position that challenged both the domestic and international perspectives of the New Labour government. This was an unusual form of 'product differentiation' – a phenomenon more often consisting of 'scoops', competitions and giveaways – but not an entirely unreasonable one given signs of growing resistance to the Blair government. David Seymour argues that the move 'upmarket' was certainly in response to 9/11 but also reflected a more general critical engagement with the Blair government, as 'the *Mirror* is more radical now than it's ever been'.[2]

The relaunch and new radical tone was not just in response to a changed political climate but also was a much-needed measure to address the long-term circulation decline of the *Mirror* and to close the gap with its principal competitor, the *Sun*.[3] In May 2002, the *Mirror* (averaging around 2.1 million copies a day) cut its price from thirty-two to twenty pence a day in order to steal readers from the *Sun* (average circulation around 3.5 million copies a day). The latter's response was swift and vicious: an even more substantial price cut that neutralised the *Mirror*'s move and cost both titles an enormous amount of money, a situation that the *Sun* was more able to bear given the deep pockets of its owner, Rupert Murdoch's News International. By the end of 2002, neither the price-cuts nor the more radical news agenda had stopped the decline in sales, which were hovering just above the two million mark.

The relaunch of 2001/2 was the latest in a long line of *Mirror* 'rebranding' exercises. The newspaper was founded in 1903 as a 'boudoir paper for – and produced by – women',[4] but when that format proved to be unsuccessful, it rapidly turned into a Liberal-supporting 'picture paper'. In the 1930s, the *Mirror* was further transformed into a socially aware, mass-circulation tabloid specifically aimed at workers. The decision to throw its weight behind Labour in the following decade was, according to one historian, taken as 'little more than a marketing calculation that its appeal to a working-class audience meant that [in the words of *Mirror* chairman Cecil King] "the politics had to be made to match".'[5]

When the Conservatives won three successive elections in the 1950s, the *Mirror* was once again forced to adapt to new circumstances. James Curran argues that the paper watered down the class rhetoric of the 1940s and took on a more middle-of-the-road political stance in order to attract the 'young and upwardly mobile readers' sought by advertisers.[6] Finally, the recently-appointed editor Piers Morgan oversaw a £16 million relaunch in 1997 which sought to modernise the *Mirror*, adding colour, celebrity features and 'racy' front pages that would position it as the 'paper for the new millennium'. This attempt to invigorate and renew the paper's readership was most graphically illustrated by the controversy surrounding Morgan's choice of ACHTUNG! SURRENDER! as the cover story on the day of a football match between England and Germany in the 1996 European Championship. According to Morgan, 'the Achtung thing was a joke that people didn't get, that's all. We did it to get the youth on side. We've got droves of readers over sixty-five. We've gotta get the youth.'[7]

These continuous rebranding exercises demonstrate the uncertainties of the political and economic environment in which the *Mirror* finds itself. It has long held progressive views that threaten to alienate advertisers; it has based itself on an identification with a single political party whose own fortunes have fluctuated and whose supporters have aged thus making them less attractive to advertisers. At a time when party political affiliations are declining, the *Mirror* is still the paper with, by far, the most loyal political base – 71 per cent of *Mirror* readers voted Labour in the 2001 general election, six per cent more than the number of *Telegraph* readers who voted Conservative.[8] In an increasingly competitive market, therefore, the politics of a particular newspaper title are bound to be more tactical than ever, determined partly by editorial tradition, proprietorial intervention and marketing assumptions concerning how to connect with the opinions and interests of the target audience.

The *Mirror* and the build-up to war

The *Mirror* followed up its hostility towards the British and American bombing of Afghanistan in 2001 with a series of articles that warned against going to war with Iraq as a distraction from the real fight against international terrorism. The problems involved in challenging George Bush and Tony Blair's war plans soon became clear. The *Mirror* celebrated American Independence Day with the headline MOURN ON THE FOURTH OF JULY (*DM*, 4 July 2002, figure one) and a two-page article by John Pilger that described the US as 'the world's leading rogue state . . . out to control the world'. In response, the fund manager of one of Trinity Mirror's large American investors, Tweedy Browne, phoned up the *Mirror*'s chief executive to complain about the article. According to Roy Greenslade in the *Guardian*, the fund manager

> told me he had simply wanted to register his disappointment about the *Daily Mirror*'s coverage to its owners. He stressed that he had opened his remarks by saying he was strongly committed to the freedom of the press but that the 'right' to that freedom required that it be used responsibly and fairly. 'The *Mirror* wasn't fair and wasn't accurate,' he said.
>
> (*Guardian*, 15 July 2002).

Morgan defended Pilger and emphasised his popularity with *Mirror* readers (if not American investors) but the episode showed that an anti-Bush, let alone an anti-imperialist, position would generate real flak.

Through the rest of the year, the paper developed its argument that an attack on Iraq would be counter-productive and would 'make us less secure, not more' (*DM*, 1 January 2003). Responding to opinion polls showing a lack of popular support for an invasion of Iraq, the *Mirror* attempted to articulate this anti-war sentiment in bold and imaginative ways. On 6 January, the paper adapted a cartoon by US labour cartoonist Gary Huck, that suggested that Bush's motive for attacking Iraq lay with his desire to control oil resources in the region, and ran it on the front page. As preparations for war intensified, the *Mirror* escalated its own anti-war profile by launching its 'No War' petition – that allowed it to feature pictures of celebrities signing the petition every day – and distributing a free 'No War' poster. The first six or so pages of the paper each morning became devoted to the subject of the impending war and how to resist it. Morgan sanctioned further polemical, campaigning and highly controversial front pages, including one featuring Blair with BLOOD ON HIS HANDS (*DM*, 29 January 2003) that David Seymour remembers as being particularly 'close to the line'.

The *Mirror* did not simply challenge the arguments for going to war but helped to mobilise opposition to the US and UK governments. It reported on the global anti-war protests in January and firmly identified itself with the national demonstration due to take place in London on 15 February. Two days before, it published a four-page guide to the march that included a map of the route and contact details of local transport to get to London. The *Mirror* paid for the video screen in Hyde Park at the end of the march and printed thousands of 'No War' placards with the paper's logo at the top. Such was the enthusiasm for the protest amongst ordinary *Mirror* staff, according to David Seymour, that many turned up to distribute the placards and to participate in the march. 'There was a strong feeling that we were on the side of right and standing up against not just the government, particularly the Bush government, and against the might of the rest of the press.'[9] The following Monday, the paper featured ten pages on preparations for war as well as a twelve-page commemorative report on the protest march. By the time the war started, the *Mirror* was devoting up to fifteen pages a day in a popular tabloid condemning the arguments of the US and UK administrations and urging the public to raise its voice against a war.

The *Mirror*'s coverage in the early part of 2003 failed to stem the decline in circulation but did, at least, win it critical acclaim and much-needed publicity.[10] Seymour recalls that the anti-war position was 'overwhelmingly supported by the readers' and that editorial staff were encouraged by opinion polls showing an anti-war majority in the UK.

> I was at a conference with the political editor of the *Sun* in the run-up to war and he said to me 'how many readers have you lost because of your stance on Iraq?' I said 'why should we lose readers when what we're saying is what the British public is saying?' It was the *Sun* that was flying in the face of British public opinion.[11]

This confidence encouraged the *Mirror* to venture into other controversial areas, most notably over the issue of asylum seekers and refugees. On 20 January, the paper ran a full-page feature on 'Why immigration is good for Britain' and followed this up in early March with a three-page special exposing the myths and reality about asylum seekers and pointing out Britain's poor record of accepting refugees despite the contribution they make to the country (*DM*, 3 March 2003). The *Mirror* was, for a time, the model of an accessible, popular, campaigning and challenging daily newspaper.

There were some ambiguities in the *Mirror*'s anti-war position, particularly in its attitude towards Tony Blair. One day it would accuse Blair of 'breathtaking arrogance' for ignoring a potential United Nations veto (*DM*, 7 March 2003) while the next it would admire Blair's resilience. 'Tony Blair has been the strongest and most powerful prime minister of modern times . . . He started down this road [of war] with the best intentions. But he has found himself in a dead end' (*DM*, 12 March 2003). The conclusion was that Blair was an admirable and determined leader who was making a tactical mistake in allying himself with the real cowboy, George Bush. Furthermore, the *Mirror*'s opposition to a war did not include the withdrawal of support for British troops should they be involved. Two days before the war started, Seymour wrote a two-page leader in which he attacked the idea of war without international backing but added that our troops 'need to understand very clearly that once the fighting begins, the Daily Mirror unequivocally supports them' (*DM*, 18 March 2003).

This contradiction – of supporting the army but opposing the war – echoed a deeper political ambiguity about how best to secure British interest. Seymour argues that 'had the circumstances and timing been different, we would have supported military action to remove Saddam'. The problem was this was a US-led initiative led by 'warmongers' who wanted to seek revenge for 9/11. 'We just couldn't see what the advantages of going in like that in the way they did go in. Had there been a grand alliance of nations as there had been after 9/11, I think it would have been difficult for us to completely oppose it.'[12] In the run-up to the war, the isolation of the British and US administrations, together with public backing for the anti-war position, was enough to convince Piers Morgan and David Seymour that opposition was justified and that pursuing an anti-war position was in the *Mirror*'s interest. To what extent would this last once the war had started?

The *Mirror* during the war

The *Mirror* continued to provide a voice for the anti-war movement even when British and American troops launched their invasion of Iraq on 20 March. Despite, or perhaps because of, the jingoistic coverage of its main competitors, the paper refused to change its opinion that the war was illegal and unjustified. Faced with accusations that to be against the war was unpatriotic, the *Mirror* filled its front page on 24 March with pictures of innocent civilian casualties and the headline STILL ANTI-WAR? YES, BLOODY RIGHT WE ARE! Along with a minority of other papers like the *Guardian* and *Independent*, the *Mirror* carried regular reports that condemned US and UK propaganda, the bombing of civilians, the appalling conditions in Baghdad and the instances of 'friendly fire'. It hired the veteran war reporter Peter Arnett, who had been sacked from MSNBC for speaking to state-run Iraqi TV, and turned this into a front page: 'Fired by America for telling the truth . . . Hired by the Mirror to carry on telling it' (*DM*, 1 April 2003). Between fifteen and twenty pages of an eighty-page tabloid newspaper were devoted to covering the war from a perspective that was generally critical of Blair and Bush's motivations.

Yet there were many areas in which the *Mirror*'s coverage dovetailed with that of the rest of the press, particularly in focusing on the details of war. The paper ran a daily 'BATTLE TIMETABLE' filled with *Boy's Own* graphics, and aired the military analysis of former SAS soldier and thriller writer Andy McNab. The *Mirror* also went along with the highly problematic system of 'embedding' journalists inside military units. Tom Newton Dunn, embedded with forty Commando, provided regular reports of the bravery and benevolence of British troops as they 'pacified' southern Iraq. In a fairly typical report, Dunn describes a conversation during the 'liberation' of a small town called Abu Al Khasib as follows:

> 'What's your name?' asks one teenage boy wearing a tatty Inter Milan football shirt. 'You should be wearing a Manchester United shirt,' says Sgt Gary Evans, 31, from Chester, pulling out a packet of energy-packed sweets. 'Here you go son, have one of these. We've come to be your friends.' The locals speak only the odd word or phrase of English but the boy didn't need to understand, he just smiled.

This valorisation of British troops was the most visible evidence of a change of emphasis for the *Mirror*. Once the war had started, it was no longer seen as appropriate to undermine British military objectives and risk sapping troop morale. Readers' letters opposing the war were replaced by messages to the troops from family members and an increasing number of stories reporting on the success of the military campaign or praising the initiative of British soldiers. David Seymour argues that the

Mirror was simply reflecting a shift in public attitudes. 'Since Suez, the accepted wisdom is that however much you campaign against military action, once it's started you have to fall in line behind your troops.'[13] Piers Morgan goes further, claiming that the *Mirror*'s coverage *had* to change.

> I personally slightly misjudged the way that you could be attitudinal on the front page in the way that we were, once the war actually started . . . I have never seen such a switch in public opinion . . . It's entirely down to the natural sense in this country – particularly among the tabloid readership – that once a war starts, if we're involved, we must unequivocally support our boys and girls.[14]

This was not the reaction of the hundreds of thousands of people who took direct action and marched demanding an immediate end to the war. The *Mirror*, at least initially, reflected *both* responses. On the day bombing started, Seymour's leader spoke of a 'horrible sense of helplessness for everyone back home here in Britain. All we can do is watch the television news and entrust our military leaders to do their job efficiently, speedily.' Yet over the page, John Pilger reported on the resistance to war, giving full details of protest groups and activities, under the headline of 'So what can YOU do? The polite term is civil disobedience . . . and the street term is rebellion' (*DM*, 20 March 2003). Yet when half a million people protested in London later that week – the biggest ever demonstration in Britain during wartime – there was no twelve-page supplement welcoming it but an attack from the *Mirror*'s regular Monday columnist Tony Parsons: 'Being against this war when British soldiers are fighting and dying seems cheap, grubby and inappropriate' (*DM*, 24 March 2003).

Another area in which the ambiguities of the *Mirror*'s political position were intensified by the outbreak of war concerned its attitude to Blair. Having previously accused Blair of having 'blood on his hands' and of being a 'PRIME MONSTER' (*DM*, 14 March 2003), the paper praised the 'passion and conviction' with which Blair addressed the nation and 'justified sending thousands of British troops into war' (*DM*, 21 March 2003). After a month of war, the paper was even more effusive. 'The past few months have seen Tony Blair unshakeably hold to the courage of his convictions . . . he has shown remarkable courage and leadership . . . he is entitled to receive recognition of his single-minded determination and relentless pursuit of his convictions' (*DM*, 17 April 2003). According to leader writer David Seymour:

> My feeling, which Piers [Morgan] supported, was that even if we thought that Blair was wrong, it would be wrong for us to deliberately accuse him of lying. We never accused him of lying over weapons of mass destruction since the story broke. We've always been at pains to make the separation between misleading and downright lying. But I also thought that just as you need to support your troops in time of war, I think there would have been a real problem – particularly for the *Mirror* with the most Labour-supporting readers – to have attacked Blair, a Labour prime minister in the middle of the war.[15]

The *Mirror*'s solution to the dilemma of how to connect to anti-war sentiment without alienating British troops (and readers) was to distinguish between what it saw as the honourable (if misguided) objectives of Tony Blair and the dishonourable, imperial ambitions of President Bush. The paper's front page on March 27 addressed Bush's love of war in no uncertain terms. 'Dead British troops paraded on Iraqi TV, 14 civilians killed in Baghdad market and Bush whoops it up. War? HE LOVES IT' A *Mirror* editorial followed this up by arguing that 'Blair's stand will help win the peace' and praised Blair for standing up to Bush by insisting on a United Nations presence in Iraq and arguing against military action in Syria and Iran. The 'poodle' has turned into a 'terrier' (*DM*, 3 April 2003). The continuing agreement between George Bush and Tony Blair over weapons of mass destruction and the rationale for war in Iraq suggests that no such canine transformation ever took place.

These changes in the *Mirror*'s coverage were stimulated not so much by a perception of a general shift in public opinion as by evidence that the paper's circulation was still declining. 'Do I think our anti-war line is to blame for any of the drop?' asked Morgan. 'Possibly a bit among our older readers who think it's unpatriotic to continue criticising the war now it's started. But the overwhelming reaction to our coverage from our readers has been totally supportive.'[16] However, a poll published in the *Guardian* on 31 March showed that while 38 per cent of *Mirror* readers disapproved of the military attack, 49 per cent approved of it.[17] Worse news was to follow. On 11 April it was revealed that the *Mirror*'s circulation had fallen below the two million mark and that its anti-war stance had contributed to this decline. Morgan was clearly under great pressure to 'ameliorate'[18] the coverage, to lessen the paper's critical attitude to the war and to shift the war off the front pages and restore a more traditional tabloid balance of hard news and celebrity stories. Commercial considerations dominated over political principles.

Seymour claims that it was not the anti-war position but simply wall-to-wall coverage of the war itself that was the problem for the *Mirror*. He argues that the change

> wasn't about politics. We're in the business – amongst other things – of wanting people to read our newspaper. And a newspaper which is so unremittingly negative or grey is not going to do the job we want it to and it's not just selling copies, it's also getting a message over . . . The *Mirror* is a mass market product which is read by five million people every day and you have to be very very careful not to offend or turn off too many people.[19]

Hard-hitting anti-war covers were therefore replaced with ones attacking Saddam Hussein (SADDAM CHEEK, April 5), marking the courage of British soldiers (BORN TO SERVE, April 8) or celebrating military success (STATUE OF LIBERTY on the fall of Baghdad, April 10). Five front pages inside two weeks were devoted to the *Mirror*'s campaign to help twelve-year-old Ali Abbas, who lost his family and both arms in an American bombing raid on Baghdad, to seek medical attention in the UK. 'What the Ali story did', according to Seymour, 'was it humanised the conflict.' Ali was one way of covering the war but in such a way as 'not to make it appear so negative'.[20] The Ali appeal was certainly well intentioned but it signalled an approach to the war with which Tony Blair and the rest of the British press could scarcely have disagreed. By 12 April, two days after the collapse of the

Iraqi regime, the war had disappeared off the front page entirely to be replaced by a photograph of television personality Ulrika Johnsson and a story about the Prime Minister appearing on an edition of *The Simpsons*.

In the months following the war, the *Mirror* has returned to a more familiar look where celebrity surveillance shares the limelight with the aftermath of the invasion and other (mostly domestic) news stories. The coverage of Iraq continues to be more critical and thoughtful than most of the rest of the British press but the project to make the *Mirror* into a distinctive and socially aware popular tabloid appears to be somewhat half-hearted and fragile. *Mirror* readers are now more likely to be addressed in terms of their leisure interests than their political aspirations, while the imaginative features on asylum seekers have been replaced by a more traditional tabloid interest in crime [. . .] The well-established tabloid balance between 'soft' and 'hard' news has been resuscitated, the radical rhetoric tamed and corporate nerves soothed by a small increase in circulation.

Conclusions

There are some key lessons about the role of the press to be learned from the *Mirror*'s performance during the Iraq war. The first is that at a time of profound social crisis when elites are divided amongst themselves and the public is willing to challenge and mobilise against these elites, a space can open up in which radical ideas start to circulate. In the context of a mass movement against Tony Blair's attempt to involve Britain in a US-led invasion of Iraq and serious international disagreement about the legitimacy of such military action, the *Mirror* was able to articulate and reinforce the views of this movement and to air opinions that would otherwise have been marginalised in the mainstream media. When the movement was on the up in the months preceding an invasion, the *Mirror* was happy to draw on a wide range of anti-war voices and to organise opposition to an invasion. It shifted from a newspaper that addressed its readers in fairly passive and restricted terms to one in which readers were conceptualised as active, thoughtful and capable of making an informed contribution to both the paper and the wider world. The significance of a mass-circulation tabloid newspaper taking on such a perspective should not be underestimated.

Although the *Mirror*'s circulation continued to decline during the war (which still involved some two million people choosing to buy a radical, anti-war paper every day), there is little evidence that its position on the war was the main contributor. David Seymour argues that, while some people did stop buying the paper because of the anti-war stance, others started taking it precisely *because* of its views. 'I got quite a lot e-mail from people who said "I used to be a *Sun* reader but I switched to the *Mirror* because you've got a good attitude to the war" '.[21] For Seymour and other media commentators, the precise political inflection of a tabloid paper is less of a factor in sales than its price. For the whole period leading up to and during the war, the *Sun* was able to maintain a price differential and therefore buy its way into a widening sales gap between the two papers. In any case, according to former *Guardian* editor Peter Preston, Trinity Mirror should have expected a decline in sales as one of the consequences of trying to push the *Mirror* upmarket. Rebranding, or as Preston calls it 'resurrection by differentiation', takes time, especially when it involves a serious attempt to win new and different readers. 'This is real long haul territory, with a smaller but better-resourced readership for advertisers at the end of journey. It needs resources, dedication, heavy marketing – and the management will to change the *Mirror*'s core identity over a decade.'[22] In the end, the *Mirror*'s anti-war position proved to be a convenient scapegoat for critics (inside and outside Trinity Mirror) who were demanding editorial changes, even though more money was lost in the fruitless price-cutting exercise with the *Sun*[23] than in the small decline in sales over the period of the war.

When 'differentiation' takes a highly political form that has already antagonised investors, shareholders and government itself, it becomes clear that a newspaper whose ultimate responsibility is to make a profit is not a reliable ally for a radical anti-war movement. Although the *Mirror* was initially keen to express the overwhelming anti-war sentiment in the UK, when military action started and opinion polls revealed a more ambivalent attitude towards the war amongst both its own readers and the general public, the *Mirror* was less willing to be identified with what it saw as minority views. Constrained by a 'responsibility' towards the bottom line, the paper was unable to maintain a consistent opposition towards the war and was forced to 'ameliorate' its coverage. Such is the logic of the newspaper business. Moments of social crisis can open up spaces for innovative and radical coverage but they sit uneasily with the market disciplines of a 'free press' that privilege, above all, profitability and competitiveness.

Notes

1　David Seymour, interview with the author, 14 July 2003.
2　Ibid.
3　The *Mirror*'s circulation peaked at over five million in the mid-1960s but declined following the relaunch by Rupert Murdoch of the *Sun*.
4　Colin Seymour Ure, 'Northcliffe's Legacy', in Peter Catterall, Colin Seymour-Ure and Anthony Smith (Eds), *Northcliffe's Legacy: Aspects of the British Popular Press, 1896–1996*, Macmillan, London 2000, p 10.
5　James Thomas, 'The "Max Factor" – a Mirror Image? Robert Maxwell and the *Daily Mirror* tradition', in ibid, p 214.
6　James Curran and Jean Seaton, *Power Without Responsibility*, Routledge, London 1991, p 111. Curiously this 'deradicalisation' is the precise opposite of the most recent example of the *Mirror*'s rebranding where 'radical politics' was seen to be a central plank of the strategy of product differentiation.
7　John Pilger, *Hidden Agendas*, Vintage, London 1998, p 438.
8　MORI poll, 'How Britain Voted in 2001', 20 July 2001, available at www.mori.com/polls/2001/elections.html.
9　Seymour, op cit. Despite huge popular opposition to a war, the bulk of the British daily press supported the proposed attack. It was predictable that the News International and Hollinger titles would line up behind a war given the ideological preferences of their proprietors (Rupert Murdoch and Conrad Black respectively), but the decision of the more liberal-minded *Observer* to support Tony Blair

was more surprising – possibly stemming from a desire not to lose circulation as it had when the paper opposed the British occupation of Suez in 1956.

10 The *Guardian* (17 February 2003) reported that the *Mirror* gained £100,000 worth of free publicity with its sponsorship of the 15 February demonstration. 'Thousands of marchers carried Daily Mirror "No War" posters on Saturday, resulting in a double whammy of brand promotion among the 1 million-strong crowd and in news coverage on TV and press.'

11 Seymour, op cit.

12 Ibid.

13 Ibid.

14 Quoted in Ian Burrell, 'Morgan's dilemma', *Belfast Telegraph*, April 2003, available at http://www.belfasttelegraph.co.uk/iraqcrisis/uknews124.jsp.

15 Seymour, op cit.

16 Owen Gibson, 'Mirror readers turn off war stance', *The Guardian*, 3 April 2003.

17 Poll results are at www.IMAGE. Guardian.co.uk/sysfiles/politics/documents/2003/03/25/03251 CM.pdf.

18 Seymour, op cit.

19 Ibid.

20 Ibid.

21 Ibid.

22 Peter Preston, 'Bore-bore not war-war is turn-off', The *Guardian*, 3 April 2003.

23 Price-cutting cost Trinity Mirror £23.5 million in 2002 alone (Trinity Mirror plc, *Annual Report and Accounts 2002*, p 13).

1.7

Photojournalism and the tabloid press [1]
by Karin E. Becker

Photography has a long and uncomfortable history within Western journalism. Despite its very visible presence in the daily and weekly press of the past century, photography is rarely admitted to settings in which journalism is discussed, investigated, and taught. Whenever the distinction is drawn between information and entertainment, or the serious substance of a journalism appealing to an intellectual reading public is defended against the light, trivial appeal of the popular, photography falls within the popular, excluded from the realm of the serious press. Nowhere are the consequences of this position more evident than in the pages and discussion of the tabloid press. There the display and presumed appeal of the photographs are used as criteria for evaluating, and ultimately dismissing, tabloid newspapers as 'merely' popular.

The history of this link between photography and the tabloid press can be traced to photography's successive adoption by three distinct types of publications: first in the elite periodical press with its established tradition of illustration; then in the tabloid press with a more popular appeal; and almost simultaneously, in weekly supplements to the respected organs of the daily press. Examining this history reveals the development of discourses about photojournalism, including beliefs about the nature of the medium, that continue to inform photography's positions in the contemporary press.

Beliefs that photographs supply unmediated pictures of actual events could have been the foundation for treating photographs as news by institutions whose credibility rests on the facticity and accuracy of their reports about the world. Yet there is a contradiction, because photography, when constructed as a purely visual medium, is also thought to bypass those intellectual processes that journalism will specifically address and cultivate. Photography's more immediate, direct appeal is seen as a threat to reason, and to the journalistic institution's Enlightenment heritage. The tension inherent in these reconstructions of photography and journalism permeates the discourse in which these practices coexist. Tracing the history of this discourse, and particularly journalism's ambivalence toward photography's popular appeal, one finds patterns of use and journalistic structures that refer to photography and exploit its popularity, while simultaneously insulating the elite segments of the daily press in exclusively verbal forms of journalistic practice.

Analysing the role of photography in the press can thus help illuminate the simultaneous problems of the 'political' and the 'aesthetic' in contemporary communication studies, and offers insights into the relationships among representation, historical knowledge, and value at the heart of the postmodern debate. This chapter engages these issues first, by examining the historical development of the use of photographs in the Western press, and secondly, by analysing the tabloid press as the contemporary context in which photography continues to be a primary means of representing the news.

The early picture press

In the early 1840s illustrated magazines were launched almost simultaneously in several European countries. The *Illustrated London News*, founded in 1842, was a well-written weekly magazine which hired illustrators to portray important current events (Hassner, 1977; Taft, 1938). Its success[2] was echoed by *L'Illustration* in France and *Illustrierte Zeitung* in Germany (both founded in 1843) and which were soon followed by others. *Frank Leslie's Illustrated Newspaper* (1855) and *Harper's Weekly – Journal of Civilization* (1857) were the first such publications to appear in North America.

These magazines were all using wood engravings to illustrate the news. Well-known artists were hired to 'cover' events, and competed to be the first with their reports. *Leslie's*, for example, sent an illustrator to the hanging of the anti-slavery movement leader John Brown in 1859, with instructions to take the first train back to New York where sixteen engravers worked through the night to meet the press deadline. The text published with the engraving stated that it was 'from a sketch by our own artist taken on the spot', invoking the authority of the eye-witness (Hassner, 1977: 170).

At that time the publication of actual photographs was technically impossible, but wood engravings were preferred for other reasons. The camera's 'likeness' apparently was considered stiff and too dependent on the luck of the machine, in contrast with the hand-drawn image that reflected the artist's perspective and the engraver's craft. When a photograph was used (often quite loosely) as a referent for the engraver, a statement like 'from a photograph' frequently accompanied it, lending the machine's authority to the artist's work. By the 1860s, the engraving was considered 'a meticulously faithful reproduction of reality' within a 'sphere of objectivity around the medium itself' (Johannesson, 1982).[3]

Thus, the periodical press had established patterns of visual reporting several decades before the half-tone process was developed to facilitate printing photographs and text side by side. The topics that were covered, the ideals of immediacy and accuracy and the competition valorizing both the journalistic process and its product (both the hunt and its trophy), were well established on publications that carried an aura of quality and distinction. The 1890s saw these conventions of illustration gradually being adapted to photography.

Histories of photojournalism trace a heritage to a limited number of prestige periodicals, locating a tradition of photographic reportage in the work of a few editors and photographers (Hassner, 1977; Edom, 1976; Kobre, 1980). *Collier's Weekly*, a 'cultural magazine emphasizing literary material', is often named as one of the first to shift from illustration to photo-reportage. Photographer James Hare, *Collier's* primary correspondent throughout the Spanish–American War, is seen as the chief reason for the magazine's success.[4] Hare's assignment to investigate the sinking of the battleship *Maine* is among the earliest examples used to present the photojournalist as hero: 'He snapped the wreck of the *Maine* from every point of the compass. He caught divers still busy at the somber task of bringing up the drowned. . . . With the aid of an interpreter, Jimmy prowled through reconcentrado camps. He photographed swollen bodies with bones breaking through the skin; he took pictures of the emaciated living, and of babies ravaged by disease. Every ship that passed Morrow Castle enroute to New York carried a packet of snapshots. Their influence upon public opinion can hardly be overestimated' (Carnes, 1940: 15; Edom, 1976: 38).

The rapid expansion of weekly magazines in the United States was due in part to the overheated atmosphere and competitive coverage of the war with Spain. Technical innovations and new legal privileges were also encouraging growth, and most important, with industrialization and the shift to a market economy, advertising began to provide significant support for the weekly press. As many magazines cut their purchase prices in half, a potentially nation-wide market suddenly opened up and the so-called 'general interest mass circulation magazine' arose. Advertising volume grew from 360 million to 542 million dollars between 1890 and 1900 (Kahan, 1968; Hassner, 1977: 216–17). The availability of large advertising revenues and the assumption of a mass appeal would become foundations of the picture magazines in the 1930s.

At the turn of the century, however, there are few indications that photography actually increased magazine sales (Kahan, 1968: 194; Hassner, 1977: 218). Nevertheless, 'the weekly photo-news magazine concept' had been established, and the heroic construction of its news photographer had begun.

The tabloid = sensationalism = photography

Daily newspapers did not have an established tradition of illustration predating photography, which helps to explain the slow introduction of half-tone reproduction in the daily press. Daily deadline requirements also meant that the early half-tone process was too cumbersome for newspaper production routines. By the late 1890s, more than a decade after the process was invented, many papers only occasionally published photographs. The exception was the United States' 'yellow press', and particularly the fierce competition between two New York papers, Joseph Pulitzer's *World* and William Randolph Hearst's *Journal*, where pictures were seen as a key to successful and sensational coverage. The *World*, for example, carried what is claimed were 'the first actual photographs of the wreck' of the *Maine* in 1898, and which were in fact drawn simulations of photographs (Time-Life, 1983: 16).

It was in the tabloid press of the 1920s that large sensational photographs first appeared, with violence, sex, accidents and society scandals as the major themes. United States press historians point to this as a low point for the press, an expression of what they consider the loose morals and loss of ethical standards that threatened public and private life. It was a time 'made to order for the extreme sensationalism of the tabloid and for a spreading of its degrading journalistic features to the rest of the press' (Emery, 1962: 624). The *New York Daily News* was a primary culprit, and by 1924 had the largest circulation of any US newspaper. Its main competitors were the *Daily Mirror* and the *Daily Graphic*. England's *Daily Mirror* (founded 1904) had established 'a genre making public the grief of private individuals', and in the 1920s was, together with the *Daily Express*, among the newspapers influenced by the US tabloids' use of photographs (Baynes, 1971: 46, 51).

'Sensational' journalism breaks the press' ascribed guidelines of ethical practice with the intention of attracting attention in order to sell more papers. In this process, journalism's audience – its 'public' – is reconstructed as a mass, undifferentiated and irrational. The 'sensational' occurs within journalistic discourses that are also bounded by cultural, historical and political practices that in turn position the ethical guidelines around different types of content, an important point to remember when examining the tabloid press of different countries.[5] Yet, a component common to the various constructions of the sensational is that attracting attention takes precedence over other journalistic values, including accuracy, credibility and political or social significance. In the US, the sensationalism of the tabloid press was intensified by 'photographs of events and personalities reproduced which are trite, trivial, superficial, tawdry, salacious, morbid, or silly' (Taft, 1938: 448). It was not the subject matter, in other words, but the ways the photographs reproduced it which appealed to the emotions and thereby created the sensation.

Herein lies the rationale for prohibiting the photographing of newsworthy events that take place where reason and order are seen as crucial, that is, within most judicial and legislative bodies. Newspaper violations of these prohibitions have been held up as examples confirming the need for exclusion (Dyer and Hauserman, 1987) or, conversely, within photojournalistic discourse to point to the need for self-regulation (Cookman, 1985). One frequently cited case was a New York divorce trial in which the husband, a wealthy white manufacturer, wanted to annul his marriage on the grounds that his wife had concealed from him that she was part African-American, which she in turn claimed was obvious to him at the time of their marriage. At one point in the trial, when she was required to strip to the waist, the courtroom was cleared and no photographs were permitted. The *Evening Graphic* constructed what it proudly called a 'composograph' by recreating the scene using actors, then pasting in photographs of the faces of actual trial participants (Hassner, 1977: 282; Kobre, 1980: 17). No discussion of this obvious montage as a dismantling of photographic truth is offered in today's texts, nor is the outcome of the trial itself. They do note, however, that such practices led to the *Graphic*'s nickname, 'the *Porno-graphic*' (see Time-Life, 1983: 17).

The *Daily News* is seen as the leader of that 'daily erotica for the masses' (Kobre, 1980: 17), particularly for heating up competition, and thus increasing the excesses of sensationalism among the tabloids. The execution of Ruth Snyder, found guilty of murdering her husband after a much publicized 'love triangle' trial in 1928, is often given as an example. Although reporters were allowed to witness the electrocution, photographers were excluded (Time-Life, 1983: 17). The day before, the *Graphic* had promised its readers 'a woman's final thoughts just before she is clutched in the deadly snare that sears and burns and FRIES AND KILLS! Her very last words, exclusively in tomorrow's *Graphic*' (cited in Emery, 1962: 629).

The *Daily News*, however, had a Chicago press photographer, unknown to New York prison authorities and press, in the execution chamber with a camera taped to his ankle. At the key moment he lifted his trouser leg and made an exposure using a cable release in his pocket. 'DEAD!' was the simple heading over the photograph in the *Daily News*' extra edition. The caption gave it scientific legitimation as 'the most remarkable exclusive picture in the history of criminology', and described details ('her helmeted head is stiffened in death') difficult to distinguish in the heavily retouched photograph. The edition sold a million copies, easily beating the *Graphic*'s non-visual account of the event (Emery, 1962: 629).

Within this journalistic discourse, the photograph itself had come to mean sensational journalism. In his history of photography in America in 1938, William Taft claimed:

> Such prodigious and free use of photographs in picture newspapers and magazines has in a measure defeated their own object, presumably that of disseminating news. Such journals are carelessly thumbed through, the reader glances hastily at one picture – looks but does not see or think – and passes on to the next in the same manner and then throws the periodical aside – a picture album with little purpose or reason.
>
> These criticisms and abuses the pictorial press must meet and correct if it is to command the respect of intelligent people.
>
> (Taft, 1938: 448–9)

Here we see, if not the origins, then a full-blown expression of the historical antagonism between the liberal and the popular press, and photography's exclusive identification with the inferior, the popular, side of that antagonism.

The daily press 'supplements' the news

With the exception of the tabloid press, photographs rarely appeared in the daily newspapers of Europe and North America until 1920. Technical and time constraints offer a partial explanation for this delay. However, by the time daily photojournalism became practical, conventions of press photography had already been established. On the one hand, the abundant illustration in the magazines of the late nineteenth century had a broader content than 'the political, legal and economic matters [that] constituted the primary news in the traditional newspaper' (Hård af Segerstad, 1974: 143). On the other hand, the leading role photography was playing in the tabloids' abuses of press credibility made it increasingly difficult to see the photograph as a medium for serious news.

Photographic realism as an ideal had entered the *verbal* codes of the daily press shortly after photography's invention. Metaphors of the American newspaper as 'a faithful daguerreotype of the progress of mankind' were common from the 1850s, with the reporter employed as a 'mere machine to repeat' each event as a seamless whole, 'like a picture'. According to Dan Schiller (1977: 93) photography 'was becoming the guiding beacon of reportorial practice'. Although the conception of photographic realism had become intertwined with the roots of objectivity in the occupational ideology of American journalism, press photography itself had been enclosed in a different and conflicting discursive field.

Daily newspapers instead had begun to print weekly supplements on the new gravure presses. The first of these appeared in New York and Chicago in the 1890s and were illustrated predominantly with photographs. Many, such as the *New York Times Midweek Pictorial*, provided substantive complements to the newspaper's daily coverage of World War I. By 1920, New York's five major newspapers had rotogravure supplements to their Sunday editions (Schuneman, 1966, cited in Hassner, 1977: 279). Established during the period when half-tone reproduction became feasible, these magazines were a response to the popularity of photography. Material was gathered and packaged with a weekly deadline in a magazine format on smooth paper that raised the quality of reproduction. Within this format newspapers had succeeded in developing a way to use photography that complemented the structure and appearance of the daily news, while insulating and protecting the newspaper's primary product from being downgraded by the photograph. Contemporary examples of this phenomenon persist,[6] offering a showcase for 'good' photojournalism, pursued separately from the daily news product.

Photography had followed three distinct routes in its entry into the Western press, establishing separate and overlapping discourses of photo-journalism which, by the 1920s, were serving as three models. One may argue that this construction is based on secondary sources, the received histories of journalism and its photography, without looking at the primary material, that is, the press itself. Yet received histories undeniably serve as models for practice, indeed that is their power. It is the memory of how things were done in the past as reconstructed in contemporary discourse – not the day-to-day production process from any specific or actual period of time – which informs today's practice.

The picture magazines' legacy

Before turning to the specific case of the contemporary tabloid press, it is important to mention briefly the mass-circulation picture magazines. Although they have had little direct influence on tabloid photojournalism, their histories and the trajectories they established continue to inform photojournalistic discourse, including standards of practice and aesthetic value (Becker, 1985).

Mass circulation picture magazines emerged between the wars, first in Germany, soon thereafter in other European countries, and by the late 1930s were established in England and the United States (Gidal, 1973; Hall, 1972; Hassner, 1977; Eskildsen, 1978; Ohrn and Hardt, 1981). Not only did these magazines establish new genres of photoreportage – notably the photo essay and the practice of documenting both the famous and the ordinary citizen in the same light. More important, they emerged during a period when, in various ways in each of their respective countries, what Victor Burgin has described as 'a dismantling of the differentiation between high and low culture was taking place' (Burgin, 1986: 5). The notion of 'mass' art – referring to both the production and consumption of the work – had emerged to challenge the notion of 'high' culture as the sole repository of aesthetic value. Photography, in particular documentary photography, became accepted as popular art, and made its first major entry into the museum world.[7]

Walter Benjamin's predictions (1936) that the mass production of photographic images would bring about a defetishization of the art object had very nearly been reversed by the postwar years. Instead, we find an 'aura' reconstructed to privilege particular spheres of mass production and popular culture, including in this case, photojournalism. Within the magazines, photography was bearing the fruits of becoming a mass medium in a form that was popular and respected. Supported by consistently rising circulations and mass-market national advertising, and operating in a cultural climate which could accept the products of mass production as popular art, the status of photojournalism and of the men and women who produced it reached unprecedented heights. Several specific elements of this photojournalism continue to be seen as meriting the institutionalized culture's stamp of value: the formal structural properties of the ideal photo essay; the determination of the single photograph as an idealized moment – fetishized as 'the decisive moment' either alone or at the centre of the essay; and the reconstruction of the photojournalist as artist.[8]

The elevation of photography's status continued to exclude the tabloid press. The ideology of cultural value which had shifted to admit photojournalistic documents into museum collections, gallery exhibitions and finely produced books has persisted in treating tabloid press photography as 'low' culture. This meant, with few exceptions, not considering it at all.[9] The vacuum which has persisted around the tabloid press would be reason enough to examine its photojournalism. This is, after all, the daily press where photography continues to play a major role.

The contemporary domain of the tabloid

Many very different kinds of newspapers are published in a tabloid format. The present investigation, based on examples from the United States, England, Australia, Austria, Norway, Sweden and Denmark,[10] found wide variation in the degree to which the different papers overlapped with news agendas of the elite press and, in the cases of overlap, distinctly different ways of angling the news.[11] The few characteristics these papers have in common include an almost exclusive reliance on newsstand sales, a front page that seems to work like a poster in this context – dominated by a photograph and headlines referring to a single story – and photographs occupying a much larger proportion of the editorial content than one finds in other segments of the daily press.

The particular 'look' often associated with the photography of the tabloid press – where action and expression are awkwardly and garishly caught in the flat, raw light of bare bulb flash – is relatively uncommon. Far more frequently, one encounters photographs of people posed in conventional ways, looking directly into the camera. Celebrities, including entertainers and sports figures, in addition to the pose, are often portrayed performing. Occasionally famous people are also 'revealed' by the camera, drawing on a set of stylistic features that have long been thought to typify tabloid photojournalism. Coverage of political events, that category of coverage which overlaps most with news in the elite press, is constructed using photographs following each of these forms. But this is also where one is more likely to see photographs that exhibit the traditional look of the tabloid press.

These three broad and occasionally overlapping categories of coverage – of private or previously non-famous persons in circumstances that make them newsworthy, of celebrities, and of events that correspond to conventional constructions of news – provide a framework for analysing this photography in terms of its style, communicative value and its political implications.

Plain pictures of ordinary people

Most photographs in the tabloid press are in fact very plain. They present people who appear quite ordinary, usually in their everyday surroundings: a family sitting around a kitchen table or on their living room sofa, couples and friends embracing, children with their pets. Sometimes the people in the photographs are holding objects that appear slightly out of place, so that we see the objects as 'evidence': a woman hugging a child's toy, or presenting a photograph to the camera, for example. Sometimes the setting itself is the evidence behind the formal pose: a woman standing next to a grave, or a man sitting in the driver's seat of a taxi. Their faces often express strong emotion, easy to read as joy or sorrow. These are not people whom readers recognize as famous. One would not be likely to pay much attention to them in another context.

From the words we learn what has happened to them, why they are in the newspaper. 'Pals for years', the two happily embracing women never dreamed that they were sisters who had been separated at birth. The family sitting in their kitchen has just had their children's stomachs pumped for narcotics, amphetamine capsules the pre-schoolers had found on the playground. The woman with the child's toy continues to hope her kidnapped son will be returned safely. The little girl hugging her chimpanzee has donated one of her kidneys to save the pet's life. The middle-aged woman lounging on her sofa in a tight-fitting outfit is upset after losing a job-discrimination suit; despite her sex-change operation, employers have refused to accept that she is a woman.

Sometimes they are people whose lives have been directly affected by major national or international events. Rising interest rates are forcing the family to sell their 'dream house'. A man holds the framed photograph of his daughter and grandchildren who have been held hostage in Iraq for two months.

If one can temporarily disregard the impact of the text on the meanings we construct for these pictures (the impossibility of doing so in practice will be returned to at a later point), they almost resemble ordinary family photographs. Many of the settings and postures are recognizable from that familiar genre. The photographs are also characterized by their frontality, a tendency toward bi-lateral symmetry, and the fact that people are looking directly into the camera. The pictures do not mimic precisely the forms found in family photograph collections: the attention to and control over light and framing give them a more professional look, while the private or informal settings distinguish them from formal portraits with their typical blank backgrounds.

Yet the particular ways that these press photographs resonate with other forms of photography that are private and familiar, make the people in them accessible to viewers. The straightforward frontality of the photographs and, in particular, the level eye-contact between the person pictured and the person looking at the picture establishes them as equals, or at least as comprehensible to each other. The people photographed do not appear to have been manipulated into those postures and settings. Instead the form suggests that the act of making the photograph was cooperative. They seem aware of the way they are being presented, even to have chosen it themselves. It is their story that is being told. And they are not so different from us.

There are two other patterns for presenting photographs of non-famous people in the tabloids, which although less common, are significant. The first is the use of the official identification, or 'i.d.' portrait. Although this is also a frontal photograph with the subject frequently in eye-contact with the camera, it carries none of the connotations of the family photograph. Instead, the tight facial framing and the institutional uses of this form immediately link it to a tragic and usually criminal act.

The second exception appears spontaneous, often candid, and usually portrays action, an event that is underway. Such photographs are part of the tabloids' coverage of news events and usually include ordinary people who have become actors in those events. They are, therefore, considered in the analysis of the tabloids' photographic treatment of conventional news later in this chapter.

Celebrities

Of the several ways that famous people appear in the tabloid press, the plain photograph of the person posing at home is probably the most common. Sports figures, entertainers and, occasionally, politicians are photographed 'behind the scenes' of their public lives, together with family and loved ones. These pictures, arranged in the same manner that characterizes the pictures of non-famous people, lack only the emotional extremes to be read from the celebrities' faces; these people all appear relaxed and happy. The obviously domestic environments naturalize the stars. The photographs suggest we are seeing them as they 'really' are. At the same time, through angle and eye-contact with the camera, they are brought down to the viewer's level. The photographic construction which presents the private person as someone 'just like us' accomplishes the same task when framing the public figure.

The difference between how these two kinds of domestic pictures work assumes that the viewer can recognize this person as famous. It is not necessary for the viewer to be able to identify the person, only that this recognition takes place. Once it has, however, the home photograph does more than present the person as the viewer's equal, someone 'just like us'. In addition, it has become *revealing*. Recognizing the person's celebrity status establishes the photograph as a privileged look behind the façade of public life.

Performance photographs are also quite common, often published next to the behind-the-scenes photograph of the celebrity at home. The picture of the singer or rock star performing is often a file photograph, and the particular performance is rarely identified. The sports figure's performance, on the other hand, is presented in a recent action photograph usually from the game or competition which provides the reason for coverage.[12] These photographs present the recognizable and familiar public face of the celebrity.

File photographs of celebrities' performances occasionally accompany stories about scandals surrounding them. When a star is arrested on gambling charges or is reportedly undergoing treatment for a drug problem, for example, the performance photograph introduces a discontinuity. The photograph contrasts the controlled public view the star has previously presented with the revelations of the present scandal.

Candid photographs which penetrate the celebrity's public façade form a distinct genre of the tabloid press. However, like the posed photograph at home, many photographs that *appear* candid must be seen as extensions of the institutional edifice constructed around the star.[13] The apparently spontaneous flash photograph of the rock musician leaving a 'gala' event with a new lover at his side, for example, may be a scoop for the photographer or a revelation for fans, but it cannot be read as a penetration of the star's public façade. He has agreed (and probably hoped) to be photographed in this public setting and, as with the photograph at home, we assume he has done all he can to control the picture that is the outcome.

Candid photographs of celebrities' unguarded moments, on the other hand, do appear in the tabloids, although with far less frequency than one is led to expect by the reputation of these newspapers. The *paparazzi*, the name Fellini gave to the celebrity-chasing photographers in his film *La Dolce Vita*, find a larger market for their work in the weekly popular press than in the daily tabloids (Freund, 1980: 181). However, the death of a major film star brings *paparazzi* work into the tabloid press. And the film star whose son is on trial for murder or the sports star who was withdrawn from public life following a drug scandal are examples of celebrities the tabloids pursue for photographs.

The look of these photographs is awkward, overturning the classical rules of good composition. Objects intrude into the foreground or background, light is uneven and often garish, and even focus may be displaced or imprecise. The photographs freeze movement, thus creating strange physical and facial contortions. They appear to be the result of simply pointing the camera in the direction that might 'make a picture'.[14] This style of 'candid' photography is grounded, as Sekula (1984) argues, in 'the theory of the higher truth of the stolen image'. The moment when the celebrity's guard is penetrated 'is thought to manifest more of the "inner being" of the subject than is the calculated gestalt of immobilized gesture, expression, and stance' (Sekula, 1984: 29). The higher truth revealed in the candid moment is a notion that is repeated and expanded in the tabloids' photographic coverage of news events.

The news event

'News' is defined and constructed in many different ways within tabloid newspapers, yet there is a core of nationally and internationally significant events that receive coverage across the spectrum of the tabloid daily press. In addition to the posed photographs of people whose lives have been touched by news events (discussed above), photographs are sometimes published from the time the event was taking place. These are usually action photographs and appear candid, in the sense that people are acting as if unaware of the photographer's presence. It is incorrect to think of the events themselves as unplanned, for many are scheduled and the press has mapped out strategies for covering them. These strategies include obtaining spontaneous photographs of people at the moment they are experiencing events that are seen as momentous, even historic (Becker, 1984).

Many of the photographs bear a strong similarity to the candid pictures of celebrities. Like those images, these undermine the institutionally accepted precepts of 'good' photography in their awkward composition, harsh contrasts and uncertain focus. Another similarity is that candid news photographs are structured to reveal how people react when the comfortable façade of daily life is torn away. Facing experiences of great joy or tragic loss, people expose themselves, and photographs of such moments are thought to reveal truths of human nature. Examples include photographs taken at the airport as freed political hostages are reunited with their families, or those of policemen weeping at a co-worker's funeral.

These candid photographs are typically treated as belonging to a higher order of truth than the arranged pose. Yet to rank them along some absolute hierarchy of documentary truth ignores the cultural practices we use to distinguish between nature and artifice. Examples of these practices within photojournalism include specific technical effects (artifice) that are integrated into the tabloids' construction of realism (or nature).

Extreme conditions, including darkness or bad weather, can reduce the technical quality of news photographs. So can surveillance-like techniques, such as using a powerful telephoto lens to photograph from a distance, or using a still picture from a security video camera to portray a bank robbery. Technical 'flaws' like extreme graininess and underexposure have actually become conventions of the tabloids' style, visually stating the technical compromises the newspaper will accept in its commitment to presenting the 'real' story. The techniques work to enhance the appearance of candour, lending additional support to the construction of these photographs as authentic.

Many of the tabloids have a legacy of active crime reporting, and this style suggests a continuation of that tradition.[15] In contemporary tabloids, however, suspected and convicted criminals are not as common as are the faces and testimony of ordinary people caught in traumatic circumstances not of their own making. Photographs of political leaders are likely to be small portraits and file photographs, while the common people acting in the event receive the more prominent visual coverage. This is particularly marked when a photographer has been sent to cover foreign news.

Political turmoil and natural disasters are reasons for sending photographer-reporter teams on foreign assignments. Earthquakes and famine, elections threatened by violence, the redrawing of national and international borders, popular resistance movements and their repression attract major coverage. The coverage may include photographs of local officials, but the emphasis is on ordinary people, particularly children, who are affected by the events. The photographs establish their perspective, portraying their actions and reactions in the candid style typical of tabloid news photography. Yet the words often transform the style of the coverage into a first-person account, relocating the photographer as the subject of the story. Here again, we encounter the impossibility of seeing the photographs independently from the ways they are framed by the text.

Reframing the picture in words and layout

Photographs attain meaning only in relation to the settings in which they are encountered. These settings include, as this investigation hopefully has demonstrated, the historically constructed discourses in which specific topics and styles of photography are linked to particular tasks or patterns of practice (Sekula, 1984: 3–5). The photograph's setting also includes the concrete, specific place it appears and how it is presented. In the newspaper, photographs have no meaning independent of their relationship to the words, graphic elements and other factors in the display which surround and penetrate them. It is these elements which are, to borrow Stuart Hall's phrase, 'crucial in "closing" the ideological theme and message' of the photograph (Hall, 1973: 185).

In general, the text which frames photographs in the tabloid press is far more dramatic than the photographs alone. Even a cursory analysis indicates that it is the words, in particular the headlines, which carry the tone of 'sensationalism'. 'Thirteen-year-old chopped up watchman' is the headline over a photograph of the victim's widow, posing with his photograph. 'Devil's body guard' are the words next to a photograph of two masked men standing beside a coffin draped with the IRA flag. Over a dark colour photograph of an oil platform, we read 'Capsized – 49 jumped into the sea last night'. The text is large in relation to the page size, generally in unadorned typefaces. Punctuation consists of exclamation points and quotation marks, enhancing both the drama and the authenticity of the words: ' "It feels like I'm dying little by little" ' is inserted into one of the last pictures of the aged film star. Often headlines are short, as for example, the single word 'Convicted!' over the police photograph of the man found guilty of murdering the prime minister.

The relationship between text and the official i.d. photograph is relatively simple to unwind. The explicit purpose of this tightly framed, frontal portrait with its frozen expression is to identify its subject in the most neutral way possible. Through its instrumental service to institutional needs, it has acquired a primary association with law enforcement and police investigations. Any time a photograph in this form is linked with news, it now connotes criminal activity, tragedy and death. The words published with the photograph serve to strengthen those connotations by repeating the associations awakened by the photograph alone and adding details that anchor the photograph's meaning in a specific event.

The relationship between text and the photographs most prevalent in the tabloids – of ordinary people posed in domestic settings – is more complex. Typically the text contradicts the 'ordinary' appearance of these subjects; they are not what they seem. The words tell us that their lives have been struck by tragedy, confusion, some unexpected joy, or else that they are deviant, carrying some secret which is not evident on the surface. The disjunction between photograph and text is greatest for photographs that present no 'evidence' that something is out of place, and instead mimic the private family portrait without interrupting its connotations of familiar security.

In these cases the text seems to carry the greater authority; it tells us what we are 'really' seeing in the photographs. The text here *illustrates* the image, instead of vice versa, as Barthes has pointed out, by 'burdening it with a culture, a moral, an imagination'. Whereas in the case of the i.d. photograph the text was 'simply amplifying a set of connotations already given in the photograph', here the text *inverts* the connotations, by retroactively projecting its meanings into the photograph (Barthes, 1977: 26–7). The result is a new denotation; we actually locate evidence in the photograph of what lies behind the formal pose. From the photograph and the apparently contradictory text together, we have constructed a deeper 'truth'.

Candid photographs, whether of celebrities or of events conventionally defined as news, offer a third case, for their look of candour depends on visual conventions that connote unreconstructed reality. Their subjects and the messages of the accompanying texts are too varied to reveal one specific pattern capable of explaining how they work together in the construction of meaning. In general, the stylistic features of the candid photograph appear to confer the text with greater authority.

When portions of the text are marked as direct quotations, a technique often used in the tabloids, additional nuances of meaning are constructed. If the quoted text is offered as the words of the person in the photograph, it becomes a testimony of that individual's experience. The quotation bonds with the subject's 'inner being' that we see revealed in the candid photograph, enhancing the connotations of closeness and depth being produced individually within the photograph and text.

Occasionally the text also specifically constructs the tabloid's photographer. Accounts include how a certain subject was photographed, emphasizing the persistence and devotion the work required. The 45-year-old *paparrazo* who took the last photographs of Great Garbo, 'for ten years lived only for taking pictures of "the Goddess" ', and now plans to leave New York and find something else to do; 'My assignment is finished', he said.

The photographer becomes a major figure, the public's eye-witness, when the words establish the photographs as first-hand exclusive reports of major news events. The two journalists sent by their newspaper to Beijing in June 1989 found themselves 'in the middle of the blood bath' that took place in 'Death Square'. The tabloid's coverage included portraits of the reporter and photographer, first-person headlines often in the present tense, heightening the immediacy, and enclosed in quotation marks (' "He dies as I take the picture" '), several articles written in the first person and many candid photographs, taken at night, showing the violence and its young victims.

This style of coverage, while it underscores many of the news values of conventional journalism, at the same time contradicts the ideal role of the journalist as one standing apart from the events being reported. Here the photographer is constructed as a subject, an actor in the events. The valorization of the photographer, a common theme in the wider discourse of photojournalism, enters a specific news story. This further heightens the authority of the coverage as an unmediated account: we are seeing events as they happened in front of the subject's eyes, as if we were present.

These specific techniques, the first-person text together with the harsh, high contrast candid photographs, further work to establish this as a sensational story. The events were so unusual that the journalists' conventional rules of news coverage proved inadequate. Their professional role stripped from them by what they were seeing, they were forced to respond directly and immediately, as subjects. The coverage is constructed to bring us closer, through the journalists' subjective response, to the extraordinary nature of these events.

Again, one must remember that what we see in the tabloid is not the work of photographers. Despite the presence of bylines, the photographs bear little resemblance to the photographers' frames. Extreme sizes, both large and small, and shapes that deviate sharply from the originals' rectangular proportions are routine. Photographs are combined in many different ways, creating contrasts and sequences. Graphic elements are imposed over the photographs, including text, directional arrows and circles, or black bands over subjects' eyes. Montages and obvious retouching of photographs are not unusual.

Many of these techniques contradict the conventions for presenting photographs as representations of fact. According to the rules applied in other areas of photojournalism and documentary photography, the integrity of the rectangular frame is not to be violated.[16] With few exceptions (which are often discussed heatedly by photographers and editors), the frame is treated as a window looking out on an actual world. Changes in perspective should be limited to moving the borders in or out: any penetration of the frame is disallowed as a change in the way the frame 'naturally' presents reality.[17]

The tabloid press' consistent violation of these conventions confronts the persistent construction of the photograph as unmediated. Here we see the 'original' image repeatedly manipulated and altered with irreverent disregard for the standards that guide the elite press. At the same time that the text and photographs combine to support the revelation of deeper truths in the tabloid's coverage, the journalistic 'package' continually overturns the guidelines established to protect the notion of photographic truth.

Conclusions

Contemporary photojournalism has attained the status of popular art, outside the margins of the daily press. Yet those characteristics which have been used to increase photojournalism's cultural capital in other spheres we see confronted and even inverted in tabloid newspapers. Instead of cleanly edited photo essays, the tabloids are more likely to present heavily worked layouts of overlapping headlines, photographs and text. In place of the idealized grace of the 'decisive moment', the individual photograph is generally either a compositionally flat and ordinary pose or a haphazardly awkward candid shot. And instead of the photojournalist as respected artist successfully interweaving realism and self-expression, the photographers who occasionally emerge from the muddled pages of the tabloid are impulsive individuals, consumed by the events they were sent to photograph.

The dichotomies that are usually drawn to distinguish between the tabloid and elite segments of the press cannot accommodate this photography. In the tabloid press, photographs appear to both support and contradict the institutional standards of journalistic practice. The practices used to present major news events are at the same time serious and emotional. Topics that lie well outside the news agendas of the elite press are covered using strategies that conform to standard news routines. Tabloid photojournalism is framed in texts that work to establish the photograph as credible and authentic and simultaneously prevent it from being seen as a window on reality. Such apparent inconsistencies are contained within a journalistic discourse that is irreverent, antagonistic and specifically anti-elitist.

Sekula reminds us that 'the making of a human likeness on film is a political act' (Sekula, 1984: 31), and publishing that likeness in a newspaper compounds the political implications. Within the journalistic discourse of the tabloid press, photography appears anti-authoritarian and populist. There are many ways in which its specific techniques construct photographers, the people in the photographs and the people who look at them all as subjects. These subjects are accessible and generally are presented as social equals. But it is difficult to locate a systemic critique in this work.

The critique that emerges from the tabloid press, and particularly its photography, is directed instead against the institutionalized standards and practices of elite journalism. In the pages of this press, we witness the deconstruction of both the seamless and transparent character of news and the ideal of an unbiased and uniform professionalism. The photographs within the discourse of tabloid journalism work simultaneously as vehicles for news and the means of its deconstruction.

Notes

1 This chapter is a revised version of my paper, 'The simultaneous rise and fall of photojournalism, a case study of popular culture and the western press', presented at the seminar 'Journalism and Popular Culture', Dubrovnik, Yugoslavia, 7–11 May 1990.

2 *Illustrated London News* circulation rose from 60,000 the first year to 200,000 in 1855, the year the tax on printed matter was repealed (Hassner, 1977: 157).

3 Johannesson has also identified competing syntaxes that apparently rendered reality somewhat differently. Whereas in the United States engravings began imitating the syntax of the photograph, in Europe the engraving followed the other visual arts (Johannesson, 1982).

4 *Collier's* circulation doubled during 1898, the first year of Hare's employment, and by 1912 had reached one million (Hassner, 1977: 224).

5 For several examples from the present investigation see note 11, below.

6 The *New York Times Sunday Magazine* is an outstanding example, frequently commissioning well-known photojournalists to cover specific topics.

7 Maren Stange offers a convincing analysis of the political and aesthetic adjustment that occurred within the Museum of Modern Art in New York as Edward Steichen launched the first major exhibitions in the documentary style, culminating in 1955 with the spectacular popularity of 'Family of Man' and its 'universalizing apolitical themes'. This major cultural institution, she argues, had 'installed documentary photography yet more firmly in the realm of popular entertainment and mass culture' (Stange, 1989: 136).

8 The reader is referred to Becker (1990) for a full development of this point. For a discussion of the left-humanist art theory which provides the basis for the reconstruction of the photojournalist as artist, see Burgin (1986: 157).

9 Exceptions include the re-interpretation of a particular style of photojournalism –

in which elements are 'caught' in the frame in strange relationships to each other, usually with the added effect of bare-bulb flash – as surrealist art. Photographer Arthur ('Weegee') Fellig's work in the best-known example of art institutional redefinition of this style (Sekula, 1984: 30).

The Museum of Modern Art exhibition 'From the Picture Press' is another example of this tendency to 'surrealize' photojournalism. The exhibit consisted primarily of *New York Daily News* photographs selected with the help of photographer Diane Arbus (Szarkowski, 1973). Henri Cartier-Bresson has long preferred to call his work 'surrealism' instead of 'photojournalism'.

10 I am grateful to Mattias Bergman and Joachim Boes, Peter Bruck, John Fiske, Jostein Gripsrud, John Langer, David Rowe, Herdis Skov and Colin Sparks for providing copies of many of the tabloids on which this analysis is based.

11 Some contrasts may be explained by national differences in newspaper consumption patterns: in England, tabloid press readership increased during the period when people began to confine their reading to one newspaper [. . .] whereas in Sweden the afternoon tabloids continue to be used as a complement to the morning broadsheet papers.

Differences in content also suggest cultural variation in the construction of the sensational. A striking case is the conditions under which sex becomes an explicit topic, ranging from near-nude pin-ups as a regular feature in British and Danish papers, to unusual cases of sexual preference treated as news, to the virtual absence of sex in the most serious Australian tabloids. Another contrast is the extensive coverage the British and Australian papers devote to the 'private' lives of their royalty, whereas the Scandinavian papers only cover their royal families when one member is seriously ill, is presiding over some official occasion, or has become involved in a political debate. Explaining such differences, significant though they may be, remains beyond the scope of this chapter.

12 The sports action photograph in the tabloid press appears to correspond precisely to the same genre in the sports sections of elite newspapers. If true, this raises interesting issues about why sports photography in particular is found without modification in both classes of newspapers.

13 Here I have drawn on Alan Sekula's discussion of *paparazzi* photography, although my analysis and conclusions are somewhat different (Sekula, 1984).

14 Weegee, one who is credited with creating the style, said of his photograph from an opening night at New York's Metropolitan Opera, that it was too dark to see, but 'I could *smell* the smugness so I aimed the camera and made the shot' (Time-Life, 1983: 54).

15 The style was associated with a particular way of working by photographers who chased down tips from their police radios into places that were dark, crowded, confusing and where they were not wanted. Although the style is now considered outmoded, a guarded admiration survives for the photographers who still follow this work routine. I wish to thank Roland Gustafsson, who has conducted interviews among the staff of Stockholm's *Expressen*, for drawing this point to my attention.

16 This convention also constructs the photographer as the authority, the intermediary through which this view of reality is refracted.

17 See, for example, the textbook guidelines for creating a 'clean' picture layout in the style of the classic photo essays (Hurley and McDougall, 1971; Edey, 1978; Kobre, 1980: 271–81).

SECTION 3
Carnival, spectacle and excess

The work of the Russian critic Mikhail Bakhtin (1895–1975) came to international attention in the 1960s and has inspired a contemporary and continuing interest in notions of 'carnival' and the 'carnivalesque'. Bakhtin's main ideas were developed in the 1920s and 1930s but because of the political climate of the period it was not until 1968 that his book *Rabelais and his World* was published. In this book Bakhtin produced a work of literary criticism of François Rabelais' proto-novel *Histories of Gargantua and Pantagruel* (1532–64). Bakhtin's study gained the attention of modern cultural critics because it was also a cultural analysis of the popular culture of sixteenth-century France and sought to situate Rabelais' work in the context of the diversions, rituals and spectacles of the period such as those that took place in the market place and the carnival. According to Bakhtin, Rabelais' comic, satirical and grotesquely funny writing captured and rearticulated the sharp wit and cruel humour of ordinary people as it was expressed in the unofficial spaces of popular culture where they could mock authority, upturn hierarchies and revel in the vulgar and the lewd. This behaviour could be understood as transgressive in the sense that it overturned conventional oppositions between high and low, mind and body, the spiritual and the profane, culture and nature, male and female and so on.

Carnival in particular was notable as an event in which there was no division between spectators and performers but rather it was a space that broke down barriers so that traditional markers of separation or inequality between people were temporarily suspended. *Rabelais and his World* can be read as a 'hymn to the common man' (Holquist in Bakhtin, 1984: xviii) and carnival as the expression of revolutionary urges amongst the people in opposition to the stasis demanded by official culture. Bakhtin used the 'grotesque body' as revealed in Rabelais' work as a metaphor that characterized the people as the unruly collective that stood in opposition to the static 'classical body' of high culture. The grotesque body of carnival revels in its display of bodily functions and especially the functions of the lower body such as copulation and defecation. In carnival the body encapsulates the physicality of life and death with gross representations of old hag-like women giving birth, of copulation, pregnancy, physical decline and death. As Michael Holquist observes in his prologue to Bakhtin's book, Bakhtin's celebration of common folk were quite different from the folk heroes of Soviet official culture:

'His folk are blasphemous rather than adoring, cunning rather than intelligent; they are coarse, dirty, and rampantly physical' (in Bakhtin, 1984: xix).

At the same time carnival functioned as a refusal of the forces of officialdom and its celebrations could even, at times, slip into more politically oriented forms of social protest. Importantly, as John Storey (2001: 109) argues, it also offered a 'utopian promise of a better life, one of equality, abundance and freedom.' In effect, Bakhtin suggested that the medieval citizen lived two lives or operated in two spheres of life: one in which he or she was subjugated to a strict order of behaviour and one which was free from restriction. The second sphere was permitted but only within certain boundaries of time and place. The way in which time is characterized and experienced is also important here. To characterize historical time as simply a narrative of steady progress, for example, would overlook other dimensions of people's experience of the everyday including their fantasy lives (see Baldwin et al., 2004: 200–1). Bakhtin suggested that prior to the modern turn which created a divide between popular and high culture literature and popular culture were intertwined. In his view it was the onset of modernity that saw the carnival spirit, with its radical utopian character, gradually decline into a less-challenging, more conservative 'holiday mood' (Bakhtin, 1984: 33). Historically, then, Bakhtin suggests that the impulse and attitude of carnival has been degraded and where it now operates it functions as a safe, officially sanctioned outlet for people's energy; its radical edge neutralized so that it is simply another diversion. The view here is that whereas it might once have challenged the status quo, sending up political elites and elevating the lowly and the base this is no longer the case.

Having said this, Bakhtin's work still informs many cultural critics' analyses of current mass media forms and their content and consumption. Critics continue to seek out traces of the carnivalesque in both everyday activities such as car boot sales and street festivals, in media spectacles such as wrestling, in comedy and political satire and in the broad humour and vulgarity of tabloid entertainment.

Following on from Bakhtin's work the carnivalesque, then, may be regarded in the words of Tony Bennett as a 'transgressive discourse embodied in the practices of the popular classes and their preferred entertainments' (Bennett, 1986: 147). Bennett himself went on to explore how this discourse might be said to operate in the holiday pleasures of working people. Others have drawn on carnival to explore popular entertainments such as vaudeville and burlesque theatre, radio and television (Docker, 1994) and reprinted in this section, wrestling (Fiske), television sitcom (Hunt) and pornography (Attwood). John Docker (1994: 198), in particular, challenges what he refers to as the 'modernist myth' that there are no continuities between pre-industrial folk culture and the mass culture of the post-industrial era and argues that its continuing presence is especially apparent in the popular culture figures of the fool, the trickster and the clown. But it should be noted that the culture now under scrutiny from this theoretical perspective is no longer the folk or common culture of the pre-industrial era. Rather it is a popular culture that, although it has generic and symbolic roots in these early forms, emerged with the rise of commercial culture to discover firstly, a mass readership via print journalism (see Burke, 1978), and then later on mass audiences via broadcasting. The early newspaper, in particular, as a mass-produced, easily distributed and easy-to-read format was the ideal vehicle to blend the enduring threads of folk culture with the new and modern capitalist culture of information and entertainment (Conboy, 2002:

23). If we accept that there continue to be unspoken but powerful and difficult-to-challenge symbolic borderlines frequently drawn between what Bakhtin called 'official' and 'unofficial' cultures then the latter might be said to include the mainstream entertainments, pastimes and leisure activities of the majority of ordinary people including the tabloid press, broadcast and new media. In other words, those diversions that fail to conform to the intellectual and social values of the establishment. Those entertainments in themselves could be said to constitute a kind of offence against good taste and the cultural values that define good taste. Whereas the notion of 'high culture' is rooted in the belief that worthwhile cultural pursuits are often difficult to access, requiring a fair level of education, cultural literacy and cultivated or innate taste, mass or popular culture can be recognized by its accessibility in terms of format, content and language.

Within the very broad spectrum of entertainment that meets this criteria there are tabloid formats, in particular, which nonetheless appear to be especially 'low' in terms of their vulgarity and overall transgressive content. Many of these forms are essentially comic in nature and as such have been critiqued in Bakhtinian terms both because laughter conceived as a transformative act is so central to his conceptualization of carnival and because the grotesque body as the object of laughter features so frequently in comedy. Andy Medhurst (1992) explicitly refers to Bakhtin's distinction between the grotesque carnival body and the classical body of high culture in his discussion of the British *Carry On* film series (which has a remarkably long run during historical periods of profound social change), which revelled in bodily functions and base desires and in this volume Leon Hunt draws on carnival to illuminate not only *Carry On* but also other British comic institutions such as Benny Hill and the 1970s situation comedy *On the Buses*. Others, such as Lorraine Porter (1998), have concentrated on the grotesque female body in order to explore the fears and desires underpinning so many enduring gendered comic traditions such as the female impersonator and the monstrous mother-in-law or family matriarch.

But the carnivalesque need not be confined to broadly comic genres. Kevin Glynn (2000: 115), in his book *Tabloid Culture*, argues that the characteristics of carnival culture (its embracing of bad taste, the offensive, vulgar language, ritualistic degradation and parody and its emphasis upon the excess) are typical of the tabloid media and especially of journalism, which is energized by its relationship with 'disreputable popular tastes for melodrama, scandal, sexual intrigue' and so on. Glynn himself invokes carnival in his analysis of broadcast news. Martin Conboy, in this section, also deploys Bakhtinian carnival as a lens through which to understand the language and appeal of print journalism but makes the point that newspapers may actually adopt a carnivalesque tone and idiom to hold on to their authoritative status as the voice of the people, a language 'purloined from the common people's armoury.'

In this sense the tabloids' carnivalesque idiom (as opposed to a fully fledged carnival culture) can be detrimental to the very constituency it claims to serve. For example, as Patricia Holland (in this volume) notes, the fun, excess and comic vulgarity of the tabloid press is frequently maintained at the expense of women whose presence as glamour models and sexualized spectacles (as 'decorative excess') has the effect of linking women with the trivial and disempowered. John Fiske, too, takes care to note in his analysis that female wrestlers endure greater humiliations than their male counterparts and their performances are relegated to clubs and pubs. And, as Jane Arthurs (2004: 146) argues in her book on television and sexuality, the ideological ambivalence of popular forms such as scandal and comedy means that even as audiences are laughing at performers and celebrities who break the rules of propriety they may also have their long-held prejudices reinforced. It is important therefore to attend to issues of identity and difference (say gender and sexuality to stay with the current examples) and *power* when considering the application of carnival theory. Theories of the carnivalesque and the grotesque (female) body have inflected academic work not only on comedy and gender, as noted above, but have also been drawn on to examine articulations of gender, sexual behaviour and sexuality in less mainstream forms of popular media and culture such as pornography, which may be ranked as the very lowest in the hierarchy of popular forms and is the very epitome of bad taste mass entertainment. On television soft-core porn and carnivalesque celebrations of sexual excess are pushed to the margins of the broadcast schedules (Arthurs, 2004: 45) and in newsagents porn is relegated to the top shelf, out of reach of the casual customer. Yet pornography, as Attwood's analysis of the British downmarket softcore magazine *Fiesta* reprinted in this section usefully demonstrates, occupies (like many other tabloid forms) a complex ideological terrain when one considers pornography in relation to other 'mass' texts that exhibit carnivalesque sensibilities.

Further reading

Bakhtin, M. (1984, originally 1968 in English) *Rabelais and his World*, Bloomington, IN: Indiana University Press, Tr. H. Iswolsky.

Burke, P. (1978) *Popular Culture in Early Modern Europe*, London: Templeton Smith.

Docker, J. (1994) *Postmodernism and Popular Culture: A Cultural History*, Cambridge: Cambridge University Press.

Russo, M. (1994) *Female Grotesques: Risk, Excess and Modernity*, London: Routledge.

Storey, J. (2001) *Cultural Theory and Popular Culture: An Introduction*, London: Prentice Hall.

1.8

A very British carnival: women, sex and transgression in *Fiesta* magazine
by Feona Attwood

[. . .]

Vulgar pleasures

Despite an extensive and ongoing debate about pornography, surprisingly few analyses of individual pornographic texts exist. Questions of regulation, harm and 'effects' have tended to outweigh those of generic composition; pornography is most often discussed as a social and political problem rather than a mode of sexual representation. Those textual analyses that have been undertaken have tended to focus on pornography's visual content as the chief indicator of its significance; content which, as many feminist writers have noted, positions women as sexual objects or 'things' for men (Dworkin, 1999; Griffin, 1982; Kuhn, 1985). 'The major theme of pornography', writes Andrea Dworkin, 'is male power' (1999: 24), figured in its insistent portrayal of woman as an object, 'used until she knows only that she is a thing to be used' (1999: 128). However, in some recent studies the notion that pornography expresses relations of male dominance and female submission has been challenged, its potential for the transgression of sexual norms emphasized and questions of pornographic style and sensibility foregrounded (Kipnis, 1996; Penley, 1997). While each of these approaches has stimulated valuable debate, both tend to conceptualize pornography in rather abstract terms. There is clearly a need for new work that attempts to remedy this kind of abstraction by contextualizing various types of pornographic texts in relation to forms of production, distribution and consumption. This article attempts something rather more modest, the examination of a single issue of *Fiesta* magazine as an example of a popular pornographic sub-genre, the British downmarket softcore magazine. My aim is to examine the magazine's style and content in the light of those accounts that stress pornography's 'dominant' or normative characteristics, and of those that stress its 'transgressive' features. In this way I hope to accomplish three things: to locate this text in terms of its cultural status and its relation to existing forms and traditions; to examine the text as a mode of sexual representation, drawing attention not only to its status as a 'problem', but also to its regimes of visual imagery, linguistic features and ways of 'speaking sex'; and to investigate the extent to which the influential notions that pornography is *either* oppressive *or* transgressive are of use in making sense of such a text.

The question of sensibility is an important one in the attempt to understand pornography as a transgressive form, and to situate it as a mode of sexual representation which can be related to other cultural forms. While pornography's sensibility has attracted little critical attention, it is often this which is implicitly evoked as the sign of its offensiveness. Attempts to distinguish between pornography and art, or pornography and erotica, may be complicated by their similar content. They may be equally 'sexual' and equally 'explicit', in these cases, a style which is held to suggest an 'intention to arouse' enables the act of categorization to take place. The low quality attributed to the pornographic, as opposed to artistic or erotic, sensibility is clearly signified by the soubriquets 'dirty magazine' or 'mucky book', which refer not only to the genre's visualization of the body as disordered and grotesque or to its smutty and explicit language, but also to its provision of cheap thrills to an audience portrayed as 'brutish' and 'voracious' (Kipnis, 1996: 175). Porn texts are texts whose pages are stuck together, a 'realm of the profane and mass culture where sensual desires are stimulated and gratified' (Nead, 1992: 85). But while pornography can be located at the very bottom of a cultural hierarchy, beneath 'tabloid TV, the *National Enquirer*, Elvis paintings on velvet', the lowest of low-class things (Kipnis, 1996: 174), it also shares the status traditionally ascribed to forms of mass entertainment that are imagined to offer 'satisfaction at the lowest level' (Leavis and Thompson, 1964: 3) and a base style found – and denigrated – in other cultural texts and forms of entertainment. For example, its attempt to 'move the body', like 'the weepie and the thriller, and also low or vulgar comedy' (Dyer, 1992a: 121) relates it to other socially reviled popular genres, while its emphasis on and eliciting of vulgar pleasures can also be found in forms of entertainment such as the pantomime and fun fair (Carter, 1982, 1995).

It can be argued that it is the vulgarity of such pleasures lacking in 'class', concerned with physicality and sensation, spurning sophistication and intellect for excess, thrills and fun, that marks the distinction between dominant and popular aesthetics, high and low cultural forms. As Angela Carter notes, the separation of this kind of 'fun' from the more 'obscure', 'swooning' and 'elevated' delights of erotic pleasure seems to depend on the association of the former with cheap thrills and with 'the working class, as defined from outside that class' (Carter, 1982: 110–13). The vulgar pleasures of 'the straightforwardly sexual' (Carter, 1982: 113), which pornography purveys most directly, have led some theorists to categorize it as a transgressive or carnivalesque form. Laura Kipnis identifies a number of carnivalesque elements in porn; and obsession with excess, an inversion of established oppositions and of official hierarchies, and a fascination with a body that is 'insistently material, defiantly vulgar, corporeal' (Kipnis, 1996: 132), while Constance Penley notes that what connects porn with other American vulgar texts is its 'lumpen bawdiness', 'based in a kind of humor that features attacks on . . . middle-class ideas about sexuality, trickster women with a hearty appetite for sex, and foolish men with their penises all in a twist, when those penises work at all' (Penley, 1997: 99). Leon Hunt traces a similar bawdy tradition in Britain, recycled in seaside postcard art, music halls and the work of comedians such as Benny Hill (Hunt, 1998); a British tradition, according to publicity for the sex comedy *Confessions of a Window Cleaner*, of 'good, naughty laughter' (quoted in Hunt, 1998: 118). In her discussion of the *Carry On* films, Marion Jordan identifies some characteristics of this 'tradition of English working-class humour': a 'grotesque exaggeration and repetition' of stereotypes; rude puns; a 'masculine view of the world'; an anti-work, anti-middle-class, anti-education stance; a 'resistance to "refinement" '; and an 'insistence on sexuality, physicality, fun' (Jordan, 1983: 312–27). In texts such as these, anxieties about male sexuality surface, despite their masculine viewpoint. As Penley and Dyer note, men are often depicted as foolish and impotent, caught between the 'female sexual energy' of the 'harridan' and the uncontrollably arousing 'busty blonde' (Dyer, 1985: 34–5).

A recognition that pornography's bad reputation can be traced not only to its sexism, but also to its relation to these mass and cross traditions of bawdiness, is a useful starting point for considering the contradictory nature of pornographic texts. Pornography and other bawdy traditions may embody a masculine view of the world, but they may also mock and undermine it. What is more, the perceived lowness of porn may derive in part from its association with the working classes, its celebration of the physical and its determined upending of social and cultural values, in particular those of social refinement and cerebral endeavour. These features, it is argued, appear to signal some kind of transgressive potential. The notion that pornography transgresses social and cultural norms sits uneasily, however, with feminist analyses which stress its conformity to dominant ideologies of sex and gender, and it is this apparent contradiction that I want to pursue in relation to *Fiesta* magazine. In order to do this, it will be necessary to locate *Fiesta* in relation to the categories of pornography and bawdy more precisely, and to describe its particular brand of carnivalesque transgression.

The bawdy world of *Fiesta*

Textual analysis is particularly useful in debates about pornography, not only as a means of reading specific texts, but in isolating features of style and content which are shared with other forms of representation. At the same time, this kind of analysis directs attention to the variety within the pornographic genre. Sweeping statements about pornography's relentless objectification of women or its embodiment of patriarchal structures of dominance and submission can not be borne out by a detailed examination of the many different types of pornography that exist. Equally, and despite the links made above between porn and low cultural forms, not all pornographies will be transgressive, carnivalesque or even bawdy. Two examples given by Jennifer Wicke in her discussion of the pornographic genre's 'internal divisions and distinctions' clearly illustrate this. Whereas 'the intricate confessional medical mode of a publication like *Forum*' – which 'builds verbal fantasy worlds out of middle-class managerial and professional milieux, interlaced with a vocabulary of the aesthetically upscale' – can not really be located within the sort of bawdy tradition that I describe above, magazines dedicated to the depiction of enormous breasts that 'are caught up primarily in extending the genre of the sexual pun ... related to a working-class British tradition of pun and rhyme melded to sexual content' clearly can (Wicke, 1993: 68). A similar contrast can be drawn between a British 'upmarket' porn magazine such as *Mayfair*, which packages sex and women as glossy, classy commodities, and its 'downmarket' counterpart *Fiesta*, which revels in a dirtier, bawdier 'cheap and cheerful' celebration of the physical (McNair, 1996: 120). Distinctions may also be drawn *between* downmarket texts; a comparison of *Fiesta* with its American counterpart *Hustler* reveals it to be far less overtly political, less antagonistic, less 'gross' and less sexually explicit than *Hustler* is.

Such comparisons are useful in situating *Fiesta*'s brand of carnival in relation to a variety of traditions and sensibilities, and show it to be not only a 'mass', 'low', 'bawdy', 'carnivalesque', 'transgressive' or 'pornographic' text, but a form of textual carnival associated with a particular nexus of British, downmarket texts concerned with fun, 'naughty laughter', ordinary everyday life and the working class. In particular, it can be noted that while general similarities exist between texts categorized as pornographic or bawdy, variations in emphasis, focus and style can also be found within differing cultural contexts. What emerges, even from this brief overview, is the difficulty of generalizing about what pornography 'is' and the necessity of specifying which elements typify a particular sexual representation. In the case of *Fiesta*, the tendency to articulate the desire for transgression in a rather playful, awkward and self-conscious manner and to contain this within an imaginary 'everyday' world is one of the elements by which it can be located within a British bawdy tradition which encompasses both mainstream and pornographic texts. [. . .] The self-conscious 'rudeness' that *Fiesta* displays is a characteristic which Hunt describes as a '*not-meant-to-be-seen*' quality (Hunt, 1998: 93), though endlessly recycled in many British representations of sex, particularly in sexploitation films, sex comedies, seaside postcard humour, and in the *Carry On* and *Confessions* films. In all of these, sex is a vulgar and naughty pleasure to be pursued in the context of ordinary everyday life, but one in which 'the promise . . . of sexual freedom' is signposted as 'a fleeting aberration' (Jordan, 1983: 317); a carnival paradoxically represented as commonplace and forbidden territory.

Fiesta announces its particular brand of sexual carnival through the visual style of its cover page, which is eye-wateringly bright and garish. A half-dressed female model displaying the 'come on' look traditionally associated with softcore pornographic address is set against a pulsating background of fierce red, yellow and blue. There are no subtle, erotic overtones here; standing at the gateway to a world of treats and greedy consumption, she invites the reader to 'Go On, Give Your Trousers A Treat' and 'Slaver over FOOD & SEX'. Inside, the treats of softcore photosets, reviews of sex shows and interviews with porn stars are set alongside more mainstream magazine fare; book and music reviews, cartoons, jokes, competitions, a horoscope and crossword. 'Reader input' is prominent in the form of letters and pictures of 'Readers' Wives'. The combination of mainstream editorial categories and sexual content creates an overall effect of a 'bawdy world', an effect heightened by *Fiesta*'s downmarket, lighthearted and vulgar 'comic-book' tone (Hardy, 1998: 52). While the fantasy world of many magazines – pornographic and non-pornographic – is constructed as a world of exotic, affluent celebrity, *Fiesta*'s realm is one of resolutely 'ordinary', accessible, physical, everyday pleasures. Outside or inside, models are displayed in the most mundane settings; living rooms, bedrooms, front drives, amongst roadsweeping equipment. Readers are introduced to other 'Readers' Wives' who are 'thrusting their bums up from Glasgow to Sidcup' (*Fiesta*: 3). Sex takes place within the routines of work, domestic and social life, at office parties, in the suburban home, at friends' houses. If this is a carnivalesque scenario where every encounter leads to messy, rude, noisy pleasure and where every body gapes, squirms, pounds and gushes, it is a carnival with its feet firmly on the ground. Peopled by 'bored house-wives' and handymen, *Fiesta* displays surprising common ground with other popular fictions which stress the ordinary transfigured; with the paperback romance whose characters are 'in a constant state of potential sexuality' (Snitow, 1995: 191), and with the pantomime where 'everyday discourse . . . has been dipped in the infinite riches of a dirty mind' (Carter, 1995: 384). This is a particular brand of carnival in which ordinary life becomes a fiesta because of the endless opportunities that can be filched from the routine of life for physical pleasure – for sex and laughs; a utopian and vulgar practice of everyday life.

Although it is possible to locate *Fiesta*'s version of carnival in terms of its ordin-ary, everyday working-class and British characteristics, its frame of reference is not contemporary British life, but the British bawdy tradition itself. 'Real' and fictional low worlds collide throughout the magazine; the Assistant Editor greets a reader's account of the sexual encounters of plumbers with the cry, 'Fuck me, it's Robin Asquith!' References to the 1970s star of the *Confessions* films, to mothers-in-law, 'cracking birds' bored at home, their 'hubbies' at work 'on the rigs' and to 'nookie', give the *Fiesta* world a curiously outdated, backward-looking, nostalgic feel. Many of its cartoons and jokes reproduce the conventions of the seaside postcard, though they are more explicit, and photosets are framed by text dripping with wordplay, puns, and dirty jokes, which call to mind an older tradition of British comedy with its slightly anxious, robustly chauvinistic, naughty tone. Here is an account of a meeting with photoset model 'Justine'.

> We met at the shoot, got on like a house on fire, and went for a little romantic wander prior to her sodding off forever. One thing led to another and, before you know it, we were getting intimate in a way I'd hardly ever experienced without paying for the privilege. 'Tell me, Julie', I said, in my most seductive voice, 'how do you like the feel of a real man's cock?' 'It's Justine', she said. 'Well it's as far in as it'll go, love', I replied, 'so you'll have to make do.'
>
> (*Fiesta*: 105)

This tone of voice, like the dirty jokes it recycles, betrays a view of the male body forever in search of pleasure, but forever foolish and failing to deliver (Dyer, 1985: 36). Despite this, it persists in its mockery of other sexual styles of presentation; of the romantic, the beautiful and the erotic. The *Fiesta* investigation into 'sploshing', the practice of combining food and sex, makes this clear.

> To some there is a gentle, delicate relationship between sex and food. The divinely suggestive vulva-like appearance of mussels and the phallic impudence of aspara-gus tips dripping with white sauce fuel flights of fantasy. Erotically-charged foods pre-empt long evenings of languid seduction. Not in *Fiesta*. The closest *we* get is having a woman in a butcher's shop taking a chopper to an over-sized salami or

giving a frankfurter a gob-job. You see, when it comes to sex and food, there is another school of thought to all that sublimated psycho-symbolism gubbins. [. . .]

(*Fiesta*: 23)

Fiesta's carnival style is constructed within a frame of reference that encompasses an existing repertoire of British low culture texts and through the rejection of other sexual styles and sensibilities. The effect is to bring sex down to earth, make it basic, cheap, ordinary, easily available – not mussels and flights of fantasy, but baked beans in the gusset. Yet its transgressiveness has clear limits; it is not so crude and excessive as to down tools and have a real holiday, and while it asserts its vision of sexual utopia as one which is so self-evidently base as to be 'real' and 'true' about sex, its self-conscious naughtiness and obvious anxieties about female pleasure hardly suggest repression cast aside. If this is a fantasy of fun, it is one in which 'half the fun of the thing is the guilt' (Carter, 1982: 111) and one in which even carnival, even sexual utopia, cannot secure pleasure for women. 'Justine' is still left to 'make do'.

'You make my pants damp!': women and sex in *Fiesta*

Many feminist accounts of women's representation in pornography emphasize their 'graphic depiction' as 'vile whores' (Dworkin, 1999: 200) and the obsessive spectacularization of their difference and sexual pleasure (Kuhn, 1985; Williams, 1990). In downmarket porn texts, the representation of woman as whore and as sexual object has a specific significance, upending the convention of woman as beautiful object and repository of domestic value. Downmarket porn like *Fiesta* overturns idealized views of women as asexual and refined, wiping these out through a fascination with a female body composed of 'leaky' orifices rather than 'laminated' surfaces (Kipnis, 1996; Nead, 1992), and through their portrayal as sexually insatiable. In *Fiesta*, the figure of the 'reader's wife' is particularly significant in this respect. Far from connoting women's maternal, familial and domestic significance, the reader's wife represents the sexualizing of these roles and the sexualizing of all possible relationships with, and indeed between, women. Age, occupation and kinship are no obstacle to women's inclusion in *Fiesta*'s world: 'Wives, mistresses, girlfriends, aunties, grannies, even the mother-in-law – they're all in the wonderful Readers' Wives' (*Fiesta*: 123). Professional or amateur, celebrity pornstar or girl next door, whore or virgin, the place of women in *Fiesta* is always and only ever sexual.

This erasure of differences between good and bad women, so crucial to many other mainstream representations of femininity, clearly and transgressively turns all women into sexual spectacle: 'all social constraints . . . deliciously sacrificed, dissolved by sex' (Snitow, 1995: 195). Notions of sexual ownership of individual women or of marital fidelity are also undermined; the reader's wife is clearly for sharing, as the captions 'This is your wife' and 'Readers' wives striptease' indicate. The conventional significance of the heterosexual couple is overturned; its 'private' and exclusive sexual relationship becomes promiscuous, public and accessible within the world of the magazine. These transgressive elements do not simply work to upend ideals of domesticity and romance, but also appear to enact a fantasy of sexual equivalence. The depiction of *Fiesta* women shows them to be as sexually eager and active as their male counterparts, represented visually in a desire to 'show off' to readers, and through their narration of explicit stories of sexual adventure. While *Fiesta*'s imagery may be understood in terms of the convention of woman as spectacle and of a fascination with sexual difference (Kuhn, 1985), the narratives set out in the form of readers' letters work rather differently. Whether attributed to male or female authors, these feature roughly the same number of male and female narrators, the same number of male and female sexual performers, and tell virtually the same story. *Fiesta* narratives appear to demonstrate male and female sexual similarity; indeed it can be argued that a key feature of the *Fiesta* fantasy is the insistence that women's sexual desires are *the same as* men's.

Andrea Dworkin's description of the pornographic portrayal of women as 'vile whores' is interesting in this context. Clearly, the 'dirty', 'filthy', 'cunts', 'bitches' and 'sluts' figured in *Fiesta*'s advertising and the 'lovely lasses' of its photosets embody an insistence that all women are whores, yet the fantasy of promiscuous sexual equivalence and the absence of clear positions of male dominance and female submission within the text undercut any sense of the objectification and degradation of women for men which writers like Dworkin and Kuhn identify. What is more striking is the use of women's bodies and voices to personify a carnival world which celebrates the vulgarity and lowness of bodies, relationships, sex and pleasure. This world is also characterized by a type of 'dissolved' utopianism which Linda Williams identifies in some hardcore porn films, achieved through women's sexual agency and insatiability, through endless sex, through the 'banishment of the ill effects of power in pursuit of cheerful pleasure' (Williams, 1990: 178). All the same, as the figure of 'Justine' indicates, all is not well in this 'paradise'. This sexual utopia, where desire appears to be satisfied without complication, envy, disappointment or failure, is shot through with anxieties which surface, predictably, in *Fiesta*'s jokes and cartoons. The joke 'Why is a blow-job like a plate of lobster thermidor? They're both very nice, but you don't often get them at home', draws attention to the 'fleeting aberration' of *Fiesta*'s sexual carnival, while images of an old man unable to perform sexually and of a 'young brickie' who 'cemented his prick' in a wall offer an interesting contrast to the sexual abundance and success celebrated elsewhere. Men's pricks are 'all in a twist' after all. In another cartoon, 'Nobbem Hall', a young couple are attacked in a wood by a pack of sexually voracious 'dogs' – hairy, scrawny, muscular harridans with huge biting mouths – an image which seems to cry out for analysis using the 'psycho-symbolism gubbins' that *Fiesta* mocks.

Perhaps what is most remarkable about *Fiesta*'s depiction of women is the way in which they are used to represent its utopian *and* dystopian fantasies, to stand for sexual difference *and* equivalence, and to embody convention *and* its overturning by carnival. 'Woman' becomes a sign of pleasure-seeking, release from the constraints of domesticity and respectability, bodily celebration *and* of fearfulness and distaste. The concept of objectification still pertains here, not particularly in the sense of woman as an object to be sexually abused by man, but in the broader sense of woman as an 'object' which stands for sex. This use of women as representational currency appears to extend to the whole range of sexual practices referred to in *Fiesta*, from the 'soft' sexual display of the photosets, through the narrated accounts of group sex and 'lesbian' sex, to the adverts which offer kinkier, more perverse pleasures. Differences between sexual practices become erased in the sense that women are used to represent them all; to stand for desire, the body, pleasure, sex itself in all its variety. An advert for 'phone sex sums up the elasticity that women's bodies appear to possess representationally for their male viewers: 'We will perform every sex act imaginable. Wank with us as we live out your fantasy' (*Fiesta*: 46).

Talking dirty

As I have indicated, the representation of sexuality within a magazine like *Fiesta* depends not only on its sexual content but on the representational style employed, an element generally overlooked in discussions of pornography. An examination of *Fiesta*'s 'dirty', 'naughty' style is crucial in terms of locating its carnivalesque sensibility and in making sense of its representation of sexuality and gender. *Fiesta*'s dirty style depends heavily on a self-conscious notion of propriety transgressed; the debasement of romantic, aesthetic and domestic ideals, the transfiguration of the ordinary and everyday, a commitment to the pleasures of the body and a sense of submerged guilt and anxiety. It is expressed in the downmarket 'homemade' presentation of women's bodies in everyday settings, in the visual language of garish colour and cartoon, and also in the linguistic features of the magazine. *Fiesta*'s linguistic features, its narrative structures and styles and its mode of dirty talk are particularly interesting in terms of their construction of a very specific bawdy sensibility.

The 'porn narrative' has been characterized both as an absence that simply provides 'as many opportunities as possible for the sexual act to take place' (Carter, 1979: 13) and as the goal-directed narrative par excellence (Dyer, 1992a: 127), a structure in which narrative 'climax' is overwhelmingly important. Much of *Fiesta*'s speaking of sex may be understood in terms of a journey towards climax, most economically in the narrative structure of advertising which exhorts its readers to 'Phone, wank, spurt', and at a more leisurely pace in readers' stories which amplify that journey through the orchestration of a variety of partners, sexual positions and orgasms. The notion of 'narrative as goal' is dependent to some extent on the visual depiction of women's bodies as the landscape for the journey taken by the male subject, yet the use of female narrators and the presentation of women as active subjects in pursuit of their own pleasure work to undercut any clear association of masculinity, subjectivity and dominance. Moreover, while the spectacle of women's bodies throughout the magazine appears to employ the notion of woman as a necessary object for the achievement of male pleasure, the particular linguistic low style of dirty talk used in *Fiesta* may undercut what is often seen as the dominant specularity of pornography – its emphasis on the visual distance between an active male surveyor and passive female object – through an attempt to represent 'what sex feels like' on a visceral level.

Fiesta's dirty talk is characterized paradoxically by an apparent transparency of sexual style which relates it to a notion of 'hardcore' or 'real' sex and to a heavy reliance on the innuendo, double entendre and cultural references which link it to a British bawdy tradition. Its transgressiveness is inflected in both of these directions. The use of a transparent style composed of plain and vivid terms emphasizes the dirtiness, hardness, immediacy and vitality of sex in marked contrast to the languid, hazy prose of erotica. This reinforces a sense of sex as overwhelmingly physical and

straightforward, appearing to strip away 'meaning' and 'emotion' from act and sensation, and evoking sex as a tactile and noisy practice firmly rooted in flesh. It is a kind of
carnivalesque poetry of the body which celebrates its rudeness, its gushing, slurping,
grunting and panting, and which relates *Fiesta*'s carnival to the 'Rabelaisian transgression' which Laura Kipnis identifies in *Hustler* (Kipnis, 1996: 133), and perhaps also
to the desire to embody what a sexual utopia of energy, abundance, intensity and
transparency 'would feel like' (Dyer, 1992b: 17–34). The journey towards climax is
fragmented and shortcircuited through the repetition of dirty words and phrases,
overwhelmed and interrupted with moments of 'premature', incoherent pleasure.
This dirty talk is also crucial in overcoming the severe legal limitations surrounding
the production of British pornographic imagery. In *Fiesta*, crude and explicit language functions to incorporate a sense of 'hardcore' or 'real' sex into a visual regime
which necessarily depends on softcore images of female sexual display, however
'downmarket'. It is sex *talk* which comes to signify real sex and sex-as-transgression.
Advertising text becomes the repository of the sexual 'perversions' which literally can
not be depicted and the prevalence of adverts for 'phone sex underlines the limited
pleasures of visual representation which can be offered within the magazine itself.
Indeed, the magazine offers itself as a bridge between the reader and the really dirty
sex he is imagined to desire; the 'dirty talk' of 'phone sex is 'guaranteed' to do what the
magazine's visual imagery can not. In this move, aural sex becomes the 'real thing' in
which, as one ad puts it, 'Hearing is believing'.

Dirty talk may be understood in terms of its transgressive, sexualizing function,
but in *Fiesta* that talk also depends on linguistic cues which relate it back to a British
carnivalesque sensibility that is always mindful of the taboos it appears to be breaking.
Comic innuendo and double entendre serve as a kind of verbal striptease in which the
crudity of sex is endlessly revealed and obscured, marking off what is apparently
celebrated as straightforwardly sexual as actually improper, comical, naughty, guilt-
ridden. This insistent signposting of the magazine's textual 'dirtiness' plays a major
part in drawing attention to its own transgressive status and in constructing the '*not-
meant-to-be-seen*' quality of this type of pornography. Seen but not-meant-to-be,
spoken but not-meant-to-be, sex is recuperated both as a straightforward pleasure
and a source of distaste and guilt. In particular, it is women's bodies and voices which
are made to signify in this contradictory and self-conscious way. *Fiesta*'s women hold
out the promise of pleasures that are always marked as dirty and always somehow
'elsewhere'. Its sexual carnival is offered as a 'fleeting aberration', real and fantastic,
accessible and out of reach, everyday life and outlaw country.

'Readers' wives'

Throughout this discussion, I have tried to emphasize the contradictory nature of
Fiesta which is expressed through the very particular kind of carnival world it constructs. Although the text is clearly marked by a desire to transgress all manner of
social and sexual norms, my reading of *Fiesta* suggests a great deal of ambivalence
about that desire. Indeed, the more *Fiesta* revels in its transgression of social and
cultural values – sophistication, intellect, sexual propriety, domesticity, sexual difference – the more it reveals an anxious awareness of the boundaries it appears to be

breaking, and an inability to imagine this as more than a fleeting moment of naughtiness. Women's bodies and voices become crucial signifiers of this ambivalence; of bodily pleasure and a squeamishness about the body, of cheerful transgression and its anxious recognition, of an insistence on speaking sex plainly and on the unspeakability of sex.

For *Fiesta*, the figure of the reader's wife bears the particular burden of this ambivalent signification as its principal object and its representative subject, the point at which the carnival is apparently anchored in real life. Here, women appear to be incorporated as real participants in the carnival they represent, not only as visual objects but as subjects asserting the right to speak sex. The transgressive potential of this downmarket strategy is clear, yet its main function seems to be, as Simon Hardy notes, to provide men with imaginary access to women, 'both in the conventionally understood sense of objectifying the female body through the image and in the generally overlooked sense of representing the subjective aspects of female sexuality through the text' (Hardy, 1998: 69). It is the framing of women's sexual speech which perhaps betrays the real limits of *Fiesta*'s transgressiveness and the tremendous anxieties that underpin its construction of a sexual carnival. For, while the magazine appears to enact a fantasy of equivalence in which both men and women celebrate the body and its pleasures, its incorporation of readers' voices tells a different story. Readers' letters are segregated by sex; men's letters provide a point of 'Interchange', while women's letters occupy a space entitled 'I confess'. This marking of men's talk as plain speech and women's talk as confessional currency is further emphasized in the magazine's appeal to women to provide 'your raunchiest confessions' for a phoneline aimed at 'our readers'. In contrast, male readers are invited to 'Listen . . . as they confess the sordid details of their most outrageous sexual encounters' (*Fiesta*: 123–9). This dual address both frames and underscores the ambivalent and contradictory nature of *Fiesta*'s carnival, its insistence on pleasure as guilt and, in particular, on women's pleasure as outrageous. This is not merely the 'methodological defect' of porn written by and for men – 'a manual of navigation written by and for landlubbers' (Carter, 1979: 15) – but a sleight of hand in which *Fiesta*'s apparent celebration of female sexuality is recast as sordid detail and the female subject is transformed into subject matter. It is also, finally, in this positioning of its carnival in the marketplace, that *Fiesta* maps out its relation to women, to readers and to the real.

As Linda Williams points out, 'the modern age's compulsion to make sex speak' (Williams, 1990: 30) has a long history, yet elsewhere in contemporary culture 'the mere fact' of women speaking desire 'is not enough to sustain a story' (Williams, 1990: 31) any longer. In *Fiesta*, despite the marking of sex *talk* as the 'real thing', the intersection of a magazine fantasy of sex and a real sexual fiesta beyond its pages, it is ultimately men's talk that is framed as real speech about real sex – male readers' letters are 'real alright' (*Fiesta*: 11). In contrast, the reader is advised to approach the women's letters with caution: 'Just how true they are is something you'll have to decide for yourself' (*Fiesta*: 95). In this very British carnival it is women's bodies, stories and voices that are required to 'speak desire', yet despite their visibility they are not meant to be seen, and despite their verbosity they are not meant to be believed. As 'readers' wives', women are transformed into fantastic creatures telling fabulous tales. The 'mere fact' of female sexual desire is only a dirty joke after all.

1.9

Carnival and the popular press
by Martin Conboy

The public sphere has always functioned as a predominantly serious space, with an emphasis on 'communicative rationality'. Popular journalism has always rivalled that space, particularly in its connections to the traditions of popular culture and its more riotous elements. The popular press as it has developed in the twentieth century has a much closer rapport with laughter and the lighter side of life. This invites comparison with the influential writings of Mikhail Bakhtin on laughter and, in particular, its popular form, carnival. For Bakhtin there are two sides to the laughter of the carnival: first, 'the positive regenerating power of laughter' (1984: 45) and, second, the corrosive laughter which threatens the status quo. Through the ages, Bakhtin says, there has always been a laughing chorus (1984: 474); now it takes the form of the popular press. Its communicative strategies, though effective in the extreme, do not depend on rationality for their appeal, but more on their ability to entertain and employ the discourse of popular culture to make themselves and their interventions more plausible.

The contemporary generalizing of popular culture in postmodernity leads this discussion to a closer consideration of the ways in which two key concepts concerning the effectiveness of popular aesthetics and formats impact upon the popular press and the ways in which these depend also on traditional connections within the genealogies of the popular for their appeal. First, the carnivalesque. We may well compare aspects of popular contemporary newspapers to the carnival, which Bakhtin theorizes in relation to the work of Rabelais. The leading contemporary British popular tabloid emphasizes in its own promotional material that it is a 'fun' newspaper: '. . . The *Sun* has not only presented itself less as a newspaper and more as a "fun"-paper, but has done so by consciously comparing itself to the broadsheet press. For example, the paper recently parodied the *Financial Times*'s advertising copy-line, "No FT, no comment", with "No Sun, no fun" ' (Bromley and Tumber, 1997: 373).

It is through a carnivalesque laughter, strangely suspended between the traditional attractions of the mocking of authority and the conservative exigencies of the political economy that the popular press functions as an institution. A superficial yet obsessive attraction to the bizarre is part of the appeal of this form of popular journalism. It is what Kelvin MacKenzie and Wendy Turner once coined the 'Cor

Doris Look At This' appeal. It belongs quite clearly to the oral tradition of sensational and hyberbolic gossip:

PRIEST BOOTS DOG IN HEAD
Cops arrest cruel Rev (*The Sun*, 29 March 2000)

Another example which highlights the grotesque and bodily humour of the carnivalesque is the following story, accompanied by a photo of the man in question displaying his distended belly and eating one of his curries.

KORMA TRAUMA
Keith gains 5st eating leftovers from his curry firm
CURRY seller Keith Bryson is a lot tikka round the waist – after being forced to EAT the leftovers of his failed delivery firm.
   He said: 'The only way I can pay what I owe and still eat is to work my way through what's left in my freezers.'

Carnivalesque is the temporary suspension of hierarchies of status, taste and behaviour; it allows a utopian glimpse of a community of plenty, freedom and creativity. Its uncrownings and inversions, the transformations into a new existence, unfettered by the exigencies of the everyday, are in the popular press returned into a cycle which redirects these impulses back into a circle of consumption and commodification. The transformations are imaginary via the reflected glories of celebrity; the uncrownings, particularly of celebrities, politicians and sports stars, are returned into a cycle of elevation and reduction. Fortunes are won but the recipients continue within the ethic of financial reward and the stereotypes of wealthy lifestyle so fetishized in all other parts of the popular press.
   Celebrity gossip can be successfully mixed with the carnivalesque. In February 2000, in the following example, we see one genre, the gossip of celebrity, transferred into another, the photo-story, in a self-referential parody of the newspaper's own discourses and formats. The protagonists are music superstars Robbie Williams and Liam Gallagher. Self-referentially, the *Sun* launched the story on 22 February that Liam and Robbie were being publicly rude about each other's musical talents. Hostilities escalated on 24 February: 'Liam: I'll break Robbie's nose.' On 29 February we had the culmination in a lookalike photo story of the encounter between the two: 'Deidre's Photo (Fighto) Casebook'. It is because the popular press can maintain and mutate this cultural mode of the carnivalesque that it retains its success, although it is a triumph of genre over content in that it does not allow radical contestations of social or economic hierarchies to emerge.
   Throughout history, carnival has served to keep alive alternative conceptions of life and power relations. In the popular press we have a ventriloquized version of the freedom and laughter of Bakhtin's carnival table-talk. It is a carnivalesque which only allows a limited perspective of individual and miraculous change, while mimicking its tone of transgression. Employing a carnivalesque mode explains how the papers retain an authority. They maintain the stance of being on the side of common-sense, against the powerful, on the side of the little man and woman, even if, as media

1.10

The carnivalesque
by John Fiske

In his study of Rabelais, Bakhtin (1968) developed his theory of the carnival to account for the differences between the life proposed by the disciplined social order and the repressed pleasures of the subordinate. The physical excesses of Rabelais's world and their offensiveness to the established order echoed elements of the medieval carnival: both were concerned with bodily pleasure in opposition to morality, discipline, and social control.

The carnival, according to Bakhtin, was characterized by laughter, by excessiveness (particularly of the body and the bodily functions), by bad taste and offensiveness, and by degradation. The Rabelaisian moment and style were caused by a collision of two languages—the high, validated language of classical learning enshrined in political and religious power, and the low, vernacular language of the folk. The carnivalesque is the result of this collision and is a testament to the power of the "low" to insist upon its rights to a place in the culture. The carnival constructs a "second world and a second life outside officialdom" (Bakhtin 1968: 6), a world without rank or social hierarchy.

> Carnival celebrated temporary liberation from the prevailing truth from the established order: it marked the suspension of all hierarchical rank, privileges, norms and prohibitions. (p. 10)

Its function was to liberate, to allow a creative playful freedom,

> to consecrate inventive freedom, . . . to liberate from the prevailing point of view of the world, from conventions and established truths, from cliches, from all that is humdrum and universally accepted. (p. 34)

In carnival life is subject only to "the laws of its own freedom" (p. 7). Carnival is an exaggeration of sport, the space for freedom and control that games offer is opened up even further by the weakening of the rules that contain it. Like sport, carnival abides by certain rules that give it a pattern, but unlike sport (whose rules tend to replicate the social), carnival inverts those rules and builds a world upside down, one institutions, they belong to structures of the capitalist elite. They articulate that stance in the mocking, deflating language purloined from the common people's armoury.

We have seen the popular press's adroit exploitation of the comic and the carnival of the people's voice, and also the negative aspects and the political implications of their truncated and ventriloquized form of the popular voice. Bakhtin's carnivalesque enabled both social stability and social protest and change (1984: 197). The popular press borrows the people's voice. It borrows the carnivalesque. It embroils them in postmodernity's intensification of cultural and capital flows and exploits the heightened effectiveness of popular culture to close down popular discourses to a restricted political agenda largely supportive of the status quo, using the traditional rhetoric and appeal of the genre to the ordinary people. The desecration and dismemberment typical of the carnivalesque never attack the body of capitalism nor the central ideologies of the status quo with regard to gender, nation, community or capital.

The popular press's version of dialogue is not, as in Bakhtin, opposed to the closure of the authoritarian word, nor is carnival opposed to the official hierarchy of culture; rather they are deployed as strategies to envelop popular traditions within a rhetoric of laughter and ridicule but emptied of anything other than a hollow, ironic resistance to the all-pervasive nature of control. It epitomizes postmodernity's blank irony; parody without a final target. It constitutes a poor deal in the hegemonic bargaining. Yet, viewed optimistically, carnivalesque's resources are still there to be directed elsewhere. Here, as in other genres, it becomes apparent that style is ideologically and politically natural. It's what you do with it that counts.

Docker claims that we are experiencing 'a culture that in its exuberance, range, excess, internationalism, and irrepressible vigour and inventiveness perhaps represents another summit in the history of popular culture comparable to that of early modern Europe' (1994: 185). If this is so then we can certainly identify the role of the popular press as significant in providing exuberance, excess, range, vigour and inventiveness, but all within a rather restricted political framework and in a mainly parochial series of national settings.

[. . .]

structured according to the logic of the "inside out" that provides "a parody of the extracarnival life" (p. 7).

Bennett (1983a: 148) suggests that the white-knuckle rides of amusement parks are carnivalesque partly because they invert the extracarnival relationship of the body to machinery:

> In releasing the body for pleasure rather than harnessing it for work, part of their appeal may be that they invert the normal relations between people and machinery prevailing in an industrial context.

The same claim can be made for video games, particularly the pay-as-you-use ones, where the skill of the operator decreases the profit of the owner (see *Reading the Popular*, Chapter 2). This release is through the body: the intense concentration of video games or the subjection of the body to the terrifying physical forces of the white-knuckle rides result in a loss of self, a release from the socially constructed and disciplined subjectivity. The body's momentary release from its social definition and control, and from the tyranny of the subject who normally inhabits it, is a moment of carnivalesque freedom closely allied to Barthes's notion of *jouissance*.

Carnival is concerned with bodies, not the bodies of individuals, but with the "body principle," the materiality of life that underlies and precedes individuality, spirituality, ideology, and society. It is a representation of the social at the level of materiality on which all are equal, which suspends the hierarchical rank and privilege that normally grants some classes power over others. The degradation of carnival is literally a bringing down of all to the equality of the body principle.

Rock 'n' Wrestling

Rock 'n' Wrestling is television's carnival of bodies, of rule breaking, of grotesquerie, of degradation and spectacle. Barthes (1973) alerts us to the function of wrestling as a popular spectacle in terms that are remarkably similar to those used by Bakhtin to describe carnival. Both authors refer to the *commedia dell'arte* as an institutionalized form of popular spectacle; both point to the centrality of the body, to excess, exaggeration, and grotesqueness; both refer to the spectacle as an important principle, and to the way that wrestling or carnival exists on the borderline of art and not-art (or life).

Bakhtin (1968: 5, 11) finds three main cultural forms of folk carnival:

1 ritual spectacles
2 comic (verbal) compositions—inversions, parodies, travesties, humiliations, profanations, comic crownings and uncrownings
3 various genres of billingsgate—curses, oaths, popular blazons

The spectacular involves an exaggeration of the pleasure of looking. It exaggerates the visible, magnifies and foregrounds the surface appearance, and refuses meaning of depth. When the objects is pure spectacle, it works only on the physical senses, the body of the spectator, not in the construction of a subject. Spectacle liberates from subjectivity. Its emphasis on excessive materiality foregrounds the body, not as a signifier of something else, but in its *presence*. Barthes argues that the physicality of the wrestlers *is* their meaning: Thauvin does not *stand for* ignobility and evil—his body, his gestures, his posture *are* ignobility and evil. The wrestlers in *Rock 'n' Wrestling* have excessive bodies and the rituals they perform are excessively physical—the fore-arm smash, the flying body slam, the hammer, the pile driver are movements whose meaning is the clash of flesh on flesh. The forms the rituals take emphasize the spectacular, the physical force, rather than their effectiveness in "winning" the context; the immobility of a wrestler in a hold is "the spectacle of suffering" (Barthes 1973: 20), for they are moments of ritual, not the skills of sport. As Barthes says, the function of a wrestler is not to win or lose, but "to go exactly through the motions which are expected of him" (p. 16). The humiliation and degradation of defeat exist only in the body and helpless flesh of the fallen wrestler, not in a structure of moral and social values that gives them "meaning." Hence the audience, and the "victor," is licensed to gloat over and glory in the crumpled body, and indeed the victor will frequently continue his attacks and degradations of the vanquished body after he has been declared the winner, after the bout has officially ended. In defeat,

> the wrestler's flesh is no longer anything but an unspeakable heap spread out on the floor, where it solicits relentless reviling and jubilation.
>
> (Barthes 1973: 21)

A bout between Andre the Giant and Big John Stud finished with Andre the "winner." King Kong Bundy, Big John's partner in "tag wrestling", tore into the ring, apparently in an uncontrollable rage, and Big John suddenly grabbed Andre's legs, throwing him onto his back. Bundy, a gross figure with a bald head and wide expanses of smooth white flesh, then executed a number of body slams upon the Giant, brushing the helpless referee out of the way as he did so. The commentator was excitedly and joyfully screaming, "This is despicable, this is despicable . . . come on referee, do something even if it's wrong. There's no way the referee . . . no way he's going to stop King Kong Bundy, who's fouling Andre. . . . he's obviously hurt, look at that sternum bone just sticking right out there!" The (apparently) broken sternum bone of Andre the Giant became an object of spectacle, divorced from the real social world of moral values and law, its meaning was its appearance as a swelling on the huge chest of Andre, which the camera zoomed in on, then and in the subsequent interview.

Earlier in the about, Big John Stud's manager had thrown him a huge pair of scissors, with which he was threatening to cut Andre's hair. The two fought for the scissors, with Andre finally forcing Big John to let them go by sinking his teeth into the wrist of the hand holding them. The cold steel of the scissors against the sweating flesh of the wrestlers, the image of sharp teeth on yielding skin, all heightened the physicality of the contest, the plane of the body on which it occurred.

The carnival form of inversion and parody is equally clearly exhibited: the main inversion is that between control and disruption. The rules of the "game" exist only to be broken, the referee only to be ignored.

A regular "character" on *Rock 'n' Wrestling* is "Lord Alfred Hayes," who provides one or two "updates" of information about wrestlers and the World Wrestling

Federation. His name, his dress, and his accent all parody the traditional English aristocrat; he is a carnivalesque metaphor of social power and status who is there to be laughed at. The social rules that he embodies are to be broken at the same time the information he imparts is accepted.

Rules organize the social and the everyday and control the sense we make of it; they determine not only behaviors and judgments, but also the social categories through which we make sense of the world. In carnival, categories are broken as enthusiastically as rules: the wrestlers' managers fight as often as the wrestlers, wrestlers not officially involved join in the bouts, the ropes that separate the ring (the area of contest) from the audience are ignored and the fight spills into the audience, who become participants, not only verbally but sometimes physically.

> Carnival does not know footlights, in the sense that it does not acknowledge any distinction between actors and spectators. . . . Carnival is not a spectacle seen by the people: they live in it, and everyone participates because its very idea embraces all the people.
>
> (Bakhtin 1968: 7)

This participation ranges from the physical—raining (ineffective) blows on one wrestler, or helping the other to his feet—through the verbal—shouting encouragement and abuse or holding up placards—to the symbolic—waving mannequin models of one's favorite wrestler, or wearing his image on T-shirts. The television camera plays on the crowd, who performs for it as much as do the wrestlers: the categorical distinction between spectacle and spectator is abolished, all participate spectacularly in this inverted, parodic world.

Wrestling is a parody of sport: it exaggerates certain elements of sport so that it can question both them and the values that they normally bear. It recovers the offensive popular pleasures that the nineteenth-century bourgeoisie struggled so hard to appropriate and make respectable. In sport, teams or individuals start equal and separate out into winners and losers. In *Rock 'n' Wrestling* the *difference* is typically asserted at the beginning of the bout. Bouts often start with one wrestler (or pair) already in the ring, dressed conventionally and minimally in shorts or tights, and given an everyday name such as Terry Gibbs. The camera then cuts to his opponent coming through the crowd, spectacularly dressed in outlandish carnivalesque costume and equipped with an outlandish name such as Randy "Macho Man" Savage, Giant Haystacks, or Junkyard Dog. The contest is between the normal and the abnormal, the everyday and the carnivalesque.

Rock 'n' Wrestling refuses "fairness." It is *unfair*. Nobody is given a "sporting chance" and anyone who attempts to "play fair" is taken advantage of and suffers as a result. Yet the commentators return us again and again to this rejected standard as a point from which to make sense of the action. The pleasure lies not in the fairness of the contest, but in the foul play that "exists only in its excessive signs" (Barthes 1973: 22).

Wrestling is a travesty of justice, or rather, justice is the embodiment of its possible and frequent transgression. "Natural" justice, enshrined in social law, is inverted; the deserving and the good lose more frequently than they win. It is the evil, the unfair, who triumph in a reversal of most dramatic conflict on television. There is a "grotesque realism" here that contrasts with the idealized "prevailing truth" of the social order: despite the official ideology, the experience of many of the subordinate is that the unfair and the ugly *do* prosper, and the "good" go to the wall.

In sport, the loser is not humiliated or degraded, but in *Rock 'n' Wrestling* he is, excessively. Sport's respect for a "good loser" is part of its celebration of the winner; wrestling's "license" for the bad to win allows also the degradation and humiliation of the loser's body. Sport's almost religious respect granted to the human body and to the individual is here profaned, blasphemed against.

And this body is almost invariably the male body. Female wrestling occurs, though rarely on television. It is interesting to note that in its nontelevisual form in clubs and pubs it frequently exaggerates the humiliation and degradation even further by being held in wet, slippery mud. In television sport the male body is glorified, its perfection, strength, and grace captured in close-up and slow motion. Morse (1983) suggests that slow motion, which is so characteristic of sport on television but used more rarely in *Rock 'n' Wrestling*, has the effect of making the male body appear large in scale, and thus more powerful, and of presenting it as a perfection of almost spiritual beauty. She cites the Greek ideal of *kalagathon*, in which the beautiful male body was linked to social and political power. Following Mulvey (1975), Morse suggests that there is a difference between the masculine gaze upon active, moving male bodies and upon passive female ones. She divides this masculine gaze upon the male into two types: one is a scientific investigative look of the will to know, which is a sublimation of the voyeuristic look and produces a repressed homoerotic pleasure; the other derives its pleasure from the slow motion replays that produce the repetition that is associated with desire. The female spectator, however, is different. She is traditionally the uninvited observer (which presumably gives her the powerful position of the voyeur), but the televising of sport has, according to Morse, eroticized the male body so that it can become an object of feminine desire and pleasure. She wonders if there has been a significant shift in what she describes as sport's precarious balance between "play and display" (p. 45). In "play," the look upon the male body is transformed into an inquiry into the limits of human performance, in "display" the look has no such alibi. In this context she quotes a warning sounded by Stone (1971) that commercialization was transforming the inherently noble *game* into the inherently ignoble *spectacle*; she comments somewhat sardonically, "The surest sign of the degradation of sport into spectacle—as far as Stone was concerned—was the predominance of female spectators" (Morse 1983: 45).

The "live" audience of *Rock 'n' Wrestling* includes many, often very participatory, female spectators (whose presence is acknowledged in the names of one tag wrestling pair—Beefcake and Valentine, and it may well be that the construction of the male body as spectacle for the female viewer is more empowering than Morse allows. Her account of the pleasures offered by the display of the male body in televised sport leaves it aestheticized and eroticized, an object of admiration that can still appropriately bear the dominant ideology of patriarchy.

But in wrestling the male body is no object of beauty: it is grotesque. Bakhtin (1968) suggests that the grotesque is linked to a sense of earthy realism; indeed, he talks about "grotesque realism." The realism of the grotesque is opposed to the "aesthetics of the beautiful" (p. 29) represented in sport's vision of the perfect body.

The grotesque body is "contrary to the classic images of the finished, completed man" (p. 25); cleansed of, or liberated from, the social construction and evaluation of the body, it exists only in its materiality. If the body beautiful is the completed, formed social body, then the body grotesque is the incomplete, the unformed. Its appeal to children (whose heroes, such as the Incredible Hulk or Mr. T, often have grotesque bodies) may well lie in the relevances they see between the grotesque body and their own childishly incomplete, unformed ones. The grotesque allies their incompleteness with adult strength. There is a sense, too, in which principles of growth and change are embodied in the grotesque, for it is in direct opposition to the stasis of the beautiful. The grotesque is properly part of the vernacular of the oppressed.

The grotesque male body, then, offers to the female pleasures different from those of sport. Seeing masculine strength and power embodied in ugliness and engaged in evil distances them from social power (*kalagathon*) and sets up contradictory pleasures of attraction and repulsion. The excessiveness of this strength, in alliance with its ugliness, opens a space for oppositional and contradictory readings of masculinity; the grotesqueness of the bodies may embody the ugliness of patriarchy, an ugliness that is tempered with contradictory elements of attraction. There is a sense, too, in which this grotesqueness liberates the male viewer from the tyranny of the unattainably perfect male body that occupies so much of the "normal" television screen. Wrestling's carnival inverts televisual norms as successfully as social ones.

The third component of folk carnival is its billingsgate, its curses, oaths, and imprecations. In *Rock 'n' Wrestling* these are both verbal and nonverbal, carried in what Barthes calls the "grandiloquence" (literally, the "excessive speech") of gesture, of posture, and the body. The wrestlers "swear" kinesically at each other, at the referee, at the spectators: the spectators similarly curse and cheer, hold up placards. The breaking of linguistic conventions is obviously "modified for TV," in that actual obscenities and blasphemies are not permitted, but the process of bad-mouthing, of insulting, is enthusiastically entered into. The interviews between the bouts consist largely of wrestlers lauding themselves and bad-mouthing opponents. This billingsgate is typically delivered not to the interviewer, but directly to camera, involving the home viewer in the process as actively as the live audience. Billingsgate is oral, oppositional participatory culture, making no distinction between performer and audience.

Bourdieu (1984) picks up on a similar point when he contrasts middle-class with working-class culture and the role of the body and of participation or distance in each. Briefly, middle-class cultural forms and the appropriate responses to them are characterized by distance, by critical appreciation. Bodily participation is confined to applause (a distanced, controlled trace of real participation) and occasional calls of "encore" (whose foreignness for the anglophone is a strong marker of distance). Working-class cultural forms, on the other hand, involve intense verbal and bodily participation, strong partisanship and involvement. Cheers, jeers, and all forms of billingsgate, "invasions" of the sporting arena or stage, the literal transformation of sporting conflict in the ring or on the field into social conflict on the terraces or in the aisles, the wearing of team/pop group/star favors, dress style, or images all typify what Bourdieu calls working-class participation in cultural forms as opposed to middle-class appreciation.

[. . .]

1.11

From carnival to crumpet: low comedy in the 1970s
by Leon Hunt

[. . .]

An obvious stopping-off point for any reclaiming of low British culture is George Orwell's 'The Art of Donald McGill' (1941), the most frequently cited text in defences of the tradition of mass-produced low comedy. Orwell was unexpectedly ahead of his time in celebrating some of the most despised aspects of the low-popular. First, there was *familiarity*, as opposed to the new and innovative – seaside postcards were 'as traditional as Greek tragedy' (a concession to 'proper' culture), 'a sort of sub-world of smacked bottoms and scrawny mothers-in-law which is part of Western European consciousness' (1941: 144). Second, there was their *vulgarity*, taken as a sign of their good health. Third, there was a revelling in *irresponsibility*, an irresponsibility which was the by-product of a predominantly repressed, compliant culture – the jokes appealed to an 'unofficial self, the voice of the belly protesting against the soul' (*ibid.*: 152).

Some of these themes and priorities were updated over thirty years later in a book which went very much against the grain of most critical writing in the 1970s. Jeff Nuttall and Rodick Carmichael's *Common Factors/Vulgar Factions* (1977) – 'bafflingly neglected', according to Medhurst and Tuck (1982: 44) – virtually invents cultural populism, with all of its weaknesses but also some of its refreshing, canon-baiting traits well to the fore. Here was a book about Blackpool, sex, pubs, sport, Harry Ramsden chip shops, 'laffs'. On the minus side, Nuttall and Carmichael's handling of taste and culture now seems simplistic – high culture represents death, an 'elephants' graveyard' reflecting 'the pale levels of good taste', while the repressed 'ruling class' will 'form a bulwark against the vigour and vinegar of the ascendant working class, a wall built of respectability' (1977: 4). Gender is even more of a problem – this is a muscle-flexing, masculine populism, and the writers find signs of resistance in the most ghastly violence and misogyny.

It comes as little surprise that Orwell is silent on matters of gender and ethnicity, and even class has a way of slipping in and out of this British low self, a 'lazy, cowardly, debt-bilking adulterer who is inside all of us' (1941: 53). Class is to the fore in Nuttall and Carmichael, however – the survival of vulgarity romantically parallels that of the 'ascendant working class'. But vulgarity has given way to ugliness and obscenity, and the former, in particular, is valued in two ways. First, it is linked to survival and identity: 'We use ugliness to fight back the smothering blankets of refinement. We use ugliness to revenge ourselves on the inevitability of death' (1977: 5). *On the Buses* is worth citing here, and we need look no further than the destination of the number 11 bus, which goes to the cemetery gates. That's the ultimate terminus, after all, and Stan and Jack drive there several times a day to remind themselves to have a good 'laff' first. Lest they forget, there's also the waxen-faced, sunken-cheeked inspector, Blakey, to signify death, a body devoid of the flatulent, guffawing lechery which functions like a life-support machine.

Second, ugliness becomes an aesthetic criterion, a kind of low-sublime, in its own right: ' "Ugliness" is not so much the absence of the aesthetic but constitutes an alternative aesthetic. A cultural force whereby the vulgar can embrace their intrinsic merits, whereby the living can spit in the face of devastation' (1977: 9). Perhaps their richest intervention is in the specific field of comedy. Their distinction between 'me' and 'us' humour stands in for a number of oppositions – south versus north, wit versus 'necessity', cleverness versus community. Mikhail Bakhtin makes a similar distinction between 'official' laughter, private and individual, 'cut down to cold humour, irony, sarcasm' (1984: 37–8), and the public, collective laughter of carnival: 'Carnival is not a spectacle seen by the people; they live in it, and everyone participates because its very idea embraces all the people' (*ibid.*: 7). High theory/low culture caveats notwithstanding, it would be difficult to keep Bakhtin apart from the *Carry Ons, On the Buses* or Benny Hill, with their insistence on the 'lower bodily stratum' – he does give us some purchase on the politics of vulgarity. Nevertheless, Nuttall and Carmichael's 'survival' humour allows more scope for the coexistence of subversive and reactionary practices and ideologies. Bakhtin, roughly contemporary with Orwell (*Rabelais and his World* was written between the late 1930s and early 1940s), is one of the first romantic populists – he is unequivocal about the noble vulgarity of 'the people' and his longing for peasant folk cultures sometimes suggests Leavis in a Kiss-Me-Quick hat.

'Me' humour is founded on wit, an important sign of cultural capital:

> a witty man is always in some way demonstrating his superiority. He has the skill to bend words, he has the special knowledge to make the right obscure reference that only you or I, of course, will recognise, in our deeply exclusive way . . .
>
> Wit is ambitious, it courts finesse. It seeks to leave behind human fallibility for which it holds an ultimate contempt . . .
>
> (Nuttall and Carmichael 1977: 24–5)

On the other hand, 'us' humour, 'survival laughter', 'the humour of necessity', rests on 'the perpetual celebration of common factors':

> Survival humour clings to the rock, embraces its own imperfections, settles for living at any price on the off-chance of pleasure or relief at some future date. Survival humour clings together with other folk, whilst for the best wits there is no safety in numbers or anything else, except escape.
>
> (*ibid.*: 25)

On the face of it, this marks out the celebrated and the critically marginalised in British comedy – the 'raucous' laughter despised by *The Daily Mail*. 'Me' humour encompasses, most obviously, the Oxbridge (and later 'alternative') tradition – by the 1970s, *Monty Python's Flying Circus* was obviously clever humour for clever people; the comic reference points had an almost unprecedented exclusivity (European philosophers, art cinema). But the more populist programmes in the 'great tradition' (*Hancock, Steptoe and Son, Porridge*) hinge on the wit of a central character, and, by implication, the writing team. 'Us' humour is trickier, already disappearing into the past. Even the *Carry Ons* cannot be viewed as pure 'us' humour, for all their music hall smut. Talbot Rothwell's 1960s scripts, like his work on *Up Pompeii*, combine familiar, recycled puns and innuendo with historical/generic parody, which implies the presence of a degree of 'wit' (the Latin jokes in *Carry on Cleo*, for example). Not for nothing is *Carry On Up the Khyber* (1968) the 'one *Carry On* that almost gets its foot in the door as a classic of respectable British cinema . . . a film that crosses the boundaries' (Ross 1996: 73) – its burlesquing of British imperialism is at least knocking on the door of satire, even if it runs away when the door opens. Nuttall and Carmichael, in any case, cast Kenneth Williams in the 'me' camp – 'literacy, articulation, rambling inventiveness . . . innuendos that "only you and I" can understand' (1977: 37). This, of course, raises other issues about who 'only you or I' might be. As Medhurst (1992) and Healy (1995) have shown, Williams's use of the gay slang *parlare* on the radio show *Round the Horne* perhaps constructs a more specific, locally defined 'us'. Sid James, on the other hand, was the *Carry Ons*' most consistent invocation of a more traditional 'us', and the most frequent to enjoy top billing. In other words, by the 1970s, 'me' and 'us' humour were already strains within British comedy rather than entirely separate textual domains. Nevertheless, there is a predominance of 'us' over 'me' in the texts considered in this chapter, even if, in the 'race' sitcoms of the period, it becomes harder to determine who 'we', the subjects of comedy (and 'Britain') are – exclusively white? White and sometimes Afro-Caribbean, but never Asian? Middle-class and liberal, not working-class and bigoted?

Carrying on

The *Carry Ons*, 'the last major cinematic flourish of "us" humour' (Medhurst 1986: 183) are often seen at one remove from cultural history, already a little anachronistic when they began in the late 1950s, increasingly so as 'the sixties' happened. The series can be broken down into three overlapping phases. The early, institution-based films such as . . . *Sergeant*, . . . *Nurse* and . . . *Teacher* featured anecdotal plots in which 'the causal logic of classic narrativity is replaced by a more loosely motivated plot, less developmental than episodic . . . weak in dramatic accumulation, functioning more as a thinly disguised pretext for the display of comic set-pieces' (Hill 1986: 142). During the second phase, generic/historical parodies offer the series even more of a holiday from social and cultural change – the sequence of . . . *Jack* (1963), . . . *Spying* (1964), . . . *Cleo* (1964), . . . *Cowboy* (1965), . . . *Screaming* (1966), *Don't Lose Your Head* (1966), *Follow That Camel* (1967) and . . . *Up the Khyber* (1968) is broken only by a return to bedpans and blanket baths with *Carry On Doctor* (1967). It's the third phase with which we are especially concerned here, beginning with *Carry*

On Camping, the most successful British film of 1969 and an unexpectedly self-reflexive one.

That ... *Camping* marks a shift is rarely disputed, and one scene is usually taken as emblematic of this turn: 'After Barbara Windsor's brassiere had at last burst ... where was the humour in teasing about the possibility of such an occurrence?' (Medhurst 1986: 183). But two points need to be made here. First, nudity and innuendo had coexisted in British popular culture for some time outside the cinema. The Windmill Theatre in Soho, from 1932 to 1964, combined nude tableaux (and later striptease) with stand-up comedy – Morecambe and Wise, Dick Emery and Harry Worth all passed across its stage, while Benny Hill, inappropriately, failed the audition.

Second, when the *Carry Ons* first capitulated to (brief) displays of nudity, they did so not by looking forward, or even sideways, but backwards. Babs's breast-propelled bra does indicate a point-of-no-return, but the opening and closing of the film suggest that the film's lowbrow determinants are more historically complex.

We are at the cinema – it ought to be a Jacey or a Compton, but in fact it's the Picture Palace. The poster announces *Nudist Paradise*, and the dialogue refers to *Naked – As Nature Intended*. Inside the fleapit are Sid James and Bernard Bresslaw with their 'dates' Joan Sims and Dilys Laye – it goes without saying that they all have ice lollies. Sid can't wipe the grin off his face, nor suppress delighted guffaws; Bresslaw's jaw is touching carpet. Dilys Laye is nauseous – a condition later linked to motion sickness, appropriately enough for a film considering a journey into new territory. And Joan Sims is equal parts outrage and indifference at all that judiciously staged volleyball:

Joan: It's disgusting, that's what it is, it's disgusting!
Sid: What are you talking about, disgusting? It's artistic.
Joan: Artistic?
Sid: Certainly!
Joan: What, with all those big bottoms bobbling about all over the screen?
Sid: Ah, you wouldn't think anything of it if we were walking about like that all the time – free, unfettered, unashamed.
Joan: Oh no? I suppose you'd rather we all sat here stark naked.
Sid: Wouldn't bother me.
Joan: It would if your ice lolly fell in your lap.

The nudist film is perfect for *Carry On* – a British institution in which high (surface) ideals masked base lechery. But by 1969, they were already consigned to history – the 'nudies' had fizzled out six or seven years earlier. The nudist camp, however, had been institutionalised as a comic locale in seaside postcards by the mid- to late-1960s, now displaying naked breasts – a helpful 'Nudist Camp' sign was always visible to explain why the British were taking their clothes off. The comic potential of (invisible) male genitals found new generic outlets – 'Ginger Nuts! I knew I'd Forgotten Something!' exclaims a woman as her red-headed husband bends over to stir the soup. Sid and Bernie take their partners to the camp featured in the film – 'back to nature, all that freedom!' – but find that it's no longer a naturist club. There they are joined by suburban Terry Scott and his wife, with her neighing, honking car-accident of a laugh, hanger-on Charles Hawtrey and a bus full of St Trinian's jailbait from 'Chayste Place' presided over by Kenneth Williams and Matron Hattie Jacques. We're back on familiar ground until the arrival of a Hippy Free Festival in an adjacent field, successfully expelled but not before they make off with Babs and the other girls. The camp is a socio-sexual space in transition – naturism has moved on, free love is on its way: the former takes itself seriously enough to be debunked, the counter culture is an unknown quantity and visibly Not Welcome.

Carry On Loving (1970), . . . *At Your Convenience* (1971), . . . *Matron* (1971) and . . . *Girls* (1973) require some comment as the most of-their-moment of the 1970s entries. . . . *Loving*'s parade of miserable couples, linked by Sid and Hattie's dating agency, are contrasted both with commercialised sex ('Everyone's Raving About – SEX!' 'Twice Nightly' declares a bus display) and uninhibited youth – a running gag finds the same teenage couple on a bus, in the back of a car, in a lift and in a telephone box ('Please be quick. Others may be waiting for it'). . . . *Matron* is about a plot by a working-class gang to steal the contraceptive pill, a felicitous metaphor for hijacking the permissive bus. The Family Planning Act was passed in 1967, and ITV was screening family planning advice in 1970, the year that the pill was officially available to the unmarried, and available on the National Health from 1973. But its use even by married couples was limited – a 1970 survey revealed that only 19 per cent of couples under forty-five used it, 29 per cent used condoms and 37 per cent didn't use anything (Marwick 1982: 117). According to Jeffrey Weeks, 'its incidence of use decreased down the social scale and in a movement from the south-east of England towards the north-west' (1989: 260). But the pill was a totem of social change, largely from a male definition: 'The eroticisation of modern culture could focus on the female body without most of the consequences which in earlier days had been feared and expected' (*ibid.*: 260). The motivation in . . . *Matron* is ostensibly to sell the contraceptive pill abroad, but there's an enduring sense of the lower orders redistributing permissive wealth.

As the 1970s *Carry Ons* returned to the institution, they also seemed to have relocated to a place called Planet Smut, a region (a lower region) populated by towns like Much-Snogging-on-the-Green and Fircombe and landmarks such as the Finisham Maternity Hospital and Rogerham Mansions. The institution, according to Marion Jordan, cannot accommodate 'the animal nature of human beings: their sexuality . . . their excretory functions, their preference for idleness as opposed to pointless physical strain' (1983: 316). But the institution is now largely given over to 'animal nature' – the hospital was always a safe bet for this, and the toilet factory in . . . *At Your Convenience* certainly doesn't function as the body-denying institution Jordan is talking about. In . . . *Matron*, Sid is preoccupied with his pill-snatch, so it's left to Terry Scott's Dr Prodd, 'the taxidermist' (there are trophies celebrating each sexual conquest), to keep the lecher's end up, not least when sexually harassing a dragged-up Kenneth Cope. The film plays fast and loose with gender, even by the standards of the series. Cope, posing as a nurse, changes his name from Cyril to Cyrille ('It's a surreal . . . a real name!') – 'Cor, I could really fancy you,' says Bresslaw admiringly, later donning a dress himself. Kenneth Williams's hypochondriac doctor learns that he has an unusually large pelvic cavity and convinces himself that he's changing sex. 'Your mail,' says Matron Hattie, handing him some letters – 'Yes, I am,' shrieks Williams, 'and I can prove it, do you hear me? Prove it!'

One consequence of carnivalising the institution is that the 'spoilsports' have to be found elsewhere – the targets become more specific (feminism, trade unions) and the community less easy to hold together. The earlier films, John Hill observes, ultimately unite authority and the group into a collective, unified effort 'binding together diverse social types through an "imaginary" dissolution of real authority relations' (1986: 143). In . . . *At Your Convenience* and . . . *Girls*, this becomes harder to do: . . . *At Your Convenience*, very much a Heath era movie, was an unexpected flop at the box office, a failure attributed by Rigelsford (1996) and Ross (1996) to its *I'm All Right Jack* anti-union stance. Kenneth Cope's Vic Spanner (in the works) largely denies human 'nature' in the interests of the union rulebook. Only 'animal nature' can reunite the group, not only on a riotous Brighton outing but by the dissolution of Vic's one-man strike by a sexy new canteen girl. Even so, and for all its considerable pleasures, . . . *At Your Convenience* is a worryingly top-down narrative, playing like a grubby *Metropolis* to unite capital and labour – boss's son Richard O'Callaghan and foreman's daughter Jacki Piper stand in for Gustav Fröhlich and Brigitte Helm respectively. Sid's class affiliation – admittedly self-delusory in real terms – is the casualty. He plays a foreman who can nevertheless 'speak the language' of the workers. Earlier, he gets them laughing and almost back to work, before O'Callaghan utters the fatal line, 'All right, that's enough fun.' Having already saved the company with his racing winnings, his daughter's marriage to O'Callaghan ensures that 'you're management yourself' – 'No, no, I'm a worker!' he protests, but to no avail. One can only speculate on the reasons for the film's commercial failure, but it is worth contrasting with the trade union populism of *On the Buses*, whose first cinematic offshoot enjoyed very different fortunes in the same year.

Carry On Girls, meanwhile, fragments fascinatingly before our eyes. This time, the plot is a confrontation – a beauty contest versus women's libbers, led by June Whitfield's Augusta Prodworthy. Interestingly, it's the latter who win, and, while Sid's trademark laugh is the last sound we hear, there's a slightly desperate ring to it. The feminists are a diverse group, older than popular representations of second wavers tended to be. Augusta combines women's rights with puritanism, and seems ripe for a humiliation that never arrives – 'there can never be anything proper in young women being shown off like cattle for the sexual gratification of drooling men'. 'Proper' is killjoy talk in *Carry On* land, and the sabotage is appropriately called Operation Spoilsport. Second in command is Angela, coded lesbian with her bobbed hair, shirt-and-tie and cardigan – a policeman calls her 'this gentleman' by mistake. There's even a bra-burning ritual which swiftly deteriorates into a conflagration. But the feminists offer empowerment to a familiar Carry On type – the put-upon wife or partner, here represented by Mayor's wife Patsy Rowlands, who joins the group, and, by implication, the taken-for-granted Joan Sims who has her revenge on Sid by stealing the takings during the beauty contest fracas. Augusta is mocked for opposing a men-only toilet – 'We will squat on this erection to man's so-called superiority' – but Rowlands's weak bladder politicises bodily functions; for her, there is truly something at stake. Unusually, as Frances Gray suggests, 'joining the women's movement has been a way into humour, not a way out' (1994a: 9), and the film allows her considerable pleasure at the humiliation of husband Kenneth Connor.

Regular rises and Bus Driver's Stomach: *On the Buses*

> I think fuckin' laffing is the most important thing in fucking everything. Nothing ever stops me laffing.
>
> 'Joey', *Learning to Labour* (Willis 1977: 29)

The word 'raucous' recurs in descriptions of *On the Buses* (LWT 1969–73), the word applied both to its audience and to the show itself, 'filled to the brim with noisily unlikeable stereotypes' (Crowther and Pinfold 1987: 71). Certainly, the show's most enduring image is of driver Stan (Reg Varney) and conductor Jack (Bob Grant) laughing, endlessly, terrifyingly – nothing can stop them. At work, it's the sign of their power over the Hitler-moustached Blakey (Stephen Lewis), while at home it's usually directed at Stan's lank-haired, milk-bottle-spectacled sister Olive (Anna Karen), who is funny simply because she is unattractive. But Stan and Jack have another reason to laugh – no oil paintings themselves, they never go short of 'crumpet', and Jack, in particular, has his pick of the sexy young clippies. As Jordan says of the *Carry Ons*, 'there is no need . . . for *men* to be attractive' (1983: 332). This is the epitome of permissive populism – anti-authority, based on male camaraderie (like all those 1970s ads showing ugly men drinking beer), delighted at the availability of modern young women. Few short scenes in British film history empower the male gaze quite like the opening of the first *On the Buses* film (Harry Booth, 1971). Wherever they look, there are cleavages to look down and miniskirts to look up – Stan is so distracted by one such 'view' that he drives through a puddle, sending an ejaculatory spray over Blakey. In 'The New Uniforms', one of the most popular episodes, first transmitted in 1970, they are forced to wear bell-bottomed trousers and flared tunics. They mince about in a mock fashion show, but their disgust turns to delight when their pulling power increases as a result. The uniforms put them up a class – they're mistaken for pilots by two Swedish girls – and down a generation.

Paul Willis's *Learning to Labour* (1977), a classic cultural studies text, follows a group of working-class 'Lads' from school to factory floor. Along the way, Willis provides some incidental but valuable insights into comedy and power. The Lads, boisterous and disruptive, distinguish themselves from another group, the 'Ear 'oles', effete and conformist, who have capitulated to the formal hierarchies of school or work. For the Lads, on the other hand, the informal must be asserted against the hegemony of the formal, and a crucial vehicle for doing so is the 'laff', 'the privileged instrument of the informal, as the command is of the formal' (Willis 1977: 29). Blakey is very much the 'Ear 'ole', utterly subservient to the bus company while forever bleating out ineffectual commands – his famous catchphrase, 'I'ate you, Butler!', is the very embodiment of powerlessness. He's the weak link in working-class masculinity, the portal through which women drivers, poncey uniforms and bureaucratic interference gain entrance.

Willis could easily be describing *On the Buses* when he characterises the 'laff' as: 'part of an irreverent marauding misbehaviour. Like an army of occupation of the unseen, informal dimension, "the lads" pour over the countryside in a search for incidents to amuse, subvert and incite' (*ibid.*: 30). Bakhtin's notion of the 'carniva-lesque' revels in the reversal of hierarchies of power, debunking and humiliating authority, just as Blakey is tormented so ritualistically – in 'Foggy Night', they amuse themselves by throwing peanuts into his snoring mouth until he wakes up, choking. Jack, in particular – a leering hedonist, cigarette in one hand, head thrown back like a shark on laughing gas – is the maestro of 'marauding misbehaviour'. It's particularly significant, therefore, that he is also Shop Steward. Apart from modulating his voice to 'speak' from this position, there is no indication that the union rulebook interferes with beer, 'birds' and laffs; rather, it bolsters up the (male) working class's right to physical pleasures, to fun and misbehaviour. Writers Ronald Wolfe and Ronald Chesney had incorporated trade unionism into an earlier sitcom, *The Rag Trade* (BBC 1961–3) – 'Everybody out!' was Miriam Karlin's catchphrase. In the very first epi-sode of *On the Buses*, there's already an impending strike over the canteen – 'We're the bosses now, you know,' Stan tells Blakey. When Tom Lappin describes the show as 'a telling witness to the Britain of the Heath era', he doesn't mean it as a compliment – rather patronisingly, he describes it as 'all vulgar fumbling and struggling to come to terms with the wider world' (1994: 18). But its vulgar populism contextualises it as part of that moment – did the miners make Heath look like the proverbial 'Ear 'ole'? *Carry On At Your Convenience* recoils from 1970s militancy, and, while picket line duty isn't much fun in *On the Buses* – Stan has to get up earlier than he would for work – it acknowledges that the working classes might have to fight for their pleasures, good-natured skiving and clippie-pulling included.

Of course, these 'laffs' aren't equally distributed – when are they ever? If the *Carry Ons* contain more diverse representations of women than tends to be acknow-ledged, *On the Buses* constructs its biggest boundaries around gender. The point of the clippies seems to be that they don't need to be seen as workers; rather, as busmen's perks. When Stan's girlfriend becomes a driver (in the 1971 film), she's off limits to him until she's demoted again, whereupon Jack gives him the green light – 'She's crumpet, mate – she's available.' In so far as the film has a plot, it deals with Blakey's scheme to bring in women drivers, who pose a threat to Stan's overtime as well as the sexual economy of the depot. Middle-aged and 'masculine', they are humiliated in a particularly vicious way, tormented with spiders and laxatives, subjected to homophobic innuendo:

Blakey: They'll be able to do your job properly, and they won't waste time trying to
         pick up the clippies.
Jack: By the look of 'em, I'm not so sure.

But it's Olive who is the butt of the show's domestic cruelty – she is, quite simply, the most abject female figure in British comedy. The more she attempts to accentuate her sexuality with false eyelashes ('They're too big – every time you blink, you'll knock your glasses off') or an improbable blue frilly mini-nightie, the more we are invited to recoil. When she puts on a bikini in *Holiday on the Buses* (Bryan Izzard, 1973), the camera looks her up and down as though it can't believe its eyes – when she dives into the pool, the bottom half inevitably comes off, to much ribaldry. Married to the lugubrious Arthur (Michael Robbins), she inhabits the most extravagant version of the sexless, discontented comic couple:

Olive: My wedding dress was very beautiful.
Mum: Yes, love, it did something for you – made you look very glamorous.
Arthur: The veil did.
Olive: What do you mean by that?
Arthur: Gawd, that veil was so thick you didn't know which way you were facing. Half the time you'd got your back to the vicar.
Olive: It wasn't the veil. It was so hot my glasses got all steamed up. And when the vicar started talking, I thought I was gonna sneeze.
Arthur: I must be the only bridegroom who lifted up the veil of his bride to kiss her and found an inhaler stuck up her nose.

The treatment of Olive is truly merciless and unremitting. Unlike Yootha Joyce's Mildred or the 'bad' wives in *Carry On*, she is never the subject of humour, only its object. But she is also the central site of the show's 'aesthetic of ugliness', its prime grotesque body. She first enters the series coughing, a constant inscription of corporeal frailty and intestinal determinants – 'Watch it love, you'll burst your boilers.' The grotesque female body gets pride of place in Bakhtin's carnivalesque aesthetic, not least in the terracotta figurines of pregnant, cackling hags. Mary Russo is more cautious – these female grotesques are 'more than ambivalent . . . loaded with all of the connotations of fear and loathing around the biological processes of reproduction and of aging', but at least 'exuberant' (1994: 63), not the word which comes to mind with Olive. But she accommodates (a suitably ambivalent word) the series's most sublime aesthetic reversal in 'Brew It Yourself', where Stan's home-made beer initiates a carnivalesque transformation of the largely desire-free zone of the Butler household. Arthur, in his drunken stupor, finds Olive 'a bit of all right!' and they kiss passionately, she in her baroque nightie, curlers and Stan's cap. 'Blimey, mate, she'll kill him!' marvels Stan – Arthur has had an unspecified but much-cited 'operation' – as they go upstairs for a rare and presumably riotous taxing of the bedsprings.

The carnivalesque body operates as a kind of anti-abject, celebrating its precarious borders as empowering rather than identity-threatening. The mouth, the genitals, the bowels and the womb are privileged sites in this anatomical agenda:

> the grotesque image ignores the closed, smooth, and impenetrable surface of the body and retains only its excrescences (sprouts, buds) and orifices, only that which leads beyond the body's limited space or into the body's depths.
> (Bakhtin 1984: 318)

These 'sprouts' and orifices belong to a polymorphous body, so that sex, eating and defecation are not fully distinguishable from one another. In one of Benny Hill's sketches, he hides a goose down his trousers and it keeps popping out, front and back, to steal food, pinch bottoms and generally misbehave; an unruly penis one minute then an animated turd or a hungry mouth. In *On the Buses*, everything comes back to the digestive system, recalling Nuttall and Carmichael's description of comedian

Frank Randle as 'a visibly overflowing sewerage system', a reminder to the audience that they were 'mere alimentary systems, mere overgrown infants, mere flesh and blood' (1977: 38). Male sexuality is not phallic, but situated, instead, in the stomach – ' 'Scuse fingers,' apologises Stan as he gropes a clippie on her way into his cab. The very first image in the first episode is sausages being cooked for breakfast, and by episode six we've been through the full high-cholesterol diet just in the opening scenes. No episode is complete without a meal-time discussion, words and half-chewed food flying every which way. But while a stomach full of fried food keeps the cemetery gates symbolically at bay, it also brings them literally closer, as evinced by 'Bus Driver's Stomach', the combined consequence of excessive fry-ups and bad posture. Stan complains that the bus 'puts a froth on my gastric juices', while Arthur warns him that 'You've got enough acid in your stomach to burn a hole in the carpet.'

In the 1971 film, Jack stops off for some quick trousers-on sex with 'Turnaround Betty' – 'Breakfast in bed' – while Stan eats his breakfast in the cab. The editing parallels these two 'meals', cutting at one point from Jack nuzzling a shoulder to Stan greedily biting into a juicy orange. The trio of bodily functions is completed by Blakey's unexpected arrival and Stan's claim that Jack is answering 'a call of nature':

Blakey: Do you mean to say he's been using that lady's facilities?
Stan: Well, you *could* say that.

This representation of women as perishable goods – eminently consumable but quick to turn rotten – has a chilling resemblance to Hitchcock's *Frenzy* (1972), a film which might appear to be a perverse presense in a chapter on comedy – only Peter Hutchings (1986) has commented on its affinity with low comedy. *Frenzy*, too, is an 'appetite' text, filled with grotesque gastronomic imagery – according to one critic, the film 'constantly alludes to the appetite of its audience, perhaps grown too large for anyone to satisfy' (Sgammato 1973: 135). The 'necktie murderer' Bob Rusk (Barry Foster) is as jauntily laddish in his pursuit of women as Jack, but we see the violence behind the charm. He eats an apple after the rape-murder of one victim, to whom he describes his sexual philosophy as 'Don't squeeze the goods until they're yours', and hides another's body in a potato truck.

Where does the carnivalesque stand in relation to the permissive, the increasingly official voice of the unofficial? In one sense, it doesn't – sitcoms aren't folk culture, regardless of the laugh track, 'the vestigial reminder of the music hall audience, the electronic substitute for collective experience' (Medhurst and Tuck 1982: 45). Stasis, nostalgia and change are all part of *On the Buses* – authority is mocked but accepted as inevitable (and, in mocking it, desirable), fried food, fag ends in the toilet and dirty nappies are as important as washing machines and family planning, 'liberation' is fine for separating clippies from their knickers but threatening if women become more than unskilled labour.

We need to look to a BBC sitcom to see carnival accommodate more radical changes in Britain's sexual culture, namely *Are You Being Served?* Murray Healy argues that the *Carry Ons* 'opened up a space for a carnivalesque critique of dominant sexual discourse, and queers got in' (1995: 247), a coup cemented by *Served*. If Williams and Hawtrey were 'narratively straight but semiotically bent' (Medhurst

1992: 19), John Inman's Mr Humphreys was unambiguously out, 'not just homo-sexual', but '*gay* at a time when the word was still radically political' (Healy 1995: 253). And while he was still an 'eccentric' stereotype contained within the sitcom group, he was 'allowed to acknowledge some sort of gay scene, a network of other gay men (he even gets to have a drink with some transsexual friends in the . . . (1977) film)' (*ibid.*: 255). Healy assesses the show: 'from a position and cultural perspective of queer confidence. It would have been hard for most contemporary gay viewers to read comfortably beyond the heterosexual imperative of these comedies' (*ibid.*: 256). But *Served* opens up a space – not found in the ITV sitcoms – within the reclaiming of 1970s smut. Catchphrases count for a lot in popular comedy, and 'I'm Free!' was a significant, if ambiguous, addition.

[. . .]

PART 2

Aspects of tabloid culture

SECTION 4
Celebrity

Perhaps the best known description of the celebrity is Daniel Boorstein's assertion that 'the celebrity is a person who is well-known for their well-knowness' (in Turner, 2004: 5). They achieve well-knowness by virtue of their ability to differentiate themselves from other potential celebrities in a crowded media marketplace. Critics insist on the essential modernity of celebrity as a cultural form and its intimate association with and dependence on the growth of the mass media industries. Indeed, the celebrity's creation and expansion is a 'phenomenon of mass-circulation newspapers, TV, radio and film' (Rojek, 2001: 16), for celebrity as concept and set of cultural practices is integrally related to mass distribution, technical enhancement in photography and print culture, the growth of the public relations and promotions industries from the beginning of the twentieth century, and more recently the technological possibilities of cross-media convergence enabling the marketing of celebrities on the Internet and via mobile phones (De Cordova, 1990; Marshall, 1997).

There is a complex network of media practices that currently produce and market the celebrity figure and lifestyle. Since the early 1990s, celebrity has become a powerful focus of self-reflexive interest in the media with debates aired about the amount of media space devoted to celebrities. That the celebrity is now the subject of not only tabloid print, TV, radio, and Internet columns dedicated to entertainment gossip, but also is increasingly an integral element of much 'hard' news and current affairs coverage feeds into anxieties about the 'dumbing down' of media output. Celebrity culture pervades many aspects of cultural life today from business and corporate culture, politics, professional sports and music industries. Turner (2004: 131) notes the broad social influence of the 'smiling professions': that of public relations and media management. The prolific use of media management means that divisions between different spheres of public life are being eroded. For example, the public persona of the politician is increasingly generated by the same mechanisms and systems used to produce entertainment and sporting celebrities. 'The need for the successful politician to build a public face means that the conventions of celebrity must collude with those of party politics' (Turner, 2004: 103). One politician who has taken the conventions of celebrity fully on board is Italian Prime Minister and media magnate Silvio Berlusconi. Ahead of the April 2006 general election he sent 11 million Italians a glossy 160-page magazine

entitled *The Real Italian Story*, which celebrated the successes of his Forza Italia administration. The magazine included dozens of flattering photographs of the premier
embracing rock stars and sporting champions as well as the usual press conference
photographs of Berlusconi alongside prominent world leaders.

As Kellner (2003: 4) notes, to become a celebrity in any arena 'requires recognition
as a star player in the field of media spectacle'. Thus Boris Yeltsin sang on Russian TV,
Bill Clinton played the saxophone at public events and many less well known politicians
find themselves performing for photo-opportunities at political rallies that resemble
talent shows. In tune with the broader demands of tabloid media, the emphasis is
increasingly on the personality of the celebrity politician. The danger of this focus on the
political personality can of course be detrimental to the politician and to detailed factual
coverage of social, economic and political issues. Tabloid scrutiny of politicians' personal lives, their lifestyles, habits, family relations, financial affairs and even sexuality
can undermine the authority of their political role. As Connell suggests, tabloid stories
about 'personalities' often turn the tables on public figures who usually set the media
agenda, confronting 'the same protagonists with themes that they thought safely buried
beneath and obscured by their positions in the public domain' (Connell, 1992: 73).
Others have noted that tabloid coverage of 'personalities' entails revelations and
exposés of personal facts that serve to mount a populist challenge to privilege (Connell,
1992; Hartley, 1996).

For critics, such emphasis on the famous personality is exemplary of the cultural
decline of the media and is aligned with the tabloid predilection for human interest and
the sensational (Franklin, 1997: 4). Even the newspaper editors of quality review pages
are being pressured to select mostly books written and reviewed by celebrities. Speaking
of the success of proprietor Rupert Murdoch's stable of mid-market newspapers, journalist Henry Porter has suggested that, in Britain at least, Murdoch astutely tapped into
'demographic developments' and 'a certain intellectual passivity', which has required
virtually all newspapers to compete for the mid-market. This has led to an expansion
of mid-market material: 'show-business coverage, interviews, scandal, human interest
stories, sports, health and fitness, and book chat' (Porter, 1999: 45).

A study of Australian celebrity in the media in 1997 measured the increase in
celebrity coverage in a sample from print and television news media, popular magazines
and daytime TV chat shows. It found between two to three times more coverage of celebrities than 20 years before in all of these media products (Turner et al., 2000: 16–23). In
the late 1980s and early 1990s, one of the key catalysts for change in the British
women's mass magazine market was competition from the rise of celebrity weekly
magazines (Gough-Yates, 2003). Magazines such as *Now*, *Chat* and later *Heat* (discussed by Su Holmes in this section) now dominate the British market. With an
emphasis on picture-led spreads (informed partly by Spanish *Holá*) these magazines
rely on photographs of actors, pop stars, minor aristocrats and the 'D-list' category of
minor celebrities often spawned from the reality TV programmes that have dominated
television schedules since the mid-1990s (Palmer, 2005: 37–8).

In the *State of the News Media 2006 Report* (SNM, 2006), an annual report on
American journalism, the growth of entertainment and celebrity news magazines was
declared 'staggering'. This growth was linked to tabloidization. In the United States,
tabloidization refers particularly to the supermarket tabloids, of which the most contro-

versial is the *National Enquirer*. This magazine has transformed its coverage from the highly popular bizarre coverage of alien abductions, Elvis sightings and contemporary 'freak' tales (Fiske, 1992: 49) to a growing dependence on celebrity coverage concentrating on scandalous, salacious and irreverent ridicule of celebrity figures (Turner, 2004: 72–3). Whilst a few years ago, there were regular reports that the print market in this area was 'fully mature' with little space for growth in titles or readership, new titles like *Ok!* (already with successful sister titles in Britain and Canada) entered the US market in 2005 to join popular titles like *People*, *Us* and *The Star*. Like the British market leaders *OK*, *Heat* and *Hello!*, much of the content of *Ok!* has been openly purchased from the celebrities themselves. This overt embrace of cheque-book journalism signals the dependence of this sector of the industry on the promotional industry for a steady supply of pictures, stories and interview material (Turner, 2004: 73). This tactic, which *OK!* calls 'relationship journalism', has ensured that the magazine has enjoyed exclusive access to celebrity stories in the past, including the 2002 wedding of Hollywood stars Catherine Zeta-Jones and Michael Douglas – images of which were infamously published by rival magazine *Hello!* leading to legal claims for redress by the couple in the British courts the following year. This merging of tabloid and entertainment forms of journalism is exemplified by the relaunch of tabloids such as the *Star* as glossy magazines (see discussion below). Such journalism brings with it the ability to charge higher cover prices and to attract a younger, impulse purchase driven readership. For example, Marc Paretsky, general manager of celebrity title *Life and Style Weekly*, suggests that the average age of his readership is 30 rather than the average age of tabloid readers at 50 (SNM, 2006: 5).

As Sanders (2003) has noted, 'Questions about values, principles, right and wrong behaviour, are an inescapable part of journalism'. Historically, gossip columnists, the predecessors to the contemporary celebrity journalist, have been widely despised since their consolidation as a modern profession within the mass entertainment industries during the 1920s and 1930s (Ponce de Leon, 2002). Often derided by the famous people that they cover, nonetheless celebrity figures and the media are in many respects mutually constitutive. And, sometimes courting their own sort of celebrity persona, some celebrity journalists, echoing the prior treatment of gossip columnists, can become the subject of the same type of coverage they inflict upon others.

In justifying their work, celebrity journalists, like many of their peers, will appeal to 'the people's right to know', the uncovering of truth, and stress the importance of 'the story'. They will also draw upon the role of humour, the use of vernacular language and an irreverence for hierarchy associated with the popular press. Media onlookers often point to the popularity of the format. In the United States, the 'godfather of the celebrity genre' *People*, sustained a healthy circulation of 3.7 million five years after its inception in 1999 despite increased competition (SNM, 2006: 5). Correspondingly, the mainstream press, many of which have incorporated aspects of celebrity journalism into their own pages, are frequently the source of criticism of celebrity coverage and the celebrity journalist often becomes elided with the seamier underside of the entertainment industry itself. For example, in August 2004, *The Economist* (US edition) focused on Bonnie Fuller, editorial director of American Media, who had been hired to reinvigorate a company whose 'racy tabloids' (including the *National Enquirer*, the *Globe*, and the *Star*) were publications which had suffered from years of falling circulation figures. *The Economist* noted that Ms Fuller's strategy with the supermarket tabloid the *Star* was to do celebrity journalism better than its rivals (unlike for example the rival *People* magazine, there was no space given to ordinary people). Taking the magazine 'upmarket' Fuller shed its tabloid format and cheap newsprint, redesigning the *Star* as a glossy magazine calculated to appeal to clever professional women in their mid-20s to mid-40s who would read a gossip sheet without embarrassment if produced along the lines of the British magazine *Heat*. *The Economist* commented on the *Star*'s twin-pronged approach of aspiration and denigration in that it both treated 'celebrities as people to envy (better clothes, better dates, better sex and, inevitably, better body parts)' but also, 'as people who are just as wretched as you'. They suggested this type of celebrity journalism 'has the magnetic appeal of the proverbial car wreck', and, as such, circulation under Fuller's leadership had grown from 800,000 readers in 2003 to 1.2 million the following year.

Celebrity journalists, media proprietors and editors, talk-show hosts and gossip columnists often defend celebrity coverage with the argument that celebrity culture represents a kind of populist democratization of the public sphere. Seen from this perspective, celebrity and public fame are part of a Western ideal of personal freedom. Celebrity culture itself is validated as a reward for the hard work of self-improvement and the labour of self-development by those in the public limelight, instead of the privileges gained through inherited status and the nepotism of elite networks. Seen thus, celebrity represents the skills, strength and force of the unique individual. And tabloid coverage of the celebrity often feeds into the narratives of enterprise and individualistic achievement that dovetail with the celebrity persona. As Jessica Evans argues: 'Fame typifies a particular idea of personal freedom and motivation to succeed that all should share' (Evans, 2005: 15). Your unique characteristics can become the resource upon which you draw to construct your celebrity persona.

Recently, there has been a distinct revival of media interest in controlling all aspects of the celebrity's portfolio, a process that echoes earlier ownership of the Hollywood film star and postwar development of the pop star. However, what is distinct about current manufacture and ownership of the celebrity-product, is the extent to which some sections of the media have used 'ordinary people' with no obvious talents, specialized performance training or history of performance (Turner, 2004: 53). The use of popular culture as a springboard to real or imaginary success is not new and historically the music hall, boxing ring, talent or beauty contest or the quiz/game show provided a space for working- and lower middle-class people to speak about public visibility (Turner, 2004: 61). What is new is the discourse of self-disclosure and authenticity enabled by new television formats such as docu-soaps, reality TV and lifestyle programming that allow ordinary people a narrative of self-improvement and empowerment via personal self-disclosure and revelation of one's authentic self (Dovey, 2000; Bonner, 2000; Biressi and Nunn, 2005).

Some critics argue that the new electronic media have enhanced both the individual's and the audience's ability to decide who should become a celebrity. Reality television programmes such as *Big Brother* and *The X Factor* enable the public's direct vote for their winning aspirant celebrity. Indeed, in January 2006, the winner of the UK's *Celebrity Big Brother* (C4) was Chantelle Houghton, the only noncelebrity amongst housemates that included a British politician, actors, a US soap star, a sport celebrity and pop stars. The following month, Chantelle, whose only prior claim to fame was being a Paris Hilton lookalike, went on to star in a six-part British TV mini-documentary series that followed her through the ups-and-downs of new found celebrity, *Chantelle: Living the Dream* (E4). Newspaper and magazine coverage was prolific and three months after the end of *Celebrity Big Brother*, newspapers were still reporting on Chantelle's engagement to housemate Preston and in April she fronted a new lifestyle makeover and dating show, *Chantelle's Dream Dates* on youth-orientated channel E4. In 'The especially remarkable: Celebrity and social mobility in Reality TV' we chart and assess the systems of media judgement and classification that position many 'ordinary' participants on Reality TV as 'classed subjects'. We argue that the participants are positioned and judged within many programmes and their personas scrutinized for their taste, clothes, disposition, banal conversation, interactions with other contestants, ambitions, and everyday behaviour. We suggest that such judgements are integral to the narrative of social mobility offered by celebrity status as a complex mediation of class and performance.

As Su Holmes argues in her chapter here, ' "Off-guard, Unkempt, Unready?" Deconstructing Contemporary Celebrity in *Heat* magazine' (2005), the magazine's status as the authoritative guide to contemporary celebrity rests partly on its status as a text in which the commercial mechanisms of celebrity construction are treated with a sense of irony and irreverence. At the same time, a number of formulaic strategies – the stress on the visibility of the celebrity captured in a public space; the revealing of the ordinary person through the image of the celebrity 'unkempt' or 'unready' for the camera; the exposure of the commercial machinery that surrounds the celebrity – all signal the complex negotiation of authenticity and manufacture that define the contemporary celebrity's iconic status. She argues that by acknowledging the fabrication of the celebrity through an ironic or irreverent tone, the magazine sidesteps the difficult question of why celebrity is such an object of fascination and debate.

Kevin Glynn (2000) analyses the tabloid coverage of the trial of African American football hero and movie star O. J. Simpson for the alleged murder of his ex-wife and her male friend. In this extract he focuses on coverage of the murder case by supermarket tabloids the *Globe* and the *Star*. He stresses the ways in which they drew upon popular counternarratives and counterknowledges to construct a sense of incredulity towards official versions of appropriate juridicial evidence. Against a racially inflected backdrop of white middle-class backlash and moral panic he argues that the validity of the trial's evidence is undermined through the tabloid's fusion of diverse factual and fictional texts – crime scene pictures, police reports, testimony from psychics, movie stills, readers' letters and so on – to interrogate the guilt or innocence of O. J. Simpson. This use of excluded perspectives and forms of knowledge spoke to the tabloid readers' feelings of alienation or exclusion from institutional power and legitimated forms of information. It revealed the ways in which tabloid coverage can subject the criminal justice system to levels of scrutiny judged inappropriate and voyeuristic by many mainstream journalists.

When Anna Nicole Smith, former *Playboy* model, minor Hollywood film star, and host of glitzy chat-reality TV show *The Anna Nicole Show* (*E!* channel from 2002–4) was found dead in her Hollywood hotel room from a drug overdose in February 2007 the media coverage was extraordinary. She was declared by the *Washington Post* 'a postmodern pin-up for a tabloid age', they claimed she had 'got under our skin' (Wood, 2007: 42).

Famous for her role as *Playboy Playmate of the Year*, multi-million dollar contracted promotional figurehead for *Guess* jeans adverts and bride to octogenarian billionaire J. Howard Marshall II, she manipulated the media with aplomb. The widespread fascination with her mediated adult life led a *New York Times* columnist to declare that 'her career ultimately says more about the culture's fascination with celebrity than it does about Anna Nicole Smith' (Wood, 2007: 42). Presented in media coverage as 'an American Tragedy' she represented for many cultural commentators, an embodiment of the contemporary obsession with celebrity. Like the definitions of celebrity discussed in Turner, Bonner and Marshall's extract here from *Fame Games: the Production of Celebrity in Australia* (2000) Smith represents one of the primary characteristics of celebrity: 'the ultimate in unauthenticity through the perceived artificiality of their personality, their reputation or even their bodies'. They argue that public interest in such personalities is aroused by the desire to penetrate (through media coverage) that construction and gain access to some essential truth about that celebrity.

John Gray is one of a number of critics who sees this 'cult of celebrity' as the culmination of a process of democratization intertwined with the development of a late capitalist market society. He argues that, in an economy spurred by the need to manufacture need in a relatively affluent society such as Britain where many people possess basic commodities, fame has become the new prize held out by the entertainment economy: 'In the past, luxury goods were sold to the masses by linking them with the lifestyles of the famous. Today, it is the belief that anyone can be famous that sustains mass consumption. Celebrity has been made into a sort of People's Lottery . . .' (Gray, 2002: 2). For Gray, programmes such as *Big Brother* are emblematic of a broader culture of celebrity in which mass consumption is tailored to a multitude of shifting niche markets, each catering to a 'carefully crafted and continually refined illusion of individuality.' Such media products sustain the illusion that 'celebrity is a universal entitlement that everyone can enjoy if they are lucky enough to be selected by everyone else' (Gray, 2002: 3).

Further reading

Evans, J. and Hesmondhalgh, D. (eds) *Understanding Media: Inside Celebrity*, Maidenhead: Open University Press.

Marshall, P. D. (1997) *Celebrity and Power: Fame in Contemporary Context*, Minneapolis: University of Minnesota Press.

Ponce de Leon, C. L. (2002) *Self-Exposure: Human Interest Journalism and the Emergence of Celebrity in America 1890–1940*, Chapel Hill, NC: University of North Carolina Press.

Rojek, C. (2001) *Celebrity*, London: Reaktion.

Turner, G. (2004) *Understanding Celebrity*, London: Sage.

Turner, G., Bonner, F. and Marshall, P. D. (2000) *Fame Games: The Production of Celebrity in Australia*, Cambridge: Cambridge University Press.

2.1

The meaning and significance of celebrity
by Graeme Turner, Frances Bonner and
P. D. Marshall

All around me were women who seemed to be wanting gossip; they wanted to know more about Elvis, and his first grandchild, and Elizabeth Taylor, and Hazel Hawke, weddings on *A Country Practice* . . . nothing nasty; not the horror stuff.

Nene King, Woman's Day

The concept of celebrity is a little slippery, partly because its constitutive discourses have leaked into such a wide range of media formats and practices (not to mention everyday life: the best soccer player in the local under-10s is widely referred to as 'a legend', while his 10-year-old sister wins a shopping centre competition for a Spice Girl look-alike by lip-synching to 'Do You Wanna Be My Lover'). Today, we hardly notice the high degree of personalisation that is used routinely within media reports as a means of producing drama. Further, given that news necessarily individuates its subjects, foregrounding the major players in all kinds of stories (perfectly ordinary businessmen, for instance, become 'corporate raiders' whose dealings are injected with personality), it can be difficult to satisfactorily determine what is a celebrity story and what is not. There is a syllogistic logic lurking behind discussions of celebrity: celebrities are people the public is interested in; if the public is interested in this person, they are a celebrity; therefore, anyone the public is interested in is a celebrity. Alberoni's well-known account of 'stars' reads a little like that when he claims that they are especially remarkable, not because they possess a particular level of economic, political or religious power but because 'their doings and ways of life arouse considerable interest'. While they enjoy some of the social privileges of an elite, however, Alberoni argues that they are, institutionally, a 'powerless elite'. Celebrities, to some extent then, are the objects of an interest over which they have no control.

Control, of course, is exactly what the celebrity industry aims to achieve. And it is possible to see the discourses of celebrity – the visual, verbal and rhetorical means of signifying celebrity in the media – as accessing power, not surrendering it. John Langer has implied precisely that by pointing out that even those who *do* possess institutional power can – and do – choose to represent themselves through the modes used to represent celebrities. Politicians are surrounded by party press officers, or 'spin doctors', intent on massaging the political message reaching the electorate. At the same time, the press officers are concerned with constructing the politician's personal image. Especially where it concerns the representation of political leaders, the construction of the political image – as distinct from the marketing of political policies – is indistinguishable from the marketing of the latest film or CD. The promotion of former premier Jeff Kennett, through the jeff.com celebrity website during the 1999 Victorian election, is a precise demonstration of this point. As his fate in that election also demonstrates, however, the deployment of practices used within the celebrity industry, while thoroughly integrated into the contemporary performance of politics, does not necessarily guarantee success in terms of either votes or consumption. Federal politicians Amanda Vanstone and Natasha Stott Despoja have both promoted themselves through, for instance, appearances on *Good News Week*, but only Stott Despoja is a celebrity.

That said, it is not easy to be confident about such statements. In practice, the distinction between celebrity and other kinds of social or political elite status is becoming less clear as the signs of celebrity drive out less powerful alternatives. According to Langer, today virtually any kind of construction of an elite proposes the individuals concerned 'as especially remarkable simply by featuring them in terms of their "doings and ways of life" – that is, through an individuated account of their personal lives as a means of acknowledging or proposing their importance'. This has the important implication of suggesting, as does David Marshall in *Celebrity and Power*,[1] that celebrity is not a property of specific individuals. Rather, it is constituted discursively, by the way in which the individual is represented. Through what Langer, after Monaco, calls a 'calculus of celebrityhood', celebrity is constructed rather than immanent:

> A calculus of celebrity is relatively flexible and can be operationalised 'down' as well as 'up', in the direction of those who have neither power in an institutional sense nor any kind of elite standing as celebrities but who, through specific personal achievements – their doings, rather than their ways of life – gain an appearance in the news and concomitantly considerable albeit fleeting public attention.[2]

This 'calculus' of discourses, then, passes through the living, breathing individual as if they were a temporary host to the desires of the audience, and those of the cultural industries whose interests are served by the celebrity's promotion.

It is important to understand this dual aspect of the production of a public personality. For example, the figure we recognise as Ray Martin presents this complex twinning of audience desires and commercial interests. As a television host, Martin is, for a large portion of the public, a reliable figure who presents a concerned and informed voice which speaks for some of the needs and desires of his audience when he interviews John Howard or Tom Cruise. Here, the celebrity stands in place of the audience and their cultural power is related to their ability to successfully occupy that role. But, for many years, Martin was also the principal public face of the Nine Network. Like network news anchors in the United States, he perfectly represented the 'ultimate integrity of the network' as his institutional identity merged with the constructed personality.[3] The celebrity is therefore a combination of the commercial interests of a cultural industry – in Martin's case, a television network – and the

Newsagency windows advertising magazines, using posters of their covers dominated by famous faces.

shifting desires of an audience. The celebrity's personality must negotiate between these differing, sometimes competing, conceptions of a public. Serving different political ends for each component of this relationship – as a means of reaching a fragmenting mass market (for the production industry), and as a means of comprehending a fragmented and confusing culture (for the audience) – the celebrity is at their most active and significant when they mark a point of convergence or, as Marshall puts it, when they can provide 'a bridge of meaning between the powerless and the powerful'.[4]

Among the defining attributes of the signifying system which produces celebrity is the dissolving of the boundary between public and private lives. By this, we mean that a key marker of celebrity treatment is evident when someone who has been newsworthy due to, for instance, the part they play in the public domain – they may be contestants in a legal case, say, or victims of a natural disaster – also attracts interest to their private lives. What the discourses of celebrity characteristically do is go beyond the primary public activities into the personal and private in order to elaborate on what Dyer has called 'the authentic self' of the individual.[5] On the one hand, the celebrity might represent the ultimate in unauthenticity through the perceived artificiality of their personality, their reputation or even their bodies (think of, for instance, Pamela Anderson), but, on the other hand, audience interest is nevertheless aroused by the possibility of penetrating that construction and gaining access to some essential knowledge about that celebrity.

While the effect of such media treatment (rumours, gossip, paparazzi shots) may be unpleasant and destructive in many instances, it also carries some benefits for its objects. Far from enrolling them in Alberoni's 'powerless elite', the achievement of celebrityhood is a means of signifying and establishing success in a wide variety of domains: business, sport, entertainment, the arts, and so on. While the individuals concerned may sacrifice their privacy to this achievement, celebrity status 'confers on the person a certain discursive power within the society . . . the celebrity is a voice above others, a voice that is channelled into the media system as being legitimately significant'.[6] Such people are a natural topic for news. What Langer calls their 'very-being-as-they-are' becomes a readily available source of occurrences that require only the slightest 'twitch' (the excitation of mild surprise, as in the headline, 'Melanie Griffith's cosmetic surgery shock') to generate news stories.[7]

The effect is, of course, to turn celebrities into commodities, products to be marketed in their own right or to be used to market other commodities. The celebrity's ultimate power is to sell the commodity that is themselves. This fact has been thoroughly integrated into contemporary popular culture and the marketing of the celebrity-as-commodity has been deployed as a major strategy in the commercial construction of social identity. Within a highly fragmented but increasingly globalised mass market, the use of celebrities has become a very efficient method of organising cultural significance around products, services and commercially available identities.

Their combination of commercial and cultural function remains, though, highly contradictory. Celebrities are brand names as well as cultural icons or identities; they operate as marketing tools as well as sites where the agency of the audience is clearly evident; and they represent the achievement of individualism – the triumph of the human and the familiar – as well as its commodification and commercialisation. Like all commodities, however, their trade needs to be organised and controlled and, as a result, the production and commercialisation of celebrities has become an industry too. Typically, the celebrity industry is structured around the need to acknowledge conflicting objectives: the commercial objective of maximising the income generated by the celebrity-commodity, and the celebrity's personal objective of constructing a viable career through the astute distribution and regulation of the sales of their self-as-commodity.

Marketing this self-as-commodity is not a simple matter, of course. The nature of public interest in the celebrity is itself highly contradictory. As signs of the potential for ordinary people to transcend their condition, celebrities are inspirational; as signs of the unauthenticity and superficiality of success, they are consoling. The legitimacy of celebrity is always radically provisional. While celebrityhood can represent success and achievement in the social world, it can also be ridiculed and derided 'because it represents the centre of false value. The success expressed in celebrity is seen as . . . success without the requisite association with work.'[8] Indeed, this is fundamental to the desirability of celebrity status. Even when they are engaged in activities that are patently 'work', such as promoting their new record, film or stage production, the actual representation of celebrities' behaviour will often deliberately elide any contextualisation that might foreground what they are doing as promotion. So, a celebrity will 'meet with reporters' in a leisure location, like a golf course or a resort.[9]

According to Ian Connell, there is a heavy weighting of scepticism in the public consumption of celebrities. For him, the display of celebrities through the popular media satisfies the 'oppositional resentment' of the popular audience. On the one hand, the success of celebrities who claim no special entitlement to their privileged position can appear to be especially valorised for maintaining their intrinsic 'ordinariness' and disavowing their elite status. On the other hand, the success of such celebrities 'encourages and nourishes scepticism about the legitimacy of the . . . personalities to act as they do'.[10] Connell argues that the thirst for stories about celebrities is fuelled by a vision of them as 'members of a privileged caste' against which the typically cheeky and iconoclastic stories of the tabloid press mount a 'populist challenge'.[11]

Contradictory and tainted with unauthenticity as they may be, it seems clear that celebrities perform a significant social function for media consumers. Langer argues that examination of the discourses used to represent celebrity can teach us a great deal about how 'values and attitudes are assembled and disseminated at particular historical conjunctures'. Echoing Dyer's argument that the 'star' represents 'the type of the individual' within their culture, Langer suggests that the 'celebrity can operate as a site from which key ideological themes can be reiterated and played out'.[12] Marshall, too, sees the celebrity as tightly articulated with the value systems of democratic capitalism, 'wedding consumer culture with democratic aspirations' while participating in the 'active construction of identity in the social world'.[13]

Constructing identity seems to be getting a little more complex and a lot more public than it used to be, requiring as it does the negotiation of key aspects of Hartley's postmodern public sphere: the dissolution of the boundaries between the public and the private, and the elevation of the personal, in media discourse. McKenzie Wark has long argued that we inhabit a world structured by unstable categories and fluid identities, for which the media is an indispensable navigational tool. As his second book argued, there is nothing surprising about the notion that the Australia we inhabit is a 'virtual republic', created by collective acts of imagination and facilitated by the communication technologies which enable us to share words, images and sounds across the nation.[14] In *Celebrities, Culture and Cyberspace*, Wark, like Marshall, argues that the representations of celebrities operate as a kind of bridge between the private world and public debate. For him, too, celebrities become crucial elements in the formation of individual and collective identity:

> Australians have many different ways of thinking and feeling, but nevertheless share a cyberspace within which cultural differences are not only negotiated and adjudicated, but creatively combined. The most visible signs of this process are celebrities. They embody not just the particular cultures from which they come, they embody also something beyond. We may not like the same celebrities, we may not like any of them at all, but it is the existence of a population of celebrities, about whom to disagree, that makes it possible to constitute a sense of belonging. Through celebrating (or deriding) celebrities, it is possible to belong to something beyond the particular culture with which each of us might identify.[15]

A key factor (although not only in cyberspace) is simply 'talk', and there is a rich literature on the social function of gossip as one of the means through which we construct, modify and negotiate our individual and collective identities.[16] Robin Dunbar claims, hyperbolically, that 'language evolved to allow us to gossip',[17] while others have argued that gossip operates as a form of social bonding, that it helps to negotiate norms for social behaviour, and that it plays an important role in providing information and social knowledge. As a consequence of their familiarisation through the media, it seems that the celebrity is (virtually) added to our social circle, and gossip about the celebrity serves similar functions to that about other (non-virtual) members of the social group. The connection between the production of celebrity and the construction of community, then, may be far more direct than is customarily accepted.

In a useful example from an earlier phase of celebrity production, Jackie Stacey's *Star Gazing* provides detailed evidence of the cultural roles played by Hollywood stars of the 1940s and 1950s for women in postwar Britain.[18] The women upon whose experiences she draws speak of the importance of their interest in stars such as Rita Hayworth, Lauren Bacall and Doris Day in constructing their identities, in exploring the pleasures of consumption, and in dealing with the pressures of a particularly austere everyday life. The rise of the gossip magazine in recent years must tap directly into this kind of potential too.

It is the celebrity's complex entanglement with, and contribution to the augmentation of, the discursive or meaning-making structures of their society that dominates most contemporary academic accounts of the cultural function of celebrity. Crudely, it is argued that the mass media celebrity is folded into our ways of making sense of our world.[19] A clue to how that might work within a world where traditional structures are shifting, and where the pace of change and the notification of that change have accelerated dramatically, can be found in Colin Sparks' discussion of the British tabloid press. Sparks acknowledges the importance accorded to individual experience within the contemporary press, even as a means for understanding large, complicated and structural social change. As he says, this is a problem for contemporary culture, that the focusing on 'the experiences of the individual as the direct and unmediated key to the understanding of the social totality' has become a common, deeply embedded feature of social-democratic popular journalism.[20] Indeed, it may well be that the more dramatic, rapid and disruptive the rhythm of social change, the greater the recourse to the personal, the domestic, the melodramatic and the sensational as a means of explanation. Gripsrud's analysis of the uses of melodrama in popular journalism comes to that conclusion, quoting Elsaesser's observation that 'popular culture has resolutely refused to understand social change in other than private contexts and emotional terms'.[21] The role of the celebrity may well be to deal with the gap between the social and the private, between stability and change. While it is probably just as well something is serving this purpose, one has to admit that the commodification of the celebrity would not have been an ideal first choice. Nevertheless, the fact that such arguments are made indicates the importance of understanding these issues better than we do now.

Whatever the explanatory power of these arguments, they have the virtue of approaching the media shifts we have been describing in something like their own terms, rather than seeing them as a subsection of arguments about media ethics or media fashion. The clear indication of the work on celebrity today is to regard the interest in celebrities as another symptom of the media's gradual disarticulation from a model of media practice that foregrounds the dissemination of information, and its increasing alignment with a model that more directly participates in the process of disseminating, interrogating and constructing identities.

[. . .]

Notes

1 D. Marshall, *Celebrity and Power: Fame in Contemporary Culture*, Minneapolis and London, University of Minnesota Press, 1997.
2 Langer, *Tabloid Television*, p. 46.
3 Marshall, *Celebrity and Power*, p. 124.
4 Ibid.
5 R. Dyer, *Stars*, London, BFI, 1979, p. 24.
6 Marshall, *Celebrity and Power*, p. x.
7 Langer, *Tabloid Television*, p. 59.
8 Marshall, *Celebrity and Power*, p. ix.
9 Langer, *Tabloid Television*, p. 55.
10 I. Connell, 'Personalities in the popular media', in P. Dahlgren and C. Sparks (eds), *Journalism and Popular Culture*, London, Sage, 1992, pp. 66, 82.
11 Ibid, p. 74.
12 Langer, *Tabloid Television*, p. 51.
13 Marshall, *Celebrity and Power*, p. xi.
14 M. Wark, *The Virtual Republic: Australia's Culture Wars of the 1990s*, Sydney, Allen & Unwin, 1997.
15 M. Wark, *Celebrities, Culture and Cyberspace: The Light on the Hill in a Postmodern World*, Sydney, Pluto, 1999, p. 33.

16 Compare Jennifer Coates and Deborah Cameron (eds), *Women in Their Speech Communities*, New York, Longmans, 1989; Deborah Jones, 'Gossip: Notes on women's oral culture', in Deborah Cameron (ed.), *The Feminist Critique of Language*, London, Routledge, 1990; Neal Gabler, *Gossip, Power and the Culture of Celebrity*, London, Macmillan, 1995; R. Dunbar, *Grooming, Gossip and the Evolution of Language*, London, Faber & Faber, 1996.
17 Dunbar, *Grooming, Gossip*, p. 79.
18 J. Stacey, *Star Gazing: Hollywood Cinema and Female Spectatorship*, London, Routledge, 1994.
19 Ibid, pp. ix, 51.
20 C. Sparks, 'Popular journalism: Theories and practices', in P. Dahlgren and C. Sparks (eds), *Journalism and Popular Culture*, London, Sage, 1992, p. 42.
21 J. Gripsrud, 'The aesthetics and politics of melodrama', in P. Dahlgren and C. Sparks (eds), *Journalism and Popular Culture*, London, Sage, 1992, p. 92.

2.2

The especially remarkable: celebrity and social mobility in Reality TV
by Anita Biressi and Heather Nunn

[. . .]

Introduction: celebrity in the modern social realm

With New Labour's inception in 1997, arts and entertainment celebrities gained prominence as exemplars of a new meritocratic and essentially *modern* democratic social realm.[1] The administration at Number 10 Downing Street actively sought the endorsement of musicians, actors and movie stars in its attempts to deploy a new, more inclusive and populist lexicon as part of its electoral address and managerial style. As a consequence, it was those who had succeeded in entertainment, rather than, say, industry or finance, who were often held up as exemplary figures 'close to' New Labour. Such entertainers and sports people, some originally from very disadvantaged social backgrounds, came to the fore as people of influence and social standing.

In the same cultural moment, the notable success of new TV forms – docusoaps such as *The Cruise* and hybrid 'reality' shows such as *Big Brother* and later *Pop Idol* – enabled the transformation of the terrain of media culture which, in turn, showcased ordinary people as potential media stars.[2] The modern social realm was, it seems, further expanded to accommodate a new band of celebrities, of ordinary people rendered remarkable through their encounter with new hybrid media forms and by their imbrication with the complex processes of identification and voyeurism that made them household names. These new media stars appeared to be able to 'make it big', to not only become wealthy but, more importantly, to sustain a transformation into celebrity stardom without overtly drawing on education, entrepreneurial skills or even any obvious talent.

Reality television's development of new iconic personas and their facilitation into a media-driven social mobility was, of course, partly anticipated by longer-established media narratives of class mobility. Biographies and news coverage of celebrity British footballers, pop performers, comedians and film stars have been central to the mythologisation of working-class social mobility in media culture. So too, narratives of football pools wins, bullion heists and lottery jackpots have long provided fantasy avenues of escape that were independent of the cultural capital gained through education, birth, entry into the professions or even talent (aside from the talent, that is, to entertain).[3]

The successful launch of the television drama series *Footballers' Wives* is a good example of a public fascination with the transformation of ordinary people into a new media-ocracy through fame, personal achievement and stunning affluence. The focus of the series, which has its roots in tabloid women's magazines such as *Hello!* and *OK*, did not dwell on the skills of players but on the fame and fortune of the newly affluent and media-savvy footballer and his wife as celebrities.[4] The depiction of Victoria and David Beckham and their family life as 'popular royals' (resident in 'Beckingham Palace') was one clear influence on the programme. Their lives are exemplary too of a doubled agenda that famous working-class celebrities need to negotiate if they are to remain in favour. They must maintain the much-mythologised 'down-to-earth' values of working-class family culture and authenticity while fulfilling the expectations of glamour and overt consumption that sustain their public personas. They operate as an important counterpoint to those born into celebrity during a period when, for example, the public no longer feels obliged to look to the monarchy or other elite persons for role models of exemplary domesticity or overt consumption.[5]

The popular impact of these and other celebrities seems to reside precisely in their very disconnection from traditional structures of influence (inheritance, education, etc) together with their intimate connection with the media and the consumer lifestyle which the media privileges and foregrounds.[6] Although celebrities have been described by some media critics as a 'powerless elite'[7], they wield a form of power formerly unrecognised as such. Graeme Turner *et al* have argued, for example, that:

> . . . the celebrity's ultimate power is to sell the commodity that is themselves. This fact has been thoroughly integrated into contemporary popular culture and the marketing of celebrity-as-commodity has been deployed as a major strategy in the commercial construction of social identity.[8]

In this context, the *accoutrements* and *appearance* of celebrity are paramount. Although the celebrity is a figure of consumption writ large they must also retain the individualism that marks them apart and renders them remarkable and commercially marketable. What might be called 'classed cross-dressing' becomes one overt and instantly recognisable expression of both their agency and their success. The sartorial and material signifiers of class transformation mark both working-class origins and the move away from them; the pleasurable and playful excess of financial escape from those origins and a rebuke or an offence against respectable 'taste'.[9] This move up is also problematised because class mobility is dependent on consumption or the unstable transformation of stardom. The dual dynamics of transformation and submerged 'real' classed identities that appear in many media representations of the socially mobile 'media-ocracy' are crucial. Focusing on the representation of social mobility and celebrity in Reality TV[10] we will consider the complex interdependence between class and performance, the freedom of taking on new identities and the notion of some hidden essence or 'true' working-class identity concealed beneath the 'glitz'.

Critical responses: disgust, democratisation and desire

Reality TV is not the end of civilisation as we know it: it is civilisation as we know it. It is popular culture at its most popular, soap opera come to life.[11]

Current responses to Reality TV coalesce around several themes. One common strand is that of derision. This response is encapsulated in Germaine Greer's much cited quotation above. In her article on Reality TV, Greer jeers at the mass audience of these shows and predictably situates them within a 'dumbed down' tabloid TV arena in which, she claims, a mixture of banality, exhibitionism and character-play guarantee audience ratings and therefore their domination of the schedules.

In keeping with broader attacks on tabloid culture and of the 'feminisation' of factual programming, a number of cultural critics (often championing a lost cause which is implicitly 'high culture') decry those who produce, watch and perform for Reality TV's cameras. Here, the ethics of what is acceptably represented in the mass media is linked to broader debates about the decline of more privileged objective factual reportage and programming. In Britain, this debate is specifically linked to the role of television in an arena in which the public service ethos has been diminished. Objectivity, fact and debate are bandied about as lost values of a formerly intellectually curious journalistic age.[12]

The Reithian theme of self-improvement and a broadcasting service that strove to use television to take viewers outside their realm of immediate existence, to educate and inform, is lamented as a lost educative ideal in an increasingly commercially pressured media environment. Reality TV, it is claimed, replaces this intellectual adventure with the limited exhibitionist challenges of the game show or the emotional outpourings of confessional culture in which the biggest challenge is to get on with a small bunch of housemates/prisoners/competitors for a limited period.[13] With Reality TV the aim is not to take viewers outside of their own experience but to present them with a fully recognisable and familiar realm of the ordinary and the everyday. The ethic of self-improvement seems, for media sceptics, to be parodied; as those without the traditional markers of media role models are seen to succeed – if not in Reithian terms, then at least within the terms of the populist media.

The disdain for the entertainment-led audience is matched by distress about changes to televisual form and genre. Frequently, the documentary becomes the marker of quality filming based on rational investigation of historical or socio-cultural fact. The detached but committed observational gaze of the documentary maker of the past has, it is claimed, been replaced by a slow slide through the docu-soap of the 1990s to the current Reality TV show. An anxiety about the decline of documentary proper is often articulated to an anxiety about Reality TV's dependence on spectacle linked to a manipulative misuse of the camera. Here, the prominence of, for example, the 'close-up' is highlighted. This fear of the seductive image is captured in language that stresses the distraction of the viewer from rational viewing: 'we *cannot think straight* . . . if our *emotions* are being *jerked up and down* by . . . zoom lenses'.[14] Underlying this anxiety about 'easy' pleasure is recognition of the destabilisation of the distant and powerful documentary camera and the move towards televisual intimacy.

In contrast to the above criticism, others have celebrated this cultural phenomenon as part of the contemporary expansion and democratisation of public culture. It is argued that Reality TV's popular expression of social concerns and everyday events, conflicts and traumas within a highly managed environment signal the opening up of the public sphere to ordinary concerns and ordinary people who, if they are popular enough and lucky enough, can become famous. Where celebrities are already a pre-requisite of the show – for example in the recent adaptations of survival shows for celebrity participants – the authenticity of the show is marked by the supposed provi-sion of insights into the hidden 'real' aspect of celebrity personality. Phil Edgar-Jones, the executive producer of *Big Brother*, described the second *Celebrity Big Brother* as a stripping away of celebrity personas: 'With normal *Big Brother* we're making ordinary people extraordinary. With this, we're making famous people very, very ordinary'.[15] In short, Reality TV is celebrated as a democratisation of public culture and the deconstruction of the components of fame that partially constitute the celebrity media subject and the construction of social identity more broadly.

The process of constructing celebrity and stripping it away can be captured in John Langer's notion of 'the especially remarkable'.[16] In his analysis of tabloid culture, he highlights the prominence in current media culture of the 'other news': a form of cultural discourse intimately connected with gossip, story-telling and the scrutiny of the newly famous as well as those with a longer-held celebrity persona. Langer situ-ates his celebrities within a co-dependent media context in which celebrity status is both ratified by media presence but also operates as a privileged authority in media culture. Celebrities have increasingly taken on the role as 'primary definers' of news. The very force of representation of the celebrity gives their actions and statements a kind of privileged authority in a world increasingly characterised as divided by those who have access to image-making and the rest.[17] This other news does not represent elite persons within the context of their institutional backdrop and does not primarily consider their role as power brokers or decision makers – but rather values their informal activities, public rituals of display and consumption, and their private lives.

This 'calculus of celebrity'[18], then, is flexible, and focuses not only on celebrities but those who have achieved possibly fleeting public attention through specific per-sonal achievements.[19] For example, the 'ordinary' stars of Reality TV shows suddenly acquire massive media visibility but possess very little in the way of institutional power or control and, unless they obtain excellent PR management, they often have little experience in media spin. It could be suggested then that Reality TV both proves and extends the mythic belief that traditional versions of mobility and success, once closely associated with economic or social terms, are increasingly implicated in and subsidiary to the mass media processes of publicity. Langer suggests:

> On the one hand ordinary people are constructed as especially remarkable for what they do. How they breach expectations, their remarkableness, is lodged in the extraordinary acts they perform. This separates them from us, makes them different and transcendent; they start where we are but move beyond. On the other hand . . . The implication is that, although these people are assigned espe-cially remarkable qualities based on what they do, such qualities and perform-ances could just as easily be within our grasp. If those seemingly mundane occupations and enthusiasms . . . can become the springboard from which those

ordinary people ascend into the realms of the especially remarkable, it could just as easily happen to us as well.[20]

The appeal of Reality TV lies partly in how seemingly unremarkable people are suddenly 'especially remarkable' and how that celebrity status is endorsed by the spectacle of their widespread public presence. For example, the UK series *Pop Idol UK*, which ran in the summer of 2002, screened countless auditions of would-be pop celebrities. The show attracted over 30 million viewers who watched and voted for those singers who would remain until the final contest between Gareth Gates and the ultimate winner Will Young.[21] These two contestants have both become chart-topping pop singers with massive media coverage.[22]

The 2002 spin-off *American Idol* warned potential contestants that their appearance on TV may be 'disparaging, defamatory, embarrassing or of an otherwise unfavourable nature which may expose you to public ridicule, humiliation or condemnation'.[23] Nonetheless its popularity with would-be idols and audiences alike ensured a second series in 2003. *American Idol 2* appeared on Fox TV and concurrently in the UK on ITV2 in March 2003. It followed the structure of the UK predecessor and the final 12 contestants were introduced to their audience through pre-recorded video cameos that emphasised their 'ordinariness', their small-town America homes and the support of their local schools, military barracks, church or family. These to-camera testimonies by family and friends and shots of the contestants feeding the ducks, visiting their old workplace at a hair salon or supermarket, or training with ordinary soldiers, located them as 'no-one particularly special', as 'regular' or 'all-American' young men and women. But, at the same time, the 'folks' that spoke of them and their singing skills, as a child amateur performer, in the Church choir, in a local bar, served to elevate their status. These subsidiary characters, like the live audience for whom the contestants then perform, function textually as a sign of public acclamation: 'the especially remarkable are seen (by us) to be seen by others in the public domain'.[24]

These short video narratives of personal triumph over ordinary obstacles and *over obscurity itself* anticipated their live stage performance singing before music industry judges and audience. The appearance in front of TV cameras before a voting TV audience was constructed consequently as the tangible reward for their accomplishments *per se* despite the lure of winning the competition. In such competitions, the ordinary masses of viewers who follow the course of the contestant's path to fame are crucial. They serve a similar role to the subsidiary characters present at the edges of the frame in TV camera or paparazzi shots of the star persona, for their presence 'watching, waiting, attending or serving' the ordinary celebrity endorses his or her status.[25] Furthermore, this identification with the 'especially remarkable' individual allows for the possibility of a sense of activity for the TV spectator, of a hand in the elevation of the ordinary person to celebrity status.

Correspondingly, Peter Balzagette, creative director of Endemol Entertainment UK, the creators of *Big Brother* in the UK, argued in the 2001 Huw Wheldon lecture to his media industry peers that Reality TV is 'diverse programming, and access to the airwaves for a more diverse spread of people'.[26] He declared that this democratisation, also signalled by the audience's ability to contribute to the elevation or elimination of the stars, goes hand in hand with a change in social attitudes about television and identification. He characterises this as a desire for 'emotional investment' latched onto the appeal of interactivity and audience participation. For Balzagette, audience figures clarify this desire to participate in and determine a programme's conclusion; a motivation which ensured that over the first two series of *Big Brother* around 34 million phone votes were cast for who should stay and who should go in the *Big Brother* house.[27]

This investment, articulated through constant media, especially tabloid press, coverage, is apparent and increasingly dominant in the most recent *Big Brother* production.[28] This third series which ran in the summer of 2002 followed the standard formula of isolating 12 voluntary participants in a house without media contact with the outside world for 64 days. These were gradually eliminated and ejected by telephone poll until the winner remained. In the final week of the programme, 8.5 million votes were cast, signalling for some media commentators that the series epitomised 'the model of participatory programming'.[29] The press measured the extent of its success by competing for exclusive interviews as the final four to emerge from the house were deluged with cash offers; the figures offered often dwarfed the £70,000 prize collected by the eventual winner, 22-year-old Kate Lawler.

But the issues we have raised about the seemingly unremarkable subject of Reality TV and their entry into the celebrity matrix are best exemplified by Jade Goody. Jade Goody, a 21 year old dental nurse from South London, fourth from last to be expelled from the house, received wildly fluctuating media coverage from the press whilst in the house and was the subject, halfway through the series, of vitriolic attacks from the tabloids. Goody was undoubtedly 'marked' negatively as working-class by her body, her voice and her supposed intellectual ignorance. She was loud, apparently uneducated, bibulous, excessive, overweight and getting fatter as the series progressed. The press revelled in quoting 'Jade-isms', the stupid things said by Goody in the course of the series. She displayed the bodily excesses that marked Roseanne Barr as a blatantly working-class woman but without the wisecracking humour that protected Barr from the worst misogynistic criticisms. Dominic Mohon, editor of the *Sun*'s showbiz column 'Bizarre', urged readers to evict Jade with the deeply misogynistic slogan, 'Vote out the pig'. He informed readers that 'Jade is one of the most hated women on British TV and life will be hard for her when she leaves the house'. She seemed to exemplify Annette Kuhn's observation that:

> Class is something beneath your clothes, under your skin, in your psyche, at the very core of your being. In the all-encompassing English class system, if you know you are in the 'wrong' class, you know that therefore you are a valueless person.[30]

However, tabloid attacks were upturned by positive viewer support for Goody resulting in tabloid battles for exclusive rights to her when she emerged from the house. Ironically, Rupert Murdoch's *Sun* and *News of the World* outbid rival tabloids and paid £500,000 for exclusive interviews with her. Since then Goody has been re-branded as a 'national treasure'.

Jade Goody's success fits the pattern highlighted for the 'especially remarkable' in that when the ordinary celebrity is prone to setbacks, these setbacks are played out before the public gaze. She won through only after a dialectic of ill-fortune and effort had been played out. And crucially her success was attributed to powers beyond her grasp or ken: she was subject to the inexplicable hand of fate, the power of the TV audience and the manipulations of the TV production crew. When she exited from the House she appeared dressed in a glamorous evening gown three sizes too small and was soon confronted by *Big Brother* host Davina McCall with a montage of clips revealing her excessive behaviour and her apparent stupidity. She was greeted by talk show comedian Graham Norton, who reclaimed her as a camp icon, the plump, giggly and dense dental nurse reminiscent of a 1950s *Carry On* film.

Subsequent media coverage focused on the re-education of Miss Goody. The TV programme *What Jade Did Next* (Channel 4, October 2002) followed her as she worked with a personal trainer, learned how to deal with the media, learned how to drive and was schooled in the very demanding work of public appearances. Her background with her single mother on a working-class social housing estate was contrasted with the opportunities on offer to her since her appearance on the reality show. She was a stark signifier of the possibility of self-transformation and social mobility in spite of class origins and limited social skills. Jade's narrative of desired transformation also reveals how class plays a central role in the production of femininity and the regulation of it. The escape which Jade articulates in *What Jade Did Next* reveals a knowledge on her part about the attainment of not just economic wealth but the cultural artefacts of taste and knowledge; of cultural capital. The possession of the 'right' car, of literacy, of designer clothes and private property are signifiers of social mobility hedged with the dangers of the disreputable: the trashy dress, the uninformed opinion, the too-loud laugh. In keeping with earlier fictional fantasies of achievement, Reality TV offered Jade Goody a way to exhibit incipient talent for performance, 'rough at the edges but with the potential for learning'.[31]

The vitriolic attacks on Jade and the manipulative techniques used on the participants of the third *Big Brother* generated popular debates about the ethical and moral conundrums spawned by some Reality TV programmes. For example, in this series the participants were frequently stimulated into exhibitionist or adversarial behaviour having been plied with vast quantities of alcohol which replaced former routine activities such as reading books, a pastime removed from the contestants. Games were devised to generate tensions between house members. Penalties involved the enforced separation of participants who had formed emotional ties and a fast-or-feast division in which the losing group were subjected to deprivation of food and basic facilities whilst the winners celebrated with plentiful food and other treats. The clear aim was to initiate volatile emotions: guilt, jealousy and paranoia ensued. Viewers were treated to simmering feuds, which resulted in one contestant, Sandy, escaping from the house not to return and another, Sunita, walking out. Sexual tension and jealousy were provoked and a number of cultural commentators were prompted to question the slippage towards exploitation illustrated by scenes such as a drunken Goody, filmed stripping naked amidst seemingly less impressionable fellow housemates.

Such displays yielded larger audiences and advertising revenues. The second instalment of the show (in the post-watershed slot 10–11.30pm) attracted an average of 9.4 million viewers: a 49% share of the audience and the channel's highest daily audience share in its nineteen-year history. These figures peaked on the final night at 9.9 million (the previous year had peaked at 8.8 million) according to unofficial figures. However, there were concerns that Reality TV was, in its search for innovation, increasingly fostering the brute forces of our psyche. The *Guardian* noted that, 'When it started, Big Brother had lofty pretensions to examine the company of strangers', but, it contended, 'social observation has yielded to darker impulses – to stir conflict, polarise and humiliate'.[32] This trajectory to disturb, provoke the base emotions and to humiliate contestants is one which celebrity aspirants need to negotiate with care.

Celebrity hybridity and packaged demotic culture

The address to the Reality TV audience varies depending on the format of the show. But across the board there is a shared assumption that the audience possesses the media-literate capabilities to judge the contestants/participants of the Reality TV show – even though the criteria of judgement are often unformulated and unspoken. These criteria are grounded in vague notions of identification, appreciation and also crucially of dislike and disdain. Participants of *Big Brother* or *Pop Idol* or *The Club* (ITV2 2003) knowingly present themselves to a judgmental audience. Their task is one of interaction and the overt immersion in the competitive structure of the show. Selected on the basis of contradictory criteria, participants are often stereotypes of the diverse identities that populate contemporary media culture – lesbian or gay, black, heterosexual bachelor, twenty/thirty-something white 'Essex' girl or boy, stud, tart, shy loner. These types share (are presented as sharing) two features: an everyday commonality and a hunger/persistence for celebrity status. The winning formula for appearance on the Reality TV show appears to be a combination of the typecast, the banal and the exceptional.

Frequently, the participants are presented as classed subjects. Whilst the boundary between working class and lower middle class is now often blurred, the participants generally are presented as residing somewhere in this region: they are clerical workers, mechanics, bar keepers, service industry workers and so on. They are also frequently aspirant media celebrities. In many Reality TV shows there is a submerged narrative about escape across classed boundaries. Also the production and editing of the show reveals a level of unacknowledged cultural capital at play. The taste and disposition of the contestants is under scrutiny; their clothes, banal conversation, interactions with other contestants, ambitions, everyday activities as related to the audience are markers of their position within the class hierarchy. The importance here is to appear not *too* wealthy, *too* cultured or *too* tasteful. Yet, as with Jade Goody, to appear too trashy, too sexual, too uncultured can also provoke media opprobrium and infamy.

A strategy of violence, then, is encouraged in the Reality TV community, for the decisions on which contestants should stay and which should go is structured as a demotic decision. This is a system of judgement and classification. A vote determines who is unworthy of respect or esteem – for the contestant the outcome of the vote makes overt the fact that one's performance on the show is readable for others: the people watch you, observe you and decide upon your fate. Here, we would argue, the seemingly more fluid opportunities of celebrity identity fuse with the traces of a class-based system. There is both a celebration of aspiration (or the desire for escape from the limitations of ordinary life) and a judgmental scrutiny of the participants' behaviour – to appear too ambitious, too outrageous, too performative is to invite audience disdain. Yet to appear too dull, too isolated, too introverted, is to also invite the vote off. The conventional markers of class identity alone are inadequate here to predict who will survive and thrive in this media environment. Yet the Reality TV competition often takes place around two axes rooted in economic and social capital – that of material goods (prize money, media contracts) and that of less tangible phenomena such as popularity.

Crucial to the possession of the celebrity status that comes with popularity is a particular form of distinction in which the contestant, as he or she appears before the media audience, can be outrageous, bold, greedy, bitchy or ruthless but they cannot appear pretentious. Pretentiousness is primarily a classed charge which calls aspirant working- or lower-middle-class identities to order: 'who does she think she is kidding', 'we can see right through him'. As Steph Lawler suggests: 'pretentiousness is a charge levelled at people in whom what they *seem to be* is not (considered to be) what they are: in whom there is a gap between *being* and *seeming*'.[33] One of the pleasures of Reality TV for the audience, then, is trying to spot the gap, to see through the contestants' inauthenticity. Yet inauthenticity – the ability to put on a show – is at the same time part of the skill of the celebrity persona.

Here, as mentioned before, 'classed cross-dressing' carries with it pleasures for the aspirant celebrity subject and the media audience, but also dangers. Arrogance, outrageous or overtly ruthless behaviour can be construed as part of older established narratives of transformation in which the working-class boy or girl who wants it badly enough eventually has it all. Consequently, such behaviour signifies a desire to escape limits, to be someone, to grab a status and power normally denied. Attendant on this performance is an inevitable lack of nuance or sophistication *within the terms of class by which the contestants are constrained.* To successfully take on markers of 'cultured' identity would be to underline too clearly that class and power can be vestments or trappings rather than some integral part of one's essential identity. Classed cross-dressing then involves always the danger of discovery, of passing as one of a 'higher order'; and the attendant pleasure for the audience of unmasking someone's hubris.

The institutionalised cultural management that is at the core of celebrity culture was wedded to a new development of the Reality TV show: *The Club*. Here, we argue, the distinction between the real celebrity and the would-be celebrity and between the reality of the game and of the game as a packaged show have been further muddied. This was launched in early 2003, when Carlton broadcast a new show staged in a City bar: Nylon, a retro-themed, two floored bar in London's square mile. Each week for the duration of the six-week show, three celebrities took control of one of the bars at Nylon and their team of bartenders would battle it out to make their bar the coolest one. Each week the celebrity nominated a member of his or her team to get the sack; viewers were witness to the nomination and to the celebrity's appraisal of their staff. TV viewers were also asked to vote for the team member that they wanted to lose their job and the sacking took place live on TV. Open auditions were then held and those who voted *or who attended* the club could, if they chose, ask to be nominated to replace the sacked bar member.

Chrysalis-owned Galaxy radio network teamed up with Carlton to promote the show and when it started, its presenters, celebrity bar managers and team members featured on the dance music stations, and Galaxy DJs managed the decks at Nylon. The club had the capacity to pack in over 500 revellers.[34] It was promoted using the now-common media practice of 'emotional branding'.[35] In this case, the commodity was associated with the subjectivities of everyday working-class life. The three celebrities selected to run the bar were emblems of working-class culture made good. Samantha (Sam) Fox, the former *Sun* 'page three girl' of the 1980s, who, as the official website profile stresses, started work on the *Sun* at sixteen years of age and has gone on to make a wide-ranging showbusiness career for herself. Fox has accrued an iconic status as a former tabloid star and still signifies a brash hedonism and visual excitement combined with a determined desire for celebrity success.[36] She was presented throughout the programme as a tough achiever who combined glamour with tabloid's populist appeal. Her climb to success is marked by a significant gender and class realignment in which working-class women resist discourses of sobriety in the unashamed use of their sexuality to accrue celebrity status; a positioning which sits easily with the personas and self-professed ambitions of Reality TV's contestants.

The second bar manager was Dean Gaffney, who started work on the long-running British TV soap opera *Eastenders*, again at the early age of fifteen. Gaffney is presented as a working-class success story, which melds real-life with his soap persona. The website states that Gaffney is 'no stranger to hard and unglamorous work, and he vividly remembers pounding the pavements on his paper round as a boy'. This is immediately juxtaposed with tales of his current penchant for fast cars and drinking sessions at *Stringfellows* nightclub: 'the trials of celebrity lifestyle!' Gaffney's bar eventually won the £15,000 prize money. The third bar manager was Richard Blackwood, a former MTV presenter turned Channel 4 presenter then pop star. The web profile again presents Blackwood as a person who wants to be remembered as 'a real personality that came from nothing'.

All three bar managers reveal the use of celebrity to represent the emotion of the cultural product: they signify the importance of ambition, exceptional personality and a drive to achieve success from nothing. What is interesting is the elision between their celebrity personas and their real-life status. All three are presented as working-class without specific reference to these terms. Gaffney's soap persona is melded with his personal media achievement whilst Sam Fox exemplifies how being a working celebrity means interpreting economics in sexual as well as financial terms.

There are a number of points to be made about the innovation and self-referential and often hybrid status of *The Club*. The contestants too are mainly from fairly mundane jobs as clerical workers, bar men or women, supermarket workers and so on. They share the common desire to succeed in media terms. *The Club* breaks down the division between would-be and successful celebrity that had heretofore been maintained in, for example, the *Big Brother* and *Survivor* shows. Celebrities work alongside ordinary contestants in the bar and are overtly constructed as cultural workers with shared ambitions. Whilst the division in power is maintained – through the hierarchy of the bar managed by the established celebrity – there are moments when this breaks down. At one point, Fox's crew chastised her in the appraisal session for drinking too much and jeopardising their chances – a scene in which Sam walks off camera twice and later apologises to her team.

The contestants and celebrities challenge any easy notion of classed identity. Both in a sense occupy ersatz class positions – drawing too easily on narratives of gritty success that, in the case of the celebrities, obliterate the distinctions between their public and private personas. Both perform for camera whilst also baring their more 'authentic' anxieties about other team members in by-now well-rehearsed confessional to-camera moments that supposedly characterise Reality TV's glimpse of the authentic person.

Finally then, *The Club* erodes the division between the audience and the performers. Shows such as the USA-based *Survivor* have operated a no-fly zone over their island competition-space to exclude the danger/chaos of outsiders breaking into the reality of the mediated event. *Big Brother* shuts contestants away from the physical presence of ordinary others and opens them only to the televisual/computer gaze. In contrast, *The Club* was open to the public who could visit the club every night of the week including the televised nights. For a minimal fee they could join in the media event, buying drinks at the bar, talking with and assessing the contestants and celebrities and, if lucky, appearing on the TV screen itself. It was a rewriting of the local and particular experience of the local bar into the global distanced voyeurism of television land. If you were young enough, had some money, dressed smartly and lived in London you could inhabit a Reality TV space. This was a marked extension of the viewers' exercise of their discrimination in voting and offered the even more fleeting few seconds of media fame as the camera caught them at the bar or nearby amidst Nylon's consumers. This was Reality TV writ large, revealing how people routinely select and weave mediated, publicly available symbolic representations and discourse into their everyday lives and revealing how that participation can be packaged and sold. It points to an extension of the fantasy role that Reality TV can play in articulating social aspiration within media culture.

Notes

1 We are choosing to use the term 'celebrity' in its broadest sense of people who are objects of pronounced media attention over which they may have only a limited amount of control. We are also excluding elite persons who, for example, first come to the attention of the media and are newsworthy through their work in the traditional 'masculinised' public sphere of politics, big business or the City.

2 There is much debate about how 'new' the new forms of programming actually are. Chris Dunckley in 'It's not new and it's not clever', Institute of Ideas (ed.) *Reality TV: How Real is Real?* Hodder and Stoughton, London 2002, argues, for example, that these programmes have their roots in popular programming dating from the 1960s. Dunckley suggests that the novel aspect of these shows is that they humiliate the ordinary people who feature in them. In contrast Graham Barnfield's 'From Direct Cinema to car wreck video: Reality TV and the crisis of confidence', also in the Institute of Ideas collection, has shown how this

programming has been influenced by the more respectable forms of Direct Cinema and ciné-verité and that its novelty lies in its testament to a prevailing loss of faith in objective truth. Although these writers disagree about Reality TV's origins they both, at least, point to the ways in which these forms are innovative in their emphasis on subjective representation and relative truth, the private sphere of the personal and the emotional (on the latter see also Liesbet van Zoonen, 'Desire and resistance: *Big Brother* and the recognition of everyday life', in *Media, Culture and Society*, Vol. 23, 2001, pp669–677.

3   See for example Vivian Nicholson's well-known autobiography *Spend, Spend, Spend* (with Stephen Smith), Fontana, London 1978, which chronicles her football pools win and the subsequent notoriety that made her a media celebrity. The National Lottery was established in Britain in 1994. For accounts of lottery winners and their encounters with the media see Hunter Davies, *Living on the Lottery*, Warner Books, London 1996.

4   Photospreads of the characters from the series have, appropriately enough, appeared in *Hello!*, 14 January 2003, pp14–18.

5   *Mirror* editor Piers Morgan has described Victoria Beckham, for example, as 'the new Diana' (*Tabloid Tales*, BBC1 2003).

6   See John Langer, *Tabloid Television: Popular Journalism and the 'Other' News*, Routledge, London 1998.

7   F. Alberoni, 'The powerless elite: theory and sociological research on the phenomena of the stars', in Denis McQuail (ed.) *Sociology of Mass Communications: Selected Readings*, Penguin, Harmondsworth 1972.

8   Graeme Turner, Frances Bonner and P.D. Marshall, *Fame Games: the Production of Celebrity in Australia*, Cambridge University Press, Cambridge 2000.

9   Yvonne Tasker, *Working Girls: Gender and Sexuality in Popular Cinema*, Routledge, London 1998, p40.

10   There are a number of conflicting definitions of reality television. In the context of this article we are excluding programmes recorded 'on the wing' via CCTV or lightweight video equipment or where dramatic reconstructions play a central part e.g. *Crimewatch*, *CCTVTV* or *999* (see Richard Kilborn, 'How real can you get? Recent developments in "reality" television', in *European Journal of Communication*, 1994, Vol. 9, pp421–439). Our focus is on programmes such as docusoaps and reality game shows where filming is more sustained and packaged in hybrid formats that marry reality-style filming with, for example, soaps, games shows, lifestyle shows and so on.

11   Germaine Greer, 'We are Big Brother', *The Australian Media*, 12 July 2001, republished in Harold Mark (ed.), *Scum at the Top, Australia's Journal of Political Character Assassination*, Vol. 5, No. 13, Melbourne: Australia, 2001 http://members.optushome.com.au/thesquiz/greer.htm accessed 3 October 2002.

12   Bob Franklin, *Newszak and News Media*, Arnold, London 1997.

13   Barnfield, op cit, p51.

14   David S. Broder in Kevin Glynn, *Tabloid Culture: Trash Taste, Popular Power, and the Transformation of American Television*, Duke University Press, Durham and London 2000, p22.

15   Julia Day, 'Channel 4: thinks big for celebrity reality show', *Guardian*, 4 November

2002, http://media.guardian.co.uk/Print/0,3858,4539336,00.html accessed 19 May 2002.

16 Langer, op cit, pp45–73.

17 Ibid, pp50–51.

18 Ibid, p46.

19 Not only achievement but also dramatic failure will bring individuals into the celebrity matrix. Most recently the attempt by Charles and Diana Ingram and their accomplice Tecwen Whittock to defraud the British quiz show *Who wants to be a Millionaire?* transformed them from celebrity winners to celebrity criminals. The documentary *Millionaire: A Major Fraud* (ITVI), which broadcast the show and revealed the fraudsters' methods, shown on 21 April 2003, attracted nearly 17 million viewers, the biggest audience ever for a factual television programme on ITV.

20 Langer, op cit, p72.

21 *Pop Idol* won the prestigious Golden Rose of Montreux in 2002. It was cited by the judges as 'perfect television' (http://www.elstree.co.uk). Will Young and runner-up Gareth Gates were both given recording contracts with BMG.

22 The appeal of the competition and its lure as a springboard to celebrity status are illustrated by the number of applications to audition for the 2003 *Pop Idol*. The programme-makers Thames TV/19 TV production received over 20,000 applications just prior to the 28 February 2003 closing date. See *Pop Idol* official website 2003 http://www.itv.com/popidol/accessed 18 March 2003.

23 Elstree Studio website http://www.elstree.co.uk/ accessed 3 October 2002.

24 Langer, op cit, p63.

25 Ibid, p72.

26 Peter Balzalgette, The Huw Weldon Lecture 2001, '*Big Brother* and Beyond', http://www.rts.org.uk/rts/html/magazine/weldon.htm accessed 3 October 2002, p8.

27 Ibid, p2. Indeed, the figures for *Big Brother* productions are impressive. The November 2002 final of *Celebrity Big Brother* attracted nearly 50 percent of the overall primetime TV audience.

28 Fans of the third *Big Brother* spent an average of three and a half-hours a week watching the action on computers at work and home. For the 2002 *Celebrity Big Brother*, BT Broadband teamed up with Channel 4 to offer 24-hour coverage of the six celebrity housemates over their ten-day incarceration, and special desktop software was developed to update office workers with the latest significant scenes within the house. Extra footage of *Celebrity Big Brother* was streamed live on E4, the digital interactive service, and the Internet.

29 'A case for expulsion: *Big Brother's* challenge for Channel 4', *Guardian* 31 July 2002 http://MediaGuardian.co.uk/bigbrother/story/0,7531,766576,00.html accessed 03/10/2002.

30 Annette Kuhn, *Family Secrets: Acts of Memory and Imagination*, Verso, London 1995, p98.

31 Angela McRobbie, 'Dance Narratives and Fantasies Achievement', in *Feminism and Youth Culture: From Jackie to Just Seventeen*, Macmillan Education, Basingstoke 1991, p215.

32 *Guardian*, 31st July 2002, op cit.
33 Steph Lawler, 'Escape and Escapism: Representing Working-Class Women', in Sally Munt (ed.), *Cultural Studies and the Working Class: Subject to Change*, Cassell, London 2000, p121.
34 Julia Day, 'New reality show joins The Club', *Guardian*, 22 January 2003 http://media.guardian.co.uk/broadcast/story/0,7493,879478,00.html accessed 14/05/2003, pp1–2.
35 James Lull, *Media, Communication, Culture: A Global Approach*, Polity Press, Cambridge 2000, p170.
36 Patricia Holland, 'The politics of the smile: "Soft news" and the sexualisation of the popular press', in Cynthia Carter, Gill Branston and Stuart Allan (eds.) *News, Gender and Power*, Routledge, London 1998, pp24–25.

2.3

'Off-guard, unkempt, unready'? Deconstructing contemporary celebrity in *Heat* magazine
by Su Holmes

A recent report on ITV1's *News at Ten* (13 Sep. 2003, UK) featured the latest developments in the changing marriage plans of stars Jennifer Lopez and Ben Affleck. The 'expert' used to explain the unfolding narrative was a representative from the British celebrity gossip magazine *Heat*. For many, the mere presence of this item, and perhaps the entire concept of a celebrity 'expert', would doubtless speak to contemporary debates about the 'tabloidization' of contemporary television news which, at the level of content, has often been lamented as a prioritization of 'the intimate relationships of celebrities' (or the Royal family) at the expense of 'significant issues and events of international consequence' (Franklin, 1977, p. 4; see also Turner, 1999; Langer, 1998). Yet in terms of understanding the construction of contemporary fame, this article is precisely interested in the fact that *Heat* should appear in a news report, foregrounding as it does the magazine's status as a 'popular' but authoritative cultural perspective on celebrity. Becoming an increasingly familiar sight on contemporary British television, the discourse and 'expertise' of the magazine is now woven into everything from the sitcom (e.g. *Absolutely Fabulous*), the celebrity documentary, television coverage of Reality TV, to general entertainment or magazine programmes. Described elsewhere as 'the bible of contemporary celebrity culture' (Llewellyn-Smith, 2002, p. 114), in 2002 *Heat* was the fastest growing magazine in Europe, with an increasing international circulation. This reach is indicative of the magazine's growing cultural penetration over the last few years, and in this respect *Heat* can be conceived as a particularly productive site for thinking through the construction, circulation and consumption of contemporary celebrity culture.

[. . .]

'The province of the cellulite bottom': *Heat* as celebrity text

Heat magazine was launched in 1999 as an entertainment magazine by EMAP where it was initially conceived as a British version of the US *Entertainment Weekly* (Llewellyn-Smith, 2002, p. 116). With circulation struggling to reach the 50,000 mark, it was not an immediate success. Editor Mark Frith then aimed to re-fashion the direction of *Heat* by shaping it into a 'true celebrity magazine', with an equally clearer address to a female audience. With its articulation as 'gossip', women have traditionally been conceived as the primary market for celebrity magazine coverage, a link which is inextricably related to perceptions of its 'low' cultural value. Celebrity gossip magazines have historically had the lowest cultural status of all women's maga-zine genres (Hermes, 1995, p. 142), and in deliberately making a 'trendy' intervention in the genre by pursuing a younger market, *Heat* can in part be seen as a response to this. While not to suggest that it is aimed exclusively at a female audience, the promotion for the magazine conceives of the primary *Heat* reader as '18–34, urban, up-market and intelligent, a social butterfly who loves pubbing, clubbing and eating out', as well as a 'fashion-conscious shopaholic' (EMAP, 2003) (and the interweaving of celebrity, fashion and consumption sits at the core of the magazine). Frith expands how: 'I have a strong idea of who the readers are . . . and there's a strong part of me that's a twenty-five-year old showbusiness fan from Norwich called Julie' (Llewellyn-Smith, 2002, p. 116). Although tempered by the insistence that this province is still culturally defined as female, there is also a potential nod here, perhaps given the increasing ubiquity of celebrity journalism, to a possible de-gendering of its audience. Either way, key here in terms of the address of *Heat* and *Now* was the 'twenty-something market for celebrity' (Llewellyn-Smith, 2002, p. 116). In rejecting 'exclu-sive' deals to cover celebrity weddings or events concerning minor royals, particularly visible, for example, has been the extent to which such magazines have developed a symbiotic relationship with the celebrity culture of Reality TV, and Frith claims that TV 'is the key to celebrity culture' (Llewellyn-Smith, 2002, p. 116). Yet in negoti-ating a market space, it is also *Heat*'s attitude towards and conception of celebrity which is important here. Frith explains how '*Heat* features stars in the way we want to see them . . . which is not up on a pedestal' (cited in Llewellyn-Smith, 2002, p. 120), while journalist Caspar Llewellyn-Smith argues that the magazine's 'guiding principle . . . was to show [celebrities] . . . off-guard, unkempt, unready, unsanitized. This was the province of the cellulite ·bottom, the rogue nipple' (Llewellyn-Smith, 2002, p. 120).

It is certainly problematic to describe this, as *Heat* seems to do, as a 'new' dis-cursive formation in the construction of celebrity. The descriptions above closely echo conceptions of the shifts in mass celebrity journalism in the postwar period, as defined, for example, by the US *Confidential* and its followers which coincided with the increasing industrial decentralization of Hollywood and the rapid growth of other media forms (such as television) (see Desjardins, 2002). However, while the rhetoric of 'expose', or 'unapproved' pictures is crucial to *Heat* and the subsequent history of celebrity journalism, it would be misleading to draw a closer connection here on other levels. For example, *Confidential*'s cultural impact and circulation was marked by its 'revelation' of scandals which could (and often did) ruin or end a star's career. *Heat*'s province, as the descriptions above suggest, is rather the playing out of how the public visibility of celebrity now saturates the 'everyday'. As the tag-line makes clear, this is the rhetoric of the 'unkempt and unready': the unflattering snap of a celebrity sun-bathing on holiday, eating lunch in a café, or walking home drunk from a night out. This is not least of all, of course, because much of the magazine depends upon the cooperation of the celebrities themselves, and in general terms it is, of course, com-mercially dependent upon, and part of, the production of celebrity as a capitalist enterprise. While *Heat* points to the ever more tenuous line that such magazines walk in balancing both the construction and 'deconstruction' of contemporary celebrity, it nevertheless is clearly also part of the way in which celebrity coverage, as Dyer (1986) argues, operates through a 'rhetoric of authenticity'. We are perpetually encouraged to search the persona for elements of the real and authentic, and while we may be aware of the constructed nature of this framework, 'the whole media construction of stars encourages us to think in terms of "really" ', what is the celebrity 'really' like? (Dyer, 1986, p. 2). However, while this structure is certainly still in place, what has been described as the magazine's 'boisterously democratic' approach (Llewellyn-Smith, 2002, p. 121) towards the famous is worth some thought in relation to *shifting* conceptions of fame.

From unique greatness to sausage maker?: textual trajectories of fame

Gamson's (1994, 2001) work has suggested a picture in which certain positions on, or explanations of, fame have had a historical significance in vying for cultural visibility. In tracing this trajectory, he poses the following question: how did this 'central American discourse migrate from fame as the natural result of irrepressible greatness to celebrity as the fleeting product of a vacuum cleaner/sausage maker?' (Gamson, 2001, p. 259). Although the contours of these narratives must be swiftly drawn here, in its early stages fame was largely limited to figures such as political and religious elites, with discourses constructing it as the province of 'the top layer of a natural hierarchy' (Gamson, 2001, p. 260). Yet with the growth of arts and technologies with a wider range of public access, by the middle of the nineteenth century celebrity was becoming established as a mass phenomenon (see Gamson, 2001, p. 261). Public visibility became increasingly detached from aristocratic standing, with discourses of democracy, as epitomized by the American context, increasingly coming to the fore. This did not, of course, render the concept of 'uniqueness' redundant, but rather constructed a discursive framework which mediated between the concepts of an elitist meritocracy and an 'egalitarian democracy' (Gamson, 2001, p. 261). With the Hollywood studio system representing celebrity's later period of industrialization, and with a controlled production system producing celebrities for a mass audience, the earlier theme of 'greatness' became muted into questions of 'star quality' and 'talent' (Gamson, 2001, p. 264). While the focus may now have been predominantly on the culture of the 'personality', the primary narrative was still one of 'natural' rise (Gamson, 2001, p. 264). However, what is crucial here is that the increasing visibility of the *publicity machine* itself gradually began to pose a threat to this myth. Gamson's argument is that attempts to diffuse this challenge shaped a discursive shift in the construction of celebrity, primarily as articulated by the popular magazine. Coinciding with the increasing de-glamorization (and 'demotion') of the famous in the first half of the century, Gamson suggests that:

> By embracing the notion that celebrity images were artificial products and inviting readers to visit the real self *behind* those images, popular magazines partly defused the notion that celebrity was really derived from *nothing but* images. Celebrity profiling became parked in exposé gear, instructions in the

art of distinguishing truth from artifice . . . The public discovers and makes famous certain people because it (with the help of the magazines) *sees through* the publicity-generated, artificial self to the real, deserving, special self.

(Gamson, 2001, p. 270)

This is crucial in the 'fusion' of what are popularly perceived as opposing explanations of celebrity: its status as an artificial production or a natural, mystifying phenomenon. Shaped by industrial and cultural shifts such as the decline of the Hollywood studio system and the emergence of television, as well as the increasing growth of celebrity journalism, the second half of the twentieth century witnessed the increasing prevalence of the 'manufacture' discourse, where it henceforth becomes what Gamson describes as a 'serious contender' in explaining celebrity (Gamson, 1994, p. 44). This is not to suggest that the older ideological myths of fame are entirely obscured but rather that, perhaps as never before, the two positions *jostle* for visibility in the same space. Indeed, Gamson suggests that by the late twentieth century it was possible to discern strategies intended to cope with the increasing potential for disjuncture here. In particular, he points towards the twin devices of the 'exposure' of the process and the construction of an ironic and mocking perspective on celebrity culture, both of which can be seen to offer the audience a flattering position of power (Gamson, 1994, p. 276). As he explains: 'Through irony, . . . celebrity texts reposition their readers, enlightened about the falseness of celebrity, to "see the joke" and avoid the disruptive notion that there is nothing behind a fabricated, performed image but layers of other fabricated, performed images' (Gamson, 1994, p. 276). This seems precisely the point at which *Heat* should enter the stage door. It is certainly a space in which the textual approach to celebrity is perpetually 'parked in exposé gear' (Gamson, 2001, p. 270). It is undoubtedly a text in which the commercial machinery of celebrity represents *part* of the narrative itself and—duly the province of irony and 'knowingness'—*Heat* describes itself as 'brimming with tongue-in-cheek humour' and as exhibiting a 'trademark irreverent style' (EMAP, 2003). It is within these contexts that *Heat* has managed to forge a highly successful and visible negotiation of contemporary fame which clearly resonates with (while also helping to shape) popular attitudes towards celebrity. The implications of this in the context of theoretical and historical conceptions of celebrity are discussed below.

'Being in public': searching for 'the self'

Emerging from a wealth of images, articles and columns, as well as the readers' letters page,[1] a key strain running throughout the magazine is an emphasis on what we can call the *visibility of celebrities in public spaces*. 'The Week in Pictures' devotes the most editorial space to this, and is comprised of approximately 10–12 pages of large photographs (with minimal explanatory text) of celebrities in various forms 'being in public' which is subject to detailed public scrutiny (King, 2003, p. 53). These can be images snapped at press conferences or premieres, but are just as often organized around television, music or film celebrities in more 'mundane', 'everyday' contexts, whether loading up the car at a shopping centre, exiting a DIY store, or walking with their children or dogs in a park. These contexts, in particular, are all represented through the rhetoric of candid photography, the blurred focus and grainy aesthetic of which trades not only on an aesthetic of realism but also the belief in 'the higher truth of the stolen image' (Sekula, 1984, p. 29, cited in Becker, 1992, p. 142). In terms of celebrity, this promises to manifest more of the 'inner being' when compared to the calculated pose, stance or expression (Sekula, 1984, p. 29). As their titles immediately suggest, shorter sections such as 'Scandal!', 'Look closer' and '100% unapproved: stars making *utter* fools of themselves', are based upon the 'capturing' of the celebrity through a more explicitly unflattering lens. This may simply be an unforgiving facial expression, pose or situation ('Martine McCutcheon's mini-skirt flies up!') (29 Nov.– 5 Dec. 2003, p. 72), or images displaying everything from a protruding stomach ('Spillage'!—well if Britney will insist on squeezing into an outfit the size of a couple of flannels') (13–19 Dec. 2003, p. 71), to spots ('Yoga and a fiddly fat-free diet may have given Geri Halliwell a buff little body, but no amount of exercise can stop the unwelcome arrival of a celebrity spot') (15–21 Jun. 2002, p. 28). The regular column 'Spotted: they can't get away from us', although including selected images, is based predominantly upon the *verbal* disclosure of celebrity sightings. These are printed in a continuous bullet-point form with minimal explication: 'A glamorous Susan Sarandon spending a fortune . . . in Portobello Rd, . . . Chris Martin and Gwenyth Paltrow ambling arm in arm up Rosslyn Hill in Hampstead, *Big Brother*'s Jade Goody and boyfriend Jeff Brazier eating like animals at Cafe pasta . . .' (22–28 Nov. 2003, p. 74). Here, it is the *recollection* of the *moment* of public visibility which is enough to be reported in its own right, regardless of the presence or absence of any evidential 'proof'.

The coverage organized around the visibility/presence of celebrities in public spaces is clearly saturated with the rhetoric of exposé, particularly in terms of penetrating the celebrity image by catching them 'off-guard'. At a theoretical level, this textual representation of celebrity, and the entire question of 'authenticity', has been understood as having a much broader cultural and ideological significance which centres on ideas of the *self*. As indicated in the introduction, in terms of his bid to ask questions about the social and ideological function of stars, a crucial element of Dyer's work was to explore how stars articulated ideas about personhood. Working from a broadly Marxist perspective which exemplified the then prominence of an Althusserian conception of ideology (in which its crucial function was to make individuals misperceive themselves as autonomous subjects) (see Lovell, 2003), Dyer argued that 'stars articulate what it is to be human in society: that is, they express the particular notion that we hold of the "individual" ' (Dyer, 1986, p. 8). Supporting the notion of individualism upon which capitalist society depends, Dyer suggested that the continual insistence on 'authenticity' in the star image, the perpetual attempt to lay claim to the 'real self', was organized around a desire to suggest a 'separable, coherent quality, located "inside" consciousness and variously termed "the self", "the soul", "the subject" . . .' (Dyer, 1986, p. 9). While Dyer appears to take a broad historical sweep here, such discourses on the elevation of an 'inner' or 'core' self can also be linked to elements of a pre-modern discourse on identity with its emphasis on a greater degree of fixity which is then subject to the uncertainties of modernity and postmodernity (see Kellner, 1992). However, post-structuralist and postmodern strands of thought have undermined and critiqued the very concept of identity and clearly made a 'depth' model of the self unfashionable, while broader theoretical shifts questioned the concept of ideological uniformity and coherence in media texts. Barry King's argument, for example, can be seen as an implicit challenge to Dyer's when he draws attention to the changed 'existential parameters of stardom . . . Today's stars . . . epitomise the postmodern self, a decentered subject, deeply reflexive and disdainful of claims to identity' (King, 2003, p. 45). In what is part of a larger questioning of Dyer's emphasis on the relationship between stardom and ideological resolution, Alan Lovell has recently challenged the very origins of his model by arguing that 'stars are improbable candidates for carrying out the ideological task [Dyer] assigned to them' (Lovell, 2003, p. 261). He argues that their notorious 'capriciousness' and superficiality represent the very antithesis of the concept of a unified, stable identity. 'In the popular imagination', Lovell suggests, 'stars are the polar opposite of the solid bourgeois citizen . . .' (Lovell, 2003, p. 261). However, Dyer seemed to acknowledge this when he suggested that:

> It is one of the ironies of the whole star phenomenon that all these assertions of the reality of the inner-self . . . take place in one of the aspects of modern life that is most associated with the invasion and destruction of the inner self and the corruptibility of public life, namely the mass media.
>
> (Dyer, 1986, p. 15)

In fact, in revisiting Dyer's argument here it seems important to emphasize his view that it was *because* of the apparatus of mediation, manipulation and 'hype' that stars could operate as a site for the working through of discourses on the construction of identity. For example, if we were to apply the questions we ask of celebrities to the broader context of human identity, they explore 'useful' issues surrounding selfhood—is there a distinction between our 'private' and 'public' selves? Do we have any 'unique' essential, 'inner' self; are we simply a site of self-performance and public presentation? In this respect, Dyer pointed not only to the shoring up of the concept of the individual but also the ways in which stars work through its anxieties, articulating both the promise and the *difficulties* of its status. Furthermore, any argument regarding a 'new configuration in the existential parameters of stardom' (King, 2003, p. 45) is also crucially in part a question about *reception*—the reading strategies used to approach and consume the celebrity text which clearly cannot (as the Althusserian models of ideology implied) be read off from the text alone. How we would pinpoint the shift that King outlines remains unexplained here. At least on a *textual* level, it is difficult to dispute the fact that *Heat* is organized primarily around a bid to negotiate authenticity in the celebrity self. As such, while its irreverent and cynical attitude towards celebrity may appear antithetical to such an earnest project, arguably it can still be accommodated within the concept of pursuing an 'inner core self' and hence, in Dyer's terms, working through discourses (and anxieties) surrounding individualism. While this does not necessarily determine how they are received, the illusion of access and 'intimacy' clearly remains the dominant structuring force in celebrity texts. This constitutes a beckoning which, on some level at least, continues to arouse audience interest.

'The media saga started on . . .': negotiating the publicity machine

Nevertheless, in qualifying what appears to be 'new' about *Heat*, it is certainly the case, as Gamson suggests, that the commercial machinery which surrounds fame has become part of the celebrity text itself. Given the continual quest for 'authenticity' in celebrity coverage, this is a discourse which requires careful negotiation. Many of the stories in *Heat* are as much about the media's wider construction of a celebrity 'event' as they are about the celebrity themselves. In reporting how 'Posh and Becks are putting their marriage back together', an article explains the narrative in terms of its wider mediation: 'The gossip machine gathered speed as . . .', 'Most reports by this time suggested that . . .' (11–17 Oct. 2003, p. 4). Similarly, the question: 'Is Britney dating a married man?' is worked through via a recounted relay of its media construction: 'This was the point at which Britney found it hitting the headlines . . .', 'The media saga started on . . .' (11–17 Oct. 2003, p. 13). But not only does the commercial machinery of celebrity form part of the narrative itself but there is also a persistent acknowledgement of how the presence of the media often actively *precipitates* an 'event': 'When a pop star with a new single to promote is photographed on a night out, the cynics among us may suggest that it's nothing but a cheap publicity stunt . . .' (15–21 Jun. 2002, p. 27). The notion that the media effectively define and hence bring *into being* a celebrity status is partly suggested by the fact that one of the generic questions in the regular interview feature 'My showbiz life' is to ask celebrities when they were last photographed ('When was the last time you were papped?'). In fact, the commercial nature of fame is often paraded in the magazine, with the concept of the celebrity-as-commodity a discourse in many interviews. Questions such as 'are you really rich now?', 'Are you a millionaire yet?', 'Were you desperate to be famous?' are routine in this respect, particularly in terms of celebrities who have experienced a rapid rise to fame, or an accelerated shift in class mobility. In a feature focusing on the makeover 'transformation' of contestant Jade Goody from *Big Brother 3* (British Reality TV's first millionaire)[2] we are told:

> Besides brushing shoulders with celebs, Jade's also been splurging in posh store Harrods and checking out flights for a trip to New York on the proceeds of the media deal she's made since leaving the house. With this fabulous acquisition of money for nothing, this brings us nicely to our first question: 'Do you even realize how much you're worth now?'
>
> (17–23 Aug. 2002, p. 65)

Given *Heat*'s conventional bid to negotiate 'authenticity' in the celebrity text, this increasing acknowledgement of the commercial machinery which constructs and perpetuates celebrity culture is necessarily carefully worked through in the magazine. Hence, celebrities who threaten to disrupt this logic are thus duly criticized for threatening the illusion of 'access' on which this negotiation of authenticity is based. In the 'Psst: you've got mail' section, *Heat* prints a fantasy e-mail to a celebrity they with to criticize. Jennifer Ellison, former *Brookside* actress turned pop star, is chastised on one occasion in ironic tone: 'How we enjoyed these "not at all posed for" "paparazzi" shots of you washing your car wearing typical car-washing clothes highly suitable for the job . . . Don't insult us girl!' (25–31 Oct. 2003, p. 60). The logic here may be that if *Heat*, and by implication, the reader, can distinguish 'truth' from 'artifice' where the visual evidence of celebrity is concerned, then its negotiation of authenticity remains intact. It is also worth emphasizing here that, despite the expressions of anger and distress which are sometimes evident on the faces of those 'genuinely' photographed for the candid sections, the magazine works to absent itself from the concept of media intrusion. (Articles in which celebrities discuss 'nuisance photographers' or 'intrusive paparazzi' are reported by *Heat* with the objectivity and autonomy of a bystander.) By the same logic, regular features such as 'Spotted! They can't get away from us!' may in part indicate a potential lack of complicity between pursuer and pursued (in so far as the title indicates the concept of a chase), the exclamation marks and inclusive address suggests more of a jovial familiarity, downplaying the more sinister connotations of what is effectively a regime of visibility made possible by surveillance. Conversely, while the magazine may well incorporate an acute awareness of the role and power of the 'publicity machine', in part it copes with this by seeking to set itself apart from any of its less desirable associations—such as falsity or manipulation. A highly typical example of this is offered by an article on the alleged breakdown of the marriage between Kym Marsh, ex-band member from the first UK reality-pop group Here'say, and Jack Ryder, former *Eastenders* star. With the conventional intertextual claim to set 'straight' other media reports (Dyer, 1986), we are told 'Kym Marsh has opened up to *Heat* . . . of course, the papers made up their own version' (25–31 Oct. 2003, p. 37). This would appear to be paradigmatic of Gamson's suggestion that, as the claim to go 'behind' the 'public' image has increased, such celebrity texts necessarily 'acknowledge that a gap between image and reality exists, but [they] deny that bridging it is a problem' (Gamson, 2001, p. 272). At the same time, *Heat* is still validating the authenticity of its coverage in a highly traditional way. Through the conventional rhetoric of exclusivity, *Heat*, of course, lays claim to 'the real' Kym Marsh (and so the cycle of searching for the 'authentic' self continues) (see Ellis, 1992).

Ordinary/extraordinary: the paradox of celebrity

Heat's pursuit of authenticity also extends to what I have argued is its appetite to reveal the 'ordinary' person 'behind' the famous self. While, as suggested below, this is clearly not new in itself, this textual strategy does appear to have witnessed a more aggressive acceleration in celebrity journalism. As with the ubiquity of the manufacture discourse, in part this poses a threat to the economic basis of the celebrity system. After all, if celebrities are so much like the rest of us, then why are so they set apart—so elevated and admired? (Gamson, 2001, p. 266). Of course, this may be less of a problem than a pleasure in that the 'exposure' of the 'ordinary' self appears to pivot on the delight in 'penetrating' the usual celebrity façade, and thus closing the potential gap between 'them' and 'us'. This in turn immediately indicates the continued presence of the 'ordinary/extraordinary paradox' which Dyer (1979) and Ellis (1992) suggested was so fundamental to the textual construction of stardom. This is thus an important discursive concept to revisit here.

While some critics have used this paradox to refer to a broad cultural fascination with stardom ('extraordinary, because the star will of course be unique . . . but ordinary, in that the star must be someone with whom the spectator can identify') (Clarke, 1987, p. 141), others use it to refer to a more specific relationship between on-and-off-screen lives, and the discursive construction of this through intertextual circulation. This may foreground, for example, the combination of 'some special talent or position' with an emphasis on ordinary hobbies and feelings (Ellis, 1992, p. 95), or a contrast between their 'glamorous' lifestyle yet 'the surprisingly ordinary domestic life of the star' (Geraghty, 2000, p. 184). In the period of Classical Hollywood cinema, however, this was primarily the product of a tightly controlled system where the off-screen construction of the stars was as much a creation of the studios as the on-screen image. Following the decentralization of the authorship of celebrity texts, and the central role played by the photographic image in celebrity journalism, contemporary magazine constructions, with their emphasis on spots, sweat patches or unkempt hair, are arguably evidence, as suggested, of a *more* brazen attempt to 'expose' the 'ordinary' self at a *visual* level. However, in terms of the tempering of this threat it is crucial, not least of all in terms of the economics of celebrity, that such items continue to co-exist in *Heat* with coverage which constructs celebrities as fabulous models of glamour and aspiration. Regular items such as 'Star style' and 'Steal her style' insist on celebrities as icons for the female reader to emulate. Although equally jostling for space with the 'democracy' of fashion critiques (e.g. 'What were they thinking?', 'The best and the worst dressed'), in the other contexts above, the celebrities of course look truly stunning and gorgeous, mystifyingly more so than 'we' *ever* could. As a result, this duality may arguably leave unresolved the long-standing question or paradox: is there something 'naturally' special or beautiful about celebrities, or is it simply their access to a particular kind of wealth and lifestyle which distinguishes them?

Furthermore, aside from the magazine's visual juxtaposition of the 'unkempt' and 'unready' self with the perfection of the glamorous image, the ordinary/extraordinary paradox continues to be articulated discursively in columns and interviews. One of the most interesting and recurrent ways in which the magazine constructs this paradox is through articles expressing approving attitudes towards celebrities who appear to be fundamentally *unchanged* by wealth and fame. For example, Hollywood film star Cameron Diaz is described as 'the hottest blonde in Hollywood, adored by everyone, because she seems every bit as funny and down to earth as she is beautiful' (11–17 Oct. 2003, p. 79) while, in an extended interview, British TV presenter Cat Deeley is perceived as lacking the airs and graces which can characterize 'normal celebrity behaviour. But then, you kind of get the feeling [that] Cat hasn't succumbed to the delusions of celebrity grandeur . . . despite the fact that . . . she is one of television's hottest young presenters' (20–26 Jul. 2002, p. 76). This discourse is particularly apparent in the construction of celebrities from Reality TV, where the basis of the celebrity as 'ordinary person' clearly has a particular currency. In an interview with Brian Dowling, winner of the second UK *Big Brother*, the magazine comments how: 'In just over 12 months he may have gone from Ryanair steward to bona fide celebrity, but he's still the same warm, irreverent and bitchy character who won *Big Brother* last summer' (21–27 Sep. 2003, p. 76). When asked if he had any advice for Kate Lawler, winner of the third series of the programme, Brian explains how: 'I just told her to be herself and not to change', to which *Heat* replied approvingly, 'wise words indeed' (ibid.). Similarly, in an interview with Cameron Stout, winner of the fourth UK *Big Brother*, the magazine commented how:

> He certainly doesn't look like the £70,000 winner of Britain's biggest Reality TV show. But that's exactly what made viewers vote for him to win BB4. Cameron's down-to-earth attitude, friendly manner and—dare we say it—ordinariness were, for many, his most appealing qualities . . .
>
> (9–15 Aug. 2003, p. 4)

As Anita Biressi and Heather Nunn have argued, Reality TV stardom is often structured within discourses of class, and its subjects become iconic through their 'newly found social mobility' (Biressi & Nunn, 2004, p. 44). As they note, this is certainly anticipated by a longer history of class rise where narratives of fame are concerned, but it has arguably come to the fore more explicitly in Reality TV. In the examples above, it seems that discourses of class rise remain somewhat submerged beneath a deliberately abstract and evasive articulation of 'ordinariness'. As Dyer explained, one of the ways in which the ordinary/extraordinary paradox can be understood is that stars can be seen as ordinary people 'who live more expensively than the rest of us but are not essentially transformed by this' (Dyer, 1979, p. 49). These are people who are perceived as bearing 'witness to the continuousness of their own selves' and, returning us to the ideology of the self, the appearance of sincerity and authenticity are two qualities which have historically been 'greatly prized' in stars (Dyer, 1979, p. 11). Indeed, a star who (as part of their persona) is valued for 'being themselves' can be seen as both endorsing the notion of the individual, while simultaneously registering the doubts and anxieties which surround it (Dyer, 1986, p. 10). In fact, in ideological terms, part of the approval the magazine expresses towards Reality TV stars may precisely circle around its implicit suggestion that we have already 'known' them as 'ordinary' people, making their 'celebrity' self somehow more sincere, trustworthy and 'closer' to the 'real' them. (Equally, as Jo Littler notes, in our celebrity-saturated culture, it has increasingly been constructed as 'ordinary' to want to be a celebrity (2004, p. 12)—a discourse which Reality TV stars perpetuate.) Concurrently, celebrities who represent the antithesis to the examples above, either by revelling in the excesses of conspicuous consumption or by exhibiting 'diva-like' behaviour, are often duly chastised in the magazine. The widely circulated narratives about Jennifer Lopez's celebrity entourage provide evidence of this, and a more specific instance, decidedly ridiculed by *Heat*, is a report on her insistence that her company 'ditch 25,000 bottles of her new perfume when the scent wasn't quite right' (20–26 Jul. 2002, p. 41). Such examples are seen as representing the undesirable nature of the superficial (shallow) self, so defined by the 'trappings' of wealth and fame as to render the question of an 'inner' or 'ordinary' self problematic.

The examples above *do* suggest some kind of desire for a stable, coherent celebrity self, based largely on a reassuring sense of ordinariness, and a coincidence of 'private' and 'public' personae. In many ways this is paradigmatic of the ordinary/extraordinary paradox, but at the same time, with the increasing acceleration of the 'manufacture' discourse and attack on the concept of 'talent', just what now constitutes the 'extraordinary' part of the equation is rather ambiguous. While this has *always* been necessarily elusive as part of the ideological and commercial construction of celebrity, whether there is any space for a sense of 'uniqueness' or 'special talent' (Ellis, 1992, p. 95) in *Heat*'s highly contradictory and irreverent approach to celebrity is complex. In the case of Cameron Diaz, 'ordinariness' is perhaps counterposed to what is represented as her natural beauty, while in the case of Cat Deeley and Brian Dowling there is at best the suggestion that they display sufficient skills to succeed as generic entertainers. All that appears to make Cameron Stout 'special' (as well as, of course, 'ordinary') seems to be that his 'natural' 'personality' was appealing enough to enable him to win *Big Brother*. For many of its critics, this would doubtless exemplify the ways in which Reality TV has epitomized the regrettable 'democratization' of fame and with it the further divorcing of the concepts of 'talent' or 'hard work' from a somehow more deserving kind of visibility. However, as I have suggested elsewhere (Holmes, 2004a, b), this is a rather simplistic conception of the relations between Reality TV and contemporary celebrity and, perhaps more significantly, it ignores the differences between particular programmes or subgenres in this respect. In fact, it is around particular elements of the relationship between Reality TV and celebrity that *Heat* seems most confident about articulating the 'extraordinary' distinction of the celebrity self—when this elsewhere appears to be less sure.

[. . .]

As a pervasive and significant site in the production and consumption of contemporary celebrity culture, an analysis of *Heat* suggests a number of implications for the analysis of fame. Firstly, despite the increasingly apocalyptic and generalized conceptions of contemporary celebrity as the province of 'famous for being famous', one of the most illuminating aspects of the magazine is the evidence that discourses on fame continue to negotiate significant contradictions. In fact, *Heat* provides exemplary evidence of the ways in which celebrity continues to explore the tensions between the two claims-to-fame stories (Gamson, 2001, p. 277). In many ways the magazine may well *embrace* the decline of more traditional myths surrounding fame where questions of merit, 'talent' or 'work' are concerned, revelling in the superficiality of a world based on performance, manufacture and 'hype'. However, its highly irreverent and ironic approach at times jostles for space with an avowedly sincere approach to the politics of fame, where traditional myths are re-peddled for contemporary popular consumption. Intrinsic to these contradictions are the long-standing tensions between the concepts of the democratic and the aristocratic (Gamson, 2001, p. 277). As Gamson enquires, do the producers of celebrity 'push in anti-democratic directions by building mystifying myths of meritocratic fame' (ibid.) or—in the increasing decline of such narratives—is there an expanding space for their deconstruction, and hence a greater possibility for democratic participation? To a degree, *Heat* confirms the presence of both possibilities. If there is arguably less emphasis on a sense of talented, 'special' self (and certainly 'extraordinariness' seems more ambiguous than ever), then perhaps this *is* potentially more democratic in terms of the gatekeeping mythology of public visibility. However, more recent innovations such as the Reality pop programmes suggest a bid to reinvigorate 'mystifying myths' of celebrity, certainly on the part of celebrity producers, but also perhaps in terms of a culture ill at ease with the decline of meritocratic ideologies of fame.

Secondly, in considering *Heat* as a site for revisiting approaches to, and conceptions of, contemporary celebrity, a key aim here was to bring these historical discourses to bear on staple aspects of star theory—particularly notions of the self. On a broad level, it is certainly true that the negotiation of authenticity sits at the very core of *Heat*, continuing to exemplify Dyer's argument about how fame works through discourses of selfhood and identity. If (despite the above) this seems in fact more fervent than ever, then the quest to glimpse the 'real' celebrity self—to 'gain access to some essential knowledge' about their being (Turner *et al.*, 2000, p. 12)—is not dependent on the belief that this 'inner' self is indeed truly special or extraordinary. Certainly, *Heat* seems to acknowledge that 'authenticity' needs more careful negotiation than ever, although its primary ethos here seems to be that with so much artifice around, we just need to sharpen the tools we use to 'see through' it. Although the search for authenticity in the celebrity self must be a quest without resolution (both at a textual level and in terms of the commercial logic of celebrity itself), it is perhaps no surprise that, while constantly doing battle with the discourse of manufacture, its presence continues to hold sway. After all, if celebrity *does* work through discourses surrounding individualism, the possibility that reality and artifice are indistinguishable threatens our own sense of self (Gamson, 2001, p. 276). It may well be that the magazine's use of irreverence and irony works in part to negotiate these tensions. It acknowledges the discourses of fabrication and falsity but, in suggesting that 'we' all know that celebrity culture is not to be taken seriously, it evades or obscures the difficult question as to why it is nevertheless so fetishized, debated and admired. At the same time, it is crucial to note that, while it may offer readers the chance to flatter their knowledge of celebrity construction and even register their disapproval at its perpetuation of inequalities, the magazine's ironic distance from celebrity culture offers an example of a discourse which is channelled straight back into feeding it—reselling fame for contemporary popular consumption (Littler, 2004, p. 22). In this way, *Heat* speaks to a number of discursive shifts in the negotiation of contemporary fame, while there is much that remains traditional in its construction of celebrity. On a broader level, it suggests the need to continually revisit explicit core aspects of star theory within the contexts of its historical circulation.

However, the ways in which the representations of authenticity in celebrity texts are actually negotiated is a question of reception, which cannot be answered here. Even the most cursory survey of the letters page in *Heat* is indicative of a variety of possible reading positions, ranging from those who invest in the 'real' self of the celebrity, those who reveal in and applaud the apparently superficial nature of the celebrity performance, to those who do not see a distinction between fact and fiction as meaningful and who, as Gamson has argued, 'don't need to believe or disbelieve the hype, just enjoy it' (2001, p. 273).

Notes

[. . .]

1   My discursive analysis here is based on a sample of 30 *Heat* magazines from the period 2001–2003.

2   A 21-year-old dental nurse from South London, Jade was initially the subject of vehement ridicule by the British press which, as Biressi and Nunn note,

exemplified the ways in which her rise to celebrity was entrenched within discourses of class. Her apparent intellectual ignorance, voice and overweight body were 'marked negatively as working class' (Biressi & Nunn, 2004, p. 50). While disapproval for this upward mobility is exemplified by criticisms of Jade's celebrity, *Heat* here displays no such concerns about the decline of older myths of fame ('talent', 'hard work'). As discussed below, however, this is not always the magazine's attitude.

2.4

And postmodern justice for all: the tabloidization of O. J. Simpson
by Kevin Glynn

[. . .]

African American [O.J.] Simpson, a former football hero, movie actor, and media pitchman, was tried for (and, in 1995, acquitted of) the brutal 1994 stabbing deaths of his ex-wife Nicole and a male friend of hers, Ronald Goldman, both of whom were white. Opinion polls consistently demonstrated a wide gap between U.S. whites, a clear majority of whom accepted the state's "truth" and thus believed firmly in Simpson's guilt, and African Americans, a clear majority of whom *didn't*. As Simpson's trial progressed, this gap grew ever wider. Consequently, Americans argued over the possibility that O.J. was yet another target of a racist police force and a criminal justice system that seems hell-bent on putting as many African American men as it can behind bars. They argued over the validity of scientific evidence that purported to demonstrate with near certainty that O.J.'s blood was present at the crime scene along with that of the murder victims. Such claims as those, rooted in the supposedly "objective" findings of DNA scientists, push whites' emotional buttons by stimulating the widespread white fear of blacks that has been well documented and, at a more implicit ideological level, by tapping into white anxieties about the inter-mingling of racially different blood. Indeed, one is forced to wonder whether the murders and the investigation and trial of O.J. Simpson would have spawned anything like the kind of high-visibility media event that they did were it not for the racial identities of the victims (and especially of Nicole). Because the white majority in the United States has proven both its intense fear of black men and its relative lack of concern for the fate of black women, we can surmise that had Simpson been accused of murdering, say, his first wife (an African American), the accusation would prob-ably not have provoked the most sustained media event of the decade.[1] This is not, however, to say that this tabloid media event was sustained only by white interest in it, for as we shall see, the case came to have great significance for many African Americans who saw it as a test of the capacity of the *criminal justice system* (a punning phrase that means very differently for blacks and whites) to produce fair outcomes not just for Simpson but for black men in general. For if even a rich and famous black man could not get fair treatment before the law, then what could possibly be done for those struggling with the police and courts under more ordinary circumstances?

The media event provoked by the murders gave rise in turn to a sustained moral panic over media tabloidization,[2] and the outcome of the trial itself engendered a conspicuously racialized and middle-class backlash that was aptly characterized by Alexander Cockburn as "white rage."[3] The line between the moral panic and the backlash is difficult to discern. I would argue that both were fundamentally expressions of anxiety about the troubling multiplicity of perspectives on U.S. society that the Simpson case brought to the fore. Quite tellingly, supermarket tabloids such as the *Globe* and the *Star* were among the most-visible media sites where these perspectives could be readily glimpsed in all their troubling multiplicity. In particular, these publications are notable for the play they gave to explanations of the murders that contradicted the one offered by the LAPD, the criminal prosecutor's office, and a large proportion of the Euro-American population.[4] In this way, the Simpson incident gave rise to tabloid media circulation of a variety of popular counterknowledges and counternarratives that are typically relegated to the margins of, or excluded altogether from, the mainstream press, which is generally much less open to socially delegitimized perspectives than is the tabloid press. This is not to deny the presence of reactionary and racist knowledges in tabloid journalism – clearly they are rife there (as they are throughout U.S. society). In particular, the tabloids were not shy about circulating images and stories depicting the gory murders and detailing the history of O.J.'s propensity to violence in his relationship with Nicole (a reportorial choice that exposes domestic violence, albeit sometimes fetishistically, while reinforcing racial stereotypes, about which I shall have more to say). However, at the same time, many tabloid stories explained the murders and their investigation in ways that implicated the LAPD, the California criminal justice system, and *white* assailants rather than a black man. Such stories clearly went against the grain of the dominant white-power-bearing perspectives on the event. The Simpson case is thus aptly illustrative of the way in which the multivocality and contradictoriness of tabloid journalism often results in a collision between dominant knowledges and a variety of popular counterdiscourses.

The terms "discourse" and "knowledge" deserve some attention here.[5] In my usage, discourse comprises both language and knowledge as they are socially practiced in particular situations. Discourse always carries both the accents and interests – political and material – of its users. It is inevitably power bearing, as it necessarily advances the sociopolitical standing of some discursive communities over and against others. Thus discourse establishes relations of power and control as it determines the ways in which events, objects, and people are inserted into systems of social sense making. The insertion of events and objects into socially established (but contested) ways of making sense of them necessarily entails choosing between the different discourses available to the sense-making agent, for events and objects "in themselves" are incapable of determining which discourses will be brought to bear on (and therefore produce and circulate a sense of) them. The choice between competing discourses is therefore one that *always* has an irreducible political dimension and thus is governed finally by the social interests that benefit from the advancement of this or that way of making sense and not by the "truth" or "nature" of the event or object subjected to this process of sense making.

Discourses operate socially by activating particular systems of knowledge, a word

I use to designate one or another coherent way of knowing. This use pluralizes the concept of knowledge and therefore rejects the meanings of the term as it is used within philosophies derived from the Enlightenment. There are many different knowledges in the world. My use of the word "knowledge" thus differs from that of the sciences, which reserve the term to describe things known on the basis of a supposedly accumulative body of "facts" purported to be demonstrably and absolutely "true." The sciences use the concept of knowledge monopolistically to exclude systems of belief that diverge epistemologically from the broad contours of scientific rationalism.[6] From the poststructuralist perspective I adopt here, by contrast, all conceptual systems produce knowledges, which are applied through socially materialized discourses and inevitably apply social power in the process of their materialization. Discourse is thus a product of the relationship between a knowledge and the social circumstances of its particular applications. Different discourses often activate different knowledges and thus produce different "truths," though they do not do so under conditions of equality. Some knowledges are more socially powerful than others, and their social power entails both the power to assert that their own "truths" are "better" than others, and the power to marginalize and repress the "truths" produced by competing knowledges.

Tabloid journalism often proliferates popular knowledges considered woefully inadequate and even disruptive of the solemn responsibilities of the "fourth estate." It often playfully and sometimes earnestly circulates counterdiscourses that question the adequacy of official ones and therefore destabilize officialdom's capacity to produce socially powerful "truths." Perhaps the most socially effective of these official modes of knowledge is scientific rationalism, which has developed a variety of sophisticated strategies for representing its epistemological assumptions and methodological protocols, if not all instances of their application, as if they were beyond question. Tabloid knowledges often express an ambivalent and conflicted incredulity toward scientific rationalism and its power to produce authoritative truths. The flip side of the tabloids' contradictory popular skepticism toward scientific rationalism is the space they create for the investment of belief in alternative ways of knowing. Both this popular skepticism and its corollary production of spaces for belief in alternative knowledges constitute one of a series of focal points for the articulation of both moral panic and backlash.

A useful example of tabloid incredulity toward official knowledges comes from a *Star* story headlined "O.J. Trial Bombshell: I've Found Murder Weapon, Psychic Tells D.A. – and Simpson Didn't Do It." This story undercuts the white majority's "truth" of O.J.'s guilt by invoking a form of knowledge that is as socially marginalized as the black minority's "truth" that proclaims Simpson was framed for the murders. It describes how a well-known psychic named John Monti came to conclude that a gang of three, one woman and two men, rather than O.J. Simpson actually committed the murders. Monti, the story tells us, is famous for solving a well-known New York kidnapping case and for predicting the attempt to assassinate Ronald Reagan in 1981. As well as to the *Star*, Monti has given his elaborately detailed (and seemingly quite plausible) account of the murders (which is based on a "psychic vision" he had "as he stood in the dried blood of the two victims") on Sally Jessy Raphael's eponymous tabloid TV talk show. Lead prosecutor Marcia Clark, however, will (not surprisingly) have nothing to do with Monti. In the view delineated by the tabloid, Clark is so narrowly and rigidly devoted to DNA science that she refuses even to take Monti's phone calls. Monti, for his part, explains that he "doesn't care" about O.J. Simpson, who was, in Monti's words, "a bad husband who beat his wife, but that doesn't mean he should be tried for two murders that he didn't commit."[7] What interests me about Monti's chronicle of the murders is its inclusion in the tabloids (where such stories are typical), its circulation of a "truth" that contests the received (and politically powerful) wisdom, and its role in both reproducing and helping to sustain a form of knowledge that persists as a socially living alternative to the dominant one. Rather than simply excluding the psychic's narrative a priori, the tabloid, unlike the mainstream media, presents the story alongside the knowledge of scientific rationalism, explicitly depicts the antagonistic relationship between the two, and demonstrates their unequal social power to determine which explanations typically come to be treated as true ones.

[. . .]

The *Globe* and the *Star* were two key print media sites for the circulation of popular discourses concerning the O.J. Simpson affair. While both tabloids presented stories that, as noted, "implicated" O.J. in a variety of (often implicit) ways – sometimes, for example, focusing almost obsessively and with disturbing racial undertones on his violent rage and purportedly voracious sexual appetites – they also did something the mainstream press did not: they took popular counterknowledges around the case *very* seriously. In doing so, they both exploited and exemplified aspects of the postmodern condition discussed in the previous sections of this chapter. In particular, the tabloids' rapid weekly succession of alternative constructions of "the truth" of O.J.'s "guilt" or "innocence" – [. . .] gives their readers an object lesson in postmodern truth making and so gives the lie to claims that either journalistic or judicial truths are discovered rather than produced. The tabloids maximally exploited the ultimate unknowability of exactly what happened on the night of the murders by enacting a profusion of plausible alternative scenarios that collectively demonstrate that in such cases the truth *must be produced* rather than merely "discovered." Their coverage of the Simpson affair thus deserves careful examination here.

A key discursive strategy mobilized by the tabloids is that involving processes of articulation, a concept associated with both the work of Stuart Hall and that of more postmodern theorists such as Gilles Deleuze and Félix Guattari.[8] Hall explains that the concept of articulation exploits the dual meaning associated with the word in British English. There, the term denotes both "language-ing" or "expressing" *and* the construction of a contingent and breakable linkage, as in an "articulated lorry," a truck whose "front (cab) and back (trailer) can, but need not necessarily, be connected to one another."[9] Articulation thus expresses the idea of meanings that come into being through a contingent conjunction of different signifying elements. The process of articulation creates an expressive unity that derives from the specific combination of meaningful elements that are linked to one another in a particular discourse. It complicates older theories of ideology, therefore, by contesting the idea that ideologies are either organically whole or necessarily attached to specific social locations. On the contrary, the theory of articulation proposes that both the elements of an ideological discourse and its connection to particular social formations and political interests can always be broken (disarticulated) and reformed (rearticulated) in a variety of ways.[10]

What I'd like to suggest here, is that in a postmodern culture where boundaries between "reality" and "representation" are ever more fluid and, in social practice, increasingly irrelevant, the field of potential articulations and rearticulations undergoes something of an expansion of possibilities and intensities. In their coverage of the O.J. Simpson affair, the *Globe* and the *Star* can be seen as both symptoms and agents of this expansive process. For example, by eliding the differences between "fictional" characters and "real" people, the tabloids were able to articulate bits of both together in ways that expressed different explanations of the murders and their investigation. Thus tabloid stories about star prosecution witness Mark Fuhrman discredit his key role in the investigation of Simpson as well as his devastating courtroom testimony by exploiting the uncertain difference between the "real" cop and the corruptly racist "fictional" police officer character he was helping a Hollywood scriptwriter to create.[11] By the same token, however, another tabloid story deploys seven-year-old movie stills of Simpson *in character* to implicate the actor. The photographs are from a fiction film in which O.J. plays a character who, "in a blind rage," uses "frightening commando knives" to conduct a "bloody one-man war." According to the *Globe*, Simpson "played the part so convincingly" that "he terrified the set photographer." The report moves fluidly between production information about the movie and forensic evidence from the murder scene.[12] Of course, forms of cultural production that combine the "real" and the "fictional" are hardly anything new (an observation that does not render the concept of the postmodern "silly," as some pomophobes would have it). What I call "postmodern" about the current moment is the expanding volume, availability, and promiscuity of images, the growing permeability of boundaries that accompanies this expansion, and the increasing indifference to, and uncertainty regarding, the integrity of epistemological categories that is a symptom of both processes. The concept of postmodernism helps me to name the encroaching qualitative shift in cultural processes that is linked to a quantitative expansion of representational diversity and fragmentation.[13]

Each week, the *Globe* and the *Star* recombined diverse elements of the Simpson story in a way that did not so much produce the emergence of enduring or long-term ideological formations; rather, their ongoing rearticulations of story elements showed the instability or unfixity of both "truths" and signifying practices under postmodern conditions. The tabloids thus expertly demonstrated for their readers that "the truth" of O.J.'s guilt or innocence is a function of the way in which particular evidentiary and narrative elements are articulated to one another and so made to speak. Having said this, though, it is crucial to point out that their stories often spoke to popular suspicions toward the LAPD in particular and contemporary policing practices in general – suspicions that are deeply rooted in the material and social experiences of people of color in the United States. This should warn us against pushing the theory of articulation to the point that it reaches in *some* postmodern thought, where "there is no reason why anything is or isn't potentially articulatable with anything" else.[14] To say that the rapid reconfiguration of "the truth" by weekly supermarket tabloids covering the Simpson affair is expressive of postmodern signification is not, therefore, to say that there are no discernible patterns to either the knowledges they circulate or the social conditions of which they make sense. Because supermarket tabloids target excluded social formations as their primary market, they must therefore mobilize excluded perspectives, many of which are typically granted little if any visibility in the main-stream press. This does not mean that the tabloids give play to all socially marginal-ized knowledges, for they clearly do not. Their profit motive does, however, push them to include whatever stories their producers think are likely to resonate with readers who have little interest in the mainstream perspectives of the conventional press.[15]

This interest in reaching socially marginalized target markets through appeals to certain forms of excluded perspectives and knowledges is made manifest in some of the predominant styles and tones of voice that are characteristic of the tabloids' cover-age of the Simpson affair. For example, the *Globe* and the *Star* appeal often to feelings of alienation and exclusion from the circulation of information. Promises to reveal that which is known and done by the socially powerful – that which takes place behind the scenes, as it were – have a potentially immense resonance with readers who are routinely denied access to information by dint of the very structure of power relations and therefore of communication flows in an unequal society. Consequently the tab-loids' reports are often framed in terms of the revelation of various forms of insider information. Indeed, along with the recurrent motif depicting a tragic vision of the California couple (*each* was shown to be obsessive and capable of extreme manipula-tion of the other, despite the immense bonds of love and devotion that endured between them), this commitment to the liberation of insider information is arguably as close as the *Globe* and *Star* come to the construction of a stable viewpoint that persists over the course of their coverage of the Simpson affair.[16]

This viewpoint takes different forms, however. For example, it supports the for-mer football hero in the *Star*'s April 4, 1995, story that ran under the headline "O.J. Couldn't Have Done It." This report articulates a mountain of evidence into a coher-ent case for the claim that the murders were a consequence of mistaken identity, for the real target of the killers was Nicole Brown Simpson's friend and confidante Faye Resnick. Having made a commitment to its case against O.J., however, the *Star* reports that the "D.A.'s office is now scrambling to try to nail him," despite its awareness of a growing accumulation of evidence that undermines their case – evi-dence that had been kept from the public but is revealed here by the tabloid.[17] Such stories speak to popular suspicions directed toward the greedily vindictive manipulations of the legal system undertaken by its highest prosecutorial officers.

Inside angles on the Simpson case cut in another direction, however, in *Star*'s report on "O.J.'s Life of Luxury behind Bars." This story and others like it speak to class-based resentment of the "special privileges" enjoyed by "America's most pampered prisoner," including better meals and more privacy than others receive in jail, entry to private showers and libraries, and unlimited access to communication technologies such as TVS, VCRS, and private telephone lines, which ordinary inmates are denied.[18] Hence, the tabloids' impulses toward the revelation of secret inside angles drifts in *favor* of O.J. Simpson when he is cast as a target of institutional power and *against* him when he is shown to benefit from the privileges bestowed on the wealthy by powerful institutions to the detriment of weaker others. For in their renderings of such stories as these, the tabloids typically express sympathies for the underdogs and the disempowered, whomever they might be in the particular situation at hand.

To take a final example along these lines, Simpson and the LAPD are both cast into the same kettle of rotten fish in an insider's exposé of "O.J.'s Sex and Drug Parties for L.A. Cops." In an interview with the *Star*, a former West Los Angeles Division officer provides a detailed account of the "guys' nights out" frequently attended by him and other policemen, "some of them very high-ranking," at Simpson's Brentwood mansion during the 1980s, where the cops were "treated like kings." The story suggests that the cozy relationship that consequently developed between police operatives and O.J. helped to facilitate the situation that prevailed throughout his relationship with Nicole, during which officers received at least *eight* "911" emergency calls from the latter and yet arrested her partner for spousal battery only *once*. This report thus provides a behind-the-scenes look at the Brentwood boys' club whose decadent and hypocritical ethos contributed immensely to the suffering of Nicole Brown Simpson throughout her marriage to the Juice.[19] This is underlined by the retired officer's revealing descriptions of the ways in which women were objectified at O.J.'s parties. These descriptions resonate tellingly, though not through any intention on the interviewee's part, with the tabloid's points about cops who repeatedly looked the other way when confronted with violent domestic abuse at the Simpson home:

> O.J. said when he was playing with the Buffalo Bills he'd had most of their cheerleaders.
>
> He told me, "They're all gorgeous and great in the sack. I'll get some over to one of my parties – and you're invited."
>
> And sure enough, I turned up for one party at the Rockingham mansion and there were about 20 women there. All gorgeous and sexily dressed.
>
> There were about the same number of guys. Some other ballplayers I didn't recognize, a few Hollywood types, a couple of other cops and two guys who said they were lawyers, but didn't tell me their names.
>
> O.J. was a perfect host. He told me, "Come on in and E-N-J-O-Y." Then he slapped me on the shoulder and said, "Take your pick. Whichever one you want is yours."
>
> I was dazzled by one long-legged brunette who told me she was a dancer. And she certainly looked it. I stuck close to her. There was plenty of booze and coke. It was a status symbol in those days for a host to have cocaine so readily available for party guests.
>
> It was a rich man's plaything and O.J. loved to play.

In this way, the *Star* provides a revelatory glimpse into attitudes toward women shared by both O.J. and members of the LAPD that helps to clarify for readers how violent abuse might have developed within the Simpsons' relationship and been ignored or dismissed by officers like the one quoted. Furthermore, this informant's tales of drug-dealing and drug-doing cops, of going "back on duty with two or three shots of O.J.'s liquor in me," and of Simpson's links with high-ranking police department officials all speak to popular skepticism toward the institutional forces that exert so much control over our lives yet are incapable of controlling their own corruption and hypocrisy – and toward the excesses and privileges of the rich and powerful in general. The story's final sentence, another quote from the former cop, emphasizes its strategy of reader engagement through the revelation of the kinds of insider information that public agencies normally prefer to repress and conceal: "I'm sure my former colleagues will try to discredit me. But I'm telling the absolute truth about O.J. I'd be happy to repeat what I told STAR to police internal investigators – under oath."[20]

The tabloids therefore constantly promise to deliver repressed information to those who resent being kept in the dark about what goes on behind the walls that conceal the activities of the powerful and the privileged. Their desire to expose any inside angles they can generates a kind of fluidly mobile suspicion whose objects and targets may shift radically from story to story and week to week. This leads to a multiplication and dispersion of both perspectives and their political implications. In some reports, it is the corrupt bureaucracies of law enforcement and the criminal justice system whose misdeeds and incompetencies have led to the mishandling of evidence or the formulation of a conspiracy to frame an innocent man that must now be made public. In others, it is the hidden details of Simpson's violently abusive and obsessively jealous attempts to control Nicole that constitute the secret to be unveiled. In some reports, it is the representatives of foreign drug cartels who are indicted for their ruthless terrorization of O.J. and shown to be responsible for the murders of Nicole and Goldman. In still others, it is Nicole who is exposed as an irresponsible and flirtatious "sex addict" who cruelly taunted and manipulated O.J. for years. In all such instances, the tabloids target for interrogation some force that they associate with power exerted unjustly, be it the official power of the state and its agencies, the illegal muscle of drug kingpins, the naked masculine violence and controlling aggression of O.J., or the sexually aggressive and manipulative "feminine wiles" of Nicole.

The glaring instability of their constructions of the "truth" of the matter therefore opens the tabloids' coverage of the Simpson affair to a plurality of alternative explanations that is striking in its contrast with mainstream (read: white) reactions to the murders. The tabloids were unremitting in their willingness to entertain seriously a whole variety of popular counterknowledges that work, through their skepticism toward the official view, to erode the heavily racialized grooves into which most mainstream thought and coverage of the case had been slotted.[21] Their stories therefore often attacked the LAPD and the prosecutor's case by proffering hidden facts to those who are continually denied access to the truth about what the established institutions and their agents are up to. This appeal was frequently enhanced with claims that the insider information being delivered by the tabloids may never even be heard by the Simpson trial jury because of one or another conspiracy or legal technicality that threatens to corrupt the pursuit of the truth in the courtroom. These tabloid reports on the Simpson case often work through a process of postmodern articulation that fuses together diverse elements – crime scene pictures, police reports, diary entries, data from official personnel files, testimony from psychics, scientific test results, letters from tabloid readers, movie stills, personal or publicity photos of the Simpsons, and a host of other types of evidence – without discriminating between them according to modernist epistemological categories and hierarchies of credibility. It is in this way that the tabloids produced and disseminated popular counternarratives through the assemblage of eclectic arrays of signifying fragments.

The August 2, 1994, edition of the *Globe* provides a useful print media example of the tabloidization of the O.J. Simpson case through the articulation of diverse

Tabloidtruth.

source elements to produce a unified counternarrative. Inch-high bright-yellow block letters on its front cover promise the story of "How Cops Framed O.J." Alongside these words are pictures of the famous bloody glove, the white Ford Bronco, and Simpson's (undarkened) police mug shot, taken the night of his arrest for the murders of Nicole and Goldman.[22] Above this headline appears a picture of a stiletto knife and a promise to reveal "new clues" concerning "lies and planted evidence." Beneath the headline is an offer of a million-dollar reward. Inside, we learn that the reward will go to the reader who can provide the tabloid with information leading to "the arrest and conviction of the real killer or killers."[23] In connection with this contest, the newspaper's cover announces the publication of "dramatic new evidence from *Globe* readers" on the matter of "who really killed Nicole."[24]

Pages 36 and 37 of the tabloid feature a close-up of Detective Mark Fuhrman under large block letters proclaiming that a "Cop Framed O.J.," and smaller bright-yellow ones stating that the " 'troubled' detective once said he wanted to kill his own wife!"[25] The low-angle half-page picture of Fuhrman is set perfectly adjacent to an equally large blowup of the bloody glove as it lay at the back of Simpson's home; the detective is using a wooden pointer to gesture toward something outside the frame of the photograph. The pointer is cut in half by the shared border between the picture of Fuhrman and that of the glove. The page layout allows the two photos to blend into one that appears to depict an action that both the text of the story and the towering headline looming over this composite image invite us to imagine: it is the "overeager" cop as he leans over to plant the key piece of evidence against Simpson. This composite image thus disarticulates the bloody glove from its associations with O.J. and quite literally rearticulates it to Fuhrman. Moreover, the image not only *illustrates* the accusatory headline to which it is articulated here but also fills the headline with meaning beyond that which it carries semantically and thus makes it "real."

The accompanying story recounts in detail the checkered history of the " 'rogue' cop" Fuhrman and his suspicious role in the investigation of the Goldman and Simpson murders. It draws heavily on Fuhrman's psychiatric evaluations, which are articulated with carefully selected quotes from Simpson's legal defense team, from police documents, and from Fuhrman himself, to depict the veteran LAPD officer as a dangerously violent racist who, as one police personnel report had it, spent "the greater portion of time . . . trying to make the 'big arrest.' "[26] The detective's career is shown to be haunted by "a long history of problems on the job," including violent attacks on people of color and the use of excessive physical force to subdue crime suspects. These points serve not only to discredit Fuhrman but also to enhance popular skepticism toward the LAPD's knowledge of the Simpson case by metonymically articulating that case to the ignominious recent history of the department and

The Globe: planting suspicion.

particularly to the beating of Rodney King. All of this then bolsters the story's claims that Fuhrman, who was (according to "insiders") "furious at being replaced by more senior investigators" at the crime scene, decided to frame O.J. by planting the glove whose subsequent "discovery" would make him the hero of the investigation. The tabloid notes, furthermore, that beyond "the dubious circumstances surrounding Fuhrman's case-building discovery," both incompetence and corruption in the Los Angeles coroner's office may cast further doubt on the evidence against Simpson.[27]

This story of an elaborate frame-up is then articulated to alternative explanations of the murder taken from letters sent to the *Globe* by its readers and placed in a sidebar alongside the Fuhrman report. The Fuhrman exposé and the popular counterexplanations thus work together to undermine both the LAPD's account of the murder and the well-worn cultural narratives concerning the threat of miscegenation and of the black male body that has escaped (white) control that lie just beneath the surface of that account. This is not to say that reactionary racial politics do not enter into the tabloid discourse on the Simpson case. For example, some readers' theories about the murder merely displace the racial threat from African Americans to Latin America. Thus Neil Vinetz writes to the editors of the *Globe* that "the *savage* brutality used to kill Nicole Brown Simpson and Ronald Lyle Goldman has all the earmarks of a Colombian drug cartel assassination." Vinetz explains that O.J. and Nicole were cocaine addicts who had become deeply indebted to Latino drug dealers whose patience ran out. Because the former football star brazenly ignored persistent demands for payment of perhaps as much as $2 million, the dealers "decided to kill Nicole and frame O.J. for the murders."[28] Another *Globe* informant adds that O.J. was forced by drug dealers to witness the execution of his wife and her friend. "He was bound and taken to the murder scene by drug-connected Colombians, who were upset because of his involvement in a drug deal gone bad." Thus, "only after both victims were repeatedly stabbed and slashed to death was O.J. taken from the scene and warned that the same would happen to him and his children if he ever revealed what he had seen."[29] Variations on these accounts of the Colombian connection to the Simpson and Goldman murders enjoyed widespread popular circulation in the wake of the police investigation and the Simpson trial.[30]

[. . .]

Notes

1 E. R. Shipp reports that this view was widespread throughout the black media. See "O.J. and the Black Media," *Columbia Journalism Review* (November–December 1994): 40.

2 See, e.g., Neal Gabler, "O.J.: The News as Miniseries," *TV Guide*, 30 July 1994, 12–17; "Don't Mean Diddly," *New Yorker*, 11 July 1994, 4, 6; Frank Rich, "Another Media Morning After," *New York Times*, 30 June 1994, A23; Frank Rich, "Judge Ito's All-Star Vaudeville," *New York Times*, 2 October 1994, sec. 4, p. 17; Walter Goodman, "The Summer's Top Crime Drama, Continued," *New York Times*, 4 July 1994, sec. 1, p. 40; Jon Katz, "In Praise of O.J. Overkill," *New York*, 25 July 1994, 12–13.

3 Alexander Cockburn, "White Rage: The Press and the Verdict," *Nation*, 30 October 1995, 491.

4 Examples abound. In addition to the ones I discuss in the text, these include "Who-dunit?" *Star*, 26 July 1994, 5, 27; "The Picture That Could Free O.J.," *Star*, 18 April 1995, 5; "Drug Gang Killed Nicole," *Globe*, 21 March 1995, 1; Bob Michals, "OJ: Autopsy Shocker: How New Evidence Could Rip Lid off Simpson Case," *Globe*, 14 March 1995, 24–25. Suspicion toward the alternative accounts of events circulating in tabloids was sometimes expressed as bewilderment in the face of a widespread popular, and particularly African American, refusal to accept Simpson's guilt. One commentator writes that "serious people, unwilling to accept what on the face of it seemed to be the facts, offered theories, even to strangers in checkout lines." See John Gregory Dunne, "The Simpsons," *New York Review*, 22 September 1994, 36. Here the invocation of checkout lines (where tabloid newspapers are most commonly found) is tellingly symptomatic of the imaginary proximity of disreputable popular knowledges and the most disreputable branches of the popular press. Another account, this one produced after Simpson's acquittal, tellingly targets "an unreasonable suspicion of law enforcement authorities" harbored by "a paranoid, conspiracy-minded sector of the population that would honestly though irrationally have rejected the state's argument virtually without regard to the evidence." See Randall Kennedy, "After the Cheers," *New Republic*, 23 October 1995, 14.

5 The ensuing discussion of these terms, in this paragraph and the next, is heavily indebted to John Fiske, *Power Plays, Power Works* (London: Verso, 1993), esp. 14–15; and Fiske, *Media Matters*, 3–6, both of which are paraphrased in places here.

6 Fiske, *Power Plays*, 14.

7 Martin Gould, "O.J. Trial Bombshell: I've Found Murder Weapon, Psychic Tells D.A. – and Simpson Didn't Do It," *Star*, 22 November 1994, 6–7.

8 Lawrence Grossberg, ed., "On Postmodernism and Articulation: An Interview with Stuart Hall," in David Morley and Kuan-Hsing Chen, eds., *Stuart Hall: Critical Dialogues in Cultural Studies* (London: Routledge, 1996), 131–50; Gilles Deleuze and Félix Guattari, *A Thousand Plateaus: Capitalism and Schizophrenia*, trans. Brian Massumi (Minneapolis: University of Minnesota Press, 1987).

9 Grossberg, "On Postmodernism and Articulation," 141.

10 Hall gives as an example the Jamaican Rastafarians' disarticulation and rearticulation of elements of Christian religion (generally a reactionary social force) with those of contemporary music culture and social rebellion, and thus the creative production of both a new expressive and ideological formation and a new social movement. As Hall explains, "they did not go back and try to recover some absolutely pure 'folk culture,' untouched by history, as if that would be the only way they could learn to speak. No, they made use of the modern media to broadcast their message. 'Don't tell us about tom-toms in the forest. We want to use the new means of articulation and production to make a new music, with a new message.' This is cultural transformation. It is not something totally new. It is not something which has a straight, unbroken line of continuity from the past. It is transformation through a reorganization of the elements of a cultural practice,

elements which do not in themselves have any necessary political connotations. It is not the individual elements of a discourse that have political or ideological connotations, it is the ways those elements are organized together in a new discursive formation" (Grossberg, "On Postmodernism and Articulation," 143).

11   "The Fuhrman Tapes Uncensored," *Star*, 5 September 1995, 36–37, 39; Ken Harrell, "Fuhrman Race Tapes Shocker," *Globe*, 1 August 1995, 5. Interestingly, in terms of the concerns of this chapter, both the incriminating evidence on Fuhrman and the uncertainty regarding its "reality" or "fictionality" stem from a series of interviews he gave in his capacity as a "consultant on a reality-based movie project about L.A. cops" (Harrell, "Fuhrman Race Tapes Shocker," 5).

12   Ken Harrell and Bob Michals, "O.J. Shocker: Killer Used Two Knives," *Globe*, 21 February 1995, 24–25, 41. Something similar occurs in a story about a 1989 Paramount pictures promotional film starring O.J. Simpson and Leslie Nielsen. In the promo short, Simpson repeatedly tries to stab Nielsen with a large knife. The *Globe* places stills from the film alongside a photo-recreation of the LAPD's scenario of the Simpson and Goldman murders; the placement of the photos creates a seamlessly fluid movement between O.J.'s fictitious character and the tabloid's grisly re-creation. See "The Mad Slasher!" *Globe*, 27 June 1995, 10–11.

13   To those who can only imagine the "postmodern" and its associated concepts in the most grandiose and epochal terms, and who are therefore dismissive of attempts to make use of those concepts, John Fiske offers a helpful formulation: "The postmodern promiscuity of images swamps any attempt to control them; it overwhelms any neat distinction between representation and reality, between fact and fiction. It refuses to allow 'truth' a place in reality alone, for it cannot see that reality still has its own place for truth to make a home in. An image-saturated culture differs from a culture of controlled and organized representations not just in degree, but in kind. And this, postmodernism tells us, is what characterizes its world as generically different from the modern. But we don't live in a completely postmodern world, we live in a world where the modern and the postmodern (and the premodern) coexist uneasily" (Fiske, *Media Matters*, 62). By the same token, we might note the existence of very old cultural forms that prefigure the postmodern.

14   Grossberg, "On Postmodernism and Articulation," 146. Hall makes this criticism of Ernesto Laclau and Chantal Mouffe, *Hegemony and Socialist Strategy: Towards a Radical Democratic Politics*, trans. Winston Moore and Paul Cammack (London: Verso, 1985).

15   S. Elizabeth Bird conducted an ethnographic study of supermarket tabloid readers and concludes that "the tabloids clearly offer millions of Americans something they do not find in other media." In 1992 the Star had a circulation of 3,562,367. Because tabloid buyers typically share the papers with family and friends, however, estimates suggest that each issue was read by approximately 11,756,000 people. During that same year, the circulation for the *Globe*, before sharing, was around 1.6 million. Bird notes that the "combined weekly circulation" of the United States' six national supermarket tabloids "hovers around ten million," although their actual readership is "estimated at fifty million." See *For*

Enquiring Minds: A Cultural Study of Supermarket Tabloids (Knoxville: University of Tennessee Press, 1992), 7, 35, 37.

16 For a sense of the instability of tabloid perspectives on the Simpson case, consider the difference between the *Globe*'s front covers for July 5, 1994, and October 17, 1995. The former, which appeared not long after Simpson's arrest, features large block letters that read "O.J. Was Framed!" The latter, which appeared not long after Simpson's acquittal, features similar block letters that promise to show "How OJ Got Away with Murder!" These extreme examples, though published more than a year apart, nevertheless demonstrate a pattern of oscillation that was evident from week to week and even within the same tabloid issue. They also suggest that the tabloids' anti-officialdom is stronger than their belief in either the guilt or innocence of Simpson: here, the *Globe* is on his side when the cops are holding him prisoner, and against him when the courts declare his innocence.

17 "O.J. Couldn't Have Done It," *Star*, 4 April 1995, 5. Similar examples include "Hunt for Nicole's Mystery Lover," *Star*, 14 March 1995, 24–25; "Stunning Evidence That Jury Won't Be Told: What O.J.'s Little Girl Heard on Night of Murders," *Star*, 25 July 1995, 29, 44. The latter reveals "fascinating clues that investigators seemed to ignore in their rush to arrest O.J. – instead of searching for any other suspects" (29). Further examples include Paul Francis, "Two Madmen Killed O.J.'s Wife & Her Pal," *Globe*, 26 July 1994, 36–37, 44; Ken Harrell, "3 Surprise Witnesses Will Set O.J. Free," *Globe*, 11 October 1994, 17; Paul Francis, "Nicole Was the Victim of Deadly Thugs Out to Kill Faye Resnick," *Globe*, 28 March 1995, 24–25, 41.

18 Tony Frost, "O.J.'s Life of Luxury behind Bars," *Star*, 11 July 1995, 6. Similar examples include "Mother's Love," *Star*, 11 October 1994, 2–3; "O.J. Invites Family to Jail for Holiday Get-Together," *Star*, 10 January 1995, 10.

19 "The Juice" is a nickname from O.J.'s days of football stardom and is based on the initials by which he is best known.

20 Tony Frost, "O.J. Gave Sex and Drug Parties for L.A. Cops," *Star*, 6 September 1994, 36–37, 39.

21 This is not to deny that many of the tabloids' stories slotted neatly into those very same racialized narrative grooves but rather to suggest that unlike mainstream media coverage of the case, the tabloids also produced a profusion of stories that went against the racial grain of the serious press and of mainstream white belief in the idea that O.J. commited the murders.

22 My parenthetic mention that the *Globe*'s representation of O.J.'s police mug shot was undarkened is a reference to the infamously darkened image of the mug shot used on the cover of *Time* magazine subsequent to Simpson's arrest. The famous bloody glove was the main piece of evidence linking Simpson with the murders. Prosecutors claimed that it was discovered behind Simpson's house by detective Mark Fuhrman. The defense claimed that Fuhrman planted it there. Its twin was found at the murder scene. The defense's claims were bolstered when in a moment of high courtroom and media drama, Simpson tried to put the glove on his hand but couldn't because it was too small.

23 "Who Really Killed Nicole: Dramatic New Evidence from Globe Readers: $1 Million Reward," *Globe*, 2 August 1994, 44.

24 Ibid., 1.

25 Mike Kerrigan, "Cop Framed O.J.," *Globe*, 2 August 1994, 36–37.

26 LAPD report, quoted in Kerrigan, "Cop Framed O.J.," 37.

27 Kerrigan, "Cop Framed O.J.," 37, 44. The coroner's incompetence is noted often by the tabloids. For example, *Globe* notes that the entire prosecution case may crumble under the weight of fully *sixteen* mistakes made by the coroner's office; see Lo-Mae Lai, "16 Mistakes That Could Set Him Free," *Globe*, 9 August 1994, 36–37. In another issue, the paper reports similarly on ten clues missed by the LAPD; "*Globe* Finds 10 Key Clues Cops Missed," *Globe*, 20 September 1994, 5.

28 Neil Vinetz, quoted in "Who Really Killed Nicole," 44; italics mine.

29 Anonymous informant, quoted in "Who Really Killed Nicole," 44.

30 Reports that Colombians committed the murders also played extensively in the tabloids. See, for example, Bob Michals, "O.J., Drugs, the Mob – & Murder!" *Globe*, 19 July 1994, 36–37, 40; Tony Frost, "How O.J. Trapped Nicole into Life of Cocaine," *Star*, 30 August 1994, 24–25, 29.

SECTION 5
Gender and sexuality

In this section we have selected research on tabloid newspapers, men's magazines and stunt TV. These focus on gendered, sexualized content and deliberate on the different ways in which such tabloid content addresses the 'liberal' reader or viewer. Whilst these chapters focus on different media outputs, they share an interrogation of tabloid culture's address to the imagined consumer through sexualized imagery of fun. They all raise important questions about tabloid media from the late 1970s offering a popular intersection between public and private life. They illustrate the role of humour, fun and irony as elements of a tabloid discourse that contests the serious journalistic values of detachment and objectivity through a playful deployment of sexualized content that often refuses conventional notions of taste, decorum and seriousness (Glynn, 2000: 7). Furthermore, they intersect with much work on popular media undertaken by feminist analysis over the previous thee decades, once again foregrounding the relevance of underlining the relationship between media texts and the broader construction of masculinities and femininities.

Two of the most influential areas of research into the representation of gendered and sexual identities in popular media culture have been that of feminist media and cultural studies. Discussions of tabloid media representations of gendered and sexual identities have inevitably circled around their place within broader cultural notions of power and politics. Early focus on the textual representation of gender drew on semiotics, psychoanalysis and Marxist theory. This led to research into the ideologies of texts within cultural context; the importance of audience address and audience pleasures; the politics of taste and the political, cultural and economic determinants of the production, circulation and consumption of gendered and/or sexual representations in popular culture. Work on the media address to consumers of girl's, women's and then men's magazines importantly interrogated the popular magazine as a cultural space in which different forms of gender could be defined, explored, challenged and idealized. Similarly, work on the gendered role of stereotypical representations on screen in the formative years of feminist TV analysis opened out to an exploration of progressive TV texts in the 1980s and then to analysis of the diverse niche audiences addressed by the multi-channel TV environment of the late twentieth to early twenty-first century.

One of the central ways in which gender has been discussed more generally in relation to tabloid culture has been through debates about the 'feminization' of journalism and factual TV formats; a move associated with the trend towards more personal, human-interest focused, informal styles of content and coverage. Van Zoonen identifies the pronounced emergence of 'feminine' and 'masculine' styles (adopted by either female or male media producers) with traditional, fact-based, serious media coverage defined as masculine and consumer-orientated, human-interest, sensationalist or celebrity/lifestyle focused coverage deemed feminine (Van Zoonen, 1998: 45).

The gendering of news across a hard/soft division is addressed by Patricia Holland in her chapter, 'The politics of the smile: "Soft news" and the sexualisation of the popular press' where she interrogates the transformation of the *Sun* newspaper in Britain after its purchase and relaunch by Rupert Murdoch in 1969. This change was in tune with the populist permissive discourses of the time and the paper addressed its readers through a legitimating discourse of pleasure and an abandonment of prior notions of class and social deference. She argues that following the *Sun*'s example, the popular tabloids became increasingly sexualized with the depiction of the page 3 female pinup in the *Sun* swiftly mimicked by other British tabloid newspapers; their inclusion of a range of improper, highly sexualized material in news stories and editorial columns copied by other newspapers from the 1970s. She locates this sexualization of news within a media culture wherein there was a fusion of news and entertainment in the popular press. This fusion, seen by some as a loosening of older notions of sobriety and cultural deference, has been defended by journalists and cultural advocates as a sign of the democratization of the news and an expansion of the terms in which we can understand the content and address of the mediatized public sphere. This turn to the sexual, the personal and the intimate has been characterized as a feminization of news. Holland contends that these sexualized representations contain, and in fact negate, any such positive potential expansion of the public sphere as they reiterate long-established constructions of the female body as a depoliticized site of pleasure and enjoyment.

Distrust and scepticism about sexual pleasure and sexualized imagery has frequently informed debates about the role of the popular media in the expansion of the public sphere. It is often claimed that the citizen's democratic right to information and education has been depleted by the impetus of the market and the commercialized pressures of a deregulated media environment. The turn to more explicit mainstream sexual imagery is seen as one element of a broader cultural emphasis on the personal, the emotional and identity within a revelatory and narcissistic confessional culture.

Patricia Holland's work is frequently informed by second-wave feminist politics. There have been heated debates since the 1980s about the relevance of this feminism to contemporary women and of the role of feminism within popular culture (Hollows, 2000; Whelehan, 2000). The rearticulation of feminist ideas as postfeminist is one outcome of some younger women's alienation from the language and objectives of their feminist predecessors. Some critics suggest that the clash between old and new forms of feminism can be read alongside generational clashes about the relevance of social democratic politics within the context of a broader triumph of the discourses of neoliberalism which have powerfully argued that the diverse tastes and interests of individual consumers are best catered for by the market. Furthermore, the emergence of 'cultural intermediaries' employed in media-related jobs have brought about a sea change in notions of tasteful representations. This new section of the aspirant middle classes sought to establish their cultural credibility by defining themselves against the 'old-fashioned' notions of lower middle-class respectability, instead adopting 'an ethic of fun' to signal their contemporary liberation (Jancovich, 2001: 6; Arthurs, 2004: 44–8). This new class formation is responsible for the expansion of 'lifestyle' journalism and TV programming including the range of more sexually explicit genres on TV and in print (Jancovich, 2001: 7; Arthurs, 2004: 45–6). McRobbie situates these trends within a broader cultural moment in which popular culture sells a younger generation of women and men new forms of identity centred on hedonism, consumption and provocative sexualized behaviour (McRobbie, 1997). She indicates how a particular form of post-feminism has become equated with the celebration of raucous sexual behaviour, and a market-led adherence to consumerism and style. Analysis of the pronounced shift to 'soft' news and consumer/lifestyle stories in TV and print journalism in the 1990s, tended to produce a list of features now characteristic of contemporary popular media output: openness, irony, playful incoherence and self-reflexivity (Chambers et al., 2004: 217). These characteristics inform voyeuristic, frequently sexualized media content aimed often (but not exclusively) at the youth or twenty-something markets that covered 'new' forms of male and female identity founded on pleasure, fun-seeking individuals who refused adult responsibility with a knowing ironic take on gender conventions (Tincknell et al., 2003).

In the case of journalism, women's magazines selectively seized the postfeminist discourse of materialism and consumerism that came to the fore in the late 1980s onwards and infused this with knowing references to the therapeutic language of emotions and personal crises. As Chambers, Steiner and Fleming argue, postfeminist journalism is exemplified by the rise of two 'girl' types in the 1990s: the 'ladette' (a female version of the 'bloke' or 'lad') preoccupied with seeking thrills, a laugh and sexual encounters and the self-absorbed, thirty-something 'singleton' captured in the popular TV series, Sex in the City (Chambers et al., 2004: 217; Arthurs, 2004: 130–44). They suggest that the 'singleton' appeared in 'girl columns' such as Candice Bushnell's New York Observer columns, whose central heroine is a journalist with Bushnell's initials; a character (like that of Carrie Bradshaw in Sex in the City) pre-occupied with sexual conquests and designer shoes. This style of writing – captured in Helen Fielding's Bridget Jones's Diary published in the Independent and the Daily Telegraph – emphasizes female zaniness, lack of any social or political reflexivity and defines gender through the lens of self-interested scheming over work, friendship and primarily heterosexual relationships. Feature journalist Zoe Heller argues that these girl columns 'all tended to an extreme perhaps ill-advised candour – regularly divulging details of marital breakdowns, sexual peccadilloes, depressive episodes, family rows and disgusting habits' (Heller, 1999: 10–11). Chambers, Steiner and Fleming argue that this new style of 'girl writing' of the 1990s and 2000s has inspired and endorsed a media iconography of new femininity (implicitly antifeminist) 'in which it is now permissible to expose one's own and other women's personal insecurities and vulgar habits, sexual conquests and defeats, and abuses of substances and people' (Chambers et al., 2004: 217). Importantly, in relation to Holland's critique of the Sun, they foreground humour as a key strategy in making this type of journalism entertaining and join other critics who question this trend as 'regressive'. Emotional self-indulgence, confession, the exploration of sexual taboos and respectability are the subject of a self-absorbed journalism that illustrates the slippery boundaries now between tabloid and broadsheet newspapers and magazines with the latter filling its weekend supplements with a plethora of personal stories of everyday trauma, shopping and sexual success or marital failure. Critics consider this turn in journalism as the ever-increasing questionable publication of 'the bizarre and the prurient' (Christmas in Chambers et al., 2004: 219).

Feminist critics have discussed the purported 'feminization' of media with reference to its 'intimization', turn to human interest and the personal with a certain ambivalence noting that it has produced almost contradictory results (Van Zoonen, 1991: 217; Macdonald, 1998; Arthurs, 2004). Whilst this turn has been acknowledged as a corrective to historically founded ideals of the rational public sphere as a masculine space (Fraser, 1992) and for some critics represents a 'democratisation of desire' (McNair, 2002) the supposedly emancipated gendered sexual identities on display in tabloid formats such as reality TV, 'lad's mags' or talk shows raise questions about the ethics of exposing intimate lives to public scrutiny. It seems that any political potential for these new playful sexualized identities is nullified in the core emphasis on individual dilemmas and pleasures devoid of any discussion of social or political or cultural context.

Good taste is a concept that is central here. Some critics have argued that tabloid culture eradicates old class-bound distinctions of high and low culture. Sexualized media content, for example, could be viewed as counterhegemonic in its refusal of class-defined notions of propriety and transgressiveness, acceptable and unacceptable symbolic representations of the body. Brian McNair (2002) in *Striptease Culture: Sex, Media and the Democratisation of Desire* proposed that modern distinctions of taste and propriety no longer hold sway in postmodern consumer culture. Anxieties about 'tabloidization' are, for McNair, an expression of a disgust that has dominated British and American media throughout the twentieth century. He suggests that an important aspect of the newly sexualized media is the space it offers to women as consumers of liberal sexual lifestyles.

One way in which liberal unfettered sexual lifestyles have been imagined in popular tabloid culture is via nostalgia for the recent past. Hunt argues that the early 1990s saw a media recirculation of 1970s popular culture which 'became a reference point for a kind of unfettered straight masculinity' defined against the widespread image of the feminized 'New Man' of the 1980s (Hunt, 1998: 7). In the early 1990s, a new type of roguish heterosexual masculinity appeared in the media: the 'New Lad'. The New Lad, a consumer category, was 'middle class (or trad-rock *nouveau riche* like Oasis), but in love with working-class masculinity and irresponsible hedonism' (Hunt, 1998: 7). The 'New Lad' included pop stars (Blur), TV comedians (Baddiel and Skinner's *Fantasy Football League*), the writing of Nick Hornby and the lad's magazine epitomized by *Loaded*, the most successful men's magazine of the early 1990s (Hunt, 1998: 7; Heller, 1999: 11). *Loaded*'s success spawned a raft of lad's mags including *Maxim, FHM* and *Nuts*. Kate Brooks' chapter in this collection, 'Loaded with meaning; men's magazines and the appropriation of tabloid talk', interrogates this marketable form of masculinity. She locates this media-mobilized masculinity within the context of cultural narratives of the 'New Man', naughtiness and nostalgia, which, she suggests, are framed by two overarching discourses: 'masculinity in crisis' and the carnivalesque. The language of naughtiness and fun (Hunt, 1998: 8) mobilized by Loaded segues with tabloid uses of the carnivalesque. Brooks argues that one way to understand the hedonistic, shameless masculinity on display in these magazines is as a carnivalesque reappropriation of the 1970s as a reaction to authoritative middle class feminism. However, 'New Laddism' ultimately became the object of media parody itself.

The same cultural context subtends Jason Kosovski's analysis of mediated masculinity in 'Performing masculinity: reflexive-sadomasochism in MTV's Jackass'. As with the other two chapters in this section, Kosovski highlights the importance of the series' celebration of fun through the male performance of pranks and stunts on screen. Jackass, targets the male youth market and shares with the men's magazines of the 1990s, a barely implicit juvenile masculine rebellion against the perceived political correctness of feminism and other representations of adult authority. Kosovski is most interested in the male performance of sadomasochistic abuse that takes place in the programmes in which young men beat, cut, and penetrate their bodies with objects for the camera and each other. He sees this performance as an attempted restoration of patriarchal masculinity. These men expose to the public what is usually kept private: nudity, public urination/defecation, body piercing etc.

Writers such as Laura Kipnis have analysed the transgressive potential of low popular cultural forms such as the men's porn magazine Hustler. She has argued that, from its inception, Hustler, attempted to 'disturb and unsettle its readers, both psychosexually and socio-sexually' by interrogating men's magazine codes and conventions of sexual representation and displaying the body in all its unromanticized corporeality: 'It's a body, not a surface or a suntan: insistently material, defiantly vulgar, corporeal' (Kipnis, 2005: 225). She reads Hustler as violation of not only bourgeois mores but of men's magazine conventions of sexuality (p. 226). If Jackass is a challenge to the prudish mores of mainstream culture, then, perhaps we need to locate such programming, alongside the humorous tabloid treatment of sex as fun identified by Holland and the laddish posturing of Loaded magazine. As these chapters illustrate, all three occur within a media market in which there is a marked increase in the volume and diversity of sexualized imagery in recent years. It could be argued that such 'permissive populism' has challenged hide-bound notions of taste and cultural deference but, as these writers indicate, they have also often reinforced notions of the division between men and women that had been challenged in previous decades.

Further reading

Arthurs, J. (2004) Television and Sexuality, Maidenhead: Open University Press/McGraw-Hill Education.

Gamson, J. (1998) Freaks Talk Back: Tabloid Talk Shows and Sexual Non-conformity, Chicago: University of Chicago Press.

LeBesco, K. (2004) 'Got to be real: mediating gayness on Survivor', in S. Murray and L. Ouellette (eds) Reality TV: Remaking Television Culture, New York: New York University Press, 271–87.

McNair, B. (2002) Striptease Culture: Sex, Media and the Democratisation of Desire, London: Routledge.

Pullen, C. (2004) 'The household, the basement and *The Real World*: gay identity in the constructed reality environment', in S. Holmes and D. Jermyn (eds) *Understanding Reality Television*, London: Routledge, 211–32.

Whelehan, I. (2000) *Overloaded: Popular Culture and the Future of Feminism*, London: The Women's Press.

2.5

Loaded with meaning: men's magazines and the appropriation of tabloid talk
by Kate Brooks

Introduction

Despite assertions during the 1980s that 'men don't buy magazines' (*Campaign* 29th August 1986), *Loaded* became the success of the UK magazine industry, as new men's lifestyle magazines became the fastest growing of all consumer magazine markets. In the 1990s, *Loaded* was outselling the most popular women's magazines, *Marie Claire* and *Cosmopolitan* (see our study in Jackson *et al* 2001). This phenomenal success generated a vast amount of media commentary around the magazines and masculinity, mostly concerning the apparent shift from the so-called, politically correct 'New Man' to the more hedonistic form of laddism and the 'New Lad'.

Loaded in particular generated a whole set of cultural narratives around this 'new' form of marketable masculinity. New Lads were – to quote *Loaded*'s infamous by-line – 'men who should know better', men who were interested in 'car, beer and sport', the man who – as Sean O'Hagan defined – 'aspires to New Man status when he's with women, but reverts to Old Lad type when he's out with the boys. Clever eh?' (*Arena* May 1991).

Our study set out to explore these new cultural narratives as discursive spaces in which various forms of masculinity could be discussed, defined, labelled, champoined and critiqued. Masculinity here should be understood not as a biological given but a discursive construction which takes different forms at different times in different cultural contexts (cf. Jackson 1991; Butler 1990, 1993). Thus what we wanted to investigate in our study were the various ways in which the new men's magazines' masculinities were discursively 'made sense of' in various popular forms.

This revised look at that study will unpack the loose term 'retrosexism' which is commonly applied to lad culture (cf. Whelehan 2000), by examining four key cultural narratives: those narratives involving definitions of the New Lad, and of the New Man, and those involving notions of 'naughtiness' and nostalgia. The cultural context of these narratives is framed by two overarching discursive repertoires – that of 'masculinity in crisis' (cf. Brod 1987; Whelehan 2000; Connell 1995), and by the discursive strategy of the carnivalesque (cf. Conboy 2002; Attwood 2002; Gregson *et al* 2001). Both these discursive repertoires work, it will be concluded, to close off the potential ambiguities and ambivalences of the cultural narratives surrounding contemporary masculinities and what it means to be male.

New Lads and the reactionary return

In this, the popular press – the tabloids – play a key role. As Conboy has argued, tabloid discourse is 'powerful . . . located within the rhetoric of the everyday and the commonsense of popular culture' (2002: 180). Tabloid discourses work to make sense of the broad cultural patterns of everyday life, circulating, drawing on and generating popular myth and shorthand vernacular for current cultural trends.

During the 1990s, one of the more dominant themes in the popular press, was the notion that since masculinity and what it meant to be a man was in question, masculinity must therefore be in crisis – a phrase which became so common-place it was discussed in places as diverse as academic texts (cf. Nixon 1996; Edwards 1997; Mort 1996) to *US Business Weekly* to *Take A Break* magazine and (then) TV chat show *Kilroy*. Franks links this sense of 'crisis' with the backlash against feminism and 'the culture of victimhood' (1999: 137), which is certainly prevalent in the literature of the Man's Movement, whose manifesto blames 'unrestrained feminism' for the 'human rights violations' of modern men[1].

However the ways in which the tabloids and men's lifestyle magazines initially mobilised this notion of crisis, were markedly more upbeat. In the 1990s, the tabloids championed *Loaded et al*, and in doing so contributed to their commercial success as well as their cultural resonance.

For the tabloids, the 'new Lad' was the real thing: a reactionary return to happy heterosexual hedonism, 'at last' men could be men again, after the apparent oppressive regime of 1980s feminism and political correctness. Masculinity, *The Times* believed, had been 'the issue of the nineties' as feminism had left men 'struggling for an identity' (31 May 1991). By 1995, New Lads were so well established as to have their own list of 'Lad Facts in the *Mail on Sunday*: what they liked (Quentin Tarantino, 'a laugh') what they ate ('pub snacks') who were 'top lads' (George Best, Primal Scream) and what was to be avoided (marriage, snobs) (*Mail on Sunday* January 1 1995).

Both the tabloids and the men's magazines share what Hunt has referred to as 'permissive populism and a particular discursive notion of fun' (Hunt 1998: 26) a 'merry violence' of jokey, blokey colloquialisms. The *Sun* for example has not travelled far from its 1969 intention to provide scandal, 'saucy' humour and sex (Holland, cited in Carter 1998: 17), and similarly, the media commentaries on the new men's magazines' contents hardly varied no matter where they were listed: from 'beer, birds and bad language' (*The Guardian* 10 October 1994) to 'Women, fast cars, sport' (*The Australian* 18 June 1997) to 'birds, beer and football' (The *Big Issue* 23–9 March 1998).

Both the *Sun* and *Loaded* parodied their more highbrow shelfmates: whilst the *Sun* has parodied the style of the *Times* and the *Financial Times* (see Conboy 2002: 168), *Loaded* frequently parodies the conventions of women's magazines, with satirical problem pages and fashion features. Both visually and verbally, men's magazines borrow conventions from the *Sun's* Page Three – the soft porn, smiling image and the associated pun: ('is that her? Corset is – pun courtesy of our dad' (*Maxim* December 2004).

These narratives of saucy fun and bawdiness are part of a wider tradition of English working class humour, from the theatrical innuendos of Victorian music hall ditties to *Carry On* films and the suburban sex comedies of the seventies (frequently featuring working class stalwarts such as plumbers, window cleaners and the ubiquitous milkman (Hunt 1998: 25). The magazines drew on these narratives: emphasising the 'authenticity' of an exuberant, self-gratifying blokiness (Attwood 2005).

The New Man

For the tabloids, the New Lad was seen as a refreshing, and importantly, sexual alternative to what the *Mail on Sunday* referred to as the 'apologetic and feeble' New Man (1 January 1995). According to *Achilles Heal*, the radical men's journal, the New Man was 'professional, usually white, heterosexual . . . [and] having somewhat of an identity crisis as his girlfriend(s) discover feminism' (Winter 1992–3). A popular 80s image of the New Man was the famous (now infamous[2]) Athena Poster, *L'enfant*, showing a bare chested strong-yet-sensitive young man cradling a newborn baby. This poster sold in its millions, although by the mid nineties, *More!* Magazine was warning its teenage readers off the New Man as potential boyfriend: 'his lack of spontaneity will drive you potty' (15–28 January 1997).

Critics of the New Man focused on two set themes: firstly, he was product of the 80s yuppie, too concerned with what to wear. Notably, the more upmarket men's lifestyle magazines, *Arena*, *GQ* and *Esquire*, were seen as 'laughably out of touch' by one-time *Loaded* editor, Tim Southwell (1998: 17). Secondly, the politically correct man was by definition, 'pathetic. .po-faced' (*The Independent* 7 February 1995). If he rejected the sexism, racism and homophobia now enjoying its 'ironic' renaissance in *Loaded*, it was because he was scared of what 'the missus' might say. The more upmarket magazines joined the *Loaded* trend: Rosie Boycott, then *Esquire* editor, claimed that 'women can't *bear* the idea of a bloke who goes to the supermarket to buy nappies . . . you want equality in the office, but who wants equal sex?' (*Mail on Sunday* 1 January 1995).

No red-blooded, 'normal' heterosexual woman, it must be assumed[3]. Thus so-called New Man's self consciousness, his inherent middle classness, and his apparent sympathies for feminism, had rendered him a fake, a wimp, sexless.

The idea that 'middle class' means phoney and pseudo is a continuing discursive theme in these cultural narratives. In the *Observer*, Kathryn Flett for example vilified the New Man's 'phoney nappy changing ways' (13 November 1994), and the *Mail on Sunday* (again) applauded the fact that young men were 'coming out of the politically correct closet and admitting all that nappy changing stuff was baloney' (1 January 1995)[4].

So to be conscientious, either about one's appearance, relationship or children, and to be self conscious here equals lack of spontaneity, just as wanting to be 'equal' takes the 'fun' out of natural sexual desires.[5]

So the 'fake', eighties New Man was finished, and the crisis of masculinity – if it ever existed – was over . . .

'Crisis', and the cultural narrative of naughtiness

This discursive concept of the 'crisis' worked on two levels. On the one hand, it became part of popular anecdotal history that in the Dark Ages of the 1980s, men weren't allowed to be men[6]. On the other, this notion of a crisis was constructed as a feminist myth – another case of feminists over-analysing – which needed refuting. Despite the real economic, social and cultural changes in work patterns, conventional family structures, gender relations and identities (cf. Franks 1999), AA Gill's comforting assertion in the *Mail on Sunday* that: 'the whole notion of masculinity in crisis has been dreamt up by crew cut North London feminists . . . [and] academics with ideological hang ups' (1 January 1995) was an extreme but not uncommon media observation.

This idea that feminism was the big spoilsport[7], and equality and sexual pleasures do not go hand in hand is again, key to tabloid discourse, as Holland (2002) and others have observed. Clare Short's accusation that Page Three was sexist and demeaning (Short *et al* 1986), is now parodied by *The Sun*, which 'allows' Page Three girls to comment on world events ('the news in briefs'). If these magazines are championed as 'harmless fun' then any critique or attempt to analyse that is simply and pointlessly spoiling fun: '*Loaded*'s not sexist, it's into sex . . . the people who read *Loaded* worship women' (Porter, editor *Uploaded*, interview, cited in Jackson *et al* 2001: 69).

So analysis is seen as the antithesis of pleasure, of naughtiness. A notion of nostalgic naughtiness appears frequently in men's magazines, such as *Maxim*'s assertion that 'we haven't been this naughty since that time in PE!' (*Maxim* December 2004). As with so-called downmarket porn mags such as *Fiesta* and *Reader's Wives*, 'you' the reader of *Loaded*, *Maxim* and *FHM* are invited to send in pictures of willing girlfriends, particularly if she is 'out of your league – you spawny git' (*Maxim* December 2004). Similarly, *Loaded* is searching for the '100 naughtiest girls' as well as the 'sexiest barmaid' (December 2004). This is constructed as both about 'real' sexuality, and about being naughty and outrageous: as according to *Loaded*'s then editor, 'academics and sensitive feminists saw *Loaded* as Beelzebub's shopping list in print' (Tim Southwell 1998: 42).

As McRobbie has noted, the media tend to invoke feminism 'only in order to dismiss it' (2004: 259). Yet its presence is necessary here as the disapproving authority/mother figure – as Hunt puts it, the New Lad doesn't want to separate from the mother – on the contrary, 'he needs her to tell him that "yes, he is a very naughty boy" and should know better' (Hunt 1998: 8, see also Benwell 2003). The *Guardian* similarly observes that newer men's magazines such as the weeklies, *Zoo* and *Nuts* – both incidentally 'closer to their tabloid cousins than to other men's magazines' – are 'fuelled by a childish notion of hedonism – pills, thrills and bellyaches' (16 June 2004).

Thus masculinity is constructed as 'naturally' child-like, about play rather than work – a notion the magazines themselves promote with their denial that putting a magazine together is 'proper work'. According to Southwell, working for *Loaded* was like 'the best party you'd ever been to' (Southwell 1998, back cover) a sentiment echoed by a typical editorial that *Loaded* 'operatives' just 'get out into the world, grab it by the throat and have a laff' (Editors letter, *Loaded* December 2004).

Nostalgia and the 'Golden Age'

The permissively populist tabloid Sun of the '70s (Hunt 1998) promoted Page Three as an example of how women 'were free to be sexual'. These girls, as in *Loaded*'s recent hunt for 'Britain's sexist barmaid' were 'ordinary young women . . . invited to . . . drop their inhibitions . . . by many a nudge and a wink' (Holland 1998: 23–4). Following Tannock (1995), Hunt (1998) writes that for *Loaded et al*, 1970s popular culture has become a popular memory reference point for 'a kind of unfettered straight masculinity' – a Golden Age before the Fall brought about by feminism and the New Man of the 1980s.

During the 1990s, *Loaded* in particular regularly drew on this kind of nostalgia for the unsound popular culture of the 1970s[8], a nostalgia which can be linked to the 90s trend for 70s retro fashion. For example, *Loaded*'s October 1997 fashion section featured old men behind East London market stalls, modelling 'Del Boy' sheepskin coats, whilst November's *GQ* focused on 'old skool' grey Farah trousers and skinny-rib jumpers (November 1997). 1970s cult viewing, in-jokes and catch phrases appear in *Loaded*, alongside the fashions for 'ironic' wearing of 70s working class clothes and uniforms, both work[9] and 'old skool'.

The 70s revisited here are about play, and about sexual playfulness: as Gregson *et al* (2001) have pointed out, politics and political unrest – such as The Women's Liberation Movement – are notably absent. Thus this 'return' to the 1970s as a reference point is not so much nostalgia (after all, those nostalgic for it – the readers and writers of *Loaded et al* – are likely to have been children then, if not yet born) as a reappropriation; less about a masculine nostalgia for a supposed lost Golden Age, and 'rather more about revisiting the 70s through the discourses and dispositions of knowingness and the carnivalesque' (Gregson *et al* 2001: 21).

The idea of 'low or vulgar' forms of popular culture as 'carnivalesque' borrows from Bakhtin's notion of fun and laughter inverting the serious business of every-day life, and celebrating the excesses of sensual pleasure and theatrical spectacle (Attwood 2002). This is one way we can understand the discursive spaces of men's magazines and the media commentaries they generated: that a more carnivalesque notion of masculinity – as sensual, hedonistic and shameless – is constructed as a reaction to the restrictions of authoritative middle class feminism – a 'blokelash' (Jackson *et al* 2001: 36).

However, the counter cultural cleverness of ironic celebration of low culture was lost on its critics. By the late 1990s, men's magazines were being critiqued for celebrating these 'witless' versions of masculinity, and *Loaded* (by then eclipsed in sales by *FHM*) came to represent a whole genre of magazines and readers: in April 1998 for example, Jack Straw referred to delinquent youths as 'part of *Loaded* generation' (*Independent* 30 April 1998).

Where *Loaded* had represented a more honest, back to basics post-new-man masculinity, it now came to represent a particular form of male malaise – men were no longer behaving badly, but sadly: both the *Independent on Sunday* (8 June 1997) and *Bella* magazine (June 1997) ran features on the increasing number of male

-

anorexics, linking the disease to 'glossy magazines for men'. The *Independent* argued that magazines like *Loaded* had:

'provided a popular solution to the identity crisis for today's man . . . but there's something sad about it . . . [with] the media celebrating male youthful behaviour there is no encouragement for men to leave their laddish phase, which sets up the potential for future crisis'.

(*Independent* 3rd February 1997)

Despite the efforts of more 'grown up' men's magazines such as the short lived *Deluxe* (for the man who wants to 'party hard' but look himself in the eye in the morning) and *Later* (for the man who 'likes a laugh but has responsibilities')[10] 'real' men are still assumed to be interested in those old staples; beer, sport and sex[11]. Essentially, Lads were 'witless, porn obsessed, drunken serial shaggers' (The *Independent*, 28 April 1997). Even *More!*, once 'Mad for Lads', lost its enthusiasm, wondering 'do you want a lout for a lover?' (15–28 Jan 1997) whilst the *Sunday Times* more recently dismissed the Lad as having turned into the Dirty Old Man (March 17 2002).

So whilst laddish masculinity is 'out', the idea of masculinity – particularly that of new fatherhood – as 'naturally' childlike remains, both on TV sitcoms and in the popular press. *FQ* (the 'essential dad's mag') for example defined fatherhood as 'a lifetime of worry and the chance to play Scalextric again' (*FQ* issue 04 2004), an image echoed by Jamie Oliver's portrayal of 'new lad dad' (Hollows 2003) and the 'lad, dad, gay icon, player' that is David Beckham (*Observer* 2 February 2003).

Conclusions

In conclusion, these 'new' forms of masculinity surrounding the new men's magazines and circulated in the tabloids, can be understood as hegemonic, in that some constructions – such as the New Lad – become socially dominant, become the natural, 'common sense' form of masculinity, as part of the historically changeable practice of patriarchal dominance (Connell 1995). Thus, these cultural narratives are inevitably articulated in relation to a wider set of gender and power relations, which can be read, essentially, as a backlash to the supposed gains of feminism (Faludi 1992; Whelehan 2000; McRobbie 2004). Such quotes as AA Gill's concerning how academics with 'hang ups' have invented the 'crisis of masculinity' thus function to close off the potential ambiguities and possibilities of the debates around what it means to be male. So, the 'crisis' becomes not about questioning what it means to be male, but a 'crisis' of oppressed masculine expression.

In economic terms, the traditional masculine workplace is changing, and the problem of today's young males is frequently debated in the press. Despite the media successes of Oliver, Beckham and other 'new' celebrity dads, it is widely assumed that with no work opportunities, and no moral obligations to get married to the mothers of their children, men are not just unwilling but unable to 'grow up' (Franks 1999). *The Observer* reports on Bob Geldof's assertions that it is women who are to blame for 'disenfranchised' dads, thanks to a divorce system which favours the female (10 October 2004).

So whilst in the media, 'feminism is cast into the shadows' (McRobbie 2004: 255), this 'crisis' is not immediately visible in the realities of the legal system or the world of work. Women are still underpaid in the labour market and underrepresented in the boardrooms, and if the labour market *is* 'feminised', it is because now the 'masculine' industries have gone, it is the low paid, low status service sector 'feminine' jobs that are left (Franks 1999). Yet it is popularly assumed that women now have it all, or at least the upper hand, as they gain in the workplace and men, who should know better, go and play, even if they're fathers.

As Tinknell *et al* have argued, men as part of the consumer market are represented as grown up only in the sense of their entry into the consumer economy rather than in the adoption of emotional responsibility – thus masculinity as represented in these magazines is one of 'extended adolescence' and lifestyle consumerism (or 'neat shit to buy' as Michael VerMeulen, founder editor of GQ, succinctly defined[12]) and by the refusal of adult responsibility (Tincknell *et al* 2003: 50). As Franks also puts it, in this unstable, unreliable world of work, the magazines had 'offered the temporary solution of regressing' (1999: 170). How this 'regression' is discursively constructed, I would argue, is through the reappropriation of carnivalesque.

Conboy has argued that the popular press 'maintain and mutate the cultural mode of carnivalesque', in order to exploit and frame the working class culture it purports to celebrate (2002: 170). *Loaded*, in its attempt to appear 'anti PC', a reaction to the 'threat' of over-analytical, puritanical feminism, borrows from this discursive repertoire. Here, the carnivalesque is not just a form of masculine, nostalgic (mis)-remembering the 70s but a discursive reappropriation of the 70s as representing a particular kind of carnivalesque masculine heterosexuality.

This notion of the nostalgic carnivalesque is thus employed as a discursive device to stabilize these hegemonic forms of masculinity: by appearing to ironise and invert the dominant order, constructed as the present 'crisis' of oppressive political correctness and feminism, whilst maintaining it by setting up laddish masculinity as the natural order of things.

And ultimately this knowing reappropriation of the carnivalesque is limited – what could have been a radical shift in men's consciousness, new discursive spaces for men to explore what it meant to be male, became a glossy, satirical version of tabloid culture and eventually, ironically, the parody of the popular became a tabloid culture caricature itself.

So the crisis was not just a popular press construction, but nor can it be mapped unproblematically onto wider social and economic changes: we need to see the construction of the crisis and the carnivalesque response as part of a wider hegemonic struggle played out in media representations and the ways in which those representations are made sense of in popular culture. In this way, *Loaded*'s by-line is more loaded than it appears.

Notes

1   http://www.ukmm.org.uk accessed 4th July 2005. The writers, The Cheltenham Group, also described feminism as 'the greatest evil of this century' (*Independent* 4 February 1997).

2   According to the *Daily Mail*, the 'curse' of this poster 'blighted the lives of those involved' (11 April 2004). *Minx* magazine, in an article entitled 'I scored with the

Athena Poster Man' also claimed the model Adam Perry was in reality 'sordid and horrible' (*Minx* April 1998).

3 It must be noted here that Boycott, with Marsha Rowe, launched Britain's first feminist magazine, *Spare Rib* in 1972, which makes her assertion all the more depressing.

4 Since then, 'dad lit' has become a popular, lucrative genre, as lads humorously struggle with the joys and terrors of all that nappy changing stuff – see for example bestsellers Hogan (2002), Hornby (2003) and Parsons (2002).

5 See Leroy (1993) and Segal (1994) on representations of female sexuality.

6 See Jackson *et al* 201: 123–125, and McRobbie 2004, for a more detailed account of this 'misremembering'.

7 Although . . . 'Good looking feminists give me a real rise . . . they're a challenge . . . [but] most of us couldn't cope with her in real life' (*GQ* March 1992).

8 It is notable, then, that it's the 70s which are seen as the Golden Age of unfettered masculinity, not the 50s. As Cohan has argued, the 1950s 'playboy' discourse had a radical impact on 50s US culture, with its representations of carefree, consumerist heterosexuality, the lady-killer bachelor out to seduce in his 'bachelor pad' (1997: 271). Yet it is the British 70s, not the US 50s which are seen as the Golden Age, and key to that, are these notions of naughtiness and playfulness (Hunt 1998).

9 See Gregson *et al* (2001) for a discussion of the iconography of 70s 'workman's shirt made cool' as retro fashion.

10 Both cited in Jackson *et al* 2001: 43.

11 For example, *FQ* magazine, for 'modern dads' offered readers 'top tips' in how to get the 'minx' back out of your newly post-natal partner. (*FQ* Issue 03 2003).

12 *The Guardian* 8 November 1993.

2.6

The politics of the smile: 'soft news' and the sexualisation of the popular press
by Patricia Holland

'What makes a woman smile?'

The *Sun* newspaper aims to make women smile. Where it has total control, in the photographs which give its pages such graphic impact, its success is, literally, spectacular. Smiling women appear on the news pages and the celebrity pages. They appear in the glamour pictures; the pictures of royalty and of television personalities; in the pictures of ordinary people whose everyday lives have brought them good fortune, and, above all, they appear on Page Three. The woman who proudly displays her breasts is almost always smiling.

[. . .]

Popular newspapers seek to amuse as much as to inform, to appeal to the emotion as much as to the intellect. The smile has been established as part of a package which continues to reach out to real women and men in an invitation to buy the paper and engage with its informal address. Increasingly over the twentieth century the aim of the popular press has been to 'tickle the public' with entertainment values. Matthew Engel took the title of his book on the history of the British popular press from an anonymous verse that went round Fleet Street in the nineteenth century:

Tickle the public, make 'em grin,
The more you tickle the more you'll win.
Teach the public, you'll never get rich,
You'll live like a beggar and die in a ditch.

(Engel 1996b: 17)

From the 1880s and 1890s, the introduction of lightweight features and all types of trivia, including the domestic, as well as a move to a 'softer' more ticklish type of news, has been seen as a *feminisation* of the new mass-circulation press, brought about by its desire for a broad appeal. In seeking out a mass audience, there was a need to recognise women as an influential segment of the potential readership, and the feminine had long been identified with the popular and accessible. But the changes initiated by the *Sun* in the 1970s pushed the meaning of 'popular' in a new direction. The

Sun was no longer feminised, but *sexualised*. Central to its appeal was the provocative image of a woman's body. Breasts were added to the smile. Instantly this implied a readership sharply divided along gender lines. Men and women readers were separately addressed, through a language and imagery which carried the full power of sexual, as well as gender, difference. The smile on the face of the Page Three girl conveyed a double message, 'After a lifetime of learning to establish eye to eye contact during conversation, the glamour girl has to learn to accept eye to breast contact' explained ex-Page Three girl, Jackie Sewell (Wigmore 1986: 13).

[. . .]

The sexualisation of the *Sun*

'What I like to do first thing in the morning is to sit up in bed and have a really good look at Vanya' wrote Colin Dunne in the *Sun* in September 1977.

> Sometimes she has a rose in her hair. Sometimes she wears a dainty necklace. Occasionally, the odd ribbon. Those apart she is always naked and I wonder how it is that she and Ena Sharples can possibly share the same sex.

A sea change in the very definition of a newspaper came about when Rupert Murdoch bought the *Sun* in 1969 and decreed that its selling points should now be 'sex, sport and contests' (Engel 1996b: 253). A year later, editor Larry Lamb introduced the topless models which became the paper's best known feature. Its predecessor, the trade-union backed *Daily Herald*, had endeavoured to create a sense of tough working-class community amongst its readers in the interwar years (Curran and Seaton 1991). From the 1970s, the *Sun* set out to create a different sort of communality by addressing the new working-class prosperity, in which pleasure was legitimised and the culture of deference put aside. The promise of uninhibited personal gratification was compatible with a rapidly expanding consumer-based economy, and went together with an open contempt for established authority and those who would keep you in your place (Holland 1983).

Larry Lamb decreed that sex in the pages of the *Sun* was to be linked not to pornographic images, nor to highly groomed models, not even, primarily, to celebrities, but to tastefully posed, ordinary young women, smiling at the reader and revealing their breasts. They must be 'nice girls', he is on record as saying (Chippendale and Horrie 1992). In those days of innocence, the *Sun*'s brash hedonism seemed to be sharing something of the freedoms argued for by feminism. Despite its unashamed commercialism, the change in style and content was in tune with the liberatory mood of the times. This was the era of *Cosmopolitan* magazine which opened up a public discussion of sex for women. Sex was explicitly dealt with in feminist magazines, notably *Spare Rib*, and even *Parents* magazine, which dealt with childcare issues, indulged in daring presentations featuring natural childbirth and a considerable amount of nudity. Rupert Murdoch was said to admire the 'serious' broadsheet, the *Guardian*, because of that newspaper's readiness to deal with issues of sexual behaviour on its women's pages. (The *Guardian* was later referred to by *Sun* writers as 'the World's Worst'.)

The *Sun*'s class and gender realignments echoed a wider set of social changes, resisting the 'discourses of sobriety', trade unions, BBC news and old fashioned politics. It valued itself as a rebel, in reaction to the remnants of postwar stringency and narrow morality. Page Three was launched as an image of defiant liberation. Its message to men was age-old, but its message to women was that women are now free to be sexual. Generations of Page Three 'girls' encouraged women readers to join them, to be proud of their bodies and to have fun. The address to women, often in major features such as the amply illustrated adaptation of Joan Garrity's *Total Loving* (July 1977), was along the lines of, 'loosen up, discover sexual pleasure'. Images of naked men joined those of naked women.

The brashness, visual excitement and downmarket appeal of the *Sun* meant that no newspaper that aimed for a mass readership could ignore it. It was imitated by the long-established *Daily Mirror* – which introduced Page Three-type topless models for a brief period – and the newly established *Daily Star* which determinedly scattered bulging breasts throughout its pages. Finally it opened the way for the *Sport*, a tabloid which claimed to be a newspaper but which dispensed with all pretence to offer anything but fantasy and soft porn. The 'softening' of the news had taken a new turn with the reassertion of the female body as spectacle. The sexualisation of the popular press had brought a different set of alignments between public and private domains, and between masculine and feminine concerns in its pages.

On the one hand, sexualisation could be seen as a logical development of feminisation, continuing to draw into the wider debate issues of sexuality and sexual relations that had been hidden but which women themselves, not least in the feminist movement, now insisted were of public importance. On the other hand, there was a deep contradiction in the presentation. Although women were invited to enjoy themselves, to follow their desires and to drop their inhibitions, the divided address, accompanied by many a nudge and a wink, made it clear that *this* women's pleasure is above all a pleasure for men. In this context, the visual is no longer associated with women and with a less linear style of understanding, but with a masculine insistence on the inalienable right to a lustful gaze.

The *Sun*'s visible culture of sex invaded every part of the paper, including the pages it has from time to time run for women. In the paper's own version of its history:

> The *Sun* called its women's pages 'Pacesetters' and filled them with sex. They were produced by women *for* women. But they were subtitled 'The pages for women that men can't resist' acknowledging that there are plenty of topics that fascinate both men and women. Like sex.
>
> (Grose 1989: 94)

But the sex remained male oriented. Chippendale and Horrie write of the 'laddish' culture amongst young women journalists on the paper, outdoing the 1990/1992).

As the years progressed, the *Sun*'s assertive vulgarity became differently aligned to the cultural and political map of the day. When Kelvin Mackenzie took over the editorship in 1981 the paper became strident in its radical Conservative sympathies, expressed as two fingers to the establishment and an insolent individualism. The Page Three image was part of a rightward move in a political and cultural consciousness confirmed by the years of Conservative Government. The central image of the semi-naked 'nice girl' and her welcoming smile was developed as a politics of disengagement. 'Page Three is good for you' was the caption which headed a Page Three picture in 1984.

> P3's titillating tit-bits are just what the doctor ordered – as a tonic against all the world's gloomy news. Research has shown that the *Sun*'s famous glamour pictures are a vital bit of cheer for readers depressed by strikes, deaths and disasters.

'A London psychologist' is quoted as saying:

> When you think how gloomy and threatening most of the news has been lately – strikes, assassinations, hijacks, starving millions and the falling pound – you need Page Three as a shot in the arm. I am sure the *Sun*'s famous beauties are a vital safely valve for the country's men when things in general seem to be getting out of hand.

The embrace of the 'loadsamoney' culture, of jingo and bingo, was in tune with a mood which crossed the social classes. Other popular papers and the burgeoning magazine market had followed suit. The culture of sex-for-fun was echoed in advertisements and on television. By the mid-1990s, the *Sun* had lost its rebellious spice. Now its sexual obsessiveness had been overtaken by a host of 'laddish' magazines on the news stands, and by raunchy imagery on the advertising hoardings. On television *The Good Sex Guide* (1993–4) had kicked off the schedules of the new ITV company, Carlton, and inaugurated a genre of 'trash television' which was partly youth-oriented, partly masculine sex fantasy. Kelvin MacKenzie himself left the *Sun* and launched *Topless Darts* (1996–) on the cable channel, Live TV. In the pages of the *Sun* the humour could all too easily harden into malice and the sexual fun into a leery, sneery soft misogyny.

A relaxation of restraint also came to mean less restraint on intolerance. It made possible the intemperate abuse of those whose sexuality and lifestyle does not conform. In the daily mosaic of the newspaper, the image of the sexy woman continues to be laid against female demons like single mothers, lesbian teachers and ugly women, such as Ena Sharples, the *Coronation Street* character whom Colin Dunne had thought could not possibly share the same sex as Page Three girl Vanya. Although the excesses of the Kelvin MacKenzie years are now rare, the obverse of the culture of hedonism remains a theatre of cruelty, which takes pleasure in the distress of the targeted individual.

Women's visibility in the public realm has involved repeated reminders that (hetero)sexuality is always an issue between men and women, from the demand to see newsreader Angela Rippon's legs (Holland 1987), to a preoccupation with Prime Minister Margaret Thatcher's wardrobe. Which brings us back to the image of the smile and to the relationship between the body and the face in the iconic Page Three image.

Body and face

Much has been written about the use of the female body as spectacle and as commodity (Mulvey 1989; Coward 1984). Carole Pateman has drawn the issue even more firmly into the political realm in the unlikely context of the theory of contract which, for liberal thinkers, secures the legitimation of civil society. The theory proposes that free social relations take the form of a series of contracts freely entered into between autonomous individuals. Contracts, such as those involving employment, are governed by law, and structure daily life. Pateman points out that women have been largely overlooked by classical contract theorists, and that, although a contract is seen as the paradigm for an equal agreement, in those contracts which are of necessity between women and men – as in marriage – the parties begin from an unequal position. Such contracts always imply a politicised *sexual* difference and reinforce what she describes as men's 'sex-right' over women's bodies (Pateman 1988: 3).

It is important for her argument that we should not lose sight of this potent *sexual* inequality, as its specificity can too easily be lost in a discussion of other categories of inequality less subject to taboo, such as those of power or gender. Men's sex-right is central to contracts, from marriage to prostitution and surrogacy, 'in which the body of the woman is precisely what is at issue' (Pateman 1988: 224). Despite the liberal doctrine that 'everyone owns the property in their capacities and attributes' men still 'demand that women's bodies in the flesh and in representation should be publicly available to them' (1988: 13–14). A fanciful analogy might pose the Page Three smile as a form of contract which reaches out to the male reader. It appears to secure an unproblematic agreement between men and women which promises access to a sexualised body.

There are many possible types of smile. The *Sun* specialises in the 'lovely to see you!' smile, one which comes straight off of the page, the gaze of the smiler entangling with that of the viewer. It is cheerful, commonplace and relaxed, and it aims to elicit smiles from the readers, men and women.

> Try to avoid a toothy grin or a Bardot pout. This sort of expression can make you look self-conscious. It's best not to copy anyone. Just be yourself.

was the advice given to aspiring Page Threes (*Sun* October 27 1981).

This smile is familiar from the snapshots of friends and family treasured by almost everyone in the Western world. Ever since the introduction of the Box Brownie in 1900, the domestic snapshot, taken 'as quick as a wink', has sought to capture a smile which builds a bond of companionship between photographer and subject, quite different from the confrontational tension created in formal portraits taken by a professional photographer (Holland 1997a; Parr 1997).

This pictured smile is part of the familial ritual, a family masquerade. It is a welcome convention which expresses a longing for happiness and togetherness even when, tragically, it may conceal the opposite (Williams V. 1994; Spence and Holland 1991). It is an affirmation of belonging and fitting into place, an acquiescence underpinned by pleasure. The work of the newspaper smile is to create an engagement with its own special public, built on the analogy of family warmth.

Much of the text of the *Sun* is organised around the presence and absence of such a smile. In the tradition of the popular press it seeks out good news in contrast to the 'gloomy and threatening' news of the 'serious' broadsheets. As an object lesson to its readers it offers contrasting images of women who will not smile ('Mrs Misery', a betting-shop cashier, 'was sacked because she was so grumpy she drove punters away' (*Sun* 3 September 1996). Such surly refusal on the part of spoilsports, moralists and the bad tempered deprives every one else of their pleasure and undermines the security of the metaphorical family structure.

With this relaxed and familiar smile firmly in place, the *Sun* has gone on to forge an indissoluble link between the welcoming face and the revelation of women's breasts. 'Lovely to see you!' was the headline over a Portsmouth crowd greeting the fleet on its return from the Falklands in June 1982. A smiling young woman, an ordinary girl, just one of the crowd, pulls up her shirt to reveal her breasts. 'A pretty girl reveals how happy she is to see Britain's heroes home – by baring her charms for the delighted sailors', the text confirms (*Sun* 12 June 1982). Sexuality is both affirmed and its danger defused in the ordinariness of the presentation.

For those who refuse the link between smile and female sexuality, the threat of humiliation is always present. When, in 1986, Labour MP Clare Short brought in a Parliamentary Bill to ban Page Three, the response was personalised abuse against 'killjoy Clare'. The *News of the World*, at the time edited by ex-Page Three caption writer, Patsy Chapman, set out to find a picture of the MP in her night-dress (Short, Tunks and Hutchinson 1991; Snoddy 1992: 110). This metaphorical attempt to undress Clare Short was symptomatic. Women who refuse to smile tend to be fully clothed, but once the clothes come off the message of the body cannot be denied. A face, even a smiling face, carries the potential of speech. The revealed body calms and defuses the challenge of that potential.

The Page Three image is an active, working image, layered with mythological resonance (Warner 1987). It displays a 'body that matters', to echo the title of Judith Butler's exploration of the discursive construction of real, material bodies. It works to reiterate the 'regulatory norms with which sex is materialised'. But as Butler goes on to point out 'sex is both produced and destabilised in the course of this reiteration' (Butler 1993: 10). The exposure of a woman's breasts needs strong legitimation, and that legitimation is achieved by the acquiescent smile. Page Three models repeatedly emphasise the point by speaking of the pleasure they take in the role.

Page Three has changed over the years. The models have become more knowing and the presentation has lost something of the exuberant celebration of the early days. Perhaps more importantly, the context in which it is to be understood is different. The women in the pictures are no longer timeless. The well-known models have grown older, and their public personae have developed. Some have had children; some, like Linda Lusardi and Sam Fox, have tried to build up show business careers; others have become unemployed and disillusioned. Their personal accounts of their experiences, published from time to time in newspapers as diverse as the *News of the World* and the *Guardian Weekend*, range from the maudlin to the insightful. Many give a very different picture from that portrayed in the jokey features which fill the pages of the *Sun*.

The highly visible image of a sexualised woman has brought into question the role of the popular press as a potential space for the expression of women's democratic aspirations and public participation. And yet an army of invisible women, journalists, photographers, researchers and editors has been steadily encroaching into hitherto-protected masculine preserves. Could it be that the reassertion of the irreducible differences on which *sexual* relations are based is partly a response to an increasing equality in *gender* relations?

Democracy, women and the public sphere

Rozsika Parker and Griselda Pollock have documented the historic relationship through which the status of male painters has depended on a distinct role for women in the world of art. While women were excluded as artists – the eighteenth-century Royal Academy banned them from its prestigious life-classes – their visible presence was necessary to the very concept of 'art'. The idealised image of 'woman' for centuries represented the archetypal subject for easel painting (Parker and Pollock 1981).

Just like the painted odalisque, the baroque visibility of women in the *Sun* is part of a fantastic excess with which the paper engages its readers. Repeating many similar ironies, the transformation of the popular press into a more accessible, more demo-cratic medium – potentially more feminine – has been carried out through an image which works to temper women's equal participation in those public spaces. A vocal feminist opposition to Page Three has argued that the circulation of the image, as a fantasy for men, would put real women at risk in the physical spaces of the streets. My argument is that by reinforcing sexual difference, the nature of the democratic dis-cursive space is brought into question. Democratic discourse, which needs to be feminised, reaches a different sort of limit when it becomes sexualised. This limit will always need to be negotiated, but negotiation is closed off if sexual difference is always presented in a way that reinforces sexual inequality.

It has been demonstrated in relation to a variety of historical contexts that the exclusion of women from public activities has been structural rather than a mere contingency. This means that the imbalance cannot easily be rectified by equal-opportunities legislation or positive-discrimination programmes, however important such initiatives may be. Carole Pateman has mapped out the ways in which the very concept of a liberal 'individual' implies a notion of sexual subordination, and 'civil freedom depends on patriarchal right' (Pateman 1988: 38, 219). In Hannah Arendt's account of the Greek polis, the private domestic base was needed to create a public space in which *men* could participate as citizens (Arendt 1989). For Nancy Frazer, the concept of a 'public sphere' which could make possible a free and equal exchange of views, was a 'masculinist ideological notion' (Calhoun 1992: 116). Joan Landes argued that 'the exclusion of women was constitutive of the very notion of the public sphere' in the age of the French Revolution (Thompson 1995a: 254).

It is consistent with these analyses that the 'serious' broadsheets, with their claims to objectivity and universal values, have excluded women even more firmly from positions of power. The first women to become editors of national newspapers (apart from the first, abortive, *Daily Mirror*) have run the most scandalous of scandal sheets, rather than upmarket papers with liberal credentials. Wendy Henry and Patsy Chapman, both editors of *News of the World*, learned their trade on the *Sun*. Hence the paradoxical position that women who lay claim to the exercise of power in the public arena of tabloid news must themselves oversee the fantasy image of a sexy woman.

The entertainment values which, in the popular press, now invade all parts of the paper, need to be reconciled with 'public sphere' objectives, where participation depends on the restrained statement of competing opinions, and where there is an assumption that all can contribute without regard to status or other identity factors (Calhoun 1992). A viable 'public sphere' would be a democratic space where, in the words of Anne Phillips, we can 'leave ourselves behind', and:

> We do want to 'leave ourselves behind' when we engage in democratic politics: not in the sense of denying everything that makes us the people we are, but in the sense of seeing ourselves as constituted by an often contradictory complex of experiences and qualities, and then of seeing the gap between ourselves and others as in many ways a product of chance.
>
> (Phillips 1991: 59)

The sexualised image of a woman is a constant reminder of the utopian nature of this goal.

Excess and the politics of fun

A consideration of the position of women in the popular press points to the need for an evaluation of the *political* implications of this interplay between fact and fantasy, 'information' and entertainment. This means that the visual presentation of a newspaper, the size of the headlines, the style of language used are never side issues. Hard news is always dependent on soft.

For that reason, rather than exploring the accuracy, bias or otherwise of the popular press, I have, in this chapter, been concerned with other aspects of its democratic role. Its role in circulating vocabularies, images and concepts with which to make sense of the contemporary world and the place of men and women within it, is of prime importance, but it also plays a role in offering a space in which people may see themselves, their views and their interests reflected, both as individuals and as groups. Bearing in mind these two aspects, rather than trying to isolate the informational content of the popular press from its entertaining presentation, a political critique would note the ways in which the news content is structured and shaped by entertainment values, while the information is itself filtered through the entertainment material (Curran and Sparks 1991). 'News' and 'entertainment' become ever more entwined as the entertainment matter colours the reader's understanding and itself carries important forms of information. James Curran has made this point in relation to the media in general, arguing that 'Media entertainment is one means by which people engage at an intuitive and expressive level in a public dialogue about the direction of society. Media entertainment is in this sense an integral part of the media's "informational" role' (Curran 1991a; 1991b: 102). Far from neglecting the political role of newspapers, this refocusing of attention is essential to an understanding of the downmarket tabloids as the most influential media of political communication.

The relentless push towards entertainment values has meant that the definition of what makes 'news' is itself constantly changing. The carefully established distinction between fact and opinion is now less easy to maintain. The need for accuracy has become dissolved into the excess of the headline, through a joke, an ironic exaggeration or an expression of outrage. It is part of my argument that, in the downmarket tabloids, the 'Page Three principle' has been a crucial element in this transformation. Images of women – seductive, spectacular yet naturalistic – have been central to a cultural and economic change which is also a political one. 'Samantha waving from the top of an armoured car as it was driven through the picket lines at Wapping was one of the defining moments of the 1980s', wrote journalist Peter Martin of Page Three icon Samantha Fox (Martin 1997: 16).

The long association made by the *Sun* between spoilsports, sexual puritans and a Labour Party now rejected as 'old Labour', has been a highly political campaign, filtered through the association of sexuality and a hedonistic lifestyle. As part of its violently anti-Labour stance during the 1992 election, the *Sun* replaced its usual Page Three with a bulgingly fat 'flabbogram lady', captioned 'Here's how Page Three will look under Kinnock! Fat chance of fun' (Seymour-Ure 1995). Political discourse of this kind appears to transcend party politics. The *Sun* dramatically changed allegiance for the 1997 election, supporting the Labour Party in its 'modernised' form under Tony Blair. On that occasion, its latest Page Three 'superstar', Melinda Messenger, 'Blairs all' and tells readers why she backs Tony Blair. Clearly the party-political switch had had no impact on the 'Page Three principle'. A politics of sexual fantasy which opens up a gap between women and men by reinforcing men's 'sex-right' over women's bodies continues to imply a political allegiance which ultimately undermines democratic participatory rights, and which continues to link the feminine with the trivial.

The *Sun* continues to reiterate that women's bodies matter, and it repeatedly demonstrates that the materiality of those bodies will always subvert women's claims to seriousness in a world where they need not smile. And yet, in the spirit of a sexuality which aims to be less under male control, many ordinary women have made it clear that they value the right to smile, even if, for the moment, they cannot smile entirely on their own terms. In a 1987 television debate, ex-Page Three model Linda Lusardi asserted that she had turned the Page Three image to her own advantage. She used it as a sign of the proud independence it had brought to her, rather than a sign of subordination to men's fantasies (BBC Community Programmes Unit 1987). That smile continues to be directed at women, too, even if it is instantly recuperated into the service of a masculine framework of understanding (Norris 1997).

But while real, embodied – if invisible – women continue to have only minimal roles in the shaping of our popular media, the men who produce the pages will continue to build their power on the decorative excess of the women who are pictured on them – just like the eighteenth-century academicians and their voluptuous models. Interestingly, a debate in the pages of the serious broadsheets during June and July of 1997 on whether a lightening of the news content of those papers constituted a 'dumbing down' or a feminisation, was largely conducted by women journalists and quickly took up the issue of women's writing. Smiling or not, the need is for participation on women's own terms. This, of course, will have consequences for the concept of 'news' and for that of 'entertainment'.

2.7

Performing masculinity: reflexive-sadomasochism in MTV's *Jackass*
by Jason Kosovski

In addition to introducing the concept of the music video, acknowledging and helping to define youth culture, and blurring yet further the distinction between program and advertisement, the MTV network contributed to the explosion of reality-based programming. Series such as *The Real World* [1992–], *Road Rules* [1994–], and *Taildaters* [2002–2003] constructed a youthful (or immature) world view, all of which are informed by emotional and physical violence. One of the more recent MTV offerings, *Jackass*, combines pranks and stunts in an effort to test the border of acceptable behavior. Parental groups as well as individual litigants have charged that the show promotes violent and dangerous behavior that children can easily mimic.[1] Indeed, the show not only enthusiastically and insistently violates standards of good taste and proper public behavior but also engages in personal and physical violations. The shows' stunts often place cast members in situations in which they could receive great bodily harm if not permanent injuries. Sigmund Freud's [1919, 1924] theory of reflexive sadomasochism is especially helpful in analyzing stunts such as these, stunts that require men to inflict real damage to their bodies in an effort to prove that they can take it, that they are real (albeit foolish) men. *Jackass* delimits its borders through a violent performance of masculinity, creating a completely male domain which women may observe and admire but in which they may not participate. This chapter unfolds the ways in which the notion of reflexive sadomasochism informs *Jackass* and how the show fitfully engages in a defensive display of masculine performance.

While the television lifespan of *Jackass* [2000–2002] was rather short, it was enormously popular on MTV, propelling its star, Johnny Knoxville, into a movie career. The show also gave rise to two spin-offs – *Viva la Bam* [2003–] and *Wild Boyz* [2003–]. *Jackass* aired on MTV for three seasons and was made into a feature-length, uncensored film in 2002. The film grossed over $22 million on its opening weekend on a budget of only $5 million, clear testimony to its popularity. I refer to the television show and film interchangeably because both were produced with the same content and the same visual technique found in many reality shows.[2] With no major celebrities or special effects, the television show and film consisted largely of pranks and cheap but dangerous stunts. Pranks on the show often poked fun at the general public's reactions to outrageous behavior or local naïveté, such as interviewing residents of a town named Mianus.[3] This chapter will focus on the stunts of *Jackass*, stunts that ranged from the deviant to the dangerous. Deviant stunts, for example, often involved attacks on male genitalia. Dangerous stunts ranged from jumping in raw sewage to being hit with a bean bag fired from a shotgun. Using the theory of reflexive sadomasochism theorized by Freud and outlined by David Savran [1998], I wish to look at the way in which masculinity was performed on *Jackass*. As a text, *Jackass* mixed the homoerotic with the mainstream, the absurd with the inane and fantastic performance with reality television. I feel that understanding *Jackass* as a text is essential to engage with its nuanced and complex enactment of gender. The simplicity of *Jackass'* narrative (a disjointed series of video clips) stands in stark contrast to its complicated masculine performance, a performance that relied quite heavily on inwardly directed masculine violence.

Defining *Jackass* as a text

Half naked men are paraded on screen consistently, if not persistently, on *Jackass*. These men perform astonishing acts on their own bodies and on the bodies of others. They seem, at times, to derive pleasure from their own pain, the pain of others, or simply from the spectacle in which they participate. The presence of *Jackass* on MTV and its marketing as a mainstream film and television show, however, place it distinctly outside of the homoerotic world. That is, while *Jackass* has been appropriated by gay subculture, the show is not aimed directly or exclusively at a gay audience. The men of *Jackass* seem eager to display the limits of their own bodies in a distinctly non-sexual performance. This masculine bravado resembles the kind of masculinity found in heavy metal videos, music often played throughout *Jackass*, along with punk and alternative artists. Dan Rubey assesses heavy metal masculinity in the MTV video:

> There's a great deal of macho posturing in MTV interviews, and the violent, sadistic imagery of many heavy metal videos—the leather, whip, chains, bare chests, and biker gear—is perhaps a defense against sexual ambiguity. (879)

The violent male performance on *Jackass* is also an unconscious defense of gender, but here it is a defense against the feminized position linked to objectification. Rather than occupy a feminized space, these men violently attack themselves and each other proving they are true men independent of their status as feminized objects within the show.

Male nudity and a preoccupation with male genitalia have led some fans, especially those on the Internet, to view *Jackass* as a homoerotic spectacle. Richard Scott writes that "*Jackass* and its creator have a huge gay following and you could be mistaken for thinking that it's aimed purely at gay men seeing as the crew of aging skater dudes parade around the set in nothing but jockstraps" (rainbownetwork.com). That is not to say that *Jackass* as a whole or selected segments cannot be read as homoerotic, but I offer that this reading is both oppositional and negotiated and not the reading intended or suggested by the text. I will argue later that homoeroticism on *Jackass* is displaced by the kinds of violent behavior exhibited by these men, just as I contend that some men may act out violently on reality dramas in an effort to displace their own objectification and thus, their own feminization. There is no question that *Jackass* participates in a homosocial spectacle – its narrative is one produced by and about men. The show's exclusion of women from its text speaks only to the homosocial act of men acting out in front of other men and does not speak to any kind of homosexual subtext. While I wish to engage with several readings of *Jackass* (including my own) that may not comport with the intentions of producers or participants, I feel it is also necessary to position the mainstream readings of this text.

At its core, *Jackass* is a juvenile performance by men who would clearly rather be boys, irking "grown-ups" at every turn, undercutting the establishment whenever possible. Kent Williams describes *Jackass* as "a televisual clubhouse with a 'NO GIRLS ALLOWED' sign nailed to the door, [a] repository for boys-will-be-boys shenanigans" (citypaper.net). Frequent objects of ridicule include businesspeople as well as authority figures, though the average citizen shopping or walking down the street is by no means considered off-limits. It would be an understatement to say that the show tests the limits of what would be tolerated by the average person, as almost everything done by the cast of *Jackass* is beyond the tolerance of normalcy. *Jackass* also goes out of its way to expose publicly what is generally kept private. Nudity is not the only part of *Jackass* that reveals that which is normally personal; the intimate is also exposed through the depiction of public urination/defecation, intricate tattooing, or unusual piercing. As none of these acts or exposures is performed for sexual pleasure, *Jackass* stands apart from both eroticism and homoeroticism. While *Jackass* may be irreverent and obscene, it is neither pornographic nor expressly erotic.

Both the text of *Jackass* and its presence on MTV place the show squarely within youth culture in the United States and abroad. Several histories of MTV assert not only the network's centrality in youth culture but also its ability to establish, modify, and reaffirm popular youth consumption (Feinstein 2000; Starr 2003; Banks 2005; Grossberg 1989; Lewis 1990; Williams, Kevin 2003; Denisoff 1988). Chip Walker comments that "MTV is probably the most impressive global TV youth phenomenon" (42). MTV found itself both influencing and influenced by the predominant youth culture. In delineating the production history of MTV, Tom McGrath states

> Despite its size, the company [MTV Networks] continued to be a place where young people ruled. It wasn't entrepreneurial any longer—that era had died when the pioneers left the company in the mid-1980s—but with a constant influx of twenty-something minds, it was still a place that was skeptical of the status quo. (203)

Jackass delights in bucking not only the status quo, but also the perceived establishment – the business and professional interests mocked relentlessly for their participation in the "adult" world. Of course, there is a fair amount of irony in noting that the participants of *Jackass* are adults themselves – adults behaving like children.

Jackass initially grew out of a culture of youth skateboarders. Many future *Jackass* stars were featured in a series of CKY (Camp Kill Yourself) videos that featured skateboarding tricks and stunts. Michael Willard marks skateboarding as a youth phenomenon that is characterized by both artistic expression and youth resistance. For Willard, skateboarding is about "the social construction of space," "the spatial construction of youth," and "how skaters reproduce the global scale of youth itself, according to the values created through skating" (333). While *Jackass* is not entirely devoted to skateboarding or its culture, *Jackass* draws on the same youth culture characteristic of both skateboarding and MTV. The connection to youth culture and to skateboarding as a youth phenomenon allows *Jackass* to occupy a space that is both mainstream and underground.

The cast of *Jackass*, like their skateboarding counterparts, often find themselves driven from public spaces. *Jackass'* presence on MTV and in movie megaplexes gives it renewed public exposure, but the acts performed often have to be done covertly or in private spaces. *Jackass* inadvertently calls into question a notion of what is public, harkening back to its skateboarding roots:

> Moments when undesirables such as skaters or the homeless are ejected from such places also show that the "public inclusion" projected so invitingly by post-modern plazas of high finance, in fact, is a "public illusion" limited to narrow definitions of who may enter and how they may participate in this fiction of public space.
>
> (Willard 334)

Much of what occurs on *Jackass* is deemed unsuitable for the public space – defecating in a toilet displayed at a hardware store or applying electric shocks to one's testicles – and thus, must be done in disguise or in the private space of a home. *Jackass'* mainstream performance in film and on television is complicated by its often underground production. While *Jackass* utilizes the public space for performance, it is often driven underground by its content and desire to remain covert.

Jackass is reality television. Much of the uncertainty and spontaneity found in the genre exists on *Jackass*. Stunts go awry – cast members have to be stitched up and bandaged, clearly unplanned consequences of their dangerous and unpredictable behavior. As a reality program, the violent performance on *Jackass* requires further scrutiny. These are real men performing real acts on their bodies and the bodies of others. The show carries with it a disclaimer that the stunts are not to be reproduced by viewers, that these acts are performed by "trained professionals." While there may be some question as to whether these men are either trained or professional, they are not actors or stunt men. As a reality show, *Jackass* works to deflect the objectification of men, objectification inherent in the genre. What makes *Jackass* unique is the way in which violence is used to both deflect the feminized position of the object and for these men to demonstrate that they are hyper-masculine masochists. The preceding construction of *Jackass* as a text allows for a more nuanced analysis of the kind of violence found in the show and film.

Jackass as reflexive sadomasochism

In his chapter titled "The Sadomasochist in the Closet," David Savran comments that modern man is often read in neoconservative circles to be the victim of feminism (173). Male performance, for Savran, is a kind of anti-feminist endeavor where men act out not against women but against the kind of subjectivity imposed on them by feminism. Savran theorizes a cultural space for masculine performativity that allows for the male body to become spectacle so long as it is in some kind of physical danger. Savran cites *Rambo* [1985] as an example of this spectacle. More recent films such as *Die Hard* [1988] and *Fight Club* [1999] suggest as well that the male body can be the object of an erotic gaze, a gaze that both mitigates and displaces homoerotic desire. For Savran, reflexive sadomasochism is part of a "relentless flirtation with pain, injury, and death" and "goes beyond heroism and bravery to a kind of self-torture" (163). The men of *Jackass* often inflict great pain and injury on themselves and each other and in some cases come close to death. For these men, self-torture constitutes a continual increase either in the amount of pain they endure or in the danger they face. Savran characterizes this kind of behavior as embodying a "particular kind of maso-chistic male subjectivity—dubbed reflexive sadomasochism by Freud—which has become hegemonic in American culture over the course of the past twenty years" (163). This anxiety is characterized by the men of popular culture – lost and anguished in films such as *Bad Lieutenant* [1992], *Falling Down* [1993], *Magnolia* [1999], violent towards themselves and others in films such as *Fight Club* and *Lantana* [2001]. Pat Gill describes these films of "suffering men [where] protagonists despair at what they feel and suspect about themselves, and despair prompts them to agon-ized acts of displacement and amelioration" (160). There is not a sense of despair in the men of *Jackass* but the masculinity they perform is somewhat uncertain, an uncertainty informed by violent (and naked) behavior.

Notable in Savran's formulation of reflexive sadomasochism is the absence of women. For Savran, the "new man validates himself less by turning against women . . . than by turning against himself" (176). This claim perfectly describes *Jackass* because there are no women in physical danger, no women throwing themselves in raw sewage, no women being shot with fire hoses, no women testing the limits of an athletic supporter. In sum, the women of *Jackass* perform supporting roles and are never put in danger. This is analogous to Cassie Kircher's characterization of rock videos on MTV where "women appear and men act" (41). *Jackass* shows men per-petrating acts of violence against themselves and each other. Laura Mulvey theorized that the body as an erotic object is inherently feminized. Savran writes that "reflexive sadomasochism functions as a kind of fantasmatic machine that relentlessly repro-duces a tough male subject who proves his toughness by subjugating and battering his (feminized) other" (190). The male body in *Jackass* is a feminized spectacle that must be attacked in order to restore patriarchal masculinity. The men of *Jackass* punish their bodies in astonishing ways – with tazers and electrodes, with bowling balls and baseball bats. Following Savran's logic, each time the body is attacked, the men are further masculinized. The injured male displaces his status as erotic other allowing him "to play the part of victim and yet be a man" (195).

There are countless instances of this behavior in both the television show and the film. At times, we see the consequences of this dangerous behavior. The cast members are followed to hospitals or stitched up on site. *Jackass* is not, however, about gore. *Jackass* is about pain and, to some degree, humiliation. In a particularly telling moment, a cast member inserts a toy car wrapped in a condom into his rectum. The idea of this stunt/prank is to have an unsuspecting doctor take an x-ray of the rectum, revealing the toy car. While the punch line of the prank comes at the end, for my purposes, the key moment is the insertion. In a motel room somewhere in America, another unwitting cast member stumbles into the room to find the insertion in progress. At that moment, the cast member inserting the car into his *own* rectum cries out "Just tell me I am a man, Manny!" For me, this foregrounds the very nature of the prank – it reveals just how far a man is willing to go to be thought of as a "man." This is not the only case of bodily invasion, though it best illustrates the theory of reflexive sadomasochism.

In psychoanalytic terms, this performance is as much a hystericization of the male body as it is an indication of reflexive sadomasochism. Unsure whether he is a man or a woman, the hysterical male is terrified by his body – both because it may be his and it may not be. Thus, the hysterical pushes his body to physical extremes, simply because he can participate in this kind of gendered performance. I do not believe that the hysterical male and the reflexive sadomasochist are mutually exclusive. It seems to me that the reflexive sadomasochist is hysterical, testing the limits of his body in an effort to define himself as masculine. The hysterical male is bizarrely troubled by his own objectification and his reaction is this particular performance of masculinity.

If one wishes to draw a distinction between gendered performance and gendered display on *Jackass*, this distinction would entail distinguishing pranks from stunts. The pranks can be read as displays, some gendered, some not, and the stunts as performances. The prank serves as a narrative for the audience. Pranks, such as pretending to bleed out of one's ear while talking on a cell phone, function entirely as displays. I do not want to suggest that the prank is a passive display or is at all feminized. I make this distinction because the narrative of *Jackass* is so clearly bifurcated. While I do not wish to ignore the pranks (a considerable part of *Jackass*), I am less interested in them because they do not involve real assaults on the male body. Participation in a *Jackass* prank is a display of obnoxious, obscene, and offensive behavior but it does not require any kind of performative assault on the body. Because the stunt is so closely linked to the body of the cast member, however, it is a performance. The stunt is often a dangerous act that requires the male body to be malleable and resistant; the stunt necessitates the real threat of injury, damage, or scarring of the body, a necessity not found in the *Jackass* prank. The moments when cast members are in real physical danger implicate both the audience and the performer. On a narrative level, then, these moments engage both the performer and the audience. On a psychoanalytic level, they are as much about defining the cast member's masculinity as they are entertaining the audience. For the observer, there is an unsettling fear, revulsion, and interest involved in the *Jackass* stunt. *Jackass* performers rarely are humiliated by their behavior. They leave it to the audience to be humiliated for them. If the *Jackass* prank tells a story, then the *Jackass* stunt makes the audience complicit.

The men on *Jackass* survive these stunts, sometimes after cracking ribs, suffering concussions, or requiring stitches. They do not die and they are not permanently injured. For Savran, their ongoing attempts at re-masculinization derive not only from the stunts themselves but from their ability to overcome danger in a continuing search for what Savran terms the phallus[4]. By phallus, Savran means the desire for an ever-elusive, stable, structuring masculinity. The phallus is not knowable or fully attainable yet desire for it continues unabated. In speaking about *Rambo*, Savran notes, "his heroically scarred body thereby serves, ironically, as a reminder that he does not finally 'have' the phallus, and that his desire can be fulfilled only through a sado-masochistic reiteration which commemorates ad infinitum both his limitless desire for pain and his perpetual victory over pain" (201). These comments are just as applicable to a discussion of *Jackass*. In fact, Savran's comments have a heightened significance when considering *Jackass* as reality television. These are real men doing real damage to their bodies. Their pleasure in pain maps on to a psychoanalytic model much more palpably than fictional characters whose actions not only must be read psychoanalytically but narratively as well. In the psychoanalytic model, *Jackass* can be read as a homoerotic text. This approach is one way to explain why half naked men attach electrodes to each other's scrotums. Savran does not reject this reading but posits that the incorporation of pain and torture undercuts the homoerotic elements. For the *Jackass* participant, "his insistent self-production as a victim of torture works to protect him from being an object of male desire" (203). *Jackass* successfully displaces male desire through pain.

Notes

1   Widespread coverage of these lawsuits and complaints can be found in the popular press, including, but not limited to, Todd Hollingshead's "3 Cited in MTV Copycat Stunt" and Will Batchelor's "Police Probe Over *Jackass* Copycat Boy".
2   These visual techniques include, but are not limited to, the use of first and third person gazes and a reliance on hand-held cameras.
3   Individual townspeople are asked questions like "Are there a lot of fun things to do in Mianus?" and "Is there a lot of meat in Mianus?"
4   Savran is using a model of the phallus originally derived by Jacques Lacan.

PART 3

Tabloid culture, production
and consumption

SECTION 6

Producing tabloid culture: behind the scenes

There is a growing body of work on media organizations and production that makes the case that knowledge of the everyday practices of the media and culture industries is essential if we are to understand the processes of 'mediatization' and the broader relationship between media and society (e.g. Tumber, 2000; Croteau and Hoynes, 2002; Cottle, 2003: Hesmondhalgh, 2005 and 2007). It could be said, however, that media and cultural studies scholarship has been relatively neglectful of the *specific* working practices of media professionals and the ways in which tabloid media, in particular, are produced. The main exception, perhaps, is in journalism studies where one of the key areas of investigation has been how journalists, editors and producers operate in terms of established working behaviours, protocols, conventions and standards and the ways in which they negotiate the institutional structures they inhabit. Much of this scholarship originates from a sociological perspective that attends to the study of the history, development, organization and problems of people working and living in social networks (see Schudson, 1989; Zelizer, 2004: 45–5). Its emphasis lies in understanding how the news is made, how decisions are arrived at about the selection, ordering and presentation of news and how these decisions impact on the overall agenda-setting functions of the news.

'Serious' journalism, in particular, has always occupied a privileged place in the hierarchy of media forms and has been regarded as authoritative by virtue of its commitment to providing timely, truthful and informative news and opinion. Many journalists value this role highly and work hard to maintain these ideals within a demanding workplace culture characterized by pressures of time, space, commercial needs and other institutional factors. One interest common to sociological inquiry in the United States, the United Kingdom and elsewhere has been, therefore, 'the systemic actions, practices, and interactions by which journalists maintain themselves as journalists' (Zelizer, 2004: 47). From the 1970s onwards these interests were evident in a range of studies concerned with newsroom practices and the views of journalists themselves about what they do (e.g. Tunstall, 1971; Chibnall, 1977; Schlesinger, 1978; Golding and Elliott, 1979; Reese, 1990; De Burgh, 2000; Rhoufari, 2000; Kovach and Rosenstiel, 2001; Deuze, 2005a and 2005b). These have been concerned with unpacking the relationship between working practices, professional ideology, institutional constraints and the manufacture of news. One of the perennial issues that arises is that of the everyday conflict between ethical journalistic standards held up as both attainable and essential in public debates and, on the other hand, the embedded professional practices of people who have to deliver the news in a highly competitive market. Mathieu Rhoufari (2000) illustrates this point well following his interviews with 'serious' and tabloid newspaper editors and reporters. He concludes that tabloid journalists are forced to work with a Darwinian model of competition between colleagues and that they are relatively disempowered in terms of the influence they can wield both collectively and as individual employees (Rhoufari, 2000: 172–3). In this working environment, and in the context of a marketplace in which newspapers strive to outshine or discredit their rival papers and grab the public's attention on a daily basis through scandal and sensational-ism, it is extremely difficult for journalists to reconcile the gap between journalistic ideals and their everyday practice.

Tabloid journalists become embroiled in public debates about journalistic responsi-bility quite regularly. This partly occurs because there clearly are commonsense assump-tions on the part of audiences and professional values championed by journalists themselves regarding the values and social role of news (values such as objectivity, truthfulness and roles such as facilitating public debate or revealing political or cor-porate misdemeanours) which cannot always be sustained. In reality it is inevitable that some journalism will fall short of these ideals. But these assumptions and values have led to journalism being viewed as a distinctive and frequently privileged cultural form and, in the words of Brian McNair (1998: 4), therein lies the 'sociological significance of journalistic communication'. McNair (p. 6) also makes the point, along with others, that journalism is an *authored* narrative, a product of human agency, which is therefore always and essentially ideological. In other words, it transmits information marked by the assumptions, attitudes and convictions of newsmakers and the institutional contexts within which they operate.

Scholarship in the United Kingdom has led the way in incorporating questions of ideology and hegemony into sociological inquiry. It has sought to show how ideology becomes transformed into 'commonsense' notions of the world that are difficult to challenge and that news should be understood not as a reflection of the world but as a way of reordering the reality and framing it in ideological ways. A number of researchers who became known collectively as the Glasgow University Media Group (GUMG) pub-lished a set of research into news bias, which supported this understanding of ideology as central to the ways in which news is framed and presented. Called *Bad News*, the original project mixed sociological approaches with linguistics, semiotics, and ideo-logical critique to analyse British TV's linguistic and visual coverage of industrial action and class politics. It produced two volumes (GUMG, 1976a, b), which showed that neutrality was difficult to sustain in even the most reputable journalistic output. It argued that the structure and framing of news sustained society's culturally dominant assumptions about the relationship between industry and labour (to take just one example) and that these were produced through the decision-making processes regard-ing interview methods, framing, choice of locations and so on. As John Eldridge (2000: 114–15) recalls, this empirical research undertook a complex and multifaceted critique of news production and provided evidence to show that across both public and commercial news bulletins similarities overrode differences, which in turn reflected a common journalistic culture and shared codes of TV news production. The GUMG's decoding of news also sought to show how codes were deployed though agenda-setting, gatekeeping and news values and concluded that journalistic culture was far from neutral.

The works of the GUMG and soon after the Birmingham Centre for Contemporary Cultural Studies (CCCS), together with later sociology of journalism, have been consistently critical of the 'liberal pluralist framework' for understanding the production and consumption of news (McNair, 1998: 26). This work has built on and developed the argument that the so-called free market of ideas and media production that circulates them and that characterizes Western societies actually masks the ways in which capitalism itself is an ideology which promotes and seeks to maintain a certain kind of social stratification. The coauthored book *Policing the Crisis* (Hall et al., 1978) is perhaps the best known of the CCCS studies into media and social control that develops this viewpoint, addressing the ways in which the media articulate ideas about law and order, crime and deviance. Here the authors sought to show how the professional rules of news gathering and reportage favoured the viewpoints of those in authority (the 'primary definers' of news) and how these in turn were bound to promote a public consensus in which it was 'common sense' that liberal pluralism worked and that the status quo must be maintained. The argument here is that those high up in institutional hierarchies are routinely turned to by journalists as the source of primary definition or interpretation of news events and those that have opposing views are always forced to counter what seems to be the prevailing, most strongly mobilized view. Many analyses of workplace culture and the production of news therefore have generally been aimed at supplementing and opening out these debates about the manufacture of news, ideology and social consensus in both 'serious' and tabloid contexts.

Other kinds of scholarship of media production is quite varied and far less easily summarized. For example, some media professionals have offered invaluable self-reflective commentaries on the philosophy of working in a particular sector or genre. This is particularly notable in the areas of television drama, documentary and reality TV where producers, writers and directors such as Peter Balzalgette, Jimmy McGovern, Lynda Laplante, Roger Graeff, Penny Woolcott and Paul Watson have spoken at conferences, have been extensively interviewed or have directly contributed to academic collections. Many of these names should be regarded as authors or else 'auteurs': that is people whose output is recognizably their own and bears their hallmark or 'signature' rather more than being the product of collective labour. There are far fewer voices of ordinary media workers to be heard in academic studies of the media with the exception being a growing body of work that debates the place of women in the media industries and often draws on female professionals' own accounts (e.g. Baehr and Dyer, 1987; Arthurs, 1989 and 1994; Steiner, 1997 and 1998; Chambers et al., 2004). Other approaches include participant or nonparticipant observation or the strategic use of interview material in order to enrich critical accounts such as Rhoufari, discussed above. Deborah Jermyn's (2007) work on reality crime television is another example of this last approach as the author integrates production and industry perspectives into a mainly textual and ideological analysis. These perspectives are garnered from both her own experience as a crime appeals press officer and through interviews with leading production personnel. Jermyn's agenda here is to flesh out the institutional and medium-driven priorities that shape the programmes for those that actually make them in order to illuminate further her own critique of an evolving television genre.

It can also often be useful to turn to documentary journalism and non-academic memoirs by media professionals to learn more about the tabloid media environment (e.g. Chippendale and Horrie, 1999; Horrie and Nathan, 1999; Brenton and Cohen, 2003). Although some of these include anecdote and hearsay they still furnish readers with an insider's view and may even overturn assumptions about the tabloids and their functions. Entertaining and highly detailed exposés, such as S. J. Taylor's (1992) account of the tabloids in the United Kingdom and the United States since the 1980s are also great for providing an insight into the atmosphere and personal attitudes of those working in the industry. Taylor's book emerged from a substantial amount of primary research including numerous interviews with editors, journalists and photo-journalists. In a wide-ranging study she investigates diverse aspects of the tabloid industry including a 'page 3' topless model photosession for the *Sun*, the gendered hierarchy of the daily press and the career ladder for female journalists, and the proto-cols of chequebook journalism. She even provides a glossary of tabloid terminology for the uninitiated. A useful insider's view of the American weekly supermarket tabloids is provided by investigative reporter Bill Sloan's (2001) history of the tabloid newspaper industry. Among his many jobs Sloan worked for the *National Enquirer*, perhaps one of the most notorious tabloid papers, and he presents a lively account of the changes undergone by the tabloid industry since the 1970s. He chronicles not only the values of the journalists involved but also the broader changes in content and presentation, the arrival of Rupert Murdoch and subsequent commercial battles and the conditions under which tabloids have been 'outsleazed' by mainstream media. Interestingly, Sloane (p. 195) also makes the case that tabloids have been badly underestimated with regard to their investigative functions and reminds readers that they have beaten the mainstream press to many of the best stories. He points out, for example, that the *Enquirer's* scoops and considered coverage of the infamous O.J. Simpson case (which is discussed by Kevin Glynn in this volume) won plaudits from both the *New York Times* and the *Los Angeles Times*.

In this section we have included two quite different studies that integrate observa-tion and interviews to produce considered accounts of the working practices of tabloid journalists. For his article 'Popular journalism and professional ideology' Mark Deuze interviewed journalists working for leading tabloids in the Netherlands in order to pro-duce an analysis of the 'interpretive repertoires' deployed by journalists in discussing their own work. With admirable clarity Deuze organizes these discussions into categor-ies such as 'ethics', 'gossip' and 'skills and standards' and then draws inferences concerning the kind of ideological framework that supports journalists' own investment in the profession and more especially in the popular press sector within which they work. In Elizabeth Bird's piece she asks quite directly 'who writes the tabloids?' and speaks to workers at Globe Communications (the group responsible for many of the best known 'supermarket weeklies') to learn more. She economically sketches the hothouse environment in which staffing changes on a regular basis and the pool of reporters and editors, which can include overseas journalists with tabloid credentials as well as Americans with extensive experience of more mainstream journalism. The piece is especially illuminating in its account of the creativity and storytelling skills of journalists who need an eye for a news item or even a historical event and the ability to transform it into an entertaining narrative.

Laura Grindstaff's piece is quite unusual as it is an academic analysis of American talkshows informed by participant observation that she undertook as a student intern working on two programmes that she calls *Diana* and *Randy*. Her central concern here is with the ways in which these shows are marked as scandalous by virtue of their guests' revelations and shocking disclosures. Drawing on the language of filmed pornography Grindstaff refers to these dramatic moments, which are crucial to the success of the shows, as 'the money shots'; these are the 'lynchpin' of the production work and drive forward the planning and choreography of the show. Her account of production processes from sourcing guests to orchestrating the show's dynamics makes riveting reading. Victoria Mapplebeck's essay also refers to the money shot but questions easily made assumptions that the exhibition of the private self and its invitation to voyeurism is necessarily exploitive. Many of the characteristics of tabloid television (and indeed journalism) have made an impact on other, more culturally approved forms, such as investigative journalism and documentary. In Britain, for example, from the 1980s onwards, documentaries adopted what later became recognized as reality TV characteristics. These led to the development of hybrid genres such as the 'docusoap' or documentary formats that included heavy use of CCTV footage, hidden cameras, video diaries and which laid an emphasis on personal revelation and the private sphere rather than the public world of politics or society at large. Mapplebeck writes as the author and director of a five-part documentary called *Smart Hearts*, which drew on reality innovations such as 24-hour webcam streaming and explores the dynamics of making television that is dependent on the cooperation and indeed performance of ordinary people for its success.

Further reading

Beck, A. (ed.) (2002) *Cultural Work: Understanding the Cultural Industries*, London: Routledge.

Cottle, S. (ed.) (2003) *Media Organization and Production*, London: Sage.

Croteau, D. and Hoynes, W. (2002) *Media/Society: Industries, Images and Audiences*, 3rd edn, London: Sage.

Hesmondhalgh, D. (2002) *The Cultural Industries*, London: Sage.

Hesmondhalgh, D. (2005) *Media Production*, Maidenhead: Open University Press.

Tumber, H. (ed.) (2000) *Media Power, Professionals and Policies*, London: Routledge.

3.1

Popular journalism and professional ideology: tabloid reporters and editors speak out
by Mark Deuze

Media culture and popular culture are increasingly difficult to classify; the ongoing blurring of boundaries between information and entertainment can be termed 'infotainment' and is generally attributed to market forces, commercialization and commodification of media content (Dahlgren and Sparks, 1992; McManus, 1994; McChesney, 1999). Particularly in the realm of journalism, concerns about infotainment or tabloidization have been voiced by scholars and professionals alike throughout elective democracies with shared histories of journalism professionalization.[1] Although there are several ways to study the articulation of popular culture with journalists and journalism, this article specifically interrogates this development by analyzing the perceptions of reporters and editors in the field of popular journalism regarding their work and values. A range of expert interviews with journalists working for the leading tabloids in the Netherlands were conducted in order to further study and understand the relationships between working for an archetypical infotainment genre and the various ways in which practitioners give meaning to their professional identity in contemporary (popular) journalism.

Authors like Hallin (1992) and van Zoonen (1998b) identify the tabloid as the prime example of a popular medium where one cannot draw a meaningful distinction between 'information' and 'entertainment'. Connell (1998) also argues that the news discourse in broadsheet and tabloid media is largely similar. Bird (1992) showed how journalists working for supermarket tabloids in the United States can be considered as the same (kind of) people who work for mainstream newspapers. Tabloid reporters and editors operate in the margins and along the edges of professional journalism, while also located in the middle of this peer group in terms of their professional identity as journalists (van Zoonen, 1998a). I am fascinated by the ways in which journalism as a profession with a certain (real or perceived) power position in contemporary society defines and organizes itself over time. Listening carefully to those within the profession who operate in the margins and thus (sometimes) deviate from what the current consensus about what good or real journalism is offers us insight into how journalism organizes and defines itself, how this process of definition is structured, and how, in turn, this influences how journalism functions (Deuze, 2002).

[...]

Expert interviews

In order to determine who to interview, I used the definitions of tabloid and popular journalism by Sparks (2000: 14–15), where he considers as the 'ultimate' form of popular journalism the supermarket tabloid – a genre non-existent in the Netherlands (apart from a brief and unsuccessful experiment with a magazine called *De Nieuwe* in the early 1990s, and a second failed magazine called *Prenza*, which appeared for only a few months during 2001–2), but well established in the Anglo-American media sphere. [. . .] Whereas the Dutch media market has no tabloids, it does have its fair share of weekly celebrity and gossip magazines, breakfast and daytime TV lifestyle talk shows and lifestyle sections in newspapers. For the in-depth interviews all the (chief) editors of the main news-stand tabloids (*Privé, Story, Weekend, Party, Talkies, Glossy, Beau Monde*) and serious-popular press (*Aktueel, Nieuwe Revue, Panorama*) were selected. These magazines have a long history in the Netherlands (*Story*, for example, was the first gossip magazine and started in 1974; *Panorama* put out its first issue in 1913), and have significant readerships (*Story, Weekend, Privé* and *Party* together had a total circulation of almost 1 million copies at the time of writing; the six other magazines together have a market share of approximately 600,000 copies). These magazines have also undergone some changes in recent years because of increased competition from other media – notably commerical television and the 'quality' press – and from other tabloid titles, most recently *Talkies, Glossy* and *Party* entered the market in the 1990s (Meijer, 1999: 42). [. . .]

The editorial departments of the 10 selected magazines were first sent a formal letter (dated late May 2001) describing the research project, and were then contacted by phone to make an interview appointment. Only the editor of *Talkies* refused to cooperate, claiming he did not have time for 'academic pursuits'. All other editors (some of these magazines have more than one editor; and *Aktueel, Glossy* and *Weekend* in fact shared the same editor-in-chief) agreed, resulting in 14 expert interviews. The results section starts with an overview and description of the full range of topical categories the participants talked about, and concludes with an analysis of the interpretative repertoires these journalists used when talking about their work. A characteristic of all interviews: the atmosphere was very informal and pleasant. Almost all of the editors said they enjoyed the fact that academics would spend time on research into popular journalism. The editors seemed to consider our interviews as some kind of intellectual acknowledgement of their work.

Analysis

As a first remark, one must note that on several occasions the interviewed editors of serious-popular magazines *Nieuwe Revue* and *Panorama* expressed different concerns from their colleagues. These are not gossip magazines, and several notions mentioned in the analysis pertain specifically to their views. On the other hand, I found that these editors do talk about more or less the same issues, questions and topics as their counterparts in the gossip press; they use the same yardsticks to evaluate themselves, address similar trends and developments in the market for infotainment media, apply the same repertoires to give meaning to their work (see also Bird, 1990, 1992). All of the interviewed experts addressed a total of seven recurring topical categories when talking about their work. In this analysis the full bandwidth of these categories is first explored; thereafter the ways the journalists give meaning to the various categories are discussed.

Category I: the gossip or popular journalistic attitude

The editors would often describe the way they go about their work as a distinct process of gossip or popular journalism. These accounts were set against experiences most of the interviewees had while working for other (non-gossip) media. In other words: the way they go about their work is instrumental in distinguishing themselves from the 'other' journalists and journalisms. The various ways in which interviewees describe their work indicates that they actively negotiate what is considered to be journalism – revealing their own marginalized or deviant position within the profession. Two colleagues at one magazine felt that these supposed differences are what define gossip journalism – a sort of raison d'être even:

> Gossip magazines are in a way just magazines like any other. But a gossip magazine should have a kind of 'mean' or 'sneaky' aura, like something you cannot really put your finger on, so if you take that away, you do not have a magazine anymore, right? Yes, it is kind of a forbidden fruit . . .

Several editors went out of their way to position themselves as 'regular' journalists, even though they would readily admit that what they do and the way they do it is not generally considered to be anything like 'regular' journalism.

> People should not think we are just making things up here. We don't do that, we just get our news not in an 'everyday-like' fashion. People do not have a clue that we work in a normal office building with regular adult people who are happily married . . . hahaha . . . Sorry I have to laugh . . . haha [Interviewer: What are you laughing about?] No, now you can't come and work here, otherwise you would have asked about that a long time ago, haha.

Sometimes editors would explicitly address this process as their motivation for doing this type of journalism:

> We try to visit a lot of educational institutes to explain how fascinating this type of journalism is, how journalistic the work is that gets done, because there are still many people that question that, which really annoys me.

Category II: skills and standards

Indeed, what does a gossip reporter need to know in order to be a real tabloid journalist? An interesting question – and one that features topically in the discussions we had with the interviewees. Several participants lamented the omission of popular journalism from the curricula of journalism schools and training institutes. One question is, what specific skills could or should a journalist learn in the popular press? A selection of statements about this sheds some light on what specific skills are expected of a gossip reporter:

> You have to be the kind of reporter Dutch celebrities talk about at parties, saying: 'Look, there is that asshole again', you should not be too friendly and positive. . . . I have to write really hard-hitting stories about people, but that does not mean I have something against those people personally – that is just how the story should be.

An important aspect of such remarks is the way these are framed versus what other news people supposedly do, emphasizing what these editors feel makes them and their genre extraordinary:

> A normal reporter tends to be very careful, but we have to write an exciting headline and a teasing lead, that makes a story different.

A discussion of skills and standards not only serves to define what tabloid-style journalism is, but also functions for the interviewees as a way to specify a concept of 'quality' in the genre.

> What we do is combining information. We protect our sources, but ask them everything to make sure we are accurate, and that is good journalism. Combine everything, use all information at your disposal: call that person, he might have heard this, and you have read that, seen this somewhere, and as you work along this way, you might even decide to put a photographer somewhere for a night on stakeout to see whether that person indeed comes home alone or with someone else, and yes . . . then you did a good job.

The framework of delineating popular journalism's skills extends to specific standards acknowledged throughout the profession, like reporting both sides of a story, or defining oneself in a position of critical acclaim throughout the profession as 'investigative reporter'.

> What we do is a kind of investigative journalism. . . . We are searching for the truth. Look, if you are a parliamentary reporter it's easy, just wait for the press conference, do some short corridor interviews, and nobody thinks that is odd. But as a gossip reporter you have to know everything about a person's private life and there are no press conferences for that, there is nothing to help you – except just researching, investigating like a detective.

The various comments on skills and standards of media practitioners in this field reads like a particular description of investigative reporting, with emphasis on (potential) conflicts with the traditional rules of the profession. One of those golden concepts – or, as Kovach and Rosenstiel write, 'the first and most confusing principle' (2001: 36) – is: truth.

Category III: truth versus 'untruth'

Other dualistic category titles could be: fantasy versus reality, lies versus truths, deceit versus honesty, rumors versus facts. The participants used these and other similar binary oppositions throughout the interviews to such an extent that one could analyze them as a topical category. Reality and truth seem to be phenomenological concepts the popular press are quite familiar with, concepts with which they actively negotiate in the daily routines of newsgathering and reporting. One of the editors offered an explanation for this approach, specifically locating truth in the story aesthetic, as in the way it can be written and presented:

> Yes, well, if . . . I assume that the gossip magazines also strive for some kind of truth, they have limits as to what they can write, those limits are a bit more stretched with phrases like 'it could be that' or 'we have heard that', but . . . ehh . . . they aim for the kind of truth they feel the public needs to know and it is of course nice to read.

This reflection comes from an editor of one of the serious-popular magazines, and is to some extent mirrored by a colleague in that category, also using a distinction between the gossip press and his own publication, seeing a perceived conflict between true and (potentially) false information as a deliberate strategy:

> It's the journalistic approach we choose, we do not exaggerate beyond all proportions. It must be something concrete, but if that is so we move in fullsteam! That is what we do. The moment such a story turns into a lawsuit all kind of extra publicity follows, our sales increase, so that is good.

Several of the gossip editors declared that what they do, is in their view part of the journalistic task of truth-finding. A complex concept of truth is common to all participants, and it is strategically used to distinguish one's own product from the competition. In this last quote, explicit reference is made to publicity and sales as aspects of evaluation and a perception of the audience as customers (rather than, for example, citizens).

Category IV: the public/readers/people

Several editors consider the weekly sales figures 'holy'. In making decisions about content or laying down cover policy, considerations of audience are core. Throughout the interviews the participants would also refer to certain characteristics of the people who buy their magazine. Such references varied from general comments ('Our readers are mostly men, their wives buy our magazine at the grocery store') to very specific ones ('Our reader eats microwave food'). Doing audience research – several journalists mentioned qualitative research like focus group discussions in particular – also seems to be part of the whole 'popular journalism experience' for these editors.

Looking more specifically at the comments made about (members of) the audience, it seems that such statements are used specifically when making editorial decisions on the visualization of content (writing style, choice of illustration or pictures, cover policy), not on newsgathering processes (like whether or not harass people to get information, or which news to print). Examples of such statements on visualization (as it relates to status):

> We are making a much more respectable magazine than a couple of years ago. Now we also have covers that you can put on the table, covers you don't have to feel ashamed about. Sometimes covers are a bit more explicit, but that does not matter.

And on style (as it relates to know-how and attitude):

> We write for the big masses, so we cannot go too far . . . you have to be carried away by the story, you should be teased to read on, like 'Hey I did not know that, wow'. That is the tone of voice of your magazine, we take a certain position, a bit tongue-in-cheek, sometimes with humor, now and then really sharp.

When it comes to the role of the audience in editorial decision-making processes, it seems that editors attribute people in the Netherlands with a certain 'Dutchness':

> Yes, sure I like the big scoops, but the larger audience will not like that. And then you should not do it, which is obvious. That is the weird thing about the Netherlands, compared to, for example, England. We have the same target group as the British tabloids, but Dutch people do not want to read about hard-hitting scandals involving the big celebrities. If it goes too far, nobody wants to read about it. Dutch people don't want to know about the fallacies and wrong-doings of their favorite stars.

Dutch tabloids are described by van Zoonen (1998b) and Meijer (1999) as relatively 'decent' forms of popular journalism – especially when compared to their British, German or American counterparts. The statements on the audience suggest this has more to do with images of audience than a specific journalistic attitude or style of newsgathering. This is also reflected in the various audience-related goals the editors talk about:

> We want to offer people a bit of distraction, entertainment. People do not have to learn from what we write, no . . . a bit of gossip, which is also enough. What is nice is that you notice how people talk about what you've published at parties.

Images of audience are also evoked when commenting on perceptions of the added value of popular journalism as compared to the mainstream news media.

> Just negative news does not work, people want to have a bit of fun reading as well. The popular magazine has a function of entertaining. Like when someone has worked hard all day and just wants to lie down at night and relax, he or she can read the magazine.

Category V: ethics

The ethical perceptions of infotainment journalists have been used as sensitizing concepts in the interviews, both by interviewers and interviewees (following Silverman, 2000: 65). The participants would address ethical issues and dilemmas when discussing the daily practices of working as a gossip journalist:

> We always say: we want to know everything, but that does not mean we publish everything. This has to do with ethical rules. We know much more about celebrities than the people know, but if we published that it would ruin careers . . . but it is becoming more acceptable now. If you knew who is calling us, tipping us off . . . Sometimes I think people are not born good but evil.

Other editors would position themselves more modestly regarding ethical rules or norms, and refer to themselves as the yardstick for measuring ethical decisions without making generalizing normative claims, linking ethics with (perceptions about) the audience:

> No, of course not, I am not here to change the world. The ultimate goal is to sell a lot of magazines, whereby you have to be able to look in the mirror each night and say: 'I have not hurt anybody today.'

The emphasis put on selling magazines has to do with the week-to-week battle for the reader, as editors explain. According to them, most readers buy these magazines impulsively, and readership diversifies across the different titles (one week buying *Aktueel,* next week *Story* or *Privé,* and so on). Interviewees furthermore added third-person comments on the ethics and trustworthiness of 'serious' journalists, now that those media are considered to be moving into 'their' terrain of news:

> Daily newspapers are writing about human interest and personal stuff more and more, but that is not bad for us. The more they talk about it, the better, because people think of the gossip press as the place to really find this news. The gossip magazines are increasingly used as an 'alibi' for the good papers to write about celebrities for example. If such a celebrity makes it onto the front page of *De Volkskrant* [national quality newspaper], which causes trials and the destruction of that person's career, then the editor of *De Volkskrant* says: 'Yes, but what he said is written in my notebook.' Well, I can show you notebooks full of quotes by people, but we can never use them, no judge will allow us to use that argument. This shows you how rocky the credibility of mainstream newspaper journalism is.

This kind of distinction regarding ethics, norms and values further contributes to the strategy mentioned earlier, of participating editors distinguishing their own particular field of journalism from 'other' journalisms in the Netherlands: discerning the popular from the serious.

The most interesting thing about what we do is the combination of creativity and management. The development of new initiatives . . . and the ability to do things, that normal journalists – put 'normal' in brackets here – consider impossible, that you can make those things happen. . . . You constantly look for those borders, yes. And sometimes you can only say with hindsight whether what you did was crossing the line too much . . . but, oh well.

What this topical category also shows is heightened awareness of continuously working on the edges of what is considered 'appropriate' in (popular) journalism. This awareness does not seem to reflect a need for a code, nor an attitude attuned to prescriptions as to how to do popular journalism, and can therefore be seen as a plea for a contextualized and situational ethics, offering ways of interpreting specific ethical dilemmas. This does not mean that these journalists are not ethical, or do not share a sense of ethics; on the contrary, the interviews suggest that ethical perceptions are actively negotiated as a means of distinguishing oneself from competitor-colleagues and 'other' journalisms. Ethical sensibility seems to function as an instrument for drawing a boundary between mainstream and popular journalism. But it is also used (together with notions of true versus false information) to discern 'good' from 'bad' tabloid-style media:

> You know what we do, that is really different than for example what *Party* does. *Party* is the youngest. That is real 'thumb suck journalism'. The weirdest thing is that it's rebellious and it's popular with a younger audience. But listen: 'thumb suck journalism' is the lowest when it comes to quality, it is not even journalism anymore.

Category VI: the magazine *Party*

Journalists seem to share very specific views on certain benchmarks in their profession. Whether this is to do with the absence of a consensual, theoretical or academic concept of quality in journalism or not is beyond the scope of this particular analysis (see Costera Meijer, 2001). But it is striking to notice that the relatively 'young' gossip magazine *Party* serves as a shared reference of 'how not to do popular journalism' for most of the participants. The notions of age, of being younger, as well as a concept of telling the truth seem to be tied in with the criticism of *Party*:[2]

> There is also a . . . a group of young people or students, but those people read magazines like *Party* . . . magazines which are completely . . . well not completely, but it is a magazine which goes too far in our line of work, they do not hesitate to, ehh . . . to write complete nonsense.

Other comments also explicitly address this issue: 'Where they really lie about everything, that is at *Party*, hahaha . . . the real dirt among the gossip press', or for example: 'I do not consider *Party* gossip journalism. . . . No, it belongs to an outside category, it is really nothing, I cannot understand that it has already existed for five or six years.'[3] When we put these comments to the editors of *Party*, they responded with an acknowledgement of the arguments about telling the truth: 'There does not have to be a core of truth in a story.' About the critical comments about the magazine: 'We make *Party* for our readers, for no one else. . . . After all these years you develop an elephant skin, whatever, it is just all about selling magazines, the salary and having a good time.'

But whether working for *Party* or any other magazine in this genre, all editors expressed to some extent a sense of unease among journalists and editors working in different genres of the Netherlands media – addressing a particular awareness of professional (*informal*) hierarchy.

Category VII: (low) status in journalism

The status (or lack thereof) of gossip and popular journalism is a topic of concern for most interviewees (see also Bird, 1990 and Rhoufari, 2000 on similar notions of unequal status of the gossip press in American and British journalism). Although this has been noted in the literature as well (see in particular the volume on tabloid journalism edited by Sparks, 2000), some of the editors indicated recent changes with regard to the status issue.

> I am getting more and more interview requests, so yes I am also in *Netwerk* and *Nova* [two quality newscasts on Dutch public television]. They consider us experts, as extraordinarily well-informed people, for example, when it comes to royalty. Which we are. . . . I think that they will still look down upon us, even though they also know that it is not a kind of 'thumb suck journalism', but that it is really investigative journalism. Then it is just a question of whether or not you are interested in topics like celebrity divorces.

Yet, on the other hand, several interviewees still feel they have to fight their lower status in journalism – which defense affirms that there does seem to exist a shared perception of professional hierarchy in journalism.

> What we really have to get rid of is the misconception that it is not journalism what we do around here, or that it is not ethical. It should not be so, that we are not taken seriously by our colleagues – colleagues in newspapers and so on – that is a kind of 'illusory supremacy', thinking that you are better. It irritates me.

This hierarchical notion is echoed in a somewhat frustrated discussion of the internship policies of the Dutch schools for journalism (a discussion particular to the gossip press editors):

> Coincidentally, yesterday two girls called for an internship, they were students of the journalism school in Zwolle. Normally these students are not allowed to do an internship at a gossip magazine, I hate that attitude. That is ridiculous, it should not be that way. Also at the Utrecht school for journalism and the universities: gossip magazines are not taken seriously in journalism.

Such a thirst for acknowledgement is generally ratified by pointing to similar reporting practices, sales figures ('We make money for all the other magazines of our publisher'), and a suggested 'complacency' of colleagues at other news media. The way tabloid editors are held accountable each week for the number of copies sold is something that keeps them more alert than their colleagues at the newspapers for example, editors would argue:

> A lot of those colleagues do not have that, I think if you work at a newspaper you stop worrying about whether or not people like to read what you write, you think 'Well, now I am intelligent and intellectual', you think you have made it. But you have never made it; every day is a new day to prove yourself. Yes, satisfaction kills creativity.

This last comment links status with intellectualism and may be seen as an element of a 'high-brow' versus 'low-brow' culture debate. Apparently the popular press uses the same discourse to defend itself, as the 'quality' media who use this discourse to distinguish themselves (as argued by Winch, 1997). In this overview of topical categories, that must be the overarching conclusion indeed.

Themes

From the various propositions applied by the participants when discussing the topics mentioned above, four more or less distinct themes (or repertoires) were distilled. These can be summarized as irony, morality, commercialism and popular journalism.

Irony

Popular journalism is all about having fun, according to our interviewees. This not only reflects the relaxed and open atmosphere in most of the interviews, it also serves as a strategy for these journalists to give meaning to a wide range of issues facing them in their work. Questions about competences, about ethics, about competition from other media or about taste, were sooner or later all answered by referring to 'having fun':

> Well, hahaha, personally . . . I think that is the fun part, to put a bit of humor in stories, like 'Look at that!' . . . In a way you work in a schizophrenic way because most of the time you do these really serious in-depth interviews with celebrities, but you write these funny stories so it is a kind of role you're playing, which is good fun. That is what is really fun every day, yes.

Fun is also used to determine quality in this genre of journalism, or even to distinguish gossip from journalism altogether:

> I think what we do is sometimes more like 'fun journalism', it is something you should really want to do as a journalist, but is a real difference with. . . . I sometimes write a column on gossip, then it is okay to skip the news like, ehh . . . just your own ideas.

The references made to having fun and the good laughs from time to time when responding to (critical) questions seem to serve as a somewhat ironic step away from the issues at hand for these editors. Instead of directly confronting issues like the objectivity or ethics of certain news-gathering and storytelling practices, participants would sometimes retreat into an ironic repertoire with which they avoid clear answers or specific statements regarding their work.

A story should be exciting, it should have some kind of emotion to it . . . hahaha [Interviewer: You really seem to enjoy talking about this?] . . . haha, yes. . . . It should have emotion, there must be something to it, it should not be some boring story which just goes on and on about nothing, about 'Oh, he is so happy with his children, blah blah blah', that is not what I am waiting for.

Irony further contributes to judgments about mainstream news journalism as being too repressed – a comment also made frequently by the *National Enquirer* reporters interviewed by Bird (1990, 1992).

It is just a really fun business to be in, and it is different every week. It is wild, things happen all of the time and the journalists working here are not so boring. . . . There are crazy photographers, crazy reporters. . . . Everyone is much more loose, it is like working for a newspaper but also making a magazine. . . . We are really a newspaper in magazine format, which is funny, it is good fun to work this way.

Bird showed that many weekly tabloid reporters expressed frustration about the 'seriousness' of mainstream newspapers, especially regarding restrictions on their creativity. According to these journalists, working in popular genres of their profession allows them more freedom to tell stories – whether 'true' or 'untrue' – and to have fun in doing so. Irony functions as a way to put some distance between 'them' and 'us' in popular journalism. The interviewees indicated that dominant topics they work with – lifestyles, celebrities, royalty, sex – are not exclusive to popular journalism anymore, which suggests that what distinguishes them from other journalisms, in their view, has to do with certain ways of reporting and storytelling, and with not being too strict (or serious) about certain traditional journalistic values. Editorial autonomy, for the tabloid editor, seems to mean not being too restricted by conventions. It almost seems a bit like a pubescent preoccupation with 'breaking the rules': seeing how far you can stretch rules laid down by parents, without actually inventing new rules.[4]

Morality

Douglas Coupland defined in his account of the 30-something generation in the early 1990s (the so-called 'Generation X') the concept of celebrity *Schadenfreude* as: 'lurid thrills derived from talking about celebrity deaths' (1991: 78). This term can perhaps be applied – in a less morbid fashion, that is – to the connection between morality and irony in popular journalism: having fun with calamities involving celebrities. As celebrities have increasingly made it to the headlines of the mainstream news media in recent years, the interviewees consciously add an element of *Schadenfreude* when covering celebrities. Celebrity is a diversified category, though. For the tabloid editors, a celebrity is someone successful, rich, living their private life in the public eye, while the serious-popular journalists also consider the 'normal' individual as a celebrity the moment he or she becomes an actor on the pages of their magazine (such as a popular *Big Brother* or *Idols* candidate, for example). The question is, why these celebrities – rich or poor, luxurious or normal-looking, jobless or movie star – enter the popular news story at all? The answer: when they breach the (fine) lines of civil morality, particularly regarding how we ought to behave in society regarding sexuality, religious practices and life politics. Examples interviewees offer are all set against a conflict of morality.

> You know, the story I am still most proud of is . . . I was working at the *Privé* at the time when we got a lead on an extramarital affair a well-known politician sup- posedly had. And then I went out and staked out his house one Sunday morning. When he came out in his car I followed him, and a bit down the road a woman and two children got in – turns out this was his mistress, and she was married too! And his own wife was back home, she was sick, yes, I mean, really . . .

The ranges of topics that are mentioned with moral indignation generally fall in the category of 'love life', ranging from marital affairs (divorce, cheating, death in the family, a baby when it is unclear who the father is), and relationships (emphasizing breaking up and getting together again, breaches of monogamy) to sexuality (extra- ordinary sex, extreme sexual preferences, physical beauty, promiscuity). I have to note that, within this range of potential breaches of morality, little or no mention is made of specific topics or issues outside the dominant, heterosexual and family- oriented view of civil life. Editors also indicated they deliberately keep certain infor- mation out of their magazines to protect certain celebrities, thus making them more willing to cooperate as sources. The readers are fitted into their moral iconic frame- work of 'good' versus 'bad' as a mass, regardless of how reader characteristics are addressed specifically (as a topic). This seemingly (moral and professional) superior attitude or 'higher ground' serves as a further delineation for the interviewees – another way to draw a line in the sand between popular and 'other' journalisms: between one's own morality and somebody else's, whereby popular journalism seems to serve as the guardian of civic morality.

Commercialism

The weekly hardship of putting attractive magazines out, making decisions based on sales figures, addressing perceived preferences of a fickle audience, were frequently mentioned in the interviews. The morality repertoire indeed reflects a specific view on the audience as a rather homogeneous, heterosexual civil 'mass' of middle-class people wanting to be entertained and informed about celebrities (overstepping the bounds of the dominant morality). This development contributes to a shared percep- tion of the interviewees regarding their market position in today's media-sphere. Now that the topics concerning life politics – notably the forming and dissolving of social relationships – have entered the mainstream news media, archetypical popular journalism genres like the tabloids are redefining their approach, especially their style:

> Newspapers cover the topics that originally come from the gossip magazines, I guess they like that as well, they are doing that now as well. . . . So we are becoming much harder. You move up a bit in gossip journalism from being nice to a bit harder, another bit harder, harder still. . . . Then there is a chance that a newspaper cannot do that anymore.

Editors did not suggest new or different topics, but emphasized a genre-wide 'hardening' of tone of voice and newsgathering methods, coupled with previously signaled moral indignation. I found a striking consensus among participants about the increasingly blurred lines so easily drawn between gossip or popular journalism and other journalisms. This poses a clear challenge to the tabloid editors, as another participant remarked (see below).

> It is kind of a problem, yes I think it is a problem. If you now hear about a royal wedding or whatever you have to fight regular newspapers which appear daily, and everywhere, who also cover this with 8 to 10 pages full-color. Until four years ago you had, as a weekly gossip magazine, the sole rights to these kinds of things. The mainstream media are taking over the topics that used to be restricted to the gossip press. . . . So we are getting harder, you have to move up a bit in gossip journalism, become tougher, because a newspaper cannot allow itself to print rumors – at least, not until now . . .

Commercial considerations indeed seem to prevail any discussions regarding ethics (or moral reflections for that matter):

> How far can you go? . . . you cannot cause any real damage, that is something you learn over the years . . . and there is also the role of commercialism, that is also important. So all those elements together determine whether it is right or wrong. It is never just one aspect; there are always more aspects involved . . . such a decision also depends on the way they ['they': i.e. celebrities trying to prevent a potentially damaging publication] approach you, about what is explained. If someone asks very nicely, please, yes, and explains why. Then you can sometimes. . . . But it is still a matter of debate. Yes, if the other magazines are running the story and selling well, then it is just commercial.

An explicitly commercial attitude is clearly held by some as the be-all-end-all of their work, indeed adding to the perception of the audience as a 'mass':

> We respond to the sentiments of the day, each day begins with checking ratings for television programs to see what is a hot topic in the Netherlands as a whole.

Commercialism for these editors also means day-to-day decision-making about news selection, gathering of information, telling stories, choosing a format and sticking to a certain all-encompassing (and ideological) popular journalism formula.

(Popular) journalism ideology

Working in popular journalism was described as working holistically – making a popular magazine means being a jack of all trades. When describing the attitude of tabloid journalists, the participants would refer to being an all-rounder as a defining quality of their trade:

> We all have our own specialties, but people need to be multifunctional here, they have to be able to do everything: reporting, writing, editing, lay-out, cover policy. . . . It is more fun for those people as well, otherwise it just is the same all the time.

The explicit use of this argument by the interviewed tabloid editors may have to do with their particular position, or can be attributed to the line of questioning pursued in our interviews, following up on issues of perceived difference between popular journalism and other journalisms. Although skills and standards are a topic journalists would talk about, a more general notion of what this genre of journalism is and how it should be understood in the context of journalism in the Netherlands serves as a system of meaning for the participating editors.

> You should learn to look differently at journalism, gossip journalism. . . . You know, what we do is a lot more creative and hard to do than the rest of journalism in the Netherlands.

Popular journalism, 'the gossip world' and the popular press are some of the terms used by the editors to describe their corner of the Dutch mediasphere. This varies from detailed descriptions of how the making of a magazine works, via elaborate definitions of what gossip 'really' means, to profiles of what a 'typical' reporter in this genre is made of. Working for a tabloid-style magazine not only requires a certain mindset, according to some it is also a choice one makes for a lifetime, which connects this career to the perceived status it has in the profession as a whole:

> After you worked for a well-known gossip magazine, it makes you a tainted person, it becomes much harder to work elsewhere if they see that on your resume. So generally people are sticking to these magazines for 20 years or more.

Indeed we found that all of the interviewees at some point worked for either *Privé* or *Story*, and several of them had connections with one or more other magazines in the field. For the participants, this clearly has to do with the 'uniqueness' of their field, the specifics defining what popular journalism is – as opposed to the rest of Dutch journalism. The sense of being a necessary all-rounder, of 'doing everything yourself' as one editor explains, may serve the same purpose as, for example, irony: it is a way for the participants to distinguish their work from other journalisms. One must note that the perceived multiplicity of tasks is further affected by the fact that the interviewed experts are magazine editors – people who can be considered to have more than one responsibility on their hands (managerial as well as journalistic responsibilities).

Discussion

The analysis of these interviews sheds light on the ways in which the tabloid editors and reporters construct their professional identity – both as Dutch journalists as well as distinctive popular journalists. In doing so, these journalists use the same discourse of journalism's professional ideology as their colleagues elsewhere (Dahlgren, 1992; Winch, 1997). Journalists in the more entertaining sector of the media share notions of ethical sensibilities, servicing the public, editorial autonomy and public credibility in order to position themselves as a distinctive genre. The differences between the applications of journalism's ideological values are embedded in the respective meanings these concepts have in popular or infotainment journalism. The ideal of servicing the public is strongly connected to commercial interests in the sense of evaluating weekly sales figures against editorial content and the cover policy of the magazine. This suggests a strict awareness of shifting wants and needs of the readership (rather than the advertiser). It also reveals the domination of the many over the few, as public awareness in this respect exclusively relates to a common or 'mass' denominator.

The preoccupation with reader statistics does not seem to infringe upon the popular journalists' perception of professional autonomy. In fact, editorial autonomy – as in the freedom to write creatively without the constraints of mainstream newspaper conventions – is cited self-reflectively as the motivation for being in the tabloid business. On the other hand, editors clearly indicate a strict adherence to a certain formula. One participant indicated he could not explain what exactly this formula is, as: 'you just know after a while'. Whereas autonomy in mainstream news media is often articulated to commercialism and perceived inroads on editorial policy made by marketers and advertisers, this is considered not to be of any relevance to the daily work at a popular magazine by our interviewees. Weaver and Wilhoit (1996: 61–2) consider autonomy to be articulated to the freedom journalists have in selecting and writing about particular subjects and stories, and, according to the participants, it is exactly this lack of freedom in the mainstream news media that prompted them to opt for popular journalism. The tabloid story may be based on similar newsgathering methods and investigative reporting practices; a paradoxical notion of freedom to write creatively around the retrieved information is central to the interviewees' understanding of autonomy.

Ethics, credibility and trustworthiness feature prominently in the way tabloid editors talk about their work and the various ways in which they give meaning to what they do. Yet, perhaps a bit unlike their colleagues elsewhere in journalism, ethical issues are continuously under critical discussion. Ethical considerations have to do with competitor-colleague relations, to autonomy ('we can do things the others cannot do') and especially to morality – sometimes assuming a higher moral ground ('we decide when to publish or not'). This particular conception of ethics is contextual: ethical decision-making is dependent on morality (considering the publication of details on an 'extreme' sex-life for example), on competition and on personal norms and values ('Have I hurt somebody today or not?'). As in earlier research in the United Kingdom, the bottom line in any kind of editorial (and thus moral-ethical) decision-making is outright audience-revenue commercialism: if the competitor-colleague is running the story, they print it as well (Rhoufari, 2000: 172).

The topics and themes all reveal an active construction of distinction: of finding new ground in a profession that is fast becoming a hybrid between different genres and formats in the perception of its professional practitioners (and academics as well). What is both interesting and perhaps troubling is the emphasis put on 'toughening up' in this process of distinguishing oneself in popular journalism: editors seem to think they have to push the limits of what is possible or 'moral-ethical' in journalism in order to survive the competition of other, notably mainstream news media. As they consider *Weekend* the best gossip magazine because it is 'the hardest' and *Party* the worst because it does not tell 'the truth', this makes for an interesting future perspective, featuring a journalistic attitude that reads like hard-hitting investigative (and creative) popular journalism.

A second and final conclusion to this article considers the various repertoires in particular. What I would like to suggest is an overarching concept of utilitarianism with regard to the function of irony, being all-round, a strict focus on weekly sales and the assumption of a moral-ethical higher ground. This utilitarian attitude seems to function as a strategic ritual to explain why and how one does his or her work in popular journalism.[5] The evaluation of this kind of utilitarianism, of tabloid editors being right or wrong solely based on the consequences of their own actions (in the opinion of the participants, reflected predominantly in number of copies sold), the distinct emphasis on pleasure (be it ironical), including a moral notion of (preventing) pain or unhappiness (in relation to both celebrities and publics) can be seen as encompassing the core defining characteristics of Bentham's moral theory of utilitarianism. An important note to be made here regards the highly personal and contextual application of the theory to the lifeworld of the tabloid editors: they talk about their own happiness, not necessarily the happiness of their (mass) audience. And one can argue that popular journalism's happiness is interdependent with the 'unhappiness' of celebrities. The ideology of journalism can therefore be seen as being actively constructed by professionals working in popular journalism genres, using a similar discourse from a different theoretical perspective: instead of professional ideology, a kind of personalized utilitarian ideological framework is applied to give meaning to being a journalist – and in particular to being a (popular) journalist other than the ones working elsewhere in the Dutch news media.

Notes

1   'Tabloidization' is a term generally related to processes in the print media sector, 'infotainment' is a term coined to describe broadcast media developments. In this project, 'infotainment' is considered to be an overarching concept, in which the blurring of information and entertainment can be located (see also Brants, 1998). Gripsrud (2000: 290–2) argues that tabloidization can be seen as a subcategory of popular journalism, and remarks that 'infotainment' is in fact a new term for a much older development of quality popular journalism such as, for example,

family-oriented variety shows on television. Infotainment is used as the over-arching (contemporary) concept in the context of the project at hand.

2   One of the serious-popular magazine editors offered us a different explanation for the widespread disatisfaction regarding *Party*. He suggested that all editors have had (verbal) fights with the current chief editor of *Party*, Ton de Wit, which has led to their disenchantment with the performance of the magazine, according to this source. A colleague of this particular editor also suggested that the editors of the other three magazines of the 'big four' (*Story, Privé, Weekend, Party*) did not like *Party* because it has invaded their market a couple of years ago and is taking away their (younger) readership. Interesting, but largely unsubstantiated, sugges-tions. What is also interesting is that most journalists in this field at some point worked for 'the competition': almost all tabloid editors at some time in the past worked for *Story* and/or *Privé*.

3   *Party* entered the market in 1994, and had been around for seven years at the time of these interviews.

4   One could almost claim that this reads like typical 'boyish-rebellious' behavior; here I would like to note that of the 14 interviewed editors, five were women. *Weekend*, described by competitor-colleagues as the 'hardest' gossip magazine in the Netherlands, exclusively employs male journalists and editors.

5   Compare this utilitarianism to the use of objectivity as a strategic ritual in 'hard' news journalism, as argued by Tuchman (1971).

3.2
Writing the tabloid
by S. Elizabeth Bird

Who writes the tabloids

For the checkout counter browser, perhaps the most common response to tabloid headlines is incredulity: who are these people, and where do they get this stuff? The very words "tabloid reporter" conjure up images of "sleaze" personified—the slimy, pushy nuisance working in shabby offices who will do anything to dig up dirt and invent preposterous stories. In this chapter, I aim to answer some of the questions, looking at who writes tabloids, where stories come from, and what relationship tabloid practices have to mainstream journalism.

A visit to the offices of Globe Communications reveals a prosperous operation doing business from a spacious office block on the outskirts of Boca Raton, Florida. Tabloids are now a multimillion-dollar industry, and the working conditions for their staff are more attractive than those of most newspaper journalists. Tabloid writers tend to be secretive about their day-to-day operations, citing intense competition among the various publications as well as irritation at having constantly to defend the way they work. The *National Enquirer* is particularly secretive: "the tab is run with the fervor, secrecy and determination of an efficient intelligence agency . . ." (Ressner 1988, 56).

Globe Communications, especially the staff of the *National Examiner*, has been the most open in allowing access to outsiders. Members of the staff have appeared on several television news shows, and they seem well rehearsed and eager to state the point of view of the tabloid writer. After requesting permission to visit and observe the operations of the tabloid, I was originally invited to visit the *Examiner* offices for one day in February 1986. After I had interviewed several members of the editorial staff, I was then permitted to return for a second day of interviews. I was not, however, allowed to attend editorial meetings or watch staff at work for extended periods. During the two days, I interviewed *Examiner* Editor Bill Burt, Associate Editor Cliff Linedecker, Photo Editor Ken Matthews (Burt, Linedecker, and Matthews have since left the paper), Staff Writer and Advice Columnist Sheila O'Donovan ("Sheela Wood"), and Psychic Adviser Anthony Leggett. In addition, I spoke casually with other staff members who happened to be present. All formal interviews were tape-recorded;

any information attributed to *Examiner* staff was obtained from transcripts of these recordings.

The writers were extremely cooperative, spending several hours discussing their work with me. After some initial suspicion, as it was established that a "hatchet job" was not my intention, rapport developed easily. I believe a more complete picture would have been obtained through some prolonged observation; writers were obviously aiming to promote the most positive account possible of tabloid journalism. The interview, while a useful methodological tool, provides information made up from the self-reflexive accounts of participants. As Bruner points out, "There may be a correspondence between a life as lived, a life as experienced, and a life as told, but the anthropologist should never assume the correspondence nor fail to make the distinction" (1984, 7). I quickly gained the impression, for example, that tabloid life as told by my informants was a rather more noble and altruistic enterprise than it might have appeared to a fly on the wall. In addition to my interviews, several "inside" accounts of tabloid life have appeared (Barber 1982; Corkery 1981; Gourley 1981; Ressner 1988), and these helped provide some useful corrective to the accounts I obtained.

Although the tabloids proclaim themselves to be highly competitive with each other, they often cover the same stories in very similar styles, occasionally using the same sources and identical quotes. At least in part this is because the papers share, in effect, a constantly circulating pool of writers and editors, who move between the papers often and tend to know each other. *Examiner* Editor Burt, for instance, is a longtime friend of *Enquirer* Editor Iain Calder, a fellow Scotsman.

The careers of writers on any one paper can be short, and many move from paper to paper or free-lance for any of them between jobs. The *Enquirer* under Pope was notorious for the pressure placed on writers to produce a constant stream of good stories; Gourley (1981) writes of how Pope pitted teams of writers against each other, firing those who failed. Since my 1986 interviews at the *Examiner*, Linedecker, Matthews, and Burt have all been fired—Burt after five years of apparent success as editor (Linedecker now works at the *Sun*). Mike Nevard, formerly editorial director for all three Globe papers, was also fired, and now works at the *Enquirer* (having at various times also worked for the *Star* and the *Enquirer* under Pope). The *Examiner*'s new associate editor, Joe West, was formerly with the *Weekly World News*. As Ken Matthews put it, "What's happened all these years is we've just traded people up and down the East Coast from the Globe papers to the *Star* to the *Enquirer*—we need new blood badly."

Examiner staff bemoan the small number of young American journalists who want to work for tabloids, in spite of the lucrative salaries. Rather than rely on American journalists, all the papers have a core of writers whose backgrounds are in British or Commonwealth daily tabloids which, though more "newsy" than American weeklies, provide training in the desired style. At the *Examiner*, Burt, Senior Editor Harold Lewis, O'Donovan, Leggett, and others are British. British staff at all the Florida tabloids tend to know each other and socialize together as part of the now large expatriate community in the Lantana area. "The Fleet Streeters began arriving in droves during the 1970s, enough of them to field cricket teams, fill dart rooms and prompt some local eateries to include bangers and mash on their menus" (Smilgis 1988, 13).

Scottish-born Burt, who worked for local and national papers in Britain, later for the *Enquirer,* "prefers places that are a bit scrungy" to his palatial *Examiner* office. He explained his preparation for tabloids: "I've been told to bug off so many times that I'm totally insensitive to it. . . . I spent too many years going up and down tenement buildings and getting punched in the mouth and hit over the head and getting involved in car chases—I was brought up in a really good school."

When available, American journalists are in demand, and many have worked for several tabloids. Associate Editor Linedecker's background seems fairly typical of American tabloid writers; he has considerable experience of "straight" journalism, including many years with the Philadelphia *Inquirer.* Matthews's credentials include the Washington *Star* as well as papers in Connecticut and California and six years as a correspondent in the Far East: "I didn't come to this because I was not acquainted with ordinary journalism. I did come to work for the *National Enquirer* when I came back from Asia and they were offering me much more money than anybody else was." While salaries were an incentive for both, they, like Burt, find tabloids a respite from the "burn-out" of regular journalism. Matthews explains: "When you've been in the business a few years, you feel like you've done everything and written every story. When it stops being exciting it's pretty much a dull job, I think."

Tabloid writers not only enjoy pleasant working conditions and large salaries, they rarely have to venture outside the newsroom—unless they are celebrity "stake-out" specialists. As Burt sees it, the successful tabloid writer is one who is not ashamed of the particular techniques he or she must use but who can revel in the "fun" of tabloids without being cynical. A tabloid writer has to be able to adapt: "We couldn't hire a Bob Woodward or Carl Bernstein here. Number one, they'd think they were too good for tabloids; number two, they'd be no good for tabs; and number three, you've got to enjoy it, you've got to get into the fun and excitement the paper can be. . . . If you're a total cynic and don't have a sense of humor, you'll never get on in a tabloid." The key to tabloid writing? "Let's flag it, let's do a bit of Barnum and Bailey. . . . If you don't get a chuckle yourself, the reader's not going to get a chuckle out of it." And most of the *Examiner* staff do indeed seem to "get a chuckle" out of their work, seeing it as a welcome change of pace from daily journalism.

Getting the story: celebrity legwork

Celebrity reporting is the main area in which there is real "legwork"—interviewing, chasing contacts, trying to beat the competition. Tabloid reporters track down the "untold story" of celebrity spats and dalliances with the tenacity of investigative journalists on the trail of a political exposé. Ressner describes tabloid reporters and photographers swinging through trees, dangling from helicopters, and staking out celebrity homes. Describing paparazzo Phil Ramey, he comments, "it's Ramey's abnormally boorish behavior and persistence that have landed him hundreds of exclusive snapshots" (1988, 53).

Audrey Lavin, a full-time free-lancer who has worked on the *Star,* the *Globe,* and the London *Sun,* is described as "a natural stake-out queen." She "has nailed stories by sliding into Prince Rainier's limousine in New York to ask about his personal relationships; by bargaining with John McEnroe for an interview after watching him publicly bawl out his pregnant wife, Tatum O'Neal; by sweating out a three-week Liberace deathwatch in Las Vegas" (Ressner, 54). Corkery describes the *Enquirer* operation that swung into action with the death of Elvis Presley, culminating in a front-page photo of the singer in his coffin, taken by a family member who was paid by the tabloid. The issue was the paper's biggest ever, selling out the press run, and starting "a new *Enquirer* tradition . . . the dead celeb in his box on page one" (1981, 21). *Enquirer* reporters began to go to great lengths to get such pictures: "When Bing Crosby died, the religion reporter disguised himself as a priest and helped get a picture of Bingo in his box. On the way out of the chapel, still dressed in clerical black, he granted an interview to Geraldo Rivera, cautioning the ABC reporter against intruding on the privacy of the mourning family" (Corkery, 21).

Celebrity specialists make it their business to know as much as possible about their subjects' lives; even if the most damaging information may not surface in the paper, it can be used. According to Ressner, "One of the most powerful weapons in a tabloid's arsenal is leverage—quashing an item on a celebrity's deep secrets in exchange for cooperation on another, less sensitive story." Of course, such threats may be hollow: "the *Enquirer* would probably not use the more explosive information anyway, since it thinks of itself as a wholesome family paper that shies away from sick sex or depressing drug stories" (Ressner, 64).

Obviously, then, the relationship between tabloids and celebrities is often confrontational, with many celebrities spending a great deal of energy avoiding such people as the "stake-out queen." The Carol Burnett libel suit, along with actual or threatened action by other celebrities, does reflect the hostility felt by some stars (Schardt 1980; Levin and Arluke 1987). The other side of the coin is that the entertainment industry and the tabloids often work symbiotically in keeping celebrities in the public eye. As mentioned already, the majority of celebrity stories are favorable, even if not all were given willingly. According to a study by Levin and Arluke, 46 percent of *Enquirer* celebrity stories are "upfront" interviews. Many tabloid stories do come direct from celebrities' publicists, who will sometimes offer a story on a major star in return for tabloid coverage of a less well-known personality (1987, 85). In addition, certain stars maintain good relationships with the tabloids and are accorded the status of "friends" (Ressner 1988). Reporters may read back quotes to "friends"; some may even be allowed full copy approval. Michael Jackson, who received extensive tabloid coverage for some of his eccentricities, apparently had his representative give photos of him in his "hyperbaric chamber" to the *Enquirer*. "One of his people called up and said, 'You can do me a favor—would you please call this bizarre? He wants the word bizarre used' " (Ressner 1988, 64).

Similarly, the tabloids have been largely responsible for hyping the excitement about "cliff-hanger" episodes of prime-time TV soap operas. Over the last few years, a tabloid staple has been the "exclusive" on the forthcoming season's story lines, appearing during the summer hiatus. Thus it suits program makers to maintain interest in their shows, and tabloids oblige, often paying large sums to get inside information. The *Star* and *Enquirer* are the main competitors for this information, using specialists with connections, like the *Enquirer*'s Sammy Rubin: "I may buy the material from the janitor, but the producer gave him the scripts and my phone number" (Ressner, 54).

For these and other show business stories, people like Rubin rely on their connections and a large expense account: "We don't rummage through people's garbage anymore. . . . We don't have to. I haven't done a formal stakeout in three years. I can call" (Ressner, 56). Rubin reportedly spent $7,000 in cash in one evening on inside tips, the end result being the scripts to the cliff-hanger episodes of three major soap operas (Ressner, 54).

Celebrity reporters' networks of contacts may be huge, including such people as relatives, lawyers, hairdressers, and secretaries—"anyone and everyone with information to peddle" (Ressner, 64). On the *Enquirer*, payment for information is routine, with fees ranging from $50 for a small gossip item to $1,600 for information that leads to a front-page story. "For really explosive stories, payoffs can soar into the high five figures" (Ressner, 64).

Getting the story: newsroom creativity

While the high-profile celebrity stories may require investigation and supplies of cash, most tabloid stories, including those on celebrities, are considerably more routine. The popular image of a tabloid writer may be the sleazy nuisance who relies on eavesdropping, intrusion, and harassment as basic research methods, but in fact most of the staff rarely leave the newsroom; their days of "legwork" are behind them. For some, that in itself is a central attraction of tabloid work. For tabloid stories, wherever they might originate, are made in the newsroom. Although they admit the existence of "top-of-the-head" stories, tabloid writers publicly deny they "make up" most of the material. So where do those stories come from and how are they written?

The key to tabloid technique is the recognition and transformation of run-of-the-mill news filler into the kind of gripping narratives whose headlines can produce an irresistible cover—the bait that turns the mildly interested browser into the buyer. To achieve the perfect mix, the staff spends hours sifting through other publications from the United States and abroad, ready to take a story "nugget" and mine it into a tabloid narrative. Freed from the constraints of timeliness that a news reporter works with, they see their role as more similar to that of a feature writer, who may develop the human-interest angle of a news story. Some stories are simply rewritten in tabloid style while others may involve some follow-up research: "We take that story nugget and then we have a reporter who will call authorities, individuals, police or whatever, get some more quotes, and then develop it in our style. We'll take a story that is two paragraphs in some paper and through phone calls and our kind of questioning, we'll have the story," says Linedecker.

Editor Burt is unabashed as to what "our kind of questioning" entails. "You've got to put words into their mouths. Say you get somebody who can only speak about ten words of English and you want to get a first-person account of what it was like floating for twenty-four hours with sharks circling their rubber dinghy or whatever. Not just the tabloids, but *Reader's Digest* or anybody. . . . Are they going to sit down and say, 'My God, it was hell' (point, new paragraph) 'The black fin of the shark spun around mercilessly and I thought it was only a matter of time. I dreamed of my little village back in blah blah blah. . . .' No! They don't talk like that, of course they don't." So instead, "you ask them a question phrased that way. I make no apologies for it, I think it's fair journalism."

Linedecker elaborates: "If we have a story line, of course we'll try to get comments that will back it up if it's a good one, but if it's just absolutely not true then you drop the story." Dropping the story is a last resort, however, and sometimes a little persuasion helps: "Just because they're a little hesitant at first to give you that good-money quote doesn't mean that you give up, because a lot of people maybe do agree with you but don't want to be quoted right away, and if you're persistent you can usually come up with that good-money quote unless your whole story is just absolutely wrong and then there's no place to go."

Questioning the participants in the story is just one way to come up with the "good-money quote." Like all journalists, tabloid writers have stables of sources who can be contacted to provide expert opinion on any issue. Like other reporters' sources, these may be doctors, psychologists, or university professors, but they may also be psychics, seers, or students of alien life forms.

In a more conventional story, reference sources and medical experts might provide background and additional details, as in a story. Burt recalls about an eleven-year-old girl who gave birth to twins: "We thought it was quite remarkable—but we were way off. You know, it was a true story but there've been cases of girls of eight giving birth to triplets." According to Burt, "we go to a doctor and find out how rare it is—that's interesting—then we go into our own files for case histories of other unusual or extremely young births and in the course of which we might find out there's a much younger one, and we develop that one, hold it for a later date."

Except for more fast-breaking celebrity stories, timeliness is not a major tabloid news value. Indeed, human-interest features in regular newspapers are also frequently timeless; all journalists are familiar with the profiles and "soft" features that get printed when space is available. Tabloids are almost all "soft" news; human-interest stories that first appeared in daily newspapers may surface in tabloids weeks, months, or even years later. As Burt explains, "People don't care. . . . Take our story on girl, 5, has baby, one of our first over the 1 million mark. It did happen in 1939, and it was the youngest recorded then." Many tabloid stories are generated from such file material, from medical reports in magazines and newspapers, census and other demographic data—much of the same background material as any feature writer might use.

Less familiar to the conventional reporter might be the "expert" in the occult and paranormal. The tabloids have their source files for these stories, too. A perennial favorite is the UFO story: "Every province in Brazil, for example, has got a UFO society, so you go and phone up the chairman. He'll give you anything you want, and if you can't find the local UFO buff there's always somebody who knows. To find out about UFOs in Caracas, for instance, I can get you a contact in five minutes," says Burt.

According to Linedecker, the paper's "specialist" in the paranormal, experts can always be found to back up his stories. Discussing several stories dealing with reincarnation, Linedecker asserts that the experts quoted do exist: "We frequently interview Indian authorities. . . . Reincarnation of course is a big part of the Hindu religion and they're aware of these cases when they occur. The universities over there seem to be far more likely to take them seriously and investigate them, so a lot of our reincarnation stories come from India."

However the story is generated, the particular stamp of the tabloid is given to a story in the writing, and *Examiner* staff members are quick to describe this as a creative process. According to Matthews, "we're constantly looking for these kernels, nuggets, and it's very satisfying when you make one grow, so it's a much more creative process than most people are engaged in."

This creativity follows well-defined lines, of course. All tabloid stories are reshaped in the newsroom, and they show the mark of a formulaic pattern of story-telling. Reporters, though they work on a story alone, must follow those formulae. Sheila O'Donovan, a reporter who doubles as advice columnist "Sheela Wood," explains that ideas go through an editor before being written up. "A lead sheet comes back and he'll write the lead or the angle that he wants you to follow on it, and then you just sort of evolve the story around that. But you basically have to follow his guidelines."

Once a tabloid story's characteristically clear point of view has been established, information is used to tell that story rather than any other that may be generated from the same sources. Corkery explained how stories were generated at the *Enquirer*, with different teams of editors and reporters bringing them to Gene Pope for review. "If he approves an idea, it gets typed up on a special form, is given a file number and becomes an entity. Once an idea is approved, you must turn in a story. It is very hard to kill an idea once it's okayed by The Boss" (1981, 20). Barber agrees, writing that stories often have less to do with what is really happening and more to do with what "the editor wishes to have happen" (1982, 49). At the *Examiner*, the same basic process operates, although apparently without the cutthroat competition that prevails at the *Enquirer*. As Matthews puts it, "you approach these things with a certain point of view, a frame of mind, and then you fashion it to fit that formula."

The formula for writing style is easily recognizable, characterized by Burt as "short and pithy" and by Linedecker as "plenty of drama and pathos." Matthews adds, "all of our stories are rewritten no matter where they come from—it's just a matter of style, you have to put in a lot of amazings and startlings and incredibles." The "brand loyalty" of the reader is constantly solicited. As Matthews puts it, "Whenever I could use the phrase 'the vast family of *Examiner* readers' you can be sure I stuck it in somewhere, because we encourage that identification." The language and style of tabloids has not changed greatly since the 1930s. As D. A. Bird writes, "each tabloid article normally is limited to a single theme or metaphor. Elaboration usually repeats the same point in different ways" (1986, 4). Stock clichés, some of them part of a larger "journalese" common in other newspapers, give tabloid writing a consistently familiar look. Apart from the torrent of adjectives—all the stories that are amazing, baffling, untold, secret, incredible, startling, etc.—certain story types generate the same words over and over again. Heroes are always "spunky," "gutsy" and/or "plucky"; a male celebrity may have a "gal pal" or "cutie"; females may have a "toy boy," or possibly a "hunk." Small children are always "tots," often "heartbreak tots," dogs are "pooches," husbands are "hubbies." Unsavory, un-American types are "punks," "creeps," or "sickos." And so it goes on. The "creativity" employed by tabloid writers often entails little more than combining and recombining information in familiar patterns, a point to which I shall return.

The creative freedom enjoyed by tabloid writers shows in other ways, too. For instance, all the staff deny that photos are ever staged and then misrepresented as an actual event, a practice that apparently was not uncommon in tabloids twenty years ago. But they are free to produce "creative" photos in a way other papers would not be. Burt recalls an extremely successful "whiz" cover story that reported on the possibility of Nazi war criminal Josef Mengele living as a woman in South America. According to Burt, the story came from AP or UPI agency reports about a group of Nazi hunters and one member's theory that Mengele is still alive: "That's been his theory for years, and that's not a new story. . . . He takes his theory one step further and he says Mengele is living as a woman. . . . We took the picture issued by the agency that says this is how he looks now, superimposed it with a woman's hair and got the art department to soften the features and from the picture of Mengele issued by all the news services, we explained that's how he would look today if he were a woman."

However, not all artwork is unambiguously labeled. Illustrations of UFOs, aliens, and similar phenomena are often obviously line drawings, but occasionally pictures are used that appear to be photographs, such as an apparent photo of the Mount Everest "Abominable Snowman" (*National Examiner* July 2, 1985, 17). Although the photo is not actually identified as the Yeti supposedly seen by an "expedition of crack mountaineers," neither is it labeled as an artist's conception or composite, as it must be.

Tabloids and journalism

Bill Burt is proud of his success in building the *Examiner*'s weekly circulation to over one million in less than three years, and he resents what he sees as elitist criticism that "sneers at the tastes of millions of people." He and his staff maintain that critics misunderstand the nature of tabloids in comparing them unfavorably with "straight" newspapers. Rather, Burt argues, they should be considered an entertainment medium comparable to television shows like "Entertainment Tonight," "Lifestyles of the Rich and Famous," or "Ripley's Believe It or Not." Tabloids, says Burt, are primarily for fun and should not be taken too seriously. The staff agree that, above all, tabloids are in the entertainment business, even though they also publish informational articles. According to Matthews, the tabloids' competition is not newspapers but fellow tabloids, magazines like *People* and *Us*, and even all the other items competing for consumer dollars in the supermarket: "It's also the chewing gum and the dogfood, and there probably are people who say, I can buy the premium dogfood for Mitzi if I don't buy the tabloid. That's the competition, not the *New York Times*, not the *Miami Herald*."

Burt, probably more than anyone else on the staff, celebrates the "fun" of tabloids, which seek only to amuse and intrigue their readers: "We're fun, we're fascinating. When you don't want to be bored, you turn to your tabloid. . . . We're providing them with an alternative, relieving them from the barrage of boredom that hits them every day. The magazines that scoff at us, like *People* magazine, like *Us* magazine, they're doing exactly what we're doing, only they're trying to disguise it. We yell it, they whisper it."

Yet at the same time, he and his staff frequently compare tabloid reporting methods with those used in newspaper journalism, arguing that the differences are less than might be imagined. They contend that "respectable" journalism has little relevance to the lives of many Americans, and that their product offers an alternative view of the world that intellectuals might prefer to think does not exist. They argue that tabloids print many informational articles on diet, self-help, and other topics familiar from any newspaper's life-style pages. *Examiner* writers maintain that the clear line journalists like to draw between "real" journalism and "sleaze" simply does not exist. Tabloids are entertainment that also informs; newspapers are informational, according to traditional journalistic standards, but they must also entertain to survive. While asserting that their product is basically entertaining fantasy, tabloid journalists are not prepared to call themselves fiction writers, and they are eager to show that in many respects they have not abandoned the methods of objective journalism. And indeed, the end product owes much to the basic philosophy of objective, "detached" reporting, albeit strongly laced with a dose of "creativity" that gives the tabloids the flamboyant style that is their pride and their critics' despair.

Objectivity

A standard constantly invoked by *Examiner* staff is the journalistic tenet of objectivity. As so many scholars have noted (Schiller 1981; Schudson 1978, 1982; Tuchman 1978), objectivity has become a central "strategic ritual" of journalism, which, although increasingly under fire, is still a cornerstone of the profession. As Jensen (1986) puts it, the news genre incorporates a stance that stresses the role of the journalist as an independent observer, gathering information to be presented to the audience as fact. Typically, that information takes the form of quotes from sources, which the journalist assembles in recognizable generic form, offering information aimed at proving the source's credibility.

Tabloid writers, most of whom have training or experience in regular journalism, claim to apply the same basic strategy. Ken Matthews, photo editor at the *Examiner*, uses the philosophy of objectivity to explain stories that many people would find incredible or ludicrous. He stresses that whether the reporter believes the "expert," who may be a psychic or UFO hunter, is irrelevant. "I've said the same thing about covering the White House. You ask the secretary of state if he has done or intends to do something and you record his answer. You don't say, I've established on my own that there are no American troops in El Salvador, you ask the secretary of state and if he says there aren't, that's the news today. We do the same thing."

As Roshco writes, "Giving sources the responsibility for supplying content freed reporters from the need for extensive knowledge about subject matter" (1975, 42). A story is "accurate" if it faithfully reports what was said or written by sources. By this standard, much of what is written in tabloids can claim to be accurate. In fact, the *National Enquirer* has been touted in *Editor & Publisher* as "the most accurate paper in the country" (Barber 1982, 49). The paper maintains a research department headed by Ruth Annan, a sixteen-year veteran of *Time* magazine. According to Annan, "We police the copy. We verify the quotes that are in the stories, the background information" (Levin and Arluke 1987, 119). Levin and Arluke, who spent time interviewing at the *Enquirer*, mention the paper's verification procedures approvingly, in contrast to other newspapers: "They [newspapers] do not ask their reporters to use tape recorders, to verify the accuracy of quotations, or to check the veracity of credentials"

(1987, 120). Indeed, it was an absence of any systematic verification procedures that allowed Janet Cooke's infamous "Jimmy's World" story to end up winning a Pulitzer Prize (Goldstein 1985). In general, reporters' honesty and accuracy are simply taken for granted.

However, accounts by former tabloid writers show how the much-touted "accuracy" sometimes worked. Jeff Wells, writing about the "nightmare" experience of covering a celebrated UFO sighting, describes how information was selected and organized: "The polygraph man said it was the plainest case of lying he'd seen in 20 years, but the office was yelling for another expert and a different result" (1981, 51). Even after Wells produced a memo detailing why the case was obviously fraudulent, the *Enquirer* filtered enough "facts" from the data gathered to run a major feature on the Travis Walton UFO abduction (Dec. 16, 1975).

As Barber writes, the research department does indeed check facts, "And yet it regularly lets through palpable inanities. . . . If the tapes and copy jibe, and sources when contacted agree to what has been reported, the story must, however reluctantly, be granted the imprimatur of accuracy" (1982, 49). Furthermore, evidence collected in a recent "60 Minutes" broadcast (Sept. 30, 1990) suggested that at least some *Enquirer* sources are unlikely to confirm stories—they may never have actually worked on them. The "60 Minutes" team found people listed as sources who knew nothing about the stories but had received checks anyway. The suggestion was that the rules requiring three sources for a celebrity story were being bent, to say the least.

One problem of course is that, even if every quote included may be "accurate," the research department can only confirm that this "fact" was said by someone. They cannot discover what else a source said, what was left out, what sources who were not consulted would have said, what the context was, and so on. Former *Enquirer* staffers have explained how some reporters deal with the tape rule by "feeding" a source with appropriate quotes that are then given back to the reporter on tape (Corkery 1981; Schardt 1980). Barber mentions a Gene Pope memo instructing reporters to "ask leading questions," using much the same method as that described by *Examiner* Editor Burt. Thus the wording of the questions, coupled with yes/no answers, suffices to provide the quotes. Pope's memo elaborates how these questions should be phrased: "Quotes should not only be appropriate but believable. A Japanese carpenter should not sound like Ernest Hemingway, or vice versa" (1982, 49).

Burt, however, compares this type of questioning to that done by other journalists: "It's like: 'President Reagan denied last night that he was contemplating taking military action against Libya.' Now that would infer that President Reagan stood up and said, 'I am not contemplating taking any military action against Libya.' They asked a question, and all he said was 'no.' "

Getting the "good-money quote," the one that confirms the premise of the story, is the central aim. While Cliff Linedecker argues that the *Examiner* occasionally drops stories if the quote is impossible to obtain, Barber writes that, at the *Enquirer*, this virtually never happened once Pope had approved a story. He describes how Pope wished to run a story on the Three Mile Island nuclear plant leak asking "Was it sabotage?" The story eventually ran, using some quotes about a "suspicious couple" in a motel, with a can opener and a radio characterized as "weaponry" and "sophisticated communications equipment" (1982).

This type of questioning was behind one story whose subject challenged two tabloids in the courts. Henry Dempsey, a commuter airline pilot, was sucked out of his plane when a door popped open as he was checking a noise. After clinging to the plane for fifteen minutes, Dempsey managed to climb back in and survived with only minor injuries. Some time afterwards, the *Enquirer* and the *Star* ran stories about the incident, even though Dempsey had refused interviews to both (Bailey 1989). Both stories were filled with quotes attributed to Dempsey; the *Star* even gave him the byline.

Both headlines were written in typical tabloidese. From the *Star*: "The sky grabbed hold of me like a sharp cold hand—and pulled me out of the plane"; from the *Enquirer*: "My back burned . . . the wind tore at my face . . . I was trapped in a wild, wailing hurricane" (quoted in Bailey 1989, 10). The *Star* quoted Dempsey: "The urge to survive is the strongest sense of all, and I held on to that rail with all my strength, just kind of praying or at least saying 'God' a whole lot, and bracing myself against this great force trying to pitch me into the sky." The *Enquirer*'s quotes are equally colorful; many "fail the straight-face test and make Dempsey sound a bit like Sergeant Fury." Dempsey reportedly said he "stared death in the face," and "I knew that I was the luckiest man in the world at that moment" (Bailey, 10–11).

Dempsey sued both papers for invasion of privacy, claiming he had been placed in a false light and commercially exploited. In court papers, *Star* Editor Richard Kaplan acknowledged that the paper was wrong to give the byline to Dempsey and said that the quotes were pieced together from interviews with Dempsey's friends and conversations with the reporter who covered the story for the Murdoch-owned *Boston Herald*. Dempsey's suit was settled out of court for an undisclosed sum in January 1989 (Bailey 1989). However, the suit against the *Enquirer*, which had also spoken to unnamed friends, was dismissed in June 1988. The judge ruled that, although the account was fictionalized, it could not be considered "highly objectionable to a reasonable person" (Bailey, 10).

The outcome of the case suggests that, while the *Star*'s false byline went too far, tabloids—and other papers—can get away with leading questions and other "creative" interviewing practices as long as the resulting story is not defamatory. *Enquirer* lawyer Gerson A. Zweifach argued that the story accurately portrayed Dempsey's feelings, and "I thought it made him look appropriately courageous for hanging on and getting through it" (Bailey, 11).

This guiding principle also seems to be behind the tabloids' coverage of celebrity stories, following the 1981 Carol Burnett libel suit, in which Burnett was initially awarded $1.6 million (later reduced to $800,000 on appeal). Ressner (1988) confirms that the *Enquirer* now is more careful with celebrity stories, employing an attorney from the influential Washington, D.C., law firm of Williams and Connolly to go through stories every week searching for problems with libel and invasion of privacy. Other tabloids also retain lawyers for this purpose, and the generally "upbeat" coverage of both celebrities and "ordinary people" stories probably protects them, as well as pleasing their readers.

The tabloid writers are the first to agree that their story styles are formulaic, that they gather quotes and facts to construct a story with the intended structure and content. But again they compare this kind of storytelling to that used by other journalists. They argue that tabloid writers are not unique in pursuing a particular "angle" to a story, that angle in the end defining what questions are asked, which sources are interviewed, and which story is ultimately presented as "the truth." Increasingly, journalism researchers argue essentially the same point—journalism of whatever kind is storytelling that owes as much to established codes and conventions as to a relationship with "the real world out there" (see Bird and Dardenne 1988 on news and storytelling). Darnton (1975) recalls constructing quotes that were appropriate to particular types of news genre, such as bereavement stories, while Cohen writes that media descriptions of "mods and rockers" in Britain owed a great deal to the reporters' "conception of how anyone labelled as a thug or a hooligan should speak, dress and act" (1981, 275; I shall return to this point later).

Tabloid staff defend their style as simply a variant on other kinds of journalistic writing—finding "the story" within an event and shaping it to fit a particular construction of reality. According to Matthews, "American journalists do the same thing. I've been at it nearly twenty-five years in all facets and you do the same thing. You go to a speech, you go to a meeting of the town council and you sit there and it's mostly boring, and then all of a sudden someone says something and you say, that's the story. And you begin writing the story in your head. . . . It's just that we take a different view of what we want to extract from the situation." Burt agrees: "Any story—let's say, 'Mum Gives Birth to 50-lb. Baby'—I could write it in such a way that it would be acceptable in the *New York Times*, and then I would write it properly, and it would go into the tabloids." Matthews readily admits that tabloid writing is stereotyped and predictable but argues that it is essentially just one such style among many: "Tabloids are a formula just as the *Washington Post* is. Every morning they sit around a table like this and decide how they're going to fashion a product and each department reports on what they've got available to fit in and then somebody decides how we'll stir it all up together so we'll come out with the proper mixture. And we do the same thing."

Indeed, the process of creating "stories" is structurally very similar in both kinds of publication. Tabloids, working on a two- or three-week lead time, do not cover "hard news" at all. But feature writers on any newspaper would be familiar with the practice of developing "enterprise" stories—the features that spring from perceived social trends, government statistics, and so on. Reporters bring their ideas to editors, who decide which ones to pursue. Although there is tremendous competitiveness among tabloid reporters to generate the blockbuster "whiz" stories (Corkery 1981), many more run-of-the mill tabloid stories spring from medical reports in magazines and newspapers, census and other demographic data, and much of the same background material as any feature writer might use. Other ideas are more intangible, stemming from such "life-style" issues as the endless stories in mainstream media about yuppies, "DINKS," and other "baby boomers." Their tabloid counterparts may be the stories that develop ideas that are similarly "in the air" among their readership—UFOs have landed, garlic will cure everything, people win the lottery all the time. Stories that seem to make sense according to the folklore of one part of the population may seem irrelevant or ludicrous to another.

The argument that tabloid journalism is simply one genre of reporting among many is persuasive up to a point—surely only the most naive journalist would cling to the idea that newspapers simply transmit "reality" to the printed page, unaffected by preconceptions, formulaic story patterns, and other considerations. Yet at the same time, tabloid writers continue to maintain that, above all, they are in the entertainment business. Unfettered by any need to "inform" their readers, they are able to exercise their creativity in, to say the least, more flamboyant directions, and thus they can afford to neglect such journalistic concepts as "balance." After all, the best and most vivid stories are consistent and clear in their point of view; competing interpretations are anathema to a good tabloid tale.

[. . .]

3.3

Producing trash, class, and the money shot: a behind-the-scenes account of daytime TV talk shows
by Laura Grindstaff

Ordinary people on television

Ordinary people have always had limited opportunities for media exposure; historically, talk shows have been one of the few. The talk show as a broad generic category is one of the oldest and more durable electronic media forms with roots dating back to the early days of radio. While most talk radio maintained a political focus and was geared primarily toward older, affluent men, in the early 1970s the talk industry launched a new type of talk show directed at women and younger audiences, featuring light, humorous conversations about male–female relationships. Informally known as "topless radio" (and denounced as "smut" by the Federal Communications Commission), this shift marked the beginning of the genre's intensely interpersonal focus, now standard on *Oprah* et al. and on countless call-in radio sex therapy and advice programs (Munson 1993: 49).

On television, the talk show has traditionally been devoted to either light entertainment, with comedy, skits, music, and celebrity guests, or more serious discussion of news and public affairs among experts (Rose 1985). Rarely did the genre feature ordinary people; indeed, only on game shows or game/talk hybrids did ordinary people routinely play more than a peripheral role. Two such hybrid programs from the 1950s were *Queen for a Day* and *Strike it Rich*, both cited as precursors to contemporary daytime talk shows because they featured individuals willing to step forward and relate their woeful life stories on camera. On *Queen for a Day*, for example, women who provided the most harrowing tales of personal tragedy and hardship were voted "queen" by the studio audience and given prizes such as refrigerators and washing machines (Munson 1993; Priest 1995).[1]

The vast majority of daytime shows aimed at women, however, consisted mostly of chitchat between hosts and celebrity guests, along with light entertainment, cooking demonstrations, or household tips. It was not until the *Phil Donahue Show* made its debut in Dayton, Ohio, in 1967 that the concept of "homemaker entertainment" underwent a radical shift. As Rose (1985) observes, *Donahue* broke down the formal barriers of existing talk-show models, eliminating conventions such as the host's desk and opening monologue that tended to impede discussion. Guests – who were as likely to be ordinary people as celebrities, experts, or politicians – were not isolated from the studio audience but sat on stage as Donahue roamed the audience with a microphone soliciting comments and questions; viewers at home could also phone in and speak with guests on the air.[2] The formal innovation was both a cause and consequence of changes in content as well. "Donahue became a forum for exploring every issue in society, particularly the diversity of sexual lifestyles, in an open manner not previously attempted by any daytime talkshow" (Rose 1985: 338).

For almost two decades *Donahue* was the only nationally-syndicated program of its kind. By 1988, however, it had been joined by *Sally Jessy Raphael, Oprah*, and *Geraldo*, and as of the 1995–6 television season there were more than 20 different daytime talk shows on the air watched by millions of viewers worldwide.[3] This growth has sparked intense competition for ratings and refigured the genre in key ways. Most notably, relative newcomers like *Jenny Jones, Jerry Springer*, and *Ricki Lake* increasingly orchestrate conflict and confrontation in order to produce what I call the "money shot" of the text: that moment of raw emotion, from the angry denunciation to the tearful confession, the display of rage or sorrow or joy or remorse. These moments are both the hallmark of the genre and central to its trashy reputation. Talk shows are parodied on television commercials and primetime sitcoms, in comic strips and newspaper columns, in everyday parlance and discourse. Producers are called "talk-show pimps" while guests are known as "freaks of the week" or "nuts and sluts" (Kneale 1988). An essay in *Wired* magazine describes the essence of the genre as a masturbatory encounter between outraged audience and sacrificial guest, while Dr Vicki Abt, an oft-quoted media scholar, suggests that disclosing one's personal secrets on national television is like "defecating in public" (Kaplan 1995: 12). "These days it has become standard for all sorts of people to flaunt not just their physical oddities but their stupidity, vulgarity, or sinfulness as well," writes Kurt Anderson of *Time*; "they volunteer, in exchange for attention or a few bucks, to suffer sneers and outright ridicule, so long as the medium is sufficiently mass." Perhaps Jeff Jarvis of *TV Guide* sums it up best when he says, "[talk shows] are a forum for trashy people to act trashy, exhibiting their bad manners, hard hearts, and filthy family laundry before millions of viewers".

Clearly what disturbs such critics is not just the public disclosure of private events, but the manner in which these disclosures are made and the kind of person making them. Thus talk shows are "scandalous" because trashy people talk trash and let it all hang out on national television. The money shot is the focus of this contempt: ordinary people's willingness to sob, scream, bicker, and fight on television. The analogy to pornography is both deliberate and fitting. The climax of most sex scenes in film and video porn, the money shot is the moment of orgasm and ejaculation offering incontrovertible "proof" of a man's – and occasionally a woman's – "real" sexual excitement and prowess. Pornography thus performs a kind of low-brow ethnography of the body, part of the documentary impulse Williams (1989) calls "the frenzy of the visible." Like pornography, daytime talk is a narrative of explicit revelation where people "get down and dirty" and "bare it all" for the pleasure, fascination, or repulsion of viewers. Like pornography, daytime talk exposes people's private parts in public. It demands external, visible proof of a guest's inner emotional state, and the money shot – the dramatic climax when the lie is exposed, the affair acknowledged, the reunion consummated – is the linchpin of the discourse.

The money shot is also the linchpin of production efforts, informing the activities of producers at every stage of the process. All the work behind the scenes – choosing topics, finding, interviewing, and rehearsing guests, coaching audience members – is done in the service of its display. Depending on the show, the money shot might be "soft-core," prompted by grief or remorse and consisting primarily of tears (as on *Diana*), or "hard-core," involving bickering, shouting, screaming, and, occasionally, physical blows (as on *Randy*). In the pages that follow I will chronicle the career of the money shot through various stages of production, illustrating how this scandalous content is accomplished in routine ways. In doing so I hope to both reinforce and challenge the framing of talk shows as media scandal by highlighting the scandalous nature of *all* mass-mediated – especially televisual – discourse.

Talk as work: routinizing the production process

Talk shows may be trashy, but trash is just as difficult to produce as more respectable forms of television, if not more so. Producers strive to elicit the money shot because they require visible evidence of a guest's emotional state. At the same time, because they tape 200 shows per year, producers must make these seemingly spontaneous and unpredictable moments predictable and routine. As Tuchman (1973) notes, organizations routinize tasks whenever possible in order to facilitate the control of work. Routinization would seem especially important – and yet especially challenging – when the work involves the intentional orchestration of volatile situations. In the world of daytime talk, "good television" requires that the money shot be genuine and spontaneous, while at the same time consistently produced. How is this delicate balancing act accomplished?

Producers draw largely on the codes and conventions of newsgathering and late-night talk. Mark Fishman (1980) and others have detailed the ways in which journalists rely on established sources and information channels in order to produce fresh news daily under the pressure of deadlines, even when the news consists of unpredictable or unexpected events like accidents, emergencies, or natural disasters. This means exposing themselves to a few key nodal points within the vast expanse of their beat territory where information is already concentrated, and then repackaging that information according to the mandates of the news organization. The world of daytime talk is also bureaucratically organized, despite the often makeshift appearance of the programs. As one producer put it, "people seem to think we pull guests right off the street like a dogcatcher picking up strays, but that's not the way it happens."

Like reporters, talk-show producers have "beat territories" they survey on a regular basis for potential story ideas – mostly magazines, newspapers, and other television programs. There is the "tabloid beat," the "hard-news-and-current-affairs beat," the "woman's-magazine beat," the "soap-opera beat," and so forth. Just as with newsgathering, there exists a potentially infinite number of available stories; in actual practice, however, talk-show topics do not come from just anywhere, but are reflexively constituted with reference to other mass-media texts, including other daytime talk shows. "There are no original topics left in this business," one *Diana* staffer confided, "it's all just variations on a theme. When I worked at *Sally*, I must have done a dozen shows on mother–daughter conflicts alone." The heavy reliance on other media as well as certain core scripts within the genre illustrates another observation made by Tuchman (1973) in her analysis of newsgathering: Variability in raw data impedes routinization. The recycling of topics (and, to some degree, guests) is less about laziness or producers' lack of imagination than the structural demands of the workplace.

In choosing topics, producers ask themselves, will the topic appeal to the target demographic (typically women ages 18–54)? If it has been done before, does it have a fresh angle? Can "real" people be found to talk about it? Most importantly, is it visual? This last question is really about the money shot, because by "visual" producers mean visibly or obviously emotional or volatile. Does the topic involve controversy, conflict, or confrontation? If not, where will the drama come from? Getting the guest to emote is the bottom line, and it cannot be left to chance. In this sense, talk shows face a dilemma diametrically opposite to that of organizations like funeral homes and hospital emergency rooms, where the goal of routinization is to minimize rather than maximize emotional displays. In both cases, however, guests and their emotions are objectified as elements of production, things to be managed and manipulated.

Another consideration is whether the topic is consistent with the image of the host and the talk show itself, for despite their seeming homogeneity, there are significant differences between shows. *Geraldo* can tackle subjects *Ricki Lake* cannot; *Jenny Jones* and *Jerry Springer* do things *Oprah* and *Leeza* do not. Each show has a unique identity, and it is the job of the executive producer to ensure that the topics, the guests, and the way both are handled support and reaffirm this identity. The executive producer at *Diana* described that show as being "classy, but with a bit of an edge. We're not one of those sleazy, tabloid talk shows, we don't ambush people and we're not confrontational – our viewers hate that. But we're not afraid to push the envelope a little either." *Diana* thus tends to avoid overt conflict, opting instead for more subtle performances. *Randy*, on the other hand, embraces it. "We always book conflict," an associate producer told me, "it's the main ingredient. Things without conflict just don't have any bearing for the show." To go back to the pornography metaphor, *Diana* is soft-core while *Randy* is hard-core, the money shot more often than not involving physical as well as emotional displays.

Once producers have been assigned a show, they rely on a number of routine sources and channels for securing guests to be on panel, the specific channel being determined largely by the topic. For serious, current-affair, or social-issue-oriented topics, more common on *Diana* than on *Randy*, the primary channel is existing groups and organizations. Producers go to the Screen Actors Guild or various publicity agencies when seeking celebrity guests, and organizations such as Alcoholics Anonymous or the local Rape Crisis Center when seeking the help and participation of experts. These experts then put producers in contact with selected "ordinary" guests, often their own clients. (Experts are thus important to the genre as much for their connections to ordinary people as for their expertise – which is why they are typically brought on stage only in the last segment of a show.) Producers can also locate potential guests through on-line databases that cross-reference stories and sources from a vast network of local and national media, or through services such as the National Talkshow Guest Registry in Los Angeles.[4] Of course, producers also rely on their own informal networks and contacts, much as journalists and other media professionals do. Sometimes these are family members and friends, sometimes former guests with whom producers have maintained a relationship, sometimes staffers at other talk shows. When in a bind, producers may rely on "stringers," individuals producers pay to find guests on short notice whom they cannot find for themselves.[5] In many cases, once producers find one guest to fit the topic, that person serves as the stepping stone or conduit to others. In this way, certain guests themselves perform much the same function as experts do for producers, or key sources for journalists.

Perhaps the largest proportion of guests, however, come from plugs, brief advertisements for upcoming topics that air at the end of every show ("Are you constantly using food as a substitute for sex? Do you refuse to date outside your race? Does your mom act younger than you do? Call 1–800-XXX-XXXX"). Plugs are used for topics that do not necessarily have an organizational base. For example, make-over shows are standard fare on *Diana*, yet, as one producer explained it, "there is no center for make-over candidates, no group or club or whatever to call. So instead of going to the guest, the guest comes to us." As an intern I logged thousands of phone calls from viewers responding to on-air plugs about forbidden relationships, compulsive lying, medical mishaps, roommate problems, interracial romance, cross-dressing, sibling rivalry, infidelity, promiscuity, dating disasters, and family feuds, among other topics.

Not surprisingly perhaps, "plug topics" have the reputation among industry insiders as the most trashy and debased, not only because of the specific content, but because, in giving ordinary people direct access and thereby bypassing official organizations and expert contacts, they require little investigative work on the part of producers. In fact, advertising for one's sources is about as far from the respected tradition of investigative journalism as one can get. It is partly for this reason, and because *Diana* defines itself in opposition to the "sleazy, tabloid" brand of daytime talk show, that the supervising producer there discouraged producers from relying too heavily on plugs to book their guests. Conversely at *Randy* – which *is* one of those sleazy tabloid talk shows (and does not pretend to be otherwise) – producers rely almost exclusively on plugs.

The blind date

Plugs are thus one of several formal mechanisms designed to streamline the difficult process of locating the kind of ordinary people producers need – those willing to talk about their personal problems, hardships, or transgressions on national television. What is more challenging to routinize, however, is the actual performance of guests once they are found. Producers thus employ various strategies to minimize uncertainty and ensure that guests will not be boring, freeze in front of the camera, or fail to show up altogether. First and foremost is an extensive pre-interview over the phone, sometimes referred to by producers as "the blind date" because they claim to know within the first minute of conversation whether the relationship is worth pursuing. If it is – that is, if the person is energetic, articulate, emotionally expressive, and forthcoming with intimate material – there are frequent follow-up conversations to iron out the exact details of the guest's story, with producers always imposing the conventional pyramid structure used by journalists to get the most important information up front. Producers may talk to other people to corroborate the story or get additional information on the guest, and they might ask for supporting documents such as letters, photographs, or videotape to use in the show. Meanwhile, the travel coordinator will have been in contact with the guest about flight and limousine arrangements.

Depending on the show's focus, producers may, like journalists, do some background research to gather facts and statistical data, especially for "social-issue" topics like rape, battery, or homelessness – again, more common on *Diana* than on *Randy*. This research usually informs the questions producers prepare for the host, and may also help producers decide on the best combination of guests for the panel. Balance of this sort is key, and is another concept familiar to journalists and other media professionals. If the issue is controversial, are both sides represented? What other elements are needed to flesh out the story? What other guests would add interest, excitement, or diversity? For example, when producers at *Diana* put together a show on teenagers with HIV, they aimed for a panel that was varied in terms of race, gender, sexual orientation, and method of contracting the virus. On *Randy*, where more energy is devoted to digging up dirt on guests than researching facts, "balance" typically means securing as many parties involved in a dispute as possible – less in the interest of fairness than of orchestrating a dramatic confrontation. As Randy himself told me: "This isn't an educational show, other than what you learn by seeing how people relate to one another. What we're discussing on any given day is the least important thing; the subject is merely a vehicle to get people to engage in certain forms of interaction."

The primary purpose of the pre-interview and other preparatory work is to solidify a structure for the show, identify the participants, narrow their stories down to manageable bits, and determine how these various bits will come together on stage in a visually compelling way. This is not so different from the assembly of late-night talk shows, described by Tuchman (1974: 131) as "the natural history of locating, preparing, and choreographing the typified personal characteristics of celebrities for public consumption." Producers of late-night talk are also concerned with, as Tuchman puts it, "designing lively interaction." They too conduct research, do pre-interviews, and strive for the proper combination of guests, especially if the celebrities interact with each other as well as the host. For that matter, so do the producers of more serious talk shows devoted to news and public affairs. And in orchestrating heated political debates among experts – which may include shouting, finger-pointing and other displays of less than "civil" discourse – they are producing their own particular version of the money shot. But the different topics discussed by ordinary people, and the kind of money shot expected of them, mean that producers of daytime talk face certain challenges the staff on shows like the public affairs debate forum *Crossfire* do not.

Given the trashy reputation of the genre, one of the biggest challenges is convincing people who may be reluctant to participate that it is in their best interest to do so or that their disclosures will serve some higher purpose. Many potential guests rightly perceive that the television industry is driven by financial rather than philanthropic concerns, and they question the motives of producers. Thus producers must be skilled salespeople with finely honed methods of persuasion. One *Diana* staffer described how he booked the cousin of the Menendez brothers after the man initially refused.[6] "I had to figure out what was going to press his buttons, what would spark some passion in this guy," the producer told me:

> So I said to him, "you know what? This whole thing with O.J. is overshadowing the Menendez brothers, and Eric and Lyle are being forgotten. I bet people in Ohio think Eric and Lyle are sitting pretty in Beverly Hills when in reality they're sitting in prison. You should come on our show and talk about that, remind people what they're going through and how unfair it is." And you know what? He totally went for that. Because I was totally taking the side of Eric and Lyle – which I do anyway.

Because producers work in pairs, they sometimes play a version of "good cop/bad cop" with guests, where the "good" producer promises certain favors or agrees to certain conditions, and then blames the other "bad" producer when the favors fail to materialize or the conditions are not met. Depending on the situation, producers may appeal to a person's self-interest ("coming on the show may be your last chance to reconcile with your sister"; "getting this off your chest will make you will feel so much better"), altruism ("if sharing your story and educating others can help protect even *one* child, your daughter will not have died in vain") or sense of justice ("don't let your boyfriend get away with this, if you don't confront him he'll just do it again"). If a guest has initially agreed and then changed his or her mind – a common occurrence on *Randy* – producers may stress the obligations of the informal contract, wheedle, cajole, promise special treatment, offer money (in the form of "lost wages" or *per diem* stipends), or claim their job is at stake ("If you don't show up, I'll lose my job"). Sometimes, if the story is big enough, producers will fly half-way across the country in order to beg in person. In general, the more sensitive the issue, and the greater the potential for embarrassment or exposure, the more difficult the show is to book.

Of course, the use of plugs helps bypass the potential problem of persuading guests, because most people responding to plugs are essentially volunteering their services. Nonetheless, if the topic involves conflict or the revelation of sensitive or incriminating information – and many do – then guests may reconsider their initial impulse to volunteer. Even if the person who first contacts the show does not reconsider, others connected to the story often will, and often within a day or two of the taping. Several producers mentioned last-minute cancellations, or "drop outs" as they are sometimes called, as absolutely the most frustrating aspect of the job. "I can't even put words around how frustrating that was," said a former *Ricki Lake* producer:

> It was just a nightmare. I'd book my show Friday and want to go to Cape Cod for the weekend and, you know, my show would be Monday and I'd check my voice mail Saturday night and half of them had canceled. So I'd stop what I was doing – I mean, I literally walked out of restaurants in between my appetizer and my main course and went back to work from a pay phone. It was just hateful. It was horrible.

Not surprisingly, the easiest guest to book is the wronged party, the person who wants to confront someone else about a misdeed or injustice, while the most difficult is the person being confronted. Although most talk shows now have official policies forbidding producers to lie – producers cannot tell a guest the show is about X when it is about Y, and are not supposed to lure guests on panel under false pretenses – they are nonetheless adept at withholding the full details of a given situation, choosing their words carefully to frame an issue in a particular light, and emphasizing only the benefits of participating. At *Randy*, producers will tell a prospective guest, "someone you know wants to surprise you on our show. We can't tell you who it is, or what the surprise is about – it could be good, it could be bad. But you'll get a free trip out of the deal, we'll fly you out here, put you up in a nice hotel, take you around by limousine, give you some spending money . . ."

In general, producers aim to book guests embroiled in a conflict at the last possible minute so they have little time to reconsider or press for more information. One veteran of the business, formerly with *Geraldo*, told me he used to book his best (i.e. most explosive) shows the night before taping. Producers at *Diana* are also wary of booking guests too far in advance, less because the topics are controversial than because of the simple fact that the longer people wait the more nervous they get, regardless of topic. "It's like going off the high dive as a kid," an associate producer there explained. "If you walk right up to the edge of the board and jump off, it's no problem, and afterward you're usually glad you did it. But if you stand up there staring down at the water and think about it too much, then you're probably going to back down." Another *Diana* producer said that if she books a guest more than four or five days before the show, she will chat with the person on the phone every day in order to reinforce their relationship – and the sense of obligation that comes with it.

Even when guests are perfectly willing to take the plunge – and the majority are – the very fact that they are "ordinary" people rather than experts or celebrities often impedes their easy insertion into the production sphere. Appearing on national television is not part of the daily routine for ordinary people. This is, in part, what makes them ordinary. They do not have professional media training, and their inexperience can make them high-maintenance, in need of constant attention and reassurance from producers. Nor do they have agents or publicists who handle their schedules and juggle their competing obligations. Many ordinary guests on *Diana* and the majority of guests on *Randy* are working-class individuals. They have jobs to go to, partners and children to care for, and are likely experiencing some personal problem or hardship – which is why they responded to a plug in the first place and why producers find them attractive. They may be battling cancer or AIDS; they may be homeless or abused; they may be feuding with their in-laws, cheating on their spouses, or going through an acrimonious divorce. The very things that make them willing and desirable guests also make their lives chaotic and their participation problematic. All of the communication between producers and guests prior to taping occurs by phone, yet if guests are poor or destitute they may not have a home let alone a telephone. If they are sick or addicted to drugs they may not be well enough to travel on tape day; if they have lost a child in a terrible tragedy their grief may overwhelm them; if they have multiple personality disorder, the personality who is interviewed and booked for the show may not be the same one who walks out on stage. And then there are the family members and friends whom guests bring along for support, people needing airline tickets, hotel accommodation, and special VIP seating in the audience.

People in crisis create extra work behind the scenes. At the same time they are the bread and butter of the genre, the people most likely to gain entry and the most attractive from a production standpoint. As we have seen, producers attempt to routinize their participation drawing on the conventions of newsgathering and other talk-show forms. But despite the routine procedures and all the preparatory work behind the scenes, an element of unpredictability remains. At no time are producers and guests alike more aware of this tension than on the day of taping itself.

Talk as show: airing dirty laundry

Clearly the groundwork for the money shot is laid long before a guest actually appears on stage. Producers have an easier time leading guests to an emotional brink in the moments before taping if the topic is sensitive or volatile to begin with, if the guest feels strongly about it, if producers have found others with an opposing viewpoint to challenge him or her, or if they deliberately orchestrate a surprise encounter they know will shock or provoke a vulnerable guest on the air. Given these conditions, coaxing a dramatic performance from individuals may not seem so difficult, but this too is a challenge for producers – again, because the true stars of the show are "ordinary" people rather than experts or celebrities. Producers of late-night talk shows have long recognized that casual conversation is as performative as an entirely scripted affair, and that "being oneself is itself a constructed activity" (Tuchman 1974: 126), especially when one does it on national television. Celebrities on late-night talk shows thus rely on their acting skills to "play" themselves. Ordinary guests on daytime talk shows do exactly the same thing, but since they are not professionals, producers spend a great deal of time and energy preparing them for their roles. Indeed, this aspect of the work can be extremely stressful because, as Tuchman (1974: 122) puts it, "try as one might, one cannot accomplish an interaction for someone else."

Although it rarely happens, producers of daytime talk live in constant fear that guests will fall apart on stage. According to one 10-year veteran of the genre, "sometimes when you sit somebody down in that chair and the lights go on and the cameras are on them and the audience is there, they freeze. I don't know if you've ever been on TV, but it's an intimidating experience. And I'm always amazed – *amazed* – that these little people from their trailer parks don't totally freak out on camera more often." "Freaking out" typically means clamming up or shutting down, or in some way failing to follow the pyramid structure of storytelling mandated by producers: not disclosing the most information first, getting the story mixed up or confused, or losing focus and going off on tangents.

To prevent this unhappy situation, all the energy expended on guests prior to taping is intensified the day of the show. It is on this day that the presentational or theatrical aspects of the genre are foregrounded, and the backstage efforts of producers come to fruition on stage. It is a day of tension and anxiety as well as excitement and drama, for staff and guests alike. Producers are on edge, making final adjustments to the script and snapping at their associates to tie up any loose ends. At some point there is a brief production meeting to go over the use of any videotape packages, stills, or live satellite hook-ups. Small crises erupt: guest no. 2 overslept and missed his flight, so he has to be moved to a later segment, and that means guests 3 and 4 cannot mention his affair until after his wife joins him on stage. Guest 5 has to stop at the pharmacy on the way from the airport to the studio because she forgot her medication, and guest 6 has changed her mind about coming altogether because she found out her sister-in-law will also be on the show. Guest 7 is in tears because the flight attendant spilled coffee on her best suit, and anything else will make her look fat on television.

When the guests begin to arrive the tension in the air increases perceptibly. At *Diana*, all guests or sets of guests have their own individual dressing rooms or trailers complete with name tag and gold star on the door. If the rooms are still in use from a previous taping (there are two, sometimes three tapings per day), they wait in the Green Room until the changeover is complete. At *Randy*, guests go directly to the Green Room or other backstage areas reserved for the same purpose, and because the topics typically deal with confrontations and surprises, producers must take great pains to keep people separated before the show. Guests whose clothes are inappropriate for television (horizontal stripes and plain white are both forbidden) or too casual (jeans, T-shirts, flannel) receive a visit from a staffer in wardrobe, and all guests at some point have their hair and make-up done. Meanwhile the stage manager wires them for sound, and the "talent coordinator" obtains written consent for their participation, along with a signed statement guaranteeing the authenticity of their story. After all this is complete, the most important remaining task is for producers to prep the guests. According to those I observed and interviewed, it is a fine line between over-rehearsing guests and providing just enough guidance so they do not freeze up. In this particular interaction, producers make a special effort to position them as both stars and experts of a sort – stars of the show and experts on their own personal experience.

The goal of backstage coaching is twofold. First, producers go over content with guests, reminding them of key points in their story and the order in which to make them. "You want guests to be fresh and spontaneous," a *Diana* producer explained:

> but on the other hand, we have very little time with these people and if they take ten minutes to answer something, it's not going to work. So I help them get to the point, I help them understand they have to start with the highlight of the answer and once they hit that they can digress all they want. You know, if the highlight of the story is that they found Jesus, I say to them, start with "I'm here today because I found Jesus." And *then* you can go back and say, "I was living on welfare in the gutter as a wino, and went through all these horrible things because I lost my job and my car and my house in a fire and da da da da da da." You know? But it's like, say what you found, and *then* how you got there. Don't build up to a point. And with some people that takes a lot of work because they want to tell you every little detail way on back to their childhood and their highschool prom and their hobbies and everything. They think they have all this time and they really don't.

Second, producers are concerned with style and performance – especially at *Randy*, more devoted to orchestrating emotional fireworks than is *Diana*. Although to a large degree the fire is built into the topic, producers use the moments just prior to taping to light the fuse. I knew the routine by heart:

> Just relax, you'll do fine. This is *your* life, you've lived it, so there's no wrong answers. Don't hold back on those emotions because this is your big chance to show millions of people you really care about this issue. If you're going to laugh, laugh big; if you're going to cry, cry big; if you get mad, show us *how* mad. This is *your* show, so take charge! If you have something to say, jump right in there, don't wait for the host to call on you, and don't let the other guests push you around. Now, when the host asks you to describe the first time you found your husband in bed with another woman, what are you going to say?

Randy guests are often carefully segregated until taping begins so the fight occurs on rather than off stage, and so producers can appear to back both sides of an issue. To the young girl and her 70-year-old fiancé in Green Room 1, a producer will say, "the important thing is to stand your ground, this show is about the two of you proving your love for each other." To the outraged mother in Green Room 2 the same producer will say, "don't be afraid to let him have it, this show is about getting your daughter away from that pedophile!"

Eventually the audience files in, while the technical crew and support staff rush back and forth, readying equipment and attending to last-minute details. *Diana* employs a comedian to warm up the audience while at *Randy* the stage manager does this job as well as his own. Both tell jokes ("your mamma is so dumb she thinks Taco Bell is a Mexican phone company") and keep up a steady stream of idle banter. Audience members are awarded prizes for singing, dancing, or telling jokes of their own. Most importantly, however, they are instructed in the finer points of audience etiquette, which forbids wearing ball caps, chewing gum, mugging for the camera, or speaking without being called on, but encourages asking questions of the panelists and giving "big reactions" (booing, gasping, clapping, etc.) to the events on stage. During the taping itself the warm-up person will often lead these reactions from the sidelines. Sometimes he has audience members rehearse the proper procedure for asking a question or making a comment ("stand up tall, lean over and speak into the mic but don't grab for it"), and he will always lead several rousing cheers in anticipation of the host's entrance. In general, the aim is to energize the audience, and to make people feel integral to the action and crucial to the success of the taping. "You can make or break this show," audience members are told. "Get involved! Show us how you feel! Ask questions! Remember, you represent all those viewers out there who can't ask questions for themselves. You represent America."

The coaching of guests and audience members, like the choice of topics, the pre-interviews, and the research, reveals the efforts of talk-show staffers to make predictable and routine what is, in the last instance, unpredictable: the behavior of ordinary people. Coaching guests increases the probability of obtaining the preferred or desired outcome on stage, and in this sense it has a number of parallels – the locker-room pep talk before the big game, or the process by which actors psyche themselves up for a dramatic performance. In my opinion, however, the most fitting comparison again takes us back to pornography. Prepping guests is not unlike preparing male porn stars for their sex scene: It gets them all "hot and bothered" so they can go out there and "show wood." With porn films, there is even a person – typically a young woman – employed on the set for this very purpose; she is called "the fluffer" (see Faludi 1995). Just as the fluffer arouses the actor to increase the probability of the money shot, producers "fluff" guests to increase the chance that they too will climax in the appropriate way. As with the male stars of pornographic films, sometimes talk-show guests can show wood, sometimes they cannot.

Most of the time – I would say 90 percent of the time – guests can. Indeed, producers have a far greater success rate than fluffers. This has to do not only with the inherent drama of the topics, but with the fact that talk-show guests, especially those responding to plugs, tend to be talk-show viewers as well. Personal crises aside, they know what is expected of them, they know what producers want, and they know how to deliver the goods. They do not need to be told to show their emotions or move their chair or stomp off the stage in a huff, because they see other guests do these things every day on television. Producers' concern about ordinary people as competent performers is thus often misplaced, for ordinary people who watch a lot of talk shows have in some sense been coached or trained long before they ever speak with a producer. (Expert guests, on the other hand, unless they have had prior talk-show experience, are more naive about the genre and may have unrealistic expectations about how an issue will be framed and their own participation managed.)

When producers put together a show they follow the same pyramid structure they urge on their guests. Thus the most "important" guest always takes the stage first, and sets the tone and framework for subsequent events (in a conflict situation, this person is typically the heroine of the story, the person who feels victimized by a past wrong or injustice). "Important" does not necessarily mean the guest has the most sensational story; it often means she is the most energetic and the best talker, and thus the one most likely to hold viewers' interest and prevent them from changing the channel. When *Diana* producers did a show about acquaintance rape, they debated back and forth about who to lead with: the woman repeatedly raped, stabbed, and left for dead, or the woman raped once by her best friend. Ultimately they decided to go with the second woman because she was a better storyteller, even though the story itself was less harrowing. Sometimes producers will switch guests at the last minute depending on what transpires in the Green Room. If guest no. 3 proves more excitable and easier to fluff, producers may bump guest no. 1 and put no. 3 in her place. According to an associate producer at *Diana*, a given show's success or failure depended in large measure on the producer's ability to make these kinds of last-minute spot decision about guests and the direction of the show. "The key is your ability to change," the producer explained:

> So you roll in that day and there's four guests there, and all of a sudden you realize the guest you thought would be in the third segment is so compelling, they're crying in the Green Room, dammit, they should be on the show first! And as a producer, that's your most important decision. Certainly planning the show beforehand is important – but you could get to the set and they [the guests] might not look or act like the person you talked to on the phone four days ago. Maybe on this day they had a bad morning, or they're PMSing, and all of a sudden they're

really emotional about their kid being killed by gang members. Dammit, start with them! It's storytelling, so the most compelling story, however it's told, should be first.

In most cases the taping unfolds according to plan. Of course, when the plan itself calls for conflict or an emotional disclosure, there is still plenty of room for spontaneity. Ultimately, the tension between scriptedness and spontaneity is what many producers enjoy about the work. According to an associate producer at *Diana*:

> the fun part is to be out there on the floor the day of the show, you and the executive producer and the host, judging where the show is going, on the fly. Because – although generally you stick to your format – you've got to be able to change things. And some shows you will change a lot throughout; you'll say, "let this go long, dump that, move that." That's when it really gets exciting.

The most memorable show for a *Randy* producer had an additional element of unpredictability because of the topic: multiple personality disorder. "The show totally had the potential to be the best or the worst," the producer said:

> This girl had 15 personalities and she was confronting her mom who caused this, after she hadn't spoken to her in years. And there was a fear that, because she had multiple personalities, when she saw her mom again [on stage] she might suddenly become her two-year-old self and not talk at all. Instead of that she became her angry person and just went nuts! It was – this one scene is just like the best television moment you'll ever see. It was so powerful and real. But she could have been, like, totally silent and withdrawn. It was just a wild card because there was so much emotion there. It was a wild card and we got lucky.

"Getting lucky" here means obtaining the money shot. But as we have seen, the money shot is really less a matter of luck and more a matter of careful design. To be sure, things inevitably happen that producers cannot foresee or control. Sometimes guests get nervous on camera and forget their training. Sometimes they get cold feet and drop out. Guests might be willing but unable to make the taping: They can fall ill, have an accident, get arrested. Someone in the audience could have an epileptic seizure during the show and unwittingly diffuse the emotion on stage. Sometimes, as one former *Ricki Lake* producer discovered, guests resolve their differences in transit and ruin the show before it even begins. "I couldn't believe it," he told me:

> This couple, they were, you know, fighting like cats and dogs 24 hours earlier and then they arrive all lovey-dovey. They're like, "oh everything is fine now, we're going to keep the baby and, you know, I'm never going to hit her again. We made up at 30,000 feet." I was like, "oh shit, come on, you're kidding me!"

By and large, however, guests and producers alike follow the script. Where guests are concerned, the venue alone – the stage, the lights, the cameras, the audience –

helps to ensure compliance with producers' desires for a dramatic and compelling performance.

[. . .]

Notes

1   *Strike it Rich* was similar to *Queen for a Day* but did not last as long on the air. According to Priest (1995: 6), the producers came under considerable fire from health and welfare officials for luring the country's destitute of New York City, where they sometimes waited for weeks in the hopes of receiving money and gifts on the program. A third game/talk hybrid was called *Stand Up and Be Counted*. Less focused on tragedy and misfortune, it dealt with an "average" woman's personal dilemma, chosen from letters submitted by viewers: should Mrs Smith use her inheritance to travel the world or invest in a comfortable retirement? Should Miss Jones marry and move away or forgo the marriage and stay close to her roots? After a discussion of the dilemma between host and "contestant" on a set resembling a Victorian-style front porch, several members of the studio audience voiced their opinions, and then the entire audience voted on what the woman should do. Not bound to accept the vote, she returned the following week to announce her decision. Viewers at home also participated by writing letters giving advice, and the best letter each week won a car, vacation, or household appliance (see Munson 1993: 54–5).

2   According to Rose (1985: 338), "Donahue was a probing interviewer who placed great emphasis on letting his studio audience (99 percent of which were women) ask the questions." In his autobiography, Donahue himself reveals that audience participation developed somewhat by accident when women began asking good questions and offering astute comments during commercial breaks. At some point both host and executive producer realized that integrating the off-stage interaction would make for a better, more interesting show (Donahue 1979).

3   King World Syndication Company estimates that as many as 50 million people watch talk shows on a daily basis. *Oprah* alone attracts between 15 and 20 million viewers in the US daily (Squire 1994; Peck 1994) and airs in more than a hundred countries, including, most recently, parts of Eastern Europe and Africa. According to Livingstone and Lunt (1994), the audience for daytime talk in Britain and the US consists largely of folks who spend at least part of their day at home: home makers, students, part-time and shift workers, the unemployed, and the retired, with gender as the most reliable demographic predictor. Goldstein (1995) cites the following statistics from the Annenberg School for Communication: 75 percent of talk-TV viewers are women, 60 percent are under the age of 54, and more than half live in households with incomes under $30,000. In a content analysis of talk-show guests, Greenberg and Smith (1995) provide an indirect profile of viewers. They report that the demographic profile of guests reflects that of viewers, which in turn is fairly consistent with the 1992 Census figures for the actual US population – the main difference being the over-representation of women and African Americans: women comprise 52 percent of

the actual population but 63 percent of talk-show guests, while African Americans comprise roughly 13 percent of the actual population but 18 percent of talk-show guests.

4   The National Talkshow Guest Registry is essentially a large database of potential guests (both expert and ordinary) organized according to topic. Anyone with a "good" story or the right credentials willing to appear on a talk show can register for a nominal monthly fee of three dollars. For a larger sum, producers can purchase from the registry a list of suitable guests.

5   While Berkman (1995) reports that many guests procured by stringers are actually aspiring actors willing to assume fake identities, one of my informants, a retired producer formerly with *Geraldo* and *Ricki Lake*, contested this framing. He said it was not so much that the guests are lying or assuming false identities as the fact that they live in very different worlds than producers do, especially in terms of class and race, and producers have few other means of accessing them. "Stringers are used for certain kinds of shows," the producer said. "You know, if producers are looking for girls who dress like sluts, and the carts come up empty, they'll go to Newark, New Jersey or Detroit or someplace and they'll pay some girl 500 dollars and they'll say, 'find five girls who dress like sluts.' That happens all the time. 'Cause to be perfectly blunt, these lily white producers out of these preppy little schools, they wouldn't know the first thing about going to the inner city and finding guests. It's the only way they can do it. You know, when you see heroin addicts and prostitutes on these shows, how else – do you think some 23-year-old Polly Pure Bread is riding around Watts, or like, you know, South Bronx? Forget it."

6   Eric and Lyle Menendez were two brothers charged with and ultimately convicted of murdering their wealthy parents for the inheritance money. When I spoke with the producer who booked the cousin on *Diana*, it was prior to the brothers' second trial and subsequent guilty verdict.

[. . .]

3.4

Money shot
by Victoria Mapplebeck

> Now and then someone would accuse me of being evil – of letting people
> destroy themselves while I watched, just so I could film or tape record them.
> But I don't think about myself as evil – just realistic.
> > Andy Warhol, quoted in Mike Wrenn, *Andy Warhol in His*
> > *Own Words*, (Omnibus Press) 1991

Warhol wasn't evil. He was just fascinated by looking, and by people. Combine the
two and you have his movies. Up in The Factory, he stood watching as his motley
crew of stars bared their souls, his camera rolled as they had sex, fought and wept.
Warhol was just as happy with the downtime: he also stood transfixed as he filmed
his stars sleeping, eating or just sitting pretty. If he could have, he would have filmed
them 24/7.

He would have loved Reality TV for its 'access all areas' approach to life. TV
shows that don't stop, that enable you to get online and watch these new TV stars
around the clock. Not only can you view them all hours, you can interact with them
too. You can become a star of the show you consume. Truly 3-DTV. He would have
been a big fan and no stranger to the controversy these shows invariably attract.
Warhol was well used to the ubiquitous critical hype that comes when cameras go up
close and personal. 'Weigh them, don't read them,' he said of his reviews. The hype
was part of the event.

I have been there too. I wrote and directed *Smart Hearts*, one of Channel 4's first
forays into Reality TV. The series received plenty of press, good and bad. *Smart
Hearts* is a five-part documentary and online portrait of two friends of mine, Brendan
Quick and Claire de Jong. It was TV's first documentary convergence series, featuring
stories and characters that cross from TV to the net and back again. *Smart Hearts*
combined my filming of the subjects with constant webcam access which streamed
from the subjects' homes on to the *Smart Hearts* website. *Smart Hearts* was about life,
lived, live for 18 months.

The series took as its starting point the roller-coaster of documentary access and
consent. What happens when your private life goes public? This was Reality TV from
the subject's point of view. As well as providing 3-D access, *Smart Hearts* explored the

fall out. *Smart Hearts* takes its name from a Japanese Tamagotchi that bleeps when it finds your urban soul mate. The initial idea was to make a longitudinal series exploring a contemporary relationship. This was the late 1990s and everywhere you looked TV was obsessing about relationships. From *Trisha* to *Ally McBeal*, this perceived relationship meltdown was reduced to the adolescent vocabulary of *Bridget Jones*. All men feared commitment and all women were begging for it.

I wanted to explore with one couple, the complexities of changing attitudes to dating, marriage and having kids. Several relationship docusoaps had featured cartoon sad cases limping from one dating crisis to the next. I wanted to make the antidote. As well as filming over an 18-month period, I also wanted to use new technologies to consolidate this approach to increased access and intimacy. Researching online documentary for *Smart Hearts*, I'd spent a lot of time on webcam sites. Couple cam, family cam, dorm cam: the list goes on and on. In the *Independent*, David Aaronovitch said of the medium, 'Webcams . . . allow the terminally bored to entertain the fatally bored' (9 August 2001).

True, the subjects can be boring. But the access is not. No matter how dull the subject, I could sit happily for hours watching real time families eating their cereal and arguing over the TV. These sites were all about the viewers' gaze. The focus was put back on looking; the relief of being able to watch rather than be told. No voice-over, no editing. And so I put the gaze of the webcams into the mix. The *Smart Hearts* subjects' homes would be live online for a year from the pilot's broadcast. Viewers could watch the emotional highs and lows of the subjects throughout production. They could interact with them to boot. Channel 4 liked it. Now we just had to find the subjects.

We put an advertisement in *Time Out*: 'Do you want to share with someone the roller coaster of your relationship, how about the entire nation?' To my amazement we had a good response. This was pre-*Big Brother* but post-*Jennicam*. The webcam sites seemed to have had a real influence on the access subjects were now prepared to provide. Many could deliver on the access but not the content. The people who responded to our advertisement led my producer Peter Day to conclude, 'the people who want to be on TV shouldn't be.'

I was forced to draw on my own life. I approached Brendan, an artist mate of mine, married to another artist Claire. I had a hunch they would be difficult, but good. My initial phone call reached Claire. Brendan was AWOL, having just left after their first and only session of marriage guidance counselling. Hearing they had split, I felt it was a case of back to the drawing board, but Brendan said he'd still be interested. Gradually they both came on board with varying degrees of enthusiasm. Filming a portrait of a broken marriage would have been a difficult and complex situation at the best of times. Add to that my constant filming of them and webcams streaming 24 hours a day, and this was a full on pride-swallowing siege for all concerned.

Brendan and Claire would not have agreed to filming if they hadn't been offered complete editorial control. To offer it is pretty much unheard of in documentary. Given the levels of access, I didn't think I had much choice. Nothing went in the series and the website that they hadn't already approved. This levels of control was much like handing them a loaded gun, which they aimed at me on a regular basis.

Traditionally, documentary filmmakers have referred to the Stockholm Syndrome, in which the hostage falls for his/her kidnapper, to describe the apocryphal dependency subjects are supposed to have on their director. For me it was the reverse, I was their hostage for 18 months. Reality TV covers a multitude of sins. For me the definition is simple, it includes any documentary in which the format is clearly fore-grounded. Reality TV creates an obviously artificial environment, places the subjects in it, and records the results. Within the industry, the genre is also referred to as 'manipulated observational documentary'. Nothing new there – all documentary is manipulated. But Reality TV puts the artifice and agendas of traditional documentary on open display.

Smart Hearts was an authored, rather than a commercial approach to the genre. We had no phone votes, or prize money. However, webcams in the subjects' living room are a clearly artificial presence. So Reality TV it was. Reviewers of *Smart Hearts* loved it or loathed it. We were introduced by *Time Out* as, 'a radical collaborative piece of art' (30 August 2000). The *Guardian* previewed the series as, 'really hypnotic stuff' (30 August 2000), but we had plenty of the run for the hills variety of criticism: the *Daily Telegraph* hoped we would, 'help give Reality TV a bad name' (30 August 2000).

Reality TV raises the inevitable questions when cameras access the highs and lows of real lives. Is this reality or spectacle – surveillance or exhibitionism? Are these new subjects martyrs or stars?

Reality or spectacle?

Who needs images of the world's otherness when we can watch these half persons enacting ordinary life?

Salman Rushdie on British *Big Brother*, The *Guardian*, 9 June 2001

Documentary filmmakers have been endlessly preoccupied with a social and political panorama of the world. The world's 'otherness' that Salman Rushdie prioritizes over 'ordinary life'. Filmmakers have too often used the lens as a journalistic device rather than a cinematic one. Documentary had to be about fore-grounding issues over people, telling us rather than showing us. TV documentary often felt like an illustrated lecture. Once documentary focused almost exclusively on the problems in public institutions: in politics, in housing, in health care, in policing. Following the shift from public to private, epitomized by the talk shows, documentaries are now almost exclusively about personal rather than public crisis.

Documentary has always been about looking, but unlike any other lens-based media it has spent a great deal of energy disguising the fact. The online documentary gaze has changed all that. The constant close-ups of the webcam sites have put the emphasis fully back on spectacle. These sites emphasize rather than disavow the documentary gaze.

[. . .]

Surveillance or exhibitionism?

Richard Brown, a radio reviewer of *Smart Hearts*, said of the access provided by the subjects, 'I braced myself for voyeuristic detail . . . voyeuristic it wasn't: with voyeurism, you the viewer spy on the subject who is unaware of your presence . . . The people we were watching wanted to be seen . . . I didn't feel like a voyeur at all' ('The Message', BBC Radio 4, 8 August 2000).

'Voyeurism' constantly eludes a precise definition. It is used to cover a multitude of sins. Traditionally, voyeurism refers to the unacknowledged gaze, but the viewer's gaze in Reality TV is very much acknowledged. The subjects of Reality TV know they are being watched and they want to be. And yet, 'voyeuristic', is the endless battle cry of the Reality TV reviewer. It seems the consensual access subjects provide for Reality TV cameras has been mistakenly linked to the erosion of privacy in the non-consensual world of surveillance and electronic monitoring, as new digital technologies are providing a platform of wider and faster access to previously hidden areas of public life.

The once 'private' scandals of politicians, monarchs and celebrities are now played out like global soap operas. This kind of access is rarely consensual. Monica Lewinsky did not consent to the FBI accessing her private emails. Bill Clinton did not consent to the details of his sexual encounters being published online. American theorists Jeffrey Rosen and Clay Calvert have explored and criticized the increase in celebrity exposé, surveillance and electronic monitoring. Both are professors in law and examine the rise of electronic voyeurism, lamenting the erosion of privacy and the civil liberties of the subjects exposed.

In *Voyeur Nation: Media, privacy and peering in modern culture* (Westview Press, 2000), Clay Calvert is particularly critical of the rise of Reality TV, 'Discussion is replaced by watching. Indeed the flipside of the death of discourse is, I argue, the birth of voyeurism.' Many critics have worried about the 'death of discourse'. They lament the decline of the issue documentary. Documentary that could change the world. It is a TV hypochondria. The starting point for Reality TV is that the world has changed. Traditional documentary has on the whole failed to reflect these changes. The emphasis of Reality TV is unashamedly on the personal, on ethics rather than politics. This shift is seen by traditionalists as 'dumbing down', as exploitative, and as a corruption of the documentary tradition.

In all of this hand wringing, the critics miss the obvious point about new levels of access. This is not *The Truman Show*. These subjects haven't discovered the cameras, they have actively sought them out. The access these subjects have provided is consensual. They are aware of the cameras' gaze, the hum of the lighting rig. They meet that gaze, sometimes with a head butt.

Martyrs or stars?

Fucking mental and physical breakdown, all on TV . . .

(Brendan Quick, Episode Two, *Smart Hearts*)

Smart Hearts was about looking and therefore about access. What made this series different from any other is that the usual levels of documentary access had been radically increased. The repercussions of this access were not disguised. The subjects denied access as much as they provided it. Brendan and his new girlfriend Lisa regularly went on webcam strike. This would invariably be just at the moment our commissioner was demonstrating the webcams to the head of Channel 4.

Instead of live and sensational access to a 3-D relationship lab, all they got on 'Brendan cam' was a shot of an Eastend corner shop. When Brendan got fed up, he'd hang the webcams out of his window. Fortunately, Claire loved the webcams and was on all day and night. She developed her own web audience and fan base. Viewers could watch her paint, cook, sleep and entertain. At one stage Leos Carax, director of the film *Pola X*, found her in cyberspace and got his casting director to track down her phone number.

But the critics worried. *Smart Hearts*, because of its increased access, was used by broadsheet TV critics as an example of the perceived ethical meltdown and moral decline of Channel 4. Yvonne Roberts' assumption in the *Independent*, that increased access automatically leads to increased exploitation, was fairly typical of the critical response to the series. 'Channel 4's new season includes *Smart Hearts*, "a multi media experiment to record the trials and tribulations of a modern marriage recorded over a twelve month period" . . . Wow. An educational opportunity for us to learn from the mistakes of others or, emotional disembowelling, leaving (some) viewers queasy and the participants degraded?' (7 February 2000).

When I met Yvonne Roberts at a conference we were both speaking at, she admitted she hadn't seen *Smart Hearts*. This is a common feature of contemporary TV criticism. Critics regularly review the press release rather than the programme. Roberts, having not seen the series, was unaware that the project was collaborative, that the subjects had full editorial control and that they were keen to work on a second series. When Claire was asked by one of the audience in the chatrooms, 'How do you cope with your personal life being constantly on camera?', she responded, 'Frankly, I don't think its public enough.'

Although *Smart Hearts* was pitched as the antidote to the docusoap, we were still stuck with its legacy. A decade of 'factual entertainment' had created a culture of viewers and critics who had grown used to a cast of happy losers prepared to let their lives descend into sitcom farce. Brendan and Claire didn't fit the bill. Brendan in particular paid the price.

The docusoap subjects were presented as mad, bad or sad. The online chat audiences tended to side with Claire as 'sad'; she was seen as the apocryphal abandoned wife. Brendan was just 'bad', as a hard drinking philanderer he was cast as the pantomime villain. Brendan complained, 'I'm horrified at being identified as the bloke who drinks in the mornings.' His girlfriend Lisa responded, 'That's your role in the movie . . . the drunk from hell with no talent whatsoever, other than pulling pretty women' (Episode Five).

Even the broadsheet critics reviewed the subjects rather than the programmes. Polly Vernon in *The Guardian*, harked back to the perceived innocence of the docusoap A list. She said of *Smart Hearts*, 'The middle classes do not make good TV. As the title implies Brendan and his friends are becoming too smart about their programmes.' If being 'too smart' makes you a bad documentary subject, does being stupid make you a good one? Nostalgic for the comic and innocent pleasures of *Hotel* and *Airport*, Vernon continued, 'I like docusoaps. I don't think that says anything too awful about me – will the head chef at Burger King Stansted airport, cope with the disgruntled passengers from Malaga? Brilliant. It is a gentle form of voyeurism' (21 December 1999).

[. . .]

Conclusion

There has been a great deal of speculation that, post 11 September 2001, the machiavellian formats of contemporary media will lose favour. Nice will become the new nasty. This isn't the answer either. There are only so many repeats of *Little House on the Prairie* and *Friends* the viewing public can take. Grief, conflict and crisis are a part of our identity and our experience. These emotions are the stuff of melodrama. Melodrama can be good or bad. It ranges from the worst of daytime soaps to the best of Douglas Sirk. What is new is that the conflict and crisis of melodrama are being increasingly sought by documentary, news and Reality TV cameras.

The key point is how these emotional climaxes are represented. The point of *Smart Hearts* was to look and to ask how we look. To challenge why when documentary goes up close and personal, it has always been about the backward glance rather than the full-on gaze. Predictably, most critics were shocked by the level of access in *Smart Hearts*. Reviews would acknowledge the compulsiveness of this intimacy but invariably attach a prefix of guilt. 'Compulsively compelling', one critic said, 'morbidly fascinating' said another. 'Car crash TV' came up in several reviews. I always felt it was over the top, such an obvious example of journalese.

In Reality TV, viewers are not peering at death and mayhem: they are merely watching how people behave behind closed doors. In porn, the money shot marks the end of a scene, the punch line. Warhol caught these emotional climaxes, but they weren't his money shots. In Warhol films, emotional highs and lows were merely part of the bigger portrait. The best of innovative documentary includes these moments of melodrama as the starting point, not the punch line. The increased access and spectacle of Reality TV has bought documentary into the twenty-first century. Subjects and viewers are now part of the equation. It has woken them up.

I'll leave the final comment on the pitfalls and potential of Reality TV to Brendan. In one of the *Smart Hearts* live chats, Brendan was asked if he would like to become a docusoap micro celebrity, like the women from *Cruise*. He replied, 'I know who I am, I don't need to join a fucking celebrity morgue.' He signed out of the chat room with, 'Don't let this programme degenerate into who you like . . . Let the excesses of documentary, the dramatic moments of editing, let that tell you what TV is, because I can't' (*Smart Hearts* website: www.the-loop.com/smarthearts).

SECTION 7

Tabloid audiences

This section addresses a number of central themes on tabloid audiences that run through audience studies more generally. These include the conceptualization of audiences as active or passive consumers; the relationship between audiences and the economics and commercial interests of the media market place; the interaction between audience and popular media; the participation and pleasure of the audience in tabloid culture. We highlight the challenge of analysing the knowing consumer/spectator in an equally self-reflexive contemporary media environment and the possibility that tabloid genres may open up new spaces for public participation in the mediated public sphere.

Many of these themes have a long history, which is enmeshed with the developments of media industry and its outputs throughout the twentieth century – and indeed for print media some of these concerns have a much longer period of gestation stretching back to the rise of mass print markets in the nineteenth century. Frequently, critical thinking about media audiences has tended to construct 'the audience' as the same as, or mirroring, notions of 'the public' in general (Nightingale and Ross, 2003: 3). Indeed, formative work on the imagined communities of mass newspaper print culture insightfully showed the crucial link between broader notions of public identity and community and those of the reading public of daily newspapers from the eighteenth century onwards (Nightingale and Ross, 2003). If the reading public was, as Benedict Anderson (1986) convincingly argues, a concretization of broader cultural and political constructions of citizens within the democratized public sphere then that understanding of the 'reading public' has been the model for the newer industries of radio and TV, as they sought to find inclusive viewing and listening audience groups for their media in the twentieth century (Nightingale and Ross, 2003; see also introduction to Section 1 in this volume). Broadcast media have operated within general ideologies of meeting criteria of educative, informative and entertaining programming that ensures the public good. But in our increasingly commercially driven media environment, such commonplaces as 'what the public wants' rather than what the public should have justifies much format-driven tabloid content, which prioritizes entertainment values above the others and seeks to deliver audiences over to advertisers. And, it could be argued, it is precisely this link between the public, what they represent as an audience, and notions of what they should consume (how they view or listen or watch or engage with tabloid media and culture) that has infused critical attempts to analyse audiences.

The power of the media and the ways that power impacts upon the audience has been a constant theme of modern media analysis. It is a commonplace that throughout the twentieth century the media played an increasingly crucial role in people's everyday lives and the amount of time given over to consuming the media unsurprisingly led to widespread conjecture about the precise nature of the relationship between audiences and media output. In the twentieth century, the mass media sought mass audiences to underpin financially and ideologically their extension of the media industries. The development and extension of mass communication technologies were consequently entwined with the concerted effort of the media industries of print, radio and then television, to speak to, attract and harness the attention, pleasures and desires of the mass audience. In the early twentieth century, for example, Europe and the United States simultaneously experienced a rise of critical interest in the power and potential danger of the mass media to audiences who were primarily understood as vulnerable, malleable and hence controllable by media output. By the 1940s, earlier work on the propagandist nature of the media and its effects on a 'passive' audience sat alongside influential political communication analysis that attempted to measure the audience takeup of political communication in order to gauge its effectiveness. Such work did little to dispel notions of the passive audience.

In the late 1940s, media analysts started tentatively to challenge the top-down model of early effects work by attempting to observe the function of the audience's broader social connections with regard to their public engagement with mass-mediated political messages. In the United States critics began to examine the audience's relationship to political media messages such as electoral campaigns (Lazarsfeld et al., 1944) or government drives to buy war bonds (Merton, 1946). In such research, the concern was to re-explore social scientific models of political communication analysis that were primarily concerned with the measurement of message takeup by individual audience members. Lazarsfeld et al.'s study of social scientific research on voters' response to a 1940 presidential campaign in Ohio discovered the importance of the audience's *social interaction* upon the dissemination of campaign material. Some politically informed individuals were more resistant to media influence and were selective in the messages or discussions they had in order to fit in with preconceived political views. It was also noted that these people were often trusted by their peers and were more influential than the media in conveying and reinforcing their view of political information to those who were less engaged with the political campaign. Thus campaigns and political media messages needed to reach the *opinion formers* in any community in the hope that these opinions would then be disseminated to their peer groups.

Similarly, Merton's investigation of social scientific research on the success of a popular US radio star Kate Smith's appeal for listeners to buy war bonds in September 1943 sought to establish the audience's socio-psychological proclivities for responding to the media message. Such research acknowledged that audience members could be enthusiastic about political messages, wish to engage other people in their enthusiasm and demonstrate a kind of media-informed expertise. This audience research pointed the way towards 'uses and gratifications' models because it credited the audience 'with being "active" and/or discriminating in their engagement with the media in a way not envisaged by the effects model' (Brooker and Jermyn, 2003: 9). As with later work on individual audience members, (Katz and Lazarsfeld, 1955; Elliott, 1972; McQuail et al., 1972; Blumler and Katz, 1974) 'uses and gratifications' importantly for this collection of readings, signalled an attention to the audience bringing their own motivations and social relationships to bear on media engagement.

Contemporary work on tabloid audiences also has been much influenced by the cultural turn in audience studies initiated in the 1970s when critics working in the Centre for Contemporary Cultural Studies (CCCS) at Birmingham, under Stuart Hall, undertook a 'paradigm break' from earlier mass communications work. They drew upon socio-logical, semiotic and Marxist theory to consider the mode of address, or way a media text 'speaks to' its audience and crucially the way the audience recognizes, opposes or negotiates that preferred reading offered by the media text (Hall, 1970; Morley, 1980 and 1983; Hobson, 1980). Working within a broadly Gramscian model of hegemonic power, the audience responses to research questions on their viewing practices were interpreted within a politicized cultural map. Here different responses to TV program-ming were seen to be shaped by power structures *outside* the text – class, gender, ethnicity and so on – informing audience responses and interpretations and also power structures *within* the text and media institution that work to promote the audiences' preferred reading (see also Gray, 1992; Gillespie, 1995; Ross, 2001).

In the 1980s, feminist critics such as Janice Radway (1984) and Angela McRobbie (1991) led the way in analysing female readers' engagement with popular culture – romance fiction and women's and girls' magazines. Significantly, their ethnographic work was as concerned with the audiences' own interpretations of their reading and what it meant and how they used it in their everyday lives. Importantly, given this author's concern with tabloid culture, these critics validated the readers' interactions with academically neglected aspects of print culture; their concern was with the act of reading and the potential ways in which the readers could, partially at least, expropriate aspects of print culture to shape and articulate aspects of their gendered identity.

Similarly, cultural studies-informed critics have returned to the active tabloid audi-ence: one that 'poaches', or 'jams' or refashions media output or one that recognizes how hegemonic power blocs can be mocked or challenged through tabloid culture's frequently irreverent style (Fiske, 1992; Glynn, 2000). This section focuses largely on tabloid TV and print formats and acknowledges inextricable links between these two, both in their address and modes of reception on the part of critics. As S. Elizabeth Bird (1997: 65) has noted regarding the derision expressed of the tabloid press: 'Critics often place the blame for tabloidization on the journalism profession itself'. The role of the audience in shaping tabloid culture is frequently overlooked or similarly derided by detractors as part of the problem of low culture.

As John Langer (1992) has argued in relation to tabloid TV news, the professionals who produce it and implicitly the audience who consume it are frequently condemned by critics as lacking in good taste and judgement. Audiences are assumed to share with the tabloid producers a questionable penchant for the emotionally driven format and both they and the formats in question are perceived to be 'symptomatic of some major cultural failing' (see Langer, 1992: 128). Tabloid television is, according to Kevin Glynn (2000: 6–7) in his account of contemporary tabloid culture, 'the electronic descendant' of tabloid newspapers in that they share similar designation as 'insignificant' or 'trashy';

designations that are bound up with their cultural positioning as counterfoil to 'quality' journalism or entertainment or alternative politicized media. Unlike these modes, which principally speak to the educated middle-class audience, the popular tabloid media have served generally 'as conduits for the circulation of *popular* (as opposed to elite or official) ways of knowing.' They address audiences positioned as outside the cultural or indeed alternative elite. The discourses and knowledge produced appeal to subject matter that crosses the boundary between public and private life and is often presented in a sensational, sceptical, ironic or bizarre tone that aims to debunk good taste and to 'defamiliarize the ordinary and banalize the exotic' (Glynn, 2000: 7).

As noted in Section 1 defenders or critics of the tabloid media and its audiences both frequently share an underlying preoccupation with the role of the mass media in constituting a democratic public sphere. The role of the tabloid media in disrupting the idealized sphere of 'rational' public debate often highlights the tabloid media's emphasis on the 'melodramatic' and emotional (Sparks and Tulloch, 2000: 24). Scholars who have defended the tabloid media and its audiences or readers often seek to rehabilitate popular taste and to legitimate the genuine human interests and anxieties that are addressed by tabloid texts (see Sparks and Tulloch, 2000: 25). It could also be argued that for audiences, tabloids constitute recognition of the concrete and familiar aspects of social life rather than the abstract and that they are valued for this reason (Connell, 1992).

In other words deliberations on the tabloid audience invariably involves loaded debates about power and control of the media over its audience/consumers enmeshed with questions about the quality and value of tabloid formats. Whilst critics have moved a considerable distance from criticism, which assumed a passive and vulnerable audience that is offered superficial pleasures; nonetheless notions of surrender to a morally bankrupt, trivial culture still inform many popular accounts and denouncements of audiences' engagement with tabloid media. This section brings together critics who have attempted to progress the analysis of the tabloid audience beyond superficial condemnation or acclamation and who construct and engage with complex notions of the active audience negotiating tabloid formats within a pressured media market place.

The readings we have included in this section address the audiences or readers of popular tabloid magazines and newspapers, TV talk shows and reality TV. Each medium clearly possesses distinct modes of consumption, but these genres frequently attract shared assumptions about the value of their tabloid output. In the print arena there has been, since the early 1980s, widespread disquiet among media critics, journalists and media watchdogs about the state of the tabloid press (and indeed the tabloidization of the quality press). There are frequent claims that the high standards of objective professional reportage are being undermined by a new culture of irreverence, triviality, sensationalism and prurience epitomized by the wilfully irreverent playfulness of the punning *Sun* newspaper. The rise of tabloid content across print journalism has been matched by the decline of 'quality' journalism. Broadsheet newspapers continue to be the victim of declining circulation figures. New sources of news and lifestyle journalism in the print media alongside expanding entertainment-led programming have increased competition.

Mark Pursehouse's 'Looking at *The Sun*': Into the Nineties with a Tabloid and its Readers' interviews with *Sun* readers reveals that the popularity of the newspaper lies partly in the way readers integrate their reading of the *Sun* into their everyday lives and position that reading as a private leisure space. They discuss how they gain pleasure from its humorous language and commonsense style and interpret their own reading frequently as apolitical whilst demonstrating that the *Sun* can be a resource for broader already formed social relations and cultural investments and that its stories can be made to fit and give selected credibility to readers' lives and beliefs.

Bridget Griffin-Foley's 'From *Tit-Bits* to *Big Brother*: a century of audience participation in the media', contends that the central role of the participatory audience, now much hailed in response to reality TV programming, has a longer history. She tracks the significance of audiences over the nineteenth and twentieth century in popular media such as *Tit Bits* and *Bulletin* magazines with their distinctly interactive address to readers and invitation for reader contributions; the confessional magazine of the 1920s with first-person reader stories; the mass market women's magazine of the interwar years which sought to foster a personal and collaborative relationship with their readers. Early radio programming in the United States similarly permeated the lives of audiences with clubs for audiences, tours and from the 1960s the opportunity for audiences to 'talkback'. Griffin-Foley argues these all fed into the current emphasis on 'real life' in TV programming.

Discussions of audiences of tabloid television are often inflected through issues of cultural value. Debate about tabloid television in the late twentieth to twenty-first century often turns to the inevitability of responding to tabloid television as a manifestation of the current competitive market-driven arena. A consideration of the economics of contemporary television frequently includes perceptions of popular programming and popular audiences as exemplary outcomes of such a profit-driven industry. The debates circulate around both content and consumption of both tabloid print media and also TV often suggest that, in terms of content, tabloid media is marked by its purported inattention to economics, politics, social and institutional and historical context. It focuses on scandal, entertainment, celebrity, sport and particularly the private lives and foibles of celebrities and occasionally ordinary people.

Since the 1980s there has been a shift in many national television systems with an increasing pressure to privatize, deregulate and to engage with new forms of distribution (Murdock, 2000). The market place in which current tabloid TV operates is one in which the rise of multichannel television has fragmented audiences and the industry has had to respond to the demand for new forms of audience loyalty that supplant older notions of communal TV viewing. This has led to the production of adaptable highly retranslatable 'high concept' tabloid formats which are often stripped across a channel's schedule every day for a number of weeks.

For critics, the format-driven nature of much tabloid television indicates that television has bowed to commercial pressures and deregulation of the market. From this perspective it is argued that contemporary popular tabloid media are the product of a market-led political economy and therefore questions of high financial gain and high audience ratings overarch any sustained attention to the cultural and educative/informative value of programming. Increased commercial pressure and increased competition amongst the widening range of channels on offer alongside the drive to decrease production costs has led to an increased need to produce ratings-attractive programme forms.

Reality TV is one such incredibly popular, highly structured adaptable example of formatted programming that can be adapted to incorporate aspects of the game show, crime programme, quiz show, talent contest, chat show and so on. In Mark Andrejevic's

'Reality TV and Voyeurism' he focuses on the voyeuristic and exhibitionistic appeal of Fox's format-driven reality programme *Temptation Island* for both contestants and audience within an astute and adaptable market that reclaims the transgressive potential of contemporary tabloid programming and absorbs it back into the drive of the market. Drawing on psychoanalytic theory, he extends work on audience spectatorship by interrogating the mutual dependency of contestant and audience who are both ultimately contained within a highly regulated format. He argues that the voyeuristic drive that fuels *Temptation Island*'s contestants as they watch their partners on dates with attractive rivals is dependent for its unconscious force on an awareness of the audience as Other/ judge of whether they are a 'dupe' in the game. But he suggests that the viewing position offered to the audience is actually less active than it appears; for the audience is in fact as closely monitored and tracked as the contestants it observes.

Viewed more positively, an inevitable outcome of the competitive media environment has been the opening up of television space to 'ordinary people' who can make choices from the diversity of programming now of offer; can engage with a range of everyday debates and issues that touch upon individuals lives in a new democratized TV culture and can indicate their preference for particular formats or even narratives within formats through both watching but also responding to programmes via new forms of interactive engagement – live streaming; online voting and Web chat rooms; question and answer sessions online – enabled by the new media environment. The popularity of tabloid TV as exemplified by the regular high viewing figures for chat shows; light magazine news formats; popular current affairs; lifestyle programming and reality TV formats bolster the claims made for these as the outputs of a diverse, pluralistic deregulated broadcasting market where freedom of choice indicates success. We end, then, with Pamela Wilson's piece on audience interaction and narrative activism because it brings us up to date by considering the new reception practices opened up by reality TV, in particular. Wilson charts the attempts by fans of the first US season of *Big Brother* to influence outcomes and of cultural jammers to subvert the rules of the game regarding inmates' contact with the outside world. Like Mapplebeck, also in this volume, she reveals that it is increasingly difficult for the newer reality formats to control the production and consumption of their programming and that the technological innovations which support the development of this output are frequently open to counter and oppositional uses by both reality participants and their viewers.

Further reading

Ang, I. (1991) *Desperately Seeking the Audience*, London: Routledge.

Bird, S. E. (1997/2003) News we can use: an audience perspective on the tabloidisation of news in the United States, in V. Nightingale and K. Ross (eds) *Critical Readings: Media and Audiences*, Maidenhead: Open University Press/McGraw Hill Education, 65–86.

Brooker, W. and Jermyn, D. (eds) (2003) *The Audience Studies Reader*, London: Routledge.

Nightingale, V. (1996) *Studying the Audience: the Shock of the Real*, London: Routledge.

Radway, J. (1984/1991) *Reading the Romance: Women, Patriarchy and Popular Literature*, Chapel Hill, NC: University of North Carolina Press.

Shattuc, J. (1997) *The Talking Cure: TV Talkshows and Women*, New York: Routledge.

3.5

Looking at '*The Sun*': into the nineties with a tabloid and its readers
by Mark Pursehouse

[. . .]

The need is to view *The Sun* as a media product in relation to its regular readers.[1] This requires moving away from the notion that an 'academic' researcher can ideologically interpret 'a text' and 'read' it on behalf of everybody else. Such a practice, with its peculiar version of what it is 'to read', avoids all the important questions about how such a paper enters into very real areas of lived culture. After all, market research can show that despite the offence often recognised, many black people and many women do buy and enjoy *The Sun*. Trying to find something of the investments these readers find in taking the paper is getting closer to the ways everyday ideological conflicts are actually experienced. If something can be discovered about the aspects of their identity which are positively responding to the paper this could be a valuable resource for left politics.

Getting closer to the social relations in which popular culture is involved does not necessarily mean throwing away ideological critique. Rather, the critique can be formulated from more clearly defined positions.

Put another way, readers become less of a 'problem' in need of explanation (trapped as ideological victims, in a rather Althusserian way) and become more active participants in the meaning contest.

Politically, there are urgent questions for the left about its images and its culture from which the example of the relations between *The Sun* and its readers may even prove useful. Somewhat ironically, I am suggesting there may be more valuable political insights by getting away from the more overt, direct style of ideological analysis.

[. . .]

Readers of *The Sun*

Articulating themselves

Throughout my interviews with regular *Sun* readers people were talking about the newspaper in relation to their own personal lives. Talking about *The Sun* involved a context of their work and domestic arrangements, but also an emphasis on their leisure pursuits and chosen forms of relaxation. These readers did not describe themselves through a sense of social position, or sociological categories, but by their hobbies and leisure pursuits. Paul's self-description specifically articulated his sense of a dual British and Jamaican identity, but quickly moved on to explain his enjoyment of watching television in the evening and an interest in football and cricket. Martyn G told me he was an 'average working man' and then told me he 'plays a musical instrument – keyboards'. *The Sun* clearly works on this self-recognition based on forms of 'entertainment' rather than more 'serious' aspects of identity.

Most of the young people wanted to say something about going out and enjoying themselves, rather than any claims of responsibilities. Employment was mentioned with less enthusiasm. Jackie responded to the invitation to describe herself by saying she was 'very down to earth' and then added 'a boring wages clerk . . . just a boring nine to five I suppose – normal'. Martin M chose to emphasise he was 'a working class kid who had worked his way into a professional industry', but then quickly shifted his self-description to add, 'main hobbies are sport, women and cars'. Nobody articulated themselves in terms of having interests beyond their personal circumstances, with no mention of attachments to any organised groups or social movements.

Another important context in how these readers meet *The Sun* is the use of other media. It seems they all watched either the BBC or ITV news and judged newspaper coverage by this standard. Ian, who had emphasised his love of travel, the pub and football revealed, 'I watch the news on telly: so you get it straight'. Helen, a secretary in a professional office, bluntly concluded; 'I usually see the news once a day . . . it's a truer report'. There was also a sense that news on television was unavoidable; that you could be informed of world affairs without trying. Martyn M, a van driver, explained:

> 'I mean a lot of the time you don't have to even look at the telly . . . you just catch it and you know what's going on in the world – without sitting down saying "OH, the nine o'clock news is on" '.

Viewing news could be as much to do with daily routine as any wish for information. Sandra, a secretary, explained how she came home and relaxed in front of the television for the early part of the evening, watching the news 'normally 'cause there's nothing else on to watch'.

Television seemed to play an important part in 'turning off' from work. Ian, who worked awkward shifts as part of the groundstaff at Gatwick airport, provided a typical preference for comedy, music and sports programmes (with British soaps also often prevalent). In Ian's phrase, 'nothing too serious'.

Other newspaper reading strongly featured local and regional titles (while any other reading was mainly limited to some of the women taking magazines targeted at their interests). The regional evening press (chiefly the '*Express and Star*') had specific personal uses, like Jackie searching for an interesting job or the need for local information.

However, *The Sun* was not read in isolation from knowledge of other national papers. Paul, a graduate working as a metallurgist, switched between *The Sun* and the *Daily Star* as he tried to progress from the *Star*'s easier crossword. Ian and John, from the south-east, both mentioned looking at the *Daily Mail*, while Paul, Martin M and John read *The Independent* occasionally. Paul explained that he bought *The Independent* for a 'decent report' when the West Indies were playing cricket, but expressed a common frustration with 'quality' papers:

> 'I end up not hardly reading anything . . . something sort of, at the back of my mind's saying that it's gonna be too much stodge and I'm not gonna be able to get through it all – so I don't bother usually.'

Interestingly, the *Daily Mirror* was frequently rejected in comparison with *The Sun* on the grounds of being 'a bit more serious' (Jackie). Martyn G commented on the *Mirror*: 'I'll pick it up and flick through it but basically nothing catches my eye'. He admitted the *Mirror* might not 'blow stories up out of all proportion' like *The Sun*, but tellingly added, 'That's like not entertaining'.

[. . .]

Attractions and pleasures

I asked each of my readers the straightforward question, 'What do you like about *The Sun?*' and nobody mentioned the paper's political or editorial stance. Some found *The Sun* useful in relation to personal interests, such as Jackie enjoying items on health matters and diets, or Dave claiming *The Sun* was 'the best for boxing'. However, the most striking comments for me were those which showed evidence of a degree of critical detachment.

Julie, who had already explained her love of reading (uniquely amongst this group), spontaneously said:

> 'I find a lot of pleasure in the way that a lot of *The Sun* articles are written . . .
> I read a story like – like the classic "Freddie Starr Ate My Hamster" and nobody in their right mind is goin' to believe that – but as a piece of journalism to me it's – it's fun'.

The Sun was being enjoyed as 'entertainment' with an openly ironic view of the paper's reputation for misrepresentation. Martyn G said, 'I know it's mostly a load of lies like [laughter], but it's just entertaining'. Similarly, Helen noted, 'I don't think some of the stories are a hundred percent true, but they're quite fun to read'. There seems to be a pleasure in holding this temporarily ironic identity; a moment when judging the truth of a 'serious' issue or event can be suspended as unimportant. As Paul summarised: 'There's always something in there that makes me laugh . . . It's not usually the items that are meant to be funny that make me laugh'.

This version of *The Sun* as being able to make anything amusing led Martyn G to conclude, 'It's just an adult comic'.[2] Perhaps, since this phrase was repeated by a number of men, but no women, it would be more accurate to say a masculine adult comic. The sexist culture was quite confidently expressed as a source of pleasure, with one interviewee responding to my question, 'What kind of things are you looking to

get out of *The Sun?*' with a hand gesture implying masturbation! There were, however, other aspects of *The Sun* with which women found forms of pleasure. Jackie
liked the 'Sun Woman' section and Julie had special praise for the regular 'Fiona on
Friday' column: 'I would love to meet that woman because she echoes my feelings
before ever I know that I'm feeling like that. I think she's superb – from a woman's
point of view'.

The *Sun* does seem to find this kind of sociable, personable relationship with its
readers – almost a form of daily companionship, which should not be underestimated.

Scandal

Historically, *The Sun* certainly did not invent 'scandal' as part of 'working-class'
reading, but it has become part of the paper's notoriety. Indeed, the position adopted
by many of my readers suggested scandal offered a form of pleasure connected with
perceptions of their own lives.

Clearly, revelations about private lives and gossip around sex are part of *The Sun*
feeding the virtually insatiable appetite of traditional, male, heterosexual culture.
However, talking to women also showed scandal could be part of other identity formations besides the male-dominated construction of sexual titillation. In the following
quote Jackie sees scandal as on her side:

> 'You can get these papers and they're all – all this politics – on the headlines of this
> *(The Sun)* you'll get er, I don't know, for example "Teacher Sex Change" . . . The
> news that I read in it I find more interesting – it may not be as important as
> whoever's getting shot in wherever but . . .' (she broke off).

Scandal is seen as part of the personal, lived experience while more 'public' domains
(in this case politics and war are mentioned) are seen as belonging to someone else's
concern, reflecting a feeling of exclusion.

Reading scandal is also part of the ironic game people play with the tabloid genre.
There is pleasure in making a judgement about a story's credibility. Sandra explained
her liking for gossip about people she saw on television, noting, 'I read it and then
I think "Oh well that's a bit over the top" or "Yeah, I suppose that's possible" '.
Similarly, Jackie said she read about television personalities and pop stars: 'I'm not
saying it's all – it's true. It may not be – far from it – but you don't know. You can sort
of build up your own opinion of the different people.' This phrase 'sort of build up
your own opinion' needs taking seriously. It is precisely the lack of certainty, the
doubts and the gaps which create the pleasure between the genre and readers. The
paper is being recognised as a 'private' comparison, partly reflecting the same kind of
guesses, conflicts and absences which apply to anyone's experiences of trying to know
other people. Martyn G provided an account of how this process of guesswork related
scandal back into real conversations:

> 'I think everybody likes to read about scandal . . . like George Michael's out with a
> different girl or whatever . . . Although it may not be true you tek ('take' in a Black
> country accent) it in for that split second that you read it and then like – say

you're talking later and you say "Did you see that in *The Sun?*" and somebody'll say "You cor (cannot) believe what you read in *The Sun*" . . . but it may be true, it may not be true.'

The fact scandal is talked about after reading the paper is an important part of *The Sun* being able to connect with everyday life. Sam emphasised this point when, after spontaneously describing *The Sun* as 'mainly just gossip', added, 'It just makes a change from the normal gossip doesn't it?'

Scandal in *The Sun* offers a number of 'Us's', capable of forming chatty relationships with various readers. Scandal seems to actively and critically involve readers in ways which strong, factual, 'serious' reports may find more difficult. Dave pointed out with some realism that people were not heard talking about 'the world economy or anything' but, 'Put two people together and they'll only talk about scandal'.

News

Nobody answered my question, 'What do you think of news in *The Sun?*' with reference to cases of misrepresentation or bias. The key issue became the types of news that were recognised as having any validity or relevance to these readers. Much 'public' news was clearly seen as not for them. Martyn G provided an example in terms of regional identity:

> 'I don't read a lot of the serious news because it doesn't affect me . . . If I wanted to know about a cyanide scare in South London, erm, – well basically I don't want to know about a cyanide scare in South London (laughs) . . . I've got my own little space and I'll stay in it like'.[3]

Julie, despite her relatively 'public' career, as a youth training scheme officer, also denied any interest in news that was seen as of little personal relevance. This version of news as serious, distant issues and events contrasted with other forms of news with which she could relate: 'I like the little newsy items – erm, you know "Fred Bloggs of so-and-so did this" . . . My information has to come in small bite-size chunks otherwise I just can't digest it'.

The Sun's jolly, off-beat news frequently gained praise, as did some of its 'human interest' coverage. At the time of the interviews the murder of Marie Wilks on the M50 motorway touched a genuine anxiety for many women and both Jackie and Julie praised the coverage.[4]

The only other way it seemed 'public' news, be viewed with any degree of recognition was when it was seen chiefly as 'entertainment'. *The Sun*'s coverage of important incidents could catch the eye in a way which made no distinction between 'news' as a separate category from the paper's 'entertainment'.

The Sun perhaps acknowledges the lack of 'public' news with which these regular readers are able to feel concerned or involved. The point has been made sharply by Andy Medhurst in Marxism Today; 'Maybe *The Sun* is simply being commercially shrewd by turning almost every story into a joke in an era when many people don't seem to want to take the news seriously any more' (Medhurst, 1989: 41).

The Sun style

Whilst I have emphasised how readers construct 'their texts' in line with their own motivations and investments the readers themselves were simultaneously discussing 'a text'. Part of the reason *The Sun* was preferred over tabloid rivals involved matters of 'form' – choices about presentation and types of language which marked *The Sun* as different.

Julie's opening, spontaneous remarks expressed great enthusiasm for *The Sun* style:

> 'I find a lot of pleasure in the way that a lot of *The Sun* articles are written . . . I mean some of the headlines – they're incredible – love 'em – I really do. I can sort of identify with the sort of sense of humour that they must have to write headings like that'.

Most readers joined in the praise for *The Sun*'s headlines. Martyn G (by his own admission not a big reader) said, 'You just can't miss a headline – it's just impossible not to see one of their headlines'. Jackie emphasised the importance of humour in the writing process: 'I suppose you've got to sort of make – make the readers interested haven't you? Like the witty headlines – you've got to sort of catch their attention straightaway'. The phrase, 'It's the way they put things' occurred in a number of interviews. Sam used the comment in attempting to find the difference between *The Sun* and the *Mirror*, while Jackie spoke about a front-page headline referring to Boris Becker at the Wimbledon tennis championship, 'You Smart Ass Kraut':

> 'Immediately you're gonna think "Oh!", you know . . . say you're not interested in tennis you're immediately gonna think "Oh what's been going on here!" . . . It's the way they present it init (isn't it)? Witty comments. I mean I don't think you'd look at that and just turn over the page . . . I laughed when I was in the paper shop – it's the way they put things'.[5]

Such an example (one of many) illustrates a reading style based on almost instant impact. If headlines, photographs and lay-out form the basis of this construction the ability of *The Sun* to get messages across with the utmost brevity was also appreciated. Helen summarised:

> 'I think more people read it when it's short – then they don't have to get involved in massive long pages of reading'.

These readers certainly suggested that the form in which a message is put can make the difference between being noticed at all and making quite an engaged attachment.

The *Daily Mirror* was certainly seen as behind *The Sun*, failing to catch the witty nerve and the cheeky headline in which *The Sun* was perceived to specialise. Julie put it easily: '*The Sun* is always tongue-in cheek. The *Mirror* seems to me to take itself more seriously'.

This majority view contrasted interestingly with the *Daily Mirror* reader I spoke to, Damian. He spoke of his own sense of a clear Labour political background and thought this played a part in how he takes a different framework to reading the tabloids:

> 'The *Mirror* to me is written in a language that I can relate to . . . You don't have to be particularly brainy but at the same time you don't have to be, – it doesn't have to insult your intelligence like, er, it sometimes does when you're reading *The Sun*, and you think "Christ what am I reading this for!" '.

Clearly while elements of 'text' (choices of content or style) may make a difference, investment priorities, the decisive perspectives, are formed by a wider field of relations. While there are genuine 'positive' connections between *The Sun* and its readers, there are also wider assumptions underlying this enjoyment with the paper, which I attempted to discuss during the interviews.

Social issues and assumptions

Readers and politics

Overtly, at least, I encountered an entirely defensive attitude towards the very term 'politics'. When I asked, 'What about politics in *The Sun?*' Sam exclaimed abruptly 'Oh I don't like politics', Julie stated 'I am not a political animal' and Jackie pointed out politics 'don't interest me'. The term was rejected, seen as being of no relevance to them.

It could be argued that the absence of any sense of political belonging itself represented an element of the Thatcherite era, with its language of depoliticisation. While there was no evidence from these interviews of the language of Thatcherite ideology, the way they talked about their priorities within the paper did suggest satisfaction with explanations and entertainment provided in an 'apolitical', necessarily conservative, culture. If there was a lack of praise for the politics of *The Sun* there was equally a lack of criticism. This leaves open some doubts about the shared assumptions between *The Sun* and its readers.[6]

Few readers actually articulated any comment about *The Sun* being a Conservative paper, though Paul described it as 'over the top Tory-wise' and others like Martin M and Ian at least acknowledged its political bias. There were other hints at the danger of myself as researcher presupposing a unanimous version of *The Sun*'s values. Julie, who took time reading *The Sun* and was aware of its political reputation, expressed some doubts:

> 'Particularly in the editorials they quite surprise me by saying things that seem to go against the politics of what the majority of people say the paper stands for – not what I say they stand for because I don't see it as cut and dried as that'.

Martyn G's enjoyment of the paper in his van led him to deny the paper was biased and Helen was not alone in making no attempt at political recognition, deciding 'I don't know whether it slants one way or the other'.

This apolitical self-identity suggests politics is neither part of their reading relationship with *The Sun* nor seen as a priority in their everyday concerns. Ideas and assumptions are clearly taken up and lived without the label 'politics' present.

When I asked Martyn G who he thought might not be interested in *The Sun* he answered, 'politically minded people'. Similarly, Jackie said, 'down to earth people would like *The Sun* because it's not a very political paper'. It seems, from this small-scale evidence, that only the Left is termed as being 'political'.[7] Attitudes and opinions aligned with Right politics seem to be covered by terminology like 'down to earth' or 'commensense', leaving Left politics with an alienating language with which to inspire people. Martyn G provided an example of this one-sided political language. He had claimed no interest in politics or the paper's news coverage but I asked specifically if he had seen any of *The Sun*'s reporting on the 1987–88 National Health Service disputes:

> 'I read a bit of it like . . . I read the story about erm, Left-wing activists who'd broken into the ranks like and started causing aggro . . . I didn't really take a lot of notice of it because it was all over the telly'.[8]

In such a case *The Sun*'s framework and labelling had, perhaps quite inadvertently, made at least a linguistic impression. *The Sun* is recognised by its readers without its political opinions to the fore, but with its political voices merged among a variety of other positions. It enhances the opportunity to gain access to various individuals by seeking to make 'ordinary' even its most vehement political language. *The Sun* has taken the risk of belonging to various publics rather than being recognised as a fixed promulgator of political messages.

Gender

There was a strong sense that *The Sun* operated a relationship with its readers on a shared ground of stereotyped gender roles, 'norms' of heterosexuality and openly sexist representations of women. In trying to gauge the depths of entrenchment of these cultural assumptions I asked each interviewee what they thought of 'page three', hoping to find some doubts or gaps where opportunities for changing attitudes may exist.

There were men prepared to be completely honest in their chauvinism. Paul mentioned 'page three' as 'one of my favourite pages' while describing his usual route through the paper, adding, 'I always oggle the bird and – I sort of give 'em marks out of ten to see how she compares with the others that I've seen in there.' Other reactions were more complex, offering hints that other identity viewpoints were recognised, despite the continuing dominance of the 'red-blooded' male, sexual identity. Ian, young and single himself, enjoyed 'page three', but did acknowledge the opposition: 'I can understand women's point of view . . . I probably wouldn't want to sit down and be faced with a pair of bollocks first thing in the morning when I buy a paper'. This level of awareness was quickly followed by evidence that male domination was not going to be easily given away. Ian had no wish to see 'page three' banned, commenting, 'All the time we can get away with it I think we should'. Only one of my male interviewees spoke clearly against 'page three'. Martin M, who worked in the field of new printing technology, commented, 'It does tend to make – give the impression – that all women are there just for one thing'.

From the women's perspective there was ample evidence of a continuing feeling of powerlessness. 'Page three' was accepted, with some apathy, as 'normal'. Sandra had resigned herself to the fact 'It's just there I suppose', adding 'I can't really do a lot about it'. The sheer abundance of sly, provocative pictures was used as an argument against any newspaper ban, with Jackie nothing, 'It's nothing out of the ordinary to see a topless woman so I don't think it does any harm'. Amongst my interviews it was the older women, Ina and Julie, who spoke out against 'page three'. Ina spoke with strong personal feelings apparently unaware that, Labour MP, Clare Short had tried to produce legislation on the subject: 'I think it's time that page three was stopped. And anybody with any respect for society or themselves wouldn't buy the paper . . . It's a paper that is very unfair to women'. Julie's comments included some astute observations on masculine culture: 'I've got a colleague at work who is a very interesting man and a very fun guy . . . but he will literally sit for twenty minutes looking at page three and that really bugs me'. Julie continued by telling how her boss annoyed her if she had *The Sun* on the desk at work:

'He'll come "Oh, let's have a look at page three and that bugs me because he doesn't buy *The Sun*, it's just – erm, it's a pose – I think. I think perhaps many men don't really particularly get a big thrill out of it but they think it's the done thing'.

Talking about 'page three' certainly showed the importance of further progress, along a wide range of relations, concerning the solidity of the 'macho' image, the dominance of the male perspective of gender relations and the perceptions of powerlessness still held by many women. In regard to her campaign, Clare Short saw a way ahead in getting more women involved in pressuring advertisers to consider where they invested their budgets, but undoubtedly wider issues of gender politics need to continue to find accessible forms of expression. These interviews reflected some hope in that there were at least comments suggesting gender issues were on the agenda. Changing attitudes might still be difficult, as Paul illustrated:

'I get sick of these erm, feminists half the time – but I do see their point of view . . . I'm sure it *(The Sun)* is offensive to women a lot of the time . . . I find things in there that are offensive towards me . . . I know my mother buys the paper – I'm sure a lot of housewives do buy the paper so erm, it can't be that bad'.

Attitudes towards homosexuality seemed more decisively reactionary and closed, from a few passing comments. Paul provided a unique moment amongs these interviews when I asked if he thought he could have been influenced by the tabloids and he replied:

'I certainly find myself using erm, things that I've read in these papers. For instance I'm – I'm not ashamed to say I'm anti-homosexual – erm, and I will use stuff that I've read in the papers as evidence [laughs] – inverted commas – "evidence" of er, the dangers or the reasons why I shouldn't like homosexuals'.

Such a comment certainly seems to show that *The Sun* is capable of fostering such prejudice and thereby holding 'influence'. Paul went out of his way to add to his comments that he wouldn't be abusive to a homosexual – offering the hope that people might behave in their real social relations rather differently to their temporary identity positions held while reading *The Sun*.[9]

Race and nation

The fact my interviews concentrated on the relationship between *The Sun* and white readers obviously imposes limits to approaches towards issues of race, but it is worth exploring the kind of assumptions being operated by the 'white majority'. To begin with, what became strikingly apparent was that the type of reading which identifies voices of racism in *The Sun* differed markedly from many white readers' recognitions of how the paper worked. When I asked about how *The Sun* portrayed black people or if there was anything racist about *The Sun* the most common response was to deny the paper was racist. Clearly the assumptions about Britain and its people most foregrounded in *The Sun* are aligned with the white majority's perception; a framework which continues to deny recognition of a variety of identities, fails to consider specific difficulties about being non-white in Britain and lacks appreciation of varied cultures or the benefits of positively working to reduce racism. The sheer 'irrelevance' of the racist voice indicates how *The Sun* and many of its readers meet on a shared ground of hardly acknowledging the existence of black people.

This lack of white recognition encourages me to emphasise the contrasting version of *The Sun* recognised by Paul, the only black person with whom I spoke. He was strongly articulate about the types of racism he encountered in *The Sun* after I asked 'Do you get annoyed with things in *The Sun?*' Paul condemned particular columnists, noted that 'black' was still attached to people committing crimes and said of reports on South Africa, 'It wouldn't surprise me sometimes if they sort of said "Oh we think apartheid's right" '. Paul also pointed to the paper's treatment of particularly public figures, like Bernie Grant, as examples of a 'hate campaign', expressing concern that there were racists around who 'use these types of things as ammunition'.

After making such powerful, pertinent points it seemed strange to me that Paul had already spoken of his enjoyment of *The Sun* and I asked him about this apparent contradiction. He replied, laughing:

'I think I have to laugh some of the time . . . If I was so serious that I took great offence all the time with what they say – I mean I just couldn't buy it and I'd probably end up not buying a paper at all'.

Paul has to 'turn down', temporarily, the overall importance of his black identity in order to concentrate on enjoying the paper. He explained how annoying reports linking black in particular with crime were causing offence 'on my Jamaican side rather than on my British side'. He still finds enjoyment in the paper as a working,

British, 'ordinary' man, but reading it definitely involves an assimilation into the framework of white British culture. This process of activating particular aspects of identity for particular purposes (in this case wanting a rest from work) helps explain how black people (and other identity groups) can still 'enjoy' what seems in other ways offensive.

These issues of race seemed closely connected with other forms of nationalism which arose in relation to *The Sun* and its readers. Typical British values were never questioned and there was a common preference for reading national rather than international news, which Sam summarised with, 'They've got their lives I've got mine'.

However, these interviews did show some disaffection with the extremes of jingosim often associated with *The Sun*. I was surprised to find four men referring to the Falklands/Malvinas war in relation to *The Sun*, without any leading from myself. There seemed to be a critical detachment from the rather crude nationalism of *The Sun*'s coverage. Martin M had already noted, 'Nothing ever goes wrong in England for *The Sun*' and referred to the war coverage as seeming to believe, 'everything in life can be sorted out and made better as long as you can send the gunboats in'. Paul remembered the tabloid coverage making him feel stronger against the war and Ian expressed his frustration at *Sun* editorials by going back to the Falklands war for his example: 'I can't be bothered to read that . . . "*The Sun* says Maggie should go to the Falklands and bomb the bastards". It isn't what really we're . . . we're supposed to believe is it?'

John provided an extraordinary account of how *The Sun* simplified the war to form a relationship with its perceived reader:

> 'They know *[The Sun]* that most blokes go out in the evening and they have five or seven pints [sic] and they think – they talk about the Falklands and they say "Oh blow the bastards up" – and they'll – cause they get – they go for a newspaper the next morning after the hangover and see on the front page of *The Sun* "We blew them up" – "Oh good . . . Let's read it" '.

Fortunately *The Sun* does not have all its own way in constructing its version of race and national issues. There are gaps between the paper and its readers, where the paper's versions are mistrusted or even opposed. The crucial point is that on such complex issues as senses of identity neither *The Sun* nor Right politics can represent all versions and experiences. The type of representations of race and nation most offered from *The Sun* belongs to a very specific, very imperial version of British history. Most readers have only more immediate, less mythical, closer notions of their own experience on which to draw.

Sun readers on *Sun* readers

Readers have their own ideas and images about the people likely to be interested in meeting *The Sun*. In most interviews I asked a question such as, 'What kinds of people do you think like *The Sun*?' and it was interesting to see the terms by which they categorised readers and the kinds of negotiations they envisaged between readers and the newspaper.

This opportunity to comment on other readers sometimes involved labelling in class terms (though the precise meaning was often vague). Tabloid readers were most strongly identified as 'working class', which Martin M added to by describing as 'the people who just do normal day to day – everyday jobs – and go about their everyday life'. When I asked Jackie who she thought would not like *The Sun* she said, 'people of a higher class'. Perhaps 'class' is being seen as a matter of status or taste rather than effective power or privilege. Clearly the tabloids still have an image associated with this loose definition of class. When I asked Helen who she thought read *The Sun* she replied,

> 'Erm, working class people. I don't think – like I work in a professional office – I don't think people in there buy it. Well they don't admit to buying it anyway. But if it's around they probably read it. They all carry *The Financial Times* around and things like that . . . to make people think that's what they're reading'.

The relative rigidity of these senses of class divisions, and the associated alignments with reading habits, provides an insight into the continuing strength of these identity formations and assumptions. Julie told a story from a course she had been on from work, which further illustrated this sense of a class-based culture:

> 'Recently I stayed in a very nice three star hotel in Shrewsbury and I was the only person that asked for *The Sun* . . . I'm quite sure that some of the people there would probably get *The Sun* – you know – or their husbands would have brought *The Sun* home from work with them . . . but because it has got this image of being, er – you know – flat caps and pigeon racing, very sort of gutter pressy – then I think people don't like to be seen to be a *Sun* reader'.

Besides class-based formulations the connected question of images of intelligence was articulated. Damian, as a *Mirror* reader, put this most bluntly: 'I'd say that thick people would buy *The Sun* and the *Star*'. He developed this point in relation to a politically conscious class consideration when he said it would be 'working class people who buy the *Mirror* – but not thickies sort of working class people if you know what I mean'.

Overall these readers seemed to construct a version of the archetypal *Sun* reader as male, young and 'working class', with some sense of an 'ordinary' job and life-style. It is probably not too much to guess that terms like 'ordinary' and 'everyday' incorporate the white, British, heterosexual identity, with average qualifications, income and ambitions. These readers seem to have identified this narrow range of positions as the prioritized sites in being likely to enjoy *The Sun*. It is a highly specific group of positions for a multiple text which claims to be for everyone. The evidence of these readers is perhaps the most powerful suggestion that it would be unwise and unhelpful to see *The Sun* as 'open' to all cultural assumptions and social position. Readers themselves identify *The Sun* as working on certain prioritized elements of recognition above others and retains the power to offer certain voices louder than others. The fact, for instance, that non-working class owners, editors and writers are producing a body of material still being accepted, perfectly genuinely, as belonging to 'working class' people remains a relevant point.

These readers also had version of the power relationship involved between *The Sun* and its readers. I often asked if they thought *The Sun* had any effect on its readers and a common response was to express concern that some people might believe and be swayed by the opinions of the paper. Anxiety for what other people were making of the paper did not stretch to a belief they could be so duped! This reflects the genuine difficulty over what to believe and not to believe – people must have doubts about the status of their own personal version of the paper.

Many readers were quite definite about *The Sun*'s ability to influence people's ideas strongly and directly. 'Hypodermic' metaphors appeared as Martin M explained how the use of humour could 'actually inject a thought in there' and John spoke of headlines that could 'implant everything in everybody's mind'. A cautionary note was also recommended with regard to people's claims not to take *The Sun* too seriously. Jackie was aware *The Sun*'s 'fun' was only one level of negotiation:

> 'Although people make a joke about it they still take it as true don't they? . . . They'll say to their mates, "Don't believe a word of it", but it's still stuck there in the memory . . . It does with me anyway'.

Interestingly, these readers assumed to be suggesting quite a variety of ways by which *The Sun* could reach readers with its views, and giving the paper more power to control the negotiation with readers than was evident in their own comments on how they lived the paper. Even when the paper was not accredited overt power another type of influence was acknowledged. Sam reckoned that after reading the paper she thought of it no further, but then added a crucial qualification: 'Unless it comes up in conversation and you think "Oh yeah I read that" '. The fact that *The Sun* persistently arises in conversation hints at the capabilities of such a paper to set agendas, make representations personally 'alive' and put elements of language into social currency. Furthermore, it makes clear that notions of 'influence' do not belong to the process of values being 'interpreted' from the 'text', but from how readers can use the texts they construct in a much wider field of relations.

This means the paper is given different degrees of power at different moments. Readers with a real investment, in terms of wider relations in their lives, in taking a particular 'textual' moment in a way suitable to those wider needs will not have their opinion changed by the newspaper. From some identity positions there will be an already-formed agreement with *The Sun*'s assumptions and voices, which can then be used as 'evidence'. A different personal investment in an idea or issue may clash with *The Sun* and this already-formed disagreement will leave the paper to be dismissed as rubbish. The personal stake effectively decides the validity of an argument or report.

From these interviews Paul provided the sharpest example. Areas of the newspaper which came close to his personal identity as a black British person were treated seriously and the paper's representation rejected. Other areas of the paper were 'a laugh' and he felt free to construct his own more pleasurable versions of text. In other words, the paper is given selective credibility in relation to the most activated, prioritised identity locations of the reader. In this argument a paper like *The Sun* becomes a central resource for very real social investments. The paper is made to fit a variety of situations in which these readers, as people rather than actual 'readers', may find themselves.

Conclusions

Living *The Sun*

The sheer enthusiasm with which people spoke about their uses and opinions of the tabloids confirmed the sense of a lively, active engagement with such papers. 'Readings' cannot only be explained in relation to 'deep' ideological bases (identities around race, nation, class, gender, age) because the tabloids become a resource amongst all sorts of everyday experiences. In particular, the way *The Sun* seemed to offer relaxation, both at work and at home, positions the paper as a site of 'private' leisure space – perhaps in an attempt to smoothe over some of the daily aspects of identity conflict. *The Sun* offers a temporary respite from some more serious social relations and instead fits into patterns of leisure interests.[10]

In addition, the evidence from these interviews would suggest that *The Sun* is recognised as containing some important ingredients for appearing to know and get close to its readers. *The Sun*'s humour, 'street credible' sociability and simplifying 'commonsense' are important aspects to its appeal. It gains credibility, almost becomes friends with readers, through appearing to 'talk the same language'.

However, it seems important to emphasise that there are many elements of everyday experience, many ways of talking, which *The Sun* cannot satisfy. Even the most avid readers had conflicts and doubts in their relationship with *The Sun*. There was a strong knowledge of what could be expected from the tabloid genre. They criticised factual inaccuracies, identified many over-the-top opinions and did not appreciate some of the gross exaggerations of character descriptions. They expect to laugh 'at' as well as 'with' *The Sun*. Paul openly criticised the one-dimensional critique of *The Sun* which fails to account for either the scepticism or the frustration provoked in regular readers:

> 'All these people who go round slagging off *The Sun* – saying "Oh you buy *The Sun*, ha-ha-ha" and laughin', erm – well they ought to think twice about why they're laughin'. I mean, yes laugh if they – if I was buying it because I thought it was a good paper but keep your mouth shut if er, you don't really know why I'm buying it'.

The 'private' enjoyment of *The Sun* does not directly produce more 'public' approval of its apparent values. While people spoke of their personal investments in looking at the paper, they were aware other people could be reading it differently. The relationship between *The Sun* and its readers operates in this sometimes conflicting space between 'private' uses and investments in the paper and the simultaneous knowledge of other positions and considerations from a wider 'public' perspective. The relationship with the paper consequently lives and changes in relation to particular identity priorities, depending upon a variety of personal experiences, responsibilities and investments. Questions of 'influence' depend upon how readers are seeking to resolve the fragmented priorities of identity in which they have to operate in their own lives. It may well be that the only way to predict likely responses to material physically in *The Sun* is to look at the way the identity investments of people are offered as socially active outside the reading moment.

This at least offers some optimism for alternative constructions to the tabloid world of *The Sun*. There are limits to the capabilities of *The Sun*. Readers know how much there is to gain from reading a tabloid newspaper. They do not expect to find answers to life's real anxieties or features which align with many real experiences. The main site which seemed strongly relevant in real life but barely present in negotiating *The Sun* was the importance of a sense of the social, as opposed to the isolated individual. The only real group *The Sun* acknowledges is the community of *Sun* readers. In its crude classifications *The Sun* may ignore that people live by helping each other out and leaving each other room to live. Readers did not seem to recognise *The Sun* with any sense of warmth or honesty, but with an ironic distance, realising the phoney nature of much supposedly spontaneous wit and accepting stories could not always be taken as they seemed. This at least leaves room for alternative constructions to find a more relevant language – reaching the same readers with a more accurate version of everyday language, humour and people's real considerations.

While *The Sun* gets close to some aspects of how real culture is lived, there are other possibilities which it does not reach. The central focus of attention needs to be the dimensions of everyday life which contribute towards various possible relations with such 'popular' texts. *The Sun*'s ability to work from multiple positions and pay close attention to cultural movements offers lessons for those involved in disseminating a very different set of values. The important point is that *Sun* readers are not simply mistaken or wrong but that they have a variety of genuine social factors and positions giving them particular investments in what the 'text' contains. Indeed the supposed 'text' is a multiple, shifting body, existing only in relation to these other social factors and positions. It is the real social practices in which 'texts' and 'readers' are involved which need further study rather than any notion that they can be separated and held in an isolated relationship.

[. . .]

Notes

1 There are a number of books viewing *The Sun* 'from the inside' shedding some light on the production and construction of *The Sun*'s world: see Chippindale, P. & Horrie, C., (1990); Lamb, L., (1989); Grose, R., (1989).

2 The possibilities of a logical progression from boy's comics to tabloid newspapers is very well argued by Paul Hoggart, (1981).

3 The story of a cyanide scare in South London was in the edition of *The Sun* on the day of Martyn G's interview, 7 April 1988.

4 Three days before I spoke to Jackie the arrest of Eddie Browning, following the murder of Marie Wilks, made the front page of *The Sun*. See 27 June 1988.

5 The story appeared following an alleged angry clash between Boris Becker and Pat Cash. See *The Sun*, 30 June 1988.
6 While this research began to explore such questions of political influence I must emphasise it is a far larger task, involving much more detail of people's lives, political opinions and practice.
7 The only two interviewed people who claimed any sort of political identity were Damian, definitely Labour and *Daily Mirror*, and Paul who described himself as 'anti-Tory'.
8 It seems Martyn G was recalling stories headed, 'Lefties wreck nurses strike' and 'Nurse arrested as red wreckers hijack demo', *The Sun*, 4 February 1988.
9 Clare Short expressed a similar optimism in the ultimate power of people's everyday experiences:

> 'It does just show that they (the mainstream media) can pay all their money in order to try and manipulate our brains but there are social movements which will come anyway. Erm, and the sense in which women – the whole women's movement thing – is deeply entrenched and growing – and I would say by class and background and age is still spreading and deepening – and – a lot of the women who are involved in it, – it's a mood and a sense of the need for, – for the right to control your own life. And a lot of the women who are part of it wouldn't use any of the language of feminism, wouldn't call themselves feminists but they are part of the thing – so although the media is poor on women, women are moving despite them and there are all sorts of little moves afoot around the media to try and catch up with where women are moving to. So there's a long way to go but I feel extremely optimistic about all of that'.

10 Janice Radway, (1988), has noted the importance leisure pursuits can play in perceptions of self-identity; 'For many individuals and subgroups, in fact, the conceptually subordinated leisure world is the primary site for the elaboration of what is taken to be meaningful identity'. 'Reception study: ethnography and the problems of dispersed audiences and nomadic subjects'.

3.6

From *Tit-Bits* to *Big Brother*: a century of audience participation in the media
by Bridget Griffen-Foley

The *Tit-Bits* periodical, launched in 1881, and the *Big Brother* reality television show, which made its debut at the very end of the 20th century, may seem unlikely bedfellows. Discussion about *Big Brother*, in both the general media and in scholarly forums, has tended to concentrate on the sexual proclivities of the housemates, sponsorship deals, cross-promotional opportunities, attempted voter fraud and, of course, the extent to which the behaviour of the housemates is 'real' or contrived (e.g. Bell, 2001; Lumby, 2001b; Mhando, 2001; van Zoonen, 2001). While some of these issues are interesting and important, the insistent depiction of *Big Brother* as a 'phenomenon' has obscured its connections with other, older print and electronic media outlets. This article contends that just as television viewers and Internet users can vote to evict the 'real' people occupying the *Big Brother* house or the *Survivor* community, audiences have for more than a century been contributing to successful media outlets. By using a series of case studies drawn from Britain, Australia and the United States, this article surveys the history of participatory media from the late 19th century to the present day. It considers the appearance of periodicals featuring significant contributions from their readers in the 1880s; the enormous popularity of the confessional magazine in the 1920s; the way in which mass-market women's magazines implicated themselves in the lives of their readers during the inter-war years; the rise of talkback radio; and the emergence of 'real life' media genres – in magazines and television – in the 1980s and 1990s.

Late 19th-century periodicals

There is a substantial literature on the 'New Journalism' which emerged in Britain and the United States in the second half of the 19th century (e.g. Wiener, 1988). Proponents of this style of journalism sought to build mass circulations by appealing to the increasingly literate lower middle classes. They devoted less space to political and parliamentary reportage, parcelled up news into short portions, featured a brighter style of writing, and used new printing technologies and typographical devices to improve the layout and appeal to the visual senses of readers.

Stephen Kern (1983: 69–70) has shown how, in the late 19th century, some commentators anticipated that journalism would perform a democratizing function by diminishing the distance – social and geographical – between individuals. Social segregation and fragmentation were the legacies of industrialization and urbanization. It was in this environment that some publishers and editors sought to offer readers engagement, interaction and connection. As Kate Jackson (2001: 62, 74) has recently argued in her fine study of George Newnes' publishing activities, the editorial voice was a major factor in the method by which his periodicals – *Tit-Bits*, *The Million* and *The Strand* – connected with readers.

Launched in 1881, *Tit-Bits* was designed to fill a gap in the periodical market between mid-Victorian family papers appealing largely to female and juvenile readers, and the sporting papers (Jackson, 2001: 48). Newnes conceptualized *Tit-Bits* as a kind of familiar companion, integral to the very rhythms of readers' lives, and he quickly established a successful formula. In the 'Inquiry Column', appearing on page 6, short questions were published each week with answers appearing a fortnight later. Readers, now products of a system of compulsory schooling, were assured that they might 'depend upon receiving accurate replies'. 'Tit-Bits of General Information' and 'Tit-Bits of Legal Information' appeared elsewhere (Jackson, 2001: 60).

Newnes was accustomed to immersing his readers in the problems of production. The editorial column recorded the technical difficulties of producing the periodical and the patience required of readers while his employees developed their skills. Readers were led into familiarity with the technical aspects of journalistic production and invited to feel a sense of connection with the otherwise impersonal structure of the mass-market press. In 1887 Newnes was moved to assure 'our friends' that not all queries could be answered due to lack of space rather than want of courtesy. A familiar editorial tone, invariably featuring references to readers as 'friends', was the very essence of *Tit-Bits* (Jackson, 2001: 61, 63–4).

From 1885 a column entitled 'Answers to Correspondents'[1] ran on page 13. This column, conveying a sense of editorial presence and reader involvement, was the linchpin of the interactive posture adopted by *Tit-Bits*. Newnes' friend and colleague Hulda Friederichs recalled that he had a special affection for this page:

> He held that, first and foremost, all answers should be given in a manner which would make each correspondent feel that he was treated with special consideration; that here behind this newspaper page, there was somebody to whom the inquirer's affairs were of real human interest. . . . Secondly, Mr Newnes held that the answers should be couched in such terms, whenever this was possible, as to make them interesting to the general reader as well as to the individual correspondent.
>
> (in Jackson, 2001: 62)

In essence, then, *Tit-Bits* represented both a medium for personalized editor/reader interaction and a commercial product with appeal to a diverse audience (Jackson, 2001: 62).

On the front page were notices about the many and varied competitions conducted by *Tit-Bits*. With his competitions, his advertising stunts and his careful invocation of a sense of communality amongst 'loyal Tit-Bitites', Newnes created a popular movement out of *Tit-Bits*. He introduced an insurance scheme for commuters if they carried a current copy of the magazine on their person while travelling on the railway; enticed readers to take part in what became a great public treasure hunt; and urged '*Tit-Bits* canvassers' to solicit donations to the hospital funds in their towns and villages (Jackson, 2001: 68–9; Pound and Harmsworth, 1959: 84).

Tit-Bits began as a collection of excerpts converted into 'text' by a process of creative editorial synthesis. As it evolved, *Tit-Bits* began inviting readers to send in literary contributions, in return for which they would receive 1 guinea per column. In 1890, £1000 was offered for a serial of 40 to 50 chapters, to be published later in book form (Jackson, 2001: 61). *Tit-Bits*' success inspired Alfred Harmsworth (later Lord Northcliffe) to launch an imitator, *Answers to Correspondents*, in 1888 (Pound and Harmsworth, 1959: 81, 85). The periodical, which soon became known simply as *Answers*, advertised a variety of novelties, including an *Answers* pipe and coffee, and ran a plethora of contests and prizes. One offered a junior editorship; another, promising £1 a week for life, caught the fancy of the nation and became a popular sensation (Thompson, 2002: 11–13). Stephen Elwell observes that 'entrepreneurs such as Newnes and Lord Northcliffe stand out now because they discovered in the 1880s and 1890s how to define and exploit the common interest of the middle class in *inclusive* rather than exclusive terms' (1985: 40, emphasis added).

These were not, of course, the only periodicals to solicit contributions from their readers. While the influence of American newspapers on the New Journalism in Britain has received some attention (e.g. Smith, 1979: 152), little work has been undertaken on the spread of the New Journalism in colonial societies. In the Australian context, what is clear is that just as the completion of the overland telegraph in 1872 enabled direct electronic communication between Australia, Britain, Europe and North America, there were other, more physical links between Australia and the rest of the English-speaking newspaper world. Journalism is a peripatetic profession; long before the introduction of formal newspaper exchange schemes, journalists and editors were moving around the British empire and beyond. While many colonial journalists responded to the powerful lure of Fleet Street, the traffic was not always from the 'centre' to the 'periphery'; some British writers, journalists and editors worked in Australia and New Zealand (Griffen-Foley, 2002). As journalists worked their way around different countries and cities, exchanged letters with colleagues and other writers overseas, read extracts from various newspapers and cabled news published in the local press, and studied whole newspapers and magazines despatched by ship, the publications to which they contributed inevitably displayed a multiplicity of influences.

In 1880 the *Bulletin* was founded in Sydney by J.F. Archibald and John Haynes. An article marking the bright and impertinent weekly's first anniversary declared that the *Bulletin* had 'started level with our own times', suggesting that it was a sort of forerunner of the New Journalism in Australia (Thomson, 1954: 121, 125; Walker, 1976: 91). As the magazine evolved, it reduced its preoccupation with immediate political and clerical news and moved away from Sydney gossip to national issues. It was one of the few weeklies that carried reports from all the colonies, including excellent mining and financial news. But Archibald, who was also editor, came to realize that to have a national magazine it was necessary to cover the continent, and that it was impossible to employ regular correspondents everywhere. The thing to do was to invite his readers – members of a small, dispersed and itinerant population – to write for him. This was a decision made in 1886, not long after Archibald returned from an extended visit to London (Davison, 1998a: 94; Rolfe, 1979: 70).

Throwing the *Bulletin*'s pages open to his readers (Rolfe, 1979: 71), Archibald published regular notices calling for contributions – original political, social or humorous matter, unpublished anecdotes and paragraphs, poems and short stories (e.g. 'To Correspondents', 1886: 4). Contributors were encouraged to address a national readership. 'I want you to remember that Australia is a big place', Archibald advised a new recruit, A.B. ('Banjo') Paterson, exhorting him to write for 'the pearler up at Thursday Island and the farmer down in Victoria' (Davison, 1998a: 94; Lawson, 1987: 157). The life of bush people was persistently rendered back to them, both in imaginative writing and in paragraphs on incidents in country towns, mining settlements and shearing sheds. The *Bulletin* brought the world to the bush, and made the bush part of the world (Lawson, 1969: 46, 1999: 90). In 1888 the magazine began referring to itself as the 'Bushman's Bible'. The title was adopted widely, thanks partly to the influence of the English journalist Francis Adams, who heard a shearer say: 'If I'd only one sixpence left, I'd buy the *Bulletin* with it' (Davison, 1998b: 101). In the late 1880s the *Bulletin* overtook the *Town and Country Journal* as the bestselling weekly in Australia, its Christmas issue sometimes selling 80,000 copies in a society with a population of only around 3 million people (Davison, 1998a: 94).

By 1892 the general invitation for contributions was casually and cheerfully worded:

> Every man can write at least one good book; every man with brains has at least one good story to tell; every man, with or without brains, moves in a different circle and knows things unknown to any other man . . . mail your work to the *Bulletin*, which pays for accepted matter.
>
> (Lawson, 1987: 154)

Specific instructions for contributors were included from time to time. 'Write carefully and plainly on one side of the paper only, obliterating every unnecessary word'; remember that the *Bulletin* welcomes material on 'bush, mining, sporting, social and dramatic themes', that 1360 words went to a column, and that stories should keep within the column if possible. Valuing simplicity and directness, the *Bulletin* constantly instructed contributors to 'Boil it down!' (Green, 1984: 576; Lawson, 1987: 154–5).

In her sophisticated analysis of the complex interplay between editor, writers and readers, Sylvia Lawson describes the *Bulletin* as a kind of 'print circus'. Archibald as circusmaster is most evident in the weekly 'Correspondence' column, where the editor directly addressed the reader/writer. Pithy replies to matter submitted by readers using initials and *noms de plume* varied from flippant advice to serious counsel, including suggestions on the right books to read about socialism and land legislation (Lawson, 1987: 154). A correspondent perplexed in his choice of profession was advised:

'Judex': Far better to be a doctor than a journalist, if you honestly like the study of medicine. Get your diploma as a doctor first, anyhow; you can become a journalist afterwards, and all the better a journalist because you are a doctor. Journalism is anybody's profession. Lots of men and women among the outside public can write just as well and forcibly and interestingly as the professional journalist.

(Lawson, 1987: 156)

In the Correspondence column, on the inside wrappers of the distinctive crimson cover (the legendary 'Red Page'), and in direct attention to submitted copy, Archibald and the literary editor, A.G. Stephens, encouraged and refined the often raw talents of a stable that eventually included the likes of Paterson, Henry Lawson, Joseph Furphy, Miles Franklin and Barbara Baynton (Davison, 1998a: 94). It is estimated that under Archibald, who remained editor until 1902, the *Bulletin* averaged some 1000 contributions a week (Rolfe, 1979: 71).

Confessional magazines

Clearly, by the turn of the century a number of publications were based partly on reader contributions. Then, in 1919, an American bodybuilder turned publisher and his wife hit upon the idea of producing a magazine generated almost entirely by its readers. Mary Macfadden, the wife of Bernarr Macfadden, the creator of *Physical Culture* magazine, claimed that she was responsible for the 'thirty-million-dollar idea' that would turn her husband into one of the most successful magazine publishers in American history. According to Mary Macfadden, she proposed the idea of publishing a magazine called *True Story*, written by its own readers in the first person (Macfadden and Gauvreau, 1953: 218–19). While there is some ambiguity about the exact genesis of the idea, all parties agree that the confessional magazine grew from surplus mail directed to *Physical Culture* (Fabian, 1993: 59). These letters told of brokenhearted women who had followed Bernarr Macfadden's physical culture programmes yet had failed to capture a husband; others confessed their sexual errors to Macfadden, who usually had an exercise or a diet that would help them overcome their difficulties (Taft, 1968: 630).

The first issue of *True Story*, launched in March 1919, featured a photograph of a man and a woman looking into each other's eyes above the caption 'And Their Love Turned to Hatred'; Mary Macfadden recalled that swarms of people handed over two dimes at the newsstand to find out why (Simonds, 1988: 150). Designed as 'a medium for publishing the autobiographies of the unknown' (Taft, 1968: 630), the magazine portentously described itself as 'the first folk-literature since the days of the Bible – a literature written by the people themselves and responded to by the people' (Hatton, 1997: 8, 12; Marchand, 1985: 54). One *True Story* solicitation uncannily echoed the *Bulletin*'s rhetoric: 'Every man and woman has lived at least one big story which has that ring of truth for which authors of fictions strive with might and main' (Fabian, 1993: 63). Macfadden's stories were unsigned, presented as anonymous products of a collective imagination. He admitted that longer serials were written by staff writers, and professional writers obviously imitated the confessional formula and pocketed prizes for manuscripts selected for publication (Fabian, 1993: 61, 64). (In their study of American magazines, Tebbel and Zuckerman [1991: 194] found that 'some newspapermen made extra income by "confessing" on behalf of women whose stories they had covered in the course of their daily work'.) But Macfadden would maintain to the end that his texts for the people were written at least some of the time by the people, asserting a sort of democracy of production that abolished distinctions between readers and writers (Fabian, 1993: 64). The question of authorial authenticity will be further considered later in this article.

The confessional magazine genre was so successful in the United States that in 1922 Fawcett Publications launched *True Confessions*. The imitator also proved very popular, although it never performed as spectacularly as *True Story* (Kunzel, 1995: 1465). By 1925 *True Story* was enjoying a circulation of 1.5 million copies; during the Great Depression it exceeded 2.5 million and matched the popularity of the established *Saturday Evening Post* and the *Ladies' Home Journal* (Hatton, 1997: 1; Taft, 1968: 630). Early issues of *True Story* appealed across the gender lines with a mixture of sex and adventure in pieces like the explorer Martin Johnson's tale of the South Seas, 'If a Cannibal Wanted Your Wife for his Harem', which appeared in the first issue. These issues also featured many advertisements addressed to men, but by the early 1930s women's stories dominated the table of contents and advertisements were primarily directed to the figure of the female consumer (Fabian, 1993: 59–60).

Like Newnes and Northcliffe, Macfadden presented his project as a great collective enterprise. In *True Story* Macfadden sold shares in his corporation, offered a monetary reward for the best letter criticizing each issue, and assured readers that they would have a 'real part' in deciding what stories would appear in future issues. Throughout the 1920s Macfadden told his readers that *True Story* plots were all potential film scripts. He ultimately had little success with the studio system, although one story did form the basis of a film starring Rudolf Valentino (Fabian, 1993: 63, 65; Taft, 1968: 631). Macfadden added other periodicals – *True Romances, True Love and Romances, True Experiences* and *True Detectives* – to his stable, many of which emerged as radio dramas airing in prime mid-evening weeknight slots (Hilmes, 1997: 100). Foreign editions of *True Story* appeared in Britain, Australia, France, Germany, Holland and Scandinavia (Taft, 1968: 631). Women who grew up in Australia during the Second World War have recalled the popularity of the Australian editions of both *True Story* and *True Confessions;*[2] in 1946 the latter hit the list of the top ten bestselling periodicals in Australia (Montgomery, 1996: 23, 2000: 56–7).

Mass-market women's magazines

By now other Australian magazines were consciously seeking to foster a personal relationship with readers and were publishing contributory features. *Woman's Budget*, the first Australian weekly magazine published for women, established a social club which by the 1920s was organizing get-togethers and dances for members (Arnold, 2001: 278). *New Idea* asked readers to write in with problems (e.g. 'Let's Talk It Over', 1928: 1–2) and raise queries (e.g. 'The New Idea Query Club', 1928: 31), while the *Australian Woman's Mirror* described itself as 'first and last an exchange of news and views between readers' (e.g. 'Looking Backward', 1934: 3). But it was a newer women's magazine that deployed such devices in a more sustained and sophisticated fashion. Making its debut in Sydney in June 1933, the *Australian Women's Weekly* was an immediate hit with readers and advertisers. A number of reasons have been proposed for the publication's early and quite remarkable success: it began as the sole, rather than the ancillary, publication in an ambitious new publishing house; it was as much a newspaper as a magazine, with special reports on topical matters of interest to women; it soon spawned interstate editions and its features were attuned to the resonances of nationalism (Griffen-Foley, 1999: ch. 2; O'Brien, 1982: ch. 1–3; Radi, 1996: 543).

And yet what was to become the bestselling magazine in Australia's history had another distinctive characteristic. Edited by G.W. Warnecke, who had earlier been responsible for the 'Answers to Correspondents' feature of *Woman's Budget* (Griffen-Foley, 1999: 8), the *Women's Weekly* insistently treated readers not only as consumers but as collaborators. Just weeks after its launch, the magazine included a 'Preference Voting Coupon' for readers to indicate whether they wanted more or less of certain features ('Preference Voting Coupon', 1933: 43). Other issues invited readers to contribute to 'What I Like about the *Women's Weekly*', 'How I Helped the Paper', 'Constructive Criticism' and 'New Feature' competitions (e.g. *Australian Women's Weekly*, 10 June 1933: 4, 1 July 1933: 12). The *Women's Weekly* directly intervened in women's lives by providing recipes and fashion patterns to be followed at home, and by proffering advice about intimate issues in regular columns such as 'What My Doctor Tells Me', 'Louise Mack Advises' and 'For Wives and Young Mothers'.

As Foucault (1977) might suggest, whether the letters and stories reprinted in the guise of readers' comments were genuine or fabricated is largely irrelevant. In her study of *True Story*, Jacqueline Anne Hatton (1997: 8–9) bemoans the preoccupation with whether or not the stories were 'true'; to Hatton, *True Story* 'is a record not necessarily of what did happen, so much as what people believed truly could happen'. In terms of the *Women's Weekly*, what is significant is that comments were *presented* as the work of readers. The appearance of a dialogue with readers was an important component in the publication's attempts to consolidate an audience, give readers a sense of agency and project a feeling of communality (see Shevelow, 1989: 38, 49–52). Such devices became, inevitably, more important as the magazine's popularity grew; in other words, as the community of readers expanded, so too did the desire to participate in that community.

Marjorie Ferguson (1983: 11) considers how the individual reader of women's magazines, through being born a woman and by being a member of a particular sub-cult – as a reader of a certain magazine – is inculcated with a double sense of sex-based belonging. Women's magazines allowed women to feel that they were being emancipated from the withering isolation of suburban life (White, 1970: 299). The editorial on the third anniversary of the *Women's Weekly* declared that it was the ingredient of 'friendliness' that had made the publication what it was, for readers always talked about 'our paper' ('Our Paper', 1936: 12). In later years, the magazine showed photographs of mailbags overflowing with readers' competition entries, offered prizes and publication for readers' fiction and cover photographs, and established travel and fashion pattern services (Griffen-Foley, 1999).

Talkback radio

At the same time as the *Women's Weekly* was cementing its enormous popularity, another media form was becoming established. Marconi may have been the first person to send a wireless signal in 1896, but it was some decades before radio emerged as a broadcast medium. In the early 1920s hundreds of broadcasting licences were granted in the United States, laying the foundations of a commercial broadcasting system; the government-sponsored British Broadcasting Corporation (BBC) was created in 1922; and over the next few years a dual – part government and part commercial – broadcasting system was established in Australia (Briggs and Burke, 2002: 161; Jones, 1995: 7–8).

The majority of early radio programming was transferred from the stage, cinema and fiction. But one type of programming that quickly developed, and proved very popular, was the quiz show (Head, 1976: 147–8). This enabled a form of audience participation as people visited the studio, either to compete as contestants or watch as the battle of wits unfolded. In 1935 NBC aired America's first 'Town Meeting of the Air', which involved members of the studio audience expressing their views on issues of the day (Sterling and Kittross, 1978: 181). The immediate, intimate medium of radio permeated the lives of listeners in other ways, too, with the formation of clubs for women and children, performers going on tour, and so on (e.g. Inglis, 1983: 52–3, 90–1). In country towns, local radio stations became a particularly vital part of community focus (Jones, 1995: 92). As Briggs and Burke (2002: 231) have remarked, everywhere radio was ' "a good companion", consoling as well as entertaining, informing and educating, and everywhere it carried with it unique blessings for the blind, the sick, the lonely and the housebound'.

By the 1960s it could no longer be said that broadcasting was simply about 'people listening' (Miller, 1993: 43). For some years American listeners had been ringing in to radio stations to request a favourite musical selection or converse on a set topic with a programme host. This type of programming became more prevalent in the 1960s, as many American stations adopted an 'all-talk' format. This format depended on telephone calls from listeners, as well as news reports, interviews and political discussion (Sterling and Kittross, 1978: 181, 397). Prior to 1967 talkback was effectively banned in Australia, until the situation was remedied by new regulations on the use of telephones. For radio stations, talkback (known in the United States as 'talk radio') was relatively cheap to produce, it proved immensely popular with listeners cum callers, and it provided a clear way for radio to differentiate itself from television. Talkback radio hosts came to command huge salaries, particularly as stations on the AM band used talkback to distinguish themselves from newer, music-driven FM stations (Douglas, 1999: 288; Jones, 1995: 90–2).

Some contemporary commentators were enthusiastic about talkback radio's potential. In 1973, for instance, two Australian political scientists argued that talkback could play an important role in educating housewives and other people about politics. They maintained that talkback programmes provided 'house-bound women an opportunity to listen to other housewives questioning, criticizing, and discussing political subjects of interest to them'. 'These programmes are not yet the nation's referenda of the air', their article concluded, 'but they at least indicate that political apathy is neither a normal state nor a necessary one' (Aitkin and Norrie, 1973: 32–8). A pioneer of Australian talkback radio, John Laws, begins his nationally syndicated programme with the confident greeting 'Hello world, this is John Laws. What's on your mind, Australia?' and describes talkback as 'dial-in democracy'; Sydney's leading breakfast talkback host, Alan Jones, purports to be the voice of the ordinary person on 'Struggle Street'.

Unlike earlier media avenues for audience participation, radio could pick up on 'real life' events and opinions and transmit them in 'real time' (Head, 1976: 148–9). Particular sub-genres of talkback radio emerged, such as matchmaking sessions, medical and gardening advice spots, and midnight-to-dawn programmes. Keith McGowan estimates that he took about 12,000 calls a year while hosting the midnight-to-dawn shift on Melbourne's 3AW. He loved his job, saying 'It's an extended family for everyone who listens' (in Jones, 1995: 123). The talkback radio 'family' consists in part of regular callers known to thousands by name and agitated callers threatening to commit suicide. Callers who ring in and mention birthdays are often sent a gift, such as flowers or alcohol; studio tours, luncheons and film parties, sometimes hosted by station personalities, are held for listeners; and listeners are encouraged to attend special shopping centre or outside broadcasts.

Reality television

The popular format of the quiz show transferred easily from radio to television. As the years passed, some television shows increasingly provided opportunities to report on 'real life' events. This was particularly the case in news and current affairs; in the 1990s an Australian commercial network even launched a nightly show called *Real Life*, which emphasized human interest and hidden camera stories. Television designed largely for entertainment gradually co-opted the claim of news and current affairs programmes to show 'real life'. Programmes like *Cops* and *911* followed police and other emergency workers on their daily rounds, and other reality shows, including ones set in hospitals, appeared (Lumby, 2001a: 324). Specials taking viewers 'behind-the-scenes' to show the 'making of' blockbuster movies also became commonplace.

But programmes such as these depended primarily on producers following stories as they unfolded. In the 1980s and 1990s some programmes emerged which provided opportunities for more overt forms of audience participation. For instance, *America's Funniest Home Videos* and *Australia's Funniest Home Videos* relied on people submitting amateur footage of amusing or embarrassing incidents, while talk shows hosted by Phil Donaghue and Oprah Winfrey extended the confessional genre to the medium of television. In 1992 one Australian family, the Donahers, agreed to participate in a 'fly-on-the-wall' documentary series, *Sylvania Waters*, filmed in their own home by the BBC.

Interestingly, confessional magazines were also revived during this period. While established media proprietaries fret about declining newspaper and magazine circulations, one magazine genre has gone against the tide. In 1994 Pacific Publications launched *That's Life*, modelled on the British magazine *Take a Break*, in Australia. *That's Life* was promoted as 'just like a best friend you can always trust', with readers' stories winning tens of thousands of dollars in prizes each week. Despite the crowded magazine market, *That's Life* quickly surpassed its sales target of 350,000 copies a week. It is now one of the bestselling weekly magazines in Australia, and has inspired several spin-offs, including *That's Life for Kids* and a New Zealand edition (Shoebridge, 1996: 66–9).

In the mid-1990s a plethora of television shows involving the regular surveillance of 'real' people began to emerge. In the United States, MTV's *The Real World* featured seven young adults living together in a house for several months while their daily lives were videotaped in half-hour instalments; a spin-off programme, *Road Rules*, showed people performing challenges as they drove from one town to another in a caravan (Andrejevic, 2002: 252); and the *Big Brother* format, pioneered in the Netherlands in 1999 and soon embraced overseas, combined television and Internet surveillance of a group of people living in a house over a three-month period. Liesbet van Zoonen (2001: 670) remarks that the significance of *Big Brother* lies in the way it turns 'the private lives of ordinary people, with all their normal, everyday, seemingly unimportant experiences and worries, into a daily public spectacle'. What makes *Big Brother* and its contemporaries a discrete genre is the fact that they are not based on the documentation of exceptional moments, but on the surveillance of the rhythms of day-to-day life. This rhythm may play out in a contrived context, but the distinguishing element of these shows is that the surveillance of the characters is, for the period they are on the show, comprehensive. Watching unedited, 'real time' footage on the show's web site also allows viewers to check up on the construction of the television narrative (Ellis, 2001: 8).

Conclusion

In comparison with earlier audience participation formats, reality television shows such as *Big Brother* provide a more comprehensive coverage of the lives of 'real' people and deploy more sophisticated technology. Even so, there would still seem to be considerable historical resonances. *The Real World*'s co-producer, Mary-Ellis Bunim, suggests that in her programme the roles of producer and audience have been reversed (Andrejevic, 2002: 252). While this comment perhaps obscures the role played by media producers in shaping content, it is a point that could just as easily be made about the other media outlets discussed here – magazines relying in large part on reader contributions, and talkback radio programmes. All of these media outlets have addressed their consumers as textual actors, either real or potential. Many have invited their audiences to go 'behind-the-scenes' to appreciate the technical aspects of production. Most have also allowed their consumers to feel involved in determining the nature of the text: *True Story* encouraged readers to critique its contributions; the *Australian Women's Weekly* invited readers to vote on their favourite features; talkback hosts often cajole people to ring in with subjects for discussion; *Big Brother* allows television viewers and Internet subscribers to vote to evict the housemates until only one remains. These strategies have sought to foster a sense of audience engagement and agency and, by extension, create a loyal community of readers/listeners/viewers.

It might be suggested that the reality television hits of the late 1990s and early 2000s are about breaking down communities; after all, *Big Brother* and *Survivor* forge particular alliances amongst audiences as individual members of the house or the community are voted out of the race for the major cash prize. And yet an inclusive approach does, by its very nature, require a degree of exclusion. For example, the *Bulletin*'s slogan was 'Australia for the White Man'; *True Story* and *True Confessions* addressed a largely working-class, white readership (Kunzel, 1995: 1467; Simonds, 1988: 151); the woman addressed by the *Australian Women's Weekly* was overwhelmingly white, heterosexual, Anglophone and middle-class (Sheridan, 2002: 143); and it seems that talkback radio, in the United States at least, has provided lower-middle-class and working-class men, in particular, with a platform to express their views (Douglas, 1999: 293).

The media proprietaries examined here often seek to create more than just a sense of consumer loyalty; not surprisingly, many of their stunts and cross-promotional deals have represented overt attempts to boost short-term revenues. Controversy has often dogged these media outlets: *Answers* was accused of abetting national degeneration, and Northcliffe of desecrating journalistic standards (Thompson, 2002: xii, 17); in the early 1960s Allan Nevins, professor of history at Columbia University, told William Taft that no serious researcher should waste his time working on Bernarr Macfadden (Taft, 1968: 627); observers of talkback radio have become increasingly shrill in their criticism of 'the popularity of the conservative fashion for uncritical rant disguised as public discussion' (e.g. Coleman, 1998: 9); and shows like *Big Brother* are routinely criticized for being voyeuristic and for exploiting their participants (e.g. Hughes, 2001: 46). While the Internet and its surrounding technologies are beyond the scope of this article, it is worth nothing that it has also been argued that on-line political discussions are dominated by conservatives (Papacharissi, 2002: 4). The point here has not been to either condemn or praise media outlets that actively encourage audience participation, or to depict this process as a means of promoting the cause of participatory democracy. Rather, this article has simply sought to show that media producers have been blurring the notion of the passive media consumer for more than a century. This perhaps problematizes Habermas's view of the decline and fragmentation of the public sphere, in which citizen-consumers ingest and absorb passively entertainment and information (Habermas, 1989: 171; Kellner, 2000: 265). And yet there is, of course, a significant contradiction between the rhetoric of personalized journalism (for want of a broader term) and the structure of the modern, heavily capitalized mass media.

Notes

1   This was certainly not the first periodical to carry a column entitled 'Answers to Correspondents'. I am grateful to Dr Elizabeth Morrison for pointing out that in Australia, for example, the *Australian Journal* and the Melbourne *Leader* had been publishing such a column since the late 1860s. As we shall see, what was distinctive about *Tit-Bits* and later imitators was the volume and range of submitted contributions and the editorial voice's determination to engage in a dialogue with readers.

2   In Australia, *True Story* was published by K.G. Murray in conjunction with Macfadden Publications; *True Confessions* was published by K.G. Murray in conjunction with Fawcett Publications.

3.7

Reality TV and voyeurism
by Mark Andrejevic

No discussion of the burgeoning reality TV trend can be complete without a consideration of its voyeuristic appeal. The power and control associated with the voyeuristic fetish is frequently evoked in popular descriptions of the appeal of reality TV, but it is rarely more than touched upon. [. . .]

Fox's titillating, envelope-pushing show *Temptation Island* did not offer a cash prize. Instead, it based its appeal on the offer of a free trip to Belize, a stimulating "authentic" experience, and access to the truth about the cast member's "romantic relationships." In this regard, it picked up on the theme of self-knowledge and personal growth outlined in previous chapters. Moreover, in a self-reflexive gesture that has become the hallmark of television programming in the era of postmodern savviness, *Temptation Island* enacted the form of voyeurism to which it appealed. For viewers, the invitation was to receive intimate access to a relationship drama: Four couples would be split up and invited to date other people to see whether they would be willing to cheat on their significant other. The viewer was given the role of the keyhole-peeping private detective: following the cast members on their dates to see whether they would have sex with each other. At the same time, the element of voyeurism was incorporated into the show itself: cast members had to decide whether they wanted to see "highlights" of their significant others' dates.

The result was an interesting, if unintentional, exploration of the paradoxical form of impotent power associated with the position of the voyeur who participates by watching. It is this form of false control that links the position of the savvy voyeur with that of the interactive consumer envisioned by the promoters of the mass-customized online economy. In both cases, the form of control on offer turns out to be yet another form of submission. However, it is not quite enough to argue alongside Gitlin that savvy voyeurism is a form of surrender or, following Zizek that "the gaze denotes at the same time power (it enables us to exert control over the situation, to occupy the position of the master) and impotence (as bearers of a gaze, we are reduced to the role of passive witness . . .)."[1] This chapter pushes the argument a step further, arguing that the role of the savvy voyeur doubles as a performance of the desire not to be "seen" as a dupe and, in this regard, as a form of submission to an imagined, omniscient gaze (which may not remain merely imaginary for long). Just as the offer of participation in the online economy via mediated interactivity reveals itself as a ruse of rationalization, so the burgeoning genre of voyeurism TV corresponds to the increasingly important economic role of an exhibitionistic form of self-disclosure. The threefold equation of participation (empowerment), access to reality, and total transparency (guaranteed by comprehensive monitoring) align themselves in the voyeuristic appeal of reality TV.

Temptation Island ended up disappointing the dire predictions of those who anticipated (with avid indignation) that it would devolve into a decadent exercise in infidelity and gratuitous sex. The show, which featured four couples invited to a tropical island to "test" their long-term relationships by dating attractive singles, was widely received as a new low in the already bottom-feeding genre of reality television. It was variously denounced by critics as a "morally bankrupt" network-sponsored attempt to induce promiscuity and infidelity, as "trash TV," and as a "perverse 'Fantasy Island' " – "[t]he latest appalling, offensive, amoral, how-low-can-we-go TV stunt."[2] A spokesman for the Parents Television Council (PTC) was widely quoted as saying that, "The producers of 'Temptation Island' should be ashamed of themselves for trying to force the destruction of four relationships for the entertainment purposes of those lowlifes who consent to watch this trash."[3] The PTC's executive director added, "If we're putting this kind of thing on TV as a form of entertainment, we might as well throw Christians to the lions. . . . It's disgusting and appalling. The idea that any company would sponsor this is unconscionable."[4] Even the show's blandly non-judgmental host, Mark Wahlberg, conceded under questioning, 'By no means will I defend it as noble entertainment. . . . It's adult over-the-top moralitywise. . . . But it doesn't reflect my morals."[5] The uproar apparently had some impact on the show's economic success, since several advertisers pulled their support, citing moral concerns. The chairman of one media buying service, for example, explained his decision to the press as follows: "I would never put our clients in a show like 'Temptation Island.' . . . The whole show is founded on a premise that is totally distasteful. The next step is the Roman Coliseum."[6]

This collective corporate/media indignation all centered on a series that, despite the hype, featured a minimum of profanity, no sex, and a finale in which all four couples declared their long-term loyalty to each other. Any purely content-based assessment of the program would have to concede that it was tamer than much of the primetime fare that easily flies beneath the moral radar of advertisers and watchdog groups. What, then, explains the strong reaction to a show less revealing than a typical episode of *Baywatch*? Precisely the fact that it concerned not professional actors and models reading from a script but the "real" relationships of "real" people. The angry response to *Temptation Island* was ostensibly predicated on the notion that it's one thing to portray fictional sex and infidelity and quite another to manipulate the emotions of real people for the entertainment of viewers – just as it's one thing to portray Christians being fed to the lions and quite another to really send martyrs to their deaths. Of course, this parallel doesn't hold up: the *Temptation Island* couples all chose to participate in the show in exchange for a $3,000 stipend, a free trip to Belize, and ready entrée into the burgeoning world of "reality celebrity." Moreover, members of three out of the four couples went on record saying they decided to participate in the show as a means of giving their respective acting and modeling careers a boost.

If the claim to reality remains somewhat suspect – given the couples' admitted motivation for participating in the show – the assertion that *Temptation Island* undermines committed relationships and promotes promiscuity seems even more so. Perhaps the most realistic aspect of the series was its depiction of the economic potential of the exploitation of voyeurism (and exhibitionism) in an era characterized by the increasingly important economic role of electronic surveillance. Rather than attempting to plumb the depths of the reality of the couple's relationships, this chapter will explore the ways in which the logic of voyeurism enacted by *Temptation Island* traces the productivity of what Zizek (2000) describes as the "closed loop of perversion" typical of "late capitalist" market relations.[7] Drawing on the Lacanian description of the scopic drive, the goal is to demonstrate how the position of the voyeur (which recurs at several levels in *Temptation Island*) enacts not the desire to see and control so much as the drive to "make oneself seen."

[. . .]

Perversion, not subversion

The indignant reaction to *Temptation Island* as a threat to public morals implicitly assumes that perversion doubles as a form of subversion. What seems to trouble the critics, in other words, is the possibility that the portrayal of promiscuity as a form of entertainment will erode the moral fabric and that once viewers start taking pleasure in the emotional plight of "real" people, true moral decay will set in. This fear incorporates a certain willful disregard for the central role of ongoing "real" sex scandals in the mass media, obscuring the fact that the obverse of the ostensibly threatened public morality is an ongoing entertainment diet of human emotional trauma. The ideological moment, in other words, resides in the denial that the moral order championed by the indignant critics coincides with the immoral forms of entertainment that ostensibly threaten to undermine it.

To recast the argument in the terms suggested by Zizek, perversion (e.g., in the form of *Temptation Island*) cannot be equated with subversion (of the dominant moral order) *pace* those strains of performativity theory that suggest the hegemony of the dominant order can be challenged through transgressive forms of "acting out." In an era when the co-optation of transgression has become a prevalent mode of the dominant order's reproduction, this conclusion is by no means earth-shattering. Nonetheless, it provides an important qualification to those forms of reception theory as well as to those forms of cultural theory that champion the subversive character of "letting the freaks speak."[8]

Moreover, a psychoanalytic approach provides a useful set of terms for thinking through the ostensibly "transgressive" format of *Temptation Island*. Perversion, on this account, is to be viewed not as a (subversive) expression of the unconscious desire repressed by the dominant order, but rather as the expression of this order's *inherent* transgression: its "obscene, super-egotistical reverse." As Zizek puts it, "The deepest identification which 'holds a community together' is not so much identification with the Law that regulates its 'normal' everyday circuit as identification with the specific form of transgression of the Law, of its suspension."[9] In these terms, a program like *Temptation Island* ought to be viewed not as an attempt to "push the limits" of decency, but rather as paradigmatic of the moral order it ostensibly subverts. Apparent excesses of voyeurism such as the burgeoning reality genre, or perhaps the media spectacle surrounding Bill Clinton's sex life, can be viewed, on this account, as the flip side of forms of representative publicity that have come to count as politics. Given the central role of the exploitation of emotional trauma and sexual transgression to the entertainment industry, this argument seems rather more convincing than the indignant criticism repeatedly leveled against the show. *Temptation Island*, in short, is not a "new" low but the *old* one that we've been living with for quite some time. Thus, it is perhaps not surprising that the series earned Fox the highest ratings ever for its time slot, and also drew more of the coveted eighteen- to forty-nine-year-old demographic than any other Fox entertainment program of the season.[10]

[. . .]

The success of *Temptation Island* and the role played by the indignant critics in helping to guarantee this success reinforce Zizek's assertion (following Freud and Lacan) that "perversion is always a socially constructive attitude" – not a socially subversive one.[11] The following sections will attempt to elaborate this socially "constructive" role within the context of the emerging surveillance-based economy associated with "flexible" capitalism.

[. . .]

Perversion 1: the cast

The driving tension of *Temptation Island* – its incitement to transgression within the narrative frame—is provided by what might be described as a sadomasochistic deployment of the gaze. Once the couples are separated from one another, they are allowed to see each other in person only during the process of picking their upcoming dates. This selection process takes place around a palm tree-lined swimming pool, with the couples divided into two groups according to gender. Members of each group select whom they want to "date" next from a lineup of bathing suit-clad members of the opposite sex. Thus, cast members do more than select a date; they also get to see whom their significant other selects. The tempters and temptresses make the most of this fact, taking the opportunity to rub it in by hugging or kissing their future dates in front of their dates' significant others.

One episode, for example, focused on the anger of a cast member named Billy after seeing a "tempter" embrace his girlfriend and carry her away from the swimming pool at the end of the selection process. Billy, picking up on the oft-repeated theme that the tempters were just "doing their job," lashed out at his girlfriend, Mandy: "Did you see that? Bad idea right there. That really pissed me off trying to get a rise out of me."[12] The show built on this cycle of provocation and reaction. Separated from each other and unable to communicate except via a few short video recordings, cast members were left to imagine what their partners were up to. The directors ensured their imaginations would be stimulated as much as possible by providing provocative glimpses of each cast member's date to his or her significant other.

The way in which this was done neatly emphasized the sadomasochistic play of voyeurism. In the early episodes, members of one group (either the men or the women) were given a choice: they could decide whether to view an excerpt from their partners' date, with the understanding that if they chose to see the excerpt, their partners would then have to watch an excerpt from their dates. The show's host, Mark Wahlberg, highlighted the logic of these rules when explaining to the women that the men had the first choice of whether to watch a "highlight" tape, adding that some of the men had decided not to watch their partners' dates: "Maybe they don't want to see what you did, maybe they don't want you to see what they did . . . sit with that for a moment." The decision of whether to adopt the position of voyeur by viewing the highlights of their partners' dates doubled as a decision regarding whether to take on the complementary role of exhibitionist (by forcing their partner to watch their own date). This double choice helped fuel tensions between couples, since a cast member who was angered by seeing his or her partner's date could "get even" by going on a particularly rambunctious date and then forcing the partner to watch it.

One of the show's central conflicts – that between Billy and his girlfriend Mandy – was driven by this circuit of voyeurism and exhibitionism. Mandy went on a particularly flirtatious date with one of the single men and then chose to watch the video of Billy's date, thereby forcing him to watch hers. At one point Billy told the host that he didn't want to see any more of the tape, saying he couldn't bear to watch (as she prepared to lick a drink off her date's belly). The host told him that he could close his eyes, but the rules were that the tape had to be played. So the other three male cast members watched as Billy looked away. But he couldn't escape the sound track of Mandy squealing in self-castigating delight: "Oh, no, Billy's going to kill me. . . . Oh, my God, Billy, I'm so sorry."[13] Billy, who was left to picture in his head the images that accompanied this soundtrack, was visibly troubled. Immediately after seeing the video, he described his reaction on camera: "Definitely trying to get the brain under control. . . . I mean. I heard her say, 'Billy's going to kill me.' Where did the date go from there? Did I see the worst part of the date, did I see the tamest part of the date? . . . That's the part that stings most."[14] From there, the situation continued to deteriorate. Billy, clearly deciding to "get back" at Mandy by cutting loose, performed a (partial) strip tease for the single women, thereby providing a highlight clip that was shown to Mandy when she was given the choice of viewing scenes from the "after-hours" partying in the men's compound. Her response as to whether she wanted to see the video was "Just play the tape. . . . I enjoy torturing myself to death."[15]

This self-stimulating and self-torturing cycle of a voyeurism that defaults to exhibitionism neatly recapitulates Lacan's description of the sadomasochistic logic of the scopic drive. Indeed, this default fulfills Lacan's assertion that '[i]f . . . the structure of the drive appears, it is really completed only in its reversed form, in its return form."[16] It is in this sense that the scopic drive – characterized by the pair voyeurism/exhibitionism – is not to be comprehended merely as the drive to see but rather as a form of "making oneself seen."[17] This claim is borne out by the example of *Temptation Island*, but how is it to be interpreted? Zizek relates it to the self-defeating (and self-stimulating) logic of perversion, arguing that the scopic drive "is neither a voyeuristic tendency to see nor the exhibitionistic tendency to be seen by another . . . but the 'middle voice,' the attitude of 'making oneself visible,' of deriving libidinal satisfaction from actively sustaining the scene of one's own passive submission."[18] It is this role of the "impotent master" – of actively staging one's passive submission – that characterizes the savvy attitude outlined above: taking pleasure in the impossibility of achieving one's goal – in the very act of repeatedly missing it. But recall wherein this pleasure resides: precisely in not being seen as a dupe – or to parallel Lacan's terminology, in *being seen* (making oneself seen) as not being a dupe. In short, the attitude is a staged one – a performance for the sake of what Lacan terms "the gaze," which he describes as "not a seen gaze, but a gaze imagined by me in the field of the other."[19]

Tellingly, the premise of *Temptation Island* invokes a certain form of savviness – of not being duped – as the show's guiding motif. The couples who appear on the show are doing so not for a cash prize or as part of a competition but ostensibly to test their relationships: to make sure that they have not been deceived about one another – that the person they are with is really "the one" for them. Thus, the show's host repeatedly emphasized that the couples had come to the island to learn the truth about themselves and their partners: to determine whether they had been duped by someone who, given two weeks in tropical paradise, would prove unfaithful. If, as Lacan puts it, the gaze is an imagined gaze in the field of the other, the "reality" format of *Temptation Island* realizes this gaze in the form of the audience: the voyeurs for whom the spectacle of courtship and temptation is staged. The audience gaze becomes that which "sees all," in contrast to the partial gaze of the cast members, who are left to imagine what their partners are up to. Furthermore, this imagined gaze – incarnated by the cameras that follow the cast members everywhere – serves as the guarantor of whether they are being duped. In the end, the cast members will know what went on "behind their backs" – it was all on national TV, thus allowing the imagined gaze in the field of the other to be realized in the form of the imagined audience. In this sense, *Temptation Island* enacts the fantasy of the gaze: that third-person position that legislates whether we have really been duped – which guarantees, in short, that reality that we ourselves cannot see. If the gaze serves as an elusive trace of the unsymbolized Real, the promise of a show like *Temptation Island* is to realize this trace – to assign it a place: that of the omnipresent gaze of the camera/audience.

This debilitating moment in which the voyeur's pleasure turns painful – and shameful – is central to the action on *Temptation Island*, which thrived on the reaction of the cast members to the images of their significant others. For example, one of the "highlights" pulled for the show's promotions featured Billy's reaction to the Mandy video: "Now the fun is over and I'm paying for it, and I hate to say it's a mistake, but now I'm in hell." As the show's critics rightly observed, the main focus of *Temptation Island* was on the emotional trauma resulting from the fact that the couples were split up and left to imagine the infidelities of their partners. What the show unleashed, via its selective use of video clips, was the power of the cast members to imagine the worst. The contestants were encouraged to fantasize the direst of outcomes – that their partners were falling in love with someone else. To stimulate this anxiety, the couples were repeatedly invited to share their anxieties about the fate of their relationships. In every case, the fear was that affections would stray and that the two-week *Temptation Island* experience would end up destroying a long-term relationship. In each case, these worst-case scenarios crystallized around an image – a brief glimpse – of the cast member's significant other. Billy, for example, responded to the videotaped image of Mandy about to kiss her date, while the cast member Valerie kept playing back in her mind her glimpse of Kaya on his first date ("I saw Kaya laughing, having a good time with this pretty girl – her hair blowing in the wind. . . . It just made me sick").[20]

The cast members – prompted by the show's host, repeatedly referred to the torment engendered by the image they couldn't get out of their heads. Billy, for example, was asked to reflect back on his decision to watch the infamous clip of Mandy and her date, Johnny: "At first I said, I've got to see it – I thought that would be best to do because my imagination runs free. But imagination is easier to deal with than reality."[21] More precisely, it is the reality of not knowing what Mandy is up to combined with the image of her flirtation that prompts him to imagine the worst. In this respect, it is the voyeuristic quality of the cast members' interactions – the fact that the only images they have to work with are stolen, fragmentary, out of context – that allows their imagination free rein.

Thus, *Temptation Island* neatly enacts Lacan's contention that in voyeurism, "What one looks at is what cannot be seen."[22] Valerie provides a literal example of this claim just prior to the final date, when by accident she encounters the group of temptresses who, because they have not been selected to go on the last date, are being sent home (the final date selections were not made in front of all of the cast members, so the cast members did not know whom their significant other had chosen). It is the *absence* of one of the temptresses from this group that bothers Valerie the most (that most stimulates her imagination). The missing woman is the one she feared Kaya would pick for his final date – the one that she felt he was most interested in, and hence the one who posed the biggest threat to their relationship. The absence of this woman from the group unnerved her and made her "rival" loom even larger in her imagination: "I have a visual in my head of who he's spending two days with, and I just didn't want to have that," she told the camera.[23] More generally, in each case, when the cast members viewed the clips of their significant others, they were trying to see what was left out – some indication as to whether their partners had been (un)faithful.

In the end, however, all of this anxiety was expressed to the cameras. The relationship of voyeurism to exhibitionism – of, for example, Mandy's grief upon getting a glimpse of Billy's strip-tease – clearly took place with an eye to the cameras that followed the cast members throughout the course of their two-week "holiday." In general, the cameras remained invisible, preserving the identification of the television viewers with the gaze of the camera, although given the beach attire appropriate to a tropical island vacation, it was possible to catch a glimpse from time to time of the radio microphones worn by the cast members. In one of the rare exceptions to the general invisibility of the production crew, Billy was shown attempting to escape the glare of the camera lights after his traumatic viewing of Mandy's highlight tape. "Turn it *off*," he yelled to the videographer chasing after him. "Seriously, this does not concern the show. It's my *life*." To which a disembodied voice – it was unclear whether it belonged to the videographer, the sound person, or a producer – replied, "Actually, your life *is* the show right now."[24]

The sound of this disembodied voice seemed uncannily out of place—an unwonted intrusion of the seemingly neutral gaze of the camera into the show's narrative content. It may sound odd to equate the sound of the voice with the gaze of the Other, but this is precisely the equation that Lacan, following Sartre, makes: "If you turn to Sartre's own text, you will see that, far from speaking of the emergence of the gaze as of something that concerns the organ of sight, he refers to the sound of rustling leaves, suddenly heard while out hunting, to a footstep heard in a corridor."[25] These sounds – heard exactly at the moment when the voyeur is "looking through the keyhole" – take the voyeur by surprise in the form of the sudden emergence of the gaze of the other. Similarly, the videographer's voice becomes the trace of the gaze that watches Billy as he watches Mandy. Billy's anger recoils back at the gaze in what comes across as an undecidable gesture: on the one hand, he seems to recognize the role of the show in stimulating the cycle of relationship transgression, on the other hand it's hard not to read each of *Temptation Island*'s emotional displays – Billy's included – as a self-conscious performance intended for that very gaze he ostensibly wants to elude. He *should* be outraged after seeing Mandy's video: it would look odd if he weren't. Moreover, he would, in some sense, be letting the producers down. In this respect, it is the presence of this gaze that provides the incitement to transgression that is central to the show's narrative tension.

This same cycle of transgression is central to the Lacanian version of perversion. Once Mandy makes the decision to see Billy's video – and thereby to force him to watch the highlights or her own date – the cycle begins. Apparently driven to distraction, Billy is seen disappearing into the cabana of one of the temptresses. Upon his disappearance, the other male cast members speculate that he is getting even by cheating on Mandy, which is what they say they'd do if they were in his place. Of course, the clip of this conversation is played for Mandy the same evening she chooses to watch the highlight video to "torture" herself. Her predictable reaction to the video is to imagine that Billy is willing to "throw away" their relationship – a fact that in turn frees her up to behave accordingly, and so the cycle continues.

Lacan's observation that the Freudian *Schaulust* – scopic drive – provides "the key" to an understanding of masochism is illustrated by this tension between Mandy and Billy.[26] For Lacan the sadomasochistic drive turns not on pain, per se, but on a violent act: "It is a question of a . . . violence done to what? – to something that is so unspeakable that Freud arrives at the conclusion, and at the same time recoils from it, that its first model . . . is to be found in a violence that the subject commits, with a view to mastery, upon himself."[27] This formulation suggests that the perverse role of the subject of the drive is per se sadomasochistic: it combines a violent act (inflicted on oneself) with passive acceptance of this act. In Zizek's terms, the drive is characterized by the derivation of libidinal satisfaction "from actively sustaining the scene of one's own passive submission."[28]

This formulation exactly describes the moment of resignation expressed by several of the cast members on *Temptation Island* in the face of anxiety about their partners' behavior: "If he or she wants to throw away our long-term relationship, so be it – it's out of my hands." Mandy, Valerie, and Andy all voice this sentiment, which rehearses the combination of activity and passivity described by Lacan: they are in the position of passively submitting to the violence that they have inflicted upon themselves. Billy's trip to the temptress's cabana enacts a similar logic: a resigned acceptance of the violence that he is inflicting on his own relationship – almost as if it's not of his own doing, as if it's beyond his control.

This sadomasochistic submission describes the paradigmatic subject position of late capitalism in which, oddly enough, those on both sides of the production process adopt the role of *victim* with respect to the big Other of the market. Producers remain "at the mercy" of the ever more volatile whims of consumers, while consumers end up having no other choice than what "the market" provides (just as workers are at the mercy of the unpredictable job market). This double submission occurs in both the narrative of *Temptation Island* (in which Mandy and Billy are at the mercy of the game itself – rather than each other) and in its critical reception. The series was roundly treated by pundits as one more example of the market making an appeal to the lowest common denominator (adopting the position that we, the viewers, are at the mercy of the market). At the same time, the show's producers described themselves as slaves to the market. Sandy Grushow, chairman of the Fox entertainment group, defended the show to the press, saying, according to one account, that the network would be negligent not to "pursue what is obviously an incredibly powerful trend in the industry": reality programming.[29] In Grushow's words, implicitly absolving the network from responsibility for the tastelessness of *Temptation Island*, the show was a result of Fox's "responsibility as network programmers to satisfy the tastes" of the audience.[30] The role of the market, in this case, is not naturalized by being relegated to the background. Instead, it is foregrounded – and bemoaned – in the passive gesture of the nonduped: yes, we are caught in a force larger than all of us, and it's time to face that fact. So be it.

This gesture enacts the "end-of-ideology" ideology of "late" capitalism. The market is no longer naturalized as the idealized, mystical invisible hand that will lead to the optimal outcome. Rather, its negative consequences are – to a significant extent – recognized and naturalized in this very fact of recognition. The disturbing consequence is that capitalism no longer need sustain itself on the basis of its promised benefits. Rather, the process of naturalization has been accomplished so thoroughly that even when the depredations of capital become evident, they attain the status of a natural disaster: tragic, but inevitable.

This naturalization is reflected in the co-optation of critique by popular culture and the entertainment industry, which, in the post-Cold War era, increasingly casts its villains as members of the capitalist elite: greedy captains of industry and corrupt politicians (and, of course, manipulative entertainment moguls). The "triumph" of neoliberalism in the 1990s has been accompanied not just by celebratory capitalist propaganda but also, tellingly, by a savvy critique of the breathless cheerleaders of the free market. From the standpoint of the savvy, the dupes are on both sides: on the one hand, those naïve enough to believe capitalism's propagandists; on the other, those naïve enough to still believe in the potential of progressive social change.

The problem faced by the social critic, then, is not the so-called false consciousness of an uninformed public but a complacent savviness that assumes it knows all too well. In other words, it's not that critical perspectives aren't being heard (e.g., the fact that Noam Chomsky can't get on *Nightline*), but rather that they have become a staple of popular culture – that Chomsky is more effectively glossed in a Hollywood product like *Bullworth* than in his own movie. Savviness works to inoculate capitalist culture by incorporating its self-critique into its self-propagation. It is in this respect that the savvy subject stages the scene of its submission as constitutive of its inner freedom: it attempts to avoid the fate of the duped, paradoxically, by accepting capitalism at its worst – by dispensing even with the promise of the benefits of the free market, a promise that might otherwise be enlisted to highlight societal contradictions.

Lest this capitulation appear too self-reflexive – as if the subject's "self-submission" is a purely internalized gesture – Lacan highlights the fact that the structure of the drive appears only "thanks to the introduction of the other." Translating this back into the example of *Temptation Island*, we might say that the self-proliferating voyeuristic drive enacted by the cast members (in watching video clips of their partners' dates) revolves around the vortex of the audience gaze – for which the entire spectacle is staged. The ostensible goal of each cast members' voyeurism is, precisely, to see from the position of the Other/audience: to discover the objective truth of the significant other's intentions (and thereby to see oneself as one is seen – to determine whether one is, in fact, a dupe). What is productive about this threefold relationship (between seer, seen, and gaze) is the disruption of the closed circuit of the intersubjective gaze between the two lovers by the intrusion of the camera: the "objective" gaze that epitomizes the trace of the real, the blind mechanism of the big Other/symbolic order. Thus, *Temptation Island* neatly highlights not just the sado-masochistic role of the scopic drive in the interplay between the cast members, but the socially complicit role played by the voyeurism of the audience. However – and this is crucial to the format's fundamentally conservative (nonsubversive) perversion – *Temptation Island* avoids thematizing this complicity, allowing the audience to *retain* the role of neutral observer, rather than highlighting the role of its own desire in the sadomasochistic interplay.

Perversion 2: the audience

Temptation Island makes explicit one of the recurring questions of the reality-based shows that document the day-to-day lives of a group of "real" people living together: who is going to have sex with whom? One of the most publicized "behind-the-scenes" details about the show was the fact that the production company ensured that all cast members – both the couples and their tempters and temptresses – were tested for sexually transmitted diseases.[31] The repeated public insistence of those associated with the show that *Temptation Island* wasn't about sex – but rather about the dynamics of "serious relationships" – came across as both obvious and disingenuous. Obvious, because given the conventions of prime-time TV in the United States, there was no question of the show being any more revealing than *Baywatch*; disingenuous, because the show – whose wardrobe was not much different from that of *Baywatch* – revolved around the question of sexual fidelity. As a reality format, *Temptation Island* played like a version of *The Real World* with all the parts that weren't about sex removed.[32] With respect to the sexual drama/trauma staged by the series, the audience was ostensibly exempted: viewers were offered the pleasure of watching the producers and the cast members instigate anxiety, grief, and sexual tension. The format followed the conventions of "objective" documentary to the extent that the action was presented as unfolding before the neutral gaze of the camera/audience. These conventions typic-ally background the effect that the camera itself has on the action: that the entire scenario was staged for the camera's eye. The filmic conventions enlisted by *Tempta-tion Island* – the invisibility of the production equipment, producers, and technicians documenting the show and the explicit claim to "reality" – encouraged the audience to adopt the position described by Zizek as that of the "pure gaze":

> [W]hile we perceive ourselves as external bystanders stealing a furtive glance into some majestic Mystery which is indifferent to us, we are blinded to the fact that the entire spectacle of the Mystery is staged with *an eye to our gaze*: to attract and fascinate our gaze – here, the Other deceives us in so far as it induces us to believe that we were *not* chosen; here, it is the true addressee him/herself who mistakes his/her position for that of an accidental bystander.[33]

The position prepared for the viewer is, in the sense outlined by Lacan in his essay "Kant with Sade," properly perverse, insofar as the audience is invited to adopt the gaze of the object – of that which is not subjectively involved in the scene, but before which the scene is staged. The audience realizes the position of the gaze insofar as it adopts the position of what Lacan describes as the object cause which stimulates the closed loop of the scopic drive.[34] With this observation, the formal Lacanian structure of sadistic perversion comes into play: the sadist pervert is precisely the subject who takes on the role of the object. As Lacan puts it in Seminar XI: "The sadist himself occupies the place of the object, but without knowing it, to the benefit of another, for whose *jouissance* he exercises his action as sadistic pervert."[35]

The point here is not to enlist Lacanian theory to bring us back to our starting point: to write off the audience as a collection of perverted voyeurs who have hijacked entertainment television. Rather, it is to push the discussion of the audience one step further: to explicate its role in the economy that produces programming like *Temptation Island* by drawing on the relationship between the two aspects of Lacanian perversion: the subject position which "gets off" on the failure to reach its goal, and that which takes on the role of the object-in-strument of the Other's pleasure. More specifically, the argument is that the subject position enacted in surveillance-based reality programming – that of the perverted subject in the throes of the scopic drive – neatly coincides with the subject position envisioned by flexible capitalism: that of the consumer committed to "making itself seen." The Lacanian claim that these two subject positions coincide seems particularly fruitful given the conjunction of the burgeoning reality TV trend with increasingly pervasive forms of private and state-sponsored surveillance.

Pursuing this argument requires a more detailed exposition of the Lacanian claim that the pervert occupies the position of the object instrument of the Other's desire. The audience, when it takes on the role of the objective gaze, simultaneously adopts the position of the sadistic pervert, whose desire is complicit in the action from which it is ostensibly removed. Translating this observation into the terms outlined earlier, we might note that the savvy subject – the voyeur exempted from the action – is the *ultimate dupe*, insofar as this exemption overlooks the complicit role of the ostensibly objective determination that "there is nothing to be done but understand the situation as it is."

How, then, is the position of the audience as pure gaze with respect to the onscreen action to be explicated? Insofar as the audience is positioned in the role of "pure gaze," it is allowed to suppress the desire at work in its ostensible neutrality, and thereby to background its complicity in the onscreen action. The truly subversive gesture to which the perversion of *Temptation Island* can be contrasted would be one that forced the audience to confront its own complicity – to recognize the way in which its own disavowed desire renders it the dupe of the entertainment industry itself, which takes on the role of the real other for whom the audience works. Such a gesture would demonstrate to the viewer who adopts the position of the other's instrument (objective arbiter of truth/audience commodity for sale) that this position is actually that of the victim – the unknowing exhibitionist in the closely monitored and tracked audience.

Temptation Island's socially "constructive" (nonsubversive) character is evidenced by the refusal of this route in favor of a conclusion that preserves the ostensibly objective role of the audience. The desire that stains the "pure" gaze of the audience (and gives the lie to its "objectivity") is the hope that infidelity will take place: that one member of a couple will have sex with one of the available singles. In the end, the audience is left with the sole satisfaction of the *failure* to realize its desire. Which raises the question of whether a truly subversive *Temptation Island* would confront the audience with the truth of the manipulation of its desire by actually *realizing* this desire in a culmination of infidelity and broken relationships. Such an outcome would surely be much more disturbing than the actual *Temptation Island* (although viewers would likely write it off as "not really" real, arguing that people who agree to participate in such a spectacle probably aren't in meaningful relationships in any case, and may well be faking the whole thing just to get on TV).

One might make a similar point with respect to the other controversial Fox reality spectacle: *Who Wants to Marry a Multimillionaire*, in which fifty women competed to marry a millionaire they had never met (and didn't even see until he had made his choice). The current analysis suggests that the more disturbing outcome would be one in which the marriage *worked out* – rather than being annulled shortly after the fact and written off as one more publicity stunt. As it turned out, the outcome served to underwrite the very values it ostensibly challenged: according to these values, such a marriage couldn't/shouldn't work out in reality. The import of the show's ostensible failure was that rather than being staged as the inherent transgression (obscene underside) of matrimony in capitalist modernity, the display of women as prizes for the millionaire (who, in the show, adopts the position of the gaze – the unseen "spot" which looks at the women "from all angles") is portrayed as marriage's fundamental violation – as its *non*inherent transgression. It is perhaps not insignificant that the network famous for its "tasteless" and perverse programming is owned by the notoriously conservative Rupert Murdoch. The complementary relationship between Murdoch's brand of conservatism and the perversity of a series like *Temptation Island* is highlighted by the network's decision to turn down an advertisement for female contraceptives, refusing to air it during *Temptation Island* because by the very nature of the product, the ad was deemed inappropriate for family viewers.[36]

[. . .]

Notes

1   Slavoj Zizek, "How the Non-Duped Err," *Qui Parle* 4, no. 1 (1990): 2.

2 Ann Hodges, " 'Temptation Island' Gets Trashy," *Houston Chronicle*, 12 January 2001, 10; Hal Boedeker, "Viewers Deserve Blame for Success of Trash TV," *Orlando Sentinel*, 24 January 2001, E1; Matthew Gilbert, "A Perverse 'Fantasy Island,' " *Boston Globe*, 10 January 2001, F1.

3 Beverly Bartlett, "No Man Is an Island, but It's an Island That Tests Us," *Courier Journal* (Louisville, Ky.), 15 January 2001, 1F.

4 "Storm Hits Fox's New 'Temptation Island,' " *Atlanta Journal and Constitution*, 8 January 2001, 1A.

5 "Viewers Learn How Tempting Island Was," *Tampa Tribune*, 27 February 2001, Baylife, 4.

6 Bill Carter, "Some Sponsors Can't Accept Racy Reality," *New York Times*, 29 January 2001, C1.

7 Slavoj Zizek, *The Ticklish Subject* (London: Verso, 2000), 248.

8 See, for example, John Fiske and John Hartley, *Reading Television* (London: Methuen, 1978); Michel De Certeau, *The Practice of Everyday Life* (Berkeley: University of California Press, 1988); Joshua Gamson, *Freaks Talk Back: Tabloid Talk Shows and Sexual Non-Conformity* (Chicago: University of Chicago Press, 1998).

9 Zizek, "In His Bold Gaze," 225.

10 Lisa De Moraes, "Fox Scrambles to Make Ratings Hay with an Extra 'Island,' " *Washington Post*, 2 February 2001, C5.

11 Zizek, "In His Bold Gaze," 248.

12 *Temptation Island*, KDVR Denver, 22 February 2001.

13 *Temptation Island*, 12 March 2001.

14 *Temptation Island*, 12 March 2001.

15 *Temptation Island*, 12 March 2001.

16 Jacques Lacan, *The Four Fundamental Concepts of Psychoanalysis*, The Seminar of Jacques Lacan, Book 11 (New York: Norton, 1998), 183.

17 Lacan, *The Four Fundamental Concepts*, 195.

18 Zizek, "In His Bold Gaze," 284.

19 Zizek, "In His Bold Gaze."

20 *Temptation Island*, 22 March 2001.

21 *Temptation Island*, 1 March 2001.

22 Lacan, *The Four Fundamental Concepts*, 182.

23 *Temptation Island*, 18 January 2001.

24 *Temptation Island*, 22 February 2001.

25 Jacques Lacan, "Kant with Sade," *October* 51 (Winter 1989): 84.

26 Lacan, *The Four Fundamental Concepts*, 183.

27 Lacan, *The Four Fundamental Concepts*, 183.

28 Zizek, "In His Bold Gaze," 284.

29 Boedeker, "Viewers Deserve Blame."

30 Boedeker, "Viewers Deserve Blame," E1.

31 Jim Slotek, "Fox, Lead Us Not into Temptation" *Toronto Sun*, 15 January 2001, 47.

32 One of the interesting twists added by the media coverage was the widely circulated report, early on, that no one on the island had sex. The *Boston Herald*, for example, reported, "In an exclusive story posted on the Internet's WorldNet

Daily.com, writer Paul Sperry claims that none of the couples had a fling and none split up at the end of 'Temptation Island.' According to a production source quoted by Sperry: 'Unfortunately no one had sex – unfortunately because, believe me, the producers wanted them to' " (Monica Collins, "A Deuce of Reality," *Boston Herald*, 11 January 2001, O41). The fact that media critics and viewers alike continued to speculate about who would have sex with whom highlights the perverse logic of the show's perception: getting off on missing "it" – the ostensible object of the voyeuristic gaze, the sex act itself.

33 Zizek, "In His Bold Gaze," 224–25.

34 In this example, the use of the term *object cause* is meant to designate the cause of the drive (the audience gaze around which the action turns) as distinct from its ostensible object (the object of the cast member's gaze: his or her significant other). The Lacanian point to be made with respect to this distinction is that what drives the cast member's voyeurism is not the attempt to make some kind of connection with his or her significant other but the drive to avoid being seen as a dupe – hence, the gaze of the other.

35 Lacan, *The Four Fundamental Concepts*, 185.

36 "Scene in Brief," *Boston Herald*, 2 February 2001, S04.

3.8

Jamming *Big Brother*: webcasting, audience intervention, and narrative activism
by Pamela Wilson

This is the story of the first season of the U.S. version of *Big Brother* and how its "reality" narrative was almost hijacked by a motley assortment of activist on-line fans and media/culture jammers. The setting is a spectacularly conjunctural moment in media history, right at the cusp of the new millennium. A window of opportunity emerged for only a brief period of time, allowing for the invasion of a slickly produced corporate television game show by amateur narrative terrorists whose weapons were clever words rather than bombs. The intervention could perhaps only have happened once, during a period of technological and programmatic flux, when the format was new, the formula was flexible, the unscripted narrative was emerging from the psyches of the not-yet-jaded improvisational players, the events were being closely followed around the clock by avid on-line viewers, and the Hollywood set was relatively unprotected. Prior to this time, no one at CBS or Endemol Productions suspected that chaos could or would come from the skies. After it, contestants were selected more for their ratings-drawing glamour than their down-home naïveté, the formula became more fixed, and chances for narrative disruption became increasingly curtailed.

The introduction of *Big Brother*—a hybrid concept inspired by George Orwell's classic treatise on political oppression in a futuristic police state that held control over the minds of its subjects—spawned a form of media activism rooted in the intersections of a countercultural and anticapitalist social movement ("culture jamming") with the shifting technological sands of the show's dual webcasting/broadcasting. *Big Brother*'s narrative was multilayered: it emerged minute by minute on the streaming Web feeds, but was controlled, produced, and structured through the selective editing of the producers for the nightly television recap. The "characters" were real people living in a fishbowl, surrounded by cameras and creating an emerging narrative shaped partially by the producers' constraints, but open enough to allow for improvisation. Enter the culture jammers, seeking to disrupt and subvert the intentions of the corporate producers as well as to influence the outcome of the "story." A new type of intervention into television was born: *narrative activism*.

The narrative activism triggered by *Big Brother* can be seen as a form of media/culture jamming, a purposefully playful and subversive activity that reflects both the postmodern condition as well as anticorporate and anti-globalization sentiments. Culture jamming might be defined as the appropriation of new media technologies and information systems to invade, intercept, and disrupt corporate systems and their products. The earliest conception of culture jamming is attributed to William S. Burroughs, who in a seminal 1969 piece stated, "Our aim is total chaos."[1] The theory and practice of culture jamming have been elaborated most fully by Mark Dery in his 1993 essay "Culture Jamming: Hacking, Slashing, and Sniping in the Empire of Signs." According to Dery, " 'Culture jamming' . . . might best be defined as media hacking, information warfare, terror-art, and guerrilla semiotics, all in one. Billboard bandits, pirate TV and radio broadcasters, media hoaxers, and other vernacular media wrenchers who intrude on the intruders, investing ads, newscasts, and other media artifacts with subversive meanings are all culture jammers."[2] Similarly, Naomi Klein calls culture jamming "semiotic Robin Hoodism" or "counter-messages that hack into a corporation's own method of communication to send a message starkly at odds with the one that was intended."[3]

There are many forms of culture jamming, but those that focus on media consider it to be semiological guerrilla information warfare, using words as weapons (a concept attributed to Umberto Eco), turning the tools of mass media against the corporate forces themselves. This has been a movement especially enabled by the rise and rapid growth of on-line media culture and the radical possibilities of the Internet; it is part of what Kevin Michael DeLuca and Jennifer Peeples describe as the transformation of the public sphere into the "public screen."[4] For critics like Dery, culture jamming is also an intensely political act, even as it grows out of a postmodern impulse:

> I'm deeply committed to a progressive politics whose calls for social justice, economic equality, and environmental action are founded on an economic critique of the catastrophic effects of multinational capitalism. At the same time, I'm profoundly influenced by the postmodern emphasis on cultural politics (as opposed to the old New Left emphasis on political economy). The intertwined histories of feminism, the civil rights movement, multiculturalism, and gay and transgender activism remind us that hacking the philosophical code that runs the hardware of political and economic power is crucially important, too. In that light, I'm naive enough to believe that ideas matter and that intellectual activism can, in its own small way, be an engine of social change.[5]

Whether social change—or at least public cultural critique—might be produced by attempts to affect, subvert, and disrupt the well-oiled mechanisms of commercial television is a question that begs to be asked in light of the narrative activism that surrounded the multimedia corporate production *Big Brother*.

Big Brother and an innovative system of program delivery

The premise was simple: "Ten people. No privacy. Three months. No outside contact." In summer 2000, the Dutch company Endemol Productions, working with CBS television, selected ten contestants to participate in the first U.S. version of *Big*

Brother: part game show, part documentary, and part soap opera. This group would live together for more than twelve weeks, isolated in a house on a Hollywood studio lot, surrounded by corridors of surveillance cameras. Every two weeks, one contestant would be voted off the show, with the last remaining contestant winning the $500,000 grand prize.

The CBS television version of *Big Brother*, with concurrent live-streaming on-line feeds in partnership with America Online (AOL), received public regard as a moderately successful, but mediocre television event. It gained even more acclaim as an unprecedented, momentous hit on the Internet, with a remarkable crossover on-line presence along with a strong and loyal on-line audience. In fact, this became the most noteworthy aspect of the venture: journalist David Kronke reported that *Big Brother* "has changed the way television and new media can interact."[6] AOL's publicity articles touted the "unprecedented convergence between television and the Internet" achieved by the CBS-AOL *Big Brother* alliance as the "largest ongoing webcast in history," and claimed a "tenfold increase in participants [of] the streaming webcast during peak usage time in the first week."[7] The official AOL website, however, was only the tip of the iceberg in terms of on-line audience involvement in *Big Brother*. On-line fans created and contributed to dozens of private websites and portals devoted to *Big Brother*, and AOL itself sponsored more than fourteen thousand unofficial fan pages about the *Big Brother* program.[8]

While the "action" that took place in the *Big Brother* house was supposed to be naturally occurring, producers structured the daily activities of the houseguests around a series of programmed "challenges." A high degree of self-consciousness also curtailed the spontaneity of the contestants' behavior. As Endemol producer John Kalish later remarked of the U.S. contestants, "They were always talking about how they were being edited, story lines, looking into cameras, being aware of it. They never let go of what the other House Guests in other countries did, which was finally to let go of the idea of being observed. These guys never did. They always referred to themselves as 'characters' as opposed to people."[9] The only site in the house from which events were not transmitted over the live Web feeds was the Red Room, a room to which the houseguests could go as individuals for private interviews with the producers (who often used these interviews as a way to elicit plot information or otherwise manipulate the developing narrative) and where they revealed their choices for banishment.

Although the premise of *Big Brother* only required audience participation in limited and ritualized ways (the call-in votes every two weeks to oust the one member of the household), audience involvement—to the point of intervention and disruption —proved to be a hallmark of the U.S. version of the *Big Brother* phenomenon. Neither the producers nor the network anticipated the level of public involvement that the *Big Brother* TV/on-line programming innovation would incite. The opportunity to contribute to the narrative of a live television series appealed both to fans and critics of the show, and intersected with a number of personal and organizational agendas unknown to the producers.

The dramatic highlight of the first season was the escalating narrative tension in the tenth week. Increasing interventions from the outside world coupled with a "groupthink" mentality among the six remaining sequestered houseguests culminated with the houseguests planning a mass walkout from the show, ostensibly to embrace an idealistic collective solidarity. Seeking their "chance to make history" and to make a profoundly anticapitalist statement as they chose friendship over prize money, they gravely threatened the very premise of the show's competitive commercialism and the network's ability to continue its run. The planned walkout was ultimately defused and contained by the producers, and the show ended successfully by commerical standards, but the producers' hold over the narrative outcome was tenuous for a few days as chaos from outside intervention and internal rebellion threatened to radically alter the program's planned plotline.

Big Brother broke new ground in establishing a multiplicity of ways that a television program could reach its audience. In fact, one might argue that *Big Brother* consisted of several different programs, several distinct audiences, and multiple versions of its narrative. In addition to television, press accounts, and the Web feeds, the other official mode of disseminating the narrative of the program was the CBS/AOL *Big Brother* website, which posted daily summaries of narrative highlights and contained the official commentary from the producers.[10] Other, unofficial versions of the narrative were posted by on-line audience members as updates on message boards, chat rooms, and portals with links to a variety of connected sites.[11] Based on these distinctions, we might theorize that the perception of the narrative events (that is, the actions and happenings in the lives of the *Big Brother* houseguests/contestants) would be complex, and that these perceptions would vary depending on exposure to selected media forms (the TV show, on-line feeds, message boards, official *Big Brother* website, and press commentary). Endemol producer Douglas Ross noted the privileging of the on-line viewer in particular: "I think that the Internet viewer really does understand the show better than the average TV viewer. People who aren't involved in the Web, and just watching it on TV—except for the dedicated viewer who just watches it as a soap opera—I don't think the average viewer really gets it."[12]

Big Brother was highly unusual in that the circumstances of its production provided for a shared role in shaping such meanings. How did amateur culture jammers "invade" the narrative world and irreparably affect the "plot" of the series? Who, in the end, produced *Big Brother?*

Invasions from the skies and other interventions

The first outside invasion of *Big Brother* occurred when someone tossed several tennis balls containing fake newspaper articles over the fence into the *Big Brother* compound. In spite of the producers' efforts to try to prevent the contestants from seeing the balls' contents, the contestants managed to read two of these "articles" containing negative comments about the show and its participants. These pieces had an immediate effect on the contestants' morale. This, the first incursion of the outside world into the seemingly secured diegetic one of the houseguests, created enough alarm both inside the house and among the producers that the CBS/AOL website ran the following disclaimer, titled "A Statement from the Executive Producer":

> The minute we saw what was going on, we told the House Guests over the PA system to bring the tennis balls and the papers into the Red Room. We quickly

discovered that the photocopied newspaper articles were fake. We then told all the houseguests that this was a hoax and that the articles were bogus. We acted quickly to set the record straight because our number one concern, of course, is for the houseguests' safety and psychological well-being.[13]

Shortly thereafter, a Web page (ZAP Design) claimed responsibility for the intrusive tennis balls.[14]

The producers' reaction was strong. Concerned that one particular contestant might request a voluntary exit in response to this prank, Endemol broke its own rules about no outside contact and provided him with a packet of reassuring letters they had hastily requested from his family. The contestant, George, a roofer from Rockford, Illinois, had quickly become popular based on his sympathetic embodiment of a U.S. archetype of the simple, beleaguered working man. As an added bonus, the reading of the letters from his young daughters to the other houseguests supplied Endemol with some tear-filled, poignant moments for the television viewers.[15] Thus, Endemol appropriated the events and used them to their own advantage.

Day fifty marked the beginning of the intensified external campaign to shape the narrative events. That afternoon, the contestants were in their enclosed outdoor courtyard. The producers, having apparently received a phone tip about a low-flying plane with a banner, came over the loudspeaker and asked the houseguests to sequester themselves immediately in the men's bedroom. A few hours later, the banner-bearing plane returned. According to the CBS/AOL website, "The airborne prankster returned and passed the house at low altitude, proudly and clearly displaying the streaming message, 'BIG BROTHER IS WORSE THAN YOU THINK—GET OUT NOW.' "

The on-line activist group Media Jammers later claimed responsibility for this first banner. The "media jamming" plans were hatched via an on-line *Big Brother* forum on the website Salon.com. According to Media Jammers founder Jeff Oswald, "We were just goofing around trying to think of ways to get messages in. We talked about catapults, compressed air cannons like the ones they use to shoot T-shirts into the crowd at sports events, etc. We had a guy scout out the location and tell us how difficult it would be to get in range. So . . . I figured our best shot was the banners."[16] There would be more to come from Media Jammers.

A campaign by George's fans to "Save George" soon emerged as well. The website OurBigBrotherGeorge.com was set up by corporate supporters to raise money for George's family in his absence. It was rumored on the message boards that the site was either illegal or unethical, and it was eventually shut down. Nevertheless, George's hometown rallied behind its local television hero with spaghetti dinners and other fund-raising campaigns. Some fan groups used their websites to sell T-shirts to benefit George, while others mobilized massive phone campaigns to get viewers to cast their telephone votes for another contestant so that George could maintain his chances of winning the $500,000. Most of the on-line fan community scorned this attempt by supporters, especially corporate interests, to help a particular contestant win an unethical and unfair intervention.[17]

While message boards heated up with irate fans protesting the Save George campaign, tensions grew inside the house. The houseguests were bonding with each other and feeling a growing distrust against "Big Brother" (the producers), perceived as their captors and programmers. A collective ethos had developed among the houseguests; the conditions of the shared lived experience had become antithetical to the competitive spirit of the game show mentality. The tension between competitive individualism and collaborative collectivism informed the group dynamics for several weeks, and ultimately, it led to their most dramatic moments.

In the wake of the airplane banner chartered by Media Jammers, the activist on-line organization began to receive a great deal of attention. On 27 August 2000, Media Jammers' Oswald posted an update on the group's website describing its philosophy and intent for future involvement in the *Big Brother* operation:

> As our belief is that this is a universal, grass roots operation, we fully advocate and encourage anybody with a desire to engage in interloping on *Big Brother* to do so of their own accord on their own terms the best way they see fit. . . . Our ultimate goal is to make actions stick, that will generate on-going dialogue about the destructive force of this CBS debacle. . . . A unanimous [contestant] walk-out, although it would be a thing of poetic beauty, is highly unlikely right now. However, if we maintain our efforts, we're confident they will eventually see that we . . . were honest about our motives, and sincere in our belief that losers talk, heroes walk. We maintain that the message is, has been and always will be that by walking out together, they will be respected for it, salvage their dignity, and have more of a chance to accomplish their individual goals. If they stay and participate to the end, they will only be ridiculed and forgotten: *Nine losers, one wealthy loser.* . . . More planes will fly, more banners will be seen. Count on it. Have fun with it. Keep watching the skies.[18]

On 30 August, three more banners flew simultaneously, also reportedly commissioned by Media Jammers: "9 LOSERS AND 1 WEALTHY LOSER? OR 10 WINNERS?" accompanied by "LOSERS TALK—HEROES WALK—TOGETHER" and "THERE IS DIGNITY IN LEAVING." That day, Media Jammers reiterated their goal to tell the contestants to "walk out on this turkey of a production. . . . We state clearly that our ONLY target is CBS/Endemol Entertainment and the production *Big Brother*."[19] That evening, the audience voted contestant Brittany off the show. The on-line fans—especially those who did not like George—attributed Brittany's loss to the "Save George" campaigns and vowed to get retribution. The houseguests, though, were unaware of the attempt by George's supporters to vote Brittany out of the house. The dramatic tension now hinged on the irony of what viewers knew that the houseguests on the inside did not know. Would "Big Brother" tell them? Would the Media Jammers banners tell them? Would they find out? And what would they do if they found out?

The Megaphone Lady, Brittany's secret, and more banners

On 2 September, a new character known as the Megaphone Lady unofficially entered the world of *Big Brother*. Kaye Mallory, a Los Angeles-area schoolteacher and an active member of the on-line "Big Brother Watchers" fan group, had been participating as usual in the discussions and updates on the fan e-mail list when she announced that she was "getting a bullhorn and going down there to yell messages to them!"

Early that evening, Mallory drove as close to the *Big Brother* house as she could get and began shouting through a megaphone: "Fight Big Brother—the editing sucks! We love you guys!"[20] Mallory's cohorts on the Big Brother Watchers fan list were ecstatic. A half hour later, Mallory went back to the *Big Brother* house and shouted, "You're worth more as a group against Big Brother. If you walk out together, you will be famous!" The *Big Brother* producers promptly called all the contestants into the house. When Mallory returned home to her computer, she rejoined the discussion on the fan e-mail list about her actions. Although some fans criticized Mallory for interfering where she did not belong, others gave her suggestions for future drive-by shoutings, and many applauded Mallory's initiative in allowing the voice of the fans to penetrate the *Big Brother* house.

Two days later, Mallory returned to the house to reveal CBS's plan to revive the flagging audience interest in the show by bribing one of the boring houseguests to leave and replacing that person with a provocative alternate. "On Wednesday, Big Brother will offer you money to leave. Don't take the money! It's a trick! Don't take the money! We hate Big Brother! We love you guys! Don't take the money! Fight Big Brother!" Mallory yelled. On her website, Mallory reports on what followed:

> As a delightful surprise, Ms. Megaphone was featured as the opening of the Monday night BB show on TV. They even had subtitles so everyone would know what was said. Subsequently, on the live Wednesday show, BB offered them the money, but they'd upped the initial offer to $20,000 and when that was refused, they upped it to $50,000. Nobody took the offer. We're very proud of them for not selling out! . . . I'm glad the HGs had two days to think about their options.[21]

That Wednesday night brought a producer-sponsored intervention. Endemol decided to bring banished Brittany to the studio and allow her to speak to one of the remaining contestants by phone for two minutes. Josh, her erstwhile love interest on the show, was sent to the Red Room for a private conversation. In the days that she had been out of the *Big Brother* house, Brittany had gained a better understanding of the dynamics of the household and the motives of the players. She revealed cryptic pieces of information about the orchestrated campaign to save George and told Josh which contestants he should trust. When later questioned by the other houseguests, Josh refused to divulge what he had learned, but he seemed troubled.

The next day, Mallory returned with her megaphone to find security guards patrolling the *Big Brother* lot. When she got the chance, she shouted more information to the houseguests. The following description on the CBS website of her visit reflects a growing corporate attempt to discredit the narrative intrusions by the fans: "At 9pm PDT, 'Crazy Megaphone Girl' began screaming muddled messages to the House Guests. Each guest listened intently, with the hope of garnering some information from the outside world. Big Brother swiftly sequestered the group."[22] When Mallory returned once more to the *Big Brother* house, she was harassed by the security guards, who engaged her in a car chase to try to intimidate her to leave the area and not return.[23]

In the meantime, new banners had been trying to discredit George. The information from the outside was making the houseguests uncomfortable, especially George, who felt attacked, and Josh, who had secret knowledge he was afraid to reveal. While tensions rose, the houseguests tried to decipher the fragmented messages from the Megaphone Lady and the banners.

The climax: the aborted walkout

> Our first project "Jamming Big Brother" is almost complete. We have interfered with the creative direction of this CBS "reality" show to the point of altering the outcome and raising awareness of the abuses the producers have committed against the contestants, their families and the viewers of the show. We have done so by introducing outside messages to the contestants who are supposedly cut off from any contact from the outside world. Our most successful tactic has been to fly aerial banners over the "house" on the CBS studio lot in Los Angeles, with messages encouraging the contestants to walk out or otherwise rebel against the manipulative producers. We have also worked with other groups who have tried to communicate with the contestants through various means including bullhorns and delivery of written messages into the "compound."
>
> —Media Jammers[24]

On Saturday morning, Josh revealed Brittany's "secret" to George, and George then called a meeting. When the houseguests gathered in the kitchen to hear George's plan, the streaming Web feeds blacked out for about ten minutes. CBS/Endemol censored this crucial discussion from the on-line audience.[25] When the Web feeds returned, it was apparent that an impassioned George was trying to convince the others that they should walk out and split the money between them. Influenced by Media Jammers and Mallory, George explained that, "That thing with the Megaphone Lady, I put it together. Think back to the beginning, and it's obvious. . . . I'm positive, we all could have been winners long before this. The thing was there all along. We are bigger than the show and they need us. . . . we are all winners." Despite some skepticism among the houseguests, many saw the opportunity to make "television history" by undermining the rules of the game and proving that, as one stated, "*We* are more than money."

Within forty minutes, all the players agreed that they would walk out together on the following Wednesday, realizing that their action would sabotage the show. They also correctly anticipated that the producers would try to talk them out of it. Having made a pact, however, they were proud and self-congratulatory: "We have decided to make all decisions as a group. . . . It's about sticking together," said one player. According to George, the information from the Megaphone Lady and the banners helped make the outcome clear.

Endemol producer John Kalish later remarked that he and the other executive producers, Douglas Ross and Paul Römer, had gathered to watch the "riveting" actions of George and the other houseguests: "It was startling. It was engaging, but looking at the reactions of the rest of them is what alerted me to the fact that this was something completely different. This was something that needed to be dealt with. Ultimately, it was a combination of fascination, excitement, and a little bit of concern. . . . This was the greatest thing that could happen to the show, and yet potentially the most devastating. [We were] living at the edge here."[26]

After their decision, the houseguests were riding high on their ebullience. They felt defiant and independent of the control of the producers. They also realized that the world knew their plans through the program's Web viewers. As they headed outside to toast their decision, Big Brother commanded them to go inside because the Megaphone Lady was back. Defying Big Brother, they stayed in the yard, and Mallory told them to walk *that* night. The producers blasted loud music over the intercom to drown out her words, making it difficult to hear the houseguests as they discussed their walkout. At the same time, all Web feeds switched to empty rooms inside the house, so the on-line audience could not hear or see what was happening in the courtyard. Once again, the producers implemented an information blackout strategy during a moment of high narrative tension.

After the walkout decision had been made, another batch of airplane banners arrived. Some supported the rebellion, while others told the contestants to stay in the house. The houseguests began to realize the magnitude of their decision to leave, and some exhibited misgivings. In the Red Room, the producers explained to individual contestants that if everyone voluntarily walked, they would forfeit the grand prize as well as their weekly stipends. The ensuing dialogue between the contestants revealed a clash of value systems, between the "noble" act of defying Big Brother in favor of group solidarity and the competitive, materialistic desire to stay, play the game, and win the grand prize. When discussing leaving, one contestant commented, "They will ask us why we came in the first place," to which others replied, "I think the money is why we all came in the first place, but the game taught us . . . that you should not give up control of your integrity or image to someone else." One added, "It's an amazing sign of America that the six of us are so different and so cohesive. . . . If I'm gonna walk, we're showing our integrity, that even though we all need money very bad we are gonna make something bigger than that. To put a message like this to society is worth much more than money."

On Saturday evening, when the houseguests prepared to enter the Red Room as a group to confront the producers, Big Brother made them wait. About ten minutes later, they were told to come to the living room. The Web feeds were switched to the chicken coops at this point, effecting another blackout of information. Apparently, a group meeting took place during this period when the cameras were not on the houseguests. Soon thereafter, in the Red Room, contestant Jamie had a long but unrecorded discussion with producer Kalish. When she emerged, she told the others that he said they had "made a commitment to the people outside who are watching this show to be in the house, and that they are breaking that commitment if they leave."

About this pivotal conversation, Kalish later observed, "I thought, 'This is the moment of truth.' . . . We couldn't let them think they were going to undermine the show or undo us by making this decision. We had to be very strategic in how we were going to respond to it." So the producer "called their bluff" and told the houseguests that the producers were making preparations for them to leave the house. Just as a parent might react to a young child who packs a suitcase and threatens to run away from home, Kalish reportedly told the most gullible contestant, Jamie, "I'm not going to try and change your mind," just as he planted many doubts in her mind about the wisdom of the decision.[27]

After the Red Room meeting, contestants Jamie's and Eddie's support for the walkout began to waver. Fellow contestant Curtis encouraged them to stay, astutely explaining that "I can see John's point of view . . . [but] John, however, DOES work for *Big Brother*." Similarly, houseguest Cassandra suggested that the "guy in the Red Room" might not have everyone's best interests at heart.

The following morning, negotiations continued and Kalish returned to the control room to again target Jamie. Interestingly, many fans at this time believed that Endemol and CBS had engineered the walkout scenario as a publicity ploy, to trick the contestants, or to play "mind games" with the viewers. Fans were also divided as to whether the group should stay or leave.

The houseguests gathered early that afternoon for a final decision. After some negotiation, they realized that they were no longer unified. A fan post on the Updates Board summed up the situation exquisitely:

> Eddie says he came to his senses.
> The rest now have changed their minds.
> Back to routine.

The "revolution" was effectively squelched. Big Brother had maintained control.

Narrative activism and the exposure of "reality's" constructedness

The thwarted rebellion by the *Big Brother* contestants was the most dramatically compelling aspect of the series in its first U.S. incarnation. The moment-by-moment suspense of the walkout weekend was especially riveting to the on-line viewers, who watched the webcast and heard the houseguests wax lyrical about leaving en masse, even as they waffled about trading in the chance to win the game (and prize money) for a moment in television history. The audience who watched only the television program and not the Internet feeds missed this dramatic arc. Internet viewers were shocked to find that CBS did not feature the planning of the walkout on its Saturday show at all. Only on Monday, when the *Big Brother* household was safely "back to routine," did CBS air a half-hour recap of the plans for the walkout and its demise.[28]

Big Brother spawned a remarkable level of narrative activism in spite of the producers' attempts to limit contact between participants and the outside world. The emergence of disruptive and subversive elements, both within and beyond the confines of the *Big Brother* house, provides a new model for conceptualizing the interactive potential of the new hybrid television/Internet documentary–game show genre. *Narrative involvement* by an audience might be considered to be the contribution of audience members to reshaping the narrative in complicity with the program's producers. This might range from suggestions about plot developments to more activist campaigns to save a program or protest a particular story line. In the case of *Big Brother*, narrative involvement would include the invitation for viewers to call in to vote on which contestant should be banished from the show. In contrast, *narrative activism* involves audience interventions that contradict the plans or desires of the corporate producers and change the narrative outcome of a program. In the case of contrived documentary game shows such as *Big Brother*, both types of narrative intervention are potentially subversive since producers shape the so-called naturally occurring actions that produce the narratives even if the programs are seemingly unscripted. Yet it is the documentary aspect of the narrative intervention into *Big Brother* that is the most notable.

There is a well-documented history of audience activism around dramatic and comedy television series. Letter-writing campaigns and campaigns to boycott advertisers have been used in attempts to save programs with low ratings but loyal audiences, attack programs with values contradicting those of the viewers, and show other types of support for the "quality" or nature of certain types of programming. No doubt such responses have affected the way that producers and writers subsequently shaped characters and story arcs to cater to viewer likes and dislikes.[29] *Big Brother*, however, is perhaps the first time that viewer activism has focused on documentary programming. The impetus of most reality TV has been to air episodes of edited documentary action (and I use the term "documentary" in the loosest sense here) into a completed narrative that had taken place in a more distant past than that of the edited *Big Brother* footage, which was at most two to three days old when it aired, often on the same day. Most important, Web viewers could watch and hear the events as they were unfolding in the daily lives of the houseguests; viewers could also compare and contrast what they had observed via the Web feed to the edited narrative that Endemol/CBS constructed for the nightly broadcasts.

The discrepancies between these two versions of narrative reality created a major source of disgruntlement and discontent for the on-line fans and other viewers since they exposed the constructedness of this (as any) documentary narrative in a way never before revealed on a U.S. reality TV show. Rarely, if ever does a documentarian provide an audience with a parallel version with the full, unedited footage, allowing them to see what has been selected and what has been omitted to create the final "documentary." We are socialized to believe that documentary and other nonfictional (reality) forms are "truth"; however, the dual modes of sharing the *Big Brother* happenings created a disjunctive and troubling awareness for many viewers that the two audiences were receiving two different versions of the "reality" of the lives of the houseguests. The ability of fans to use the Internet not only to follow the moment-by-moment action but also to organize and mobilize as activists as well as interventionists supplied a crack in the surface of the network or producer's total control over the television product. In so doing, it inadvertently offered a space through which viewer-fans could actively participate in the production of the program and affect its narrative outcome, even (especially) having the opportunity to work toward goals at odds with those of the official network and program producers. In effect, the audience and fans caught the network and its production company off guard as they appropriated an opportunity to become, to a significant extent, coproducers of the program's narrative. Ultimately, though, Big Brother (the corporate producers) regained control of the wheel and steered the show back onto its original course.

Narrative activism and media/culture jamming take the much discussed concept of interactivity to a new level. Following Mark Dery's theory of culture jamming, we might consider narrative activism to be an act of social protest in its potential desire not only to subvert the narrative outcome of a television program but also to make larger statements about the media and capitalist globalization at a larger level.

Media Jammers exemplifies this broader intervention in its belief that Media Jammers is a grass roots "culture jamming" organization created to raise awareness of irresponsibility in the news and entertainment media through high profile stunts, hoaxes and general media mayhem. . . . We practice and advocate safe, legal means of interfering with media events, taking control of the message and exposing the incompetence, lack of integrity, distortions and abuses of the media, holding them accountable for the consequences.[30]

As Oswald remarked in retrospect, "Our 15 minutes of fame was a lot of fun, and I did enjoy the notoriety. I really liked knowing that we were making network executives sweat. I never thought it would be seen as such an impact on future 'audience interactivity.' I was amazed at how people were inspired to influence the show after we did our thing. We had control of the direction of the show for a few days, and then others stole our thunder and inspired complete anarchy." When asked about how the idea for "jamming" *Big Brother* originated, he explained that "the *Big Brother* project happened because it was just too easy. CBS provided us with all the tools we used to mock them. The live video feeds were crucial to our success. And every time we forced the producers to make a choice, they accommodated us by making the wrong one. It all played to our favor."[31]

The culture jamming of *Big Brother* came from various sources with diverse agendas—political activists, fans, pranksters. The long-term effectiveness of their interventions may arguably have been minimal due to the appropriation of the interceptions by the producers and their subsequent integration into the program's structure. Still, the short-term effects of media/culture jamming presented a jolt to corporate producers, and influenced the behaviors and beliefs of the *Big Brother* participants. In their decentralized efforts to disrupt and subvert the corporate control of the outcome of reality TV, even for a short time, the culture jammers provided new insights into the more radical possibilities of challenging the hegemonic control of the media giants by throwing small rocks with their slingshots.

Notes

1 William S. Burroughs, "My Mother and I Would Like to Know," *Evergreen* 67 (June 1969); see also "The Electronic Revolution," 1970, http://www.syntac.net/dl/elerev2.html.

2 Mark Dery, "Culture Jamming: Hacking, Slashing, and Sniping in the Empire of Signs," Open Magazine pamphlet series, 1993, http://www.levity.com/markdery/culturjam.html. See also Stephen Downes, "Hacking Memes," http://www.firstmonday.dk/issues/issue4_10/downes/index.html; and David Cox, "Notes on Culture Jamming: Spectres of the Spectrum; A Culture Jammer's Cinematic Call to Action," http://www.sniggle.net/Manifesti/notes.php.

3 Naomi Klein, *No Logo* (New York: Picador, 1999), 280–81.

4 Kevin Michael DeLuca and Jennifer Peeples, "From Public Sphere to Public Screen: Democracy, Activism, and the 'Violence' of Seattle," *Critical Studies in Media Communication* 19, no. 2 (June 2002): 125–51.

5 Http://www.levity.com/markdery/inform.html.

6   David Kronke, "Web Interaction on *Big Brother* Could Alter Reality TV," *Miami Herald*, 5 October 2000, http://www.herald.com/content/tue/entertainment/tv/digdocs/077750.htm. See also Anick Jesdaunun, "*Big Brother* Finds Fans Online," Associated Press/Internet, 28 September 2000, http:// dailynews.yahoo.com/h/ap/200000928/en/big_brother_Internet_1.html; and Mindy Charski, "TV Companion Site Creates Buzz," *Inter@ctive Week 7*, no. 28 (17 July 2000): 48. News reports indicated that the AOL-sponsored site was the most highly visited new Internet site during July 2000, the month the program premiered, with more than 4.2 million visitors. Some of the most notable of the reviews and cultural commentaries on the reality TV game show trend in the popular and academic press included Bill Carter, "Television's New Voyeurism Pictures Real-Life Intimacy," *New York Times*, 30 January 2000, 1; Robert Sheppard, "Peeping Tom Television," *Maclean's*, 10 April 2000, 58–62; Mark Boal, "Summer of Surveillance," *Brill's Content* 3, no. 5 (June 2000): 66–71, 122–25; James Poniewozik et al., "We Like to Watch," *Time*, 26 June 2000, 56–63; Steven Rosenbaum, "Peeping Tom TV: The Beginning of the End or the Birth of Meaningful Media?" *Television Quarterly* 31, no. 2–3 (summer 2000): 53–56; Edward D. Miller, "Fantasies of Reality: Surviving Reality-Based Programming," *Social Policy* 312, no. 1 (fall 2000): 6–16; Edward Rothstein, "TV Shows in Which the Real Is Fake and the Fake Is Real," *New York Times*, 5 August 2000, B11; James Wolcott, "Now, Voyeur," *Vanity Fair*, September 2000, 128–32; Rob Sheffield, "Reality," *Rolling Stone*, 14 September 2000, 138; Ziauddin Sardar, "The Rise of the Voyeur," *New Statesman*, 6 November 2000, 25–28; John Podhoretz, "*Survivor* and the End of Television," *Commentary* (November 2000): 50–52; Brian D. Johnson, "We Like to Watch," *Maclean's*, 29 January 2001, 56–58; and Brooke A. Knight, "Watch Me! Webcams and the Public Exposure of Private Lives," *Art Journal* 59, no. 4 (winter 2000): 21–26. An issue of *Variety* on 25 September 2000 had a number of articles devoted to the spread of reality TV programming in various countries, including the United Kingdom, Hungary, Switzerland, South Africa, Argentina, Brazil, the Philippines, Australia, Korea, and the United States. Also, there was an interesting BBC News-sponsored opinion forum titled "Are We Turning into Peeping Toms" on 23 July 2000, just after the premiere of both the U.S. and U.K. versions of *Big Brother*, to which viewers on both sides of the Atlantic (as well as some from Asia) posted their insights; see http://news.bbc.co.uk/hi/english/talking_point/newsid_834000/834731.stm.

7   See "AOL's Big Brother Web Site Setting Records in Unprecedented Convergence between Television and the Internet: Ambitious Alliance between Popular CBS Television Series and World's Largest Interactive Services Company Sets Webcasting Records as Largest Ongoing Webcast in History," *Hollywood Reporter*, 18 July 2000, http://news.excite.com/news/bw/000718/va-america-online.

8   Many fan sites were internationally based and served as sites for fans of the *Big Brother* series in various countries, such as the U.K.-based Orwell Project (http://www.orwellproject.com) or the Netherlands-based Big Brother Central (http://www.BigBrother2000.org). Others were specifically devoted to serving the audience of the U.S. show.

9 *Big Brother* 2000 official website (http://bigbrother2000.com).

10 See http://bigbrother2000.com or http://webcenter.bigbrother2000.aol.com.

11 For the best literary commentary on the *Big Brother* phenomenon, in a tone alternately fond, fascinated, and scathing, see the series of *Salon* articles at http://www.salon.com/ent/tv/bb/index.html.

12 Cited on *Big Brother* 2000 official website.

13 Ibid.

14 Graphic designer at ZAP Design, Los Angeles, http://www.zapdesign.net/articles/.

15 See *Big Brother* 2000 official website.

16 Jeff Oswald, personal correspondence; and *Big Brother* 2000 official website. For information on the grassroots activist Media Jammers organization, see http://www.mediajammers.org.

17 See letter titled "CBS/BB Improprieties," 1 September 2000, from "D I N Only" and posted on an AOL message board, then reposted 3 September 2000 on Joker's Commentary Board by "Kerry." The letter writer urged fans to take action against the perceived ethical improprieties.

18 Media Jammers website statement, 27 August 2000.

19 Statement made about philosophy behind banners, Media Jammers website, 30 August 2000.

20 "An Interview with Ms. Megaphone," Kaye Mallory's Ms. Megaphone website, http://bennyhills.fortunecity.com/billmurray/532/bb/meg-run1.html. The remarks from the Big Brother Watchers fan group can be found in the archives of the Big Brother Watcher e-group, http://groups.yahoo.com/group/bigbrotherwatchers.

21 Kaye Mallory's website.

22 *Big Brother* 2000 official website, CBS/AOL, article 389.

23 Kaye Mallory's website.

24 Information page (FAQ), Media Jammers website, http://www.mediajammers.org/faq.htm.

25 There was a running joke among the on-line fans that CBS/Endemol would place one or more cameras on the chicken coop in the courtyard, with close-ups on the chickens, whenever the producers did not want the on-line audience to see or hear some action happening in the house. This move was affectionately dubbed the "chicken cams" by the fans and recognized as a strategy by the producers to engineer an information blackout. In an interview on the official website, long-time Endemol producer Paul Römer discussed his use of the "panic button" by which the producers could blackout the on-line feed. In his earlier European shows, he remarked, he had tried to keep the breaking news off the Internet to "save" it for the TV program. After a while, however, he realized the advantage of showing most of the action on the Web feeds: "People saw things happening live and they wanted to see what we did with it on television. The moment I would show it on television the Internet side went sky-high because people wanted to see what happens now. I learned there was a mutual benefit. We are not competitors. We were really helping each other—but that's a big change of mindset for a television producer."

26 Cited on *Big Brother* 2000 official website.

27 Ibid. Apparently on Endemol's Spanish version of the show, *Gran Hermano*, the producers also encountered resistance by the contestants to "Gran Hermano's" authority.

28 For some popular press accounts of the aborted walkout, see Lynn Elber, "*Big Brother* Members Mull Walkout," Associated Press, 9 September 2000, http://news.excite.com/news/000909/19/big-brother; Greg Braxton, "*Big Brother* Guests Threaten Walkout," *Los Angeles Times*, 11 September 2000, http://www.calendarlive.com/calendarlive/calendar/20000911/t000085524.html; Frazier Moore, "*Big Brother* Walkout Flops," Associated Press, 13 September 2000, http://news.excite.com/news/ap/000913/22/ent-big-brother; Mark Armstrong, "Squashing Another *Big Brother* Revolt," *E! Online*, 11 September 2000, http://www.eonline.com/News/Items/0.1.7074.00.html?ibd; and Robert Bianco, "*Brother* Walkout?" *USA Today Online*, 13 September 2000, http://www.usatoday.com. Some postmortems of the U.S. *Big Brother* phenomenon included Bill Wyman, "Who Screwed Up *Big Brother?* Everyone," *Salon*, 29 September 2000, http://www.salon.com/ent/tv/feature/2000/09/29/bb_final/print.html; Gail Shister, "Lack of Sexual Chemistry Hurt *Big Brother*, Producer Says," *Kansas City Star Online*, 28 September 2000, http://www.kcstar.com/item/pages/fyi.pat?file=fyi/3774cb5a.928; Mike McDaniel, "O, Brother; At Last, the End Is Near," *Houston Chronicle*, 27 September 2000, http://www.chron.com/cs/CDA/story.hts/headline/entertainment/683555; and Antonia Zerbisias, "Big Brother Made Reality TV Real," *Toronto Star*, 29 September 2000, http://www.thestar.com/editorial/entertainment/20000929ENT11b_EN-ZERBTV.html. During the run of the program, the CBS/AOL website published extensive interviews with several of the *Big Brother* executive producers, including Paul Römer (24 August 2000), Douglas Ross (21 September 2000), and John Kalish (13 October 2000) (see http://webcenter.big-brother2000.aol.com/entertainment/NON/).

29 See Sue Brower, "Fans as Tastemakers: Viewers for Quality Television," in *The Adoring Audience: Fan Culture and Popular Media*, ed. Lisa Lewis (London: Routledge, 1992), 163–84; Julie D'Acci, *Defining Women: Television and the Case of Cagney and Lacey* (Chapel Hill: University of North Carolina Press, 1994); Henry Jenkins, *Textual Poachers: Television Fans and Participatory Culture* (New York: Routledge, 1992); Kathryn C. Montgomery, *Target: Prime Time: Advocacy Groups and the Struggle over Entertainment Television* (New York: Oxford University Press, 1989); Charlotte Ryan, *Prime Time Activism: Media Strategies for Grassroots Organizing* (Boston: South End Press, 1991); Ellen Seiter, Hans Borchers, Gabriele Kreutzner, and Eva-Maria Warth, eds., *Remote Control: Television, Audiences, and Cultural Power* (London: Routledge, 1989); Dorothy Collins Swanson, *The Story of Viewers for Quality Television: From Grassroots to Prime Time* (Syracuse, N.Y.: Syracuse University Press, 2000); and Heather Hendershot, *Saturday Morning Censors* (Durham, N.C.: Duke University Press, 1999).

30 Information page (FAQ), Media Jammers website.

31 Jeff Oswald, personal correspondence, 28 February 2001.

Bibliography

Aitkin, D. and Norrie, A. (1973) Talk-back radio and political participation, *Australian Quarterly*, 45(2): 32–8.

Alberoni, F. (1972) 'The powerless elite: theory and sociological research on the phenomena of the stars', in D. McQuail (ed.) *Sociology of Mass Communications: Selected Readings*, Harmondsworth: Penguin.

Anderson, B. (1986) *Imagined Communities*, London: Verso.

Anderson, K. (1993) Oprah and Jo-Jo the dogfaced boy, *Time*, 11 October, p. 94.

Andrejevic, M. (2002) The kinder, gentler gaze of *Big Brother*, in *New Media and Society*, 4(2): 251–70.

Andrejevic, M. (2004) Reality TV and voyeurism, in *Reality TV: The Work of Being Watched*, New York: Rowman & Littlefield.

Ang, I. (1991) *Desperately Seeking the Audience*, London: Routledge.

Arendt, H. (1958/1989) *The Human Condition*, Chicago, IL: University of Chicago Press.

Arnold, J. (2001) Newspapers and daily reading, in M. Lyons and J. Arnold (eds) *A History of the Book in Australia, 1891–1945*, Brisbane: University of Queensland Press.

Arthurs, J. (1989) Technology and gender, *Screen*, 30(1–2): 40–59.

Arthurs, J. (1994) Women and television, in S. Hood (ed.) *Behind the Screens: The Structure of British Television in the Nineties*, London: Lawrence & Wishart.

Arthurs, J. (2004) *Television and Sexuality: Regulation and the Politics of Taste*, Maidenhead: Open University Press.

Attwood, F. (2002) A very British Carnival: women, sex and transgression in Fiesta Magazine, *European Journal of Cultural Studies*, 5(1): 91–105.

Attwood, F. (2005) Tits and ass and porn and fighting, *International Journal of Cultural Studies*, 8(1): 83–100.

Baehr, H. and Dyer, G. (1987) *Boxed in: Women and Television*, London: Pandora.

Bailey, D. (1989) Ghost writers in the sky, *Columbia Journalism Review*, 28(1): 10–11.

Bakhtin, M. (1968/1984) *Rabelais and his World*, (translated H. Iswolsky), Bloomington, IN: Indiana University Press.

Baldwin, E., Longhurst, B., McCracken, S., Ogborn, M. and Smith, G. (eds) (1999/2004) *Introducing Cultural Studies*, revised 1 edn, London: Pearson Education Limited.

Banks, J. (2005) Keeping 'abreast of MTV and Viacom', in J. Wasco (ed.) *A Companion to Television*, Malden: Blackwell.

Barber, S. (1982) The boss don't like swindle make it robbery, *Washington Journalism Review*, July–August, pp. 46–50.

Barker, M. and Brooks, K. (1998) *Knowing Audiences*, Luton: University of Luton Press.

Barnfield, G. (2002) From direct cinema to car wreck video: reality TV and the crisis of confidence, in Institute of Ideas (ed.) *Reality TV: How Real is Real?*, London: Hodder & Stoughton.

Barnett, S. and Gaber, I. (2001) *Westminster Tales: The 21ˢᵗ Century Crisis in British Political Journalism*, London: Continuum.

Barthes, R. (1973) *Mythologies*, London: Paladin.

Barthes, R. (1977) The photographic message, in S. Heath (ed. and trans.) *Image, Music, Text*, New York: Farrar, Straus & Giroux, pp. 15–31.

Batchelor, W. (2004) Police probe over *Jackass* copycat boy, *Press Association*, 21 April.

Baynes, K. (ed.) (1971) *Scoop, Scandal and Strife: A Study of Photography in Newspapers*, London: Lund Humphries.

Bazalgette, P. (2001) 'The Huw Weldon Lecture, *Big Brother* and beyond' at http://www.rts.org.uk/rts/html/magazine/weldon.htm (accessed 3 October 2002).

Becker, K. (1984) Getting the moment: newspaper photographers at work, paper presented at the American Folklore Society Annual Meeting, San Diego.

Becker, K. (1985) Forming a profession: ethical implications of photojournalistic practice on German picture magazines, 1926–1933, *Studies in Visual Communication*, 11(2): 44–60.

Becker, K. (1990) 'The simultaneous rise and fall of photojournalism: a case study of popular culture and the western press', paper presented at Journalism and Popular Culture, Dubrovnik.

Becker, K. (1992) Photojournalism and the tabloid press, in P. Dahlgren and C. Sparks (eds) *Journalism and Popular Culture*, London: Sage, pp. 130–53.

Bell, P. (2001) Real new formats of television: looking at *Big Brother*, in *Media International Australia*, 100: 105–14.

Belsey, A. and Chadwick, R. (eds) (1992) *Ethical Issues in Journalism*, London: Routledge.

Benjamin, W. (1936/1969) The storyteller, in Hannah Arendt (ed.) *Illuminations*, New York: Shocken Books, pp. 83–109.

Benjamin, W. (1936a) 'The work of art in the age of mechanical reproduction', in Hannah Arendt (ed.) *Illuminations*, New York: Shocken Books, pp. 217–52.

Bennett, T. (1983) A thousand and one pleasures: Blackpool pleasure beach, in Formations (ed.) *Formations of Pleasure*, London: Routledge & Kegan Paul, pp. 138–45.

Bennett, T. (1986) Hegemony, ideology, pleasure: Blackpool, in T. Bennett, C. Mercer and J. Woollacott (eds) *Popular Culture and Social Relations*, Buckingham, Open University Press, pp. 135–54.

Benwell, B. (ed.) (2003) *Masculinity and Men's Lifestyle Magazines*, Oxford: Blackwell.

Berkman, M. (1995) Daytime talk shows are fraud-caster, *New York Post*, 4 November.

Berry, D. (ed.) (2000) *Ethics and Media Culture: Practices and Representations*, Oxford: Focal Press.

Billig, M. (1995) *Banal Nationalism*, London: Sage.

Bird, D. A. (1986) 'E.T. star's daddy is a skid-row bum'; 'Goetz gets a break'; 'Doc errs, drug perils mom-to-be': rhetorical and style of selected tabloids, paper presented at Sensationalism and the Media Conference, Ann Arbor, Michigan.

Bird, S. E. (1990) Storytelling on the far side: journalism and the weekly tabloid, *Critical Studies in Mass Communication*, 7(4): 377–89.

Bird, S. E. (1992) *For Enquiring Minds: A Cultural Study of Supermarket Tabloids*, Knoxville: University of Tennessee Press.

Bird, S. E. (1997/2003) News we can use: an audience perspective on the tabloidisation of news in the United States, in V. Nightingale and K. Ross (eds) *Critical Readings:*

Media and Audiences, Maidenhead: Open University Press/McGraw Hill Education, pp. 65–86.

Bird, S. E. and Dardenne, R. (1988) Myth, chronicle and story: exploring the narrative qualities of news, in J. W. Carey (ed.) *Media, Myths, and Narratives: Television and the Press*, Beverley Hills, CA: Sage, pp. 67–87.

Biressi, A. (2001) *Crime, Fear and the Law in True Crime Stories*, London: Palgrave.

Biressi, A. and Nunn, H. (2004) The especially remarkable: celebrity and social mobility in reality TV, *Mediactive*, 2: 44–58.

Biressi, A. and Nunn, H. (2005) *Reality TV: Realism and Revelation*, London: Wallflower Press.

Biressi, A. and Nunn, H. (2007) You are what you eat, unpublished paper at First International Conference on Lifestyle Television: The Big Reveal, Salford University, 27–29 April.

Blumler, J. and Gurevitch, M. (1995) *The Crisis of Public Communication*, London: Routledge.

Blumler, J. and Katz, E. (1974) *The Uses of Mass Communication*, London: Sage.

Bonner, F. (2000) *Ordinary Television*, London: Sage.

Bourdieu, P. (1984) *Distinction: A Social Critique of the Judgement of Taste*, Cambridge, MA: Harvard University Press.

Boyd-Barrett, O. and Rantanen, T. (eds) (1998) *The Globalization of News*, London: Sage.

Brants, K. (1998) Who's afraid of infotainment? *European Journal of Communication*, 30(3): 315–16.

Brenton, S. and Cohen, R. (2003) *Shooting People: Adventures in Reality TV*, London: Verso.

Briggs, P. and Burke, P. (2002) *A Social History of the Media*, Cambridge: Polity.

Brod, H. (ed.) (1987) *The Making of Masculinities: The New Man's Studies*, Boston: Allen & Unwin.

Bromley, M. (1998) Tickle the public : consumerism, in M. Bromley and H. Stephenson (eds) *Sex, Lies and Democracy: The Press and the Public*, Harlow: Longman, pp. 13–24.

Bromley, M. (1998a) The 'tabloiding' of Britain: 'quality' newspapers in the 1990s, in M. Bromley and H. Stephenson (eds) *Sex, Lies and Democracy: The Press and the Public*, Harlow: Longman, pp. 25–38.

Bromley, M. (ed.) (2001) *No News is Bad News: Radio, Television and the Public*, London: Longman.

Bromley, M. and Stephenson, H. (eds) (1998) *Sex, Lies and Democracy: The Press and the Public*, Harlow: Longman.

Bromley, M. and Tumber, H. (1997) From Fleet Street to cyberspace: The British 'popular' press in the late twentieth century, *European Journal of Communication Studies*, 22(3): 365–78.

Brooker, W. and Jermyn, D. (eds) (2003) *The Audience Studies Reader*, London: Routledge.

Bruner, E. M. (1984) The opening up of anthropology, in E. M. Bruner (ed.) *Text, Play, and Story: The Construction and Reconstruction of Self and Society*, Washington DC: American Ethnological Society, pp. 1–16.

Burgin, V. (1986) *The End of Art Theory: Criticism and Postmodernity*, London: Macmillan.

Burke, P. (1978) *Popular Culture in Early Modern Europe*, London: Templeton Smith.

Burroughs, W. (1969) My mother and I would like to know, *Evergreen*, 67, June.

Butler, J. (1993) *Bodies that Matter: On the Discursive Limits of 'Sex'*, London: Routledge.

Calhoun, C. (ed.) (1992) *Habermas and the Public Sphere*, Cambridge, MA: MIT.

Campbell, C. (1995) *Race, Myth and the News*, London: Sage.

Campbell, V. (2004) *Information Age Journalism: Journalism in an International Context*, London: Arnold.

Carnes, C. (1940) *Jimmy Hare, News Photographer*, New York: Macmillan.

Carter, A. (1979) *The Sadeian Woman: An Exercise in Cultural History*, London: Virago.

Carter, A. (1982) Fun fairs, in *Nothing Sacred*, London: Virago, pp. 110–16.

Carter, A. (1995) In pantoland, in *Burning Your Boats: Collected Short Stories*, London: Chatto & Windus, pp. 382–9.

Chambers, Deborah (2004) *Women and Journalism*, London: Routledge.

Chambers, D., Steiner, L. and Fleming, C. (2004) *Women and Journalism*, London: Routledge.

Chaney, D. (1994) *The Cultural Turn: Scene-setting Essays on Contemporary History*, London: Routledge.

Chibnall, S. (1977) *Law and Order News: An analysis of crime reporting in the British Press*, London: Constable.

Chippendale, P and Horrie, C. (1990/1992) *Stick it up your Punter: The Rise and Fall of the Sun*, London: Mandarin.

Coates, J. and Cameron, D. (eds) (1989) *Women in their Speech Communities*, New York: Longman.

Cohan, S. (1997) The bachelor in the bedroom, in *Masked Men: Masculinity and Movies in the Fifties*, Bloomington: Indiana University Press.

Coleman, S. (1998) BBC Radio Ulster's *Talkback* phone-in: public feedback in a divided public space, *Javnost the Public*, 5(2): 8–19.

Collins, A. (2003) *Where Did it All Go Right? Growing Up Normal in the 70s*, London: Ebury Press.

Conboy, M. (2002) *The Press and Popular Culture*, London: Sage.

Conboy, M. (2006) *Tabloid Britain: Constructing a Community Through Language*, London: Routledge.

Connell, I. (1992) Personalities in the popular media, in P. Dahlgren and C. Sparks (eds) *Journalism and Popular Culture*, Newbury Park: Sage, pp. 64–83.

Connell, R. (1995) *Masculinities*, Cambridge: Polity Press.

Cookman, C. (1985) *A Voice is Born*, Durham, NC: National Press Photographers Association.

Corkery, P. (1981) Enquirer: an eye witness account, *Rolling Stone*, (11 June): 19–21 and 62.

Costera Meijer, I. (2001) The public quality of popular journalism: developing a normative framework, *Journalism Studies*, 2(2): 189–205.

Cottle, S. (ed.) (2003) *Media Organization and Production*, London: Sage.

Couldry, N. (2000) *The Place of Media Power: Pilgrims and Witnesses of the Media Age*, London: Routledge.

Coupland, D. (1991) *Generation X: Tales for an Accelerated Culture*, New York: St Martin's Griffin.

Coward, R. (1984) *Female Desire: Women's Sexuality Today*, London: Paladin.

Cranfield, G. (1978) *The Press and Society: From Caxton to Northcliffe*, London: Longman.

Cronkite, W. (1997) More bad news, *Guardian*, 27 January, p. 2.

Croteau, D. and Hoynes, W. (2002) *Media/Society: Industries, Images and Audiences*, 3 edn, Pine Forge: Sage.

Culf, A. (1995) Talk radio told off for obscenity, *Guardian*, 2 May, p. 6.

Culf, A. (1997) BBC faces upheaval in Labour plan, *Guardian*, 22 January, p. 1.

Curran, J. (1977) Capitalism and the control of the press 1800–1975, in J. Curran, M Gurevitch and J. Woollacott (eds) *Mass Communication and Society*, London: Edward Arnold and Open University Press.

Curran, J. (1991a) Rethinking the media as a public sphere, in P. Dahlgren and C. Sparks (eds) *Communication and Citizenship*, London: Routledge.

Curran, J. (1991b) Mass media and democracy: a reappraisal, in J. Curran and M. Gurevitch (eds) *Mass Media and Society*, London: Edward Arnold.

Curran, J. and Gurevitch, M. (eds) (1991) *Mass Media and Society*, London: Edward Arnold.

Curran, J., Gaber, I. and Petley, J. (2005) *Culture Wars: the Media and the British Left*, Edinburgh: Edinburgh University Press.

Curran, J. and Seaton, J. (1991) *Power Without Responsibility*, 4 edn, London: Routledge.

Curran, J. and Seaton, J. (2003) *Power Without Responsibility: The Press, Broadcasting and New Media in Britain*, 6 edn, London: Routledge.

Curran, J. and Sparks, C. (1991) Press and popular culture, *Media, Culture and Society*, 13: 215–37.

Dahlgren, P. (1992) 'Introduction', in P. Dahlgren and C. Sparks, (eds) *Journalism and Popular Culture*, London: Sage, pp. 1–23.

Dahlgren, P. (1995) *Television and the Public Sphere*, London: Sage.

Dahlgren, P. and Sparks, C. (1991) *Communication and Citizenship: Journalism and the Public Sphere*, London: Routledge.

Dahlgren, P. and Sparks, C. (eds) (1992) *Journalism and Popular Culture*, Thousand Oaks, CA: Sage.

Darnton, R. (1975) Writing news and telling stories, in *Daedalus*, 104: 175–94.

Davison, G. (1998a) Bulletin, in G. Davison, J. Hirst and S. MacIntyre (eds) *The Oxford Companion to Australian History*, Melbourne: Oxford University Press, pp. 93–4.

Davison, G. (1998b) Bushman's Bible, in G. Davison, J. Hirst and S. MacIntyre (eds) *The Oxford Companion to Australian History*, Melbourne: Oxford University Press, p. 101.

De Burgh, H. (2000) *Investigative Journalism: Context and Practice*, London: Routledge.

De Certeau, M. (1988) *The Practice of Everyday Life*, Berkeley: University of California Press.

De Cordova, R. (1990) *Picture Personalities: The Emergence of the Star System in America*, Urbana, IL: University of Illinois Press.

DeFleur, M. and Ball-Rokeach, S. (1989) *Theories of Mass Communication*, 5 edn, New York: Longman.

DeLucca, K. and Peeples, J. (2002) From public sphere to public screen: democracy, activism and 'violence' of Seattle, *Critical Studies in Media Communication*, 19(2): 125–51.

Denisoff, R. S. (1988) *Inside MTV*, New Brunswick: Transition.

Derry, M. (1993) Culture jamming: hacking, slashing and sniping in the empire of signs, *Open Magazine Pamphlet Series*, http://www.levity.com/markderry/culturjam.html.

Desjardins, M. (2002) Maureen O'Hara's confidential life: recycling stars through gossip and moral biography, J. Thumin (ed.) *Small Screen, Big Ideas: Television in the 1950s*, London: IB Tauris, pp. 118–30.

Deuze, M. (2002) *Journalists in the Netherlands*, Amsterdam: Aksant Academic Publishers.

Deuze, M. (2005a) Popular journalism and professional ideology: tabloid reporters speak out, *Media, Culture and Society*, 27(6): 861–82.

Deuze, M. (2005b) What is journalism? Professional identity and ideology of journalists reconsidered, *Journalism: Theory, Practice and Criticism*, 6(4): 443–65.

Docker, J. (1994) *Postmodernism and Popular Culture: A Cultural History*, Cambridge: Cambridge University Press.

Donahue, P. (1979) *Donahue: My Own Story*, New York: Simon & Schuster.

Douglas, S. J. (1999) *Listening In: Radio and the American Imagination*, New York: Times Books.

Dovey, J. (2000) *Freakshow: First Person Media and Factual Television*, London: Pluto.

Dugdale, J. (1995a) Seeing and believing, *Guardian*, 4 September, pp. 12–13.

Dunbar, R. (1998) *Grooming, Gossip and the Evolution of Language*, Cambridge, MA: Harvard University Press.

Dunkley, C. (2002) It's not new and it's not clever, in Institute of Ideas (ed.) *Reality TV: How Real is Real?* London: Hodder & Stoughton.

Dworkin, A. (1999) *Pornography: Men Possessing Women*, London: Women's Press.

Dyer, C. and Hauserman, N. (1987) Electronic coverage of the courts: exceptions to exposure, *The Georgetown Law Journal*, 75(5): 1634–700.

Dyer, R. (1979/1998) *Stars*, London: BFI.

Dyer, R. (1985) Male sexuality in the media, in A. Metcalf and M. Humphries (eds) *The Sexuality of Men*, London: Pluto, pp. 28–43.

Dyer, R. (1986) *Heavenly Bodies: Film Stars and Society*, London: BFI.

Dyer, R. (1992a) Coming to terms: gay pornography, in *Only Entertainment*, London: Routledge, pp. 121–34.

Dyer, R. (1992b) Entertainment and utopia, *Only Entertainment*, London: Routledge, pp. 17–34.

Dyke, G. (1994) And now the bad news, extracts from the Mactaggart Lecture 1994, *Guardian*, 27 August, p. 27.

Economist (US edition) (2004) 'Bonnie Fuller, star of celebrity journalism', 7 August 2004, http://web.lexis-nexis.com/executive/form?-index=exec_en.html&_lang=en&ut= 3322908376, (accessed 19 April 2006).

Edey, M. (1978) *Great Photographic Essays From Life*, New York: Little, Brown.

Edom, C. (1976) *Photojournalism: Principles and Practices*, Dubuque, IA: William C. Brown.

Edwards, T. (1997) *Men in the Mirror: Men's Fashion, Masculinity and Consumer Society*, London: Cassell.

Eldridge, J. (2000) The contribution of the Glasgow media Group to the study of television and print journalism, *Journalism Studies*, 1(1): 113–18.

Elliot, P. (1972) Uses and gratifications research: a critique and sociological alternative, in D. McQuail (ed.) *Sociology of Mass Communications*, Harmondsworth: Penguin, Ch. 12.

Ellis, J. (1992) *Visible Fictions: Cinema, Television, Video*, London: Routledge.

Ellis, J. (2001) Mirror, mirror, *Sight and Sound*, 11(8): 8.

Elwell, S. (1985) Editors and social change: a case study of *Once A Week* (1859–80), in J. Wiener (ed.) *Innovators and Preachers: The Role of the Editor in Victorian England*, Westport CT and London: Greenwood Press, pp. 23–42.

Emery, E. (1962) *The Press and America: An Interpretive History of Journalism*, 2 edn, Englewood Cliffs, NJ: Prentice-Hall.

Emery, E. and Emery, M. (1978) *The Press and America: An Interpretative History of the Mass Media*, Engelwood Cliffs, NJ: Prentice Hall.

Engel, M. (1996a) Papering over the cracks, *Guardian*, 3 October, pp. 2–3.

Engel, M. (1996b) *Tickle the Public: One Hundred Years of the Popular Press*, London: Victor Gollancz.

Eskildsen, U. (1978) Photography and the neue sachlichkeit movement, in D. Mellor (ed.) *Germany: The New Photography, 1927–33*, London: Arts Council of Great Britain, pp. 101–12.

Esser, F. (1999) Tabloidization of news: a comparative analysis of Anglo-American and German Press Journalism, in *European Journal of Communication*, 14(3): 291–324.

Evans, J. (2005) 'Celebrity, Media and History', in J. Evans and D. Hesmondhalgh (eds) *Understanding Media: Inside Celebrity*, Maidenhead: Open University Press/McGraw-Hill Education, pp. 11–55.

Evans, J. and Hesmondhalgh, D. (eds) (2005) *Understanding Media: Inside Celebrity*, Maidenhead: Open University Press.

Fabian, A. (1993) Making a commodity of truth: speculations on the career of Bernarr MacFadden, *American Literary History*, 5(1): 51–76.

Fallows, J. (1996) *Breaking the News: How the Media Undermine American Democracy*, New York: Pantheon Books.

Faludi, S. (1992) *Backlash: The Undeclared War Against Women*, London: Vintage.

Faludi, S. (1995) The money shot, *New Yorker*, 30 October, pp. 64–87.

Featherstone, M. (ed.) (1993) *Global Culture: Nationalism, Globalization and Modernity*, London: Sage.

Feinstein, S. (2000) *The 1980s From Ronald Reagan to MTV*, Berkeley Heights: Enslow.

Ferguson, M. (1983) *For Ever Feminine: Women's Magazines and the Cult of Femininity*, London: Heinemann.

Fiesta (1999) Volume 33, Issue 11, Witham Gallaxy Publications.

Fiske, J. (1982) *Introduction to Communication Studies*, London: Methuen.

Fiske, J. (1989) *Understanding Popular Culture*, Boston: Unwin Hyman.

Fiske, J. (1992) Popularity and the politics of information, in P. Dahlgren and C. Sparks (eds) *Journalism and Popular Culture*, Newbury Park: Sage, pp. 45–64.

Fiske, J. (1993) *Power Plays, Power Works*, London: Verso.

Fiske, J. (1998) *Media Matters: Everyday Culture and Political Change*, Minneapolis: University of Minnesota Press.

Fiske, J. and Hartley, J. (1978) *Reading Television*, London: Methuen.

Foster, H. (1985) Introduction, in H. Foster (ed.) *Postmodern Culture*, London: Pluto, pp. xi–xii.

Foucault, M. (1977) What is an author? in *Language, Counter-memory, Practice: Selected Essays and Interviews*, Ithaca, NY: Cornell University Press, pp. 113–38.

Franklin, B. (1996) Why the sun does not shine on Mr Major, *Parliamentary Brief*, March, pp. 18–21.

Franklin, B. (1997) *Newszak and News Media*, London: Edward Arnold.

Franklin, B. (2005) McJournalism. The local press and the McDonaldization thesis, in Stuart Allan (ed.) *Journalism: Critical Issues*, Maidenhead: Open University Press/McGraw Hill, pp: 137–150.

Franks, S. (1999) *Having None of It: Women, Men and the Future of Work*, London: Granta.

Fraser, N. (1989) What's critical about critical theory? The case of Habermas and gender, in N. Fraser (ed.) *Unruly Practices: Power, Discourse and Gender in Contemporary Social Theory*, Minneapolis: University of Minnesota Press.

Fraser, N. (1992) Rethinking the public sphere: a contribution to the critique of actually existing democracy, in C. Calhoun (ed.) *Habermas and the Public Sphere*, Cambridge, MA: MIT Press, pp. 109–42.

Freedman, D. (2004) 'The *Daily Mirror* and the war on Iraq: profits, politics and product differentiation,' *Mediactive: Media War*, 3: 95–108.

Freud, S. (1919/1963) A child is being beaten, in *Sexuality and the Psychology of Love*, New York: Collier.

Freud, S. (1924/1963) The economic problem of masochism, in *General Psychological Theory*, New York: Collier.

Freund, G. (1980) *Photography and Society*, London: Gordon Fraser.

Frost, C. (2000) *Media Ethics and Self-Regulation*, Harlow: Longman.

Gaber, I. and Barnett, S. (1993) 'Changing patterns in broadcast news', unpublished paper at the annual conference of the *Voice of the Listener and Viewer*, November.

Gable, N. (1995) *Gossip, Power and the Culture of Celebrity*, London: Macmillan.

Gamson, J. (1994) *Claims to Fame: Celebrity in Contemporary America*, Berkeley, University of California Press.

Gamson, J. (1998/1999) *Freaks Talk Back: Tabloid Talk Shows and Sexual Non-Conformity*, Chicago: University of Chicago Press.

Gamson, J. (2001) 'The assembly line of greatness: celebrity in twentieth-century America', in C. L. Harrington and D. D. Bielby (eds) *Popular Culture: Production and Consumption*, Oxford: Blackwell, pp. 259–82.

Garnham, N. (1986) The media and the public sphere, in P. Golding, G. Murdock and P Schlesinger (eds) *Communicating Politics: Mass Communications and the Political Process*, New York: Holmes & Meier.

Geraghty, C. (2000) Re-examining stardom: questions of texts, bodies and performance, in C. Gledhill and L. Williams (eds) *Reinventing Film Studies*, London: Arnold, pp. 183–201.

Gidal, T. (1973) *Modern Photojournalism: Origin and Evolution 1910–1933*, New York: Collier Books.

Giddens, A. (1987) *Social Theory and Modern Sociology*, Cambridge: Polity Press.

Gill, P. (2003) Taking it personally: male suffering in *8 MM*, *Camera Obscura*, 52: 157–87.

Gillespie, M. (1995) *Television, Ethnicity and Cultural Change*, London: Routledge.

Gitling, T. (1990) Blips, bites and savvy talk: television's impact on American politics, in *Dissent*, Winter: 18–26.

Glencross, D. (1994) 'Superhighways and supermarkets', a speech to the *Royal Television Society*, 8 March.

Glynn, G. (2000) *Tabloid Culture: Trash Taste, Popular Power and the Transformation of American Television*, Durham: Duke University Press.

Golding, P. and Elliott, P. (1979) *Making the News*, London: Longman.

Goldstein, R. (1995) The devil in Ms Jones: trash TV and the discourse of desire, *Village Voice*, 21 November.

Goldstein, T. (1985) *The News at Any Cost: How Journalists Compromise their Ethics to Shape the News*, New York: Simon & Schuster.

Goodman, G. (1994) The Power to say 'no', *British Journalism Review*, 5(4): 1–4.

Gough-Yates, A. (2003) *Understanding Women's Magazines: Publishing Markets and Reader-ships*, London: Routledge.

Gourley, J. (1981) 'I killed Gig Young' and other confessions from inside the *National Enquirer*, *The Washington Monthly*, September, pp. 32–8.

Gray, A. (1992) *Video Playtime: the Gendering of a Leisure Technology*, London: Comedia/ Routledge.

Gray, F. (1994) 'A body, a bosom and a joke? The actress and the Carry Ons', unpublished paper at Leicester Film and Television Summer School.

Gray, J. (2002) Ulrika is a sign that we've got it all; Celebrity sells. But it's more than a marketing tool: it is an expression of our unprecedented democracy and prosperity – and boredom, *New Statesman*, 28 October 2002, http://web.lexis-nexis.com/executive/print?dd_jobType=spew&_m=e23d9331f107fef, accessed 18 April 2006).

Gregson, N., Brooks, K. and Crewe, L. (2001) Bjorn Again? Rethinking 70s revivalism through the reappropriation of 70s clothing, in *Fashion Theory*, 5(1): 3–28.

Green, H.M. (1984) *A History of Australian Literature, Vol 1*, London: Angus & Robertson.

Greenberg, B. and Smith, S. (1995) *The Content of Television Talk Shows: Topics, Guests, and Interactions*, report prepared for the Henry. J. Kaiser Family Foundation by the Depart-ments of Communication and Telecommunication, Michigan State University.

Greer, G. (2001) We are Big Brother, in H. Mark (ed.) *Scum at the Top: Australia's Journal of Political Character Assassination*, 5(13): at http://members.optushome.com.au/thesquiz/greer.htm (accessed 3 October 2002).

Griffin, S. (1982) *Pornography and Silence: Culture's Revenge Against Nature*, New York: Harper & Row.

Griffin-Foley, B. (1999) *The House of Packer: The Making of a Media Empire*, Sydney: Allen & Unwin.

Griffin-Foley, B. (2002) The crumbs are better than a feast elsewhere: on Australian On Fleet Street, *Journalism History*, 28(1): 26–37.

Griffen-Foley, B. (2004) From *Tit-Bits* to *Big Brother*: a century of audience participation, in *Media, Culture and Society*, 26(4): 533–48.

Gripsrud, J. (1992) The aesthetics and politics of melodrama, in P. Dahlgren and C. Sparks (eds) *Journalism and Popular Culture*, London: Sage.

Gripsrud, J. (2000) Tabloidization, popular journalism and democracy, in C. Sparks and J. Tulloch (eds) *Tabloid Tales: Global Debates Over Media Standards*, New York: Rowman & Littlefield, pp. 285–300.

Grossberg, L. (1989) 'MTV', in S. Jhally and I. Angus (eds) *Cultural Politics in Contemporary America*, New York: Routledge.

Grossberg, L. (1996) On postmodernism and articulation: an interview with Stuart Hall, in D. Morley and K.-H. Chen (eds) *Start Hall: Critical Dialogue in Cultural Studies*, London: Routledge, 131–50.

Gross, L., Katz, J. and Ruby, J. (eds) (2003) *Image Ethics in the Media Digital Age*, Minneapolis: University of Minnesota Press.

Grose, R. (1989) *The Sun-sation*, London: Angus & Robertson.

GUMG (1976a) *Bad News*, London: Routledge & Kegan Paul.

GUMG (1976b) *More Bad News*, London: Routledge and Kegan Paul.

Habermas, J. (1989) *The Structural Transformation of the Public Sphere*, Cambridge: Polity Press.

Hall, S. (1970) Encoding/decoding, in S. Hall, D. Hobson, A. Lowe and P. Willis (eds) *Culture, Media, Language*, London: Hutchinson/CCCS, pp. 197–208.

Hall, S. (1972) The social eye of the *Picture Post*, in *Working Papers in Cultural Studies*, Number 2, Birmingham: CCCS.

Hall, S. (1973) The determinations of news photographs, in S. Cohen and J. Young (eds) *The Manufacture of News*, London: Constable, pp. 176–90.

Hall, S. and Jacques, M. (1983) *The Politics of Thatcherism*, London: Lawrence & Wishart.

Hall, S., Critcher, C., Jefferson, T., Clarke, J. and Robert, B. (1978) *Policing the Crisis: Mugging, the State and law and Order*, London: Palgrave Macmillan.

Hallin, D. (1992) The passing of the 'high modernism' of American Journalism, *Journal of Communication*, 42(3): 14–25.

Hård af Segerstad, T. (1974) 'Dagspressens bildbruk: En funktionsanalys av bildutbudet i svenska dagstidningar 1900–1970' (Photography and the Daily Press), doctoral dissertation, Uppsala University.

Hardy, S. (1998) *The Reader, the Author, his Woman and her Lover*, London: Cassell.

Harris, R. (1983) *Gotcha! The Media, the Government and the Falklands Crisis*, London: Faber & Faber.

Hartley, J. (1992) *The Politics of Pictures: The Creation of the Public in the Age of Popular Media*, London: Routledge.

Hartley, J. (1996) *Popular Reality: Journalism, Modernity, Popular Culture*, London: Edward Arnold.

Hartley, J. (1999) *Uses of Television*, London: Routledge.

Hassner, R. (1977) *Bilder För Miljoner (Pictures for the Millions)*, Stockholm: Rabén & Sjögren.

Hatton, J. A. (1997) 'True stories: working-class mythology, American confessional culture, and *True Story Magazine*, 1919–1929', PhD thesis, Cornell University.

Head, S. W. (1976) *Broadcasting in America*, Boston: Houghton Mifflin Co.

Healey, M. (1995) Were we being served? Homosexual representation in popular British comedy, in *Screen*, 36(3): 243–56.

Heller, Z. (1999) Girl Columns, in S. Glover (ed.) *Secrets of the Press: Journalists on Journalism*, Harmondsworth: Penguin, pp. 10–17.

Herd, H. (1952) *The March of Journalism: The Story of the British Press 1622 to the Present Day*, London: George Allen & Unwin.

Hermes, J. (1995) *Reading Women's Magazines: An Analysis of Everyday Media Use*, Cambridge: Polity.

Hesmondhalgh, D. (ed.) (2005) *Media Production*, Maidenhead: Open University Press/ McGraw-Hill Education.

Hesmondhalgh, D. (2007) *The Cultural Industries*, London: Sage.

Hilmes, M. (1997) *Radio Voices: American Broadcasting, 1922–1952*, Minneapolis: University of Minnesota Press.

Hobson, D. (1980) Housewives and the mass media, in P. Marris and S. Thornham (eds) (1996/ 1997) *Media Studies: A Reader*, Edinburgh: Edinburgh University Press, pp. 307–20.

Hogan, P. (2002) *Parenting Made Difficult: Notes from the Alphabet Soup of Fatherhood*, London: Piccadilly Press.

Hoggart, R. (1957) *The Uses of Literacy*, London: Chatto & Windus.

Holland, P. (1987) When a woman reads the news, in H. Baehr and G. Dyer (eds) *Boxed In: Women and Television*, London: Pandora, pp. 133–49.

Holland, P. (1997a) 'Sweet it is to scan': personal photographs and popular photography, in L. Wells (ed.) *Photography: A Critical Introduction*, London: Routledge.

Holland, P. (1998) The politics of the smile: 'soft news' and the sexualisation of the popular press, in C. Carter, G. Branston and S. Allan (eds) *News, Gender and Power*, London: Routledge.

Hollingshead, T. (2003) 3 cited in MTV copycat stunt, in *Deseret Morning News*, 24 July.

Hollows, J. (2000) *Feminism, Femininity and Popular Culture*, Manchester: Manchester University Press.

Hollows, J. (2003) Oliver's Twist: Leisure, Labour and domestic masculinity in *The Naked Chef*, *International Journal of Cultural Studies*, 6(2): 22–248.

Holmes, S. and Jermyn, D. (eds) (2004) *Understanding Reality Television*, London: Routledge.

Holmes, S. (2004a) 'All you've got to worry about is having a cup of tea and doing a bit of sunbathing': approaching celebrity in *Big Brother*, in S. Holmes and D. Jermyn (eds) *Understanding Reality Television*, London: Routledge: pp. 111–35.

Holmes, S. (2004b) Reality goes pop! Reality tv, popular music and narratives of stardom in *Pop Idol*, *Television and New Media*, 5(2): 147–72.

Hornby, N. (2003) *About a Boy*, London: Penguin.

Horrie, C. and Nathan, A. (1999) *Live TV, Telly Brats and Topless Darts: The Uncut Story of Tabloid TV*, London: Pocket Books.

Hughes, J. (2001) Not really, *Eureka Street*, 11(3): 46.

Hunt, L. (1998) *British Low Culture: From Safari Suits to Sexploitation*, London: Routledge.

Hurley, G. and McDougall, A. (1971) *Visual Impact in Print*, Chicago, IL: Visual Impact.

Hutchings, P. (1986) *Frenzy*: a return to Britain, in C. Barr (ed.) *All Our Yesterdays: 90 years of British Cinema*, London: BFI.

Inglis, K. (1983) *This is the ABC: The Australian Broadcasting Commission 1932–1983*, Melbourne: Melbourne University Press.

Jackson, K. (2001) *George Newnes and the New Journalism in Britain 1880–1910: Culture and Profit*, Aldershot: Ashgate.

Jackson, P. (1991) The Cultural Politics of Masculinity: towards a social geography, *Transactions, Institute of British Geographers*, 24: 98–108.

Jackson, P., Stevenson, N. and Brooks, K. (2001) *Making Sense of Men's Magazines*, London: Polity.

Jameson, F. (1991) *Postmodernism, or the Cultural Logic of Late Capitalism*, London: Sage.

Jancovich, M. (2001) Naked ambitions: pornography, taste and the problem of the middle-brow, *Scope: An Online Journal of Film Studies*, June, http://nottingham.ac.uk/film/journal.

Jancovich, M. (2002) Placing sex: sexuality, taste and middlebrow culture on the reception of *Playboy* magazine, in the online journal, *Intensities: The Journal of Cult Media*, http://www.cult-media.com/issue2/Ajanc.html.

Jarvis, J. (1994) Ricki Lake, *TV Guide*, 2 July, p. 7.

Jensen, K. (1986) *Making Sense of the News: Toward a Theory and Empirical Model for the Study of Mass Communication*, Århus, Denmark: Århus University Press.

Jermyn, D. (2007) *Crime Watching: Investigating Real Crime TV*, London: IB Tauris.

Johannesson, L. (1982) *Xylografi och pressbild* (*Wood-engraving and Newspaper Illustration*), Stockholm: Nordiska museets Handlingar, p. 97.

Johnson, R. (2000) *Cash for Comment: The Seduction of Journo Culture*, Sydney: Pluto.

Jones, C. (1995) *Something in the Air: A History of Radio in Australia*, Sydney: Kangaroo Press.

Jones, D. (1990) Gossip: Notes on women's oral culture, in D. Cameron (ed.) *The Feminist Critique of Language*, London: Routledge.

Jönsson, A. and Örnebring, H. (2004) 'Tabloid journalism and the public sphere: a historical perspective on tabloid journalism', in *Journalism Studies*, 5(2).

Jordan, M. (1983) Carry on . . . follow that stereotype, in J. Curran and V. Porter (eds) *British Cinema History*, London: Weidenfeld & Nicolson, pp. 312–27.

Kahan, R. (1968) 'The antecedents of American photojournalism', PhD dissertation, University of Wisconsin.

Kaplan, J. (1995) Are talk shows out of control? *TV Guide*, 1 April, pp. 10–15.

Katz, E. and Lazarsfeld, P. (1955) *Personal Influence*, Glencoe, IL: The Free Press.

Katz, J. (1987) What makes crime 'news'? *Media, Culture and Society*, 1(9): 47–75.

Keane, J. (1991) *The Media and Democracy*, Cambridge: Polity Press.

Kellner, D. (1995) *Media Culture: Cultural Studies, Identity and Politics Between the Modern and the Postmodern*, London: Routledge.

Kellner, D. (2000) Habermas, the public sphere, and democracy: a critical intervention, in L. Hahn (ed.) *Perspectives on Habermas*, Chicago: Open Court, pp. 259–87.

Kellner, D. (2003) *Media Spectacle*, London: Routledge.

Kern, S. (1983) *The Culture of Time and Space, 1880–1918*, Cambridge, MA: Harvard University Press.

Kilborn, R. (1994) How real can you get? Recent developments in 'reality' television, *European Journal of Communication*, 9: 421–39.

King, B. (2003) Embodying an elastic self: the parametrics of contemporary stardom, in T. Austin and M. Barker (eds) *Contemporary Hollywood Stardom*, London: Arnold, pp. 29–44.

Kipnis, L. (1996) *Bound and Gagged: Pornography and the Politics of Fantasy in America*, New York: Grove.

Kipnis, L. (2005) (Male) Desire and (Female) Disgust: reading *Hustler* in Raiford Guins and Omayra Zaragoza Cruz (eds) *Popular Culture: A Reader*, London: Sage, pp. 223–40.

Kirche, C. (1990) The disruption of glamour: gender and MTV, *Platt Valley Review*, Winter: 18(1): 40–7.

Klein, N. (1999) *No Logo*, New York: Picador.

Kneale, D. (1988) Titillating channels, *Wall Street Journal* 18 May, pp. 1, 15.

Kobre, K. (1980) *Photojournalism: The Professionals' Approach*, Summerville, MA: Curtin & London.

Kovach, B. and Rosenstiel, T. (2001) *The Elements of Journalism*, New York: Crown Publishers.

Kronker, D. (2000) 'Web interaction on *Big Brother* could alter reality tv', in *Miami Herald*, 5 October, http://www.herald.com/content/tue/entertainment/tv/digdocs/077750.htm.

Kuhn, A. (1985) Lawless seeing, *The Power of the Image: Essays on Representation and Sexuality*, London: Routledge & Kegan Paul, pp. 19–47.

Kuhn, A. (1995) *Family Secrets: Acts of Memory and Imagination*, London: Verso.

Kunzel, R. (1995) Pulp fictions and problem girls: reading and rewriting single pregnancy in the postwar United States, *American Historical Review*, 100(5): 1465–87.

Lacan, J. (1989) Kant with Sade, *October*, 51 (Winter), 55–75.

Lacan, J. (1998) *The Four Fundamental Concepts of Psychoanalysis*, The Seminar of Jacques Lacan, Book 11, New York: Norton.

Langer, J. (1981) Television's 'personality system', *Media, Culture and Society*, 3(1) 351–65.

Langer, J. (1992) Truly awful news on television, in P. Dahlgren and C. Sparks (eds) *Journalism and Popular Culture*, London: Sage, pp. 113–29.

Langer, J. (1998) *Tabloid Television: Popular Journalism and the 'Other news'*, London: Routledge.

Law, I. (2002) *Race in the News*, London: Palgrave.

Lawler, S. (2000) Escape and escapism: representing working-class women, in S. Munt (ed.) *Cultural Studies and the Working Class: Subject to Change*, London: Cassell.

Lawson, S. (1969) Jules Francis Archibald, in D. Pike (ed.) *Australian Dictionary of Biography*, Vol 3, Melbourne: Melbourne University Press.

Lawson, S. (1987) *The Archibald Paradox: A Strange Case of Authorship*, Melbourne: Penguin.

Lawson, S. (1999) Print circus: *The Bulletin* from 1880 to Federation, in A. Kurthoys and J. Schultz (eds) *Journalism: Print, Politics and Popular Culture*, Brisbane: University of Queensland Press.

Lazarsfeld, P., Berelson, B. and Gaudet, H. (1944/1968) *The People's Choice: How the Voter Makes up His Mind in a Presidential Campaign*, 3 edn, New York: Columbia University Press.

Leavis, F. R. and Thompson, D. (1964) *Culture and Environment: The Training of Critical Awareness*, London: Chatto & Windus.

LeBesco, K. (2004) Got to be real: mediating gayness on *Survivor*, in S. Murray and L. Ouellette (eds) *Reality TV: Remaking Television Culture*, New York: New York University Press, pp. 271–87.

Leroy, M. (1993) *Pleasure: The Truth about Female Sexuality*, London: HarperCollins.

Levin, J. and Arluke, A. (1987) *Gossip: The Inside Scoop*, New York: Plenum Press.

Lewis, L. (1990) *Gender Politics and MTV: Voicing the Difference*, Philadelphia: Temple University.

Lewis, J., Inthorn, S. and Wahl-Jorgensen, K. (2005) *Citizens or Consumers? What the Media Tell Us about Political Participation*, Maidenhead: Open University Press.

Littler, J. (2004) Making fame ordinary: intimacy, reflexivity and 'keeping it real', *Mediactive*, 2: 8–25.

Livingstone, S. and Lunt, P. (1994) *Talk on Television: Audience Participation and Public Debate*, London: Routledge.

Llewellyn-Smith, C. (2002) *Pop Life: A Journey by Sofa*, London: Sceptre.

Lovell, A. (2003) I went in search of Deborah Kerr, Jodie Foster and Juliane Moore but got waylaid, in T. Austin and M. Barker (eds) *Contemporary Hollywood Stardom*, London: Arnold, pp. 259–70.

Lull, J. (2000) *Media, Communication, Culture: A Global Approach*, Cambridge: Polity Press.

Lumby, C. (2001a) The future of journalism, in S. Cunningham and G. Turner (eds) *The Media and Communications in Australia*, Sydney: Allen & Unwin.

Lumby, C. (2001b) The naked Truth, *Bulletin*, 29 May, 42–4.

Lyotard, J. F. (1984) *The Postmodern Condition*, Manchester: Manchester University Press.

Macdonald, M. (1998) Politicizing the Personal: Women's Voices in British Television Documentary, in C. Carter, G. Branston and S. Allan (eds.) *News, Gender and Power*, London: Routledge.

Macdonald, M. (2000) Rethinking personalisation in current affairs journalism, in C. Sparks and J. Tulloch (eds) *Tabloid Tales: Global Debates over Media Standards*, Lanham, MD: Rowman & Littlefield.

MacFadden, M. and Gauvreau, E. (1953) *Dumbbells and Carrot Strips: the Story of Bernarr MacFadden*, New York: Holt.

Madger, T. (2004) The end of TV 101: reality programs, formats, and the new business of television, in S. Murray and L. Ouellette (eds) *Reality TV: Remaking Television Culture*, pp. 137–56.

Marshall, P. D. (1997) *Celebrity and Power: Fame in Contemporary Context*, Minneapolis: University of Minnesota Press.

Martin, P. (1997) The sad tale of Mr Fox, *Observer Life*, 16 February.

Marwick, A. (1982) *British Society Since 1945*, Harmondsworth: Penguin.

Marchand, R. (1985) *Advertising the American Dream: Making Way for Modernity, 1920–1940*, Berkeley, CA: University of California Press.

Mayes, T. (2000) Submerging in 'Therapy News', *British Journalism Review*, 1(4): 30–5.

McChesney, R. (1999) *Rich Media, Poor Democracy*, Champaign, IL: University of Illinois Press.

McGrath, T. (1996) *MTV: The Making of a Revolution*, Philadelphia: Running Press Book Publishers.

McGuigan, J. (1992) *Cultural Populism*, London: Routledge.

McHale, B. (1989) *Postmodernist Fiction*, London: Routledge.

McLachlan, S. and Golding, P. (2000) Tabloidization in the British Press, in C. Sparks and J. Tulloch (eds) *Tabloid Tales: Global Debates Over Media Standards*, New York: Rowman & Littlefield, pp. 75–90.

McManus, J. (1992) What kind of commodity is news? *Communications Research*, 19(6): 780–812.

McManus, J. (1994) *Market Driven Journalism*, London: Sage.

McNair, B. (1994) *News and Journalism in the UK*, Routledge: London.

McNair, B. (1996) *Mediated Sex: Pornography and Postmodern Culture*, London: Arnold.

McNair, B. (1998/2001) *The Sociology of Journalism*, London: Arnold.

McNair, B. (2000) *Journalism and Democracy: An Evaluation of the Political Public Sphere*, London: Routledge.

McNair, B. (2002) *Striptease Culture: Sex, Media and the Democratisation of Desire*, London: Routledge.

McNair, B. (2003) *News and Journalism in the UK*, 4 edn, Routledge: London.

McQuail, D., Blumler, J. G. and Brown, J. R. (1972) 'The television audience: a revised perspective, in D. McQuail (ed.) *Sociology of Mass Communications*, Harmondsworth: Penguin, Ch. 7, pp. 135–65.

McRobbie, A. (1991) 'Dance narratives and fantasies of achievement', in *Feminism and Youth Culture: From Jackie to Just Seventeen*, Basingstoke: Macmillan Education.

McRobbie, A. (1997) Pecs and penises: the meaning of girlie culture, *Soundings*, 5: 157–66.

McRobbie, A. (2004) Post-feminism and popular culture, *Feminist Media Studies*, 4: 255–64.

Medhurst, A. (1992) Carry on camp, *Sight and Sound*, August, pp. 16–19.

Medhurst, A. (1996) Music hall and British Cinema, in C. Barr (eds) *All Our Yesterdays: 90 Years of British Cinema*, London: BFI.

Medhurst, A. and Tuck, L. (1982) The gender game, in J. Cook (ed.) *Television Situation Comedy*, BFI Dossier, No 17, London: BFI.

Meijer, L. (1999) Roddeljournalistiek in Nederland, in *Het Gouden Pennetje*, Amsterdam: Balans, pp. 41–9.

Merton, Robert K. (1946/1971) *Mass Persuasion: The Social Psychology of a War Bond Drive*, Westport, CT: Greenwood Press Publishers.

Methven, N. (1997) 5 news audience peaks at half a million viewers, *Press Gazette*, 18 April, p. 2.

Mhando, M. (2001) *Big Brother*: conniving lives as public events, *Australian Screen Education*, 28: 184–7.

Miller, T. (1993) Radio, in S. Cunningham and G. Turner (eds) *The Media in Australia: Industries, Texts, Audiences*, Sydney: Allen & Unwin, pp. 41–58.

Montgomery, R. (1996) The lost collections, in *Australian Book Collector*, 70 (February): 22–3.

Montgomery, R. (2000) 'We didn't know we were part of History': adolescent girls, reading and the second world war in Australia, *Oral History Association of Australia Journal*, 22: 54–9.

Moores, S. (2005) *Media/Theory: Thinking about Media and Communications*, London: Routledge.

Morgan, J. (1996) Marr hits at 'Waddling, transvestite, giggling' broadsheet rivals, *Press Gazette*, 18 October, p. 14.

Morley, D. (1980) *The Nationwide Audience*, London: BFI.

Morley, D. (1983) Cultural transformations: the politics of resistance, in H. Davis and P. Walton (eds) *Language, Image, Media*, Oxford: Blackwell, pp. 104–17.

Morse, M. (1983) Sport on television: replay and display, in E. A. Kaplan (ed.) *Regarding Television*, Los Angeles: AFI/University Publications of America, pp. 44–66.

Mort, F. (1996) *Cultures of Consumption: Masculinities and Social Space in Late Twentieth Century Britain*, London: Routledge.

Mulvey, L. (1975) Visual pleasure and narrative cinema, *Screen*, 16(3): 618.

Mulvey, L. (1975/1989) Visual pleasure and narrative cinema, in *Visual and Other Pleasures*, London: Macmillan.

Mulvey, L. (1975/1990) Visual pleasure and narrative cinema, in P. Erens (ed.) *Issues in Feminist Film Criticism*, Bloomington: Indiana University Press.

Munson, W. (1993) *All Talk: The Talkshow in Media Culture*, Philadelphia: Temple University Press.

Murdock, G. (2000) Digital futures: European television in the age of convergence, in J. Wieten, P. Dahlgren and G. Murdock (eds) *Television Across Europe: A Comparative Introduction*, London: Sage.

Murray, S. and Ouellette, L. (eds) (2004) *Reality TV: Remaking Television Culture*, New York: New York University Press.

Nead, L. (1992) *The Female Nude: Art, Obscenity and Sexuality*, London: Routledge.

Nightingale, V. (1996) *Studying the Audience: The Shock of the Real*, London: Routledge.

Nightingale, V. and Ross, K. (2003) *Critical Readings: Media Audiences*, Maidenhead: Open University Press.

Nixon, S. (1996) *Hard Looks: Masculinities, Spectatorship and Contemporary Consumption*, London: UCL Press.

Norris, C. (1992) *Uncritical Theory*, London: Lawrence & Wishart.

Norris, P. (ed.) (1997) *Women, Media and Politics*, New York: Oxford University Press.

Nuttall, J. and Carmichael, R. (1977) *Common Factors/Vulgar Factions*, London: Routledge & Kegan Paul.

O'Brien, D. (1982) *The Weekly*, Melbourne: Penguin.

O'Hagan, S. (1996) Here comes the New Lad! in D. Jones (ed.) *Sex, Power and Travel: Ten Years of Arena*, London: Virgin Publishing.

Ohrn, K. and Hardt, H. (1981) Camera reporters at work: the rise of the photo essay in Weimar Germany and the United States, paper presented at the Convention of the American Studies Association, Memphis, TN.

Orwell, G. (1941/1950) The Art of Donald McGill, in *Decline of the English Murder and Other Essays*, Harmondsworth: Penguin.

Orwell, G. (1946/1950) Decline of the English murder, in *Decline of the English Murder and Other Essays*, Harmondsworth: Penguin.

Overington, C. (1999) 'Talk back radio' in *News Extra, The Age*, 23 October.

Paletz, D. (1998) *The Media in American Politics*, New York: Longman.

Palmer, G. (2003) *Discipline and Liberty: Television and Governance*, Manchester: Manchester University Press.

Palmer, G. (2005) The undead: life on the D-list, *Westminster Papers in Communication and Culture*, 2(2): 37–53.

Papacharissi, Z. (2002) The virtual sphere: the internet as a public sphere, *New Media and Society*, 4(1): 9–27.

Parker, R. and Pollock, G. (1981) *Old Mistresses: Women, Art and Ideology*, London: Routledge & Kegan Paul.

Parr, M. (1997) 'August Sander: A Personal Perspective', talk given at the National Portrait Gallery, London, March.

Parsons, T. (2002) *One for My Baby*, London: HarperCollins.

Pateman, C. (1988) *The Sexual Contract*, Cambridge: Polity.

Peck, J. (1994) Talking about race: framing a popular discourse of race on *Oprah Winfrey*, *Cultural Critique*, 27 (Spring): 89–126.

Penley, C. (1997) Crackers and whackers: the white trashing of porn, in M. Wray and A. Newitz (eds) *White Trash: Race and Class in America*, London: Routledge, 89–112.

Phillips, A. (1991) *Engendering Democracy*, Cambridge: Polity.

Philo, G. (ed.) (1995) *Glasgow Media Group Reader Volume 2: Industry, Economy, War and Politics*, London: Routledge.

Pilger, J. (1998) *Hidden Agendas*, London: Vintage.

Pilling, R. (1995) 'Changing news values in ITN bulletins for ITV', unpublished MA thesis, University of Keele, Department of Politics.

Piper, C. (2000) Use your illusion: televised discourse on journalism ethics in the United States 1992–98, *Social Semiotics*, 10(1): 61–79.

Ponce de Leon, C. L. (2002) *Self-Exposure: Human Interest Journalism and the Emergence of Celebrity in America 1890–1940*, Carolina, NC, University of North Carolina Press.

Porter, H. (1999) 'Editors and ego maniacs', in S. Glover (ed.) *Secrets of the Press: Journalists on Journalism*, London: Allan Lane, pp. 34–47.

Porter, L. (1998) Tarts, tampons and tyrants: women and representation in British comedy, in S. Wagg (ed.) *Because I Tell a Joke or Two: Comedy, Politics and Social Difference*, London: Routledge, pp. 65–93.

Pound, R. and Harmsworth, G. (1959) *Northcliffe*, New York: Frederick A Praeger.

Press, A. L. (1991) *Women Watching Television: Gender, Class and Generation in the American Television Experience*, Philadelphia: University of Pennsylvania Press.

Priest, P. J. (1995) *Public Intimacies: Talkshow Participants and Tell-all TV*, Kresskill, NJ: Hampton Press.

Pullen, C. (2004) The household, the basement and *The Real World*: gay identity in the constructed reality environment, S. Holmes and D. Jermyn (eds) *Understanding Reality Television*, London: Routledge, pp. 211–32.

Pursehouse, M. (1991) Looking at the *Sun*: into the nineties with a tabloid and its readers, *Cultural Studies From Birmingham*, 1: 88–133.

Radi, H. (1996) Alice Mabel Jackson, in J. Richie (ed.) *Australian Dictionary of Biography*, Vol 14: Melbourne, Melbourne University Press, pp. 543–4.

Radway, J. (1984/1991) *Reading the Romance: Women, Patriarchy and Popular Literature*, Chapel Hill, NC: University of North Carolina Press.

Raphael, C. (2004) 'The political economic origins of Reali-TV', in S. Murray and L. Ouellette (eds) *Reality TV: Remaking Television Culture*, New York: New York University Press, pp. 119–36.

Reese, S. (1990) The news paradigm and the ideology of objectivity: a socialist on the *Wall Street Journal*, *Critical Studies in Mass Communication*, 7(4): 390–409.

Ressner, J. (1988) Enquiring minds: a walk on the sleazy side with the new breed of tabloid reporters, *Rolling Stone*, (30 June): 53–6, 64.

Rhoufari, M. (2000) Talking about the tabloids: journalists' views, in C. Sparks and J. Tulloch, (eds) *Tabloid Tales: Global Debates Over Media Standards*, New York: Rowman & Littlefield, pp. 163–76.

Rigelsford, A.(1996) *Carry on Laughing: A Celebration*, London: Virgin.

Rivers, C. (1996) *Slick Spins and Fractured Facts: How Cultural Myths Distort the News*, New York: Columbia University Press.

Rojek, C. (2001) *Celebrity*, London: Reaktion.

Rolfe, P. (1979) *The Journalistic Javelin*, Sydney: Wild Cat Press.

Rooney, D. (1998) The dynamics of the British tabloid press, in *Javnnost: The Public*, 5(3): 95–107 at http://www.javnost-thepublic.org/media/datoteke/1998–3-rooney.pdf (accessed 11 May 2007).

Rooney, D. (2000) Thirty years of competition in the British tabloid press: the *Mirror* and the *Sun* 1968–1998, in C. Sparks and J. Tulloch (eds) *Tabloid Tales: Global Debates Over Media Standards*, New York: Rowman & Littlefield, pp. 91–110.

Rose, B. (1985) The talk show, in B. Rose (ed.) *TV Genres: A Handbook and Reference Guide*, Westport, CT: Greenwood Press.

Roshco, B. (1975) *Newsmaking*, Chicago: University of Chicago Press.

Ross, A. (1989) *No Respect: Intellectuals and Popular Culture*, New York: Routledge.

Ross, K. (2001/reprinted 2003) All ears: radio, reception and discourses on disability, in V. Nightingale and K. Ross (eds) *Critical Readings: Media and Audiences*, Maidenhead: Open University Press/McGraw Hill Education, pp. 131–44.

Ross, R. (1996) *The Carry On Companion*, London: Batsford.

Rubey, D. (1991) Voguing at the carnival, *South Atlantic Quarterly*, 90(4): 871–906.

Russo, M. (1994) *Female Grotesques: Risk, Excess and Modernity*, London: Routledge.

Sampson, A. (1996) The crisis at the heart of our media, *British Journalism Review*, 7(3): 42–56.

Sanders, K. (2003) *Ethics and Journalism*, London: Sage.

Savarin, D. (1998) The sadomasochist in the closet, in *Taking it Like a Man: What Masculinity, Masochism and Contemporary American Culture*, Princeton: Princeton University Press, pp. 161–210.

Schardt, A. (1980) Hollywood Stars vs. the *Enquirer*, in *Newsweek*, 8 December, p. 86.

Schiller, D. (1977) Realism, photography, and journalistic objectivity in nineteenth century America, *Studies in the Anthropology of Visual Communication*, 4(2): 86–98.

Schiller, D. (1981) *Objectivity: The Public and the Rise of Commercial Journalism*, Philadelphia: University of Pennsylvania Press.

Schlesinger, P. (1978) *Putting Reality Together*, London: Constable.

Schudson, M. (1978) *Discovering the News: A Social History of the American Newspaper*, New York: Basic Books.

Schudson, M. (1982) The politics of narrative form: the emergence of news conventions in print and television, *Daedalus*, 111(4): 97–112.

Schudson, M. (1989) The sociology of news production, *Media, Culture and Society*, 11(3): 263–82.

Schultz, J. (1994) *Not Just Another Business: Journalists, Citizens and the Media*, Sydney: Pluto.

Schuneman, R. S. (1966) 'The photograph in print: an examination of New York daily news-papers, 1890–1937', PhD dissertation, University of Minnesota.

Sconce, J. (1995) Trashing the Academy: taste, excess and an emerging politics of cinematic style, *Screen*, 36: 371–93.

Sconce, J. (2004) 'See you in hell, Johnny Bravo!', in S. Murray and L. Ouellette (eds) *Reality TV: Remaking Television Culture*, New York: New York University Press, pp. 251–67.

Scott, J. (1992) Experience, in J. Butler and J. W. Scott (eds) *Feminists Theorize the Political*, London: Routledge.

Searle, C. (1989) *Your Daily Dose: Racism and the Sun*, London: Campaign for Press and Broadcasting Freedom.

Segal, L. (1994) *Straight Sex: the Politics of Pleasure*, London: Virago.

Seidler, V. J. (ed.) (1991) *The Achilles' Heel Reader: Men, Sexual Politics and Socialism*, London: Routledge.

Sekula, A. (1984) *Photography Against the Grain*, Halifax: The Press of the Nova Scotia College of Art and Design.

Sendall, B. (1982) *Independent Television in Britain, Vol 1: Origin and Foundation 1946–62*, London: Macmillan.

Seymour-Ure, C. (1995) Characters and assassinations: portrayals of John major and Neil Kinnock in the *Daily Mirror* and the *Sun*, in I. Crewe and B. Gosschalk (eds) *Political Communications: the General Election Campaign 1992*, Cambridge: Cambridge University Press, pp. 137–59.

Seymour-Ure, C. (2000) Northcliffe's legacy, in P. Catterall, C. Seymour-Ure and A. Smith (eds) *Northcliffe's Legacy: Aspects of the British Popular Press 1896–1996*, London: Macmillan, pp. 9–25.

Sgammato, J. (1973) The discrete qualms of the bourgeoisie, *Sight and Sound*, (Summer): 134–7.

Shattuc, J. (1997) *The Talking Cure: TV Talkshows and Women*, New York: Routledge.

Sheridan, S. (2002) *Who Was That Woman? The Australian Women's Weekly in the Postwar Years*, Sydney: University of New South Wales Press.

Shevelow, K. (1989) *Women and Print Culture: the Construction of Femininity in the Early Period-ical*, London: Routledge.

Shipp, E. (1994) O.J. and the black media, *Columbia Journalism Review*, (Nov.–Dec.): 39–41.

Shoebridge, N. (1996) New bid to revive the glory days of two magazines, *Business Review Weekly*, (2 December): 66–9.

Short, C., Tunks, K. and Hutchinson, D. (1991) *Dear Clare: This is What Women Feel About Page Three*, London: Radius.

Silverman, D. (2000) *Doing Qualitative Research*, London: Sage.

Simonds, W. (1988) Confessions of loss: maternal grief in *True Story*, 1920–1985, *Gender and Society*, 2(2):149–71.

Sirus, R. U. and St Jude (1994) The medium is the message and the message is voyeurism, *Wired*, (February): 46–50.

Sloan, B. (2001) *'I Watched a Wild Hog Eat my Baby': A Colourful History of the Tabloids*, Amherst, NY: Prometheus Books.

Smilgis, M. (1988) In Florida: the rogues of tabloid valley, *Time*, (15 August): 13–14.

Smith, A. (1979) *The Newspaper: An International History*, London: Thames & Hudson.

Snitow, A. (1995) 'Mass market romance: pornography for women is different', in G. Dines and J. Humez (eds) *Gender, Race and Class in Media: A Text/reader*, Thousand Oaks, CA: Sage, pp. 190–201.

SNM (2006) *State of the News Media 2006 Report* at http://www.stateofthenewsmedia.org/2006/

Snoddy, R. (1992) *The Good, the Bad and the Unacceptable*, London: Faber & Faber.

Snow, J. (1997) More bad news, *Guardian*, 27 January, p. 3.

Sparks, C. (1992) Popular journalism: theories and practices, in P. Dahlgren and C. Sparks (eds) *Journalism and Popular Culture*, London: Sage.

Sparks, C. (2000) Introduction: the panic over tabloid news, in C. Sparks and J. Tulloch (eds) *Tabloid Tales: Global Debates Over Media Standards*, New York: Rowman & Littlefield, pp. 1–40.

Sparks, C. and Tulloch, J. (eds) (2000) *Tabloid Tales: Global Debates Over Media Standards*, New York: Rowman & Littlefield.

Spence, J. and Holland, P. (1991) *Family Snaps: the Meanings of Domestic Photography*, London: Virago.

Squire, C. (1994) Empowering women? *The Oprah Winfrey Show, Feminism and Psychology*, 4(1): 63–79.

Stacy, J. (1994) *Star-Gazing: Hollywood Cinema and Female Spectatorship*, London: Routledge.

Stallybrass, P. and White, A. (1986) *The Politics and Poetics of Transgression*, Ithaca, NY: Cornell University Press.

Stange, M. (1989) *Symbols of Ideal Life: Social Documentary Photography in America, 1890–1950*, Cambridge: Cambridge University Press.

Starr, L. (2003) *American Popular Music: From Minstrels to MTV*, New York: Oxford University Press.

Steiner, L. (1997) Gender at work: early accounts by women journalists, *Journalism History*, 23(1): 2–15.

Steiner, L. (1998) Newsroom accounts of power at work, in C. Carter, G. Branston and S. Allan (eds) *News, Gender and Power*, London: Routledge.

Sterling, C. H. and Kittross, J. (1978) *Stay Tuned: A Concise History of American Broadcasting*, Belmont: Wadsworth.

Stephens, R. L. (2004) 'Socially soothing stories? Gender, Race and Class in TLC's *A Wedding Story* and *A Baby Story*', in S. Holmes and D. Jermyn (eds) *Understanding Reality Television*, London: Routledge, pp. 191–210.

Stephenson, H. (1998) Tickle the public: consumerism rules, in M. Bromley and H. Stephenson (eds) *Sex, Lies and Democracy: The Press and the Public*, Harlow: Longman, pp. 25–88.

Stone, G. (1971) American sports: play and display, in E. Dunning (ed.) *The Sociology of Sport: A Selection of Readings*, London: Sass, pp. 47–59.

Storey, J. (2001) *Cultural Theory and Popular Culture: An Introduction*, London: Prentice-Hall.

Street, J. (1997) *Politics and Popular Culture*, Cambridge: Polity.

Street, J. (1998) *Youth, Popular Culture and Moral Panics*, London: Macmillan Press.

Street, J. (2001) *Mass Media, Politics and Democracy*, London: Palgrave.

Strinati, D. and Wagg, S. (eds) (1992) *Come on Down? Popular Media Culture in Postwar Britain*, London: Routledge.

Szarkowski, J. (ed.) (1973) *From the Picture Press*, New York: Museum of Modern Art.

Taft, R. (1938) *Photography and the American Scene: A Social History, 1839–1889*, New York: Dover.

Taft, W. (1968) Bernarr MacFaden: one of a kind, *Journalism Quarterly*, 45(4): 627–33.

Tasker, Y. (1998) *Working Girls: Gender and Sexuality in Popular Cinema*, London: Routledge.

Taylor, S. J. (1992) *Shock! Horror! The Tabloid in Action*, London: Black Swan.

Tebbel, J. (1963) *The Compact History of the American Newspaper*, New York: Hawthorne Books.

Tebbel, J. and Zuckerman, M. (1991) *The Magazine in America, 1741–1990*, New York: Oxford University Press.

Thomas, J. (2000) The 'Max Factor' – a Mirror image? Robert Maxwell and the *Daily Mirror* tradition, in P. Catterall, C. Seymour-Ure and A. Smith (eds) *Northcliffe's Legacy: Aspects of the British Popular Press 1896–1996*, London: Macmillan.

Thompson, J. B. (1995) *The Media and Modernity: A Social Theory of the Media*, Oxford: Polity Press.

Thompson, J. B. (1995a) The theory of the public sphere, O. Boyd-Barrett and C. Newbold (eds) *Approaches to Media: A Reader*, London: Edward Arnold.

Thompson, J. L. (2002) *Northcliffe: Press Baron in Politics, 1865–1922*, London: John Murray.

Thomson, A. (1954) The early history of the *Bulletin*, *Historical Studies: Australia and New Zealand*, 6 (May): 121–34.

Time-Life (1983) *Photojournalism*, revised edn., Alexandria, VA: Time-Life Books.

Tincknell, E., Chambers, D., Van Loon, J. and Hudson, N. (2003) Begging for it: 'new femininities', social agency and moral discourse in contemporary teenage and men's magazines, *Feminist Media Studies*, 3: 1.

Tuchman, G. (1971) Objectivity as strategic ritual: an examination of news men's notions of objectivity, *American Journal of Sociology*, 77(4): 660–79.

Tuchman, G. (1973) Making news by doing work: routinizing the unexpected, *American Journal of Sociology*, 79: 110–31.

Tuchman, G. (1974) Assembling a network talkshow, in Gaye Tuchman (ed.) *The TV Establishment: Programming for Power and Profit*, Englewood Cliffs, NJ: Prentice-Hall.

Tuchman, G. (1978) *Making News: A Study in the Construction of Reality*, New York: Free Press.

Tulloch, J. (2000) The eternal recurrence of new journalism, in C. Sparks and J. Tulloch (eds) *Tabloid Tales: Global Debates Over Media Standards*, New York: Rowman & Littlefield, pp. 131–46.

Tumber, H. (2000) *Media Power, Professionals and Policies*, London: Routledge.

Tunstall, J. (1971) *Journalists at Work: Specialist Correspondents, Their News Organizations, News Sources and Competitor Colleagues*, London: Constable.

Turner, G. (1999) Tabloidization, journalism and the possibility of critique, *International Journal of Cultural Studies*, 2(1): 59–76.

Turner, G. (2000) Talkback, advertising and journalism, *International Journal of Cultural Studies*, 3(2): 247–55.

Turner, G. (2001) Reshaping Australian institutions: popular culture, the market and the public sphere, in T. Bennett and D. Carter (eds) *Culture in Australia: Policies, Publics and Programs*, Melbourne: Cambridge University Press.

Turner, G. (2004) *Understanding Celebrity*, London: Sage.

Turner, G., Bonner, F. and Marshall, P.D. (2000) *Fame Games: The Production of Celebrity in Australia*, Cambridge: Cambridge University Press.

Van Zoonen, L. (1991) A tyranny of intimacy? Women, femininity and television news, in P. Dahlgren and C. Sparks (eds) *Communication and Citizenship*, London: Routledge.

Van Zoonen, L. (1998) 'One of the Girls': The Changing Gender of Journalism, in C. Carter, G. Branston and S. Allan (eds) *News, Gender and Power*, London: Routledge, pp. 33–46.

Van Zoonen, L. (1998a) A professional, unreliable, heroic marionette (M/F): structure, agency and subjectivity in contemporary journalisms, *European Journal of Cultural Studies*, 1(1): 123–43.

Van Zoonen, L. (1998b) The ethics of making private life public, in K. Brants, J. Hermes and L. van Zoonen (eds) *The Media in Question: Popular Cultures and Public Interests*, London: Sage.

Van Zoonen, L. (2001) Desire and resistance: *Big Brother* and the recognition of everyday life, *Media, Culture and Society*, 23: 669–77.

Walker, C. (1996) Can TV save the planet? *American Demographics*, 18: 42–3.

Walker, R. B. (1976) *The Newspaper Press in New South Wales, 1880–1920*, Sydney: Sydney University Press.

Warner, M. (1987) *Monuments and Maidens: The Allegory of the Female Form*, London: Picador.

Wark, M. (1994) *Virtual Geography: Living with Global Media Events*, Bloomington: Indiana University Press.

Wark, M. (1997) *The Virtual Republic: Australia's Culture Wars of the 1990s*, Sydney: Allen and Unwin.

Wark, M. (1998) *Celebrities, Culture and Cyberspace*, Sydney: Pluto Press.

Weaver, D. H. and Wilhoit, G. C. (1996) *The American Journalist in the 1990s: US News People at the End of an Era*, Mahwah, NJ: Erlbaum.

Whelehan, I. (2000) *Overloaded: Popular Culture and the Future of Feminism*, London: The Women's Press.

White, C. L. (1970) *Women's Magazines, 1693–1968*, London: Michael Joseph.

Whyte, F. (1925) *The Life of W.T. Stead: In Two Volumes*, Vol 1, London: Butler & Tanner.

Wicke, J. (1993) Through a gaze darkly: pornography's academic market, in P. Church Gibson and R. Gibson (eds) *Dirty Looks: Women, Pornography, Power*, London: BFI, pp. 62–80.

Wiener, J. (ed.) (1988) *Papers for the Millions: The New Journalism in Britain, 1850–1914*, New York: Greenwood Press.

Wigmore, N. (1986) The page three connection, *Guardian*, 27 March.

Willard, M.N. (1998) Séance, tricknowlgy, skateboarding, in J. Austin and M. N. Willard (eds) *Generations of Youth: Youth Cultures and History in Twentieth-century America*, New York: New York University Press.

Williams, F. (1957) *Dangerous Estate: the Anatomy of Newspapers*, London: Longmans, Green & Co.

Williams, G. (1994) *Britain's Media: How They are Related*, London: Campaign for Press and Broadcasting Freedom.

Williams, K. (2002) 'Jackass nation', in *Philadelphia Citypaper.net*, 8–14 August at http://city-paper.net/articles/2002/08/08/cover.shtml.

Williams, K. (2003) *Why I (Still) Want My MTV: Music Videos and Aesthetic Communication*, Cresskill: Hampton Press.

Williams, L. (1990) *HardCore: Power, Pleasure and the 'Frenzy of the Visible'*, London: Pandora.

Williams, R. (1961/1992) *The Long Revolution*, London: The Hogarth Press.

Williams, V. (1994) *Who's Looking at the Family*, London: Barbican Art Gallery.

Willis, P. (1977) *Learning to Labour*, Aldershot: Gower.

Wilson, P. (2004) Jamming *Big Brother*: webcasting, audience intervention, and narrative activism, in S. Murray and L. Ouellette (eds) *Reality TV: Remaking Television Culture*, New York: New York University Press, pp. 323–43.

Winch, S. P. (1997) *Mapping the Cultural Spaces of Journalism: How Journalists Distinguish News From Entertainment*, Westport, CT: Praeger.

Wood, G. (2007) 'Chronicle of a death foretold', in the *Observer, Woman Magazine*, 13 May: 42.

Zelizer, B. (2004) *Taking Journalism Seriously: News and the Academy*, London: Sage.

Zizek, S. (1990) How the non-duped err: literature, philosophy, visual arts, history, *Qui Parle*, 4(1): 1–20.

Zizek, S. (1999) In his bold gaze my ruin is writ large, in *Everything You Always Wanted to Know About Lacan But Were Afraid to Ask Hitchcock*, London: Verso.

Zizek, S. (2000) *The Ticklish Subject*, London: Verso.

Index